Survey
of
Science Fiction
Literature

**FIVE HUNDRED 2,000-WORD ESSAY REVIEWS OF
WORLD-FAMOUS SCIENCE FICTION NOVELS
WITH 2,500 BIBLIOGRAPHICAL REFERENCES**

Edited by
FRANK N. MAGILL

Volume Four
Nio - Sho
1537 - 2050

SALEM PRESS

Englewood Cliffs

LIBRARY OF CONGRESS CATALOG CARD NUMBER: 79-64639

Complete Set: ISBN 0-89356-194-0
Volume IV: ISBN 0-89356-198-3

PRINTED IN THE UNITED STATES OF AMERICA

LIST OF TITLES IN VOLUME FOUR

page

Niourk — *Stefan Wul* 1537
No Blade of Grass — *John Christopher* 1541
noites marcianas, As — *Fausto Cunha* 1545
Noon: Twenty-Second Century — *Arkady* and *Boris Strugatsky* 1548
Norstrilia — *Cordwainer Smith* 1555
Nova — *Samuel R. Delany* 1560
Nova Express — *William S. Burroughs* 1566

October Country, The — *Ray Bradbury* 1571
October the First Is Too Late — *Fred Hoyle* 1574
Odd John: A Story Between Jest and Earnest — *Olaf Stapledon* 1583
oeil du purgatoire, L' — *Jacques Spitz* 1588
Omega: The Last Days of the World — *Camille Flammarion* 1592
Omnivore — *Piers Anthony* 1596
On the Beach — *Nevil Shute* 1603
Ophiuchi Hotline, The — *John Varley* 1608
Oraşele Înecate — *Felix Aderca* 1613
Orbitsville — *Bob Shaw* 1617
Other Days, Other Eyes — *Bob Shaw* 1622
Other Side, The — *Alfred Kubin* 1627
Out of the Silent Planet — *C. S. Lewis* 1632
Oxygen och Aromasia — *Claës Lundin* 1637

Paradox Men, The — *Charles L. Harness* 1641
Past Through Tomorrow, The — *Robert A. Heinlein* 1645
Pastel City, The — *M(ike) John Harrison* 1655
Pavane — *Keith Roberts* 1660
Pellucidar — *Edgar Rice Burroughs* 1665
Perelandra — *C. S. Lewis* 1669
Philosopher's Stone, The — *Colin Wilson* 1674
Picnic on Paradise — *Joanna Russ* 1678
Pilgrimage: The Book of the People *and* The People:
   No Different Flesh — *Zenna Henderson* 1682
Plague of Demons, A — *Keith Laumer* 1687
Planet of the Apes — *Pierre Boulle* 1692
Player Piano — *Kurt Vonnegut, Jr.* 1697
Poison Belt, The — *Arthur Conan Doyle* 1702

page

Pollinators of Eden, The — *John Boyd* 1705
Ponedel'nik nachinaetsia v subbotu — *Arkady* and *Boris Strugatsky* 1710
Poorhouse Fair, The — *John Updike* 1714
Princess of Mars, A — *Edgar Rice Burroughs* 1720
Prisonnier de la planète Mars, Le — *Gustave LeRouge* 1726
Puppet Masters, The — *Robert A. Heinlein* 1730
Purple Cloud, The — *M. P. Shiel* 1735

Quando le Radici — *Lino Aldani* 1739
Quinzinzinzili — *Régis Messac* 1742

Rakehells of Heaven, The — *John Boyd* 1746
Ralph 124C 41+ — *Hugo Gernsback* 1751
Re-Birth — *John Wyndham* 1755
Rendezvous with Rama — *Arthur C. Clarke* 1759
Report on Probability A — *Brian W. Aldiss* 1764
Republic of the Southern Cross, The — *Valery Bryusov* 1768
Retief: Ambassador to Space — *Keith Laumer* 1775
Riddle of the Tower, The — *John D. Beresford* and *Esme Wynne-Tyson* .. 1780
Rim of Morning, The — *William Sloane* 1784
Rim Worlds Series, The — *A(rthur) Bertram Chandler* 1789
Ring Around the Sun — *Clifford D. Simak* 1794
Ringworld — *Larry Niven* 1799
Rite of Passage — *Alexei Panshin* 1805
Riverworld Series — *Philip José Farmer* 1809
Roadside Picnic — *Arkady* and *Boris Strugatsky* 1817
Rogue Moon — *Algis Budrys* 1821
Rogue Queen — *L. Sprague De Camp* 1827
Rose, The — *Charles L. Harness* 1832
R.U.R. — *Karel Čapek* 1837

Sagan om den stora datamaskine — *Olof Johannesson* 1844
"Sandman, The" — *E. T. A. Hoffmann* 1848
Sanreizan Hiroku — *Ryo Hanmura* 1854
Santaroga Barrier, The — *Frank Herbert* 1859
Satana dei Miracoli — *Ugo Malaguti* 1863
Saurus — *Eden Phillpotts* 1866
Science Fiction of Edgar Allan Poe, The — *Edgar Allan Poe* 1871
Second War of the Worlds, The — *Arkady* and *Boris Strugatsky* 1879
Seed of Light — *Edmund Cooper* 1884
Seedling Stars, The — *James Blish* 1888
Sempiternin — *Lajos Mesterházi* 1892
Sepoltura, La — *Gianni Montanari* 1896
Shadows in the Sun — *Chad Oliver* 1898
Shape of Things to Come, The — *H. G. Wells* 1902
She — *H. Rider Haggard* 1908
Sheep Look Up, The — *John Brunner* 1913
Ship Who Sang, The — *Anne McCaffrey* 1917
Shockwave Rider, The — *John Brunner* 1922

LIST OF TITLES IN VOLUME FOUR

page

Short Fiction of Arthur C. Clarke, The — *Arthur C. Clarke* 1926

Short Fiction of Avram Davidson, The — *Avram Davidson* 1930

Short Fiction of Dmitri Bilenkin, The — *Dmitri Bilenkin* 1934

Short Fiction of Edmond Hamilton, The — *Edmond Hamilton* 1939

Short Fiction of Fitz-James O'Brien, The — *Fitz-James O'Brien* 1944

Short Fiction of Frederik Pohl, The — *Frederik Pohl* 1948

Short Fiction of Fredric Brown, The — *Fredric Brown* 1954

Short Fiction of Fritz Leiber, Jr., The — *Fritz Leiber, Jr.* 1958

Short Fiction of Gennadiy Samoilovich Gor, The —
Gennadiy Samoilovich Gor 1963

Short Fiction of H. G. Wells, The — *H. G. Wells* 1967

Short Fiction of H. P. Lovecraft, The — *H. P. Lovecraft* 1973

Short Fiction of Harlan Ellison, The — *Harlan Ellison* 1978

Short Fiction of Herman Melville, The — *Herman Melville* 1989

Short Fiction of J. G. Ballard, The — *J. G. Ballard* 1994

Short Fiction of James Tiptree, Jr., The — *James Tiptree, Jr.* 1999

Short Fiction of John W. Campbell, Jr., The — *John W. Campbell, Jr.* .. 2003

Short Fiction of Jorge Luis Borges, The — *Jorge Luis Borges* 2008

Short Fiction of Judith Merril, The — *Judith Merril* 2014

Short Fiction of Kirill Bulychev, The — *Kirill Bulychev* 2019

Short Fiction of Larry Niven, The — *Larry Niven* 2023

Short Fiction of Murray Leinster, The — *Murray Leinster* 2030

Short Fiction of Nathaniel Hawthorne, The — *Nathaniel Hawthorne* 2035

Short Fiction of Ray Bradbury, The — *Ray Bradbury* 2042

Short Fiction of Robert Sheckley, The — *Robert Sheckley* 2046

NIOURK
(New York)

Author: Stefan Wul (Pierre Pairault, 1922-   )
First book publication: 1957
Type of work: Novel
Time: The future
Locale: The Earth

> *Poisoned by the radioactivity on a postatomic Earth, a black child flees his tribe and gradually acquires the powers of a god, preferring to reconstruct an Earth civilization rather than join humanity which has emigrated to Venus*

> *Principal characters:*
> THE BLACK CHILD
> THÔZ, the chief of the tribe
> JAX,
> BRIG, and
> THE DOC, shipwrecked passengers from a Venusian spacecraft on Earth

Paradoxically, *Niourk* is Stepan Wul's least original novel from a thematic viewpoint, while at the same time it is his masterpiece. *Niourk* is set on a postatomic Earth where the oceans have almost disappeared. Civilized humanity, which has emigrated to Venus, has left deserted cities behind which have become the cities of the Gods for the primitives.

One day, a black-skinned child escapes from the tribe of white men into which he was born. Since his color made him a symbol of evil, the chief of the tribe had decided to sacrifice him. He flees to find one of the deserted cities in order to become a friend of the gods, but instead he finds a weapon that would enable him to guide his tribe. But a fire forces the tribe to flee before his return, and so the black child starts out after them. Eventually he catches up with them, after combating all kinds of dangers and monsters, but it is too late. The radioactivity has quickly doomed Thôz, the chief, and his companions.

After that the black child continues on his way to Niourk, the ancient New York, with a tame bear for company. There he meets shipwrecked Venusian astronauts who cure him of his radiation burns. But they also affect his brain: the child has gained an understanding of life and the Universe. With this knowledge, he uses the vestiges of the ancient Earth civilization to change the destiny of Earth by propelling it into the heart of the galaxy after placing a mini-sun in orbit around it. Then he leaves Niourk to the Venusians who cured him and goes back to live "the only life that's worth living" with the members of his tribe, which he has built up again from nothing.

As it is easy to see, the themes used by Wul have almost nothing original about them. It is the treatment that transforms the book into a masterpiece, perhaps because Stepan Wul has succeeded in making a fairy story out of it.

Niourk is a primarily visual novel: if the black child is the book's hero, the dessicated Earth is its heroine. The Earth is divided into two very well-defined settings: the jungle and the cities. The jungle has always been Wul's favorite environment, the place where he feels comfortable bringing out the monsters he likes so much. He admits to a kind of fascination for the bush and the jungle, even if he has never been there. In the universe of *Niourk*, a forest covers the former ocean floor and climbs the slopes of the new mountains which had been islands a very long time before.

The landscape is very harsh for those who try to cross it, but in its heart lies the greatest danger: a big lake colonized by giant mutant octopuses. These octopuses are among Wul's most successful monsters. One would think they were derived from the great animated cartoons of Walt Disney. After a few lines one can imagine them, enormous dark masses gliding noiselessly among the mangrove roots flashing their great luminescent yellow eyes. The reader begins to share the anguish felt by the hunters of the tribe as they attempt to deal with these monsters, who have been made powerful by radioactivity. Endowed with rudimentary intelligence, the creatures have developed the ability to come out of the water, and they are gradually surrounding the tribe. Images which stay engraved in one's memory reinforce the power of the narrative, such as that of the octopus throwing a javelin at a squirrel on a tree or the awful moment when one of the prisoners is decapitated with a quick stroke of a beak. Even if one knows that this is only pure fantasy, the realistic, terrifying description makes the picture vivid and tragic.

Another extraordinary sequence is the one where the members of the tribe, after eating the radioactive flesh of the octopuses, see their entrails become luminescent and blue in the night. The visual effect is astonishing. A similar effect is achieved when the men, undermined by radiation, suddenly die and begin to swell up and fly away in the form of monstrous gold-beater's skins. The scene would be laughable without the dramatic intensity Wul displays.

After leaving the jungle and its perils, the black child might have thought he was beyond danger, but this is not the case. Niourk, with its useless wharves and its port perched on clifftops, represents another sort of jungle, a mechanized jungle every bit as dangerous as the one on the floor of the ocean. The black child (whose brain is beginning to record flashes of supralucidity) considers it the city of the gods, but they are noticeably absent except on immense movie posters. The black child then begins to explore the place in search of food for himself and his bear. There, too, a comparison with Walt Disney is inevitable, as well as with another novel, Rudyard Kipling's *Jungle Book*, with its Mowgli, who is very much like the black child. The city, still partially automized, receives him coldly, and the black child begins to give up the hope of meeting the gods in spite of his powers, including the marvelous weapon which enabled him to overcome the octopuses, and will keep him safe from the monsters that reign in the great empty apartment buildings. Rats, also mutants, have become a thousand times more dangerous than their ancestors; they are in the city what the octopuses were in the jungle. Stepan Wul has chosen as monsters the most terrifying animals of both the marine and urban environments, animals associated with terror in the collective unconscious.

However, the gods the black child is looking for, or rather two of their descendants, are also wandering in the maze of buildings in the dying city. In fact, after leaving the wreckage of their spacecraft to explore Niourk, Jax and Brig find themselves prisoners in an apartment building with broken machinery, the same as the one in which the black child is lost. Finally, Brig manages to get out alive and rejoin the Doc in the ship. Afterwards the two men find the black child and care for him. This is the moment when the mutation begun in his brain reaches its ultimate point and turns the child into a true god, a being far superior to those he mistook for divinities.

Stepan Wul describes the city as if it is driven by the same forces as the jungle. The only difference is that space becomes vertical instead of being horizontal. Concrete and steel replace foliage and bushes, but they have exactly the same function and they veil similar perils. Far from making the novel uniform, this way of looking at the city gives it additional relief. The Earth has become entirely wild.

For Wul, it seems that man can no longer reconquer the Earth until a long time has passed, so the remnants of humanity have returned to the only social structure adapted to the jungle: the tribe. Even when he has become the equal of a god, the black child returns to this kind of existence, leaving Brig and the Doc the task of amusing themselves with the renovated but lifeless city of Niourk. At the end of the novel, the Earth is brought to the most secure place in all the galaxy, not to become a technological world again but to be sheltered from surprises. The black child proposes a total return to the Earth, a return in tranquility.

The lesson is important; after destroying everything humanity is not able to recover its power all at once, but must once again retrace the long and perilous road to civilization. The black child, who has become immortal, will guide his tribe and their descendants, trying to avoid certain errors of the past; that is what is understood in the conclusion of the book. Stepan Wul has endowed his character of the black child with divine power (since he even succeeds in moving the Earth by the power of his thought), while at the same time keeping the wisdom of childhood in him. When he has built up the tribe again, he has the wisdom to entrust its command to Thôz, an energetic man capable of change. The child watches over him from a distance as he also does for Brig and the Doc, destined to remain in their ultra-modern city because they are incapable of returning to the nomadic life.

Brig, Doc, and Jax are interesting characters because their reactions suggest the state of development of humanity which has emigrated to Venus. Culturally it seems that society has become completely hierarchical and obsessed with technology. However, from the incomprehension displayed by the new

Venusians when confronted by the mechanisms of Niourk, it also appears that the new humanity might have regressed following its migration. In short, Stepan Wul suggests information in a few paragraphs which make one regret that he did not write another novel about the men on Venus. In any case, he does not seem to have a great deal of confidence in these emigrant Earthmen. The flight of the Earth to another part of the galaxy appears, above all, the best way for them to avoid returning to their world or origin, a return whose price would be the failure of the black child's experiment and of his hopes of seeing a new and saner humanity arise.

Alongside the storybook landscapes of *Niourk* and its omnipresent monsters, another favorite theme of Stepan Wul emerges: mutation. Mutation is a necessary means of adaptation for the character who must brave the chaos of the new environment. Wul's typical hero must either transcend his condition or be destroyed by his enemy. In the case of the black child, mutation is carried out in two very distinct stages. First, he passes from the status of an animal, cursed by his own tribe, to a full-fledged human being according to the criteria prevailing in the tribal society. This transformation is only possible through the weapon, the symbol of power. This first mutation is a conscious mutation which the black child adjusts to at once. The second arises when he eats the brain of a radioactive octopus, adhering to a well-known tribal rite which supposes that the victor acquires the qualities of the vanquished by devouring his brain. Here, the qualities are amplified to infinity, since the radioactivity which gave intelligence to the octopus opens the black child's brain to universal knowledge. Finally, the Venusians' science prevents the black child's death. In that moment, the new god has in his hands the power to lead his people towards a new destiny and to circumvent the constantly growing power of the giant octopuses. The black child also has stolen the quality of chosen species by devouring the brains of his victims and becoming capable of survival.

It seems, then, that *Niourk* is a curious novel which has an extraordinarily rich texture behind an unreal, fairy-tale aspect. The evocative power Stepan Wul displays in it certainly makes it not only his masterpiece, but also a masterpiece in science fiction.

Richard D. Nolane

NO BLADE OF GRASS

Author: John Christopher (Samuel Christopher Youd, 1922-   )
First book publication: 1956 (as *The Death of Grass*)
Type of work: Novel
Time: The near future
Locale: England, from the London conurbation to Blind Gill, an imaginary valley in the northwest

A virus selectively attacks and destroys all forms of the Gramineae (grass, wheat, barley, rice), precipitating worldwide famine and the collapse of civilization

Principal characters:
    JOHN CUSTANCE, a London engineer
    DAVID CUSTANCE, John's brother, a Westmorland farmer
    ANN CUSTANCE, John's wife
    ROGER BUCKLEY, a Public Relations Officer
    OLIVIA BUCKLEY, Roger's wife
    MISTER PIRRIE, a gunsmith and marksman

Like other examples of the "world disaster" story, *No Blade of Grass* (British title, *The Death of Grass*) is about the nature of civilization. It is perhaps significant that most of the practitioners of this specialized subgenre within science fiction have been English, from H. G. Wells to John Wyndham, Nevil Shute, John Christopher, Edmund Cooper, D. F. Jones, and Christopher Priest. During the twentieth century England has become in some respects the epitome of what one could broadly call "Western democracy." England is not necessarily the most civilized country in the world, but its civilization has been subject to least challenge or disturbance. Unlike almost all European countries, with the exception of Iceland, Sweden, and Switzerland, it has not recently been invaded or conquered, has not suffered catastrophic inflation, civil war, or the rise of fascism or communism. Unlike the United States, it has until recently contained almost no ethnic minorities (minority groups thus play no part at all in *No Blade of Grass*, though they are prominent in Christopher Priest's *Fugue for a Darkening Island* written sixteen years later). And the English equivalent of the "Indian Wars" took place between nine and fifteen centuries ago. A characteristic image of this peaceful society is the British policeman, by tradition unarmed except for the wooden truncheon he is not permitted to display. These facts, together with memories of the British Empire and the *Pax Britannica*, have combined to make England (until recently at least) perhaps not the most cultured part of the Western world, but certainly the part where civilization seems to have its deepest roots and fewest competitors. The question of how deep those roots sink into human nature has, therefore, intrigued English authors in particular for close to a century.

In Chapter One of *No Blade of Grass* Ann Custance says of her husband John and his brother David that they are "both savages really," and goes on to reflect "I suppose all men are." At that stage the remark is purely casual, and

the point at issue — whether marriage is woman's destiny — is irrelevant to
the rest of the book. But at that stage the Chung-Li virus is only in its first
phase of destroying only rice, and while this has already reduced Asia to collapse, the effect on England is almost nil. The plot of the novel is based on the
increasing power of the virus, the approach of death by starvation even to
Englishmen, and their various responses to the threat. Perhaps the most striking thing about this simple plot is that the responses are indeed various. Ann
Custance remarks that her brother-in-law has lost more of his "veneer of
civilization" than her husband, but in many cases the implications of her
remark prove wildly wrong. To some, civilization *is* only a "veneer," easily
chipped off. To others, however, it seems to be bred in the bone, and cannot
be discarded. The tension between these two states give the fine details to the
story's action, and are responsible also for the developments or oscillations in
the main characters.

The main characters consist of two married couples: John and Ann Custance
and Roger and Olivia Buckley. With their children, they spend the major part
of the book (once the Chung-Li virus has openly defeated countermeasures and
extended its range to all the *Gramineae*, which make up most of the world's
food) in fighting their way from London to Blind Gill, the easily defensible
valley owned by John's brother David. The only other major character is Mr.
Pirrie, the gunsmith and marksman whom John and Roger try first to rob
(since England has exceptionally stringent gun controls, it is unusual for private citizens to own firearms), and then to persuade to convoy them across
England as guard-cum-executioner. The many other people in the book function as threats, victims, or dependents, symbols of greater or lesser adaptation
to jungle law. Even the four central characters are not strikingly individual-
ized; their role is to stage a dispute over ethics and imagination.

The dispute begins to develop as early as Chapter Two, where the four are
playing bridge and simultaneously listening to the radio. The news, which is
about the utter disaster in China, is counterpointed against a series of remarks
by Roger: "What's two hundred million? . . . There's an awful lot of Chinks
in China. . . ." and so on. The others protest, and continue to do so during the
next few chapters. But increasingly Roger defends his attitude with an argument not entirely unethical. The issues raised by the Chung-Li virus, he says,
are not simply those of total Good or benevolence against total Evil or heart-
lessness. If the Chinese could be saved by effort of will, he would save them.
But in practice the choice is between saving one person (maybe an unknown
Chinese) or another (maybe his wife, his son, himself). Is it wrong to choose
the latter instead of the former? Further, if the case is as he sees it, the concern
and charity of his friends is not creditable at all, but the product of delusion,
or, as he increasingly puts it, lack of imagination. *They* cannot imagine
England brown and grassless, with English children chewing bark. If they
could, they would become as heartless as himself. Since Roger's job is Public

Relations Officer to the Ministry of Information, he experiences daily the gap between the illusion of unshakable civilization propagated by the government, and the reality of the limits of even governmental power.

In the continuing dispute the reader's instincts are likely at first to be anti-Roger, and the author exploits this probability with occasional glimpses of the horrors Roger's policy entails: napalm, machine guns, and in the end hydrogen bombs dropped on English cities by the Royal Air Force to reduce the population. On the other hand, the logic of the events in the story support Roger's viewpoint. In particular the illusions of competence projected by press, radio, and politicians come to seem hateful; the author exploits another fact about the English situation when he points out that the land *can* just barely support the population, but only at the cost of an immense change in dietary habits, away from beef and bread to potatoes and tubers, which are immune to the virus. The politicians could save England, but they fear the angry reactions of consumer-voters if, for instance, the virus were to be defeated after the country had been committed to years of turnips. In the last analysis it is the machinery of democracy which causes the collapse of England; and insofar as John, Ann, and Olivia share the politicians' blindness, their views are unacceptable, and Roger's by contrast tolerable.

The balance begins to tip in Chapter Five, however, when (this is perhaps the least convincing part of the book) the celebrated English patience snaps and a new Prime Minister orders the R. A. F. to obliterate his own cities. Forewarned by Roger, the Custances and Buckleys try to break out of London; after initial failure, John recruits Mr. Pirrie and assists him in murdering the soldiers at a roadblock. John, therefore, has come over to Roger's "side," and Pirrie was there to begin with. Ann follows very rapidly, for as the families drive away she and her daughter are cut off, trapped and raped by a gang of men who have discarded civilization more completely and abruptly than most. Saved by Pirrie and the others, she shoots one of her attackers in cold blood. "No! You can't. It's murder!" he says; and we are directed with wry irony to the failure of the rapist's imagination, which has profited from the breakdown of civilization but not grasped that from now on "murder" will be only a word, without policeman, judge, and hangman to define it. Roger has proved his point, to his friends and probably to most readers.

At this point, however, the author begins to tip the balance back towards the ethics of civilization. John contemplates his murders, reflecting that at least some people would choose, unlike himself, to die well rather than live badly. This seems unappealing at the time, but as the Custances are forced into one act of self-preservation after another, we begin to remember the good features of civilization (gentleness and tolerance) as well as the bad (hypocrisy and folly). Regret is communicated by a series of more or less devalued kindnesses to the waifs and strays the party picks up *en route*. The possibility of voluntary as opposed to forced savagery is further highlighted by Mr. Pirrie, the strongest character in the book. From his first appearance, he is different from all his partners. He is paradoxical: he makes decisions instantly, forcefully, and without vacillation, yet he is oddly soft-spoken; he shoots his wife for cuckolding him, and enforces delicate distinctions of honor, status, even propriety, yet takes the daughter of another victim. Significantly, he claims to be half-French and so in a measure immune to the English lack of imagination; he appears to represent the future of England and the world.

In the end, John Christopher leaves the issue of human nature unsettled. The entry to Blind Gill is barred, and John Custance and his warband have to break in, killing David Custance in the process. Pirrie is also killed; does his death spell an end to murder and a return to civilization? At the close of the novel, parallels to the Biblical story of Cain and Abel, which have been hinted at from the beginning, are more definitely stated. The future belongs to Cain, by right of survival. Even though this particular Cain loves his brother and regrets his death, he still cannot lay down his arms. John's son, like Enoch the son of Cain, may be a man of peace who will live "in a city" as the Bible says, or who will refound civilization; but he will keep his father's rifle as Enoch kept Cain's dagger. *No Blade of Grass* is in the first place a warning against smugness and the illusion that liberal views can be held without payment, and in the second place an affirmation that human civilization is immensely worthwhile even if it is not *natural*.

T. A. Shippey

Sources for Further Study

Reviews:

Analog. XL, October, 1957, pp. 156-157.

Infinity Science Fiction. II, October, 1957, pp. 104-105.

Magazine of Fantasy and Science Fiction. XIII, October, 1957, p. 102.

Original Science Fiction. X, November, 1959, p. 130.

Vanguard Science Fiction. I, June, 1958, pp. 87-89.

AS NOITES MARCIANAS
(Martian Nights)

Author: Fausto Cunha (1928-   )
First book publication: 1960
Type of work: Short stories

The first collection of stories by one of Brazil's outstanding literary critics

Fausto Cunha is still better known in Brazil as a critic than as a fiction writer. Cunha earned his reputation fairly. Born in 1928, he was one of the leaders of his generation who introduced a technocultural approach to criticism that was built on solid knowledge and a deeper than customary delving into literary works. This approach was in contrast to the impressionist concept, with its subjective and emotional attitude toward art, which was much more common in Brazilian literary criticism some decades ago.

The debut of any important critic as a novelist is always greeted with surprise and interest, but when Fausto Cunha decided to come out as a science fiction writer, there was great shock at his choice of genre. Bias against science fiction was much stronger in Brazil two decades ago than it is today, although it still exists. The majority of critics then (and some now) considered science fiction not even worth a second look; it was viewed as a minor genre designed for comic books and police novels. As a consequence of this unfair judgment, *As noites marcianas* has not been as widely read as it deserves; yet the simple fact that a reputable author wrote a science fiction book imparted respect and importance to the genre.

The first story in this collection is "Sentimental Journey of a Young Martian to the Planet Earth." Written before space probes proved that the chances of either animal or plant life existing on Mars are almost nil, the story tells of a Martian explorer who lands at the South Pole and at first believes the penguins to be human beings. The story is simply curious, a mediocre tale like a hundred others published since the famous Martian invasion created by H. G. Wells. Nevertheless, its depiction of the invading Martians, its scientific logic, its situational irony, and its literary quality make it good reading even today.

"They Called Me Monster" is one of the most original pieces in the book. It tells the story of Ghrh, a being native to a very distant planet, who is usually amorphous and who has the ability to change into or absorb anything it comes across — men, animals, or objects. Almost immortal, it is astonished to find that humans die in a "fraction of a second," yet "believe that they live for a long time." Ghrh muses, "In a little town where I was a park bench, I saw a human being just about rise up out of the baby carriage into which he was put by the wet nurse, grow like a flash of lightning, and then die stretched out in a coffin. . . . I'm very sorry for the humans. They could do great things if they didn't rush to die." Ghrh tells of his transformations into human beings, men and women, and relates his memories of other worlds; the story ends with

Ghrh in the body of a science fiction writer. Stories such as this one do not pretend to forecast future technologies or examine humankind as it faces progress or confronts probable outer-space travelers. Science fiction in this case is a pretext, a new angle of observation or perception from which to describe humankind and its existence.

The story "The Return" makes use of Einstein's theory of relativity. An astronaut, in a ship traveling close to the speed of light or faster, will, upon coming back to Earth, observe that time on the planet has elapsed thousands of times more than what was recorded on the ship's chronometer. It takes Pedro Santos sixteen years to get to the constellation of Triangulum. While traveling, he receives instructions from Earth which enable him to modify and improve his communications equipment. Ordered to return, he finds a completely alien Earth. Although he has traveled for only a year and a half, centuries have passed on Earth; things and customs had changed entirely. He is like a grown-up baby whose cultural conditioning is totally inappropriate to the existing situation on Earth.

Many science fiction writers have speculated about the ability of highly developed communication technologies to control people, brainwash them, and rule them through subliminal messages. Frederik Pohl and C. M. Kornbluth in *The Space Merchants* predicted that within a hundred years, the world would not be ruled by political parties and their ideologies, but by advertising agencies. These agencies naturally predominate because they control consumer markets by selling products by the most dishonest scientific methods. Future advertisers, using all the resources and techniques of psychology laboratories and secret inventions that affect every human sense, will not only help to sell goods and services and to create consumer habits, but will also induce everyone to want or do things according to the wishes of the Establishment.

In Fausto Cunha's story "Oanzol and the Fish," a wave of suicides is precipitated by an advertising campaign which results in the death of thousands. At the end of the story, the president of the agency which created the new method of persuasion dies himself. Both in this story as well as in its predecessors, the fear of misapplication of new technological inventions always causes the death of thousands or billions of peaceful people. The implication often is that the disaster is a terrible punishment inflicted on them for becoming machine worshipers and abandoning a serene life in communion with nature.

As in realistic fiction, there exist in science fiction many repeated classical themes in which the invention is no longer important and the slant of the story depends upon a new angle of observation, a unique, different, or uncertain psychology. For example, the time machine, which offers the possibility of going into the future or returning to the past, is an inexhaustible topic in science fiction. In "The Day Just Past," a man is going to return to the previous day; however, he kills the woman he loves in a fit of anger. Will he be able to return to the past and undo his act? In a very well-known story, Ray Bradbury tells about a man who travels back in time a million years, and who unintentionally steps on a butterfly and kills it. He then comes back to the present to find a completely different reality: the death of the single butterfly a million years before set off a chain of events which radically changed the present. In "The Day Just Past," by contrast, Fausto Cunha's character goes back into the past but is unable to alter what he has already done.

Even after eighteen years, *As noites marcianas* is interesting to read. The author's erudition is evident in every story; some pieces, such as "The Light the World Put Out," in which a literary chronicler uses a dry and balanced style to analyze the story of a famous scientist, are particularly sophisticated. Fausto Cunha's stories are sometimes poetic, usually enlivened by exciting action, and always inspired by a satirical, well-tempered vision that runs throughout his plots. Even though this remains his only book in the genre, Fausto Cunha stands at the forefront of Brazilian science fiction writers.

André Carneiro

NOON: TWENTY-SECOND CENTURY
(POLDEN', XXII BEK: VOZVRASHCHENIE)

Authors: Arkady Strugatsky (1925-   ) and Boris Strugatsky (1933-   )
First book publication: 1962
English translation: 1978
Type of work: Thematically related short stories
Time: About 1985-2021 and 2119-2150
Locale: The Earth, various planets, deep space

A series of stories, sharing the same characters and presenting a many-sided (sometimes kaleidoscopic) picture of a distant future on the Earth

> *Principal characters:*
> SERGEI KONDRATEV, a space pilot, later an oceanographer
> EVGENI SLAVIN, a doctor, later a writer
> GENNADI KOMOV ("CAPTAIN"), a boy, later a space pilot
> ALEKSANDR KOSTYLIN ("LIN"), a boy, later a biologist, space pilot of the landing party, and an embryomechanic
> POL GNEDIKH ("LIEBER POLLY"), a boy, later a servomechanic and a hunter
> SIDOROV ("ATOS"), the fourth schoolboy
> LEONID GORBOVSKY, an "Assault" space pilot, a member of the Contact Commission

The first edition of *Noon: Twenty-Second Century* appeared in 1962. At that time is was a simple collection of stories set in a singular space-and-time continuum. In 1967, the book was enlarged and amended. The authors reduced the number of main characters to six. At least one of these characters appears in each story. Thus, a collection of stories has become an integral book. (In addition, every Chinese character was changed to Japanese as a result of the Sino-Soviet split.) To identify the type and style of the collection is not a simple matter. Kaleidoscopic "stop-shots" of a distant future has been changed in its second edition by the Strugatsky brothers into a streamlined and profoundly logical book. In this case, the history of the book's evolution is rather useful for further understanding of the work.

Noon: Twenty-Second Century was published five years after the first edition of *Andromeda* by Ivan Yefremov, which was, in fact, the beginning of modern Soviet science fiction. *Andromeda* was written in accordance with the canons of the traditional Utopia and was structured accordingly. More philosophical than literary, the problem of creating a majestic panorama of the Earth's future was enormous in itself. Yefremov was limited by the traditional structures of Utopian literature, which left very little space for a thorough psychological picture of the characters (psychological details are mere trifles for the general sociological scheme of a Utopia). Though *Andromeda* has been and still remains a forerunner of modern Soviet science fiction and Yefremov's profound and expansive sociological ideas have no parallels in our Utopian science fiction, the literary faults of the book are evident.

Noon: Twenty-Second Century was created as a quiet polemic not only with Yefremov's novel, but also with the traditional structure of all such books. This polemic was less concerned with ideological differences than with the means of expressing the views. Thus, besides a social task, the Strugatsky brothers set an artistic task for themselves, namely, to show a positive future world by creating live, sympathetic characters.

Written as an openly fragmentary book, the authors lead the reader into their imaginary world step by step, through the perceptions of the main characters. They change the attitude toward their imaginary world in accordance with the changes in the perception of their readers; hence, the imaginary world becomes an evolutionary process and not an initially preset model. Had *Noon: Twenty-Second Century* been written some ten years later, the authors might have quite consciously used such a fragmentary method as their methodological principle of "discovering the world," such as John Brunner so brilliantly did in his novel *Stand on Zanzibar*. But even the Strugatskys' subconscious and intuitional approach to traditional structures brought its results: this work can be called a Utopian book only because no other term for it exists. In essence the book is a structural antipode to the Utopia.

This may be why the Strugatsky brothers did not try to begin with a monumental literary work, but first tested themselves with "sketches." The initial results were stories which were quite arbitrarily united in a book under one cover. But gradually this imagined world of the book was perfected, reexamined, and widened in space and time. In turn, this change revealed that the fragmentary and kaleidoscopic style of the authors was blocking the perceptions of the reader. Upon realizing this, they "unified" the main characters, leaving only six major personalities to link the separate stories, while the rest of the characters became secondary or episodical ones.

To present their world to the reader, the Strugatsky brothers use the common method of placing our near-contemporaries into it. The spaceship *Taimyr* is involved in an accident, and the two crew members, still alive, find themselves a century and a half ahead of their time, in the noon of the twenty-second century (the book begins at the end of the present century). These two crew members are the navigator, Kondratev, and the doctor, Slavin. They differ very little from our contemporaries; therefore, the chapter which introduces Kondratev is philosophically called "Almost the Same." But the living world of the twenty-second century is a qualitatively different society. Becoming acquainted with it and adapting to it ("Homecoming") form the core of the book's plot.

Kondratev and Slavin make many friends, who are gradually presented to the reader. At the same time the authors create a parallel plot with a "wonderful quartet" of schoolboys from the twenty-second century, pupils of the Anyudin boarding school. The four juveniles — Gennadi ("The Captain"), Pol, Lin, and Sidorov ("Atos") — are presented to the reader in one of the first chapters. Entering the twenty-second century the four boys will appear throughout the book becoming more mature and experienced, learning both professions and the meaning of life. In a way they act as our guides in this future world.

The preface of *Noon: Twenty-Second Century* contains two chapters ("Night on Mars" and "Almost the Same"). In the first chapter we become acquainted with Slavin; the second chapter deals with his student years. Their "homecoming" into the twenty-second century opens the first section, which is devoted mainly to their adaptation to this world ("Old-timer," "Two from the *Taimyr*," "The Moving Roads," "Homecoming"). Thus, the first section of the book introduces a new world not only to the main characters, but also to the readers. In addition, one chapter ("The Conspirators") brings in "the wonderful quartet."

The next section of the book is devoted mainly to the world of the future. In these stories Kondratev and Slavin have changed. They are no longer strangers in this world; they have acquired friends and families, as well as new professions. By this time Pol, Lin, Sidorov, and Gennadi have grown up and become full-fledged members of society. They all live and work in an atmosphere of constant searching, creativity, and inspiration.

The final section is rather short, as is the preface. In the last chapters of the book the main characters, fully grown and mature, have tasted the bitter experience of life and become rather old, but at the same time they have remained prudent, kind, and humane, in accordance with the "conception" at the beginning of the book. In the chapter entitled "Defeat," the reader parts with the by now experienced "Atos," who has lost much of his image as a romantic "hero," striving to accomplish senseless deeds. In "The Meeting" we part with Lin and Polly. The last story is prophetically entitled "What You Will Be Like." It deals with a future of this future world, a society of almost omnipotent people, who are even greater than powerful figures of religion and mythology.

The two seemingly independent plot lines pass through the book, and the central plot of the complete book spins around them. Why was it necessary to create the plot line about "the wonderful quartet"?

If the Strugatsky brothers had limited themselves to the characters of Slavin and Kondratev, the book would have been a Utopia in the classical form: our contemporaries become acquainted with the world of a distant future. But the authors have complicated and enriched the traditional scheme by introducing a different angle of perception: the contemporaries of this future world, living and progressing in it. For this reason, the quartet of boys from the Anyudin boarding school was conceived.

Besides Slavin, Kondratev, and "the wonderful quartet," the book is full of other rich and memorable characters. Each separate story and its characters is presented as an instant flash, as a "stop-shot." They remain an episode or a developing whole. Nevertheless, the reader believes in them; they are remembered as human beings and not as personified ideas.

Though seen only in a few episodes, one character is particularly worthwhile mentioning. He successfully competes with the main characters. This is Leonid Gorbovsky, a spaceship pilot, who eventually becomes a member of the Contact Commission. Gorbovsky, the hero of the novel *Far Rainbow*, plays an important structural role in *Noon: Twenty-Second Century*. As if combining and embracing the two plot lines, Gorbovsky is an idol of the Anyudin quartet, and at the same time he becomes the best and most important friend of Kondratev and Slavin, helping them to adjust to their new surroundings.

In a number of aspects Gorbovsky acts as the authors' spokesman, expressing their credo and acting as a representative of the wonderful future the Strugatsky brothers envision. The authors openly sympathize with Gorbovsky who embodies the world in which he lives. If Slavin and Kondratev are only "homecoming" and getting acquainted with the noon of the twenty-second century, and the quartet of juveniles is growing up and maturing (in a way also adapting to it), Gorbovsky is a full-fledged representative of this world in all aspects.

But what is the world presented by the Strugatsky brothers? How is it similar to or different from a great number of Utopian pictures created prior to the publishing of *Noon: Twenty-Second Century* and afterwards?

The authors present a society based on the principles of friendship, comradeship, and fraternity among people. This is not a mere declaration but the essence of human relations in the future. There is neither private property nor the exploitation of one man by another. At the same time, this society is not an anarchic commune, such as the one presented by Ursula K. Le Guin in her novel *The Dispossessed*. In her novel we see a "Communist society of paupers," whereas in *Noon: Twenty-Second Century* every citizen is rich by today's standards, because all the treasures of the society literally belong to him, and the whole society practically works for every citizen. But today's standards are not quite applicable, because in the world of the future every member devotes his efforts completely to society.

There are no such anachronisms as "political institutes" (to say nothing of judicial or administrative bodies), and money has fallen into oblivion as well. The world of *Noon: Twenty-Second Century* is a world of abundance. The authors devote much time to their interesting deliberations about the prospects of this world of the future, particularly to its economic problems. It is impossible to enumerate all of their forecasts, but it should be mentioned that all the problems inherent to progress (such as overpopulation, ecological crisis, personality leveling in the age of automation, and so on) have been eliminated as a result of solving the main social problem. This does not mean that the future society is a serene and eternally blissful Eden. On the contrary, the authors literally charge the reader with the activities, seething tempers, and young maximalism of this world. The problems have remained, but they are of a different character; from the "outer space sphere" they have passed to the "inner space sphere," to use the terminology of modern science fiction.

As in every company of boys, the four juveniles from the Anyudin boarding school dream about heroic deeds in space, but they are shocked to learn that the most respected professions in the world are those of teachers and doctors. The Strugatsky brothers have deliberately changed the scale of human values, thus emphasizing the notion that the human race of the future — the "people-gods" — will face the problem of problems in the interrelations with nature trying to secure their "employment" centuries ahead. This immense problem concerns the final elimination of social atavisms and the irrevocable consolidation of everything humane in man.

One basic criticism is usually made about all Utopias; and not without reason. Opponents of these societies raise this question: if the world is so perfect, what is left for dynamic and creative people? To put it in a nutshell — would Utopia not be too dull?

In their novel *Predatory Things of the Age*, the Strugatsky brothers have satirically derided such a narrow-minded attitude toward the aims of social progress. Its only aim has never been simply to feed and clothe people. Nor has it been to provide permanent entertainment for degraded idlers. The authors maintain that when these primary problems are solved, humanity will have to come down to solving the basic problems of reforming the world as well as the man himself.

Even if the world becomes free from famine, poverty, exploitation and the animosity, dullness, and envy resulting from them, there will remain such suffering as unhappy love, failures of mutual understanding, limitations of human possibilities in the face of the vastness of the problems to be solved. Or simply the phenomenon of time: none of the characters is immortal, and they know the bitter taste of remorse caused by the failure to fulfill one's lifework. They also know the torments of conscience, which punish mercilessly and impartially (for instance, in the story "The Meeting," old Pol cannot forgive his one mistake in the course of seventeen years). But first and foremost all of them are human, intellectual, and brought up in the humane traditions; therefore suffering does not terminate their life and cannot turn them into brutes.

The Strugatsky brothers repeatedly stress the importance of proper upbringing. Thus, "the wonderful quartet" appears in the world and in the book right after graduation from school. From the first chapters, the reader constantly learns about the pedagogics of the future world. Two basic principles are emphasized in the book: to make each man a personality and individual instead of a "small fry" in a production process; to bring up each man realizing that he is a part of the human race. Is there not a contradiction between individual and collective trends? By no means! According to the Strugatsky brothers this dialectical unity of the two principles is absolutely organic: first and foremost the man lives for society, but at the same time he remains a unique and original personality. One cannot help bringing in a comparison with the "yin" and "yang" principle of Annares-Urras from Le Guin's *The Dispossessed*. But that novel describes two extremes, whereas in *Noon: Twenty-Second Century* there exists a unity.

It is possible that this future educational system might evoke an ironical response from some of our contemporaries. Is it not unrealistic: children are taught that the most contemptible human qualities are cowardliness, mendacity, and aggression; that the word "sportsman" denotes the person who declines any useful social activity and bears a humiliating connotation; that the most important thing in this society, work, brings joy and happiness: it is life itself and not an obligation.

However, the educational program of the authors does not remain only a program; the children in the book are given the chance to see the results of its realization in their teachers. In this world the teacher's profession is open only to the most worthy and respectable people, such as former spacepilots, scientists, or artists. The teacher receives a quartet of pupils and mentors it through the whole school program up to graduation. How does he manage it? The teachers teach no subjects at all as we understand them today; this is done more skillfully with the help of teaching machines and textbooks. But the task of bringing up small children can be carried out only by a human being, and an outstanding one at that. It is that simple.

The authors tell us about the educational system for young people (whom we are to meet further) in the first chapters of the book. This introduction gives us a chance to understand and justify the motives and actions of the main characters. They are not gods beyond our ability to understand them; they do not possess supernatural physical or psychological qualities, though in our age they would set a number of world records in several kinds of sports simultaneously. But qualitatively they are quite different people, and the Western reader might consider them more fantastic than visitors from alien planets. The authors preserve a fine balance between the known, unknown, and surprising. This explains why at one moment the reader accepts the characters of the book as our contemporaries ("almost the same"), and at another they seem almost an unattainable ideal. This relates to the book as a whole. But unified as it is, the book consists of separate, memorable chapters, which prior to being collected were separate, interesting, and quite original stories. Individually, they contain plenty of interesting and picturesque ideas, details, and situations.

In its intensity and richness of problems *Noon: Twenty-Second Century* has very few analogues in the world of science fiction. And still the most important quality of the book is not the creation of distant worlds, but the presentation of people. The book expresses the belief of the authors that one day their imaginary pictures will not be accepted as speculative sociological experiments any more. Their belief pervades every page of the book, and makes us abstain from using the term "Utopian" in relation to *Noon: Twenty-Second Century.*

Vl. Gakov

NORSTRILIA

Author: Cordwainer Smith (Paul M. A. Linebarger, 1913-1966)
First book publication: 1975
Type of work: Novel
Time: Approximately A. D. 16,000
Locale: Norstrilia (Old North Australia), Mars, Earth

The adventures of Rod McBan, who buys the Earth but gives it up and returns to his native Norstrilia when he learns the real meaning of life

Principal characters:
RODERICK MCBAN, CLI, a very rich, very bright, very eccentric
    young Norstrilian
LORD REDLADY, his first protector
THE CATMASTER, his guru
ELEANOR, his stand-in
LAVINIA, his patient true love
C'MELL, a fabulously beautiful, wise, and trustworthy cat-woman
LORD JESTOCOST, a powerful chief of the Instrumentality and ally of
    the underpeople
E'TELEKELI, spiritual leader of the underpeople

Like Frank Herbert and J. R. R. Tolkien, Cordwainer Smith dreamed a world into being. In his twenty-seven "Instrumentality of Mankind" stories, Smith developed one of the most elaborate and extensive imaginary universes in science fiction — a universe of several thousand planets, each with its own weirdly appropriate creatures, culture, and terrain. Moreover, he linked these myriad planets by more than fourteen thousand years of history, in which the Instrumentality is the dominant, unifying force. Because it encompasses such breadth of space and depth of time, Smith's dream world has a captivating density and a richness of detail which have engrossed readers since the series began to unfold in the 1950's.

Norstrilia, which is the longest and one of the last of the "Instrumentality" tales, provides a particularly illuminating perspective on Smith's inventiveness with settings. It is the only novel in the group (the other twenty-six "Instrumentality" works are all short stories) and, although Smith died before he could complete his grand design for the whole series, we know that he intended *Norstrilia* to serve as a major focal point. In *Norstrilia* Smith amplified and explored many of the themes he had introduced in his short stories; by centering his novel on the contrasting cultures of two especially important planets in his system, Earth and Old North Australia (or Norstrilia), he pointed up the dynamic antithesis that shapes all one hundred and forty centuries of his fictional history.

Most simply, this basic antithesis is between logical positivism and intuitive spirituality. Most Lords and Ladies of the Instrumentality, and indeed most people throughout Smith's vast planetary system, are logical positivists; they believe that life is precisely what the physical senses declare it to be, wholly material. From their point of view the planet Norstrilia is one of the universe's great resources, because it is the sole producer of "stroon," a life-prolonging substance which gives almost all humans a life span of several hundred years. Thanks to "stroon" and other technological improvements, the human condition in the seventeenth millennium when *Norstrilia*'s action takes place, is no longer the nasty, brutish, and messy sort twentieth century readers must endure.

Surprisingly, however, the Norstrilians themselves quietly but systematically resist the effects if not the premises of the enlightened materialism to which Norstrilian "stroon" so significantly contributes. Instead of adopting the luxurious hedonism favored by Earth's humans, Norstrilians live in spartan simplicity, denying themselves fleshy comforts in order to protect and heighten what they believe to be their truest, most important resource — Norstrilian strength of character. Because it deliberately reintroduces discomforts, uncertainties, and even dangers into the materialistic Utopia designed and administered by the Instrumentality, Norstrilian culture epitomizes the "Rediscovery of Man" movement which forms a large part of Smith's world history. To Rediscovery people, exemplified in this novel by the Norstrilians, the "perfection" engineered by the Instrumentality's technocrats can only corrode and destroy human nature and human societies, for such notions of Utopia inaccurately assume that material ease is the one object of human desires.

But to Roderick McBan, CLI, *Norstrilia*'s central character, Norstrilian asceticism and Earthly hedonism alike fail to meet essential human needs. McBan first turns to the holographic image of Shakespeare's Hamlet, then to "Reconstituted Late Inglish Language Verse," for the wisdom he finds lacking in his native Norstrilian culture. These ancients instantly show him that the human condition is fundamentally, not incidentally or secondarily, psychological — that what one thinks determines what one experiences. Energized by this radically antimaterialistic sense of things, McBan exiles himself from Norstrilia and flies to Earth, which he has bought in the initial manic flurry of his new self-assertiveness. And on Earth he completes his personal version of rediscovering mankind: he enters the underpeople's mysterious subculture and is converted to their revolutionary religious outlook:

> Now it was all different. . . . He had his own problems, but they were no longer the problems of wealth or of survival. Somehow he had a confidence that a hidden, friendly power in the universe would take care of him, if he took care of others.

McBan gains this intuitive world view by undergoing a sort of primal scream therapy under the direction of the underpeople's principal spiritual teacher, the Catmaster. Much of what he learns in the Catmaster's "Department Store of Hearts' Desires" we are plainly meant to learn for ourselves in the pages of *Norstrilia*, which recounts that each place McBan visits really signifies a psychological rather than a physical locale. So Earth represents humanity's divided consciousness, split between the pragmatic, rational thinking which dominates Western civilization and the intuitive, emotional thought processes which Westerners have traditionally associated with women, (some) animals, and the inscrutable Orient. For the first several millennia of its existence the Instrumentality, symbolizing the organizing force in human consciousness, has allied itself with pragmatic intellectuality (whose philosophy is logical positivism) and suppressed the instincts and feelings (according to Smith, the core of intuitive spirituality); now, in the time of Roderick McBan, CLI, the psychological balances are shifting, and especially astute Chiefs of the Instrumentality, such as Lord Jestocost and Lady Alice More, are beginning to liberate the underpeople — to reaffirm the value of intuitions, instincts, and feelings in the psychological universe.

Read from this perspective, *Norstrilia* provides a vivid map of what Julian Jaynes has termed the broken-down bicameral mind. Smith appears to have anticipated Jaynes's theory that all human history originates in and is explainable by the breakdown of communications between the verbalizing, rationalizing, "sensible" left lobe of the human brain and the non-verbal, intuitive right lobe. But Smith, unlike Jaynes, argues that this split can be healed. This is the significance of Norstrilia, which stands for the mind on the verge of reintegration. By emphasizing simplicity, self-reliance, and family-centeredness, Norstrilian culture requires the balanced exercise of both left-lobe and right-lobe traits, and at the same time prevents too enthusiastic an attachment to the values of either half of consciousness. Insofar as it proposes that the Norstrilian life-style is the necessary preparatory discipline we, too, must follow if we hope to become whole, *Norstrilia* is a tract, not a map — Smith's sermon on what we must do to be psychologically saved.

Unfortunately, this novel, which sets forth the case for integration with many beguiling images, memorable characters, and dramatic incidents, fails to practice the very virtue it most insistently preaches. *Norstrilia*'s plot is conspicuously disunified. In fact, the book reads less like a novel than like two imperfectly joined novellas, strikingly dissimilar in focus and style. Excluding the obviously tacked-on "Theme and Prologue," *Norstrilia*'s first seven chapters form a unit dealing with the Old North Australian rites of passage which initiate McBan into manhood; this section centers on the personality of Rod McBan, whom it convincingly portrays as a youth with enormous psychological potential. The plot of these seven chapters consists of a series of harrowing ordeals which compel McBan to acknowledge, develop, and test his capabilities as an intuitive, rational, pragmatic, and feeling person; and the seventh chapter concludes with McBan in the midst of the most difficult challenge of all — testing whether his psyche can survive when his brain has been transplanted into a new body.

Then, following three jarringly choppy "bridge" chapters which remove

McBan to Mars and introduce us to numerous new, undeveloped characters, *Norstrilia*'s second sequence of eight chapters begins. Here McBan's role is primarily that of passive observer touring exotic Earth, while the plot centers on the intrigues of Lord Jestocost, C'Mell, and other underpeople. The function of this half of the book is to explore characters and themes from "The Ballad of Lost C'Mell," "The Dead Lady of Clown Town," and "Drunkboat." Indeed, *Norstrilia*'s second half is far more a sequel to these three short stories than a coherent continuation of *Norstrilia*'s original plot. In these eight chapters McBan's initiation experiences dwindle to minor, peripheral incidents, and his initiators are infinitely more interesting than he is. As a matter of fact, the Rod McBan who visits Earth is so limp and ordinary a young man that one is tempted to conclude that his great experiment has failed, and that his grandly promising psyche died on the surgeon's table.

Paradoxically, the problems with *Norstrilia*'s overall plotting spring, it seems, from the book's strongest and most attractive feature — the intense imaginativeness which vivifies individual scenes. Both here and in his short stories, Smith's best scenes dramatize the sense of wonder — the soul's encounters with an amazingly various, intriguingly numinous universe. McBan's moments in the Garden of Death, the Gap, and the Palace of the Governor of Night all represent his retreat from the world of Norstrilian received wisdom and common sense to the private place of his own interior selfhood; by focusing on McBan's expanding consciousness and building these scenes wholly out of the images in McBan's active intuition, Smith brings his character's adventures straight into our own minds. In the scenes involving the underpeople Smith is even more demanding of himself and us: instead of working through McBan's mediating consciousness, he compels us to perceive the meanings of the underpeople's words and actions for ourselves. Smith's utter fidelity to each imaginative vision — his insistence that every such vision live on its own terms — makes *Norstrilia* an extraordinarily fascinating and suggestive — although inconsistent — work.

Smith's emphasis on imaginative vision at the expense of intellectual outline is all the more interesting when one considers his formidably intellectual background. Actually "Cordwainer Smith" is the pen name of Paul Myron Anthony Linebarger, who was until his death in 1966 one of America's most expert authorities on the politics, history, and literatures of the Far East, as well as on psychological warfare. Fluent in six languages and intimately conversant with several Oriental and Occidental cultures, he used his science fiction chiefly as a vehicle for escaping any single culture's mindset, synthesizing his extraordinary wealth of information into an almost mystical search for a transcendent understanding of human nature and human history. Because its basis is intuitive rather than intellectual, *Norstrilia*'s numerous references to mythological, literary, historical, political, and scientific figures do not exclude most readers, as scholarly allusions usually do: for example, we know C'Mell to be an earth mother goddess because *Norstrilia*'s action forces us to appreciate her primal fertility, not because we happen to remember the role of Semele in Greek mythology.

Although Smith composed *Norstrilia* as a single, novel-length work, it was not published in that form during his lifetime. Smith himself divided *Norstrilia* into two shorter units and added a little explanatory padding to each, but it is not entirely clear whether he did this simply in order to get the story quickly into print by bringing it out in science fiction magazines (which did happen; these edited portions of *Norstrilia* were published in the 1960's), or in order to improve the story's form and focus. Whatever the case, the novel-length *Norstrilia*, which Smith's widow published almost ten years after Smith's death, expresses the vitality and openendedness of a good work-in-progress. And it challenges us to speculate on what Smith might have done with it, had he lived to explore his fictional universe more completely.

Jane Hipolito

Sources for Further Study

Reviews:

Best Sellers. XXXV, August, 1975, p. 148.

Book World. June 15, 1975, p. 4.

Library Journal. C, May 1, 1975, p. 883.

Magazine of Fantasy and Science Fiction. XLIX, August, 1975, p. 46.

New York Times Book Review. March 23, 1975, p. 30.

Publisher's Weekly. CCVII, January 13, 1975, p. 61.

NOVA

Author: Samuel R. Delany (1942-   )
First book publication: 1968
Type of work: Novel
Time: Near the beginning of the third millennium A.D.
Locale: The known galaxy, including Earth and Vorpis in Draco, Ark and the other
  world in Pleiades Federation, and New Brasillia in the Outer Colonies

*An obsessive interstellar quest, a super space opera that is also an exploration of
human emotions and personal involvement in a context of art and politics, and a highly
successful self-conscious fiction about the making of archetypal, mythically allusive
fictions*

> *Principal characters:*
> LORQ VON RAY, heir to the leadership of Pleiades Federation
> PRINCE RED, heir to Red-shift Limited, lifelong enemy of Lorq Von
>   Ray
> RUBY RED, Prince's sister and loved by both Prince and Lorq
> MOUSE, a gypsy metamusician from Earth
> KATIN, a moon-born apprentice novelist
> TYŸ and SEBASTION, crew members from Pleiades Federation
> IDAS and LYNCEOS, twins and crew members from the Outer Col-
>   onies
> CYANA VON RAY MORGAN, Lorq's aunt

Nova remains, over a decade since its publication, a unique work. Its influence, or the influence of its author's extraordinary expansion of the literary
possibilities inherent in science fiction, can be felt in almost all the best works
in the genre published since then. On the surface, *Nova* is the ultimate space
opera, in which a few superior beings battle for control over the fate of the
galaxy and all its inhabitants. Still, there is so much apparently superfluous
material attracting one's attention from the violent action of the main narrative
that the reader may begin to wonder why it is important. However, a second
trip through the novel reveals that Delany has made a palimpsest, layer after
layer of rich meaning surrounding his basic driving narrative.

Nova is a great adventure story of stunning narrative force, but it is many
other things as well. It is an experiment which pushes the limits of Alfred
Bester's pyrotechnics in *The Stars My Destination* (1956) even further; it is an
intriguing mythopoeic transformation of the story of Prometheus and of Indra's
Freeing of the Waters into science fiction terms; and it is one of the genre's
most successful attempts to re-create the mood of Greek tragedy. Delaney offers subtle and dramatic explorations of character in one of the most complete,
complex, and intelligent renderings of a future society to date; he also seriously investigates the nature of political and economic power and attempts an
intellectually valid historic/economic explanation of his interstellar society.
Nova is also an engaging comparative study of two types of the artist; it is one
of science fiction's boldest self-conscious works, a novel containing an ap-

prentice novelist who not only explains many of the forms and narrative patterns being used (like the Tarol/Grail Quest) but, it appears, eventually "writes" the book we are reading.

How does Delany do all this? He does it with style. *Nova,* like all his work since *Empire Star,* is brilliant, delightful, extravagant, intelligent, passionate, and witty; it is a paradigmatic example of what he means when he insists that "put in opposition to 'style,' there is no such thing as 'content.'" *Nova* is of immense formal significance to science fiction precisely because, as a powerful adventure tale, it continually challenges and transcends the genre expectations generated by its narrative line through its poetically charged and compressed style. Rather than provide a conventional pulp-realism window onto a typical action, its language — manifesting itself in the creation of characters whose felt humanity is invested with, but never overwhelmed by, mythic and symbolic significance and in the fully realized presentation of a "secondary universe" in which such an adventure appears the necessary and natural result of historic cultural, political, and social forces — insists that we confront deeper significances than the conventions ever engage on their own.

Nova's story is deceptively simple: Lorq Von Ray, inheritor of the leadership of one third of the inhabited galaxy, seeks to secure a sufficient amount of ultra-rare Illyrion to wrest control of intersteller transportation from his bitter enemies, Prince and Ruby Red of Earth, in the oldest sector, Draco. Lorq intends to gather massive quantities of the psychomorphic power-source from the core of a novaing star. Choosing a crew for his starship composed of two "cyborg studs" from each sector — Idas and Lynceos from the Outer Colonies, Tyÿ and Sebastion from his own Pleiades Federation, and Katin and Mouse from Draco — he goes after his star, with Prince and Ruby Red in hot pursuit.

Lorq's family and Red-shift Limited have a long history of conflict based on the political struggles accompanying the opening up of the newer sectors and especially the early Von Rays' determination to win sovereignty for the Pleiades Federation at almost any cost (the Von Rays are still called "pirates" in Draco). Lorq's father thinks he and Aaron Red have finally established a truce, so he doesn't tell Lorq of the feud, but Prince, whose missing arm has branded him a half-person since his birth, renews hostilities, partly because he hates Lorq, especially after Lorq tries to woo his sister, and partly because he realizes that if the Von Ray concerns somehow ever seize the vast economic power vested in Draco and Red-shift, their historic preeminence will be lost. Prince is willing to kill Lorq to prevent his own fall but he doesn't know what Lorq is planning. All he can do is trail his enemy and attempt to stop him before it is too late; but Lorq, "suddenly cursed with a purpose," seeks to keep just ahead of Prince and then destroy him by succeeding before his eyes. The action is fraught with suspense right up to the brilliant, violent climax, but much of that suspense is built upon the background provided by flashbacks and historical discussion.

For *Nova* is not only Lorq's story; it is also the story of those two different figures of the artist, who are caught up in his obsessive quest: Mouse, the metamusician whose approach to playing the sensory syrinx is emotional and intuitional; and Katin, the novelist-to-be who insists upon developing a complete theory of the novel before he even begins looking for a subject. Delany has structured his novel with extraordinary care: it not only begins *in media res* as Lorq seeks a crew for his final assault on a nova, but it begins with Mouse, not Lorq. At this point, Mouse is as ignorant of Von Ray and his position in the galaxy as we are; therefore, as he learns, through the action and his conversations with Katin, so do we. But we learn more, faster, because we soon share Katin's and Lorq's memories and perceptions as well. Unlike the classic science fiction novel, in which authorial exposition is the norm, *Nova* provides information through the perceptions and thoughts of three of its characters; thus every description informs us both by what is perceived and by who perceives it.

Chapter One is essentially Mouse's, including the flashback which explains both the fear he has lived with "all his short, shattered life" and his attempt to pursue "the intricate process of becoming himself," whole and unafraid. Chapter Two is Katin's, and its flashback does much the same for him, suggesting why he has chosen the archaic art of the novel. In Chapter Three, the already archetypally heroic figure of Lorq (as perceived through Mouse and Katin) is humanized in a much longer and more complexly historical flashback. Because Lorq, Ruby, and Prince are members of a special and immensely powerful galaxy-wide aristocracy, they are "unique," living on a cultural plane where the rules by which ordinary people live do not apply. Like ancient half-divine heroes, they are "beyond good and evil." Or are they? Delany's great achievement in this novel is to break the heroic stereotype even as he explores its literary validity. His careful construction of certain psychologically significant scenes in Lorq's childhood and youth creates a flawed, deeply human, and sympathetic character. Lorq's decision, in the bloody moment of his triumph, to accept full responsibility, *without guilt*, for changing the political and economic structure of the galaxy is therefore all the more powerful in its impact. Nevertheless, though he fights for change and against stasis, Lorq, who like Prometheus is both culture hero and criminal, is frozen at the end in the suffering attitude of his greatest act. It is for Mouse and Katin to carry on in the utterly changed and everchanging universe which Lorq's heroic act has created.

Through their involvement in Lorq's obsessive quest, Katin and Mouse have both achieved a maturity in which they can live as they desire. Mouse has conquered his fear by facing the implications of the violent acts it has driven him to, acts he can no longer accept in himself (though at the end his proper sense of personal safety prevents him from trying to see the nova as it happens). He is now free to follow his art wherever it leads him, a wandering minstrel with a whole galaxy to wander. Katin has not only grown psychologically, he has found his subject (perhaps in the terrible glory he had the courage to view). He will now write *Nova*; and this final flash of novelistic self-consciousness newly illuminates all of Katin's pronouncements on both the theory of the novel and the archetypal patterns their adventure has followed, bringing them into new focus. They are not interruptions in the fast-moving plot but segments of a complex web of language containing both that plot and the fascinating meta-fiction of its telling. *Nova* is not only one of the finest science fiction novels but a theoretical exploration of the making of such a novel. This level of discourse causes it to transcend its generic frame even as it remains valid science fiction.

Within the generic frame, *Nova* achieves a fullness of being in its cultural extrapolation of a technologically advanced civilization matched by only a handful of science fiction novels since (and one of those is Delany's own *Triton*). Delany incorporates all his hard information through genuinely interesting conversations, casual references, and carefully natural descriptions. Even the longest of Katin's expositions have fictional propriety; like all the other forms of information in *Nova*, they fit easily into the ongoing process that is the whole story.

Delany's most important technological extrapolation is the humanized and democratic technology of "neural plugs and sockets" which enable individuals of all classes to "plug into" all the devices and machines in their environment. As Katin puts it, echoing Marshall McLuhan, "it's a totally cross-cultural phenomenon — part of the way of considering all machines as a direct extension of man that has been accepted by all social levels since Ashton Clark." Delany does not simply demonstrate the centrality of this technology through its ubiquity in work and play, he also shows the social alienation people without sockets, like Mouse's Gypsy tribe, would suffer. As well, he suggests how language (an important indicator of culture as Delany knows and shows in all his later novels) would reflect socket technology's presence. Mouse, like Katin, is a "registered, tested, competent cyborg stud," and the sexual symbolism is explicit even as it transcends gender (Tyÿ is a woman: this future is essentially nonsexist). Prince Red's impotence on all levels is symbolized by his missing arm, for he lacks one of the four sockets a person needs for full control of any cyborg situation.

Delany uses language, specifically speech, to reveal differences of class, education, and cultural background. People from Pleiades Federation speak in a certain way, for example, though Lorq generally follows Draco usage as befits a member of galactic aristocracy. Delany also provides histories for all three sectors, various suggestive insights into the forms of education and myriad subtle little details revealing how the composite culture influences everyone's behavior. Finally, he subjects this background to the philosophical speculations of various characters, implying their dynamic relationships to it and to one another. Thus the use of the Tarot, with its "symbols and mythological images that have recurred and reverberated through forty-five centuries of human history," combined with Katin's explanation of why it has become important in the post-Ashton Clark universe as a nonsuperstitious method of propagating "an educated commentary on present situations," suggests the spiritual roots and sophistication of *Nova*'s civilization. The historical analysis placing that civilization's beginnings in the twentieth century, with the major exception of the invention of neural plugs in the twenty-third, is also fascinating.

Delany has always been a highly allusive writer who often tries "to say several things at the same time." In *Nova*, he weaves a variety of Eastern and Western myths into the structure of his narrative, of which the battle between Indra and the cloud-hoarding Vritra serpent and the various forms of the Grail quest investigated in Jessie L. Weston's *From Ritual to Romance* are most prominent. Literary allusions also abound, adding to the fullness of *Nova*'s fictional future history and reminding us that it *is* fictional, the product of a mind (Katin's, Delany's) steeped in literary tradition. The short history of the naming of the planets of the burnt-out sun, "the Dim, Dead Sister," is a good example of this process. The first explorer named the outermost planet Elysium, then, seeing how inhospitable to life the worlds were, he named the middle one Dis. His fate, however, "suggests the agenbite of inwit come too late," for he crashed on the third one, which "remained unnamed, and to this day was referred to as the other world, without pomp, circumstance, or capitals." Delany then adds that "the other world's oldest city . . . had been very carefully named: the City of Dreadful Night." Though witty and entertaining, this passage also implies the power which ancient mythic dreams and nightmares retain in *Nova*'s invented future culture.

Delany's poetic imagery, his often startling juxtapositions, his ellisons of syntax, all contribute to one's sense that *Nova* is one of the most literate and literary of science fiction novels. Sometimes he strives to concentrate too many effects in one short passage — "the Serpent, animated and mechanical, symbol of this whole sequined sector of night" is perhaps a bit pretentious, and "animated" is ambiguously obscure — yet his willingness to attempt such a compressed, intense play of language more often than not yields riches too seldom found in science fiction. The image of a net — of metal links for fishing (and with which Ruby tries to kill Lorq), of historical moments, of cultural, economic, and psychological strands, of all the people of the galaxy, of art and music, and, most important of all, of language — occurs again and again in *Nova*, binding its various systems of signification into single resonant aesthetic form which ultimately transcends all attempts at paraphrase or analysis. *Nova* is a superb experience on whatever level the fortunate reader wishes to engage it.

Douglas Barbour

Sources for Further Study

Criticism:

Miesel, Sandra. "Samuel R. Delany's Use of Myth in *Nova*," in *Extrapolation*. XII (May, 1971), pp. 86-93. Miesel analyzes Delany's writings and praises him highly for his use of Indian mythology.

Reviews:

Analog. LXXXII, November, 1968, pp. 166-167.

Galaxy. XXVII, January, 1969, pp. 189-192.

Magazine of Fantasy and Science Fiction. XXXV, November, 1968, pp. 43-46.

New Worlds. CLXXXV, December, 1968, p. 61.

SF Commentary. XIII, July, 1970, pp. 9-10 and XIV, August, 1970, pp. 7-10 and XVII, November, 1970, pp. 38-41.

Speculation. III, January, 1970, pp. 17-20.

NOVA EXPRESS

Author: William S. Burroughs (1914-   )
First book publication: 1964
Type of work: Novel
Time: The present
Locale: The Earth

The plan by a gang of interplanetary criminals to cause the Sun to become a nova is frustrated by an interstellar force for good, the Nova Police

> *Principal characters:*
> INSPECTOR LEE, an official of the Nova Police
> AGENT K9, an operative of the Nova Police
> URANIAN WILLY, defector from the Nova Mob
> THE NOVA MOB, including Sammy the Butcher, Green Tony, Iron Claws, The Brown Artist, Jacky Blue Note, Limestone John, Izzy the Push, the Subliminal Kid, and others

Since the pulps of the 1930's spread their four-color glow over science fiction, writers and readers of the genre have often been defensive; authors such as C. S. Lewis, George Orwell, and Aldous Huxley have been cited time and again in answer to those who would deny literary merit to science fiction. William Burroughs presents those defenders with a quandary. It might seem pleasant to be able to identify science fiction with a figure so determinedly avant-garde, yet Burroughs — Beat, dope addict, expatriate, intimate of Jack Kerouac and Gregory Corso, *cause célèbre* for Allen Ginsberg and Norman Mailer — is for many admirers of science fiction not so much an asset as an embarrassment. Is Burroughs, as the critic David Ketterer claims, one of the few American writers of superior science fiction? No, certainly not. *Nova Express*, stripped of the pretensions of its experimental style, is not even moderately interesting. It is therefore on an analysis of that style that an analysis of the novel must depend, and with that style that an evaluation must begin.

Although only a foolish reader would claim certainty, the plot of *Nova Express* seems straight out of a Doc Smith thriller. A motley assemblage of criminals, the Nova Mob, has psychological control of the Earth. The Mob in some way duplicates its members by encoding their personalities in viruses which "possess" the psyches of those humans they infect. The members, who cannot otherwise live on Earth, use their hosts to exacerbate human conflicts. It is not entirely clear what they get out of all of this, unless they derive some pleasure, profit, or sustenance from human emotional conflict. When the conflicts rise to a certain pitch, the sun becomes a nova (don't look for Burroughs to explain why), and they move on to the next planet. They have done this in the past and will continue to do it in the future, unless they are checked by the Good Guys of the universe, the Nova Police. The Police move in, are (or are not) successful, and the Earth is (or is not) saved.

The style is the reason for the hesitancy of the last sentence. It is hard to say what the novel presents as reality, since Burroughs argues that what we think of as reality is simply a "scanning pattern" imposed in the novel (and on us, if we see *Nova Express* as a metaphor of soceity) by sinister forces. The way Burroughs chooses to break the psychic chains is to destroy the substance of which they are forged — language. And one cannot argue the efficacy of his method: language comes close to being destroyed in the book. The method he chooses, the "fold-in" technique, is explained and illustrated in the chapter "This Horrible Case." One selects an appropriate passage; in this case, a page from Franz Kafka's *The Trial*. A page of the author's own composition is then folded in half lengthwise and laid on the page from Kafka. The material is then presumably copied off, joining the left half of Burrough's lines to the right half of Kafka's. In the second step (and here we are on less firm ground) the hybrid copy is tape-recorded. This accomplished, the author then plays the tape, stopping it at random and recording short phrases, perhaps by free association. By then, little resemblance to the original remains.

Perhaps Burroughs' process is not as mechanical as the above description asserts. If folding-in consists only of juxtaposing two passages of prose, and selecting those constructions that satisfy some subconscious sense of fitness, then the author's procedure is selection and arrangement and differs only in degree from that which any writer follows. Its chief difference would be the method's restriction of the vocabulary of the writer to that limited set of words which appear in the chosen prose sample, and in throwing over the difficulties of composition for the easier task of allowing the well of the subconscious to overflow.

Whether such a method can in fact succeed at the task the author sets for it depends on the relation of language to reality. As a minimum requirement, language must at least impinge on reality. If no relation exists between the two, then changing one will not affect the other. If we examine various theories of the relation of language and reality, we may be no closer to recognizing the strange beast that is *Nova Express*, but we will have identified some of its progenitors.

Plato discusses the subject in the dialogue *Cratylus*, in which the man for whom the work is named serves as the target for Socrates' cool common sense. Cratylus believes that reality molds language, producing a short of natural correspondence between the word and the concept it names. Socrates at first agrees, and even supplies evidence: for example, the sound signified by the Greek letter *rho*, he argues, is produced with quick movements of the tongue, and is hence well-suited for use in a word like *rhoein*, "to flow." After a number of such instances, though, Socrates reverses his position and cites numerous counterexamples, leaving the whole argument up in the air.

Cratylus represents an extreme view of the relation between concept and word, one seldom encountered in linguistic theory today, that the concept calls forth or creates the associated bits of language that represent it. The exact reverse of this idea — that the word creates the concept — is prepared for by the works of the Swiss linguist, Ferdinand de Saussure (1857-1913). Central to de Saussure's system is the *sign*, the linkage of a concept and an acoustic image. (The acoustic image is not the specific sounds we hear, but our remembrance of the sounds.) In the notion of a sign, we see again a close connection between the word and the concept, so intimate a connection that a change in one of the parts will necessarily bring about a change in the other. Cratylus would certainly have agreed that an altered concept produces an altered acoustic image. However, neither his position nor a third position, that the relation between word and concept is arbitrary, can accommodate de Saussure's notion that a change in the acoustic image creates a change in the concept.

The way, then, was already cleared for a theory like that of Benjamin Lee Whorf (1897-1941), who would claim that the particular language entirely constrains the way its speakers perceive reality: the word creates the concept. The Whorf Hypothesis, as it is sometimes called, was a provocative and fertile idea for many a science fiction writer. The members of the Inner Party, creators of Newspeak in George Orwell's *Nineteen Eighty-Four* (1949), adopt it as an article of faith and use it to manipulate the inhabitants of Oceania. The founders of Anarres, in Ursula Le Guin's *The Dispossessed* (1974), embrace it wholeheartedly when they construct the artificial language that becomes their national tongue. A wizard of Breakness, in Jack Vance's *The Languages of Pao* (1958), employs the Whorf Hypothesis as his chief weapon in achieving the desires of his megalomania. As these examples suggest (and they could easily be multiplied by ten), there is something sinister in a conjunction of the Whorf Hypothesis and the power to implement it.

Can we say, then, that Burroughs builds the Whorf Hypothesis into *Nova Express*? Not entirely. He does assume the accuracy of the theory, but whereas Whorf believed in an underlying reality that languages may obscure or reveal, it seems clear that Burroughs entirely rejects the notion of "reality"; for him all is image, all is illusion. There would seem little hope, then, in trying to reform or somehow purify language to make it more transparent. Rather, since all images are false, and since all languages create images, the answer can only be silence, a tactic that is described several times as the ultimate weapon of the Nova Police.

It is an overstatement to say that Burroughs' novels attempt the destruction of language — what they aim for is the more modest goal of destruction of syntax. This end is approached by several means. One is erratic punctuation, consisting of a heavy use of dashes, the syntactically most neutral mark of punctuation. A second is the frequent, though not total, elimination of what are sometimes called function words: articles, prepositions, and conjunctions. Thus, for example, we read "Show your cards all players." The sentence becomes ambiguous. A comma would make it clear that the statement is directed to the players: "Show your cards, all players." The insertion of *to*, on the other hand, gives a different meaning: "Show your cards *to* all players." Burroughs offers something else in the place of the syntactic signals that show us the interconnections of the words.

Burroughs' folding-in method places unrelated words and phrases within the deformed structures, and, since humans make the natural assumption that language-like material conveys meaning, the readers attempt to discover (or even supply) a meaning by making associations between the words and phrases. One example will suffice. In the following passage, Uranian Willy is working with the Nova Police to frustrate the efforts of the Mob. He is about to liberate an area from their domination:

> . . . he was under sentence of death in Maximum Security Birth Death Universe. So he
> sounded the words that end "Word" —
> Eye take back color from "word" —
> Word dust everywhere now like soiled stucco on the buildings. Word dust without color
> drifting smoke street. Explosive bio advance out of space to neon.

It is possible to make sense of this passage in the context of the novel as a whole: Willy, like every other creature, is born into a universe which has entropy as its material end (the First Law of Thermodynamics). The universe may be compared to a maximum security prison, since no one can escape from it (the Third Law of Thermodynamics). Yet Willy has agreed to help the Nova Police, and he destroys the Nova Mob's false images by saying the words "Eye take back color from 'word.'" The false images controlling the area have an apparent reality (have "color") because the "eye" (the "I," the observer) has endowed them with it through language. If the eye takes back its color, if the observer withdraws that apparent reality by refusing to use the language, then the images ("Word") disappear. What they leave behind is evidence of their falsehood: "Word dust," which drifts everywhere. The exposed shams, "Word dust without color," are seen to be "drifting" like "smoke" through the "street." Uranian Willy has been changed by The Biologic Court's sentence to a more independent being: he is an "Explosive bio advance out of space," and he returns an independent view in vivid colors, "to neon," to the observer, to whom it rightfully belongs.

The difficulty with this method of reconstruction by paraphrase should be obvious. The reconstructed text will differ unpredictably from reader to reader until one wonders whether their several understandings of the text share a common kernel of meaning. If various readers find different meanings in the work, then communication, chancy under the best of circumstances, has been hindered, and hindered unnecessarily, one feels. Which audience does Burroughs write for? Consideration of the audience has disappeared, and rhetorical strategies, such as the multiplication of ambiguities, become pointless.

Where understanding ceases, plot ceases. Where actions are incomprehensible, character evaporates. Where descriptions are random, setting is lost.

So dependent are the elements of fiction on language that a shattered grammar places an enormous handicap on the writer. And if that handicap is self-imposed, one must question the writer's judgment. Although marketed as a novel, *Nova Express* is unquestionably something else; perhaps the best term for it is one advanced by the French philosopher Michel Foucault, *heterotopia*. In a passage quoted by Samuel R. Delany in an appendix to his novel *Triton*, Foucalt explains:

> *Heterotopias* are disturbing, probably because they make it impossible to name this *and* that, because they shatter or tangle common names, because they destroy "syntax" in advance, and not only the syntax with which we construct sentences but also that less apparent syntax which causes words and things (next to and opposite one another) to "hold together.". . . heterotopias. . . desiccate speech, stop words in their tracks, contest the very possibility of grammar at its source; they dissolve our myths and sterilize the lyricism of our sentences.

The heterotopia, of which *Nova Express* is a far better example than *Triton*, aims at making fiction impossible, at leaving only silence in its wake. But if fiction is destroyed, what follows afterward will not be silence, but the noise of the jungle, which was forgotten for the first time a hundred thousand years ago when one of our ancestors, sitting by a campfire, told the first story.

Walter E. Meyers

THE OCTOBER COUNTRY

Author: Ray Bradbury (1920-   )
First book publication: 1955
Type of work: Short stories

A collection of nineteen weird tales and stories about people who perceive reality in unusual ways

Ray Bradbury has had a long productive career writing short stories, novels, poetry, plays, and screenplays for both film and television. Although a great deal of his popular fame rests on *Fahrenheit 451* (1953) and *The Martian Chronicles* (1950), his earlier short stories are also indicative of his imaginative genius for creating unique and fantastic realities. *The October Country*, a new compilation of previously published short stories, appropriately appeared in the month of October, 1955. The title of the collection symbolizes the encompassing sense of weird surrealism present in most of the stories. Bradbury's people live outside of normal space and time. They inhabit a country where ". . . people are autumn people, thinking only autumn thoughts. Whose people passing at night on the empty walks sound like rain."

A story which encapsulates this image is "The Cistern." Two sisters, Anna and Juliet, sit inside on a gloomy, rainy day. Anna, staring intensely out the window, suddenly senses that there is a "dead" city in the cisterns beneath their streets. She becomes involved in a lengthy romantic daydream about the life two lovers share in this watery underground. Finally, she feels that she knows the man involved and, furthermore, that she is the woman needed to complete the picture. Acting on this knowledge, she joins him under the streets, leaving Juliet to ponder the mystery of her action. Bradbury has presented a person who, once she has arrived at the point of departure from reality, must follow the logic of the insight gained. Anna's new perception becomes her own reality, and she acts accordingly. The life in the cistern has captured more than her imagination and replaces her previous life with her sister. Bradbury is not concerned with why Anna has met this fate, only that she has met it.

All of Bradbury's protagonists are trapped by this same isolated view of life and reality. In some cases like "The Dwarf," this separation is caused by a real problem such as physical deformity; while in others, such as "The Wind" and "The Crowd," the hero is caught because he dared seek an answer to a mystery presented by life. Some victims are simple innocents who stumble into the autumn country, as in "The Scythe," "The Emissary," and "The Cistern." The twist which makes these stories so intriguing is that most of the protagonists begin life as ordinary people surrounded by ordinary thoughts in normal environments. Yet there is some unknown special quality which marks them and eventually propels them into the October Country; their uniqueness is highlighted by the presence of normal characters in the stories.

In the story "The Wind," the main character, Allin, is never actually present. The action is related through his old friend, Herb, who is spending an ordinary evening at home with his wife and some friends. Allin's perception of the wind as an evil hunter is suspect, especially since this is not the first time he has telephoned for help. Herb's wife and, to some extent, Herb believe him to be slightly insane and very paranoid. By the end of the evening Herb has acknowledged the validity of Allin's belief and mourns the loss of his friend. The reader must also accept the real menace the wind has been, although the other characters never accept it.

Bradbury continually prods the reader's perception of reality by presenting situations which begin with fact, but then ask "What if. . . ?" or "Suppose. . . ?" The answers and situations posed in these stories reveal a vivid imagination capable of building totally separate worlds next to, and within, our own. In "The Scythe," a simple family man seeking a way to support his family becomes, quite literally, the reaper of Death. Although he is innocently forced into this new grim reality, he alone is aware of the significance of his task. He still has his ordinary human feelings despite his elevation to a superhuman role, and he reacts with a maniacal fervor to the necessity of killing his family. As a result, wars and holocausts beset the real world, while his neighbors passing the field only casually wonder at his frantic pace. This final irony strengthens the overall impression created and recalls the many farmers we have passed on quiet country roads.

"Jack-in-the-Box" also depicts a parallel world in which Bradbury has constructed a separate reality out of Developmental Psychology 101. Daddy was God, killed by Beasts in the Outside. Mother is the Provider, Protector, Teacher, Keeper of the Keys, and Giver of Gifts. Mother has created this allegorical world, and the strain of maintaining eventually overcomes her. The innocent child, who had been trapped in this warped world like Jack-in-the Box, escapes at the Mother's death and crosses over into normal reality. He has carried with him an ironic tie with his past as he exlaims "I'm glad I'm dead," to the wonder of the Beasts who overhear him.

Bradbury's stories are windows through which we glimpse other realities. The reader is asked to suspend his own sense of reality and accept the view offered. Once this has been done, each story is consistent and logical within its own frame of reference. Various methods are used to create this suspension of normality. Several stories take for granted the existence of other life forms. "The Man Upstairs" is a vampire. "Uncle Einar" has green wings, and his family consists of a whole variety of spooks and witches who gather during "The Homecoming." Carnivals are also often used as a background for this surrealistic activity. Since such places are usually filled with hucksters and sleight-of-hand artists, they make a fitting locale for "The Dwarf" and an excellent starting place for "The Jar." Many of these stories were previously collected under the title *Dark Carnival*, published in 1947.

Death is another motif which runs throughout the collection. In "There Was an Old Woman," Bradbury presents lovable Aunt Tildy, who is so strong-willed that she refuses to die. After bullying the local undertaker into returning her stolen body, she inhabits it forever, proud of her triumph. We don't know whether or not she actually remains alive, but she carries on as if she does, and in this land, belief is reality. Another Bradbury character survives death by dying symbolically. After reading "The Strange Death of Dudley Stone," one wonders whether Dudley will survive physical death as comfortably. In "The Emissary" and "The Lake," the Living remain tied to the Dead and are drawn away from life into a gray uncertain fate. Bradbury often intermingles the world of the Dead with our own.

In his morbid themes, Bradbury resembles Edgar Allan Poe. He is different, however, because he has avoided Poe's singular fixation with only the macabre aspects of life and death. Bradbury uses these themes only as one form of an altered frame of reference. Each story presents a completely separate perception of reality, often only subtly different from our own. The story's development out of that norm is what traps the reader into acknowledging the plausibility of the alternate reality presented. The titles of the stories, like the title of the collection, symbolize the key image or concept around which each new reality is centered. Each title is like a picture title or a news bulletin, around which Bradbury builds his story. Although the scope of each story is limited to one major image, each story shares a common landscape: the October Country. It is Bradbury's ability to evoke vivid moods from a wealth of detail in describing his fictional territory which marks him as a major contributor to today's science fiction literature.

Christine Gladish

Sources for Further Study

Criticism:

Slusser, George Edgar. *The Bradbury Chronicle*. San Bernardino, Calif: Borgo Press, 1977, pp. 10-26. A detailed analysis of the novel is given here, providing an insight into the author's style of writing.

Reviews:

Amazing Stories. XXX, February, 1956, p. 119.

Analog. LVII, April, 1956, pp. 147-148.

Galaxy. XI, March, 1956, pp. 96-98.

Magazine of Fantasy and Science Fiction. X, February, 1956, pp. 94-95.

New Worlds. LI, September, 1956, pp. 127-128.

OCTOBER THE FIRST IS TOO LATE

Author: Fred Hoyle (1915-   )
First book publication: 1966
Type of work: Novel
Time: 1966, 1917, 425-424 B.C., A.D. 8000, and beyond human time
Locale: England, Scotland, New York City, California, Hawaii, France, Athens, Russia, and Mexico City

As Earth passes through a strongly modulated electronic signal wave, temporal discontinuities create the unprecedented interfacing of different epochs and their cultures from the past, present, and future of Earth history

> *Principal characters:*
> RICHARD _____, the Narrator, a composer-musician
> JOHN SINCLAIR, F.R.S., Nobel laureate in theoretical physics of elementary particles
> ALEX HAMILTON, a Scots musician and friend of the Narrator
> ART CLEMENTI, an American scientist
> THE PRIME MINISTER
> MELEA, Priestess of Apollo in Athens, 424 B.C., but actually a woman of the future
> NERIA, Delphic priestess and another woman of the future

Fred Hoyle is a well-known English astronomer, mathemetician, and physicist. He has to his credit many scientific articles and books, but he is best known for his research and publications in astonomy. When he is not teaching astronomy at Cambridge or doing research in the Mount Wilson or Palomar observatories, he devotes himself to one of his hobbies — music and science fiction writing. Unlike most of his other novels, *October the First Is Too Late* is not a textbook of hard science fiction. It does deal with a phenomenon of astronomy and with the confrontation of human cultures under the direction of an alien intelligence, but the mechanism of the plot is a variation of time travel and parallel world tales. In other words, *October the First Is Too Late* is a science fantasy. The qualities that make this novel a major contribution to the literature of science fiction are those which transcend the ingenious idea of the time-space discontinuities to include brilliant speculations on the interrelationship between science and art as modes of perception, a fantastic variation on the Heisenberg uncertainty principle, and in the end something like a cosmic morality tale.

There are several extraordinary features of Hoyle's story of the shuffling of human time-space coordinates. To begin with, the story is designed in a way that deliberately recalls an elaborate musical composition made up of many movements with different but interrelated themes and connected by the development of certain motifs and phrases. Beginning with Chapter One, "Prelude," and concluding with Chapter Fifteen, "Coda," the reader's perceptions, and to a considerable extent his reactions, are controlled by the movement of the story. That movement is, as the chapter headings suggest, more musical than mathematical.

Another unusual aspect of this scientific romance (Wells's term seems particularly appropriate in this case) is the viewpoint of the first person Narrator. We know him only as Richard, "Dicky" actually, in the one reference in which his friend Sinclair addresses him by name. It is through the perceptions of the Narrator that we meet the other characters and experience the strange events of a cosmic experiment in which wildly diverse and chronologically remote periods interface across boundaries that are, for a time, geographical rather than temporal. It is also in terms of the Narrator's viewpoint that we must try to interpret what is happening, how, why, and finally what it means. While these questions are all clearly related, they are also different; and the differences are directly related to the intentions of this extraordinary novel.

The effect of bringing together moments of human cultural history and having them all coexist on Earth is similar to that produced on Billy Pilgrim when he becomes unstuck from time in Vonnegut's *Slaughterhouse-Five* (1969). The effect was not only to change the way Billy experienced events, as nonsequential rather than as serialized, but also to transform his consciousness of human history and its meaning. Thus, to a certain degree, the reader's own consciousness is transformed as the imaginative byproduct of involvement in the narrative. Yet, there are important differences between Vonnegut's intentions and those of Hoyle. In Hoyle's story, it is not merely the hero who comes unstuck while everyone else experiences life in the ordinary way, but rather it is the world itself which has been taken to pieces and reassembled anachronistically as the result of the transit of a powerful, modulated energy beam from the sun. Somehow — and we are never given a clear answer to how the trick is done — history is scrambled to permit the coexistence of several historical epochs: Athens in 425 B.C.; Europe in 1917; Hawaii, Australia, and England in 1966; Mexico in A.D. 8000; and the Earth perhaps a million years or more in the future.

The unfolding of the narrative is remarkable for the way in which it brings the reader to feel, if not to understand, the implications of the bizarre changes which the world undergoes. Events proceed after the fashion of a good mystery in which the reader is constantly challenged to interpret an apparently random series of events and make some kind of plausible sense out of them. As the familiar boundaries of the world and the life experience of the characters undergo perplexing and fantastic changes, we are given two consistent guides to interpreting the seemingly discontinuous experience: science, especially mathematics, and art, especially music. The underlying theme of this novel is what science and art are finally able to make of such experiences and of such a world. The answers reveal the powers and limitations of both as they attempt to express the mind and the soul of the human species.

Significantly, the story begins as the Narrator is preparing a set of variations connected by a common musical theme for the 1966 Festival of Contemporary Music in Cologne. He is interrupted in his labors by an overpowering inspiration, "a tremendous tune, the melody of a lifetime," as he is walking along the Cornish cliffs listening to the waves. Caught up in the moment, the Narrator composes a great symphonic work for full orchestra which becomes the first of many affirmative statements of the greatness of the human spirit. This opening also introduces several other important themes. One is the Narrator's stand in the controversy of modern *versus* traditional music. This opinion is expanded in the course of the novel's development to encompass larger and greater questions than the Narrator's preference for the fuller and more romantic qualities of traditional music.

Another theme involves the Narrator's response to the events that buffet him about in the course of the story. Although, to a degree, he later becomes Sinclair's Watson in keeping a record of the events which subsequently transform their world, he is also an interpreter of those events through the music he writes and the music of the classical and romantic composers he plays. One more important theme worked into the fabric of the narrative at the outset is the question of the meaning of time and the significance of patterns or designs in the human experience of events. From the point of view of the scientist, as Sinclair declares early on, there is no such thing as the common-sense assumption of time as an ongoing stream, a steady progression from past to future. The Narrator's response to this view is to contrast the experience of music in which arrangement and sequence are the significant thing about the art form. At the beginning, therefore, we are introduced to the conflicting and yet complementary views of science and art.

The Cologne concert is a fiasco; the Narrator's composition is roundly booed because it does not conform to contemporary musical prejudices. Upon returning to England, the Narrator meets John Sinclair, an old school friend and now one of the foremost scientists of his time, a Nobel Prize-winner. On a walking tour of Scotland, they experience strange periods of blackout, for which there is no apparent explanation. Sinclair is at work on a problem relating to American space launchings, and he invites the Narrator to come with him for a week or so on a visit to the United States. This visit proves to be a furious round of work, incredible speculations designed to fit incredible events, and a round of parties designed to ease the tensions in which the Narrator's playing and choice of music reflect an increasing depth of emotion and inquiry into the great mysteries of life and death and the role of the creative imagination.

Sinclair's hypotheses grow and evolve in response to the unfolding discoveries of the American scientists. An astonishing modulation in the region of one hundred megacycles is discovered and traced to the region of the sun. It appears to be a beam of infrared radiation designed to transmit large amounts of information. Rather than resisting the implications of the theory, both the

Narrator and Sinclair seek verification. For Sinclair, the issue is simple enough: the important thing is to know that reasoning works, he tells the Narrator, not where it leads. Sinclair speculates that the modulation may be coming from an interstellar or intergalactic relay station, or that the transmissions involving an enormous volume of communications are processing biological information, perhaps information needed to construct human beings. Either way, it seems logical to assume that the signal implies the agency of some unknown alien beings who are using it for some purpose of their own which may or may not be related to Earth and human history. While Sinclair and the Narrator are at the Hawaii tracking station, they are informed that the United States has been attacked. At least, that is the assumption, because suddenly all radio and television communication with the mainland stops.

Sinclair and the Narrator take a reconnaissance flight to the mainland and find that all signs of twentieth century civilization on the west coast have disappeared, and that the area seems to have reverted to wilderness. The flight continues inland: Denver, Chicago, New York have vanished, and in their place the forests have returned. The only signs of human life are primitive shacks of America in the fourth millennium. Meanwhile, the flight continues to London, which has remained stuck in 1966. More surprises await them there. The ministers of government are trying to accommodate themselves to the bewildering transformation. The most immediate issue, however, is what to do about the great war on the continent of Europe, where it is September, 1917. The issue Hoyle raises is an obvious and yet provocative one. Britain of 1966 does not share or accept the mentality that was typical of Britain in 1917. The response is immediate and universal — the carnage must cease. The country makes its demands clear to all the parties, and the Prime Minister arranges a demonstration that convinces the continental powers of 1917 that Britain (of 1966) has the power to impose a Pax Britannica if she chooses. The demonstration is simple and convincing. A modern stereo system is played for the heads of state after they hear an early phonograph record played on one of the primitive hand-cranked phonographs of the period. The analogy is easily extended to modern *versus* early twentieth century weapons. The unexpected peace treaty is welcomed by the men at the front as a miracle, and no questions are asked. Having lived in a war-maddened world for so long, they find it an easy enough adjustment to return from 1917 France to 1966 England. Had it been Hoyle's intention to explore all the interesting variations of the potential grandfather paradoxes implied in this bizarre juxtaposition of two worlds brought together geographicaly while still fifty years apart in time, the Narrator would have remained in England. But this is more than a well-told tale of alternate history and parallel worlds.

Richard and John Sinclair take off on another reconnaissance flight to eastern Europe and the Middle East. The clouds break over what should have been Moscow to reveal what appears to be a vast ocean, which closer investigation reveals to be a plain of glass that extends beyond the horizon in every direction. Sinclair's interpretation of this phenomenon is that the plain represents the last stage of earth, long after all life forms had become extinct, and that the surface has been transformed by an expanded sun into a glasslike flux. Another flight over the Middle East reveals still another transformation into a sparsely inhabited marshy wilderness. A search for Jerusalem reveals that it is missing, or never built, because the Hebrews never reached Palestine in this world. It is a new world into which "Christ would not be born."

On the return leg to England, the flight over Athens reveals the Acropolis restored to glory and the city state apparently flourishing as it did in its Golden Age. Richard resolved to return to Athens with an exploration party that outfits a motorized sailing boat for the voyage. When the captain learns that Richard is a musician, he insists that a piano be included as cargo so that he can be entertained on the voyage. The party crosses the invisible but quite real dividing line between Europe of 1917 and the Mediterranean of 425 B.C. on the last day of September, just before a barrier is created keeping all intruders out of the area. October 1 would have been too late.

The party lands in Athens and creates a sensation. Thus begins an interlude, an idyll for Richard, whose piano performances are greeted with amazement by the population. During the winter and early spring of 425-424 B.C., Richard enjoys the most prolifically creative period in his life as a composer. The events of the preceding months seem to stimulate the deepest parts of his being, and he spends much of his time in almost obsessive composition. In the spring, word comes to him from the Temple of Apollo to prepare for a music contest with the god Apollo. There follows one of the most absorbing scenes in modern science fiction. With the priestess Melea and himself as both performers and judges, the contest goes on late into the night, as Richard matches the increasingly more subtle and mysterious music of the god with selections from classical and romantic masters: Bach, Beethoven, Schubert. The final round is reached when Richard is asked to play something of his own, and he chooses a long, choric-symphonic work that had occupied him for two months of his stay in Athens. At the end Melea and Richard are content to call the contest a draw.

After spending the remainder of the night in Melea's arms, Richard awakens to find himself in another world — Mexico City of A.D. 8000 — with Sinclair, who also managed to reach the future, but by a different means. Together, they explore the technological marvels of a house that is capable of shaping itself to the contours of its inhabitants and of providing for the day-by-day needs of the men. When Melea reappears, Richard realizes that she is a woman of the future, and that the music of the god Apollo was actually the music of the future played upon an electronic instrument capable of entirely new tones and new effects. It seems that the future world is the Utopia of which humans have always dreamed. Yet, while it is far in advance of the present, it is not advanced proportionally to the time differential of six thousand years. Sinclair and Richard soon learn why. They are shown a film which chronicles the six-thousand-year history of the race from their time until the future present. It is a horrifying catalogue of the rise and fall of technological cultures, the extermination of animal life, and the struggle to find a way of developing and maintaining a stable social order. For the first time, Richard begins to understand the note of despair, even hopelessness, in the music of the future he has heard. Although the population of this future world is comparatively small and has enjoyed peace and prosperity for a thousand years, signs of instability have begun to appear once again. Moreover, the visions of the various time-space zones seem to point the way to the future extermination of human life. Africa had been found to be without sign of human life and was believed to be a representation of a time in the future, presumably still long before the annihilation of the plain of glass.

The people of the future have made their choice. They will do nothing because they believe that nothing can change the destiny they foresee. Their philosophy is similar to Sinclair's regarding time. To them, all time is equally variable; there is no sense of development or purposeful change. In this context they find themselves largely unaffected by the bizarre time displacements. If some alien force, even a growing godlike consciousness, is responsible for the phenomenon, they will still meet it passively. Sinclair and Richard must now choose either to stay in the future world or to return to 1966, for soon the world will become stable again and for these futurians, all that will remain will be their world.

Sinclair chooses to leave, chiefly because it would take him too long to learn the science of the intervening millenniums. He also hopes to be able to influence the direction of future history by returning to the past. But here is the rub: once he returns to the past, he will not remember anything that happened from the moment he first experienced those few lost hours in Scotland. Richard's choice, finally, is to remain; he makes his choice on the basis of his music and his emotions rather than on reason. He feels at home in the future, whereas Sinclair does not. Moreover, he has something to contribute to the future, a dimension that its technology does not provide. Indeed, it is a dimension that technology cannot provide: a sense of the creative possibilities of life, a view that it is art and not science that validates the present moment.

During the course of his adventures, Richard comes to some important conclusions about the questions of time, the nature of consciousness, and the essence of music. Time and consciousness may be relative, as Sinclair and the futurians believe, and may even exist in parallel fashion, as the space-time shifts proved. However, rational and conscious powers are not the only ones that humans possess. Man is also creative, and by virtue of that power brings design, order, beauty, and finally hope into the universe.

One major question is never quite answered: who was responsible for the aberrations? The answer seems to be that they were the product of an alien force. We are free to construe this force either as similar to Arthur C. Clarke's benevolent shepherds of the universe, or as superintelligence like Thomas Hardy's "Immanent Will," a comforting Victorian notion that the universe is evolving toward some higher moral plane of understanding and action. The question "why" is easier to answer. The purpose of such an elaborate enterprise is to bring Richard into the world of the future in the expectation that his presence there will, indeed, change the future course of human history. Sinclair's brain and his science have no place in the future world; for all his brilliance and his analytical powers, he is an anachronism. As the futurians themselves realize, technology has failed over and over again to provide the stabilizing force in society. What Richard brings to the future is something it has lost — the ability to be deeply moved by the events of life and by the human condition. It is on the basis of deeply felt emotion that Richard forms his aesthetic: great music and therefore great art come ultimately out of powerful emotions called forth by the great events of life. When life itself becomes routine, the senses are dulled, and the passions loose their compelling force. Above all, it seems, the futurians need that sense of passionate response to life if they are ever to have hope in their creative energies once again. This analysis assumes, of course, that the time-space manipulation was purposeful, and that it was intended as an assistance rather than as either an experiment or a punishment.

Hoyle proposes an answer to the question of alien purposes, motivations, natures, and the like rather early in the book. Sinclair and the Narrator are discussing the possibilities inherent in the speculations of multiple time tracks and multiple but discreet conscious personalities. This leads to a consideration of aliens as they have been presented in science fiction. Hoyle argues that science fiction is necessarily anthropomorphic, that its aliens are simply costumed human intelligences. Humans will not be able to render a truly alien being until one is met. *October the First Is Too Late* is, therefore, consistent on this point: we really cannot know alien purposes with certainty unless they choose to make them known to us. Even then there may be some doubt of our ability to interpret or understand those purposes correctly.

While science fiction literature is undoubtedly now part of the mainstream, whatever else it may have been in the past, it is still rare for an author to successfully bring together elite and popular traditions. Hoyle does so with extraordinary success in *October the First Is Too Late*. This may be illustrated briefly by focusing on the speculative elements of the story. The speculative fantasy of the time-space manipulations has already been touched upon; they recall the tradition of parallel world stories beginning with Murray Leinster's "Sidewise in Time" (1934). None of those stories has anything like the complexity and resonance of theme that Hoyle manages.

Speculations on the nature of consciousness take two courses in Hoyle's story, just as time-space does. One is rational, scientific, and analytic. Paradoxically, it leads to the dead-end view that time is not developmental, that all times are equal, that consciousness is both accidental and singular. Related to this view are the future scientific speculations as interpreted for us by Sinclair as a visitor in the world of A.D. 8000. It turns out that Sinclair has nothing to offer the future, and it has nothing to offer him. Richard, on the other hand, has both his music and his own narrative account of the events since the 1966 walking tour of Scotland to teach him that meaning and value come only from patterns and sequences. For Richard the nature of consciousness is bound up with the unconscious, the artistic, and the emotional. Paradoxically, this view leads to artistic models which have progressive movement and intelligible design.

The speculative art elements are among the most original and compelling inventions in the novel. Emerging from Richard's introduction to future music is Hoyle's own speculative aesthetic, combining elements of the past in a dramatic new synthesis. Classical music tends to be gay or solemn in its expression. Classical music stresses the importance of rules over emotion. Romantic music is best suited to express passion and inspiration, and it stresses emotion over rules. Modern music, on the other hand, is professional and technical; it is best suited to express anger, frustration, and alienation. It is highly stylized, stressing forms over ideas. Future music in part depends on new electronic instruments yet to be developed, and is best suited to express melancholy and sadness. In the music of the future, rules depend upon form. Richard learns, however, that future music forms can be applied equally well to the other styles of music, although it is clear that he prefers classical and romantic music to modern. Nonetheless, it is a brilliant *tour de force* for Hoyle to create an imaginary music (which the reader never hears except in imagination), to give it a convincing musical sense of integrity as well as of difference, and to connect the whole so subtly and so ably with the structure of the narrative and with the other major themes of the novel.

October the First Is Too Late has flaws. The reader wishes passionately that Hoyle could slow down the pace and explore some of the ideas that invite further disposition but are simply lost in the time shuffle. The last two chapters do not hold up well stylistically under the heavy burden that Hoyle necessarily must place them under, and we are left with needlessly trivial questions that distract us from the main effect. Are we to believe that the loss of hope among the futurians is the result of living in a world into which Christ was never born? Is there salvation in music? It would seem that Hoyle would accept neither proposition, yet he leaves them as unanswered questions.

Nevertheless, despite its blemishes, *October the First Is Too Late* is an important science fiction work. It is not nearly as well known as it should be. Besides being an entertaining and gripping story, it proves to anyone who might entertain secret doubts that science fiction or fantasy ideas and the ideas and attitudes of traditional, elite literature can be blended together successfully. Hoyle's novel also proves to writers and fans of science fiction that the genre need not rely exclusively on science, pseudoscience, and popular story forms for its speculations; ideas from traditional, elite concerns like aesthetics and art criticism can also offer a renewed sense of value to science fiction literature. *October the First Is Too Late* sets new standards and points the way to new and more fruitful speculations that may help science fiction realize its claim of being a literature of ideas.

Donald L. Lawler

Sources for Further Study

Reviews:

Analog. LXXVIII, January, 1967, p. 167.

Fantastic Stories. XVIII, February, 1969, pp. 143-144.

Magazine of Fantasy and Science Fiction. XXXII, January, 1967, pp. 66-67.

National Review. XVIII, December 13, 1966, p. 1278.

Publisher's Weekly. CLXXXIX, May 30, 1966, p. 85.

Punch. CCL, June 1, 1966, p. 820.

Times Literary Supplement. May 12, 1966, p. 412.

ODD JOHN: A STORY BETWEEN JEST AND EARNEST

Author: Olaf Stapledon (1886-1950)
First book publication: 1935
Type of work: Novel
Time: Immediately before the outbreak of World War II
Locale: Principally England, with visits to foreign countries culminating in settlement on a nameless Pacific island

A child born to ordinary parents develops abnormal intellectual, physical, and spiritual powers which make him appear the forerunner of a new and superhuman species

> Principal characters:
> JOHN WAINWRIGHT, a developing superman
> THE NARRATOR, a journalist addressed by John only as "Fido"
> "PAX" WAINWRIGHT, John's mother and lover
> ADLAN, a deceased superman with whom John makes telepathic contact
> LO, a superwoman, John's proximate wife
> THE HEBRIDEAN BABY, a superchild of enormous power and total malignance

Odd John is one of the most challenging books in the science fiction genre and also one of the most designedly irritating. Challenge and provocation appear within the first few words of the novel, which tell us not only that its hero, "Odd John," is a superman, but also that the biographer who is supposed to be writing his story is an ordinary man regarded by John as a mere animal, and addressed by him as "Fido." Some few readers can class themselves as supermen, the rest are left to identify with this human spaniel. Stapledon is telling us, in effect, that many of the events in his novel will be beyond our capacity to judge: it is not an opening designed to endear the author to his readers.

It might be tolerable, even so, if "Odd John" would confine himself to philosophy or tales of superscience, which we could admire from a distance; but he also commits a sequence of almost wayward assaults on ordinary morality. He murders an unarmed policeman who has caught him in the act of theft. He commits acts of seduction, homosexuality, and incest (with his mother, though on this subject Stapledon was driven by the mores of 1935 to express himself in hints). One might say that since "Odd John" feels himself to be of a different species, these acts also constitute a kind of bestiality. Finally, in an almost irrelevant scene near the end, John and his fellow-supermen first rescue a lifeboat-load of survivors from a shipwreck and then, changing their minds, murder them and throw their bodies to the sharks. These are assaults on our moral sensibility, for Stapledon goes out of his way to make each incident more than predictably horrific, stressing in the murder of the policeman, for instance, that the victim had always been John's friend, that being underage John was in no great legal peril, and that the policeman had a sick and dependent wife whom he was on his way to visit. But John stabs him to death, feels no remorse, and proposes to go on and murder the wife to spare her suffering. The narrator, doglike as ever, can only comment *"Odd* John." "Odd" seems hardly the correct word.

Stapledon, of course, was well aware of the probable reactions to his book. His challenge to the reader is an entirely deliberate one, made in order to pose a series of questions and, indirectly, to make some corresponding statements. The most obvious question (set up by the continuing contrast between the reader's disquiet and the narrator's loyalty) is whether a member of a lower species can presume to judge the actions of a member of a higher one. Our normal answer would be "No" — we take no notice of the opinions of steers or battery hens. By the same logic, then, "Odd John's" various murders must be blameless. A further question is posed by "Odd John's" very existence. He is evidently a mutation, a sport, compared explicitly to the "wolf-children" of fable who are reared by animals. According to Darwinian theory, though, such mutations are the cause of evolutionary progress, forming the raw material of variation on which "natural selection" can then work. "Natural selection," however, is a term which embraces, among other things, the ability to kill competitors. Are John's murderous activities not part of the law of nature? Has he not in some sense a duty to his own emerging species to protect himself by any means in his power?

These issues of the nature of morality and the basis of judgment animate the entire development of *Odd John*, and it is Stapledon's achievement to have given the issues emotional depth by forcing the reader to take sides. Yet the novel also contains elements which seem to be less deliberately designed and to come from deeper within the author's psyche. It must be evident, for one thing, that it is a highly dangerous experiment for an ordinary person (and Stapledon, if not ordinary, was at least no superman) to try to convey the thoughts of a supermind, since failure exposes one to easy irony. Why did Stapledon attempt it? One common and obvious explanation for other such attempts does not apply to Stapledon's effort: he does *not* try to depict the inner workings of a superman's mind for the purpose of presenting Utopian ideals. For *Odd John*, though it ends in the traditional locale of Utopias, an island inhabited by supermen, has very little in the way of "Utopian" content. John and his followers do not offer explanations of the proper way to live, though they exemplify sexual freedom and a few other mildly moralistic traits. They are, therefore, not primarily a device, as are most utopians, for expressing forcibly the author's own opinions.

On the other hand, *Odd John* does exhibit a strong streak of satire. From his childhood John is brought into contact with representatives of authority and allowed to bowl them over. Mr. Magnate (a capitalist), the Bishop (a representative of orthodox religion), and sundry Communists, revolutionaries, psychiatrists, and others, are all weighed and found wanting. Their anonymity makes it plain that Stapledon is striving to make some general statement about the nature of society, and an almost entirely negative one. It is hard, though, to discover the core of the statement, and "Odd John's" perceptions are not immediately helpful. He compares humanity unfavorably with the animal kingdom, observing, for instance, that gannets have "so much more *style.*" He also consistently makes friends, not with the most intelligent human beings, who might be thought closest to him in ability, but with the simplest ones — fishermen, flirtatious children, and his own almost comically bovine mother. The idea that seems to underlie these observations is that humanity has, to use modern terminology, outgrown its ecological niche, has developed beyond a natural point. Mankind, John says on one occasion, is "a sort of archiopteryx of the spirit" — a flying dinosaur, waiting only to be superseded by the more efficient birds. But these hints and similes do not add up to a comprehensive indictment of society, still less to a program for reform. Of course, it is hardly likely that one person *could* produce a total reform program, when one considers that he would first have to master and then to reject all major fields of human endeavor. This would be possible only for a superman, like "Odd John," not for a real man like Olaf Stapledon.

Failure is, therefore, in a way built into the scheme of the book, as is the excuse for it — that the "Fido-narrator" never understood clearly what he was told. Beneath these fictional stratagems, though, we can still detect and respond to Stapledon's attempt to stir in us some recognition of the human inadequacy we all sometimes feel, and which people felt particularly strongly in the doomed years before the start of World War II. The targets of the author's social satire are often not hit with any great accuracy — his account of capitalism as represented by Mr. Magnate, for instance, is grossly onesided, while his evident sympathy with at least the goals of Russian Communism was being betrayed by Stalin.

But Stapledon's vision of the roots of social ills in biological inadequacy remains often deeply suggestive, as in "Odd John's" account of the seeds of nationalism in football matches. If people cannot even *see* the fouls committed by their own side (and it is a matter of common experience that they cannot), then what criticism can one expect them to make of national policy? Can national policies indeed be anything other than a series of shortsighted moves prompted by historical accident? The conclusions Stapledon draws may be wrong, but the insights on which he bases them are valid. It must also be said in his favor that he identified, in 1935, the "revulsion from rationality" and the neopaganism of Nazi Germany, while he had also at least an inkling of the coming development of nuclear power. The explosion that ends the book is a proto-A-bomb.

Not surprisingly, therefore, a rather evident element in *Odd John* is authorial despair. We see it relatively lightly in the impish or puckish element in the hero's character. From his childhood he delights in tantalizing would-be rescuers, in putting pseudonaïve questions to scientists, in making human beings look silly. Why? A real superman, surely, would concentrate on achieving his ends and defeating opposition, not gratuitously provoking it. One feels that Stapledon really enjoys spectacles of human humiliation and uses "Odd John" to create them for him; he had a low view of human nature. Something similar is expressed in the rather inconsistent descriptions of "Odd John" as "wide-awake," "really grown-up." If he were a mutation, these adjectives could hardly apply to him. The implication is, not exactly that John is *not* a mutation, but that the rest of humanity has similar powers but chooses willfully to stay asleep, to remain in childhood. But this thesis is destroyed by John's eleven-month gestation and peculiar physique. Ordinary people *cannot* reach his level by any development or awakening. The suggestions that they can achieve such growth are the product of a conflict in Stapledon's own mind, a kind of impatience with his own species.

Finally, despair is evident in the book's peculiar and unexpected conclusion. John has contacted several other superminds, some of them with powers even greater than his own. They have retired to their island, where they are developing unguessed spiritual and scientific talents. They then come under gentle pressure from the Great Powers (Britain, Russia America, and so on), who send cruisers to investigate. The supermen have shown no compunction previously in eliminating witnesses; and even if they felt they could not or should not fight the world, they have the option of going back into hiding. Instead, after a certain amount of contemptuous play with their enemies, they commit suicide — thus demonstrating, one might think, their unfitness to survive. No good explanation for this appears within the book, but there are two one could draw from outside it.

One explanation is that Stapledon simply knew his limitations. He had presented John as a superintelligence, and yet also had in his mind the notion that a true evolutionary leap would be, to human imagination, as inconceivable as human intelligence would be to an animal. So "Odd John" had to have something besides bigger brains, and Stapledon begins to hint at mystic powers of telepathy and control over nature. But the more these are detailed, the more they are marked and devalued by purely human thinking. "Odd John," therefore, *had* to undergo some sort of ascension. He might, however, have been allowed to survive above or beyond our awareness. To kill him off implies the second speculative explanation, which is that, as the book's subtitle so strongly suggests, Stapledon in the end lost faith in his own fantasy. He had a low view of ordinary human nature; he created "Odd John" as a corrective to this; but the low view remained, in his mind, essentially true, so that "earnest" overpowered "jest." Alternatively one could say that the fictional nature of his "jest" became too strong for him to continue to treat it "earnestly." Either way, the book's delicate balance failed, and the warships of reality sailed over the "new Adam" of Stapledon's dreams.

Odd John derives its force primarily from the author's own involvement in what he wrote, and from his ability to involve the reader by provocation and dispute. It is the most radically thoughtful of the many fictional extrapolations of *On the Origin of Species* and the least comfortable in its conclusions. Above all it exposes the flimsiness of thinking that "Superman" will always be on the side of the police, that evolution has stopped, or that from now on evolution will only take place nicely.

T. A. Shippey

L'OEIL DU PURGATOIRE
(A Look into Purgatory)

Author: Jacques Spitz (1896-1963)
First book publication: 1945
Type of work: Novel
Time: 1945
Locale: Paris

Following an injection of microbes, a man gains the ability to see the future be-
cause the time he "sees" progresses faster and faster in relation to the time he is
"living" in

Principal characters:
   JEAN POLDONSKI, a failure as a painter, who becomes a time traveler
   CHRISTIAN DAGERLÖFF, the discoverer of the microbes

L'oeil du purgatoire was Jacques Spitz's eighth and last science fiction
novel. Thanks to the previous seven, he had risen to the forefront among writers in the genre in France [see especially his *L'agonie du globe (Sever the
Earth)* and *La guerre des mouches (War of the Flies)*], but he still lacked the
great masterpiece that would crown his career. That work was *L'oeil du purgatoire.*

At first one is surprised to find that the plot is tenuous and generally unorig-
inal. Indeed, it might well be classified as the overworked story of the
scientist-who-invents-a-new-gadget and who tests it out on the person of the
guinea-pig-who-does-it-because-he-needs-the-money; and considering that
time travel is perhaps the trickiest theme for a science fiction writer to handle,
it might be thought that Spitz would have had little chance of success. However, as the pages go by, the reader experiences one of the most fascinating
fictional trips ever undertaken — travel through the realm of causality.

Jean Poldonski, a failed painter on the verge of bankruptcy, becomes the
unwilling guinea pig for an old laboratory researcher, Christian Dagerlöff,
who has prepared a new microbial culture. These parabacilli growing on Poldonski's optic nerve enable him to see the future. People and objects start to
age at a uniformly accelerated rate in the painter's sight even though, to his
other senses, they remain in their proper spatiotemporal location. Causal
movement (causality being the connection between cause and effect) is dis-
rupted, and the protagonist begins to see everything around him as it will look
in a more and more distant future. It is a weird sensation, since all his other
senses are in step with the normal flow of time. Thus, Poldonski finds a piece
of meat on his plate with the unappetizing look of already-digested food, even
though it smells like a tasty porterhouse steak.

But movement speeds up and events little by little take an increasingly
dramatic turn. Poldonski sees his familiar surroundings disintegrate around
him, eroded away by time in an unrelenting way; people first turn into corpses

and then into walking skeletons. One beautiful day the painter is present at his own death while looking at his reflection in a mirror. Then the tombstone disappears and with it the long life that came before. The world is nothing more than an empty graveyard where ectoplasms, the last traces of a vanished humanity, roam. Finally, when the painter's body really dies, his eyes see the end of time, the moment when the universe is no more than empty space, a limitless nothing.

One peculiarity of *L'oeil du purgatoire* lies in the choice of characters. In such a story one would have expected to see key characters develop, people whose status would have been important enough to exert some influence on the inexorable logic of the plot. In fact, exactly the opposite is true. While not venturing outside the scientist/guinea-pig boundaries, Spitz refuses to play the game in the usual way. Take Christian Dagerlöff. The man who plays the role of the more or less mad scientist is only an obscure laboratory researcher at the Pasteur Institute, uninspired until he has a "brainstorm" one day about the possibility of overcoming causality by means of a new strain of parabacillus. Spitz deviates from the practice of many authors, their scientists often being gradually forced into the background as their discoveries become progressively more interesting. But here a suddenly extroverted Dagerlöff walks into a print shop to order some calling cards with the descriptive word "genius."

Spitz's implicitly amused commentary on the traditional scenario of the genre is evident; and it becomes even more obvious where the main character is concerned. At the start, Jean Poldonski fits the role of the conventional guinea pig to perfection. When he meets Dagerlöff, he is at the point of no return as a Parisian artist, a common enough human experience. Poldonski is living his last hours as a human being and he knows it, since he has set the date of his death. But just before the fated hour the laboratory researcher places a parabacilli saturated compress over the painter's eyes and he is thrust into the mind-bending experience that is the core of the novel. Poldonski, then, is a guinea pig in spite of himself, although one can guess that he would have accepted a straightforward proposal from Dagerlöff if the mad scientist had made him one instead of tricking him into the experiment. In any case, when Poldonski learns the truth, he finds that his only reward for having vainly sought fame and fortune is to go down in history an utterly unknown. The novel leaves the beaten path the instant Poldonski realizes, after much indecision, that he is well on his way to the future.

The novel is sprinkled with passages in which the author displays an austere detachment and an adroit skill in the use of "black" humor. One of his most beautiful passages, and one of the most meaningful, is doubtless the one in which Poldonski watches himself die in the mirror. Rarely does Spitz attain in his fiction such mordancy in the logic of the absurd. The character's grotesquely comic pantomime relieves the tension that would otherwise have left a bitter taste in the mouth of the reader.

Each line of *L'oeil du purgatoire* is written with meticulous care in order to derive the maximum effect. Spitz is a very controlled and intellectual writer who organizes his visions with precision, unlike the writer, more characteristic of our times, who simply writes "with his guts." Is his the better approach? This is a matter of personal judgment, but it should be noted that feelings described without emotion and with a certain detachment have an often intensified impact. The picture of a man surviving his own death gains much by being described in an objective, almost clinical, way. If it is Spitz's intention to describe realistically his own reveries, he has succeeded. Spitz was something of a social and political outsider; and, elsewhere, images of decay seem to represent his sardonic commentary on the life of his time.

The book ends on a note very characteristic of modern thought in general — expressing gloomy thoughts about errant ectoplasms being the only thing left of the human race. Although a bit heartier than flesh, they are not strong enough to outlast the death of humanity for very long, and little by little even they fade away. Spirits and souls that defy time and space are nothing more than a man-made invention designed to overcome people's fear of death. Here, too, Spitz's skepticism is strikingly apparent. *L'oeil du purgatoire* is a novel of disillusionment about the entropy lying in wait for us no matter what we may do to counteract it.

Reasons for the success of Spitz's novel are obvious. It is a well constructed, well written, and original book. But, how does it fit into the framework of science fiction? In the first place, it is an extremely original treatment of the theme of a trip through time, not only concerning the means (the Dagerlöff parabacilli representing nothing more than an ingenious method of getting the trip under way) but also the outcome.

In the classic time trip story the traveler leaves one universe to arrive in another. But in this novel the traveler literally becomes a prisoner in two different universes, the one in which he is living and the one which he sees. And with both universes drawing away from each other at an increasing rate, the traveler finds himself more and more torn between his two planes of existence. Here, too, the most intellectual aspect of the work is discernible, because, had an ordinary emotionally oriented human being been put in such a situation, he would have been plunged into madness almost instantly. Jean Poldonski, however, is so detached that he not only keeps a cool head, but even permits himself the luxury of having a good time with sardonic wit and unemotional humor. The subject matter of this novel extends rather broadly into the realm of parallel universes and the problems of their relationship. The complexity and sophistication of the novel, therefore, are remarkable; and Spitz deserves credit for having produced a book that is thoroughly in tune with its historical era at a time when science fiction was barely out of its infancy.

If the originality of *L'oeil du purgatoire* stands out in a worldwide context, it shone even more brightly in the French world at a time when science fiction

was backward compared to what was being done in English-speaking countries. Jacques Spitz has written a novel that will remain one of the great
monuments of French science fiction and the first important work of its kind to
come out of France in the postwar period.

Richard D. Nolane

OMEGA: THE LAST DAYS OF THE WORLD
(LA FIN DU MONDE)

Author: Camille Flammarion (1842-1925)
First book publication: 1894
English translation: 1894
Type of work: Novel
Time: From the twenty-fifth century to ten million years in the future
Locale: The Earth

The story of Man's last great civilization on Earth, from the twenty-fifth century to its end ten million years from now

Principal characters:
OMÉGAR, a young man
EVE, a young woman

For more than half a century Camille Flammarion was a leading science fiction author and expert in Europe, an editor and spiritualist, and a world-famous astronomer. His works on astronomy were immensely popular, and his science fiction novels were translated into many languages. From a science fiction perspective he is also notable for writing the first book *about* science fiction, the now classic *Les mondes imaginaires et les mondes réels* (1865), which provides the history of science fiction from the Roman Lucian to the early nineteenth century. His importance in his time as a popularizer of science and a writer of science fiction in Europe can best be compared to that of Isaac Asimov in the United States today — although Flammarion remained an astronomer of high repute even though he devoted more and more of his spare time to writing. He also greatly influenced other leading science fiction writers of his day, particularly his friend Jules Verne, but also Maurus Jokai and H. G. Wells.

Flammarion was an astronomer and a popularizer of astronomy; but he was above all a Utopian, trying, as H. G. Wells did later, to reform the world through his writings. He was obviously not very successful, but several of his novels, notably *Récits de l'infini* (1872) (the story of a soul traveling through the universe as a ray of light) and *Omega: The Last Days of the World* (1894), made a deep impression on science fiction writers and readers at the time. Much of Flammarion's writings can best be characterized as a mixture of Stanley G. Weinbaum and Olaf Stapledon, with spiritualist preaching and astronomical lectures added for good measure. This makes for rather dense reading at times, at least for a modern reader. It is hardly surprising then that his compatriot, the pleasant teller of tales, Jules Verne, is still read and popular today, while the philosopher and lecturer Camille Flammarion is now all but forgotten even in France.

Though it has weaknesses, such as longwindedness and somewhat tiring lectures, the novel remains one of the most grandiose visions of mankind and the universe ever written in science fiction. The work is divided into two parts:

The Twenty-fifth Century, first published as a magazine serial in 1893-1894, and *In Ten Million Years*, presumably written to round off the novel for book publication and to present Flammarion's vision of the future of man and Earth. For this second part of the book, Flammarion borrowed some ideas from Jean-Baptiste Cousin de Grainville's noted novel *The Last Man* (1805), even to the point of naming his hero, the last man in the world, Omégar after the hero of Grainville's novel. The vision as such is pure Flammarion, however, and could hardly have been written by anyone else.

The Twenty-fifth Century, a Utopian tale of a type very popular at the end of the nineteenth century, tells of the magnificent twenty-fifth century where most ills are abolished. Science reigns, people are happy and free, and menial work is mostly done by trained apes who are also servants to the Utopians. All is not perfect, however. Capitalism rules hand in hand with the Pope, whom Flammarion treats with great distaste and scorn. In between long lectures on the evils of religion, and spicy descriptions of the private lives of Renaissance popes, Flammarion tells of the greatest threat ever to mankind and civilization — an enormous meteor hurtling towards Earth. Humanity is warned by the kindly Martians, and the reactions of people to the news of this impending disaster — rebellion, fatalism, religious madness, attempts to cash in on people's fears — are the main interest of this part of the book. Salesmanship triumphs in the end. As the meteor destroys a large part of Italy, an ingenious newspaper tycoon breaks the false news that the entire Vatican (including the Pope and all the cardinals) has been destroyed, only to retract everything when he has sold a few hundred million copies of his newspapers. This part of the book ends with a long treatise on famous catastrophes in history.

In Ten Million Years is somewhat less cynical and much more visionary, telling of the incomparable Utopia appearing on Earth after the great catastrophe. It starts in a very Utopian way, with all women on Earth going on love strikes *à la* Lysistrata, refusing to marry men who have ever carried weapons. After some hedging, the leaders of the world see the light and all armies are abolished, after which the true Utopia commences. Energy is abundant and the swarming billions of Earthlings live in fantastic splendor in wonderful cities that include all the time-honored Utopian hardware — moving sidewalks, television, space flight, and so on. Taxes and monarchy are abolished and capitalism is all but forgotten, as is Communism, religion, and most diseases. "By the 200th century," Flammarion says, "mankind had ceased to resemble the apes." The upper classes no longer have children; that is done for them by the common people, while all menial work is handled by the faithful apes. It is indeed a true Utopia, at least in Flammarion's eyes, and one that goes on for millions of years.

Nothing is constant, however. The sun slowly loses its heat, and the subterranean fires of Earth also die. By the 100,000th century, mankind is dying. The enormous Utopian cities are deserted and dead, energy is no longer plentiful, and a growing coldness has forced the last remnants of man's once glorious civilization into a last redoubt in two valleys near the equator: two fantastic glass cities inhabited by a handful of people. As the older inhabitants die one by one, the population of one of these cities is reduced to one: the young man Omégar, who spends his days walking the unending corridors of his Utopian city. The descriptions of his aimless wanderings in this gigantic tomb are magnificent and give, together with Flammarion's sober, almost indifferent, description of the degeneration of Earth, a haunting feeling of inevitability. It is a glimpse of a universe which cares nothing for man and is at best indifferent to him, finding no place for the human race in the great scheme. Flammarion's brief glimpses of this dying world, written in a cold, dispassionate prose, show him at his best; it is here that he resembles Stapledon most.

Meanwhile, back in the other dying city, south of what was once Ceylon, waits the only other remaining human being on Earth, who very unsurprisingly turns out to be a fair young girl named Eve. The two meet and spend a few months touring the dead Earth in an air ship, searching in vain for other survivors. They find no one and finally land in Egypt, close to the Sphinx which miraculously still stands in the eternal desert. Here they die, and their souls are, in typical Flammarion fashion, transported to Jupiter, which is now a world teeming with life and harboring a civilization even greater than that of Earth in its former splendor. Mankind, or the souls of men, lives on.

Flammarion was a philosopher fighting for the lofty ideals of Utopianism and spiritualism, and like all idealists he was prone to preach. He was the leading writer of what might be called didactic fantasticism, and many of his novels actually read like textbooks. Like Olaf Stapledon, he was a man with a great vision, but he did not content himself with making this vision available through his many novels; he also toiled incessantly to make contemporary science available to people through popular books. He believed that science would make man free, liberate him from the burden of religious superstition and belief in authority, and create a true Utopia which would allow him to achieve his final cosmic goal. Flammarion was also, surprisingly for a scientist, an ardent believer in reincarnation, which, combined with the fact that he was the leading authority in science fiction in this time, enabled him to write some of the most fascinating works of science fiction during the closing decades of the nineteenth century.

Flammarion was not a very literary writer, however. His prose is usually slow, dry, and unexciting. *In Ten Million Years* is probably his best work from a literary point of view, yet even it has serious artistic defects. It was his vision that made him outstanding, and it is the same vision that makes *Omega: The Last Days of the World* readable today. The book is not easy in any sense of the word; a modern reader, accustomed to the streamlined bestsellers of today, would probably find it painfully boring. But this is a novel where ideas count more than literary style, which probably accounts, in part, for the honored position its author held among intellectuals around the turn of the century.

Camille Flammarion's work embodies much of what is characteristic of the science fiction genre even today. *Récits de l'infini* is even more grandiose than *Omega: The Last Days of the World* in its vision of the immensity of time and space and the greatness of the human spirit; but that novel is somewhat overburdened by lectures on astronomy and reincarnation. *Omega: The Last Days of the World* has great vision, but it has an eye for the less than spectacular aspects of human life and endeavor as well, which makes it the more interesting of the two works.

Sam J. Lundwall

OMNIVORE

Author: Piers Anthony (1924-   )
First book publication: 1968
Type of work: Novel
Time: An unspecified future
Locale: The United States and the planet Nacre

A novel about first contact with an alien species beyond human comprehension, which shows how the human characters and the aliens are products of their different biological and social structures

> *Principal characters:*
> SUBBLE, an investigator for the central government
> VEG (VACHEL SMITH), one of the three members of an exploration team on the planet Nacre
> 'QUILON (AQUILON), the second member, and only woman, of the team
> CAL, the third member

Ever since the publication of Stanley G. Weinbaum's "A Martian Odyssey" in 1934, science fiction has been filled with intelligent aliens that pose not a threat to mankind but a puzzle. Such aliens are not the brutal invaders of the Earth that can be found in H. G. Wells's *War of the Worlds* or Robert Heinlein's *The Puppet Masters*, but rather they usually take the form of beings who are interested in observing and communicating with humanity. Such creatures, moreover, are often used by science fiction writers as a means of comparison by which shortcomings in the human race are pointed out. Theodore Sturgeon's "Affair with a Green Monkey" uses aliens in this fashion, as does *Omnivore*.

To say that *Omnivore* presents the aliens so that statements can be made about mankind does not sufficiently characterize the novel nor does it do justice to Anthony's accomplishment. In trying to present both the aliens and the humans, Anthony has created an outstanding example of how a good science fiction writer is able to create new worlds with consistent systems of biology, physics, and environment. His portrayal of the planet Nacre is both convincing and pleasing, and, furthermore, his description of a future Earth is equally consistent and believable.

It is important for the novel that the worlds of Nacre and Earth be credible because the point central to the work is that the aliens of Nacre and the humans of Earth are a result of their physical structures. Anthony takes the old maxim, "we are what we eat," and carries it to its ultimate conclusion. Thus, how each creature lives within its environment, how each constructs its social institutions, and how each lives with its individual identity are all determined by the biology of that being. With such a theme Anthony must carefully construct his world so that each feature will fit.

Omnivore is divided into four chapters. Within each of the first three chapters, the investigator, Subble, interviews a member of an exploration team to Nacre that has returned to Earth. The final chapter concerns Subble's own confrontation with the aliens from Nacre. Anthony has created in Subble one of the more interesting secret agents in literature. He is a human being who has been so modified that he is, for all practical purposes, identical with all the other investigators in his agency. After each assignment, moreover, all individual memories are erased so that the reaction of all investigators to any one case will be identical. This identity of form and mind should not, however, be seen as an equality in mediocrity. All of the agents share a high degree of intellectual achievement, an advanced state of concern for the people they become involved with, and a fine sense of how to use the physical capabilities they have been given through biological modifications. Subble, therefore, is not an oversexed, amoral agent incapable of making independent judgments, nor are any of his fellow agents.

The first of the exploration team that Subble interviews is Veg, a character who in every way fits the description of a rugged outdoorsman, except that he is a vegetarian with a fierce respect for the sanctity of life. Veg is not a pacifist; he is willing to take life if he or his friends are threatened; but aside from such a situation, he insists on the right of all animate creatures to live.

During the course of the interview the reader learns that Subble only knows that he must interview the three explorers and determine if any threat exists to Earth. Subble does not have any idea who these people are or what form a potential threat might take. Each agent is given only the barest details, so that any conclusion he draws will come directly from what he learns on the case. Anthony, thus, uses Subble's complete ignorance of the facts as an excuse for the exposition of the plot; by and large, the device works well.

Subble learns through the interview why Veg became a vegetarian. When he was young, Veg's older and more promising brother died of cancer. Veg could not understand why the brother had died rather than he himself. His only method of resolving this dilemma was to conclude that there was no reason for death in general, and that nothing should die. Thus he resolved to avoid killing all animate creatures. Veg, in other words, has chosen his style of life out of a need to respond to a personal crisis. His choice reflects an attempt to answer a question that has no solution, and, in this way, it is not an answer but an escape.

Once Veg has told Subble about his earlier life, he is able to speak about his part in the exploration of Nacre. Instead of simply having Veg relate his experience, Anthony uses a flashback method, with Veg as the point-of-view character. In this way he recreates the entire episode, complete with Veg's reactions to it, without having to keep up the pretense of a conversation as well. Thus, the planet can be fully described without interruption by Subble.

As Veg describes Nacre the picture emerges of a luxuriant mushroom world filled with colorful, divergent types of fungus, and Anthony's style is equal to the lush nature of the planet. Aside from the "plantlife" Nacre has three species of animate creatures: herbivore, omnivore, and carnivore. Veg's interview describes the exploration team's first encounter with the carnivore, the last of the three varieties the team encountered. The carnivores are mantalike creatures that fly at great speeds and use their thin tails as whips. The tails are extremely sharp, capable of cutting the bodies of the omnivores to shreds. The omnivores appear to be their sole source of food; however, Veg, 'Quilon, and Cal were not aware of the mantas' eating habits, and, therefore, fled the first one they saw. In fleeing, the team's vehicle burned out and the three were stranded on Nacre, forced to return to their base on foot.

Veg relates only the first stage of their journey. He tells Subble that it will be up to 'Quilon and Cal to finish the story. Clearly, the tripartite division of the adventure is geared to the three characters. Each part ends with a climactic moment for the teller. For Veg, this moment occurred when he killed one of the carnivores, believing that his and 'Quilon's lives were in danger. In order to save 'Quilon, in particular, he was forced to destroy the creature. The death of the manta at the hands of Veg ends the first chapter of *Omnivore*. From Veg's earlier conversation with Subble, the reader can be sure that this killing has had a deep and disturbing effect on Veg, but it is an effect that Veg must work out for himself. Having all the information he will get from Veg, Subble moves on.

In Chapter Two Subble and the reader are introduced to 'Quilon. After the interview with Veg it has become obvious that there is a love triangle between Veg, 'Quilon, and Cal. According to 'Quilon, the reason that the three of them are now separated is so she can make a choice between the two men. Subble, however, and the reader as well, suspects that the cause of the separation lies deeper. The killing of the manta has hurt Veg, and one starts to look for an equal injury in 'Quilon. She tells Subble that she too has become a vegetarian, but unlike Veg, her food preference seems to be an emotional response to her stay on Nacre. 'Quilon is a remarkably beautiful and intelligent woman who, as a child, was somehow made to feel guilty about her beauty. As a result, she has convinced herself that her smile is both ugly and revealing of her inner worthlessness. When she finally trusts Subble sufficiently, the episode she relates to him is centered around these feelings of self-hate.

'Quilon's story begins after the killing of the manta. Later on the trip, another manta began escorting the three explorers. It did not threaten them except when 'Quilon approached Veg. Veg was able to touch Cal and 'Quilon was able to touch Cal without any reaction from the manta, but 'Quilon was driven off each time she neared Veg. While experiencing this mysterious behavior on the part of the manta, the team was attacked by an omnivore. On Nacre it is the omnivore that is the most vicious of the creatures. It attacks all things with senseless brutality unconcerned with the destruction it causes. The omnivore is only concerned with sustaining its own life, and anything that will contribute to that single and immediate end will suffice.

In the battle against the omnivore, Veg fell over a ledge. 'Quilon quickly followed and, happy to see Veg unharmed, she smiled. Veg was immediately aware of the significance of the smile and rather than call attention to it tried to control his own expression. The result appeared to be a sneer, which 'Quilon interpreted as confirmation of her inner ugliness. Thus, Nacre has proved climactic to 'Quilon as well. At that moment her most unhappy thoughts about herself were reinforced.

'Quilon's attempt to be a vegetarian is part of her self-punishment. Before her episode on Nacre is related, she takes Subble to see an automated "farm" in her living complex. It is a nightmare of machinelike efficiency in which animals are caged, fattened, and slaughtered with complete indifference. To 'Quilon, the human race is the equivalent of the omnivore of Nacre; it destroys brutally for its own self-indulgence with no concern for the environment it must live in. It is in this chapter that Anthony portrays the overcrowded life of Earth in detail.

Life has become intolerable to many humans because of the compromises that have had to be made for the sake of overpopulation. 'Quilon is a fitting spokeswoman for this description because she strongly feels an affinity with the omnivore of Nacre and sees in the human omnivores a distinct parallel. Where Veg has turned to vegetarianism because of his guilt for not dying in place of his brother, 'Quilon turns to it because of guilt for being a human.

In the first two episodes, Subble has been a concerned and interested listener as Veg and then 'Quilon tell their stories, but when he interviews Cal, Subble must assume a new role. Veg referred to the threesome as brawn, beauty, and brains, and Cal is definitely the "brains" of the group. He becomes Subble's teacher as Subble prepares to face the mantas. Cal confirms Subble's suspicion that the three explorers have brought some mantas back to Earth. It will be Subble's task to confront them and learn from the mantas as well.

Before Cal begins his lessons, however, he ties together the story of the expedition on Nacre. Cal has a rather gruesome dietary quirk. Both previous to and during the adventure on Nacre, Cal had convinced himself that he could "eat" nothing but blood. 'Quilon had told Subble of this and included the fact that during their trip back to their base she had bled herself in order to sustain Cal. Furthermore, after the attack by the omnivore and its subsequent death at the tail of the manta, Cal had drunk the "blood" from the body of the creature.

He then explains to Subble the reasons behind each of the characters' eating habits: each of them is seeking to establish a separate identity, one that denies their humanity. Life has become far too burdensome as man, and, therefore, such habits become both a denial of the human characteristics so abhorrent to them and a claim to individuality. Cal, however, has also learned a lesson on Nacre which involves a fundamental difference between humans and the creatures of that planet. The three species of Nacre are inexorably characterized by their place in the food chain, while humans can transcend their position.

Before Subble understands Cal's point, Cal leads him on a hallucinatory dream through the fungus kingdom. Subble learns to allow the vision to shape his thought as he comprehends the importance of various types of fungi for life on Earth. Unfortunately, while the description of the dream and the events that take place are rich in detail, Anthony never fully justifies its length or most of the information that comes from it. Subble must learn something of the type of creature represented by the mantas and he must learn to control his vision under the influence of the drug. But much of the dream exists for its own sake and does appear to slow down the novel at its crucial point. The dream sequence is intensified when the Cal part of the episode on Nacre is finally brought into the chapter as an afterthought. The dream simply seems to be too long for its stated purpose and it interrupts the more important part of the chapter.

Cal's episode begins with a description of how the manta killed the omnivore by cutting it to shreds with its tail. Cal then continues by explaining the manta's attempts to keep Veg and 'Quilon separated. The manta classified Veg as a herbivore, 'Quilon as an omnivore, and Cal as a carnivore. On Nacre the herbivores are entirely peaceful, feeding off the "vegetation" of the planet. The carnivores, while not so peaceful, feed strictly off the omnivores and preserve the herbivores as a vital link in their food chain. The omnivores, however, disrupt the food chain because their food preferences are not limited. Thus, they are totally destructive, and the carnivores, by making the omnivores their sole source of food, keep them in check. Given such biological organization on Nacre, the mantas did not see Cal as a threat to Veg because carnivores do not eat herbivores. 'Quilon, moreover, could not be a threat to Cal because carnivores are fully capable of destroying omnivores. But the omnivore 'Quilon was a threat to the herbivore Veg; therefore, the manta tried to protect Veg from her.

It was this revelation that has so disturbed 'Quilon, but an even worse one was in store for Cal. For years Cal had tried to destroy any interest in preserving his own life. He had deliberately cut himself off from any positive friendship and had formed self-destructive habits. Cal was not only sick of his own life, he was sick of the human race itself. Thus, when 'Quilon bled herself for him, Cal's whole aim toward annihilation was shaken. His friends were willing to die rather than abandon him to his long-sought goal. As a gesture of his love for his friends, Cal gave up trying to die on the journey back to the base.

A second event occurs before they return which makes Cal put off his own death indefinitely. Toward the end of the adventure the three explorers encountered a group of mantas. At that moment, the cloud cover of Nacre opened and bright sunlight broke through. Since the mantas evolved in a world usually shaded by the clouds, this light blinded one of the creatures. 'Quilon ran to aid it, but the light had done its damage and the manta was completely disabled.

The other mantas quickly put the helpless one to death, and then one of them lightly punished 'Quilon for interfering. Although she was not aware of it, 'Quilon's actions prevented the freeing of the dead manta's spores into the atmosphere. The mantas, however, recognized 'Quilon's motive as compassion, and as an act of faith they gave her eight baby mantas. These are the mantas that the team has brought back to Earth with them.

What has so deeply disturbed Cal about this whole event is that he understands that the mantas see in 'Quilon a nobler quality than he has seen in his fellow man. The mantas have every reason to hate any omnivorous creature, but they are willing to trust what they have seen. Cal has refused to place any such trust in people, even his friends. Thus, the mantas have undercut the very basis for Cal's death wish, and as Cal implies in his conversation with Subble, he has learned that simple classifications will not do. But such a lesson is a hard one to absorb fully, and, like 'Quilon and Veg, Cal has needed time to appreciate what his experience on Nacre has done for him.

The final chapter of *Omnivore* is Subble's confrontation with the mantas. In many ways it is an unsatisfactory chapter. Anthony equips Subble for this confrontation with electronic gear and with a hallucinogen, and Subble does establish contact with them. But the mantas insist that Subble fight one of them to the death to prove his worthiness to "speak" with them. They are aware of the personal problems which inhibit Veg, 'Quilon, and Cal; they are also aware that they are dealing with a race of omnivores that can be compassionate. But they have refused meaningful contact with the humans because they are in doubt as to how far the race has advanced. Unfortunately, Anthony never really gives a convincing reason as to how Subble's killing of one of the mantas will prove human worthiness, nor does he explain on what criterion the mantas base their concept of advanced civilization.

Thus, while the reader is treated to a very effective battle between Subble and one of the mantas, the question as to why all this is happening is never clear. The question, moreover, changes from why to what as the chapter continues. Subble takes the hallucinogen and goes through a series of visions that start with an exposition of the manta life cycle and end with the death of the manta at Subble's hands. Subble is then killed by his own hallucination.

At this point it would appear that Anthony got tired of his work. The ending comes fast and it leaves too many questions open. Evidently the mantas have learned to respect Subble. As a gesture of such respect they radio his report to his superiors and end with a description of the mantas and the fact that Subble has killed one of them. The superiors, fearing what the spores of the dead manta will do to the ecology of the Earth, round up the remaining mantas, as well as Veg, 'Quilon, and Cal and ship them all off the Earth; and it is at this point that the novel closes.

Throughout *Omnivore* Anthony has carefully compared the products of two different biospheres. Cal, Veg, and 'Quilon, with all their hopes and fears, are perfect products of their environment. The mantas, moreover, are equally perfect representatives of a parallel evolution that has taken place on a planet with a very different ecology. But having made the comparison Anthony leaves the reader to wonder what the experience has done for any of the characters. Beliefs are shaken, but that is all. Such an ending is unfair to the reader because he has become involved in the lives of these characters. It is hard not to care about them. Thus, a lack of resolution is frustrating.

Veg, 'Quilon, Cal, and the mantas appear in two other novels which follow *Omnivore*. It is interesting to note, however, that in neither of these novels does Anthony go into the same depth of detail in characterization as in the first, nor does he ever resolve the inner problems for his humans. Perhaps this is the problem of working on a series of novels involving the same characters. A complete resolution in one novel defeats the series, but too often a series that deals continually with the same characters exhibiting the same personal problems becomes boring. Whatever the cause for the weak and unsatisfying ending to *Omnivore*, one can only regret it. Piers Anthony created two credible worlds, fascinating aliens, and sympathetic humans. Such creations deserve better treatment.

Stephen H. Goldman

Sources for Further Study

Reviews:

Amazing Stories. XLIII, September, 1969, pp. 126-127.

Analog. LXXXIV, October, 1969, p. 176.

Books and Bookmen. XIV, July, 1969, p. 38.

Observer. June 8, 1969, p. 28.

Times Literary Supplement. May 22, 1969, p. 33.

ON THE BEACH

Author: Nevil Shute (Nevil Shute Norway, 1899-1960)
First book publication: 1957
Type of work: Novel
Time: 1962-1963
Locale: Australia and on board an atomic submarine following a massive nuclear war in the Northern Hemisphere

A small band of survivors of a nuclear holocaust gradually face their inevitable deaths in Australia, despite the fact that no bombs were detonated in the Southern Hemisphere; all commit government-sanctioned suicide rather than face death from radiation poisoning

> *Principal characters:*
> DWIGHT LIONEL TOWERS, commander of an American nuclear submarine
> MOIRA DAVIDSON, a young, liberated Australian woman, who falls in love with Towers
> JOHN OSBORNE, a physicist with a passion for auto racing
> PETER HOLMES, a young Australian naval officer
> MARY HOLMES, his wife

Nevil Shute takes both his title and his epigraph from T. S. Eliot's "The Hollow Men," but his choice is ironic, since what he shows us in *On the Beach*, is neither the bang that signifies the end of the world in a nuclear holocaust nor the whimper that might accompany the death of the last of humanity. Instead, we see man's indomitable spirit making the best of a bad situation, and we come to love and respect these people who, although doomed through no fault of their own, resolve to carry on as best they can until the end. Ultimately, *On the Beach* is a novel about suicide, and Shute has extrapolated a world in which suicide is the only rational response to a completely irrational situation. It is a tribute to his skill as a writer that most readers find the orgy of suicides with which Shute ends his novel not only rational and inevitable, but also admirable.

On the Beach is a narrative of the last year in the intertwined lives of five individuals. We first meet Peter and Mary Holmes, a young Australian couple living in a suburb of Melbourne. Peter is a Lieutenant Commander in the Australian Navy, and he is to receive an assignment after having been "on the beach" for five months. As the Holmeses go through their morning routine with their baby daughter Jennifer and make plans for the day, the narrator informs us, in an offhand way, that there had been a war six months after they were married in 1961. There is no history of this thirty-seven day war, save for the seismograph records of explosions in the Northern Hemisphere. The massive irony of this understated Armageddon does not become apparent to the reader for some time, since the only apparent effect on the Holmeses is switching from an automobile to bicycles for transportation.

Peter, Mary, and Jennifer serve as touchstones for the reader as the novel unfolds. Seemingly average in every respect, they represent the norm against which readers may measure themselves. Unsure, obedient to authority, alternately comforting and frightened, they help each other face the inevitable end. We meet the other characters through them, and see much of the unfolding tragedy through their eyes.

Peter's assignment is as liaison officer aboard the *U.S.S. Scorpion*, an American nuclear submarine under the command of Captain Dwight Lionel Towers, the most important of the main characters. It is with the introduction of Commander Towers that Shute informs the reader of the nature of the war and broadens his hints about the coming radiation poisoning. It seems that Albania (one of the countries that Shute brands "Irresponsibles") obtained atomic weapons and bombed Naples for no apparent reason; then some unknown country intervened in the latest Arab-Israeli war by dropping a hydrogen bomb on Tel Aviv. The Americans and British, hoping to nip the use of atomic weapons in the bud before it could spread to the major powers, demonstrated how easily Cairo could be destroyed by staging a fly-over. The Egyptians retaliated by sending thirteen long-range bombers to Washington and London. While only three planes got through, both capitals (and, with them, the most important Western statesmen) were destroyed. Unfortunately, the Egyptian bombers were of Russian origin and carried Russian markings, so the American military mistakenly ordered massive retaliatory strikes against the Soviet Union. Naturally enough, the Russians retaliated against this apparently unprovoked attack, destroying the NATO countries, and then the Chinese took advantage of the confusion to launch an all-out attack against Russia. The Soviet Union was not unprepared for such an eventuality, however, and it launched the rest of its missiles and bombers against China. Of the more than four thousand seven hundred atomic weapons exploded, most were hydrogen bombs and many were cobalt bombs, especially formulated to destroy the population with radiation. The fallout has already killed every living creature in the Northern Hemisphere, and the line of radiation sickness is moving inexorably southward. People in Melbourne, the southernmost major city in the world, have approximately eight months to live, and nothing can save them.

As an American military officer, Dwight Towers could easily have been made a saber-rattling scapegoat by Shute, who was, after all, writing for a primarily Australian audience. Instead, Towers is portrayed as a highly sympathetic individual who follow orders and places his duty above everything. When the Captain admits that he probably would have conducted the war in exactly the same way had he been in charge, Shute intends the reader to sympathize with the character. The unasked rhetorical question is clear: how could anyone have done anything else? Once the weapons existed, they were going to be used. It was simply a question of time. For Shute, nuclear proliferation leads inevitably to nuclear holocaust.

Dwight's chief characteristic in the novel is his fantasy that his wife and children are alive and well and awaiting his return to them, at his death, in the United States. He speaks about them and acts as though he believes in the literal fact of their existence, despite his certain knowledge to the contrary. This, of course, makes him insane by our standards, but it is this insanity which enables him to continue to function. When, at the end of the novel, he takes his submarine out to the open sea to sink her rather than leave her unattended at the dock, killing himself and all members of his crew in the process, he takes with him special gifts for his wife and children, secure in his belief that he will soon join them.

At the same time, Towers repeatedly reminds the other characters that death is inevitable and that they can do nothing but stoically accept what is coming to them. His only plan is to keep busy, do his duty, and remain faithful to his principles. While doing so, he rescues another major character, Moira David-son, from the depths of alcoholic despair. Moira (whose name is a transliteration of the Classical Greek word meaning "fate") represents another way of facing the end when we first meet her. Because she cannot make sense of her situation, which both seems to be and is grossly unfair, she has tried to drown her sorrows in a whirlwind round of strong drink and cheap sex. Dwight's strength and purpose are infectious, and Moira comes to love him. She is initially puzzled by his fantasy, and somewhat frustrated by his fidelity to a long-dead wife, but her love gives her a reason for living; she drastically reduces her drinking, and by the end of the novel she accepts his fantasy as her own. Moira is the only character in the novel who changes and grows, and her adoption of Dwight's attitude instead of his adoption of hers is a clear indication of what Shute considers admirable under the circumstances.

The last of the major characters to be introduced is John Osborne, a scientist who serves a primarily expository function. It is Osborne who provides Dwight and Peter (and, of course, the reader) with the details about the war, and it is he whose authority stands behind the certainty of the radiation poisoning. But Osborne also plays a dramatic role in one of the subplots of *On the Beach*. He shares some of Moira's initial attitude of making merry on the eve of death, but without her morbid despair. Osborne takes his opportunity to do the one thing he has always wanted to do, become an automobile racer. He buys what is the probably the fastest car in the world, a Ferrari, and uses it to win the last racing championship ever to be run, thus achieving his secret life's ambition.

Throughout the novel, Shute emphasizes the importance of having a purpose. Even the secondary characters are happy when they have a purpose, and unhappy when they have none. Several of the characters express envy of those who have a reason for living, even when that reason is as personal or as trivial as winning an auto race or finishing the club's sherry and port before the end. Each character eventually faces the inevitability of his own death and chooses to dedicate the remainder of his life to the achievement of some goal. With a focus outside oneself, life and death become bearable.

The final chapter tidily wraps up all of the subplots and characters. Amazingly, not a single character, major or minor, dies of radiation poisoning. The cavalcade of suicide begins with Osborne's mother, who takes a pill obtained free of charge at the corner drug store and dies in her bed, leaving instructions for her son to see to the dog. The radiation-sick Osborne gives the animal a lethal shot (also obtained at the drug store, and just as effective on babies, as we later discover with Jennifer Holmes), then lovingly puts the Ferrari up on blocks and takes two pills himself, dying in the driver's seat. Peter and Mary Holmes also get the sickness, and although Peter's symptoms subside for a while he hides this fact from Mary, gives Jennifer a shot, and takes a pill with Mary. All three die in bed. Dwight takes the submarine out to the open sea and sinks it, killing himself and the crew. Moira's parents are last seen in bed, weak with radiation poisoning, but with the pills that promise relief close at hand. And Moira herself drives frantically along the beach to keep Dwight's submarine in sight as long as possible, timing her own swallowing of pills with his best estimate of when his ship will go down. Her dying wish is for Dwight to take her with him when he goes to his family.

Shute somewhat awkwardly makes his didactic purpose clear in the last chapter, in a conversation between Peter and Mary. She asks why it all happened, and her husbands responds that

> Some kinds of silliness you just can't stop. . . .The only possible hope would have been to educate them out of their silliness. . . . You could have done something with newspapers. We didn't do it. No nation did, because we were all too silly. We liked our newspapers with pictures of beach girls and headlines about cases of indecent assault, and no government was wise enough to stop us having them that way. But something might have been done with newspapers, if we'd been wise enough.

On the Beach is apparently Shute's attempt to help educate us out of our silliness.

On the Beach succeeds as a novel because of the strength of the characterization. Readers identify with all of the major characters, and empathy builds to the point where their frustration is ours, their sense of purpose is ours, and their loss is ours. More than twenty years after its initial publication, *On the Beach* remains the quintessential statement of the folly of atomic war and one of the best arguments against nuclear proliferation.

David Stevens

Sources for Further Study

Reviews:

Analog. XL, February, 1958, pp. 144-145.

Atlantic. CC, August, 1957, p. 80.

Chicago Sunday Tribune. August 4, 1957, p. 1.

Commonweal. LXVI, August 23, 1957, p. 524.

Galaxy. XV, March, 1958, pp. 119-120.

Magazine of Fantasy and Science Fiction. XIII, October, 1957, pp. 102-103.

New Republic. July 28, 1957, p. 4.

New Worlds. LXV, November, 1957, p. 124.

New York Times. July 28, 1957, p. 4.

Time. LXX, August 19, 1957, p. 84.

Venture Science Fiction. II, January, 1958, p. 80.

THE OPHIUCHI HOTLINE

Author: John Varley
First book publication: 1977
Type of work: Novel
Time: Approximately six hundred years in the future
Locale: Luna, Earth, Saturn, Poseidon, Pluto, and a position seventeen light-years
from the Solar System

*Forced to flee the Earth because of the invasion of superior aliens, mankind will
soon be forced to leave the Solar System*

Principal characters:
> LILO-ALEXANDR-CALYPSO, an unwilling agent of Boss Tweed
> BOSS TWEED, former president of Luna and leader of the Free
> Earthers
> VAFFA, Tweed's child, multiple clones of whom serve as Tweed's
> soldiers
> CATHAY, a disbarred teacher and unwilling agent of Tweed

The fictional world of the future presented in *The Ophiuchi Hotline* is one of the finest examples of what science fiction does best: create self-consistent, alternate worlds that address present-day concerns. John Varley portrays a world replete with dazzling technological innovations, mysterious aliens, advanced human cultures, and exciting space opera; yet each of these elements is kept in balance with one another and with the statements the author makes concerning the future of humanity.

Just how fine an accomplishment the novel is can be seen in how much Varley packs into the world of *The Ophiuchi Hotline* without destroying either its inner consistency or the reader's credibility. At some point during the end of the twentieth century, aliens had entered the Solar System. They are of a far greater level of intelligence than humans, but seemed, at first, uninterested in the planet Earth. A race similar to these aliens exists on the planet Jupiter, where the aliens first went. However, after these aliens learned of the existence of sperm whales, killer whales, and bottlenosed dolphins on Earth, creatures which the aliens consider of an order of intelligence second only to themselves, they invaded the Earth to free it from the control of man, a creature of only third-level intelligence. Mankind had no adequate defense, and those who survived the famine brought on by the invasion fled to eight planets and satellites in the Solar System.

This dispersal of humanity took place some five hundred and fifty years before the opening of the novel. Between the invasion and the first action of the novel, a second significant event had occurred: about four hundred years earlier radio signals started to be received from what was believed to be Ophiuchi 70. These signals have been constantly monitored since then. They contain scientific information thousands of years in advance of human science, and while only about ten percent of that information is understandable to man, it has caused significant innovations. Among these innovations are an exact method of recording the entire content of a human brain, procedures for gene manipulation, processes for using minute black holes as sources of energy, and force fields that allow humans to exist in the vacuum of space. Thus, while the human race has lost its home planet and exists in fear of what the Invaders might do next, it has continued to develop complex technologies that allows it to mold new environments.

One particular technological innovation, however, stands out from all the rest: man has learned how to clone exact duplicates of himself. The clones are not used as slaves or as colonizers; in fact, no clone is allowed to live if a person with the same genetic code is alive at the same time. Clones plus the brain recording device are used to ensure the immortality of the originals. Every citizen of the Eight Worlds has the right to this eternal life. Their brains are periodically recorded, and if one should chance to be fatally injured, a clone of that person is awakened and the brain record is implanted in it. In such a way, the original may die, but a type of immortal life is given to the mind of that person.

Three elements are woven together in the well-structured plot. The novel opens in the cell of Lilo-Alexandr-Calypso, who has been condemned to permanent death for a crime against humanity. Because of the universal use of cloning and of cosmetic surgery, the Eight Worlds are faced with the difficult task of defining exactly what constitutes a human being. This problem has been resolved by using as the basis of the definition the fundamental human genetic code; that is, humans are defined by their DNA. Given such a definition, human DNA becomes one of the taboo areas for genetic manipulation because, for this society, that would be tampering with the equivalent of the soul.

Lilo, however, was interested in trying to reverse the effects of the inbreeding of the race caused by the limited stock of human survivors of the alien invasion. She was aided in her research by the belief that much of the untranslated information gathered from the Ophiuchi Hotline outlines methods of manipulating DNA. But Lilo was caught with her research notes and now faces eternal death.

Because of the severity of her sentence, Lilo becomes a prime candidate for Boss Tweed's Free Earthers. Tweed sees her as useful to his plans to retake the Earth, and, immediately before her execution, he substitutes one of her clones for the original Lilo. Even though Lilo is freed through Boss Tweed's machinations, however, she has simply changed one death for another, although this one is far less permanent. Tweed is obsessed with the desire to return to Earth and throw out the Invaders. This obsession has gone so far that he has taken his only child, created multiple clones from it, and turned them all into highly efficient killers. Lilo wants no part of his schemes, and it takes the death of the original Lilo and one of her clones, before the third Lilo agrees to at least play along with Tweed for awhile.

What follows this agreement is a fine example of what a science fiction writer is able to do that a mainstream writer cannot. Varley develops three parallel elements by creating three different Lilos. Through a series of events, one Lilo ends up on Earth, and through her the reader learns of how the planet and a small remnant of humans has fared since the dispersal. By the end of this episode, it is clear that Earth can never be home for mankind again. The second Lilo becomes part of a successful rebellion against Boss Tweed. No matter how admirable his intentions, Tweed's actions are both unrealistic and inhuman. They are unrealistic because the aliens' superiority to man is not just a myth — there really is nothing the human race can do against them. They are inhuman because he has created what is in effect a prison camp on Poseidon, a satellite of Jupiter, and peopled it with condemned criminals and illegal clones. All of these people face instant obliteration if any of the Eight Worlds learns of them, and Tweed holds this over their heads as a whip to make them do his bidding. By the end of this episode the reader's sympathy is on the side of the prisoners.

It is finally left to the third Lilo to solve the problem of the Ophiuchi Hotline. Whoever is responsible for the hotline has sent a message to the humans that there is a charge for use of the hotline and that the bill is now due. No one, however, knows what that charge is or what the threatened consequences of nonpayment might be; this information is left to Lilo, Cathay, one of the Vaffas, and a pilot named Javelin to discover. Javelin has learned that the hotline originates not at Ophiuchi 70, as had been supposed, but at a point seventeen light-years from the Solar System. The trip out to this point takes ten years, and when they reach it, they meet the Traders, the "Ophiuchis" themselves, and learn that the message was meant to accomplish two things. First, the Traders wanted the humans to get to the sending station so that they could be informed of what their future holds. Second, they wished to propose to the humans a form of payment for use of the hotline.

As to the first of these goals, Lilo and her fellow travelers are told that the fate of the human race is no different from that of other land-dwelling, tool-using creatures. The Invaders are far superior to them all and has a past history of displacing these other intelligent races. All one can do is accept the displacement and find another home. Even Tweed's rebellion against the Invaders is nothing more than a repetition of what has been tried by many other species in the past. It is inevitable that the displaced race will try to regain their lost home, and it is equally inevitable that the Invaders will destroy the race as a result of the attempt.

The Traders' advice to the humans as to their future actions is painfully clear: man must change so that he can fit into the wandering life that his future holds. It is the function of the Ophiuchi Hotline to inform the endangered race of the knowledge needed to survive. The most important part of that informa-tion is the manipulation of human DNA. If man is to wander the stars, he must be physically prepared for it. The human resistance to the necessary genetic manipulation is one of its most serious handicaps, for in order to live a race must be willing to change. Thus, William, one of the Traders who runs the hotline, says to Lilo and the others:

> You can no longer afford that quirk. You will have to cease defining your race by some-thing as arbitrary as a genetic code, and make the great leap to establishing a racial aware-ness that will hold together in spite of the physical difference you will be introducing among yourselves. And you *must* define your race more successfully than you have done so far. Today, you could not tell us what it is that makes one a human being.

These words summarize, in fact, much that has happened in the novel. Tweed, for example, dreams of a return to the original homeland, but he has no feeling of remorse for the ways in which he has used people and caused them to suffer. What good is the homeland if there is no humanity in it? Cer-tainly the Earth has only a pitiful few humans living on it. But just as certainly Tweed's methods lack humanity.

Even more to the point, however, is the position of the people of Poseidon. They are given no right to life; they are not considered human by the laws of the Eight Worlds. Yet, after the reader learns their histories and their hopes, they are seen as very human indeed. Thus, Varley ends *The Ophiuchi Hotline* with one of the most often-asked questions in science fiction: what is a man? While he never gives a direct answer to that question, it is obvious that the definitions used by the majority of the characters in the novel are not accept-able.

By introducing the Traders at the end of the novel, Varley is able to tie all his elements together. The Invaders, the hotline, and the cloning are now seen as a whole. The Invaders are not just a unique event in the lives of a single race; they are a cosmic phenomenon that many, many races have had to learn to cope with. The Ophiuchi Hotline follows these Invaders, giving the knowl-edge necessary for survival to those races that will learn.

Finally, Varley examines the cost of such knowledge. The development of cloning has narrowed the human race's definition of what constitutes a human to a technical one limited in scope to what humans were in the past. The Traders offer humanity a chance to change that definition. In return, the Traders demand that they be allowed to enter the minds and bodies of human individuals to learn about human culture. Through the acquisition of new cul-tures, the Traders have been able to maintain a racial vitality. Without change a race will stagnate and die.

In both races, human and Trader, change is essential, for neither will exist long without it. In the presentation of this quintessential science fiction theme,

Varley has dramatically described a world of vast changes that is merely the prelude to further changes.

Stephen H. Goldman

Sources for Further Study

Reviews:

Analog. XCVII, September, 1977, p. 167.

Best Sellers. XXXVII, August, 1977, p. 139.

Kliatt Paperback Book Guide. XII, Fall, 1978, p. 19.

New York Times Book Review. April 24, 1977, p. 44.

Publisher's Weekly. CXI, March 21, 1977, p. 80.

School Library Journal. XXIII, May, 1977, p. 84.

ORAŞELE ÎNECATE
(The Drowned Cities)

Author: Felix Aderca (1891-1962)
First book publication: 1935
Type of work: Novel
Time: A remote future
Locale: The drowned cities of Earth

The human race struggles to survive, having retreated to the ocean floor after the Sun has gone out

> *Principal characters:*
> ENGINEER XAVIER, the General Manager of the city Marianas
> ENGINEER WHITT, the General Manager of the city Hawaii
> OLIVIA, daughter of Pi, the deceased former President of Mankind
> ENGINEER FILISTER, the General Manager of the city Ceylon
> DOCTOR HARWESTER

A novelist belonging to the school of Marcel Proust and James Joyce, a subtle and penetrating essayist, responsive to new and exotic trends, Felix Aderca is one of the Romanian writers to be attracted to science fiction between the two World Wars. A reader of H. G. Wells and J. H. Rosny *aîné*, and translator of the celebrated play *R. U. R.*, by Karel Čapek, his first brush with the genre came in a chapter of *Les Aventures de M. Ionel Lacusta-Termidor* (1928). Here the hero tells a theater manager the plot of a fantastic "tragedy in several synthetic *tableaux*," entitled *La Pastorale*. The action takes place in the year 8000. Since the Earth is overpopulated, some of the inhabitants establish themselves in a kind of bamboo cage on the bottom of the ocean. These are the Atlantides, beings who do not move about because they have no feet, and who appear as "oval-shaped as fruits, with large eyes and high foreheads." They send electric current, ideas, and music to the dry lands, and receive supplies of food in return. Determining that the Atlantides do no labor, the Land Dwellers decide to cut off the shipment of food stuffs. Dissatisfied with the fare that they are obliged to prepare for themselves chemically, the Atlantides try to frighten the Landsmen by showers of burning lights in the sky. Then the cages break open and their occupants are drowned in the Atlantic. This end "of a supreme civilisation and of a superior human type" is evoked in a page of *Oraşele Înecate* — a novel that may be considered a continuation of *La Pastorale*.

A perpetual knight-errant of modernism in literature and art since 1923, Aderca has posed a somewhat rhetorical question: Should a writer of pure fantasy, but with extraordinary talent — supposing that he should appear — be hounded out of Romanian literature merely because he does not belong to the ranks of "the nationally-oriented type"? It should be remarked that here he mounts an attack on the exclusivism of the usual traditionalists, but, in the ardor of his dispute, postulates a false antinomy. Many of the science fiction novels of Wells and Rosny are shot through with nationalism.

The prologue and epilogue of *Oraşele Înecate* are set in a futuristic Bucharest of A.D. 5000. The cameraman Ioan Doicin tells his mistress, the florist Ri, a story of the world's end. He supposes the gradual extinction of the Sun and the repercussions of that phenomenon, culminating in the movement of mankind to the floor of the oceans, closer to the incandescent core of Earth. He describes cities of glass connected by tunnels through which ultrafast trains travel; chemical tablets for food; and baths of light that rejuvenate the brain and nerves, rendering sleep unnecessary. He speaks of biological changes brought about through the control of heredity, and of selective breeding for development of the higher sentiments. All of these factors constitute the backbone of Aderca's novel.

The four undersea settlements take different forms: Hawaii, the Capital and center of scientific studies — an immense crystal globe; Cape Verde, the seat of electrical generators — two cubes upon which are set another, smaller one; Ceylon, the food city — a huge parallelopiped; and finally, Marianas, the seat of the metal workers, miners, and founders — a pyramid with three transparent sides. These structures correspond to the several dominant traits of that part of humanity that has attained an almost geometric rigor in its comportment. The inhabitants of the privileged cities of Hawaii, Cape Verde, and Ceylon remind us of the Atlantides in *La Pastorale*. They have very white hairless skin, extremely small arms, large heads, lidless eyes, and oval-shaped figures. Their blood has become a pale pink; their body temperature has fallen to twenty-five degrees centigrade, life expectancy has been reduced to forty years. Doctor Harwester bitterly declares, in a discussion with the Engineer Whitt, master of Hawaii: "We have run through almost all the circumference of Life, and we draw near to its origin: the amoeba of the ocean abysses." As regards the inhabitants of Marianas, they resemble the descendants of the Landsmen, whose appearance and customs they have inherited. It would not require a prophet to see that the latent antagonism between these two communities must certainly lead to disaster.

The action of the novel begins at a moment of crisis for the submarine society: the death of aged Pi, the President of Mankind. Who will succeed him? Who will govern Marianas, the ambitious Whitt, or the indifferent Xavier? It is not merely a choice between two men. What is at stake is the destiny of mankind. Whitt wishes to push matters to their farthest consequences, firmly believing that the only salvation is to descend even lower, toward the sole source of natural heat still available. For Xavier, the Earth is considered to be hopelessly lost; he therefore dreams of abandoning it in an aircraft propelled by rockets for launching into space. Old Pi had arrived at the same conclusion and worked for "the destruction of molecular cohesion and the attempt to seize energy from within the atom" — which would have offered the means to reach another star system. But he had died before discovering the gas necessary for the last cone of the eight-stage atomic tube.

After much fruitless work, Whitt gives up his search for the gas and succeeds in convincing the others that the only solution, confronted as they are by ever increasing cooling with the resulting loss of energy, is to penetrate into the Earth's crust. He therefore begins construction of a subterranean city. Men congregate at Marianas, leaving Hawaii, Ceylon, and Cape Verde in ruins. In the meantime, Xavier with his telescope discovers a planet that seems capable of sustaining life. But the rockets needed to reach it no longer exist, after the sabotage perpetrated by a friend of Olivia, daughter of the deceased President, because she loves Xavier and does not want him to leave.

Whitt would sacrifice Marianas and its inhabitants in order to save the diminishing supply of electricity needed to bore into the Earth's crust. The Marianasians mutiny, however, thus bringing about the death of practically all of the rest of mankind.

Escaping the catastrophe with Olivia, who again declares her love, Xavier discovers the secret of the last cone. Since Whitt and his secretary Lucia have also survived, the atomic tube will be used to actualize the heroes' dreams:

> And while two remain deep at the Earth's core, bound by their will to their destiny, another two quit the Earth, bearing the spark of life in the Universe, wheresoever they may arrive. Adam and Eve at the heart of the globe, Adam and Eve embarked on the conquest of a new Earth, in outer space.

Upon this canvas, the author has painted a picture of subtle human relations and images charged with the melancholy of the abysses, while not forgetting the elements necessary to put his novel into the orbit of classic science fiction. To those elements already cited, one must add the silver disk that spins faster and faster, turning itself into a kind of screen wherein one may see whoever carries on a conversation; the silent electric gun that stops the heartbeat and paralyzes the brain; foodstuffs in gaseous forms; and instruments with which Xavier can hear and see the sounds and faces of the past. But all of these inventions and discoveries are not used as symbols of ineluctable progress, nor, for that matter, as a pretext for a warning against forays into the future. Their role is to dramatize the fate of doomed humanity and to lay down the foundations for a final solution.

Obviously, the basic hypothesis of this novel — that it would be possible to take refuge in liquid abysses in order to substitute the heat of the Earth's fiery core for that of a moribund Sun — seems obsolete today. The author, however, takes the necessary precautionary measure of presenting the plot as a poetic invention of Ioan Doicin. Even if he seems to believe that the tragic errors of human societies will be repeated in the future, in the end he gives his optimism full rein.

Oraşele Înecate is not simply one of the books that delight the specialists because they constitute a "missing link" in some putative atomic table of themes. Because of its artistic qualities, the novel bears comparison with the best of the genre published between the two world wars. Ever since its publication, it has excited a lively interest. As the prestigious critic George Calinescu says in his *Histoire de la littérature roumaine*:

> The geographic spaciousness of thought, the ingeniosity of plastic form, the strict technology of the aquatic realm, the mechanization of every branch of activity, from birth to death, the abundance of electricity without heat — all these aspects of Faerie and Utopia are diverting. Here is added British humor, straight-faced, wrought with hyperbole and fantasies. . . .

Ion Hobana

ORBITSVILLE

Author: Bob Shaw (1931-   )
First book publication: 1975
Type of work: Novel
Time: The future, perhaps three or four centuries hence
Locale: The Earth and Orbitsville

Human explorers discover the ultimate alien artifact, a Dyson sphere, and realize that it will profoundly change human nature

Principal characters:
    VANCE GARAMOND, Starflight employee, Captain of the *Bissendorf*
    ELIZABETH LINDSTROM, President of Starflight
    THE CREW OF THE *BISSENDORF*

When people look for examples of rock-hard science fiction, they usually find works by Arthur C. Clarke, Hal Clement, or, more recently, Larry Niven. Since 1975, Bob Shaw's *Orbitsville* can be added to that list. In hard science fiction, some element of the story (often the setting) is drawn from scientific speculation; the idea is then extrapolated, with the author being careful not to violate any current knowledge; finally, the effect of the scientific element on the characters is explored, showing the interaction of man and artifact. When done poorly, hard science fiction gets tangled in its transistors, but when done well, it delivers a unique pleasure and an expansion of the mind that only science fiction can give.

The specific science fiction element in *Orbitsville* is its setting. The immense idea behind the setting began with scientists of eminence and imagination, of whom the first was probably Konstantin Tsiolkovsky (1857-1935), who in 1903 conceived of building artificial dwellings for humans in space. His notion was expanded and modified by the physicist J. Desmond Bernal (1901-1971), who discussed space colonies in his 1929 book, *The World, the Flesh, and the Devil*, and continued to develop the idea throughout his scientific career. Bernal noted that the Earth receives an insignificantly tiny percentage of the total energy radiated by the sun; if that wasted energy could be collected and used, almost nothing would be beyond human accomplishment. Bernal predicted that the first steps toward harvesting that energy would be accomplished by capturing small asteroids, say ten miles in diameter, and hollowing them out for human habitation. To these asteroids would be attached the energy collectors — they need only be thin sheets stretched on vanes, resembling huge wings, made from a material that would turn the sunlight to more usable forms of energy.

Bernal's ideas were the raw material for Freeman Dyson, a theoretical physicist born in England in 1923, who held the rank of Professor first at Cornell and then at the Institute for Advanced Study in Princeton. Dyson approached the subject from an odd direction. He wondered principally how we on Earth could detect the presence of highly intelligent aliens on planets circling other stars. With this question in mind. Dyson made certain assumptions about the alien society: that they, like us, had a growing population, and that their star had a family of planets like our solar system. Putting these assumptions together with the speculation of thinkers like Bernal, Dyson saw an abundant source of more living space: take the asteroid belt, for example, the millions of variously sized chunks of rock circling the sun between the orbits of Mars and Jupiter. Gerard O'Neill, the Princeton physicist who has done more work than perhaps anyone else on the details of space colonization, estimates that the material of the asteroid belt, reassembled into space settlements, would provide three thousand times as much land area as the Earth.

Dyson supposed that over several millennia a number of such space cities would be built, each orbiting the star, each drawing its power from the radiation of the star. From the beginning, the cities would need "traffic laws" to regulate their movements. Eventually the hypothetical alien society would have hundreds, then thousands of such huge orbiting colonies. As more and more were created, the conglomerate would begin to resemble a thin shell, a hollow sphere completely enclosing the star — hence the name "Dyson sphere."

Such a structure would, of course, completely block out visible light from an observer outside the sphere, but it would still give off heat in the infra-red range. If we want to seek signs of an advanced society in space, Dyson suggested, we should look for such "infra-red stars." And the Dyson sphere would solve two human problems for quite a long time. First, the structure would make almost the maximum profitable use of the energy from its sun; second, it would yield living space for almost any foreseeable future. A Dyson sphere constructed from the material of the solar system would provide room for a population a thousand billion times that of Earth.

Dyson's suggestions came in 1959. The sphere as he conceived of it is not a rigid shell, rather it is a multitude of separate platforms, each moving in an independent orbit. The calculation of the millions of paths in this ultimate traffic jam would need to be precise indeed. Clearly, the structure becomes much simpler if as many of the colonies as possible are joined together, thereby reducing the number of separate orbits.

A discussion of this simplification came not from science but from science fiction. Larry Niven's *Ringworld* (1970) took an exploring spaceship to a star encircled by a partial Dyson sphere. The "ring" in *Ringworld* is just that — something like a ribbon around a sun. Although the structure would appear narrow when seen from space, it nevertheless has a vast amount of room on its inner surface: the ribbon is a million miles wide. Although Dyson's theories had been circulating for over a decade, *Ringworld* caused an immense stir in science fiction circles. The concept, even in this partial form, awed reviewers and certainly contributed to the awarding of both the Hugo and the Nebula Award to *Ringworld* the following year.

Shaw's *Orbitsville* combines the concept of a complete Dyson sphere with Larry Niven's depiction of a rigid structure, and adds a twist of its own. The sphere in *Orbitsville* does not have to be assembled piece by piece by a cosmological construction company. Shaw supposes that the aliens who built it had a device like nuclear fission in reverse, a machine that directly converts energy to the desired form of matter. This "matter projector" simply "freezes" the radiant energy at a certain distance from its source at the center. The resulting sphere is immense. The first humans to encounter it know that they have found an artificial structure, but they are almost mute at its size — three hundred million kilometers in diameter. Later, they calculate that the interior of the sphere has a surface area equivalent to five billion times the usable land on Earth. No human being could confront such a structure unchanged, and when humans find it, the sphere (named "Orbitsville" by the humans) begins to work its spell on the characters of the novel.

The plot has started well before the discovery of the sphere. It begins to move under the force of human emotions, since although the novel is set perhaps three or four hundred years in the future, the people of that time still experience feelings of fear, revenge, greed, and hate.

Shaw imagines a multinational company, the wealthiest organization in the world, with a monopoly on space travel and transportation. This company, Starflight, is headed by Elizabeth Lindstrom, a woman whose appetite for imperial power matches her physical ugliness. Although interstellar travel has been possible for more than a century, only one additional planet fit for human life has been discovered, and insiders suspect that Starflight has been scanting the budget of its exploratory arm because the company is secretly reluctant to find new planets. Cheap land would cut into the huge profits it derives from transportation fees paid by immigrants to the second planet, Terra Nova, and from land fees they pay once they arrive.

The hero of the novel, Vance Garamond, is a Starflight commander of a discovery ship. As the novel opens, he is going to Lindstrom's headquarters for the ritual leave-taking she demands before one of her ships sets out. While there, Garamond has Lindstrom's only son entrusted to his care, and the son is accidentally killed. Although he is innocent of any wrong doing, Garamond knows that Lindstrom is a vicious and unpredictable woman, given to insane rages, and capable of revenging herself not only on him but on his family as well. He flees the palace, collects his own wife and child, and departs Earth in his ship, the *Bissendorf*.

Searching for a refuge against the odds, Garamond heads his ship for a region where there may or may not be a body named Pengelly's Star, which has a strange and shadowy history. It seems that one of the planets discovered in the prior century of exploration cannot support intelligent life, but did at some earlier time. The planet, named "Sagania," had a space-traveling society at about the time that civilization was beginning on Earth. But the Saganian society was destroyed in a catastrophic fire that stripped the atmosphere from the planet; human knowledge of their culture comes only from archaeological investigation. An archaeologist named Pengelly uncovered a variety of star charts which could be relatively dated by the depth of their burial. The older ones show a star (Pengally's Star) in a certain spot where the younger charts have a blank. The most recent chart of all shows the star, but this time circled by a ring. Heading for that area, Garamond finds Orbitsville.

He finds also the remains of a gigantic battle fleet clustered outside the single kilometer-wide entrance to the sphere, showing that at one time a war had raged, with the Invaders gaining the upper hand, moving inside, and abandoning their still-circling ships. The word of the discovery goes back to Earth, and the sensational news makes Garamond such a hero that Lindstrom dares not take her revenge. Instead, Starflight takes possession of the sphere, names it "Lindstromland," and begins exploiting the sphere as it had exploited Terra Nova. Despite the huge size of Orbitsville, Starflight's monopoly is made possible by its control of the single entrance.

However, Lindstrom is not through with Garamond. She hires a saboteur to destroy the navigational equipment of the *Bissendorf* while the ship is on a short exploring trip outside the sphere. When Garamond attempts to return, he discovers that he cannot slow the ship down; they will crash into the impermeable shell of Orbitsville at interplanetary speed. Using what little time and maneuverability they have left, the crew of the *Bissendorf* aims the ship for the forcefield-protected opening and strengthens the craft for the impact. They burst through with no major damage, but must slow down gradually; they crash-land five days later, more than eight million miles from the opening with the ship no longer operable.

Orbitsville begins to change the behavior of the crew immediately. It is possible for the crew to cannibalize the ship, build a fleet of fixed-wing aircraft, and set out for Beachhead City. Their chances of ever returning are slim, and many members wish to remain right where they are, living out their lives on the bounty of Orbitsville. Garamond cajoles them into building the aircraft and calls for volunteers to return with him. Revenge is now his only motive, since he believes that once he has been put out of the way, nothing will halt Lindstrom's revenge on his wife and son. The remainder of the novel describes the journey of the nine airplanes that set out on the long return journey. Fortune smiles on Garamond's persistence: 193 days into the trip, down to their last three planes, the survivors find another opening to the outside, one that has been sealed up and camouflaged. Although they have traveled only about a quarter of the necessary distance, their trip is almost over; the conditions of Orbitsville prevent radio communication, but with the discovery of a second opening, Garamond can extend an antenna outside the shell and radio for help. Help soon arrives, and Garamond returns to Beachhead City in time to frustrate Lindstrom's plot to kill his wife and child. Still more important, he has broken the Starflight monopoly on Orbitsville. They later surmise that the defenders in the battle eons past had sealed many of the openings as a safeguard against the invaders. Although the shell is itself impenetrable, these covers are not, and with numerous openings to receive immigrants from Earth, the logjam has been broken, and Starflight's power ended.

But what was the purpose of Orbitsville? Twice humans encounter aliens living inside, yet both species are strangely unassertive, passive, almost bovine. At the conclusion of the novel, it is conjectured that the sphere is a benevolent trap for aggressive races: once there, they quickly lose their territorial imperative. With always more land free for the taking, the impulse toward progress drains away, and things settle into "the quiet of that last long Sunday." The most powerful character has been the sphere itself, whose massive presence broods over the whole novel.

Walter E. Meyers

Sources for Further Study

Reviews:
Observer. February 23, 1975, p. 28.
Times Literary Supplement. March 14, 1975, p. 284.

OTHER DAYS, OTHER EYES

Author: Bob Shaw (1931-   )
First book publication: 1972
Type of work: Novel
Time: The late 1980's, early 1990's
Locale: Primarily the United States

A novel dealing with the technological and ultimately the political effects brought about by the discovery of a new kind of glass which slows down the passage of light

Principal characters:
    AL GARROD, a research scientist and director of a glass company
    ESTHER GARROD, his possessive wife
    JANE WATSON, a beautiful, part-Oriental secretary in the Department of Defense
    COLONEL JOHN MANNHEIM, an officer in the Pentagon

Science fiction seldom produces an idea that does not prove to be merely a variant of an older idea, or a simple extrapolation from already existing data. Bob Shaw's "slow glass" is a triumphant exception to the rule. It is a fine example of one of the dominant themes of traditional, "hard" science fiction: the introduction of a technological innovation, which eventually transforms totally an otherwise quite familiar near-future society. It is a paradox that change itself is the most enduring theme of science fiction.

Slow glass is glass which has been treated to slow down the passage of light. The explanation for this phenomenon is given in terms of a piezo-electric effect of the glass's crystalline structure, but this is no more than a piece of satisfying sleight of hand on Shaw's part — a typically well-managed piece of authorial reassurance calculated to soothe the reader who, if given no explanation, would regard the slow glass (officially known as Retardite) as fantasy rather than science fiction. The effect of slow glass is measured in terms of its time-width; a piece of ten-year glass, for example, will first register the image of what it sees after a ten year delay; before that it will appear black. Hence, an industry has grown up, geared to produce scenic windows. These are left in beauty spots for a period of time and then installed as windows in city houses. The occupants of the house will see for the appropriate length of time exactly what passed before the glass while it was being charged — sea, sky, mountains, drifting clouds, and perhaps the odd shepherd or wild animal.

Slow glass first appeared in Shaw's short story "Light of Other Days" (1966), which was nominated for a Nebula Award. Shaw's best short story, it is justly celebrated for the tautness with which it dovetails a fascinating scientific idea and a moving human dilemma. It turns on the point that every window has two sides. A young couple on a touring trip in the Scottish highlands pause to buy slow glass from a crofter who deals in scenic glass as a sideline. Through the window of his cottage they see a wife and child moving about; only at the end do they realize that they are watching the past from the outside of a slow glass window; the crofter lives a fantasy life alone, having to leave the house and look back to see his dead family as if alive.

The success of this story inspired two sequels, "Burden of Proof" (1967) and "A Dome of Many-Colored Glass" (1972). The former story deals with a retired judge, who has waited for five years to see the delayed evidence of a slow-glass window overlooking a playground where a murder took place. He hopes it will support the guilty verdict he brought in years before at the trial of a criminal who has been executed on the basis of circumstantial evidence. The latter story is a baroque tale of a crashed USAF pilot, and the attempts of a Chinese interrogator to brainwash him; when he is forcibly fitted with contact lenses made of slow glass which have been charged with living scenes of American atrocities in the Far East, from My Lai onwards, he retreats into psychosis.

It is typical of science fiction publishing that a successful series of linked stories should lead to a commission for a novel. Such "fix-up" novels, as they are sometimes known, usually consist of the original stories glued together with linking material; this is a common practice which explains why so much science fiction suffers from an over-episodic quality.

In *Other Days, Other Eyes* Bob Shaw adopted a different strategy. The original three stories are incorporated as what he calls "sidelights" (one of the many vision-puns of the book), unchanged, but embedded in a matrix which is wholly new; the new matrix constitutes the novel proper, and the original stories in their new context take on the weight of metaphor, reinforcing the ideas of the surrounding novel, and working through analogy like the imagery of a poem to give added resonance to the human feelings implicit in the central narrative.

The novel opens with the accidental discovery of slow glass. A new heat-insulating glass, Thermgard, has been installed in the windshields of sports cars and even jet planes. Al Garrod, the glass manufacturer, solves a series of inexplicable accidents. Through the glass, the drivers and pilots have been receiving information that has been delayed; they have seen the situation as it was a fraction of a second earlier, and their judgment of fine maneuvers has consequently been thrown off. Garrod realizes the importance of the discovery and is able to build up a multi-million dollar industry quite quickly by increasing the time-width of the glass and selling it for a variety of purposes, all described by Shaw with great ingenuity.

Garrod achieves success without any help from his wife's very rich family. His wife has enjoyed the fiscal power she held over her husband, and being a woman of few emotional resources, the collapse of this power crushes her spirit. Her downfall is mirrored in the blinding she receives when she unwisely enters Garrod's laboratory at the moment when all the light stored in one piece of slow glass is released in one searing flash. Garrod has been working on ways of retrieving information from the glass without waiting years of real time for it to emerge naturally, a point which has been illuminated by the sidelight-story "Burden of Proof"; and Esther's blinding is a direct result of this research. It is a wonderful image; the curious person, slyly seeking information which is not hers, is literally blinded by receiving it all in one shocking instant of time.

Esther now has the emotional weapon she needs; perversely, she is almost prepared to embrace her own maiming for the opportunities it gives her to emotionally blackmail her husband. Garrod, quick-witted intellectually, is unsophisticated in human relationships and accepts this clinging burden stolidly, with a dour stamina and a resentment that remains silent. He becomes involved in the inevitable love affair although his partner, Jane, is really nothing more than a conventionally attractive character of little significance. However, Garrod ultimately finds the strength to reject his wife and create a new world for himself, which parallels the new world which has been created by his invention.

Shaw has always stood out from the crowd of commercial, genre science fiction writers because of his sudden flashes of lyrical imagery, always brief and controlled, so that they do not clash too badly with the rather laconic tone of his ordinary narrative voice. These bursts of surprising color emerge rather in the manner of the similarly unexpected images of Raymond Chandler in his California detective thrillers. But in this novel most of the poetry, the strongest feeling, is carried by the three embedded short stories, and they are perhaps too slender to carry the weight. *Other Days, Other Eyes* suffers to a degree from the prosaic quality of the main plot, which though well-crafted is slightly diagrammatic.

The plot reflects two of the quirky themes which have haunted all of Shaw's fiction: blindness/perception change, and the power wielded by strong-willed women over unsophisticated men. The former theme presumably relates to Shaw's life; he has suffered from intermittent bouts of near blindness himself, often preluded by minor visual hallucinations. In the novel, Garrod has an eye problem, and ironically (given the theme) wears tinted glasses because "the light hurts." Critics who have assumed the latter theme to be connected with Shaw's domestic life have had short shrift from the author, who has more than once found it necessary, to his own embarrassment, to appear in print testifying to the happiness of his own marriage of more than twenty years. Nonetheless, the subplots of domestic discord between men and women in Shaw's work have often, as here, been strongly and grippingly rendered, and they certainly constitute, unusual for the genre, one of the ways in which his work stands out from the science fiction pack.

In *Other Days, Other Eyes*, however, the plot dealing with the outside world is the strongest, though the domestic and public plots are very cleverly woven together. Much of the story deals with Garrod's discovery of new ways, often illegal, in which slow glass is being used. He solves two murder mysteries, one involving a frame-up, the other a false alibi.

The story, which employs fairly conventional thriller elements, is considerably enlivened by its increasing blackness. Slow glass functions as a metaphor, very appropriately and prophetically just before the age of Watergate, for the increasingly sophisticated violations of privacy becoming possible in our crowded and technologically minded world.

The first "sidelight," "Light of Other Days," takes its title from Thomas Moore's 1815 song of the same name, which begins "Oft in the stilly night/ Ere slumber's chain has bound me/ Fond memory brings the light/ of other days around me." Slow glass is a form of physical memory, quite literally bringing the light of other days. But it is also, even in this first and gentlest of the three sidelights, something more. These are not private memories; anyone can share them. Hence the unbearable shame of the Scottish crofter when it is exposed that he has not only captured the past, he is captured by it.

With each advance in the plot, the function of slow glass as an invader of privacy becomes more evident. New forms of visual bugging become commonplace; spies can even carry tiny slivers of slow glass embedded in pores of their skin; secret meetings have to take place in darkness, or in rooms that have just been completely painted. The invasion-of-privacy theme satisfyingly links the marriage story with the public story in the second half of the book, as Esther Garrod makes increasingly painful attempts to capture her husband's complete attention and life, rationalizing her inevitable, reproachful presence as a "sharing." The two plots coincide literally at the point where Esther, whose vision has been partly restored by the insertion of Retardite lenses in her ruined eyes, insists that her husband program these lenses. In other words, she will experience whatever he sees twenty-four hours later; in the most terrifying way she has invaded his every waking minute, living through his vision just as a vampire exists on its victim's blood.

The final image of the book is an apocalyptic extension of this private trauma. For some time Garrod has been noticing crop-dusting planes at work in odd areas, and with a flash of intuition he realizes that they are actually, on government orders, sprinkling slow glass all over the country — eventually, all over the world. Information retrieval techniques have become such that images can be called back even from microscopic grains of powder. Now the Government can see all — the whole world becomes its big eye, in an image which renders the ever-present television screens of George Orwell's *Nineteen Eighty-Four* (1949) quite tame in comparison. It is typical of Shaw to be appalled at the government cynicism he has so powerfully symbolized; however, he is not so shaken as to be frightened of the consequences. He is, in a sense, excited by them: men will learn "to live without subterfuge or shame as they had done in a distant past when it was known that the eyes of God could see everywhere." It is a wonderful stroke, bringing the story around in a full, historical circle — both just and beautiful.

Other Days, Other Eyes incorporates too many thriller-conventions, which are too familiar and inflexible to do justice to the scale of Shaw's speculations. However, the book remains outstanding at its peak moments, flaming again and again into life.

Peter Nicholls

Sources for Further Study

Reviews:

Analog. XC, January, 1973, pp. 167-168.

Futures. IV, December, 1972, p. 92.

Observer. July 16, 1972, p. 30.

Publisher's Weekly. CCI, May 29, 1972, p. 34.

Renaissance. IV, Summer, 1972, p. 11.

Times Literary Supplement. October 13, 1972, p. 1235.

Worlds of If. XXI, June, 1973, p. 172.

THE OTHER SIDE
(DIE ANDERE SEITE)

Author: Alfred Kubin (1877-1959)
First book publication: 1909
English translation: 1967
Type of work: Novel
Time: The present
Locale: A sequestered "Dream Kingdom," somewhere deep in Asia

The account of grotesque and horrible events in a closed human community that slowly decays under fantastic metamorphoses

> *Principal characters:*
> ALFRED KUBIN, the narrator
> CLAUS PATERA, the creator and master of the Dream Kingdom
> HERKULES BELL, an American billionaire

Alfred Kubin was one of twentieth century Germany's greatest artists of the nightside of human nature. His scurrilous and demoniac drawings, that seem to evoke the hidden mysteries of the unconscious, grace many books of the fantastic. Today, first editions containing his illustrations command high prices. It has been remarked that his line-drawings are almost "literary," but this is a doubtful contention. He did, however, write a novel that has become one of the masterpieces of German fantasy: *The Other Side*. It is a classic not only of fantastic literature, but also of modern fiction, a novel that influenced writers such as Gustav Meyrink and Hermann Kasack and anticipated the aims and methods of the literary surrealists. Kubin may even have been an influence on Franz Kafka.

In *The Other Side* there is an episode which suggests this influence. The narrator tries to gain permission to see his friend Patera, the master of the Dream Kingdom, to present a petition or lodge a complaint; but he fails. At first, he is told that Patera is engaged in urgent business, and later that he is away. Then the narrator learns where he can obtain a ticket for an audience. However, when he appears at the correct place, he is ignored at first, then asked to produce all kinds of impossible and irrelevant documents, such as the certificate of his mother's vaccination. Upon mentioning that he is Patera's guest, the narrator is treated with the promptest attention and utmost civility and assumes that he will be brought into the presence of Patera at once. But he is simply led through a number of empty rooms and halls, all filled to the ceiling with reports and documents collected from all over Europe. At last he comes face to face with his Excellency, a beribboned bureaucrat, who promises to send him the necessary ticket and then like an automaton triggered by a cue, turns and begins to address a nonexistent audience on an impending improvement of the dramatic arts.

In short, the Dream Kingdom is an absurd world that obeys its own mad rules; the unexpected is the expected. Every act is soon counteracted by another; the laws of causality are suspended, and arbitrariness reigns. The hero obtains his ticket to the audience, followed the next day by a message that it has been rescinded. Every seeming success is instantly nullified. Services or goods may be obtained for next to nothing, or they may require large sums of money. The hero's wife receives a large basket of groceries for a ridiculously low amount, but the narrator is charged a fortune for a box of matches in a coffeehouse. All standards of the normal world are totally devalued.

This Dream Kingdom is the creation of Claus Patera, a long-lost school friend of the narrator, Alfred Kubin. One day an emissary of Patera arrives to ask Kubin to follow him to the Dream Kingdom. Like Kubin himself, Patera is an enemy of progress, especially scientific progress. His Dream Kingdom is protected by a high wall, and its capital, Pearl, is also surrounded by monumental walls and fortifications. A single gate allows entry to his empire. Patera's aim is not the creation of a utopia. It is also not the preservation of real values.

Only carefully selected individuals are allowed to enter the Dream Kingdom. They are characterized by extremely refined senses; they are able to perceive relationships in the real world which do not exist for an average individual, except in rare moments of heightened awareness. These qualities are the quintessence of the dream people. The people who enter this realm, which borders on life and death, sanity and madness, night and day, are predestined by birth and previous experience. Normal life and dreams are at opposite poles, and since the dream people seek to enter into the depths of being, normal joys and pains are alien to them. They live in moods, believe in nothing but their dreams, and consider material existence the raw material for their psychedelic spiritual experiences.

The entire book is marked by a remarkable visual quality (not surprising in an artist), which at times achieves a painful sharpness. Kubin writes simply and lucidly, but as a man obsessed. The geography of the Dream Kingdom and the journey to it are described exactly and in the most banal terms imaginable. A map even accompanies the book. The city of Pearl consists of four main quarters: the railway quarter, located near a swamp, contains the administrative buildings, the archive, and the postal services; the garden quarter is inhabited by the rich; the "Long street" is the business district, inhabited by the middle class; the French quarter, inhabited by disreputable Romans, Slavs, and Jews, dangerous to enter by day and night, is a place of nocturnal crime and brothels. Towering over everything is the huge and hideous palace of Patera, a castle as mysterious and strange as that of Kafka's novel or Mervyn Peake's Gormenghast.

The buildings and artifacts, often dilapidated, have been brought from all over Europe by Patera's agents, who purchase them with unlimited funds. It is later divulged that these are not common buildings that have been rebuilt there; they are buildings marked by crime, blood, and evil deeds. Patera's palace has been built out of the fragments of places that witnessed bloody conspiracies and revolutions. Everything in Pearl is touched by human misery; everything has been soaked with the emanations of that which is the most base, brutal, and abnormal in human nature.

Such qualities also characterize the inhabitants, who are, with the exception of a supremely meditative race of blue-eyed Mongols, a collection of freaks. The most harmless among them are possessed by various ticks, bizarre hobbies, religious fanaticisms, and a thousand forms of neurasthenia and hysteria. The inhabitants of this world are mostly unhappy creatures at odds with themselves: hypochondriacs, spiritualists, adventurers seeking rest, acrobats, political refugees, tricksters, wanted murderers, counterfeiters, thieves, and other types of criminals. In addition, there are many people with physical deformities, which are described in great detail. The population is kept constant by new arrivals, and children are considered an expensive and troublesome inconvenience.

No one in the Dream Kingdom looks to the future. Fashions are from the year 1860; the buildings, artworks, and artifacts are much older. The Dream Kingdom does not give the impression of venerable age, but that of a mixture of past epochs, a mad conglomeration of various styles and fashions combined in a mythical timeless world. It is a phantasmagoric vision dominated by death; a world that is, although nostalgic, not so much of the past as outside of time and normal historical processes. This impression is strengthened by the sky, which is always gray and overcast; the sun is not visible by day, nor are the stars visible at night. Everything is touched by an eternal gloom, with only a moon of doom shining over this world. In short, it is a world cut off from direct sensory contact, a world of timeless symbols, metaphors, and archetypes. It is structured like a dream, dreamt on a symbolic rather than a literal level, following a mad yet quite consistent inner logic.

As strange as the events in the first two thirds of the novel are, characterized by darkly symbolic scenes such as the narrator stumbling through labyrinthine cellars or the death of his wife, the furious culmination of the novel brings even stranger occurrences, which begin with the arrival of the American, Herkules Bell, in the Kingdom. Immensurably rich and powerfully built, he is the antithesis of the father figure Patera; he embodies the principles of life, light, common sense, and progress as opposed to the death principle of Patera, who stands for the past, madness, and destruction. Bell and Patera are not independent of each other, but various aspects of the same person, one divided personality torn into two parts.

Although Bell is the representative of life, the decay of the Dream Kingdom begins with his arrival. First there is a proliferation of all forms of animal life, especially ants, rats, cockroaches, snakes, and beasts of prey. Sexual frenzies, debaucheries, orgies, and wild mass copulation between humans and animals follow. These vitalistic excesses are but a prelude to general starvation, and eventual death. Buildings crack and fall apart, crashing in heaps of rubble. There is dirt and grease everywhere; food decays even while it is being cooked. Cannibalism runs rampant; one character ends his existence as a roast on a spit. The swamp encroaches upon the city, hidden canals and abysses emerge everywhere, and entire sections of the city collapse. The finale of the book is an apocalyptic vision, a *danse macabre* in which Kubin gives his extraordinary imagination free reign.

Alfred Kubin was a strange and troubled man. Obsessed by many fears, he perceived all life as a battle of opposing principles. He once declared that since the age of nine, he had viewed the world as a horrible hell in which beauty existed only as a contradiction which begat concupiscence and lust. As a result, his fictional world is a horrible game and a dream. He utilizes the well-known metaphor of the world as a stage, with Patera as the stage-manager — Lord and Devil of his Kingdom, creator and tormentor of his subjects.

In the grandiose finale of the novel, Patera grows to a gigantic size, a veritable demon of destruction tearing up a volcano and disrupting large rivers. The American also becomes gigantic, and the two men battle in an ocean of blood, which sometimes reveals through the churning waves a floor of feces. As they fight each other they undergo monstrous metamorphoses. Finally, Bell shrinks, with only his phallus remaining gigantic, and the "horrible member" creeps like a snake over the Earth, until it too becomes smaller and disappears in the subterranean caverns of the Dream Kingdom. After Patera's death in this orgy of transformations, he turns into a corpse of classic beauty. The military forces who enter from the outside find only a heap of ruins and a few ragged survivors, including the crazed narrator. The novel ends with the remarkable sentence: "The demiurge is a hermaphrodite."

The Other Side does not describe a fight between good and evil, rather the dichotomy of existence: the complementary nature of day and night, heaven and hell. The real hell is constantly at work in us; the sublime, and the base do not exist independently but coexist in the human subconscious. The novel provides Freudian critics with a field day. It abounds in Freudian symbols such as snakes, tentacles, holes, rats, seas of blood, and both vaginal and phallic symbols. Lesser known early works of Kubin confirm the Freudian interpretation. Some of them are of a frighteningly sexual nature, describing genital organs so large that the humans connected to them are merely appendages. There can be little doubt that many of Kubin's fears were sexual in nature.

This novel, however, is more than a collection of psychological symbols; it is a stringent phantasmagory and a fully realized and visual work of art that gives expression not only to personal anxieties but also to the anxieties of Kubin's time and place. The territory of the then Austro-Hungarian monarchy produced other writers fascinated by doom: Franz Kafka, Gustav Meyrink, Bruno Schulz, and Fritz von Herzmanovsky-Orlando. They all foresaw in their visions the fall of this Empire, which they both loved and hated, and the horrors of the barbarity to come. Compared to Kubin's haunted creation, the works of most of these other writers appear mellow; his powerful imagination joins disparate elements into a coherent apocalyptic vision.

Franz Rottensteiner

Sources for Further Study

Reviews:

Kirkus Reviews. XXXV, August 15, 1967, p. 986.

Library Journal. XCII, October 1, 1967, p. 3445.

Publisher's Weekly. CXCII, September 4, 1967, p. 51.

OUT OF THE SILENT PLANET

Author: C.S. Lewis (1898-1963)
First book publication: 1938
Type of work: Novel
Time: The present
Locale: England and Malacandra (Mars)

The first book in the Ransom trilogy — the others being Perelandra *(1943) and* That Hideous Strength *(1945) — in which Lewis uses science fiction as the vehicle for a mythopoeic discussion of good and evil*

> *Principal characters:*
> RANSOM, a Cambridge philologist
> WESTON, a physicist
> DEVINE, a materialist
> HROSSA, seal-like Martians, poets, singers, and dancers
> SERONI, angular, human-shaped Martians, thinkers
> PFIFLTRIGGI, toadlike Martians, artists and artificers
> ELDILA, lesser spirits which do Oyarsa's bidding
> OYARSA, the spirit which governs Mars
> MALELDIL THE YOUNG, the Creator
> THE OLD ONE, the being with whom Maleldil lives

Combining religion and science in the same narrative can be a difficult task. Early science fiction writers, for the most part, either ignored religion or claimed that future man would no longer need it. In many cases, where both science and religion had thematic import in the same story, religion was depicted as a haven for the deluded, the foolish, and the unrealistic. However, more recent science fiction, especially that written since the beginning of the 1950's, has been able to bring science and religion into a working, if not always harmonious, literary relationship. C.S. Lewis was one of the writers who demonstrated how this could be accomplished; in *Out of the Silent Planet*, he uses the genre as a means of bringing the reader to a thoughtful contemplation of the mythic nature of the universe.

Dr. Elwin Ransom, a Cambridge philologist on a walking tour of the English countryside, is kidnaped by Weston, a physicist, and Devine, a former schoolmate whom Ransom dislikes. The two are making their second journey to Malacandra (Mars) and take Ransom along in the mistaken belief that the ruler of the planet wants a human for sacrifice. This mistake is typical of Weston's and Devine's inability to perceive what they find on Malacandra. Ignorant of his role in this enterprise, Ransom is delighted to find that space is not a cold and dark emptiness but an "ocean of radiance" which should be called "the heavens." He finds himself mystically attuned to what he sees, and his thoughts turn to images from Greek mythology and to lines from Milton. At this early point in the book, Lewis is already changing the focus from the scientific vehicle in which the three are traveling to the mystical realm through which they are voyaging.

When the ship lands on Malacandra, the scientific portion of the book is virtually over. Weston and Devine are about to hand Ransom over to six *seroni* when a larger water beast attacks. Ransom, who has overheard the other two discussing his fate, uses this moment of confusion to escape. From this point on, Lewis develops a mythopoeic fantasy in the manner of David Lindsay (*Voyage to Arcturus*) and George MacDonald (*Phantastes* and *Lilith*), both of whom Lewis acknowledged as formative influences. Ransom's journey, then, becomes not a journey to discover new places, things, theories, or people, but a journey to discover the self and its relationship to the rest of creation. In addition, Ransom will discover the mythic nature of his own planet, Thulcandra (Earth), and its place in the Field Arbol (the solar system).

For almost two days, Ransom flees every living thing he sees. While resting on a riverbank, he comes face to face with a *hross*, Hyoi. They attempt to communicate, and Ransom finds that his philological knowledge enables him to decipher the Malacandran language. Hyoi takes Ransom by boat to a *hross* village down in a *handramit* (valley) where he spends several weeks getting to know the *hrossa* and learning about Malacandra from them. He also discovers that the *hrossa* know of his own planet, which they call Thulcandra, the silent planet. He learns that Malacandra is ruled by an Oyarsa, a different order of being, and that everything was created by Maleldil the Young who lives with the Old One, two spirits of the highest order without "body, parts or passions." But the *hrossa* cannot tell him more than this; they are but poets, singers, and dancers. For answers to his questions, he must ask the *seroni*, who "would know such things," or Oyarsa himself.

Ransom's life among the *hrossa* is idyllic, and he finds them living the kind of life to which men and women on Earth aspire but rarely attain. Since Ransom spends little time with either the *seroni* or the *pfifltriggi*, the inhabitants of Malacandra must be judged by the actions and attitudes of the *hrossa*. These creatures are by nature temperate, monogamous, and peaceful. The Malacandrans do not even have a word for evil in their language; the closest Ransom can come to a term for such a concept is "bent." That the *hrossa* are the microcosm of Malacandra is made obvious by Hyoi. He links all three major groups — *hrossa*, *seroni*, and *pfifltriggi* — together as *hnau*. What is true of one group, insofar as moral or ethical standards are concerned, is true of all. Lewis, as is made clear later in the book, seems to be presenting a picture of what Earth might have been like if the Edenic state had not been lost by the Fall.

Ransom journeys to meet Oyarsa at Meldilorn guided by a *sorn* named Augray. Ransom and Augray spend several days traveling together, they learn much from each other. Ransom discovers that Oyarsa has ruled Malacandra for all of its existence and that each planet, including Thulcandra, is ruled by an Oyarsa with the help of many *eldila*. Augray also explains that Earth is called Thulcandra, the silent planet, because no communication comes from it. Ransom learns even more about his own planet's singularity when he is questioned by a group of younger *seroni* who are greatly puzzled by Earth's violent history; an older *sorn*, who cannot conceive of a bent Oyarsa, suggests that Earth is as it is because the people there, in trying to rule themselves without an Oyarsa, are like someone trying to lift himself up by his own hair. Ransom, like so many literary travelers before him, finds his own world and race somewhat difficult to explain to these superior beings.

Once in Meldilorn, an island of great beauty inhabited by many *eldila*, things move much faster for Ransom. It is within these pages that Lewis brings the major social and mythic themes to their climax; this climax, however, is not so much a climax of action as a climax of thought and philosophy. It is here that Lewis states the ideas for which he has been constructing examples in the previous chapters. These ideas are articulated in a confrontation between Oyarsa and the other two Earthmen, Weston and Devine, who have been brought before Oyarsa for killing Hyoi and two other *hrossa*. Ransom acts as translator during this encounter and attempts to explain Weston's and Devine's comments to Oyarsa.

Weston and Devine are the spokesmen for attitudes which Lewis find abhorrent. Devine's reason for coming to Malacandra is materialistic; gold is abundant and easy to acquire there, and he plans to make his fortune. His previous speech to Ransom about expensive boats, women, and vacation homes and his lack of anything but a working knowledge of Weston's space vehicle were preludes to this. Devine is evil because he is willing to step on anyone, as evidenced by his earlier willingness to sacrifice Ransom in order to make his fortune; to Devine, making money is the most important thing in life. Oyarsa recognizes Devine for what Lewis believes him to be, a talking animal whose body should be "unmade" since the spirit in it is already dead.

Weston's evil is much more serious. Weston believes in sacrificing anything for science and for the future of the human race in general. He believes that it is science and technology which make humans superior and which will enable them to spread throughout the universe; he believes it is the right of humans, as superior beings, to supersede such lesser beings as he perceives the Malacandrans to be. Ultimately, he believes in a Life Force, but he believes it to be evidenced solely in the humanity of Earth which, as a race, will live forever. Weston does not even care for his personal fate and says that if Oyarsa kills him the spread of humanity will take place all the same.

Weston's philosophy seems to be taken almost directly from J.S.B. Haldane's *Possible Worlds* (1927) and Olaf Stapledon's *Last and First Men* (1931), both of which depict future man taking over adjacent planets for himself and slaying the natural inhabitants to make those planets more like Earth. Lewis has prefigured Weston's speech here; earlier in the book, Weston was contemptuous of Ransom's branch of learning, suggesting that such studies used money which should go to science, and Weston was quite willing to sacrifice Ransom to proceed with his scientific inquiry. Ransom's translation of Weston's speech into Malacandran shows just how parochial Lewis finds such a philosophy; moreover, Ransom has already learned from Hyoi, from Augray, and from Oyarsa that Maleldil the Young did not create these worlds and races to last forever. Weston comes off as a nineteenth century nationalist in scientific trappings. His lack of concern for his own fate raises him above Devine's animal status in Oyarsa's eyes, but Oyarsa still judges him bent. It is ironic that Weston, as an agent of the bent Oyarsa of Thulcandra, has made this journey to Malacandra; the journey breaks Thulcandra's quarantine and will cause the bent Oyarsa serious defeats.

On both sides of the confrontation with Weston and Devine, Ransom has time to discuss matters with Oyarsa, and it is here that Lewis delineates the mythic dimensions of the solar system. From the *hrossa*, Ransom has learned of the Old One and of Maleldil the Young, the Creator. Ransom now learns that all of the planets except Thulcandra are united under Maleldil. The Oyarsa of Thulcandra, however, became bent and was subsequently bound to his planet. The Oyarsa of Malacandra explains to Ransom that the bent Oyarsa and the *eldila* who serve him are largely responsible for the state of affairs on Thulcandra, but he also believes that Maleldil the Young has not given Thulcandra up to the Bent One. In fact, there are rumors that Maleldil has "dared terrible things" and may have appeared on Thulcandra at some point to struggle with the Bent One. Thus, Ransom discovers not new truths but the one, universal truth of which Thulcandra's philosophies and religions glimpse or remember only a part.

This theme is the basis for the Christian readings of this book and of the rest of the trilogy. However, students of comparative religions will see that Lewis' structure is so generalized that it could well be interpreted as the basic structure of a number of religions. In fact, this structure can also be observed in many of the world's ancient myth-systems, and this is why the novel is mythopoeic — it reaches beyond a specific doctrine and toward the awe-inspiring and the numinous. Ransom learns a great deal about the "true" nature of the universe. By extension, Lewis seems to be hoping, so also does the reader.

The ending of the book retreats, temporarily, from these considerations as Weston, Devine, and Ransom are allowed to return to Thulcandra. The conflicts are left unresolved and are to be continued in *Perelandra* and *That Hideous Strength*. Critical opinion on *Out of the Silent Planet* and the rest of the trilogy varies considerably; the harshest critics, however, still acknowledge it as an important book, while those who favor it find it extremely moving. In any case, it is a well-written, thought-provoking novel which attempts to deal cogently with the "greater truths" behind or beyond our everyday affairs.

Charles William Sullivan III

Sources for Further Study

Criticism:

Devoe, Alan. "Scientifiction," in *American Mercury*. LXXVII (August, 1953), pp. 26-29. Devoe discusses the work of Lewis and compares it to that of Ray Bradbury and other major figures in science fiction.

Green, Roger Lancelyn. *Into Other Worlds: Space Flight in Fiction from Lucian to C. S. Lewis*. New York: Abelard Schuman, 1958. Green establishes Lewis' work as the prototype for other science fiction writers dealing with the theme of space flight.

Hillegas, Mark. *The Future as Nightmare: H. G. Wells and the Anti-Utopians*. New York: Oxford University Press, 1967. Hillegas makes a concise but acute analysis of the influence of Wells's "cosmic pessimism" upon C. S. Lewis.

Hilton-Young, Wayland. "The Contented Christian," in *Cambridge Journal*. X (July 1952), pp. 603-612. This critic views *Out of the Silent Planet* as an allegorical depiction of the three parts of man.

Moorman, Charles. "Space Ship and Grail: The Myths of C. S. Lewis," in *College English*. XVIII (May, 1957), pp. 401-405. Moorman comments on the function of Lewis invented mythology in the Ransom trilogy.

OXYGEN OCH AROMASIA
(Oxygen and Aromasia)

Author: Claës Lundin (1825-1908)
First book publication: 1878
Type of work: Novel
Time: 2378
Locale: Gothenburg and Stockholm, Sweden

A satiric Utopian novel of the almost perfect society of the year 2378

Principal characters:
>AROMASIA DOFTMAN-OZODES, a young woman, a famous artist on the "scent-organ"
>OXYGEN WARM-BLASIUS, a weatherman, Aromasia's fiancé
>APOLLONIDES, a poet
>MRS. SKARPMAN-STORMFÅGEL, a scheming old lady
>MISS ROSENDOFT, a young lady, madly in love with Apollonides
>GIRO, a banker
>HEMISFÄRION, a scientist
>KARL JOHAN KVIST, a time traveler from the year 1878

The late Victorian era was the scene of unparalleled technical and scientific development which, during a few decades, completely changed the Western world. From 1870 on, many of the inventions appeared that have formed our present world: gasoline and battery powered cars, streamlined trains, heavier than air airplanes, wireless telegraphy, electric bulbs, wireless telephoto, cinematography, the Dussaud television, telephone, wire recorder, and phonograph. This was Jules Verne's era, a time of unbridled optimism during which the shadows thickened so imperceptibly that few appeared to notice them. Revolutions and world wars would soon come, as technological advances were followed by vast sociological changes, but at the time it seemed as if Schlaraffenland was indeed coming true. Vernian optimism reigned absolute, at least in science fiction, and Utopianism reached its apotheosis with Edward Bellamy's book *Looking Backward 2000-1887* (1888), in which all citizens, men, women, and children, are privates in the great and glorious industrial army of the world.

Lofty Utopianism inevitably bears the seed of its opposite, however, and in the midst of this jubilant optimism intellectuals voiced their growing uneasiness. Thus appeared works such as Samuel Butler's *Erewhon* (1880), Albert Robida's *Le vingtième siècle* (1882), and William Morris' *News From Nowhere* (1890). One of the first works voicing a growing discontent with the Utopian ideals of the time was Claës Lundin's *Oxygen och Aromasia.*

Oxygen och Aromasia describes a Utopia where things are almost, but not quite, perfect, where people are shown as human (although somewhat caricatured), and where progress and failures are part of everyday life. This is a society in change, not the rigid utilitarian world of the usual Utopias. In other words, Lundin's picture is an unusually convincing description of the future, at least for the time, written with much humor and wit, even vicious satire at times. This alone makes the novel stand out from the uniformly greyish bulk of Victorian Utopias.

Claës Lundin was a celebrated journalist and popular historian, Sweden's first war correspondent and the author of a number of books on Stockholm. He witnessed the Paris Commune of 1871 as journalist and saw at close hand the slaughter which ended this attempt to revolution and the creation of a new society. He also visited the World Exhibition in Paris 1878, where all the wonders of the new machine age were shown in all their cast iron splendor. All this appears, in various forms, in *Oxygen och Aromasia*.

Claës Lundin was not a science fiction author; *Oxygen och Aromasia* was his only attempt in the genre, and actually his only novel, even though he knew personally many of the leading science fiction writers of the day, including Jules Verne, André Laurie, and Kurd Lasswitz. *Oxygen och Aromasia* was written after Lundin had read Lasswitz's science fiction book *Bilder aus der Zukunft* (1878), which evidently gave him an idea or two; he borrowed the idea of a Utopian society a few centuries hence, several situations, and the names of some of the protagonists and proceeded to write his own commentary on his time and the glorious future. But whereas Lasswitz's story, "Zum Nullpunkt des Seins," was a rather slight piece, mixing irreverent slapstick and student's jokes with lighthearted depictions of the wonders of the future (although they have serious implications), Lundin used the groundwork not only to satirize the society of his times, but Utopianism in general. The result was eminently satisfying and the novel is very readable even today. It was, indeed, reprinted as late as 1974.

Oxygen och Aromasia takes place in Gothenburg, the future capital of Sweden, and in Stockholm, in the glorious Utopian year 2378 where almost anything is possible and only the improbable is commonplace. All the usual Utopian hardware is present — space ships, television, moving sidewalks, communal kitchens, even time travel — and also several rather unusual marvels, like invisibility drugs and the fantastic "brain organ," a new musical instrument which stimulates the senses by hammering on the skull; the organ is necessary because Wagnerian music has made everyone deaf.

Aromasia, the heroine of the novel, is what we might call a liberated woman, a famous artist on the "scent-organ" and a member of the Swedish Parliament. Her lover, the heroic Oxygen, is a weathermonger, creating and selling all sorts of weather to needy customers. Aromasia also has an ardent admirer, the poet Apollonides, who loves her dearly but without much success; Aromasia treats him like a pet, refusing to take him seriously. This trio moves through a Utopian society which on the surface appears to have all the time-honored traits of a true Utopia, but which, on closer examination, turns out to be somewhat less than perfect.

In Lundin's society, the bureaucracy is unbelievable, capitalism rules, and everything can be bought and sold, including the future. The leading newspapers, with names like *The Rapacious Wolf*, *The Ravenous Tongue*, and *Next Week's News*, fight violent battles with one another, with the government, and with anyone else in order to boost circulation; and in the world outside Sweden, world war is closing in. An enormous fleet of Chinese flying fortresses is defeated off the California coast by "air cannons," but an even greater battle between the United States and Russia is imminent and might destroy the entire world. Corruption is rampant everywhere, and hideous poverty lurks behind the gleaming Utopian facades.

However, Aromasia, Oxygen, and their poet friend Apollonides only move in the best circles — among the industrial barons, government members, "machine authors," musicians, and other members of the Utopian jet set, constantly traveling around the world in search of new, untasted pleasures. No one ever questions the world order, least of all this trio of protagonists. Apollonides longs to return to an older, simpler life, hopefully together with Aromasia; his idea of a simple life is that of a nineteenth century country squire with some Utopian frills added.

Lundin manages, in his description of life and endeavors in his Utopia, to describe the uncaring, unconcerned, and nonchalant life of a few amiable nitwits in a Utopian world standing on the brink of catastrophe. This is no mean feat, especially considering the rather naïve state of Utopian novel-writing in his day. Lundin was a good friend of August Strindberg, with whom he collaborated on one book about Stockholm, and one indeed recognizes much of Lundin's razor-sharp satire in Strindberg's first novel, *Röda rummet*, which appeared one year after *Oxygen och Aromasia*. Lundin emerges as a brilliant satirist, particularly in two passages — the Poet Apollonides meeting with the news media of Utopia, especially the Bureau for Propagation of Useful Untruths; and the magnificent sequence in which a group of businessmen divide the future into shares and sell it to one another. Aromasia works untiringly for the amelioration of the common man's situation, agitating for the "social issue," but to little effect.

The novel culminates in a way that would have pleased Michail Bakunin. Aromasia composes a scent sonata about the "social issue" in order to describe "its final solution through the perfection of the machines." But when she plays this masterpiece for the ruling elite in Stockholm, the scent organ breaks down, a terrible stench pervades the hall, the public is forced to flee, the organ starts to burn, and the building explodes. The poet Apollonides flees in a Moon rocket and dies in space, while Aromasia decides to spend her life in politics, leaving her weathermonger Oxygen whose wrath leads to months of violent storms over Sweden. Nothing has really changed; the industrial barons go on as before, the literature factories continue to spew out machine-manufactured poetry and fiction, and the world war mounts in intensity.

This novel is far less harmless than most Utopian novels of the time, and might even have had some impact on science fiction as such if it had been written in a language more widely read than Swedish. As it was, the book's success was confined to its native country, and its author returned to journalism. *Oxygen och Aromasia* proved to be of some importance for other writers of satiric prose in Sweden, such as Strindberg; and later Swedish science fiction authors owe a great and obvious debt to Lundin's novel.

The idea of presenting an apparent Utopian society which upon closer scrutiny turns out to be quite imperfect is now "old hat" in science fiction; but Lundin was one of the first to realize the fundamental ambiguity of the Utopian dream. He gives us the benefit of a wider, more cynical perspective, and deserves to be remembered as one of the first true science fiction satirists.

Sam J. Lundwall

THE PARADOX MEN

Author: Charles L. Harness (1915-   )
First book publication: 1953
Type of work: Novel
Time: 2177
Locale: Imperial America, a Lunar Observatory, and the surface of the sun

An extravagant novel of lost identity, ideological conflict, and the fate of human-kind

Principal characters:
ALAR, a thief
BERN HAZE-GAUNT, Chancellor of Imperial America
KEIRIS, his wife and slave
THE MICROFILM MIND, a manipulator of possibilities
GENERAL THURMOND, Police Minister and duelist
LORD SHEY, a sadistic psychologist

The Paradox Men belongs to an easily recognizable subgenre of science fiction and carries clear evidence of its literary ancestry. It is one of the gaudy and "intensely recomplicated" melodramas which were first made popular by A. E. van Vogt. The plot contains several deliberate echoes of van Vogt's style and even of passages from van Vogt's own work, particularly *The World of Null-A* and the "Weapon Shops" series.

The background of the novel is one of decadent civilization, where swordplay coexists with superscience, and the plot is a combination of Ruritanian romance and space opera. The central character, Alar the Thief, shares the predicament of van Vogt's typical protagonist: he is a superhuman being whose powers lie dormant, waiting to be released by psychological pressure and the threat of extinction. He is also without identity and must find out who and what he is while events unfold around him. The supporting characters gradually focus all their attention on him, trying desperately either to help or to destroy him. His importance, of course, transcends the petty plans of emperors and warmongers, for upon his fate hangs the future of the entire human race.

Van Vogt himself was so enchanted by this formula that he used it time and time again and is still doing so. Its psychological appeal is so strong, and its flexibility so workable, that two of the most capable writers in the field, Charles L. Harness and Ian Wallace, have borrowed it and employed it repeatedly. Van Vogt apparently constructed the plots of his classic works in this vein entirely by intuition, with relatively little preplanning. Despite a tendency to be devoid of any sensible structure, these plots are effective because of fast pacing and the creation of an intensely paranoic atmosphere. The author skillfully exploits the fact that the hero, like the reader, not only never knows what is going on (in particular, why those guiding and persecuting him are acting as they are) but also need never actually find out. As the plot rushes to its climax, he will come into his superhuman inheritance and render the whole net of menace and confusion redundant, logical flaws and all. Because of this uncontrolled aspect of his work, van Vogt has become a rather curious literary phenomenon, a writer of considerable influence within his genre whose most prolific imitators are better than the master. Harness and Wallace are both more capable writers, and Harness, especially in *The Paradox Men,* shows an ability to construct a plot of van Vogtian complexity which is nevertheless tight and makes relatively good sense. Because of Harness' adeptness in using van Vogt's technique, he has become something of an influence in his own right, though not in his own country. It is also notable that Harness uses the van Vogt formula toward ends more ambitious and more humanly pertinent than those featured in the standard van Vogt power-fantasy, which, for all its mesmeric thunder, is essentially empty of anything except extravagant responses to feelings of personal frustration.

The Paradox Men is set in a future America following a third world war. An elite group has taken control of America's depleted resources, enslaving the remainder of the population. Though the Empire has the aged empress Juana-Maria as its figurehead, the actual leaders are a political "Wolf Pack" led by Chancellor Haze-Gaunt and Thurmond, the Police Minister. They are opposed by a subversive organization called the Society of Thieves, founded by Kennicot Muir, a scientist who has developed a process for harnessing the sun's energy by means of "solarions" set outside the surface of the sun to manufacture the prolific source of power, Muirium. He originally intended to use this power to regenerate the general living standard of the world and free the slaves, but was thwarted by Haze-Gaunt, who is using the power to maintain the system and to prepare for war against the Eastern Federation as a step toward world domination.

When the book begins, Muir has been missing for some years but from his hiding place still controls his organization, which is dedicated to the redistribution of capital by organized theft. The Thieves thrive because they are equipped with energy shields, which render them immune to bullets (though not to blades, thus providing the logic of the emphasis on swordplay). The Society has several friends in the Imperial Palace (notably Kennicot Muir's ex-wife Keiris) now owned by Haze-Gaunt and the Microfilm Mind, a man with features blistered into anonymity whose brain is capable of assimilating information at high speeds and synthesizing conclusions by intuition.

Alar, the hero of the novel, has a past which extends only five years, to the moment when he was rescued from a river following the crash of a mysterious spaceship (Earth's first spaceship, the T-22, has yet to be launched as the book begins). Under the aegis of the Society, Alar has become an expert Thief. He comes under threat when Haze-Gaunt, prompted by the Microfilm Mind, sets out to track him down, in the belief that his plans for war and world dominion can be thwarted only by Alar. The attempts to eliminate Alar are confounded one by one as Alar develops his superhumanity. He escapes the torturer Shey and flees to the moon, but is gradually steered to a rendezvous with fate when he faces Shey and Thurmond on an energy collector which is hurtling out of control into the heart of the sun. Meanwhile, the other major characters rendezvous with their destiny on Earth, as Imperial America and the Eastern Federation rain nuclear missiles upon each other. Haze-Gaunt competes with the Microfilm Mind to take flight in the T-22, which is fated to circle the galaxy, moving backward in time as it accelerates beyond the speed of light, eventually to splash down five years earlier, carrying the evolved Alar. One of the two must *become* Alar, and the actions of the being which Alar becomes through the transcendental metamorphosis which follows his death depend on which one is victorious.

This skeletal plot is embellished by numerous clever touches. There is the creature, physically resembling a spectral tarsier, who emerged from the crashed spaceship with Alar and who sits throughout the plot on Haze-Gaunt's shoulder, perpetually imploring him with the words "Don't go." There is a throwaway invocation of the limitations of the principle of the excluded middle; the anti-Aristotelian accusation on which van Vogt uncomprehendingly built an awesome mysticism in *The World of Null-A*. There is at one point a brief but clever discourse on some of the imaginative implications of relativity theory, which casually refers to galaxies being torn apart by the close passage of the T-22 on its epic flight. (The T-22 is possessed of near-infinite mass as it circles the universe to arrive before its departure.) There is also a discussion of Toynbee's theory of historical reiteration which is apparently thrown in as mere background coloration, but which is actually crucial. It is the psychological motor of the Toynbean cycle, which dooms all civilizations to eventual destruction, that Alar in his transcendent role must obliterate from human nature if the race is to survive. The novel is full of these ideational flourishes, but each is handled with confident authority and every one fits into the whole in such a way as to enrich it. When it comes to the deployment of scientific jargon as a device to make the most ambitious and outrageous ideas seem plausible, Harness has no peers. There are other writers who are as spectacular, but none who can so cleverly contain their most spectacular scenes within a framework of imaginative implication drawn from real scientific theory.

The van Vogtian style of romance is a deliberately naïve literary construction. It is primarily costume melodrama, colorful and fast-moving. It provides, however, an ideal matrix for bold ideas. It is a framework in which anything can happen and in which the most spectacularly improbable ideas are perfectly at home. For this reason it is ideal for the presentation of certain motifs which come across poorly in more realistic futuristic scenarios, particularly the motif of superhuman transcendence, which is central to the best novels in the van Vogt tradition: van Vogt's own *Masters of Time* and *The World of Null-A*, Harness' *The Paradox Men* and *The Ring of Ritornel*, Bester's *The Stars My Destination*, and Wallace's *Croyd* and *Dr. Orpheus*. The motif exists elsewhere, of course, and its importance in modern science fiction goes far beyond novels of this species, also occupying a crucial place in such novels as Arthur C. Clarke's *Childhood's End*, Theodore Sturgeon's *More Than Human*, and Harness' *The Rose*.

The Paradox Men deserves special attention within its subgenre for the neatness of its plotting, its ideational enterprise, and its narrative verve. However, the quality of its prose does not measure up to the standard later set by Bester, and its paranoic atmosphere does not have the intensity of that clothing van Vogt's best work. In view of its considerable merits it is difficult to understand why *The Paradox Men* never attained great popularity in America. John Campbell and the readers of *Astounding Science Fiction* were so enthusiastic about van Vogt that one can only wonder why they failed to react enthusiastically to Harness. After the novel's appearance as half of one of the earliest Ace Doubles, it was not reprinted again until it was resurrected in Britain as a result of the enthusiasm of several British writers (the new edition published by Faber in 1964 contains a laudatory introduction by Brian Aldiss, who coined the term "widescreen baroque" to characterize its subspecies). It is, in fact, a novel which deserves to be far more widely read. It is historically notable as one of the earliest as well as one of the most skillful examples of the transcendent superman story, which has become postwar science fiction's most prominent salvation-myth.

Note: The shorter magazine version of this story appeared under the title *Flight into Yesterday* in *Startling Stories* during 1949. The first book edition retained the magazine title but all subsequent editions have borne the title in current usage.

Brian Stableford

Sources for Further Study

Reviews:

Analog. LVI, February, 1956, pp. 147-148.

Infinity Science Fiction. I, February, 1956, pp. 121-123.

New Worlds. XLVI, January, 1965, pp. 112-114.

THE PAST THROUGH TOMORROW

Author: Robert A. Heinlein (1907-   )
First book publication: 1967
Type of work: Stories and novels
Time: Approximately 1950-2150
Locale: Earth, the moon, deep space, and a few other planets

The major collection of Heinlein's shorter fiction, including two novels, comprising the "Future History" series, originally published between 1939 and 1963, and arranged in order of fictional chronology

Principal characters:
HUGO PINERO, whose invention predicts the instant death of Harriman
DELOS ("D. D.") HARRIMAN, administrator and salesman extraordinary
RHYSLING, "the Blind Singer of the Spaceways"
JOHN LYLE, a young soldier who revolts against a theocracy
ANDREW JACKSON ("SLIPSTICK") LIBBY, an intuitive mathematical genius
LAZARUS LONG (alias WOODROW WILSON SMITH), an immortal vagabond

Robert A. Heinlein and John W. Campbell, Jr., editor of *Astounding Science Fiction*, are generally credited, or blamed, with inventing something called "modern" science fiction. This book includes a number of stories, and their linking concept, that show why. Not really a continuous series, the stories (or most of them) are set within a "Future History" chart (reprinted and revised in this volume) originally published in *Astounding Science Fiction* in 1941. Not simply a guide to the works of the once and future Heinlein, the chart suggested a model for the kinds of stories Campbell wanted to see in his magazine. More than once he asked for tales that would seem examples of contemporary realism ("mainstream" in science fiction jargon) once the future they projected came into being.

Heinlein never took the chart so seriously that he had to fill in all the blanks or even all the stories once intended. But he did take seriously the underlying concepts. Progress is assumed in both technology (transportation, power sources) and society (culminating in "The First Human Civilization") with some cross-over (psychometrics, semantic science), but not in a straight line. He took it for granted that power would be abused and setbacks would occur, with pendulum swings between freedom and enslavement (in both physical and psychological terms). Against that large-scale movement, individual human dramas would be played out which might illustrate or counterpoint the slow cultural fall and rise.

In variant versions, the chart placed up to twenty-seven works of fiction against some seven hundred or so years of history. Some were never written

[*], others are not included, and two are present that do not really fit, so that the present volume has twenty-one stories, arranged according to the time they are supposed to take place. Although the intent is laudable, the inclusion of the two interlopers, the aesthetic distance between the author's prewar and postwar fiction, and the sketchy continuity between stories mar the balance of this volume. Still, it shows off the bulk of Heinlein's early work and the Future History concept, which operated (often consciously) as a background to other fiction of Heinlein and many other writers of the 1940's and 1950's.

"Lifeline" (*Astounding Science Fiction*, 1939) is an appropriate introduction to the omnibus, although its characters and devices have no noticeable impact on later stories (Lazarus Long in *Methuselah's Children* (1941) claims to have run into them). Heinlein's first published story, it ostensibly concerns a machine, invented and advertised by Dr. Hugo Pinero, that can predict the exact instant of a person's death. The real subject is the implication of such a device for scientists, reporters, insurance companies, gangsters, even lovers. The satire cuts both ways, however, both at those who fear such knowledge (all of us?) and at those who would produce it. Thus the story points us toward the future at the same time that it questions how much we ever really want to know about it. Appropriately, in its present position, it also introduces such continuing themes as the forgotten genius, the insanity of complacency, the value of empirical proof over orthodox theory, and the powerful motivation of financial gain.

The next three stories explore the psychology of power — technological, economic, and psychological. The first two are *Astounding Science Fiction* stories from 1940, emphasizing action and resolution, with the melodrama, pace, and conventionally clipped dialogue so common to popular fiction and cinema of the period. The third, a short novel first published in a book of the same title, suggests what Heinlein could — and could not — do a decade later, without an editor and a habituated, specialized audience looking over his shoulder.

"The Roads Must Roll" is memorable for its inaccurate projection that private cars would so clutter the world that another transportation system would be developed shortly after midcentury. Closer to home, perhaps, was its assumption that the transportation monopoly would have to be watched over by

---

*At least five titles on the various charts have not been used. In "Concerning Stories Never Written: Postscript," *Revolt in 2100* (1953), Heinlein explained why three of them were never written. The plots outlined in 1955, however, bear distinct resemblances to materials used in *Stranger in a Strange Land* (1961), *The Moon Is a Harsh Mistress* (1965) and the novelette, *Free Men*, published in *The Worlds of Robert A. Heinlein* (New York: Ace, 1966). He made no excuses for the nonexistence of two others, "Word Egewise" and "Fire Down Below." Three stories on the chart which were published, but are missing from the present volume, are: "Sky Lift" and "Columbus Was a Dope," available in *The Menace from Earth* (1959), and "Let There Be Light," in *The Man Who Sold the Moon* (1950). The last story on the chart, "Da Capo," the title being a musical term for repetition, can also be fitted in several ways to Heinlein's last novel (as of 1979), *Time Enough for Love: The Lives of Lazarus Long* (1973).

a faceless paramilitary class more threatening in a way than either labor or management traditionally conceived. The description of the moving roads themselves is vague and confusing, the lectures that halt the action are obtrusive, and the final confrontation between the perfectionist administrator, Gaines, and the labor leader, Van Kleeck, is overblown and melodramatic. No doubt an effective propaganda piece at the time and for the audience it was aimed at, this story has not worn well, though it has often been reprinted.

The problem of who will watch the watchers is even more central to "Blowups Happen," another frequently anthologized story. The story is not so much about atomic power plants as it is about the custodial psychology adumbrated by Gaines and his Transportation Corps. The problem posed is that to avoid atomic accidents, psychologists must watch technicians, and be themselves observed, making temperamental flareups all the more likely. A world-famous expert, both physicist and psychologist, is consulted; he sees the situation as impossible, and it becomes even more so when evidence surfaces that the Moon once suffered a nuclear Armageddon. Rather than risk the economic chaos of a shutdown, however, the directors of the power fire the superintendent and relocate the plant in orbit, using an atomic fuel coincidentally developed by two plant technicians in their spare time. This facile ending and subplot were dictated by editor Campbell, a tireless crusader for atomic energy and spaceflight, neither of which were in sight at the time, but Heinlein's vision of an insoluble problem still haunts the world today.

"The Man Who Sold the Moon," though oversimplified by contrast with the real American space program, is still readable and enjoyable despite its being dated. The chief reason is its main character, D. D. Harriman, the millionaire huckster and administrator who harnesses all his resources to a dream he can only realize vicariously. Beneath the wheeling and dealing, as power brokers swap and wager billions like Monopoly pieces, a sharp satirical blade separates Harriman's grandiose dreams (which go far beyond a mere moon landing) from the mundane realities of selling people something they do not really want.

Given the actual mass media treatment of the space program in the 1960's, it is not much of a stretch of the imagination — in retrospect — to consider using the Moon as a gigantic billboard, or making up the last few dollars of a tight budget through faking lunar-cancelled postage stamps and seeding the lunar landscape with smuggled diamonds. Harriman's gamesmanship enables him to play off against each other the avarice and self-interest of rich and poor alike and gives him a place in literature within striking range of the confidence men of Melville and Mann. His greed for accomplishment, however, also leads him into the financial trap which keeps him, like Moses, from ever reaching the promised land. The sense of a legend in the making haunts every scene, most of which are handled with wit and practical wisdom, and the pace for a change is almost leisurely.

With space opened up, many of the stories following are anticlimactic. The next eleven, fictionally bracketing the year 2000, are for the most part compactly and carefully crafted, but dependent for their impact on a slick manipulation of sentiment, as is appropriate for publication in mass-circulation magazines of the postwar period. Financially but not intellectually ambitious, they show a more mature (and cynical? or just practical?) Heinlein manipulating a general audience relatively unfamiliar with the conventions of science fiction and presumably intolerant of the punch and melodrama of the narratives in the science fiction pulps.

"Delilah and the Space-Rigger" (*Blue Book*, 1949) describes the building of a space station in orbit, but its plot turns on the device of permitting women to be part of the work crew. Merit is more important for building a future than sex or race or class, though conventional expectations and miseducation based on these differences may get in characters' way (and sometimes in the author's). "Space Jockey" (*Saturday Evening Post*, 1947) concerns a rocket pilot whose job conflicts with his home life. These are followed by an early story, "Requiem" (*Astounding Science Fiction*, 1940), concerning how an aging D. D. Harriman outwits his heirs and the law, and manages to get to the Moon after all, with the aid of two calloused space bums and a rickety rocket ship. His triumph is shortlived, since he dies from the physical strain of the flight, though not before he sets foot on the lunar surface, giving a special treat to those who have read the story about his earlier exploits. Sentimental, crudely expressed, clumsily executed, "Requiem" has a raw power the later, more accomplished stories do not, resulting partly from its archetypal main character who stands in for every science fiction fan (and writer) who ever dreamed of making that final pilgrimage.

"The Long Watch," intended for the *Saturday Evening Post*, seems perfectly tailored for its actual first audience (*American Legion Magazine*, 1949). It offers a detailed sketch of how a political and military *naif* surprises his hunger for heroism by sacrificing his life to foil a right-wing military takeover of a lunar base for atomic missiles. "Gentlemen, Be Seated" (*Argosy*, 1948) also takes place on the Moon, amid civilian colonization; its point is the efficacy of plugging an air leak with the seat of one's space-suited pants. Another lunar rescue story, "The Black Pits of Luna" (*Saturday Evening Post*, 1948), depends on our sentimental concern for a lost child and his brother, the teenage narrator, who rescues him.

Completing this lunar series, " 'It's Great To Be Back' " (*Saturday Evening Post*, 1947) is the best of the lot, working on the reader's understanding that you can't go home again. A young scientist couple dissatisfied with the regimentation of life on the Moon serve out their terms and return to New York City, then to the suburbs. Unable to cope with the weight, the noise, the dirt, the insanity of their friends and relatives, and the unreliability of machinery and repairmen, the MacRaes finally go back "home," to the Moon. The satire is crisp, the characterizations precise, the dialogue perfectly caught, and the future, surprisingly for someone familiar only with the later Heinlein, is attractively packaged as a welfare state.

The next story, " — We Also Walk Dogs" (*Astounding Science Fiction*, 1941), is another of Heinlein's best, though it does not belong in this line of Future History. Despite its presence on the chart, it introduces gravity neutralization, aliens from other planets in the solar system, and a "corporate hero," General Services, Inc., which have no connections with other stories in the book. Thematically, to be sure, the story exhibits the faith in technology and in self-serving behavior which are Heinlein hallmarks. By its position here, surrounded by lunar enterprises, it suggests, moreover, that Earth is not completely stagnant all this time. Depending on how seriously we take GS as a model, the story might even be said to foreshadow the chart's prediction of a "First Human Civilization."

Built up by the desire of people to have things done for them, General Services is called upon for something that strains even their capabilities: an order to find a way to hold an interplanetary conference on Earth. The nullification of gravity required is theoretically impossible, but one man might be able to do it. To get his cooperation, however, since he is only interested in his own research, GS must do something else impossible: replicate a famous bowl in the British Museum and give him the original. All of this must be, and is, accomplished quickly and without publicity, and the caper proceeds as competently as a segment of *Mission Impossible*.

The real focus, however, is on people and motivations. Like D. D. Harriman, the GS people are interested in making money, in seeing a job well done, and in getting something extra for themselves. They cynically manipulate a rich dowager, opportunistically rig contractual rights to the gravity neutralizer, and treat the whole operation as a matter of course. But they are humanized, as is the crotchety inventor, by their reverential possessiveness toward the coveted bowl, once it is in their hands. "The Flower of Forgetfulness" tempts even them to withdraw into abstract contemplation.

Space as a backdrop returns in three more stories, oddly juxtaposed. "Searchlight" (for a 1962 advertisement) asks our unearned sympathy for a blind girl, a musical prodigy, lost and found on the Moon. "Ordeal in Space" (*Town and Country*, 1948) describes a spaceman's Earthbound attempts to deal with his fear of falling. The scenes that trace his fears are well done, but the miraculous cause of his overcoming them is a lost kitten on a windowledge. The manipulation of sentiment goes even further in "The Green Hills of Earth" (*Saturday Evening Post*, 1947), which recounts the adventures of the space bum, Rhysling, and asks us to believe in his doggerel, his dirty songs (clearly expurgated), his romantic visions, and his dying act of heroism, during which he recorded the final version of the title song.

A little less than halfway through the omnibus, a final "historical" sequence now begins, which unites five of the remaining six stories, two of novel length, mostly from the prewar years. They suffer from the heavy moral didacticism and clumsiness of much of Heinlein's early work, but they are concerned with matters of substance both to the author and to habitual readers of science fiction, matters for which the simple coming true or not coming true of fictional projections is not debilitating. As Alexei and Cory Panshin have indicated, these stories are concerned with how to live, and how to make meaning of one's life. They point forward to the artistically more successful novels of adolescence of Heinlein's middle period, as well as to the contorted and controversial novels of old age in the 1960's and 1970's.

The need to be free is the issue of "Logic of Empire" (1941), in which the colonial economy of Venus makes slavery inevitable, and the spirit of man makes its eventual overthrow just as necessary. The unlikely hero is Humphrey Wingate, a sophisticated lawyer of an effete Earth society, who is forced to experience the slavery on Venus which he, convinced of social progress, refused to believe even exists. On his return to Earth after some happy coincidences, he finds others as hard to convince as he had been. Earth people, imprisoned in their mental security blankets, simply do not want to believe in others' discomforts, since they might feel guilty if they did nothing to remedy them.

Wingate, besides suffering physical indignities, is guilty of psychological self-enslavement. From his initial disbelief he turns to a numbed acceptance which makes it easier for his owner to manipulate him. After escaping, he clings to a "devil" theory about the colonial slaveowners, which then modulates into scorn for the conspiracy of silence back home. Unable to find an audience except for the pseudofictional, ghostwritten "I Was a Slave on Venus," Wingate is a sometimes comic, mostly leaden, illustrative figure for a Heinlein lecture on an "unthinkable" topic which permeates the last half of the omnibus.

For a brief respite, the book takes us back to the Moon for "The Menace from Earth" (*The Magazine of Fantasy and Science Fiction*, 1957), which shows no awareness whatever of the theocratic takeover of the United States which the "Future History" chart indicates should be happening or impending at this time. The story does, however, suggest reasons why man's future should not be planned on Earth. Luna City is clean, orderly, unthreatening, relatively nonsexist, even more attractive than before. It is especially attractive to Holly Jones, the girl narrator, who corresponds to the heroes of Heinlein's contemporaneous novels of adolescence. She and the story bubble along, developing logically her provincialism, her expertise in her own back yard, her disdain for the visiting media starlet of the title, and her need to be educated about her own emotions.

The real protagonist, as Panshin once pointed out, is Luna City, whose characters and events seem to exist for the sake of giving the reader a tour of the facilities. Holly's blasé acceptance of tourists' idiosyncrasies, of the multi-leveled warren she lives in (neatly summed up by its single map, huge and three-dimensional), and of the "Bat's Cave," where everyone flies for enjoyment, provides the proper air of understatement such wonders would deserve in their own context and environment. Given Holly's self-involvement, we learn little about the people, politics, or technology of Luna City, but we get to know a great deal about how it feels to live there.

It feels great, by contrast with the stifling climate of the theocratic dictatorship which has ruled the United States for seventy years by the time the next story opens. If refusing to face discomfort helped get America into the fix, as suggested by "Logic of Empire," that story's way out is the only one left here too: fighting for freedom. As an early long narrative (*Astounding Science Fiction*, 1940), "If This Goes On. . ." is not unimpressive. Improved by rewriting for book form in 1953, it is still choppy and disjointed, though that is partially justified by the viewpoint of the narrator. To tell of events leading up to and including the overthrow of the Prophet Incarnate, Heinlein chose a young innocent, John Lyle (whose last name is the same as Heinlein's mother's). A recent graduate of West Point, he is dragged into a revolution by his romantic infatuation with an equally young and innocent priestess, or Virgin, whose virginity is demanded by the Prophet. Ten short chapters recount his fleeting romance, his induction into the local unit of the underground Cabal (which normally discourages "romantics"), his inquisitions, and the rescue of Sister Judith, followed by Lyle's disguise, travels, and escape to General Headquarters in a cavern near Phoenix. At this point, he is ordered to write the preceding events in a journal.

Continuing the journal, apparently for his own interest, Lyle devotes two long chapters to the organization's setup and his own partial reeducation, before describing as much of the warfare as he saw himself. If Lyle is typical of the populace, reeducation should be slow, since his innocence is all but invincible and the Cabal leaders reject the techniques of brainwashing. Lyle strikes blows for freedom that are simple, personal, and emotional, perhaps Oedipal, leaving theoretical concerns to others. He does, however, describe the business of revolution, the manipulation of the media, and the power of propaganda, perhaps illustrating in general his powers of common sense. The action scenes are well-handled, the illusion of (others') expertise is excellent, but the naïveté about women and romance, though perhaps commercially necessary, is only made credible by psychologically emasculating the hero.

That the re-education of the people actually does take place is apparent, since the remainder of the omnibus is set against the background of the "First Human Civilization," a dynamic kind of Utopia such as Heinlein tried to describe in *Beyond This Horizon* (*Astounding Science Fiction*, 1942, revised 1948, not included here). The Future History variant of this civilization obeys a libertarian rule called "The Covenant," exceptions to which propel the plots.

In "Coventry" (*Astounding Science Fiction*, 1940), David McKinnon, an

incompetent brawler educated only in "romantic" literature, learns to appreciate the net of civil interdependence by having to live outside it in a reservation of malcontents, consisting of three societies, all more repressive than what
he left. McKinnon's failures provide low comedy, until he is rescued by an
undercover agent, and proves his own reconditioning by a heroic act of loyalty
to the Covenant society. The point of the sermon is obvious: that liberty is
only made possible by responsible cooperation. Like Wingate and Lyle,
McKinnon provides an object lesson in right living for a competent man in a
future society.

The next-to-last entry in the omnibus is the second one Heinlein published,
"Misfit" (*Astounding Science Fiction*, 1939), which looks forward formally to
the postwar series, with its matter-of-fact, detailed sketch of everyday behavior under special future circumstances. Youths outside the Covenant, or dis-
obedient to it, are pressed into service in the "Cosmic Construction Corps."
On one such job, converting an asteroid into a space station, one boy whose
talents are not utilized on Earth is Andrew Jackson Libby, an intuitive mathematical genius, whose idiosyncratic skills and stubbornness prove highly valuable. Even "The First Human Civilization" will not provide for everyone, in
other words, and an untrained youth, like so many *Astounding Science Fiction*
readers, might turn out to have some invaluable talents. Of course Libby was
born outside the Covenant through no fault of his own, and he does happen to
be a verifiable genius.

If you cannot have innate genius, a healthy longevity may serve just as
well, according to the last piece in the book, the novel *Methuselah's Children*
(*Astounding Science Fiction*, 1941; revised 1958). This time we have an entire
subculture of misfits, the Howard Families, products of a voluntary program of
breeding for longevity of ten generations (from 1874 up to 2136, when the
novel begins). If "Life-Line" was an appropriate introduction to the Future
History, this is an even more appropriate conclusion. It picks up a number of
threads from other stories in the omnibus, such as freedom and slavery, practice over theory, progress through experimentation, and the value of administrative competence. References to the Prophet and the Covenant, to Pinero and
Harriman and Rhysling, to the rolling roads and the colonies on the Moon and
Venus provide continuity. One character is even carried over, "Slipstick" Libby, who turns out to be able to develop a handmade "light pressure" drive
which converts to faster-than-light travel.

The general thrust of the Future History away from Earth and from arbitrary
rules and constraints is extended beyond the solar system in this novel when a
hundred thousand people escape persecution by commandeering a starship
designed to support generations of human life. This act is made necessary by
their society's suspension of the Covenant in order to pry loose from them the
"secret" of their longevity, believed to be some sort of chemical treatment.
Planning and escape take up the first half of the story, after which the sequel is

more leisurely. The families experience aimlessness aboard the *New Frontiers* and on two alien planets, before going home to seek a lost sense of meaning. In their absence, the people of Earth have perfected the nonexistent treatments they sought, making everyone potentially "Methuselah's Children."

The story comes full circle, only to close on an open note. If the Howard Families can find no meaning in life, what will it profit the rest of the race to have the gift of longevity? If the purpose of man is to fare forward, as most of the Future History stories imply, why does the *New Frontiers* come home again, without having met the challenges posed by the aliens? These questions are given even more point, but no answers, in the person of Lazarus Long, the major unifying character in the novel, and an enduring Heinlein *persona* who surfaced again in 1973 in *Time Enough for Love*.

Although the novel is ostensibly about one hundred thousand people, it focuses on a handful, and this man, alias Captain Aaron Sheffield, born Woodrow Wilson Smith (in 1912) is at the center. The stuff of legends, he has already lived through many careers, but not to the point of boredom or passivity. Action-oriented, where his relatives are security-conscious, he is capable of carrying out that action, as he proves. Far older than any other surviving member of the Families, he is a precursor of what longevity could bring. He has problems of memory storage, but his zest for life is undimmed by having already lived several lifetimes.

But he has no immediate or long-range purpose except to survive. He leads the Howard Families out of bondage, but not into the Promised Land. Unlike his friend, Mary Sperling, he does not seem to get old, so he cannot accept her merging into an immortal alien hive-mind in a virtual Garden of Eden. But loss of individuality is not all that Lazarus and his "cousins" can not accept. When the "Little People" prove capable of improving the human breed by manipulating its germ plasm, the majority decide it is time to leave. About three hundred want to move on to newer frontiers, but most want to go home, despite their uncertainty about what awaits them on Earth.

Even though they are welcomed back, the novel's ending is inconclusive. Having experienced what they have, they can hardly stay home complacently. If they cannot get away like the MacRaes in " 'It's Great To Be Back,' " they will be as dissatisfied as Wingate in "Logic of Empire." The return may be only another pendulum swing before a new wave advances into space and the future. But if this is simply another restless tossing and turning of Western, Faustian man, two basic questions are unanswered: Does he lie awake or asleep? What is this movement for?

On such an open end the omnibus closes, as does the Future History, if in fact it ever ends. "Universe" and "Common Sense" (*Astounding Science Fiction*, 1941) pursue an alternate path for the generations-long space journey, which ends with a new beginning on a distant planet for the select few who have seen through their shipboard society's mythology. Many of Heinlein's other stories would be equally at home on such alternate paths of the Future History framework, including the novels of adolescence which frequently end with the hero ready to make a mature, adult decision. Even *Time Enough for Love* essentially just resurrects Lazarus, again and again, reassuring him at the end, "You can not die, beloved," which many of us long to hear, in contrast to the information available from Dr. Pinero in "Lifeline."

The Future History as a whole, if we can truly identify the boundaries of where it stops, provides a paradigm for "modern" science fiction which deals more in probabilities than in values. Every story about the future, at least since *The Time Machine*, has been an imaginative bid for longevity, even immortality, but not at the cost of giving up what we are. Though we may vicariously take on alien forms, we remain readers and writers, bound to the here and now. For those who are satisfied to be, rather than to become, Heinlein offers confirmation of the rightness, if not the wisdom of that choice.

He also offers, in this volume, a mixed bag of stories. Written and rewritten at different times, out of differing needs or compulsions, they are of uneven quality, of course. But they illustrate both his concerns and his ability to make those concerns central to the science fiction tradition. And they show how a determined craftsman can not only work within, but also go beyond the conventions of popular literature.

David N. Samuelson

Sources for Further Study

Criticism:

Samuelson, David N. "Frontiers of the Future: Heinlein's Future History Stories," in *Robert A. Heinlein*. Edited by Joseph D. Olander and Martin H. Greenberg. New York: Taplinger, 1978, pp. 32-63. Samuelson explores the future events that Heinlein has blocked out in his short stories.

Slusser, George E. *The Classic Years of Robert A. Heinlein*. San Bernardino, Calif.: Borgo, 1977, pp. 9-24. Slusser explores Heinlein's ideas on the destiny of man.

Reviews:

Analog. LXXX, September, 1967, pp. 162-164.

Booklist. LXIII, July 1, 1967, p. 1134.

Books Today. IV, April 9, 1967, p. 8.

Galaxy. XXVI, October, 1967, pp. 191-192.

Kirkus Reviews. XXXV, February 1, 1967, p. 164.

Library Journal. XCII, April 15, 1967, p. 1643.

THE PASTEL CITY

Author: M. (Mike) John Harrison
First book publication: 1971
Type of work: Novel
Time: The distant future
Locale: The Earth, various regions of the Viriconium empire

The Viriconium empire, built on the ruins of the last of the Afternoon Cultures, is torn asunder by civil warfare in which the destructive technology of the past threatens the annihilation of all human life

Principal characters:
> TEGEUS-CROMIS, a Byronic knight of the Methven Order and the best swordsman, a would-be poet
> NORVIN TRINOR, Methven master of strategies who defects to the northern enemy and leads their armies
> TOMB THE DWARF, a Methven specializing in engineering and energy weapons
> BERKIN GRIF, the most warlike of the Methven
> QUEEN METHVET NIAN, the young queen of Viriconium
> QUEEN CANNA MOIDART, the usurper of the north
> CELLUR OF GIRVAN, "Lord of the Birds," a kind of wizard, mentor to Tomb

The Pastel City is a romance of the future, a science fantasy that has acquired a large number of passionate devotees. The appeal of this romance lies chiefly in the author's powerful rendering of a distant future in which a new feudalism has grown out of the dark ages following the collapse of the most highly advanced of all technological civilizations. Reflections of this great culture remain, but since its fall, humans have reverted to more primitive social structures and to a prescientific state of mind. The ruins of this last of the Afternoon Cultures of Earth are visible everywhere. Indeed the new feudal empire of Viriconium, which has emerged after nearly a thousand years, depends largely upon salvaging metals and other remnants of that lost technology. While understanding of the technology of the Afternoon Cultures may have been lost, some of the technology has survived and remains operational after a thousand years. It is primarily the weapons of the earlier culture which have been preserved, chiefly the *baan*, an energy force blade about the size of a dagger. Airships have also survived. They are called crystal launches and fly by an antigravity or other exotic energy source. These and other terrible weapons are brought to bear in the War of the Two Queens.

The War of the Two Queens was but the last phase of a thousand-year struggle between the inhabitants of the northern and southern lands of the post-Afternoon Cultures. The northern tribes held the Great Brown Waste and as their major industry, salvaged the large deposits of metal and machinery left from the ruined cultures of the past. Over the centuries, the south threw off the oppressive rule of the northern tribes and renovated Viriconium, the Pastel

City, and the hub of the last of the Afternoon Cultures. The city was restored to its former glory and became the capital of the empire to which it gave its name.

For half a millennium Viriconium remained secure, but peace brought complacency and stagnation. At last a new hero emerged, Methven Nian, who resolved to reverse the signs of an approaching Dark Age. He formed the Order of Methven, or "Northkillers," who beat back the encroaching northern tribes. He also halted the social decay, and began the development of a new science independent of the old technology, hoping thereby to wean his people from dependence on the diminishing supply of ancient machines and materials. His one mistake came out of his desire to establish a lasting peace with the north through a blood alliance. So it was that his brother, Methvel, was married to the Queen of the northern tribes, Balquhider, who murdered him in his sleep and fled with their daughter Canna Moidart. Thus, when Methven died, there were two Queens who claimed the throne. One was Methvet, Methven's sole heir, and the other was the warlike and treacherous niece, Canna Moidart.

Ten years later Canna Moidart moved against Queen Methvet of Viriconium. Meanwhile the Methven knights had scattered to pursue their various interests. Tegeus-Cromis, the greatest swordsman among the Methven, retired to a solitary life devoted to reflection and writing poetry, but his retirement was brief. Without Methven leadership, there had been little organized resistance to the maraudings of the northerners. Viriconium had barely escaped capture. The army of Canna Moidart was advancing from the north, and only a hastily organized army supported by militia rushed into the field to block its advance.

Bearing one of the Queen's rings as authorization, Cromis sets out to rally as many of the remaining Methven as can be found and to take command of the army before the great battle begins. When he attempts to find Norvin Trinor, Methven master of strategies, he discovers that Trinor has left his wife and defected to the north. Cromis, however, joins forces with Berkin Grif and his band of smugglers, Theomaris Glyn, the eldest Methven, and Tomb the Dwarf, master of engineering and the technology of the old cultures. En route, Cromis is intercepted by a lammergeyer, a metal vulture, which bears a message warning Cromis to beware the *geteit chemosit* and to undertake a journey to the tower of Cellur. The bird promises to remain with Cromis until the warning is heeded and proves to be a useful ally.

The first crisis occurs on the Metal-salt Marshes on which the company has camped on its way to meet Queen Canna's army. There, Cromis fights the first of the *geteit chemosit* he has seen. Although he drives his attacker off, he is left shaken and dispirited. His own famous weapon, the nameless sword, was cut to pieces by the energy blade of his foe, and Cromis has suffered many flesh wounds from the struggle. Worst of all is the fear that the confrontation has instilled in him, the fear of the warrior who knows he is overmatched. The *chemosit* are seven-foot black robots with three eyes and a murderous single-ness of purpose; Cromis recognizes the irresistible power of the ancients in them.

Although the party catches up with the army, the commander haughtily refuses to recognize the leaders as Methven and denies their claim to lead the defense of Viriconium. During the night the battle begins with the northern forces under the leadership of Norvin Trinor employing a leading wave of *geteit chemosit*, whose ferocity and appearance panic the defenders. These northern forces are invincible, but during the action there is room for individual heroics on the part of the Methven fighting as irregulars. Cromis encounters Trinor, challenges him to single combat, and defeats him but spares his life. Eventually as pockets of resistance are assaulted by overwhelming forces, the four Methven take their stand and prepare to die, while the *chemosit* go about the battlefield doing their grisly work of removing the brains of the slain. When it looks as though all is lost, an unexpected rescue is effected by Queen Methvet and her airships, but the rescue is costly. Theomaris Glyn is killed, and the airship of the Queen is severely damaged.

Viriconium is lost, and almost without hope Grif, Tomb, Cromis, and Queen Methvet head south for Girvan Bay to find the mysterious man who sent the metal vulture to warn Cromis against both delay and the *chemosit*. They find Cellur of Lendalfoot, called "Lord of the Birds," for it was he who made not only the metal vultures, but a hundred other varieties as well. Cellur is very old: he has lived in his tower by the sea for more than a millennium and possesses the secret of how the *chemosit* may be stopped. He trains Tomb the Dwarf how to shut down the electronic brain that controls them, and the company leaves in quest of the central control just as the patrols of the enemy begin an assault on the tower.

While exploring the first possible site of the brain, the company is captured by Trinor and his soldiers who are hoping to stop the *chemosit*, which have begun slaughtering their former allies. The central brain is located beneath the floor of the Lesser Rust Desert, and Tomb succeeds in opening the door to the underground vaults by reading the mysterious ideographs and giving the correct series of passwords. Tomb descends with Trinor and his guards who bring Queen Methvet along as hostage.

After nearly a week of confinement, Grif and Cromis make their move, killing the guards and invading the vaults in search of Tomb and the Queen. In the subsequent battle Grif is slain in a duel by Trinor, who in turn, is killed by Cromis. Tomb appears in the nick of time to save Cromis and the Queen. He leads a company of soldiers, whom he has resurrected by manipulation of the central brain. Tomb then reveals that he had neutralized the *chemosit* almost at once, spending the rest of his time discovering the secret of resurrecting those soldiers of the Afternnoon Cultures whose brains had been preserved by the computer. We then learn the true origin of the *chemosit*, which were designed to salvage the brains of slain warriors so that eventual reconstruction of the body of the dead could be completed by the central electronic brain.

The War of the Two Queens is resolved favorably by Tomb, who leads a host of resurrected Afternoon Culture soldiers against the forces of Queen Canna Moidart, defeating them and recapturing the Pastel City. Queen Methvet finds Cromis brooding in the Tower of Balmacara, and she persuades him to return with her to Viriconium to assist in the building of a new world order which will combine the scientific and technological genius of the resurrected men of the Afternoon Culture tempered by the understanding of past mistakes that has been gained by the post-Afternoon Culture.

The kingdom of Viriconium is one of those fictional rarities: a successfully rendered future world in which the clash of two cultural experiences of the human race reinforce each other. The remnants of the Afternoon Culture, the great wasted areas of earth, the spectacular rusting ruins of the last of the metal cultures are vivid images and compelling symbols of folly and wisdom mixed together in nearly equal measure. The effect is rather like that of one of the great Germanic epics, except that the outcome is not a Twilight of the Gods but something more like their resurrection.

The reader will find a host of ready literary parallels, all of which seem apt enough, perhaps because their authors were touching upon the same or similar patterns of reader response. One senses the presence of Edward Gibbon's *Decline and Fall of the Roman Empire* together with two contemporary science fiction classics: Frank Herbert's *Dune* and H. G. Wells's *The Time Machine*. Certainly Wells seems to be the godfather of the Pastel City, which reminds us of the great ruined emerald city of *The Time Machine*. Harrison's romance also suggests analogues to writers in the sword and sorcery tradition of science fiction like Fritz Leiber (especially Fafhrd and the Grey Mouser series) and Leigh Brackett. The story is rich in mythic parallels to the Arthurian legends as well. These and the other elements of the romance are brought together harmoniously with a tone that mixes Byronic melancholy with the traditionally more affirmative cadences of science fiction.

The weaknesses of Harrison's novel are as patent as its strengths. Like so many science fiction and fantasy novels written for popular consumption, the plot does not resolve some of its own inherent contradictions. The new world promised by the blending of the two cultures seems too easy a solution for the kind of complex issues raised in the story. Characterization is often sketchy and superficial. The reader is never quite certain how to take the relationship between Cromis and Queen Methvet, for instance, and Cromis' own brooding, Byronic nature is the merest sketch of what it might be. Perhaps the most serious weakness of the work is the haste with which the story is told, the author's silence in many areas where the reader hopes for further development.

If Harrison could handle the vagaries of his characters and the implications of some of the weightier themes, the reader would find himself wishing that this science fantasy could be rewritten in a more appropriate length. To give the best elements of *The Pastel City* the full treatment they deserve would be to produce a work at least the length of *Dune*; but perhaps that is asking too much from what is, after all, highly imaginative entertainment. As it is, *The Pastel City* is the sketch of what might have been a masterpiece.

Donald L. Lawler

PAVANE

Author: Keith Roberts (1935-   )
First book publication: 1966
Type of work: Thematically related short stories
Time: 1968-c. 2000
Locale: England

Six stories of a world in which Queen Elizabeth I was assassinated in 1588, result-
ing in the successful invasion of the Spanish Armada, the reimposition of the Catholic
Church as the guiding force of European politics, and the retardation of technological
progress

One of the more interesting and peculiar subgenres of science fiction is the alternate history, in which the known facts of past human existence are altered just enough to bring about a different result in the modern world. Hence, we have worlds in which the South won the Civil War (Ward Moore's *Bring the Jubilee* and MacKinlay Kantor's *If the South Had Won the Civil War*); in which the Nazis won World War II (Eric Norden's *The Ultimate Solution* and Philip K. Dick's *The Man in the High Castle*); in which the atom bomb never went off and the United States actually invaded Japan (David Westheimer's *Lighter Than a Feather*); and even a novel in which the Arabs defeated Israel (*If Israel Lost the War*, by Richard Z. Chesnoff, Edward Klein, and Robert Littell). But perhaps the best-conceived and most human of these enterprises in destiny is Keith Roberts' *Pavane*.

In 1588, Queen Elizabeth I is shot down by a Catholic fanatic. As a result, the Spanish Armada successfully invades England, Philip II becomes King, and the Catholic Church is restored. With the power of the English people, the popes subdue the forces of Protestant resistance throughout Europe, and once again make themselves the political masters of the civilized world. The Inquisition is introduced into England and the other ex-Protestant states. The Americans remain under Spanish rule.

Roberts choreographs his stately dance into six "Measures," each originally published separately, and loosely connected to form a picture of a society in transition. The first story, "The Lady Margaret," is set in 1968, but this is a time that bears little resemblance to the year in which Martin Luther King and Robert F. Kennedy were assassinated. The Church has retarded technological progress: electricity is outlawed, and the internal combustion engine is banned. Society is restricted through a series of closed guilds and family enterprises.

Strange and Sons is one such business, a shipping firm which hauls its goods over the English countryside in six- or ten-car railless steam-powered trains. *The Lady Margaret* is the magnificent engine driven by Jesse Strange, owner of the company, on the last run to the coast for the winter season. Jesse's father, Eli Strange, has recently died, and with the death of one driver, the firm is shorthanded; Jesse himself must make the last trip. The haulier's twin enemies are the cold and the *Routiers*, Norman bandits who roam the countryside, looking for easy prey. But Jesse is intensely loyal to the ideals of hard work, tradition, and responsibility to his company, and he pushes on, in spite of the harsh conditions. Near the end of his journey he is attacked by the bandits, led by one of his old school chums; Jesse lets them have the last carriage in line, saving the rest of his train. As he drives off through the night, the darkness is lit by a flash of light and a loud explosion: the bandits have been destroyed by their own greed.

The second measure, "The Signaller," is the tale of Rafe Bigland, a poor boy who has always been fascinated by the semaphore station located near his town. With electronic communication devices banned by the Church, the popes and the state maintain chains of semaphore stations throughout all of Europe. The Guild governing the signallers is one of the strongest in England; only twelve commoners are allowed admittance annually into the Guild's training school. Rafe is determined to be one of the twelve, and with the help of the sergeant at his local station, he obtains the proper forms, studies diligently, and wins a place in the school through a nationwide exam. The College is located in Londinium (the Latin name for London), and there Rafe learns all of the basic languages spoken in the realm (Norman French for the upper classes, Latin for the Church, modern English for commerce and trade, middle English, Celtic, Welsh, Gaelic, or Cornish for the peasant classes), in addition to signal codes and techniques, mechanics, and composition.

After several years of work, Rafe passes his exams, and is posted to a training station, a major switching center called St. Adhelm's. The final test is a daylong ordeal in which two trainees must transmit from one to the other an entire book of the Bible, signing on and off at the end of each verse. Rafe has finally become a Signaller, and is posted to his first assignment, a small personal station located in one of the great family estates. After a year's service there, he receives his first independent command, a small station located in the hills of Dorset, a lonely command isolated from the next nearest post by two rugged miles. The winters are harsh and fierce in the uplands, but the signallers still must maintain vigilance. On one of his daily walks during an off-duty period, Rafe is suddenly attacked by a wildcat, and badly clawed. He crawls back to his station, and falls in his bed. There he is comforted by the Fairies, a race older than mankind, before succumbing to his wounds and the cold. His body is found in the spring by his replacement.

The third tale, "Brother John," examines more closely the workings of the Church. John is an engraver in the monastery of St. Adhelm, in Dorset. One day he is summoned by his Abbot, and told to report to the head of the Court of Spiritual Welfare, as the Inquisition is now called in England. The Church wants a record made of the torture sessions used to extract "truth" from heretics, criminals, and political dissidents. But the sessions with the court destroy John's artistic sense, and nearly drive him mad. When he leaves the city,

John heads for the hills, plagued by visions, noises, and memories of the screams and pleadings of the victims whose sufferings he so faithfully recorded for the Pope. There he starts a revolution aimed at Church and state, and quickly gathers a following among the peasant class. Soldiers are assaulted, and insurrections spring up around the countryside. The Cardinal Archbishop of England excommunicates the monk and puts a price upon his head in a letter dated June 21, 1985. But John escapes his pursuers when the commoners hide him from the searching soldiers, and the price rises quickly to two thousand pounds. John gathers a huge peasant army, and marches to the coast, where he addresses the people, telling them of the great new age approaching, when the Catholic Church will ease its grip upon the land, and when progress will east the lot of the people. He turns to the sea, steps into a boat, and sails into storm-tossed seas, on his way, he says, to see the Pope. The waves wash in the boat's keel the next morning.

"Lords and Ladies" features Margaret Strange, niece to Jesse Strange, and his ultimate heir after her father. Jesse is dying, and Margaret remembers her own adventurous life as she waits for the old man to expire. Margaret as a young woman had helped a poor fisher boy whose hand had been mangled in a winch; her erstwhile companion, Robert Purbeck, son of Lord Purbeck, drives her home to his castle, dominating the pass called Corfe Gate. After a brief courtship, Margaret finds herself in Robert's bed, but awakens to find him gone; the Seneschal tells her Robert has been called away on King's business. As she rides away from the massive walls, she spies an old man sitting amid ruined pillars, a representative of the Old Ones, the Fairies. He tells her the Church has a purpose that will be fulfilled, and should not be despised: "The great Dance finishes, another will begin." And then he vanishes. She returns to her home, finds her uncle on his deathbed, and waits for his death. Shortly thereafter Lord Robert comes for her, flogging his horse to a frenzy.

"The White Boat," the fifth measure, was published a year after the main sequence of stories, and was not included in the British edition of *Pavane*. In tone and in texure the mood of this tale differs from the rest. Becky, a young peasant girl, lives on the coast not far from the point where Brother John had met his end. One day she sees a white boat sneak into the harbor, unload some cargo, and then move off. This pattern continues for several weeks, off and on. Finally, the girl, driven by her father's brutality, sneaks aboard the craft, and is taken by it to France, where a cargo is loaded and men paid. They are obviously smuggling some secret goods into England. When she pries open a case, she finds a heretic device, a manufactured object not sanctioned by the Church; she hides one under her clothing, and takes it with her when she leaves. When she shows it to her priest, he calls in government troops to intercept the boat on its next pass. But Becky has second thoughts, and grabs the lanyard of a cannon, setting it off prematurely. The white boat, forewarned, turns away from the coast, laughing at the guns.

The sixth and last tale, "Corfe Gate," was actually the first written. Eleanor Purbeck, daughter and heir of Lord Robert Purbeck and his wife Margaret, now both deceased, and granddaughter and sole heir of Timothy Strange, Jesse's sole remaining brother and head of Strange and Sons, has succeeded temporarily to Lordship of Corfe Gate on her father's accidental death; pending her marriage, she rules the great castle standing astride the pass into Dorset. Shortly after her accession, Pope John XL levies new taxes on an already strained economy, and Eleanor declines to pay: her people, she says, will starve if she hands over the grain. A rakish knight is sent against her, but she meets him at the portcullis, and when he threatens Eleanor and her people, she herself ignites the break cannon that kills a score of Papal soldiers. Soon the castle is invested, and the countryside in arms. Sir John Falconer, Seneschal to Eleanor and her father, is one of the Old Ones, the Fairies, a nonhuman race which has been helping man from before recorded history.

In the end, King Charles returns to his lands and appears before the Castle, and she surrenders it to her Lord; Corfe Gate is dismantled, and Eleanor retires to obscurity, later being assassinated in her old age by the King's agents. In a brief "Coda," Falconer ties together the loose ends: the Church deliberately slowed technological progress until man's racial maturity had advanced to the point where atomic power would not result in mass destruction. There had been an earlier rise of mankind, an earlier Renaissance, an earlier Armada, and a civilization which had ended in flames. Only the popes and the Old Ones knew the whole story. The siege of Purbeck had been the Church's last gasp: within ten years, Charles had gained sufficient independence to throw off the chains, and much of Europe had followed. A new Utopian Age had dawned.

Roberts' lyrical story cycle is intensely British in theme and outlook. Much of the story derives directly from the real-life history of the Isle of Purbeck, which is still dominated by the enormous ruin of Corfe Castle. During the English Civil War, Lord Bankes placed the defense of Corfe in the hands of his wife, Lady Mary; her courage and resourcefulness were such that she was allowed to retain her lands at the end of the struggle. The castle itself was destroyed. Roberts imbues his tale with the best qualities of the English people, a curious blend of honesty, loyalty, love of tradition, and ironic dourness. Throughout the cycle we continually experience the loyalty of major characters to strongly felt beliefs: Jesse Strange follows his ideals, even when they result in the death of his friend; Rafe Bigland is loyal unto death to the Guild of Signallers; Brother John follows his visions into the sea; Margaret Strange returns to her uncle's deathbed, and Robert Purbeck follows his love as far as he must; Eleanor surrenders her castle only to her liege lord, the King.

Indeed, the very title of the book suggests its theme: the stately dance between Church and state holds together an artifically retarded society that would otherwise disintegrate. In six clearly delineated snapshots, Roberts combines his love for the Dorset people with the grand theme of societal and cultural regeneration. "The great Dance finishes, another will begin." And so it has always been.

R. Reginald

Sources for Further Study

Reviews:

Analog. LXXXIII, April, 1969, p. 164.

Galaxy. XXVIII, April, 1969, pp. 116-118.

Library Journal. XCIV, March 15, 1969, p. 1347.

Magazine of Fantasy and Science Fiction. XXXVI, April, 1969, pp. 44-45.

New Worlds. CLXXXVI, January, 1969, pp. 62-63.

Observer. February 16, 1969, p. 29.

Worlds of If. XX, April, 1970, pp. 155-156.

PELLUCIDAR

Author: Edgar Rice Burroughs (1875-1950)
First book publication: 1923
Type of work: Novel
Time: 1914
Locale: At the Earth's core

> *David Innes returns to Pellucidar, rescues Dian the Beautiful, reunites his empire,*
> *and begins bringing the benefits of civilization to the people of the interior*

> *Principal characters:*
> DAVID INNES, a wealthy young mine owner and Emperor of Pellucidar
> ABNER PERRY, his elderly companion, an inventor
> DIAN THE BEAUTIFUL, his mate, princess of Amoz
> HOOJA THE SLY, his principal adversary

Pellucidar is the second of seven novels that Edgar Rice Burroughs situated on the interior surface of a hollow earth. The history of the "hollow earth" theory, whose most notable recent adherent was Charles Manson, is outlined in more detail in the first work of the series, *At the Earth's Core* (1914). Burroughs, never one to let a good idea lie fallow, continued to use the setting in *Tanar of Pellucidar* (1929), *Tarzan at the Earth's Core* (1929), *Back to the Stone Age* (1937), *Land of Terror* (1944), and *Savage Pellucidar* (1963).

As the dates show, Burroughs' second use of the setting closely followed the publication of *At the Earth's Core*. *Pellucidar* was finished in January of 1915, and published as a five-part serial in Frank A. Munsey's *All-Story Cavalier* that same year. Although it did not see book publication until 1923, it has been reprinted frequently since, as have most of Burroughs' novels. It formed part of the author's incredible early productivity: *Pellucidar* was the sixteenth novel-length work published since he had begun writing in 1911. Even more astonishing is the variety of the work that Burroughs turned out in that short span. In four years he used African settings five times (three of them with Tarzan as the central figure) invented the world of Barsoom, and employed his celebrated Martian setting in three novels. He wrote two novels with contemporary settings, one realistic and one adventurous, wrote two set on Pacific islands, wrote a Ruritanian romance, set a historical novel in thirteenth century England, and adapted the hollow earth theory for the world of Pellucidar inside the Earth.

Although Burroughs did not long maintain this level of productivity, he always lavished his imagination on his settings, as this remarkably diverse record shows. In fact, one might say that the center of interest of a Burroughs novel is not the taciturn hero or the nubile and courageous heroine, not the stereotyped chase-and-grab-'em plot, not the usually workmanlike but often wooden dialogue, but the setting. And if we take the slight liberty of considering his exotic aliens as part of the furniture, then the setting is certainly the star.

The typical Burroughs adventure is enclosed within a frame story designed to ease the transition from the reader's world to the strange tale to come, and *Pellucidar* is no exception. It has a magnificent framing device, one which the critic Richard A. Lupoff believes to be one of Burroughs' finest creations. The frame begins, as many of the author's works do, not in *Pellucidar* itself, but in an earlier book in the series. Burroughs was as much a conservationist of plot as of setting, and he provided many of his novels with a hook at the end to which the narrative of a sequel could be linked if desired. For example, *The Gods of Mars* (1913) ends with John Carter's wife, Dejah Thoris, caught in a cell with a sort of timelock, the supplies in which will be exhausted before the cell will open again. Her rescue comes in the sequel, *The Warlord of Mars* (1913).

In the same cliff-hanging way, *At the Earth's Core* concludes with David Innes stranded in the Sahara; he has brought the mechanical prospector that had taken him to Pellucidar back to the surface. But as a result of treachery, he has not returned triumphantly with Dian, his mate, but with a Mahar, one of the reptilian creatures that rule the lands of the core. Determined to return to Dian, he plans at the novel's end to load the prospector with gear of various sorts and technical works, and burrow through to Pellucidar once again, stringing a five-hundred-mile telegraph cable behind him as he goes.

As *Pellucidar* opens, an unnamed narrator — Burroughs himself, it is implied — tells of receiving a letter from a traveler, Cogden Nestor, in Algiers. In Nestor's Saharan travels he has discovered a box buried a few inches in the sand. It contains a telegraph key clicking away, and a wire running from it downward into the sand. Since Nestor cannot understand the Morse code, the noise means nothing to him. But he has read *At the Earth's Core* — he considers it "impossible trash" — and he realizes the significance of a small piece of paper within the box, bearing the initials "D. I." He writes to the narrator for urgent confirmation that *At the Earth's Core* is pure fiction. In one of the admirably laconic responses in literature, the narrator cables: "Story true. Await me Algiers." The narrator and a telegrapher join Nestor, and they begin communicating with the person at the other end of the wire, who is indeed David Innes, and the messages they receive form the major part of *Pellucidar*.

As a story, *Pellucidar* is inferior to *At the Earth's Core*; its plot is fast-moving but predictable. At the end of the earlier novel, Innes had united the nearby tribes into an empire with himself at its head. Since his return to the surface, however, the union has fallen apart, and Dian has been captured by Hooja the Sly. Innes' task is therefore twofold: first to put his empire back together, and second to rescue Dian from a villain whose sole purpose in both novels seems to be the frustrating of the hero. With the aid of Abner Perry, the inventor of the mechanical prospector, Innes succeeds at both endeavors, and at the end of the novel he is busily engaged in bringing more and more cultural advantages to Pellucidar. Having given the stone age inner world bows and arrows, the cannon, and the like, he is dismayed to realize that Perry's and his chief function has been to increase the efficiency of warfare, making it possible to kill more Pellucidarians at a much faster rate. So in addition to his earlier gifts of the sailing vessel, the compass, and other peaceful innovations, Innes establishes regular trade, invents a Pellucidarian writing system, founds shipyards, coal mines, colleges, and printing presses — everything but money, which he refuses to institute. The story ends with no obvious hook for a sequel, chiefly because Innes has taken a fatal step for the hero of an adventure novel: he has settled down.

There are signs of haste that help to diminish the standing of *Pellucidar*. When Innes enters the territory of the Thurians, he sees one of their villages, and describes it as being walled by logs and boulders; it lacks a gate, but "ladders that could be removed by night led over the palisade." Burroughs has forgotten that only in the previous chapter he had situated the Thurians in "The Land of Awful Shadow," where it is always night.

One innovation does brighten the novel (again, one concerned with setting), but even that change raises problems. A frequently occurring theme in *At the Earth's Core*, one which continues in *Pellucidar*, is a meditation on the nature of time. The interior of the earth is perpetually lighted by a central miniature sun; hence, Pellucidar enjoys a continuous noon. There are no months or years, because the motion of heavenly bodies, by which people of the upper Earth can measure accurately and repeatedly long periods of time, are absent in Pellucidar. Innes and Perry make conjectures about the passage of time being subjective. Innes takes part in adventures that seem to him to last weeks, even months, yet when he returns to Perry, the old man has been reading the whole time, and perceives Innes' absence as consisting of a matter of minutes. Again, when Innes returns to the surface, he is amazed to find that his journey, which he believes to have lasted at most one year, has in fact taken ten.

To be sure, there is some kind of biological clock that continues to function: characters eat and sleep (though not with any regularity), the natives of Pellucidar are born, grow old, and die. But neither Innes nor Perry (nor the natives, who have no conception of time) can be sure of duration. This uncertainty irritates Innes and Perry, and in *Pellucidar* they discover a way to measure time objectively.

It turns out that Pellucidar has a satellite, a "pendant world" that hangs eternally suspended about a mile above the inner surface. Because this moon rotates upon an axis parallel to the surface, and because its topography is clearly visible from Pellucidar, Innes decides to establish an observatory to note the recurrent appearance of a marked surface feature and to use the period of rotation of the pendant world as a measure of time. Later, after he has developed radio transmission, the observatory broadcasts time signals to the rest of his empire.

Although the pendant world can give Pellucidar an objective standard of time, it presents a problem for some of the inhabitants, who must live in darkness. The period of rotation for the pendant is the same as that of the earth-shell, so it hangs suspended always over the same spot ("The Land of Awful Shadow," covered always by a dusky gloom). Burroughs never gives an estimate of the magnitude of the satellite, but it is obviously of considerable size because from the surface Innes can see mountains, valleys, rivers, forests, plains, and even oceans.

Perhaps Burroughs himself was beginning to weary of Pellucidar, or to feel his invention flagging within the Earth. The second novel in the setting had capitalized on the popularity of *At the Earth's Core*, yet *Pellucidar* was not to see book publication for eight years, preventing immediate comparison between the two novels. Whatever the reason, a full fourteen years passed before Burroughs had Tarzan visit the setting. Despite the pendant world, despite the use of dinosaurs as mounts (á la Alley Oop), despite a newly invented race of agricultural apemen, *Pellucidar* shows a falling off from the inventiveness of the book to which it was a sequel. *Pellucidar* does not show Burroughs at his best.

Walter E. Meyers

Sources for Further Study

Criticism:

Green, Roger Lancelyn. *Into Other Worlds: Space Flight in Fiction from Lucian to C. S. Lewis.* New York: Abelard Schuman, 1958. Green attempts to place Burroughs' science fiction writing in its proper critical perspective.

Krneger, John R. "Names and Nomenclature in Science Fiction," in *Names.* XIV (1968), pp. 203-214. This interesting article reveals Burroughs' systematic pattern of indicating rank and occupation through names.

Reviews:

Galaxy. XXI, June, 1963, p. 137.

PERELANDRA

Author: C. S. Lewis (1898-1963)
First book publication: 1944
Type of work: Novel
Time: The early 1940's
Locale: England and the planet Venus, called Perelandra

The saving of the planet Venus from an Adam and Eve-like fall from grace

Principal characters:
 DR. ELWIN RANSOM, a Cambridge philologist
 EDWARD ROLLES WESTON, a physicist
 THE GREEN WOMAN, the "Eve" of Perelandra

The second novel of the famous space trilogy is certainly C. S. Lewis' most beautifully written book. Given his genius, it should have been, for Lewis had set himself the incredibly difficult task of writing a novel, the setting of which is Paradise itself — a fresh, just-born innocence on the planet Venus before the Fall — before sin, death, corruption.

The last novel of the trilogy, *That Hideous Strength*, is a remarkable fantasy, a satiric study of our own very fallen planet. The first, *Out of the Silent Planet*, introduces the main character of the trilogy, Dr. Elwin Ransom, a Cambridge philologist, in a novel which is formally a fairly traditional voyage-to-Mars work of science fiction. Ransom is kidnaped by an evil physicist named Weston who wants to colonize and corrupt the planet Mars. Ransom helps to foil Weston's scheme as he learns about Mars, a planet coming to the end of its life. Ransom also learns to overcome his human fears of the alien — a key theme in Lewis' work — as well as to accept death, his own and even the death of a whole world.

Ransom's education takes place within a very traditional Judeo-Christian cosmology: God's creation of the worlds and their inhabitants, their later fall from innocence and the role of the fallen angels led by Satan, and the consequences of that fall are all part of the scheme Lewis employs. He renames the angels *eldila*, gives the planets other names (Mars is Malacandra; Venus, Perelandra; and Earth, Thulcandra) and calls God Maleldil; but generally his universe, for all its spaceships and modern physics, would be readily familiar to, say, John Milton or Dr. Samuel Johnson.

The kidnaping that took Ransom to Mars was an apparent accident. But the *eldila* send him from Earth on his second space voyage and the difference is important. The second novel is concerned, philosophically, with the question of free will and predestination. Ransom is sent to the young planet of Venus in order to help prevent, if he can, the fall from innocence of its first morally responsible creatures. He meets a Green Woman, who is, of course, the "Eve" of this planet. She is tempted by Satan who has taken — literally taken, in diabolic possession — the body of Weston, still determined to preserve his limited conception of life (that is, simply human life as it is known on the planet Earth). On Mars, Weston had tried merely to subdue the natives, like a conquistador, to make room for Earthlings. But on Venus, he cooperates with Satan to reduce the Green Woman, and thus the children she will later have, to the fallen moral level of his own species. Though a fallen mortal himself, Ransom is given the extraordinary chance to do battle with Weston-Satan for the soul of the Green Woman and the destiny of Perelandra. This chance also enables Ransom to learn about the nature of destiny and to ask, in both a general and profound way, what kind of thing life itself actually is.

Perelandra can be seen as seven separate but unequal sections (or movements: Lewis himself described the book as "operatic" — even Wagnerian). Indeed, it has something in common with the epic. It involves a long journey by a single man, who, after a hand-to-hand battle, receives an Achilles-like wound in his heel. Moreover, it is told in a kind of epic flashback. The first section offers the "frame" for the rest of the work. A narrator, identified as "Lewis" himself, learns of Ransom's mission in the first two chapters. Ransom asks him to assist in his departure from and his return to Earth. Thus "Lewis" must wade through, almost literally, a swamp of fear — the basic human condition — and learn that the fight with Satan could be a real, that is physical, fight. (Lewis insists that moral realities are not to be regarded as "merely" spiritual.) In the second chapter, Ransom returns to Earth, tells his story to "Lewis," who then describes for us the journey.

The second section describes Ransom's arrival and first days alone on Perelandra. In fact, Ransom lives in Paradise: Lewis' description of this Paradise has a beauty so rapturously intense as to suggest almost a drug- or dream-vision. Ransom finds himself on an island which floats upon the surface of the seas like a rush mat or giant lily pad. On the floating island — there are other such islands which sometimes come together to form small continents and then break apart in a ceaseless flow of changing beauty — Ransom eats, drinks, smells, and absorbs such pleasures as to bring him to the edge of consciousness. He eats a globed fruit, for example, which is so delicious it redefines for him the very meaning of the word *pleasure*. A drink releases in his brain such fantastic sensations that he is nearly delirious with the realization of what sensations his own body is capable of in so wondrous a place.

It is no wonder that Ransom thinks this reality must be a dream and that he feels he is not merely having an adventure but is enacting myth. He wonders why he does not desire merely to consume the fruit or drink the drink and do nothing else. In particular, he wonders about the very idea of repetition and speculates on the possibility that the real root of all evil is the desire to have things again, to repeat experiences. Perhaps, he thinks, even money is valued chiefly as a means of keeping things so as to have them again.

This speculation becomes important, even central, to the novel's development of its principal theme. Interestingly, Ransom strongly desires to wake from a dream, even a pleasant dream; it is Reality he is in search of. (Indeed, much later in the novel he eats a drugweed and rejects it: Reality is not to be found that way.) The Green Woman, whom he meets in the third section, helps him to understand the possessiveness implied in our human hankering for repetition. They discuss time and the order of things, concepts she deals with easily. From her he learns that one must, in effect, know how to choose the given, not necessarily the expected good. But he can help her as well. In her innocence, she cannot understand why she is so separate from God (Maleldil); of course, as a fallen human, Ransom is able to enlighten her.

The Perelandran equivalent of the forbidden fruit in Genesis is Maleldil's prohibition against the Green Woman's sleeping on the Fixed Lands; she is to make her home on the ever changing floating islands. Ransom comes to understand the moral implications of this. First, Maleldil makes any such command in order to bring the necessary virtue of obedience into the world. Second, He makes this particular command to show the importance of accepting change and flux and to resist the impulse (born of fear and lack of trust) for permanence and its near-relation repetition.

The Green Woman is looking for the King, her Adam, and knows that Maleldil is preparing her for this marriage. She learns and thus grows less "young," that is, innocent. In this world, growth and knowledge are possible without experiencing evil. However, the maturity she needs for her destiny — to be the Queen-Mother of Venus — is not possible without knowing and rejecting evil.

Evil arrives (in the fourth section) in the person of Weston. "Westonism" — the mad dream of space colonization — is now put into a moral perspective larger than the one offered in *Out of the Silent Planet*. Westonism is the ultimate desire for Permanence and Repetition, a refusal to accept change, growth, development, even death as part of that process, an insistence that life always and everywhere be what we know on Earth. Lewis' development of Westonism, then, has cosmic implications (outward) and moral implications (inward). It can be both the dream of a mad scientist traveling through space and the temptation to save one's soul from fear and despair by taking refuge in a false hope of permanence.

It might be said that Lewis gives a very new meaning to the "Eternal Triangle" in the crucial (and longest) fourth section of the novel. Ransom and Weston (progressively taken over, however, by Satan) fight — in this part by argument — for the soul of the Green Woman. Behind Weston, as both man and devil, there lies a slowly revealed evil which is utterly imbecilic and pointless. As a particular man, he represents a vague sort of scientific religion, clearly based on the Creative Evolution devised by Henri Bergson and popularized by Bernard Shaw: Weston is always talking about the "thrust" of Life and the need to worship "Spirit." As devil, his temptations to the Green Woman are slightly perverted versions of roles — the tragic queen, the long-suffering mother, the misunderstood woman — which might be good in themselves but here are bad because they are self-obsessed and unreal. Since there is no evil yet on Perelandra there is no need for tragic resignation — although the tragic pose might be attractive in and of itself.

Ransom responds in different ways to different arguments and temptations, and all his responses have to be searched for, sometimes with difficulty, sometimes even through pain and near-despair. To the "scientific" argument that "spirit" should be worshiped, Ransom can only respond that "spirit" has no particular value in itself; as always, the question is of value itself, its source and its location. Of course, Ransom has learned, so to speak, from his own body. On Perelandra taste and pleasure are positive sources of knowledge. When Weston-Satan tempts the Green Woman with the allure of various roles, Ransom can only appeal to Reality itself. But behind it all lies pure evil, an evil which must, however, attach itself to physical bodies and which must, therefore, be fought physically.

The brilliant climax of the fourth section is a long soliloquy (in Chapter 11) in which Ransom goes through a despairing search for the Real by considering the relation of myth and history, change, and even the importance of his own name. He realizes that he is the ransom which must be paid, that there are no accidents, and yet moral actions are possible; he represents God on Perelandra, just as Weston's body is the devil's only foothold on this planet.

The fifth section is the epic fight between Weston and Ransom, rendered with surprising violence. As Ransom has learned earlier the joy that comes through physical pleasure, so he now learns the uses and the joy of righteous hatred. In addition to the physical fight, Ransom is tempted by many of the fashionable twentieth century philosophies. He deeply feels the fear of madness, of death, of pain, and is tempted to surrender (as a hunted man is tempted to give up) to despair itself. There are times when life seems what "Weston" says it is — a bit of pleasure, mostly misery, and, beyond a moment of conscious life, nothing but an eternity of nothing. Ransom must order these thoughts out of his brain even as he kills Weston.

The transitional sixth section shows Ransom alone, recovering from his fight and beginning to experience again the wild physical pleasures of Perelandra as preparation for the closing section of the novel, in which he sees myth become reality. He sees Ares and Aphrodite. He sees the marriage of the King and Queen, saved from a Fall by his action and trust. Tor, the Adamite King of Perelandra, explains to Ransom that he and his Queen did learn of evil — but directly from Maleldil, not through the experience of the Devil. Ransom learns that it is only "cold love and feeble trust" which prevent one from living with each wave that life brings and the even more profound truth that "The best fruits are plucked for each by some hand that is not his own." Ransom asks if everything is without plan. No one can answer, but the conclusion of the novel is a great dance in which Ransom seems to see a Reality in which

everything is contained in everything else, in which there are so many inter-
locking plans that only a mystic could comprehend them all.

And so this novel, an intensely interesting philosophical fantasy and beautiful prose poem, comes to an end with a celebration of movement, order, and
love and these noble words: "The splendour, the love, and the strength be
upon you."

Brian Murphy

Sources for Further Study

Criticism:

Hilton-Young, Wayland. "The Contented Christian," in *Cambridge Journal*.
X (July, 1952), pp. 603-612. Hilton-Young explores allegorically the myth
of the beginning and ending of the human race as it is depicted in *Perelandra*.

Moorman, Charles. "Space Ship and Grail: The Myths of C. S. Lewis," in
College English. XVIII (May, 1957), pp. 401-405. Moorman utilizes
Lewis' own statements on mythmaking in an examination of the authors
invented mythology in *Perelandra*.

Norwood, W. D. "C. S. Lewis, Owen Barfield, and the Modern Myth," in
Midwest Quarterly. VIII (Spring, 1967), pp. 279-291. Lewis' study of the
"true Christian myth," is the central concern of *Perelandra*, according to
Norwood.

Spacks, Patricia Meyer. "The Myth-Makers Dilemma: Three Novels by C. S.
Lewis," in *Discourse*. XI (October, 1959), pp. 234-243. Spacks traces
Lewis' treatment of Christian and classical myths in the Ransom trilogy.

THE PHILOSOPHER'S STONE

Author: Colin Wilson (1931-   )
First book publication: 1969
Type of work: Novel
Time: Chiefly the late 1960's and early 1970's
Locale: Various, but mainly Great Glen, near Leicester

An account of the narrator's successful quest for self-actualization and his discoveries about man's prehistory made by using his superior mental abilities

> Principal characters:
> HOWARD LESTER, the narrator
> SIR HENRY LITTLEWAY, a psychologist
> ROGER LITTLEWAY, his brother
> SIR ALASTAIR LYELL, a biologist

In 1962 Colin Wilson published *The Strength to Dream*, one of a series of philosophical tracts that began with *The Outsider* and continued with *Religion and the Rebel*; each in one way or another exalted the Romantic writer, the Romantic hero, or some other rebel against the supposed mediocrity of the masses. *The Strength to Dream* is a study of imaginative literature, seeking in the farther reaches of the literary imagination evidence of a new kind of consciousness and a new way of looking at the world (characterized in *The Philosopher's Stone* and elsewhere as a "god's-eye view"). One of the authors dealt with is H. P. Lovecraft, who is castigated for the production of "sick" fantasies and is offered as the cardinal example of what Wilson considers to be the "inauthentic" use of the imagination.

This treatment of Lovecraft annoyed August Derleth, Lovecraft's admirer and publisher, who challenged Wilson to write an "authentic" Lovecraftian novel. Despite his disapproval of Lovecraft, Wilson was, in fact, fascinated by his mythology of an implacably hostile universe in which any man who acquires accurate knowledge of the human predicament falls victim to the terrible supernatural power of the "Great Old Ones" who were once masters of Earth and whose return from cataleptic exile is imminent. Eventually, Wilson wrote two novels employing the Lovecraftian mythos for his own ends: *The Mind Parasites* (1967) and *The Philosopher's Stone*. A further Lovecraftian story was developed from a section omitted from *The Philosopher's Stone* and published in Derleth's anthology *Tales of the Cthulhu Mythos* as "The Return of the Lloigor." Wilson was also involved in a curious literary joke: the recently published volume entitled (after Lovecraft's celebrated imaginary text) *The Necronomicon*.

Among modern writers who have worked with the imagery of the Cthulhu Mythos, Wilson is exceptional for his complete reworking of the Mythos to fit his own world view. Wilson is essentially Nietzschean in his disdain for what Nietzsche calls (in *Beyond Good and Evil*) the "ethics of the herd"; and he looks forward to the imminent "next stage" in evolution: the superman. He finds the powers of the superman presaged in the visions and careers of a whole range of such remarkable men as Wordsworth, Wagner, and Nijinsky. In both his fiction and nonfiction he is a champion of the alienated and the unorthodox, occasionally carrying this enthusiasm to the morbid extreme of glorifying perpetrators of multiple murders, who are held to be expressing their superiority over the ethics of the herd. His favorite science fiction writer is A. E. van Vogt (he has written a van Vogtian thriller called *The Space Vampires*), and *The Philosopher's Stone* has a rather van Vogtian flavor toward the end, where the hero is being threatened, persecuted, and harassed as his latent superpowers slowly blossom into their awesome potency. The apparatus of the Cthulhu Mythos assumes its natural role as the agency of threat and harassment.

The Philosopher's Stone is the story of Howard Lester, who offers in Part One an account of his early life from 1942 to 1971, explaining how he ascended from humble beginnings in a Nottinghamshire mining village to a life of ease and intellectualism, largely through his "adoption" by the rich biologist Sir Alastair Lyell. Lyell supervises his intellectual development for some years, and then dies leaving his protégé a considerable fortune. This section recapitulates Wilson's philosophical ideas. Lester explains how he slowly became convinced that certain great men were of a finer breed than their fellows, living longer as a result of living more actively (in the intellectual sense).

After Lyell's death, Lester finds a new mentor in Sir Henry Littleway, a psychologist who introduces him to new ideas, including those of Aaron Marks. Marks's work is primarily concerned with "value experiences": moments when certain persons feel they are imbued with special insight and understanding. (This is a pastiche of the work of Abraham Maslow, the prophet of "self-actualization," who refers to such moments as "peak experiences.") Lester concludes that these value experiences are of great importance, not as ends in themselves but as windows through which a new way of being can be glimpsed by those who have the will: the new supermen. He and Littleway are, of course, such men; Littleway's dissolute brother Roger provides a cardinal example of one who is not.

While working with Littleway on the surgical treatment of mental illness, Lester finds a way to induce value experiences by stimulating the prefrontal cortex of the brain. Neurotic patients cannot take advantage of the opportunities thus provided, but Lester is convinced that he and Littleway can. The first part of the book ("The Quest for the Absolute," in ironic remembrance of Balzac's novel) ends with Lester's having undergone the operation that is to make him a superman. The second part (entitled, with similar irony, "Journey to the End of Night") is an account of the development of his new mental powers, especially the power of "time vision" that allows him to receive sense impressions from the past related to environments he visits or artifacts he handles.

While he is learning to use his time vision he quells a poltergeist and discovers that Francis Bacon did indeed write Shakespeare's plays, although he considers the matter to be of no real consequence since the plays are clearly the work of a second-rate mind too preoccupied with the commonplace to qualify as a visionary proto-superman; the Lovecraftian element enters the plot when Lester finds that he obtains strange impressions of terror and awfulness in connection with Stonehenge and Silbury Hill. He is fascinated by two artifacts that his time vision shows to be half a million years old; but some kind of interference prevents his learning more about their origin.

Lester and Littleway now find themselves the victims of supernatural hostility as mysterious forces try to bring about their death. These forces are curiously ineffective, however, and soon give up their assault, apparently without reason. For a brief period the novel seems to lose its way. Lester marries despite the fear that by doing so he is not merely giving hostages to fortune but offering the hostile forces a new way of attacking him. However, the forces do not take advantage of this circumstance, and his wife plays no further part in the story.

Lester's time vision allows him to decode the Voynich manuscript (attributed to Roger Bacon), which he finds to be a commentary on the legendary *Necronomicon*. Together with a new Mayan Codex discovered in the vaults of the Vatican, this work gives him much information about the nature of the forces arrayed against him. He is able to fill in the gaps in his knowledge when by chance he discovers an unlikely method of avoiding the interference with his time vision; he finds it is better to use photographs of the crucial artifacts rather than the artifacts themselves. He discovers how and why the Great Old Ones created men by controlling the evolution of apes: they are useful as "precision tools." He also discovers how and why the Old Ones, in attempting to control their own evolution so as to obtain more focused consciousness, created for themselves such acute psychological difficulties that they were thrown into a state of catalepsy after precipitating a chain of disasters that destroyed the civilization of Mu, which they inhabited together with their human servants. Now, it seems, the remote descendants of the survivors of Mu have the power to free themselves from their slave mentality and become godlike, a prospect that is threatened only by the possibility that the Old Ones might awake too soon and circumvent it.

This account of human evolution, embodying as it does ideas drawn from Hörbiger (whose pseudoscientific theories also fascinated the Nazis) as well as the Lovecraftian mythos, is rather confused. The account of what happened in prehistory changes direction several times; the author appears to be constantly reinterpreting his material (perhaps in a futile attempt to iron out the logical flaws). A genuine Lovecraftian fantasy has no need to worry about the lack of rationality, for the failure of reason is one of the instruments by which Lovecraft sought to bring about the mood of fear which was his sole literary objective. Wilson, however, *is* trying to rationalize his whole account, for it needs some kind of rational integrity if it is to serve its function as a kind of moral fable, teaching that Lovecraft's attitude of utter despair was not only unwarranted but was, in fact, a greater evil than the supernatural forces that he conjured up from the abyss of his imagination. Wilson's success in making this point is rather dubious.

Wilson is at his most plausible when he is at his most patronizing, name-dropping furiously and pandering to the feelings of uneasy superiority that characterize the withdrawn, alienated, imaginative intellectual. His main appeal as a *littérateur* and philosopher is that he provides reassurance for those who think they have a right to despise the members of a society from which they feel excluded, and regard their dreaming as a sign of their great calling. His writing is at once bitterly misanthropic and extravagantly self-conscious. He is an artful writer, and can be very convincing as he parades his erudition; but his work owes its success to the intensity and inexhaustibility of its implicit mythology. His interest in the occult and his rather condescending fascination with some elements in *genre* science fiction enable him to develop two archetypal species of power-fantasy: the image of the magus, possessor of arcane knowledge and mysterious potency, and the image of the emergent superman, the product of the next phase of evolution. In *The Philosopher's Stone* he tries to combine the two, with results that are not wholly convincing. What he has produced is a rather dubious hybrid. The novels in which he concentrates on the occult version of the fantasy (the Crowleyesque *Man Without a Shadow* and *The God of the Labyrinth*) flow more smoothly, because there he can take refuge from the need for rationalization in the traditional aura of mystery. Whether they are really any more convincing, however, is open to doubt.

As a fantasy, *The Philosopher's Stone* has potential for entertainment. Only if its philosophical pretensions are taken seriously does its absurdity become objectionable. Wilson would presumably argue that its philosophical pretensions *are* to be taken seriously, but many readers may feel that it then becomes the purveyor of a repellent, and perhaps even dangerous, ideology. Everyone occasionally aspires to superman status, but actually to come to believe that one's fellow men are inconsiderable mediocrities without virtue or purpose is quite another matter.

Brian Stableford

PICNIC ON PARADISE

Author: Joanna Russ (1937-   )
First book publication: 1968
Type of work: Novel
Time: The indefinite future
Locale: A winter resort planet called Paradise

Trans-Temporal Agent Alyx leads an odd group of tourists across a strange and dangerous "resort" planet

> *Principal characters:*
> ALYX, a thief, time-traveler, and survival guide
> MACHINE, a rationalist and Alyx's lover
> GUNNAR, a wishful-thinker and self-serving coward
> MAUDEY, a beauty and youth cultist
> IRIS, Maudey's daughter
> THE NUNS, religious fanatics and drug users

In 1968 when *Picnic on Paradise* appeared, very few writers of science fiction bothered to create believable female characters, and even fewer readers noticed. Women in science fiction novels were one-dimensional stereotypes — seductresses, stony ice-maiden scientists, or an occasional housewife who, as Joanna Russ remarked in her essay "The Image of Women in Science Fiction" (1970), might accidentally solve a galactic crisis by mending her slip. In part, science fiction writers did not need women characters — or so they thought — in the golden age of science fiction when menacing robots, fantastic cities, or monstrous extraterrestrials were the stuff of the novel. Usually, the plot involved the male hero who prevailed against these forces of evil. In part the audience who read science fiction would not notice or might expect female stereotypes, since science fiction readership has been overwhelmingly male, and often adolescent male at that.

Joanna Russ not only is among the first science fiction writers to recognize these caricatures of women, but she has also developed compelling female characters in her own fiction. A prize-winning short story writer and a poet, Russ also holds an MFA from Yale Drama School. This diverse literary background serves her well; her works are consistently vigorous, terse, and timely. She is considered to be one of the writers of the "New Wave" of science fiction, a movement characterized by social consciousness and stylistic innovation. *Picnic on Paradise* is her first novel, and while it is not her best — *The Female Man* (1975) is stylistically more smooth and thematically more mature — it is an important novel for anyone wishing to understand both the role of woman in science fiction and Russ's works in particular. Moreover, in its own right, *Picnic on Paradise* is compelling reading.

The action of the novel occurs sometime in the future on a winter resort planet called Paradise. But Paradise is not without peril, as the heroine of the novel, Alyx, discovers. Snatched out of her own time and planet, Alyx is selected to lead a group of vacationers across the planet. The caravan meets with external threats — bears, the harsh environment — but the real journey occurs within, and the real perils are of the soul, not the flesh. The travelers reveal themselves as they step deeper into an unknown, hostile environment; in particular, the novel follows Alyx on her metaphorical journey into the crevasses of her mind.

The portraits of the other travelers allow Russ to evaluate various aspects of her own society in the late 1960's. The novel mocks the culture which values youth and beauty, uses mood-altering drugs, and devalues emotionally intimate and familial relationships. For example, Maudey has dyed her eyebrows blue and has had extensive cosmetic surgery to retain the appearance of youth; she and her daughter Iris have molded themselves into plastic sex-goddesses. Yet when confronted with the extreme conditions of their journey across Paradise, Maudey despairs that she has made herself into a doll, and Iris reveals that Maudey is indeed her own mother, a fact she has concealed partly to shield Maudey from being thought old, and partly because family relationships are not considered fashionable in the society of that time. Two other tourists are called nuns, devotees of some nouveau-mystical religion whose major ritual seems to be the popping of pills. The nuns have a pill for every emotion, even those which eliminate the grief that the death of a loved one brings. Proffering their hallucinogenic pills to Alyx, the nuns change little in the course of the journey; their path through reality is a dead end.

Alyx herself is one of the first fully realized female protagonists in science fiction. Born in ancient Greece on the planet Earth, she was a murderer and a thief before becoming the tour guide on the planet Paradise. Her presence on the planet was occasioned when she was snatched out of her time and place by the Trans-Temp, a group of anthropologists who study other cultures by interviewing their members in person. In her last moments on Earth, Alyx was about to be drowned, having been cast into the Bay of Tyre while tied to a huge boulder, as a punishment for stealing a chess set. Since she was about to die, the Trans-Temp could ethically remove her from her time without disrupting the stream of events, a problem they scrupulously avoid. Alyx is particularly interesting to them because of her "special and peculiar skills," mainly her ruthlessness, her overwhelming instincts for survival, and particularly her talent which makes her an expert murderer: she hurls a knife expertly, silently, and lethally.

Alyx's attitudes and emotions, however, are the real interest of the novel. Her personality defies the traditional female traits; she is aggressive, fierce, and unmaternal. Her history reveals a woman who had abandoned three children, who was the lover of many but loved no one. In the course of the journey she slaps recalcitrant travelers, eliminates a huge bearlike animal, and finally kills a fellow-traveler, Gunnar, whose cowardice was responsible for the death of Machine, the man who had become Alyx's lover. Moreover, Alyx is a small, compact, dark, not at all the voluptuous stereotype. She is the sexual aggressor in that she initiates the relationship between herself and Machine, but she is not a seductress who ensnares him — the usual stereotype in science fiction. On the contrary, she and Machine have a developing relationship through which both are changed and yet through which both must learn to appreciate the ways in which each of them will not change.

The portrait of Machine parodies stereotypical notions of what a man should be. The name *Machine* itself mocks the emotionless exterior that too often characterizes the science fiction hero. The stereotype preaches that a "real" man should be cool, aloof, and remote, like the traditional Western hero, like the popular film hero played by Clint Eastwood. Too often the science fiction hero has simply been a cowboy transplanted into another time and place; an adventurer who has no woman (or leaves her) and who loves or at least prefers the company of his machine (be it robot, starship, or computer) just as the cowboy preferred his horse. In *Picnic on Paradise*, Machine has named himself because as an "adolescent rebel," he prefers to wear a television-like device called a "Trivia" on his head twenty-four hours a day; plugged in to his drug, he avoids feeling altogether.

Alyx and Machine both move from their isolationist stances and come to a full sharing. In scenes that are sexually explicit yet tender and erotic, Machine allows himself to feel passion, even love, and Alyx, far from being the meek partner of the stereotype, is his teacher and helper.

Russ's purpose throughout her fiction is to depict radical life styles, to present individual portraits of humans who are characterized as much by the way they change as by the way they remain the same. In *Picnic on Paradise* she fulfills these purposes so well that even the climax of the novel (Machine's death and Alyx's stabbing of Gunnar) is acceptable. Machine's accident came as a result of his newfound spontaneity, and Alyx's action, consistent with her former life as a murderer, was no longer criminally motivated but was in an ultimate way motivated by a primal sense of justice and caring. Modern morality does not condone such acts, to be sure, yet one of the successes of this novel is that the reader accepts the rightness of the act.

Some reservations about the novel are its rather brusk exposition and slow pace after the journey commences. A more conventional description of the characters would help involve the reader in the story. Generally, however, Russ has displayed considerable courage in her writing, particularly in her attempts to present themes and characters associated with tragedy. Until recently, science fiction has by and large avoided the truly tragic for the sad or the unfortunate. The death of Machine, while not classically tragic, brings about a kind of redemption in Alyx. She had never lost anything she really wanted, she said, and so had not until then understood her fellow humans or indeed experienced the profound emotions of anger, grief, and acceptance that such events bring.

Ultimately, then, *Picnic on Paradise* presents an assemblage, not merely of travelers but of pilgrims, who journey at first as an escape from their daily lives, but then as seekers and discoverers of their own selves. As Alyx realizes at the end of the novel, her "special and peculiar attitudes" are what define her — not what she can do or even what she can think, but what she is.

Kathryn L. Seidel

Sources for Further Study

Reviews:

Amazing Stories. XLII, March 1969, pp. 143-144.

Analog. LXXXIII, April, 1969, p. 165.

Fantastic Stories. XVIII, December, 1968, p. 141.

Magazine of Fantasy and Science Fiction. XXXV, September, 1968, pp. 35-37 and XXXVI, January, 1969, p. 41.

New Worlds. CLXXXV, December, 1968, p. 61.

Observer. December 21, 1969, p. 21.

SF Commentary. I, January, 1969, p. 10.

PILGRIMAGE: THE BOOK OF THE PEOPLE
AND
THE PEOPLE: NO DIFFERENT FLESH

Author: Zenna Henderson (1917-   )
First book publications: Pilgrimage (1961) ; *The People* (1966)
Type of work: Novelization of short stories
Time: The present and the late nineteenth century
Locale: Southwestern United States

Both books detail, in a series of loosely connected stories, the attempts of a group of extraterrestrials, possessing psionic powers and stranded on earth after their own planet is destroyed, to find the surviving members of their own race and to forge relationships with earthlings

> *Principal characters:*
> MARK AND MERIS EDWARDS, a young earth couple in *The People*
> LEA HOLMES, a depressed and suicidal young earth woman in *Pilgrimage*
> KAREN, Jemmy's sister, a teacher and one of the People
> JEMMY, an "Old One" of the People, though young in years and Valency's husband
> VALENCY CARMODY, a teacher who possesses an unusually large amount of the People's psi powers
> BETHIE MERRILL, one of the "sensitives" of the People
> DR. CURTIS, an earth doctor who learns to work with Bethie

Zenna (Chlarson) Henderson is a schoolteacher who has spent most of her life in Arizona teaching young children. She is also a very gifted storyteller. Her stories are basically stories of hope, of understandings reached often after potentially tragic misunderstandings, or of new discoveries that lend hope to a seemingly hopeless future. They assume that all intelligent life, human and alien, is morally good and shares similarities that make understanding possible. Henderson started writing her stories about "the People" in the early 1950's, a more optimistic and innocent generation, and stubbornly continued on during the 1960's, untouched by the disillusionment and cynicism of that decade. She has written only four books of science fiction. Two of them, *The Anything Box* and *Holding Wonder*, are undisguised collections of short stories previously published in science fiction magazines. The other two, *Pilgrimage: the Book of the People* and *The People: No Different Flesh*, are thematically connected collections of similar short stories. What differentiates the latter two books is not so much the fact that they are tied together by linking narratives or common themes, but that their concern is with a very special group of people.

"The People," as Zenna Henderson describes them, are a group of extraterrestrials (and their earthly descendants) who emigrated to earth sometime during the nineteenth century when their planet was destroyed (in "Deluge"). They are very similar to native earthlings except for their psionic powers (which must be concealed from most earth humans) and their genuine goodness. They settle in an isolated region of the southwestern United States and the stories tell of their adventures from the time of the destruction of their planet to the late 1960's when they often travel by flying in their pick-up truck. Since they are blessed with a kind of racial memory, those of the People alive in the 1960's have no difficulty remembering and relating a story "narrated" by one of their great grandparents.

Each story is narrated in the first person by one of its major characters. If the character has died, the story is related by one of his or her descendants, still in the words of the person who lived it, by means of the aforementioned racial memory. In *The Pilgrimage* this feat is accomplished by calling a gathering of the people to record their history on earth with a newly invented recording device. They have recently been contacted by another group from their home world who found and settled an empty planet, and they must now decide whether to join this group on their new home, or remain on earth. Three of the six stories in the second book, *The People*, take place a few generations before the stories in the first book, and concern the destruction of the home planet and the tragic first contacts between humans and members of the People. All of these stories are related to an earth couple, befriended by the People in the first story, and the only excuse necessary for such storytelling is the couple's natural curiosity about their new friends.

All of the stories (with the exception of "Deluge") take place in isolated desert country in the southwestern United States. Here Henderson's stories are too compactly written for her to spend much time describing the scenery, but when she does, the canyons and flats, rocky slopes, "scrub-covered foothills," and "pinepointed mountains" are all authentically presented. Authentic, too, are the backwoods characters that people these regions: the country doctors, miners, sheriffs, old-timers, and Mexicans who add local color to her stories. Glory and Seth, the old mining couple in the story "Return," seem as genuine as the land itself.

Unfortunately, not many of her characterizations are that vividly drawn. Her stories often concern young children and their parents and schoolteachers (generally young women). The schoolteachers are interchangeable, as are most of the mothers and fathers. The schoolteachers, whether they are earthlings or members of the People, are sensitive, intelligent, unfailingly patient and understanding of their young charges, and generally a little too good to be true. The fathers are all strict yet kindly and understanding, and the mothers are all warm and loving. Karen's mother and father in "Ararat" are almost completely interchangeable with Bruce and Eve Merrill, the parents in "Gilead"; Melodye Amerson of "Pottage" and Perdita Verist of "Wilderness," both teachers, have very little in their personalities to differentiate them. Henderson is concerned with the similarities between people and between humans and aliens, not with their individual differences. Still, after reading two books in which a great many of the characters are overly similar, one begins to wish that she stressed individual differences more.

All of the stories in *Pilgrimage*, including the thread of narrative that knits them together, explore the problems of lost people, alienated from the rest of their world because of some difference which they sense inside themselves. In most cases the difference is a real one; the People do have powers that earth humans do not possess, and their landing on earth caused many of them to become lost and isolated. With others (many of whom are earth humans) the difference they feel is one they have fashioned out of their own suffering and discontent. It is this problem alone that alienates them and makes them feel lost and alone. These lost ones range all the way from Lea, a normal earthling who is so disillusioned with the futility of her life that she wants to end it, to the whole group of People in the story "Pottage," who are so afraid of revealing their differences from earth humans that they not only deny themselves all use of their powers but all normal enjoyment of life as well. In *The People*, too, the stories are about lost and troubled individuals. In "Deluge" the People lose their home planet, and in subsequent adventures the few who survive the landing on earth are truly lost and alone. Mark and Meris of "No Different Flesh" each suffer greatly because of the destruction of an important manuscript and the death of a baby. Their individual misery alienates them from each other and the world around them. And yet all of these lost people eventually find solutions; there are no unhappy endings. Despite the tragic deaths of some loved ones and the occasional discovery that what one had earlier sought was no longer wanted once it was attained, the stories all end hopefully, full of the optimistic expectation of a bright future.

Zenna Henderson's preoccupation with a bright future for everyone, for happy endings, is tellingly stressed in a story called "Turn the Page" which appears in *The Anything Box*. In it a first-grade teacher teaches her charges about good and evil and that "everyone will finally live happily ever after because it is written that way." Unfortunately her students fail to learn the lesson, which is the same lesson that Zenna Henderson wishes to teach us through her stories: we must believe, because through believing, we can solve our problems and achieve happiness. The People do not have to struggle to believe as we earthlings do; one of their powers consists of the instinctive knowledge that there is a "Presence" that gives great joy, from whom they are separated at birth and to whom they are called back at death. They also know with a certainty that all the events on inhabited worlds must coincide with His grand plan.

Henderson does not present her religious ideas with a heavy hand. Instead she tries to show us that there is still wonder, magic, and miracles in our world. The People themselves seem magical; they can fly and "platt" sunbeams and moonbeams. And in one of the stories, "Wilderness," an earthling is discovered who has developed some of the same powers, as well as some special ones of her own. But the real magic in the stories of the People is worked by human love and understanding. This is the religion that Henderson advocates. It is the love and understanding that Glory and Seth show Debbie and her own love for her newborn child that end her cruel selfishness and assuage her grief in "Return," not any magic performed by the People. And it is the understanding of a human teacher and the love of a human girl that save the Francher child from delinquency in "Captivity."

The author's message is one of Christian love and tolerance for those who are different, for those who may not look or act like the rest of us. In "The Closest School," a story from her latest book, *Holding Wonder*, she makes this tolerance clear when she describes a new child registering for school, a child who is purple and fuzzy but who is as much a shy child as any human six-year-old entering school for the first time. If we can accept a fuzzy purple child as being essentially similar to ourselves, shouldn't it be that much easier to accept the basic similarity of children and adults of other races, religions, and nationality groups? If we can sympathize with the People and feel the pain they are made to suffer because of human intolerance, shouldn't this teach us to be more tolerant ourselves?

The People suffered greatly from human intolerance in some of their first contacts with earth humans. Lytha's family were burned as witches in "Angels Unawares" by people who were religious fanatics — the kind of fanatics who "pervert goodness, love, and obedience and set up a god small enough to fit their shrunken souls." It is the goodness, love, and tolerance that the People exhibit that Henderson would have us emulate.

The People, aside from their special powers, are very human. There are a few customs they remember from their home planet which they no longer follow, some native fruit they brought with them that they still grow and cherish, and a few words and expressions from their native language that are the only clues we are given to the life they lived before they traveled to earth. There is no detailed creation of another culture in these books. "Cahilla," the word Timmy used to refer to the little box of things he brought to earth, comes from the Spanish word *cajilla*; and the expression of surprise and exasperation used by the people, "A donday veeah," seems to come from a Spanish expression which literally means "where are you going?"

Zenna Henderson's books are not profound works nor are they great literature. They were written, as she has said, "for fun" and to make us wonder, and dream, and perhaps learn a few lessons. Her books might be faulted by some readers as being unfailingly optimistic and a bit naïve. But for those who have not become unshakable cynics as a result of the many disillusionments of the last fifteen years, for readers who still have the strength and courage to hope and dream, her stories can be quite touching and enchanting and well worth reading.

Ina S. Faye

Sources for Further Study

Reviews:

Amazing Stories. XXXV, June, 1961, pp. 140-141.

Analog. LXVIII, September, 1961, pp. 163-164 and LXXXI, April, 1968, pp. 159-160.

Galaxy. XX, December, 1961, p. 146.

Kirkus Reviews. XXXV, January 15, 1967, p. 85.

Library Journal. XCII, March 1, 1967, p. 1032.

Magazine of Fantasy and Science Fiction. XX, May, 1961, pp. 96-97.

New World. CXXIII, October, 1962, p. 127.

New World. CLXIII, June, 1966, p. 152.

Publisher's Weekly. CXCI, January 16, 1967, p. 78.

Punch. CCLI, November 9, 1966, p. 719.

A PLAGUE OF DEMONS

Author: Keith Laumer (1925-   )
First book publication: 1965
Type of work: Novel
Time: The future, perhaps thirty or forty years from now
Locale: Algeria, the United States, and a far distant planet

An American agent discovers that aliens have infiltrated human society and are carrying on some scheme that involves stealing the brains of fallen soldiers

Principal characters:
JOHN BRAVAIS, a spy for an American intelligence agency
FELIX SEVERANCE, Bravais' superior and member of the Ultimax group

Although Keith Laumer has made a career in the American Air Force, he has found enough time to become prolific as a writer of science fiction. He is probably best known for his stories about Retief, an interstellar diplomat, but in *A Plague of Demons* he has written a novel that is often richly inventive. (*A Plague of Demons* first appeared as a shorter serial in *If* magazine in November and December of 1964, but it is the fuller book version, published in 1965, that will be discussed here.)

The novel opens with the atmosphere of a next-generation James Bond story: John Bravais, a reserve Army officer and agent for an organization referred to as CBI, is in Algeria on a mission, and in preparation for it he is equipped with as many gadgets as Ian Fleming might have used in three novels. To begin with, he has an optical-effect suit, a garment that makes him the next thing to invisible; when the time comes for him to go into action, he wears a device the size of a canteen — a focused phase field generator — that neutralizes gravity around him, enabling him to fly through the air. The goggles of his suit can be tuned to adjust the magnification of its lenses and to allow him to see by infrared. His is also armed with a gun that fires poisoned darts. But this technological plenty finds use in just a single scene. After surreptitiously observing a battle and seeing some very strange things, he reports to his superior, Felix Severance, who decides he needs to be fitted with PAPA: Power Assisted Personal Armament.

Imagine a person wearing a suit of armor, with motors attached to make him faster and stronger than normal muscles can. Suppose further that the person were provided with various sorts of radio equipment and laser weaponry. Assume finally that devices could speed up his reflexes and improve his eyesight. Now imagine that all this is implanted beneath the skin, that outwardly the man looks no different than he did before, and you have PAPA.

As interesting as these innovations are, the gadgetry is not the most fascinating concept of the first third of the novel. Rather, the most provocative idea is one that Isaac Asimov would call "social science fiction," a concept of the kind that *Galaxy* was noted for, in particular: the battle that Bravais is to observe is an infantry-and-armor clash between Algerian and Moroccan forces, one that has been arranged and is being supervised by the United Nations.

Laumer hypothesizes a general agreement among the nations of the world to resolve conflicts in which diplomacy has failed by means of wars that are indeed limited: these small-scale conflicts serve as an outlet for aggressive tendencies at the same time that they settle disputes. They are carefully overseen and confined by United Nations forces, with each side apparently submitting its battle plans in advance to the U. N. Monitor-General. The system is much like a war-game with live ammunition. But those readers who find the notion a fascinating sociological concept will not be satisfied by a full treatment in *A Plague of Demons*: the whole scheme of controlled conflict serves only as a backdrop for the main action — what Bravais does when he sees alien creatures removing and carrying off the brains of fallen soldiers.

Bravais learns that the aliens, who look like large dogs, have infiltrated the United Nations Command, and he suspects that their influence may be much wider. They employ a telepathic control to keep humans from seeing them, a control from which Bravais is immune thanks to one of the implants PAPA provided him. His escape from Algeria, once the aliens have noticed him, begins the middle third of the novel, and its weakest part. As Severance dies, he tells Bravais of a hideout in Kansas in which he can find refuge, and here again Laumer supplies a novel-sized idea only to drop it without development as the plot moves on.

This second idea is the existence of an organization, the Ultimax Group; it consists of about a hundred people as rich as Croesus, as wise as Solomon, as inventive as Edison, and as secretive as Howard Hughes. Since its founding by a circle that included Benjamin Franklin, Ultimax has watched over the rest of us, nudging human events this way and that in order to bring about desirable results. Among other things, it helped to defeat George III, Napoleon, Kaiser Wilhelm, and Hitler. That Ultimax also aided in the modernization of Japan and the unification of the German and Italian states suggests that it must be composed of confirmed, though fallible, nationalists.

Somewhere beneath Coffeyville, Kansas, Ultimax has built one of its Survival Stations, and Bravais gains entrance to it. Almost bomb- and detection-proof, it contains, among other equipment, a completely automated device for the diagnosis and treatment of human ailments. The robot-doctor sedates Bravais, amputates his badly infected left arm, and replaces it with a prosthesis. After recovering from surgery (in an astonishingly short time), Bravais fears that the aliens, still on his trail, may begin to dig down after him. He contacts the other Survival Stations, but there's nobody home — at any of them. He makes his escape from another exit, and orders the station to blow itself up.

The Ultimax Group is another provocative idea, but its necessity to the plot is nonexistent. Although Felix Severance is a member of Ultimax, he sets Bravais to work in Algeria as an agent of the Defense Department. Although Severance suspects that an inordinate number of people have been missing lately, these nagging doubts reside beneath his Defense Department, not his Ultimax, hat. Although he gives Bravais the information needed to enter the Survival Station, it is hard to see why. It heals Bravais' wounds, but since he had met a human doctor on the ship which brought him to the United States, that function was not necessary. Although Severance has suggested the trip to the States for the purpose of organizing reliable individuals into a counter-alien group, the Survival Station never puts Bravais in touch with any other member of Ultimax. When Bravais leaves the station, he goes to the nearest diplomatic post, the British Consulate in Chicago. Had he been cured of his infection by the human doctor and gone directly to Chicago after landing in America, the outcome of the story would not have been affected in the slightest. The Ultimax Group neither helps nor hinders him; it simply occupies space.

Nor is there a convincing reason for Bravais to go to the British Consulate. Presumably, he wants to test the degree of alien infiltration into human society, and when he discovers that the consul is one of the aliens' androids, his suspicions are confirmed. But what purpose is served by the trip? In what way is the British Consul in Chicago more important to alien success than, say, the governor of Kansas? Or the head of the Kansas State Police? Or, for that matter, the customs inspector at Jacksonville, Florida, where he landed? The outcome of the middle part of the book is Bravais' capture by the aliens, and given their omnipresence, that could have happened anywhere. Perhaps the most convincing evidence of the disjointed nature of the middle part is this: the Ultimax Group has given Bravais their emergency number, but despite the spy-eye detector in his upper left canine, the CBI emergency band receiver in his right lower incisor, and a radar pulser transmitter in his right lower third molar, he cannot contact the Ultimax Monitor when the aliens overwhelm him: he has to use a public phone for that.

The third part begins as Bravais regains consciousness to find that he has turned into a huge fighting machine, a super-tank battling unknown forces on an unfamiliar planet. He correctly assumes that the aliens have removed his brain after overpowering him, and installed it as a small but efficient computer in one of their war machines. The aliens, like selective Valkyries, have been taking the brains of the fallen from battlefields in this way for at least 1,500 years, judging from the other units he meets. Bravais finds himself part of a galactic conflict that has been waged since before the human race evolved. Clearly, Laumer's attention in this third part is on the marriage of man and machine, and the replacement of legs by treads and senses by sensors.

The feeling of this new environment is well drawn and has a fascination of its own, but whereas the background of the first and second parts was detailed, almost oppressively so, the background of the third part, the galactic war, is extremely sketchy. The issues at stake are never clear, if they exist at all. What we have is a picture of a kind of Manichaean struggle between opposing forces that are locked in perpetual battle simply because it is their nature to do so.

Bravais, thanks to PAPA's hypnosis, remembers his past. The personalities of the rest of the brains (except for one) lie dormant beneath the control of the aliens. Yet Bravais finds it a simple matter to wrest control of his fellow units from their superiors, return them to self-consciousness, and enlist their aid in a rebellion. At the climax, he transfers his consciousness to a small housekeeping robot, kills the supreme commander on the planet, and takes over. Yet through all the rebellion and apparently after it, the enemy forces that the aliens had been locked in battle with are nowhere in evidence. After Bravais and his comrades (all of whom like nothing better than a good fight) begin their revolt, we hear no more of the enemy. Either they have been defeated just before the revolt began (unknown to the alien commander), or they have conveniently withdrawn.

After Bravais is in control, he contacts Earth and tells Ultimax about the alien menace. The humans start seeking and eliminating the aliens, and expect no great difficulty in the task. Ultimax offers to the human brains the bodies of the alien androids that they have captured on Earth, yet all of them decide that as long as there is a battle out there among the stars, they will keep on as tanks. Their decision is based on love of combat, it would seem, since nothing we have been told about the galactic war presents the slightest reason why humans should involve themselves in it.

In the final analysis, *A Plague of Demons* is three well-made short pieces that do not fit together. Parts were written in 1964, only about four years after Laumer began writing a great deal of science fiction, and Laumer's more recent works show a competence and sureness in the handling of plot that are not displayed in this early work. Similarly, the balance between foreground and background is not always under control: the first and second parts are richly detailed, almost beyond the needs of the story, but the third part seems sketchy and trite, peopled as it is by a grab-bag of unknown soldiers from the conflicts of the Western world. One wonders why, for instance, the aliens choose only male brains, not female ones; it is never asserted that something in the experience or personality of the owner of the brain is made use of once the brain is hooked up in the machine. Quite the contrary: the aliens make every attempt to suppress the consciousness of the brain. Why do we meet only the brains of soldiers, not the man or woman on the street? Why do we meet the brains only of those fallen in battle, not those endangered by accident or disease? If the first and second parts of *A Plague of Demons* are detailed down to the makes of the cars and the calibers of the weapons, why are the motivations of the third part so cloudy?

Whatever the reason for the faults of the whole, the book nevertheless contains scenes that are memorable: Bravais' night observation of the battle in Algeria, his passage on the undersea freighter, and his awakening to consciousness on the alien battlefield are noteworthy. *A Plague of Demons* will most likely be remembered for these well-realized and vivid scenes.

Walter E. Meyers

Sources for Further Study

Reviews:

Luna Monthly. XL, September, 1972, p. 21.

Magazine of Fantasy and Science Fiction. XXX, May, 1966, p. 45.

New Worlds. CLXXV, September, 1967, p. 64.

PLANET OF THE APES
(LA PLANÈTE DES SINGES)

Author: Pierre Boulle (1912-   )
First book publication: 1963
English translation: 1964
Type of work: Novel
Time: 2500-3200
Locale: The planet Soror

A grimly satiric account of an earthman's ordeal on a distant planet where apes are the intelligent, civilized species and humans are lower animals

> Principal characters:
> ULYSSE MEROU, a young journalist taken along on an interstellar voyage for his ability at chess
> PROFESSOR ANTELLE, the wryly misanthropic scientist who leads the expedition
> ARTHUR LEVAIN, Antelle's disciple, a brilliant young physician
> ZIRA, a chimpanzee scientist of Soror who befriends and aids Mérou
> CORNELIUS, Zira's chimpanzee fiancé, also a scientist and benefactor of Mérou
> ZAIUS, an orangutan, chief representative of Soror's "official science" and Mérou's principal enemy
> "NOVA," the brute but beautiful humanoid female of Soror who becomes Mérou's mate

Planet of the Apes provides plenary evidence of the coming of age of science fiction as a mode of literature. It is a wholly serious work by an internationally recognized author, first published in translation in the United States by the Vanguard Press, not a usual science fiction outlet. Within a few years it became the basis for a major Hollywood film, starring no less a figure than Charlton Heston. Reviewers respectfully traced the novel's antecedents to *Gulliver's Travels* as well as Jules Verne. But for all this, *Planet of the Apes* is undeniably and unequivocally a science fiction novel, drawing on Einstein's theory of relativity to explain certain features of interstellar travel, and extrapolating from Darwin and his successors to explain the upward evolution of a simian species and the devolution of a human species to a state of subrationality.

But to see *Planet of the Apes* as a work of science fiction in no way diminishes it as Swiftian satire. On the contrary, *Gulliver's Travels* may readily be apprehended as an early example of science fiction, both insofar as its plot relies on extrapolations from the new discoveries of eighteenth century South Seas exploration, and — more important — insofar as a major aspect of its theme, especially in Book III, is science itself. Indeed, as both *Gulliver's Travels* and *Planet of the Apes* make clear, science fiction by its very nature furnishes an especially keen satiric instrument for probing the human condition and man's illusions about himself. The essential method of satire is to establish a new perspective in which to examine human character, and no more radical viewpoint can be imagined than science fiction, which devises a wholly new setting in time and space.

Planet of the Apes, from the beginning, is encrusted with ironies. The main character and first-person narrator, Ulysse Mérou, is a "Ulysses" whose companions, like those of his heroic namesake on Circe's island, are, in a sense, turned into beasts, or at least regarded as such on a planet of intelligent apes. When Mérou finally makes his escape, he returns to earth to find, not a faithful Penelope, but an "unfaithful" world: since his departure seven hundred years earlier relative to terrestrial time, earth's humans have declined, its apes advanced, as on Soror; and when he brings the starship's landingcraft down at Orly airport, it is greeted by a gorilla in an officer's uniform.

Similarly ironic is the fate of Professor Antelle, the designer of the starship and leader of the interstellar expedition. He has chosen to journey to Betelgeuse, at a distance of three hundred light years, rather than Proxima Centauri, only about four light years away, because he wants to get far from earth and see something really different. Having grown weary of his own kind, he has no desire to return to a familiar earth, and is quite willing to return seven hundred years later (only two years for the travelers at near light speed). At first the irony is rather superficial: the three-man party finds a planet virtually identical to earth in climate and topography — hence the name Soror, "sister." But the irony deepens when it turns out that the humanoid creatures they first discover, identical to earthlings in physical appearance, are merely brute beasts, hunted by a race of civilized, intelligent simians. Confronted by this stunning reversal of roles, more of a "difference" that he had anticipated, the aloof, misanthropic scientist is shattered. After their initial capture and separation by the apes, Mérou at last finds his mentor in a zoo performing tricks for simian spectators, reduced to a mute irrationality from which he never recovers.

Boulle manages the capture and misidentification of the earthlings by the apes of Soror with economy and plausibility. Having passed over towns and cities, the three-man crew finally brings down one of the starship's launches in a dense forest. After a brief exploration the three men strip to bathe in a pool at the foot of a waterfall. Here they encounter a naked female human of striking beauty, dubbed "Nova" by Mérou. They take her for a member of a primitive tribe and attempt to communicate with her; but not only does she show no signs of intelligence, but even appears terrified by the sound of human speech and laughter. Although the young "woman" mysteriously strangles their pet chimpanzee in a terrified rage, she appears harmless and the men attempt to humor her. Soon they find themselves taken off guard by what is a *herd* rather than a tribe of these humanoid creatures, who destroy the astronauts' clothes and all other artifacts, even battering the launch to the point that it cannot be operated or repaired. Without hurting the earthmen, the humanoids of Soror force them to go along on a trek through the forest that leaves the wrecked landing craft and the other shredded remnants of their civilization behind. It is thus, naked and unarmed, that Mérou and his companions are discovered by the apes.

The third member of the crew, Antelle's disciple Arthur Levain, is shot dead by gorilla trophy hunters, Antelle is captured and later turns up in a zoo, and Mérou is captured in a net and sold to a scientific research institute, where humans are experimented on by apes even as the latter are the subject of men's experiments on earth. It is here that Mérou meets the chimpanzee Zira, who after several weeks he convinces of his superior intelligence by learning her language and drawing geometrical diagrams. Very soon Mérou becomes an important element in the academic struggle of Zira and her fiancé Cornelius against the "official science" of the orangutans, exemplified by Zaius, the director of the research institute. The demonstrable intelligence of Mérou is solid evidence for Cornelius' radical and shocking theory that humans had once been intelligent and civilized, that they had indeed originated the civilization that the apes had only imitated and taken over after the decline of the human beings as a race.

Shortly after the extraordinary phenomenon of Mérou is revealed to the simian society of Soror, Cornelius' theory is confirmed by an archaeological discovery. In the meantime it turns out that Mérou has fathered a child upon "Nova," the humanoid female with whom he had been caged at the institute. Moreover, Nova is herself beginning to manifest signs of intelligence. Zira and Cornelius, fearing for the lives of their human friends on account of the malice of the orangutans — and indeed, suddenly uncomfortable with the implications of their own discoveries — engineer the escape of Mérou, Nova, and their child in the first simian satellite around Soror — a satellite designed for experimental humans anyway. With modifications to the equipment, Mérou is able to pilot the satellite to a rendezvous with his starship, which is still in orbit.

The competition and antagonism among the inventive chimpanzees, the tradition-bound orangutans, and the pragmatic gorillas (who excel in war and administration) is an obvious satire on the racial and ethnic conflicts of human society. The barbaric cruelty of most apes toward the helpless humans of Soror, and the arrogant "scientific" explanations of simian superiority (reversed mirror images of contemporary anthropological explanations of the emergence of human dominance on earth) serve a similar satiric function. As in *Gulliver's Travels*, however, the ultimate satire lies in the fate of the central character. Like Gulliver, Mérou finds his comfortable sense of his own importance and assured place in the universe shattered.

Although his satiric method is similar to Swift's, Boulle's final achievement, nevertheless, falls short. To some extent the defect is technical: *Planet of the Apes* lacks the detailed texture and dramatic immediacy of *Gulliver's Travels*. The setting is not developed with sufficient cogency, and Mérou is not, finally, a particularly interesting character in his own right. His tragedy, unlike Gulliver's, is almost wholly a result of blind circumstance rather than his own spiritual pride.

Perhaps the crucial difference between Swift and Boulle is not, however, so much a matter of technique as of underlying moral assumptions, not only about man's future but even about his very nature and purpose. The floundering figure of Gulliver, ridiculous and despairing at the end of Swift's work, stands against a clear standard of human conduct, an unyielding norm of human significance; but the conclusion of *Planet of the Apes* appears to open an abyss of meaninglessness.

The particular *frisson* with which the novel closes requires the use of a familiar device of romantic fiction, the framed narrative, here managed by means of Edgar Allan Poe's specifically science fiction device, the "MS. Found in a Bottle." In this case the bottle is picked up not at sea, but in deep space by a couple on an interstellar pleasure cruise aboard a vessel which "sails" on the photon "wind" radiated from the stars. The vast majority of the novel, the narration by Ulysse Mérou of his adventures on Soror, is told in the manuscript found in the bottle. The framing narrative is, however, a grim and crucial element in the satire. The usual purpose of a narrative frame is to provide authorial distance (hence a sense of objectivity) from fictional events which are improbable or mysterious: for instance, the ghosts in Henry James's *The Turn of the Screw*. In the last chapter of *Planet of the Apes*, "Jinn" and "Phyllis" look up from the manuscript they have found and agree that it must be untrue, a cosmic literary hoax; obviously the notion of intelligent, civilized *humans* is preposterous. Only in the final sentences of the novel is it clearly revealed that Jinn and Phyllis, and presumably all intelligent inhabitants of the known universe, are apes.

Lemuel Gulliver, at the close of *Gulliver's Travels*, despising his family and sleeping in the stable with the horses, because they remind him of the super-intelligent Houyhnhnms, is a satiric caricature of rationalistic eighteenth century man who has forgotten his place in the order of things, whose intellectual pride has ended in despair; but the end of *Planet of the Apes* depicts a cosmos in which man has no place, and in which the only "order" is the blind, remorseless law of "survival of the fittest" (a tautology reducible to "survival of the survivors"). Boulle's problem here — and it is a problem shared by many serious science fiction writers — is to bring the work to a successful close. The "surprise" ending, so often resorted to by science fiction writers, has the air of excessive artifice and cleverness, and does not generally hold up well under rereading. Undoubtedly the cause of Boulle's use of this device in *Planet of the Apes* is inherent in any science fiction novel which, like Arthur C. Clarke's *Childhood's End* or John Wyndham's *Re-Birth*, depicts the human race as superseded by another species. The reader is left with a severe problem of identification. Writers such as Clarke and Wyndham expect the reader to make the leap and to identify with, or at least approve of, the new superior phase of human evolution. They soften the blow, however, by envisioning the next rung of the evolutionary ladder as a direct emergence, an improvement on the present human species; but Boulle's satire defies our identification with the wholly alien and not especially sympathetic apes.

If it is difficult enough to project, singlehandedly, an altogether new and evolving (and hence relativistic) value system like Clarke's or Wyndham's in opposition to the Judaeo-Christian tradition, which has sustained Western culture for centuries; then to cut the ground out from under any possibility of purposive value, as Boulle seems to do, gives rise to a literary situation that is almost impossible to bring off. The satirist especially, for all his apparent cynicism and malice, as a rule must assume, as a Swift or an Evelyn Waugh does, a firm norm against which satirized deviations are measured. But Boulle imagines a cosmos governed by evolutionary caprice. Although Boulle knows the shape and location of the targets of his satire, it is not at all clear that he has chosen any very solid ground from which to take aim.

R. V. Young, Jr.

Sources for Further Study

Reviews:

Analog. LXXIII, May, 1964, p. 85 and LXXXIII, May, 1969, p. 168.

Atlantic. CCXIII, January, 1964, p. 120.

Book Week. December 15, 1963, p. 14.

Critic. XXII, February, 1964, p. 90.

Library Journal. LXXXVIII, December 1, 1963, p. 4661.

New Statesman. LXVII, February 7, 1964, p. 219.

New York Times Book Review. December 8, 1963, p. 48.

Time. LXXXII, November 8, 1963, p. 101.

Times Literary Supplement. February 6, 1964, p. 101.

PLAYER PIANO

Author: Kurt Vonnegut, Jr. (1922-   )
First book publication: 1952
Type of work: Novel
Time: The near future
Locale: Upstate New York

A satirical yet poignant commentary on the dehumanizing influences of technology in contemporary American life, and man's struggle to gain and maintain a sense of his own identity

> *Principal characters:*
> PAUL PROTEUS, brilliant young manager of the Ilium works
> ANITA PROTEUS, his perfect hostess wife
> ED FINNERTY, Paul's best friend, an antiestablishment iconoclast
> JAMES LASHER, an anthropologist, chaplain, and rebel leader
> SHAH OF BRATPUHR, ruler of a primitive culture

Kurt Vonnegut's first novel extends and refines the fictional strategy and techniques of his early science fiction short stories, originally published in *Galaxy*, *Worlds of If*, and *The Magazine of Fantasy and Science Fiction*. His relatively straightforward story line with a traditional beginning, middle, and end serves as a literary clothesline on which to hang epigrams, fables, non-sequiturs, episodic subplots, and thematic refrains.

Vonnegut's essay "Science Fiction" (originally published in *The New York Times Book Review* and reprinted with minor changes in *Wampeters, Foma, and Granfalloons*), describes *Player Piano* as a novel about people and machines in which machines frequently get the best of people. In the essay, Vonnegut expresses surprise and anger at being labeled a science fiction writer, since in the early 1950's "serious" critics were commenting disparagingly on the genre. Despite this, *Player Piano* was reissued in 1954 as a part of Bantam's science fiction program and was retitled *Utopia-14*. Vonnegut clearly makes use of many standard science fiction themes and devices in the novel, including an examination of man-machine relationships, the scientist's moral responsibility, future shock, and paradigms of utopia and dystopia.

Player Piano satirically attacks the foibles and failures of industrial technology, big business, politics, and religion. Though the plot is borrowed, as Vonnegut himself acknowledges, from Aldous Huxley's *Brave New World* (1932) and Eugene Zamiatin's *We* (1920), it is adapted to 1952 America and extrapolated to a bitterly comic dystopian vision. The setting is the Ilium Works, an industrial complex in Ilium, N.Y., after World War III and in the midst of the "Third Industrial Revolution." The characters have been dislocated and dissociated by the "Copernican Effect," the realization that they are not created in the image of God and are not the center of the universe's meaning and purpose. Most workers have been replaced by machines, which not only are vastly improved models of physical efficiency, but which also devalue human thinking. But for sabotage, for example, the checker-playing machine, "Checker Charley," would have defeated Paul Proteus, the novel's central character and the undefeated champion of the Ilium Works.

In Vonnegut's future America, each individual's destiny is determined by how a computer scores his personality in a series of tests which reward management skills and academic intelligence and punish active imagination and physical dexterity. America has become a dystopia: an elitist, totalitarian, mechanical society in which men have been replaced by machines, superheroes by supercomputers, liberty by organization, and the pursuit of happiness by the pursuit of efficiency. It is the machine which has human organs: electrical eyes, mechanical hands, welding heads, and punch-press jaws. It is the machine which dances, does calisthenics, and creates symphonies like "The Building 58 Suite." A hierarchy of technical minds has replaced a hierarchy of money, with little or no improvement.

The main plot concerns the story of Paul Proteus, the young manager of the Ilium Works, and the most brilliant and important person in Ilium. He seems to be the ultimate company man, married to a perfect hostess (who might have been one of the Stepford wives), and living in a plastic suburban "Utopia" in which all manual chores are done mechanically. Yet Paul has doubts about the quality of his stainless steel future, and these doubts are intensified when his old friend Ed Finnerty returns to town. Finnerty questions Paul's integrity, and takes him across the river from his white-collar haven to the Homestead, a place peopled with those rejected by the machine society: the self-employed, and the Reconstruction and Reclamation Corps, who work at what little manual labor still needs to be done in Ilium. In a Homestead bar Paul meets James Lasher, anthropologist and chaplain to the "Reeks and Wrecks" (the nickname pun for the Corps), and eventually becomes a member of the rebel Ghost Shirt Society. Lasher has organized the Society (named after nineteenth century American Indians who believed their medicine men's tales that charmed shirts would stop the white man's bullets, and so were annihilated) to defend the old humanistic values and restore dignity to mankind (the machines are to almost everyone what the white men were to the Indians). Paul pretends to be a double agent for the "organization" (one must always be careful what one pretends to be, as Vonnegut shows in *Mother Night*), and becomes instead as involuntary messiah-figure created by the Society to lead a rebellion against the managers and engineers as well as the machines.

The abortive uprising is quickly quelled, however, and the faith of the Ghost Shirt followers is shown to be just as misplaced as belief in technological "progress." The Society has indiscriminately destroyed all the machines it could find, including the sewer treatment plant, the bakery, and the Museum. Of the four imprisoned rebel leaders, only Lasher never loses touch with reality; he realizes that the Ghost Shirt Society is no workable answer to their dilemma. However, the sole escape from this technological nightmare seems to be dream or death: Paul undergoes a drugged "truth dream" as part of his initiation into the Society, and his cat is killed making a "stand" against a sweeping machine in the Ilium Works. Though Paul's dream escape is only temporary, at the novel's close he is at least figuratively free of his old machine-oriented ideas and values.

As a counterpoint to this main plot Vonnegut uses his now-familiar device of a visitor from another planet or a distant country to provide a point of view outside the main perspective of the narrative. The visitor in this case is the Shah of Bratpuhr, who is in the United States on a state visit to receive financial and technological aid for his country. In the course of his travels, the Shah gains for himself and for the reader an extensive view of the mechanical culture in which Paul and the other characters are mere cogs. He brings the unintentionally comic perspective of a "primitive" society to bear on American culture, seeing Americans as prisoners, "citizens" and soldiers as slaves (his language has no euphemism like "the average man"), and democracy as communism. It is also the Shah who asks many of the adverbial questions which are common in Vonnegut's fiction: why? (why hurry with work when the only play is watching television?), and what? (what are people for? he wants to ask the ultimate computer Epicac XIV; and he will receive no answer, as he has received none to the ancient riddle he has asked it; "false god," he sneers). The Shah thus provides a means of external evaluation of the novel's primary "cosmic egg," its particular moment and value in the time-space continuum. However, the Shah never sees Paul's personal world, and this lack of interaction is one of the novel's structural weaknesses.

The tone of *Player Piano* couples satire with nostalgia. The novel condemns the tyranny of the machine and man's fascination with "progress," as well as his sentimental desire to return to a pretechnological world in which he may live "naturally." Behind the story is Vonnegut's wry awareness that this is the world which man has built, and the best thing he can do is to learn how to go on from here. One of the key lessons that Paul learns is that man has surrounded himself with machines *intentionally*, for he wants them to do the work. Another lesson is that "Nature" (in the form of an old farm Paul buys so that he and his wife Anita can return to a premachine world of books and wood-burning stoves rather than television and electricity) is in actuality coarse, harsh, hot, and smelly. Paul, like Jay Gatsby and Eugene Gant, has tried and failed to recapture the past.

Player Piano also satirizes the failure of love in the modern world to be a redeeming center for human relationships. Paul and Anita's clichéd, ritualistic love refrains ("I love you, Paul." "I love *you*, Anita") punctuate the emotional barrenness and lack of intimacy in their lives.

Partly because the novel is episodic, the reader focuses most intently on the fascinating and varied cast of characters. Despite the fact that they have seemed to some critics to be flat, stereotyped, and shallow, they function like some of the best comic-strip characters: they focus our awareness as they embody and reflect the ideas and values which Vonnegut is placing under a fictional macroscope for examination, and they invoke both our irony and our pity.

Besides Proteus and Lasher, the characters include Finnerty, the brilliant antiestablishment iconoclast and alcoholic engineer who influences Paul's decision to drop out of the technocratic society and into the Ghost Shirt Society. Finnerty explains that he will not see a psychiatrist to cure his oppressive loneliness and alienation because a psychiatrist would want him to return to the "normal" center of things, while he wants to stay close to the creative edge, where people can see "big undreamed-of things." It is Finnerty who is the live piano player, improvizing savagely on the instrument and thus embodying a reality antithetical to that implied in the book's title. There is also Dr. Ewing Halyard, who loses his Ph.D. degree, and therefore his job and social status, because it is discovered that his degree was granted by computer error (he never fulfilled his P.E. requirement); Rudy Hertz, the once-superb lathe worker whose "essence" is now on tape, a ghost running all the lathes in the Ilium Works; and "Dog Eat Dog" Shepherd, whose nickname reflects his personality, and who believes that life is laid out like a golf course, with a series of beginnings, hazards, and ends, with a clear and factual scorekeeping after each hole by which to compare oneself with others.

Other characters reflect aspects of Paul's personality and its changes: Edgar Rice Burroughs Hagstrohm, who, like Paul and his namesake, longs to escape and be a "real man" in primitive nature, although his idea of "living" is watching television; and Luke Lubbock, who changes his identity mercurially by the simple act of changing costumes and joining another organization.

Vonnegut has frequently been called a "black humorist," yet the satire in *Player Piano* is more affectionate than cruel. If man often seems puny and ineffectual when pitted against an overwhelming technological age, he still may choose (like Santiago in Ernest Hemingway's *The Old Man and the Sea*), to be "destroyed but not defeated." Vonnegut's cosmic pessimism is paradoxically countered by his personal optimism.

Player Piano shapes and focuses Vonnegut's major themes: the quest for individual truth and meaning in an absurd universe; the paradoxical contrast between illusion and reality (what he refers to in *Cat's Cradle* as the absolute necessity of lying about reality and the absolute impossibility of lying about it); and man's need to establish a personal equilibrium in a chaotic world by telling himself harmless lies (*foma*).

The dystopian vision in *Player Piano* examines the futuristic effects of alienation of labor: man's displacement by machines (the title's literal as well as symbolic meaning) in a society which has separated work and leisure, and in the process eliminated true play. *Homo ludens* is replaced by the mechanical man. Clearly, the novel is arguing, man must choose to limit the scope and influence of the machine. Man is imperfect (frail, inefficient, and stupid as well as brilliant), yet it is precisely his imperfection which needs to be accepted and even celebrated, for man is only happy when he has dignity and self-respect, and these feelings come only when he feels needed and useful.

In science fiction terms, *Player Piano* shows the results of holocaust followed by dystopia, the destruction of the world followed by a reconstruction of society without freedom or fulfillment. In the scene which effectively closes the novel, Paul (now, perhaps like Vonnegut himself, a failed Romanticist) starts a toast "To a better world." He then realizes that people have not changed; they are still eager to re-create the "same old nightmare." He shrugs, and toasts "To the record." It is this dynamic tension between Utopian possibility and historical fact, between what might be and what is, which gives *Player Piano* its structure as well as its theme.

Clark Mayo

Sources for Further Study
Criticism:

Mellard, James M. "The Modes of Vonnegut's Fiction: or, *Player Piano* Ousts *Mechanical Bride* and *The Sirens of Titan* Invade *The Gutenberg Galaxy*," in *The Vonnegut Statement*. Edited by Jerome Klinkowitz and John Somer. New York: Delacorte, 1973, pp. 178-203. This interesting article compares several novels and shows the progression in Vonnegut's work.

Reed, Peter J. *Kurt Vonnegut, Jr.* New York: Crowell, 1972, pp. 24-56. This general work on Vonnegut gives some discussion on *Player Piano* within the body of the author's novels.

Reviews:

Analog. L, February, 1953, pp. 167-168.

Galaxy. V, February, 1953, pp. 96-97.

Magazine of Fantasy and Science Fiction. IV, April, 1953, p. 98 and XXXI, November, 1966, p. 62.

New Worlds. XXI, June 1953, pp. 125-126.

Kirkus Reviews. XX, June 1, 1952, p. 330.

New Republic. CXXVII, August 18, 1952, p. 19.

New York Herald Tribune Book Review. August 17, 1952, p. 5.

Saturday Review. XXXV, August 30, 1952, p. 11.

THE POISON BELT

Author: Arthur Conan Doyle (1859-1930)
First book publication: 1913
Type of work: Novel
Time: The early twentieth century
Locale: London and Rotherfield

An account of events preceding and following the passage of the Earth through a region of "poisoned ether"

> *Principal characters:*
> PROFESSOR GEORGE CHALLENGER, an eccentric genius
> LORD JOHN ROXTON, an adventurer
> PROFESSOR SUMMERLEE, a representative of "scientific orthodoxy"
> E. D. MALONE, a reporter

The Poison Belt was Arthur Conan Doyle's sequel to *The Lost World* (1912), and is something of a testament to the difficulties involved in following up an outstandingly successful novel. *The Lost World* triumphed because of its spectacular use of monsters from prehistory and its equally fascinating characterization of the bombastic Challenger. If Doyle did not quite succeed in creating a sequel of equal impact, at least his attempt is not without a certain flair of its own.

The story begins with Challenger's reaction to an observed blurring of the Fraunhofer lines in the spectrums of the planets and stars. This he interprets in characteristically melodramatic fashion as a sign of the imminent end of the world. In a letter to *The Times*, he describes the solar system as a bundle of tiny corks adrift in a vast ocean, helpless in the grip of its waves and vulnerable to unimaginable dangers. Disaster is about to strike because of a change in the composition of space; the Earth is about to be sterilized just as a piece of equipment might be sterilized in an alcohol bath by a laboratory scientist. Faced with this approaching disaster, Challenger invites his *Lost World* companions to join him at his home so that together they might witness the catastrophe, preserving themselves with the aid of oxygen for a few extra hours.

The effects of the poisoned ether begin to make themselves felt as the narrator (Malone), Summerlee, and Roxton board a train out of Victoria station. As they are seized by a kind of intoxication, their dialogue becomes even more aggressive and feverish than usual. Through all their adventures (save those in *The Land of Mist*, 1926) these characters are never far from comedy in their conversations, but on this occasion their speech descends to outright farce. The comic relief dissolves rapidly, however, once they have sealed themselves into a single room in Challenger's house, armed with cylinders of oxygen, ready to wait out the long night while the world slows to a halt around them. (The scientific background here is shaky — the ether is presumed to permeate everything, and thus cannot be kept out; the sealing of the room is supposed to keep *in* the oxygen, which will mysteriously combat the poison in some way.)

Tension quickly builds as the companions perceive the signs of the world's collapse. The first climax is reached when the oxygen runs out, and Challenger breaks a window in order to get a last breath of air before the poison claims its final victims. The Earth, however, has by this time cleared the poison belt, and the group is saved; they journey by car through a London devoid of all life save for one old lady similarly sustained through the tragedy by her own cylinder of oxygen, used to combat an asthmatic condition.

There is a science fiction tradition which deals in anguished and often gruesome detail with the exploits of survivors of a world catastrophe. Such novels tend to be either unrelievedly morbid or extremely earnest in their pursuit of a mythology of rebirth. A party such as that assembled in *The Poison Belt*, however, would be remarkably ill-fitted for such an exercise, and Doyle would never have undertaken such a work. His science fiction is all entertainment, trading on spectacle and the shock-value of its ideas. *The Poison Belt* extends its disaster just long enough to obtain the appropriate theatrical effect before the situation is redeemed by a casual flourish.

It seems that the world is not dead at all, but merely cataleptic. So suddenly does life resume that Malone is compelled to wonder whether the whole episode might not have been a dream. Doyle, however, is too mature a writer to allow a resurrection merely of the *status quo*. He is insistent that the event is real and its consequences significant, even though it has left relatively few material scars. He returns to the perspective initially offered in Challenger's letter to *The Times*, declaring that what was previously the peculiar world view of a maladjusted scientific eccentric must now become the view of the general public.

Malone, as narrator, emphasizes that after such an event the world must be changed because people have been *shown* what they otherwise could not quite accept: their own insignificance in the cosmic scheme of things. The brief passage through the poison belt was meant to teach mankind humility. This message is repeated and reinforced by the quotation from an imaginary headline from *The Times* which closes the book, emphasizing that it is not simply an observation made *en passant* but the very core of the story.

This perspective is very much a product of nineteenth century discoveries in science, and lies close to the heart of many of the seminal works of science fiction. In the 1840's, Henderson, Bessel, and Struve measured the parallaxes of three of the nearest stars and provided the yardstick for the first accurate assessment of the likely size of the universe. In the previous decade Lyell's *Principles of Geology* had begun the work of popularizing an appreciation of the true age of the Earth, setting human history within an appropriate time scale. It was from such discoveries as these that there emerged the sense of the smallness and vulnerability of the human world which permeates so much scientific romance and which provided the main imaginative impetus for such writers as Camille Flammarion, H. G. Wells, J. D. Beresford, W. H. Hodgson, and later, Olaf Stapledon.

It is not surprising, then, that this should be the most serious note intruding into Doyle's science fiction, raising it above the level of simple adventure fiction. It is worth noting also that in several of the above mentioned writers' works, this sense of the vastness of the universe, though derived from scientific knowledge, is combined with emotions whose customary association is with religion. Though nineteenth century science did much to erode faith in the anthropocentric dogmas of traditional Christianity, it actually fed belief in mystical, pseudoscientific kind of religious sentiment. In Flammarion's work in particular, this cosmic perspective is intimately interwoven with notions concerning reincarnation and the immortality of the soul, and it is significant that Flammarion and Doyle became close friends following the death of Doyle's son and his subsequent passionate interest in spiritualism.

In this more serious aspect of *The Poison Belt* there is something which provides, if not a creative link, at least an imaginative channel which connects the first and most playful Challenger novel, *The Lost World*, to the last and most earnest, *The Land of Mist*. *The Poison Belt* is genuinely intermediate between these two. It is skillfully written and it makes the transition from the borderlands of farce to sober contemplation of larger issues gracefully and easily. It is, perhaps, an underrated work.

Brian Stableford

Sources for Further Study

Criticism:

Boucher, Anthony. "Criminals at Large," in *New York Times Book Review*, November 8, 1964, p. 68. Boucher discusses the character of Professor Challenger and finds that had Doyle written more stories, Challenger would have been the Sherlock Holmes of science fiction.

Reviews:

Book Week. December 6, 1964, p. 41.

Library Journal. LXXXIX, November 1, 1964, p. 4390.

Scientific American. CCXII, May, 1965, p. 147.

THE POLLINATORS OF EDEN

Author: John Boyd (1919-   )
First book publication: 1969
Type of work: Novel
Time: The twenty-first century or later
Locale: The Earth and the planet Flora

A beautiful and intelligent woman scientist struggles to be reunited with her fiancé on a planet where flowers rule, and in the process discovers astounding things about herself and her relationship to nature

> *Principal characters:*
> FREDA CARON, a beautiful and intelligent cystologist
> HAL POLINO, a handsome young student
> PAUL THEASTON, Freda's fiancé
> HANS CLAYBORG, a friend of Freda, also a cystologist

John Boyd continues in *The Pollinators of Eden* what he began in *The Last Starship from Earth* — a science fiction treatment of the mythic connotations of man's fall from grace — this time borrowing from the myth of Phaedra and Hippolytus. In that myth Phaedra falls in love with her stepson Hippolytus. She erects the Temple of Peeping Aphrodite overlooking the gymnasium where Hippolytus conditions himself by running, leaping, and wrestling, stark naked, and watches him with incestuous desire. She sends him a letter professing her love, suggesting that they go away and live together for awhile at least. Hippolytus is horrified and vehemently reproaches Phaedra. After leaving a note accusing Hippolytus of ravishing her, she hangs herself. When he reads the note, Theseus, Phaedra's husband and Hippolytus' father, prays to Poseidon for Hippolytus' death. His prayer is answered when a huge wave dashes Hippolytus' chariot against some rocks, and Hippolytus is dragged to death by his horses.

With the Phaedra myth as a springboard, Boyd presents his readers with Freda Caron, the protagonist of *The Pollinators of Eden* and a character he himself once described as the thinking man's ideal woman — one who could quote Shakespeare while making love. A beautiful woman whose intelligence has been attested by computers, Freda may well be the thinking man's ideal woman; but she is also a woman capable of being aroused and responding in a sensual manner.

As the novel begins, Freda, Administrative Director of the Cystological Section of the Bureau of Exotic Plants, is awaiting the return of Paul Theaston, her fiancé, from Planet Flora. He is not aboard the spaceship returning from the Planet of the Flowers, however, because he has been given an extension of duty to continue his study of the pollination process of the unique orchids discovered on the planet. In his place comes Hal Polino (Hippolytus), carrying two pots of tulips as a gift to Freda from Paul. Hal is a handsome student assistant, who is much more interested in twentieth century folkways and his guitar than he is in scientific methodology and bureaucratic authority. The tulips Hal has brought are striking in that they are heterosexual in their development, and they can also reproduce sounds that are made against their bulbs.

Freda listens to the briefing that Dr. Hector, the project's scientific director, presents. Dr. Hector, whose lectures are ordinarily marked by a flow of precise, valid, and constant data, now speaks in a passionate and irrelevant fashion that borders on the poetic. From the briefing, which includes a filmed report from Paul on his orchids, Freda learns that not only are the flowers on Flora heterosexual, but that there are no insects on the planet to help with pollination. But more than that, Freda notes that Paul, at one point in the film, inspects an orchid he has named Sally not with the eyes of an empirical scientist, but with the longing of a lovesick adolescent. Indeed, in his own private note to her, he refers to the orchids as lovable and as capable of loving him.

Freda, however, exists wholly in civilization as it has developed and is proud to be a part of its machinery. She attributes much of what Paul has written to her about his work on Flora as simply fanciful speculation that has been encouraged by Hal Polino. Even more shocked when Hal explains that Paul actually believes the orchids of Flora to be ambulatory, she begins to think that her fiancé is in need of institutional care. Nevertheless, with Hal's help, she begins a series of experiments with the tulips sent by Paul to see if she can discover the secrets of their pollination.

As Freda and Hal carry on their experiments, the line between teacher and student begins to blur, and it becomes obvious that Freda is drawn physically to the young Latin. He in turn plays the seduction game from his end. Boyd handles this aspect of the novel with a dexterous combination of subtle innuendo and not so subtle multilevel punning — all of which results in an interesting parallel to the loving flowers of Flora.

Hal's view of Flora is that beneath its beauty lurks a malevolence toward humans. He believes that the plants once destroyed all carnivorous creatures on the planet and that, if given the chance, they will do so again. Freda, though, is not ready to accept such a theory. Nor is Dr. Hans Clayborg, who supports the plan to put a permanent experimental station on Flora. His theory is that the flowers on Flora have learned to survive the death and rebirth of universes — something that man has not learned.

Freda and Clayborg are part of the deputation to Washington to testify before a Senate committee on the value of the experiments a permanent station could carry out on Flora. Confessing to him that she is afraid of being touched, she permits him to conduct a martini experiment. After four doubles, they feel she is ready for sexual adventures. It turns out, however, that Clayborg is too drunk to calculate correctly the point at which her desire to be loved balances her fear of being touched — and they end up in a cold shower.

One of the more interesting scenes in the novel takes place following the

Senate committee's rejection of the plan to construct an experimental station on Flora. Senator Heyburn, Chairman of the Senate Committee on Plant Classification, states off the record that ease, order, intellect, and enlightenment have combined to destroy the moral fiber of the United States. Echoing Wallace Stevens' view of death as being the mother of beauty, Heyburn argues that man has progressed only because he was cast from Eden. Like Captain Ahab of *Moby Dick*, he hurls curses at the dying sun and blasphemes the name of God. In short, what Heyburn would do is to rev up a starship to a velocity that would send it out of time — beyond God — and then to return after the explosion of the present universe to a new and virgin universe. Clayborg responds by saying that man cannot go beyond God, but must accept the Law of Morality and work within the cycles of creation. Only in that way can man achieve the New Jerusalem.

The experiments that Freda and Hal carry out with the tulips convince them that the plants can actually think and are, in fact, more intelligent and adaptable to their surroundings than is man. Thus, says Hal, they along with the orchids on Flora, pose a danger to men. Together, he and Freda begin to incorporate their findings into the thesis that Freda is writing on the possibility of intelligent plant life.

As they proceed with this work, Freda — like her namesake Phaedra — is attracted to Hal. She does not build a temple from which to watch him, but she is aroused by his working around the tulips in only a pair of shorts. She realizes her emotional weakness in this situation but is helpless to do anything about it and finally reconciles herself to an approaching sexual tryst with Hal. Before this tryst can occur, however, Hal is killed by a high-frequency sound wave sent off from the tulips.

Freda, aware that if it is found out that the tulips killed Hal they will be destroyed, confides in no one. Moreover, she also recognizes that the danger that Paul faces on Flora is not that of being killed, but that of having his libido taken over by the orchids. Her motivation now is not that of a scientist, but that of a woman fighting to keep her man. Her problem is how to get to Flora. Reminding herself that the best administrator is one whose symbol of authority is the second finger extended vertically from a clenched fist, Freda cleverly extorts from her superior, Dr. Gaynor, approval to join a small group leaving for Flora.

Thus Freda and Paul are reunited on Flora, where the latter delights in showing his fiancée his groves of orchids. He is unmoved when she tells him that the tulips killed Hal, and he explains to her that both he and Hal knew that the tulips could emit dangerous high-frequency sound waves.

During her first night on Flora with Paul, Freda dreams she is offered up "breech foremost" to an orchid high priest and seduced amidst "exquisite agony and searing rapture." The next day Paul takes her to a female orchid, and Freda is once more "lifted to heights of adoration," this time knowing well "what was up and who was down." Freda awakens the following morning to find Paul gone and three men approaching her with a tranquilizing gun. Because some of their private conversations have been overheard, they have been branded as defectors.

Back on Earth, Freda, confined to a kind of mental institution for officials, gives birth to a chubby, perfectly oval-shaped seed, which is sent to Santa Barbara to be planted. Using her wiles and her body, she enlists the aid of a psychiatrist, who, with the help of Hans Clayborg, obtains her release and a permanent assignment to Flora. So the novel ends.

When one recalls how Darwin devoted two volumes to orchid pollination, the plot of *The Pollinators of Eden* seems not so strange after all. But Boyd in this novel is not interested primarily in the scientific aspects of orchid pollination. What he is interested in is man's perennial desire to recapture Eden or something like Eden; but he is interested in an ironic way. While obviously there could have been no pollinators of the original Eden, Boyd does have pollinators on Flora, his new Eden. The irony is that it is man himself (woman herself) who becomes an instrument of pollination. Freda, the true Earth Mother, is gloriously deflowered by a flower and gives birth to a seed. If ever there were a culmination of the back-to-nature motif so prevalent throughout literature, here it is. A human world hopelessly ensnared in technology, bureaucracy, and behavorial psychology, and selfishly intent upon raping nature has, in some sense at least, had the favor returned.

While Boyd, as mentioned previously, uses the myth of Phaedra as a springboard for his story, a search for strong parallels between the two yields little. Freda can in a limited way be seen as Phaedra. The names are similar, as are the names Hal Polino and Hippolytus; and Freda seems to fall in love with Hal as Phaedra did with Hippolytus. Even (Paul) Theaston sounds like Theseus. But there the similarities seem to end. Anything more requires a wrenching that can only distort and diminish a rather fascinating story, a story with optimistic, not tragic, overtones. Freda has achieved her goal: to be sent back permanently to Flora, where presumably she will be reunited not only with Paul but also with nature, in the truest sense. For her, Eden will exist again; and man and nature will be one, working within the cycles of creation.

Wilton Eckley

Sources for Further Study

Reviews:

Analog. LXXXIV, June, 1970, pp. 167-168.
Kirkus Reviews. XXXVII, April 15, 1969, p. 475.
Library Journal. XCIV, July, 1969, p. 2638.

Luna Monthly. XXII, March, 1971, p. 29.

New Worlds. CC, April, 1970, p. 30.

Observer. March 15, 1970, p. 38.

SF Commentary. XXV, December, 1971, pp. 11-12.

Spectator. XXVIII, January, 1971, pp. 18-20.

Worlds of If. XIX, December, 1969, pp. 95-97.

PONEDEL'NIK NACHINAETSIA V SUBBOTU
(Monday Begins on Saturday)

Authors: Arkady Strugatsky (1925-   ) and Boris Strugatsky (1933-   )
First book publication: 1965
Type of work: Novel
Time: The present
Locale: Solovets, an imaginary town in European North Russia

A novel in three relatively independent parts linked by common heroes and setting as well as by the specific type of fantasy and the humorous, often satirical style employed

> *Principal characters:*
> ALEXANDER PRIVALOV, a computer programer
> ROMAN OYRA-OYRA, VLADIMIR POCHKIN, VICTOR KORNEYEV, AND EDIK AMPERYAN, young scientists and magicians, colleagues and friends of Privalov
> IANUS NEVSTRUYEV, Director of the Institute
> MODEST KAMNOYEDOV, Assistent Director of the Institute
> AMBROSY VYBEGALLO, PH. D., leader of a laboratory

Is science fiction a branch of literature essentially different from "realistic" prose, as well as from fairy tales, pure fantasies, and surrealistic writing, because of its exclusive use of the "scientific method," as some critics proclaim? Or is it part of a common stream of fantastic literature, in which the same magic wands and spells, fantasy symbols and fairy tale wonders are simply presented in scientific dress? The Strugatsky brothers believe that the latter is true, and have tried to embody their opinion in some of their novels, mixing science fiction with other fantasy conventions.

The first step in this direction was their short novel *Escape Attempt* (1962), in which the hero of a typical science fiction plot set in the usual future environment turns out to be a man of our century who escaped from a Nazi concentration camp into a better future by pure force of will; in the end he returns in the same way to do his duty to the future. Other novels in the traditional science fiction mode followed — among them, as a further development of problems touched upon in *Escape Attempt*, the famous *Hard to Be a God* (1964), which in a 1967 poll was chosen as the readers' favorite of all science fiction books published in the Soviet Union. The second place in this poll was won by another Strugatsky work, *Ponedel'nik nachinaetsia v subbotu (Monday Begins on Saturday)*. The work can be called a novel or a long tale, but the authors preferred to call it "a fairy-tale for junior scientists."

The text consists of three parts; in the first, "Fuss About the Divan," Alexander Privalov, a computer programer, makes a vacation trip through Solovets, a small town in the Russian European North, where Roman and Volodya (Vladimir), two hitchhikers he took along in his car, live. They arrange overnight accommodation for him at an ancient wooden hut that belongs to the scientific institute where the two work. In the hut Privalov is met by an obscure old woman and spends a very strange night, visited by a speaking cat and disturbed by a telephone call from Bald Mountain (the place where Russian witches, demons, and devils used to gather). His hostess turns out to be the Baba Yaga, the witch of Russian folklore. He also catches in a well the Speaking Pike that, according to the tradition, fulfills one of his wishes and also tells him of the Golden Fish's tragic experiences with modern times, especially with sea warfare. This night and the following day the hero meets many other characters from folklore and mythology. He gets into trouble with the police because of the Pike's gift, a coin that perpetually returns to its owner when used for payment. He sees and involuntarily experiences many strange, magic things, for Roman and Volodya's institute is the Scientific Research Institute of Sorcery and Magic. Privalov is intrigued and decides to take a job as a computer programer there.

"Fuss About the Divan" is a series of jokes built upon the mixing of old-fashioned folklore and mythology with the rationalistic spirit of modern science and with everyday life in a small Russian town. This section is both an introduction to more important events to come, as well as a tale in its own right.

The second part, "The Big Hassle," starts in the spirit of the first one, with a series of jokes on mythological themes. Privalov has already worked for some time in the Institute, learning to use some of the minor magic spells that require a knowledge both of medieval incantations and of modern mathematics. He is ordered to stay there as watchman on New Year's Eve and New Year's Day. As one might expect, the mythological bestiary collected in the Institute shows some of its tricks, and the magicians return to work (secretly, for Law and Trade Union rules forbid holiday work).

Besides the humorous anachronisms, one finds satirical remarks on life and conditions in contemporary scientific institutions in the Soviet Union. In the beginning, the satire is quite good-natured; even the stupid bureaucrat Modest Kamnoyedov (the surname means "Stone-eater") is pictured without hatred.

The story comes to a climax with an extraordinary experiment: Vybegallo, Ph. D., intends to test two of his creatures, both of them models of the Ideal and Perfectly Happy Man. The first one is a man-shaped being that gains Perfect Happiness from eating enormous amounts of herring heads. The other, an advanced model, is dangerous because of its greater power and voracious appetite: it grabs all objects within reach with horrendous speed. The thing plans to consume everything, and then to close space around itself and make Time stop, thereby remaining forever in a state of perfect satisfaction. Only by extreme magic means (a terrible jinni is pushed against it) can it be stopped and destroyed.

These events are used by the Strugatskys to give a portrait of Vybegallo, a bad magician/scientist whose ignorance about both science and magic is surpassed only by old Merlin, another unpleasant, but quite harmless member of the Institute (borrowed by the Strugatskys from Mark Twain's novel *A Connecticut Yankee in King Arthur's Court*). As a demagogue, however, Vybegallo is a master. He is the type of scientist who camouflages his intellectual impotence by political phrases, speaking of Communist ideals and man's welfare when he is really referring to his own profit. Thus, in his models (who even resembles Vybegallo), his own ideals of a paradise of consumption are embodied. The authors also show how other characters behave toward Vybegallo. Though nearly all of them either recognize him for what he is, or at least instinctively dislike him, he is tolerated — or feared — by the Institute's authorities, as well as by his colleagues, and few are willing to oppose him. In this second section, therefore, the Strugatskys turn from the ingenious but always friendly jokes of the beginning, to social satire, which is their forte.

Opposite of Vybegallo are the scientists/magicians, who take their search for ways to humanity's happiness so seriously that they cannot stop working, and make Monday begin on Saturday, thus leaving out the day of rest. One of them is Janus, the Institute's director, who has somehow been split into two persons, an administrator and a scientist. The scientist behaves quite strangely, often not remembering what he did and said the day before, but sometimes seeming to know the future. Most of the third part of the novel, "All Kinds of Hassle," is the story of how Privalov and his friends, by a detective style of reasoning, find out the truth about Janus: that his two incarnations are actually one person. Somewhere in the future, the administrator, having silently done important research work, discovers a way to invert his personal time; from then on he lives backward in time, jumping from the end of each day to the beginning of the day before.

The Strugatsky brothers succeed partially in mixing science fiction, folklore, and fantasy elements in this novel, thus illustrating the notion that science fiction is simply the twentieth century's fairy tale. The novel proves that science fiction and fantasy are analogous enough to be compatible, and different enough to create a peculiar tension when brought together. The same point has been illustrated in other works as well, such as Clifford Simak's "Goblin Reservation" and, in a completely different way, Stanislaw Lem's *Cyberiade*. But in this Strugatsky novel, the mixture is not always coherent; the balance between the components is sometimes disturbed.

It is important to mention that in the third part, there is, besides the detective plot, a chapter isolated from the rest of the story to the extent that it might stand as a wholly independent short story. It is a parody in which Privalov travels in a special time machine to the future — not the real future, however, but the future as it has been described in literature. Here the authors are at their best, wittily satirizing both ancient and medieval utopias; Soviet science fiction, with its grossly exaggerated technological hardware, its crude lyrism and empty pathos, and its propagandistic elements; and Western science fiction, with its feudalistic-style galactic empires and repetitious plots about aliens conquering the Earth.

In 1968, the Strugatsky brothers published a sequel to *Monday Begins on Saturday*, called "The Tale of the Troika," which might be considered a fourth part of the cycle. In this piece, they continue the satirical line of the second section of the novel, but now the satire is directed against bureaucracies and obscure ideologies. The hero is thrown into a frightening fantasy world that recalls Kafka or Gogol. This story is more coherent and of greater social and political relevance than the three "Hassels," but it does not belong to the original version of *Monday Begins on Saturday* since it creates a rather different atmosphere.

H. Walter

Sources for Further Study

Reviews:
Kliatt Paperback Book Guide. XII, Winter, 1978, p. 11.
Publisher's Weekly. CXII, September 26, 1977, p. 135.

THE POORHOUSE FAIR

Author: John Updike (1932-   )
First book publication: 1958
Type of work: Novel
Time: August 15, 1973
Locale: A poorhouse in the fictional town of Andrews, southern New Jersey

An ironic impression of the modern world's loss of values, seen from the vantage point of a home for the elderly poor in a near future, quasiutopian setting

> *Principal characters:*
> MARTIN CONNER, prefect of the Diamond County Home for the Aged
> BUDDY LEE, his adoring young assistant
> JOHN HOOK, a ninety-four-year-old former teacher
> BILLY GREGG, an irresponsible seventy-year-old teacher
> GEORGE LUCAS, tender of the pigs and garbage, "the Informer"
> ELIZABETH HEINEMANN, a blind, still beautiful, quasimystical lady

Throughout his career, John Updike has flirted with issues and forms commonly subsumed under the label, "science fiction." He often tries to reconcile religious belief with the findings of science which seem to contradict such belief. He is also concerned with restrictions on freedom, however trivial, which accompany social progress; if life is made more healthy and humane, it is partly by progressive rationalization, removing the justification for the irrational.

Science and technology do not operate in Updike's fiction only in the guise of aircraft, automobiles, and appliances. Scientific fantasies comprise at least three short stories: "During the Jurassic" (1966) concerns a cocktail party among prehistoric beasts; "Under the Microscope" (1968) is about another such affair among microscopic forms; "The Baluchitherium" (1971) consists of an interview, inside a computer, with one of that extinct race of giant mammals. A central symbol of *Rabbit Redux* (1971) is the Americanization of the moon, seen over the ubiquitous television set; that sterile, distant adventure counterpoints the social and moral revolution of the 1960's which "Rabbit" Angstrom is living through and processing *via* the typesetting machine he operates. Fantasies dominate *The Centaur* (1963), with its figures of classical myth in Olinger, Pennsylvania, and *The Coup* (1978), with the overthrow of its imaginary African dictator.

Science fiction explicitly appears in *Of the Farm* (1965), in which two books on the shelf in the narrator's old bedroom symbolize different ways of life. A book on flowers points toward the here-and-now life of his dying mother; his favorite old science fiction anthology, however, is now shared by his new stepson, over his second wife's objections. A story the boy is reading, apparently part of Henry Kuttner's "Baldy" series (eventually collected as *Mutant*), suggests that both males inhabit a mental world that can never exist, and are partially blind to the limitations and the glories of the present. It is in Updike's first novel, however, that he most obviously ventures into the territory appropriated by science fiction. Published sixteen years before Ursula K. Le Guin used the term, *The Poorhouse Fair* is a remarkable example of an "ambiguous utopia."

The narrative occupies some fifteen hours of August 15, 1973, (the third Wednesday of August in the year before the "crystal" — fifteenth — anniversary of the St. Lawrence Seaway, opened in 1959), in what is now an "alternative future" contradicted by history. Our cars, for example, are not almost fully automated, nor have moon landings been limited to animals. A Democratic President has been assassinated in addition to the three Republicans cited in the book, and we have not yet had a Jewish President. The federal government has not become a one-party system, lower electoral offices have not become civil service sinecures, and bloody wars have been fought during the era the novel sees as dominated by peace. Party similarities have been accentuated, to be sure, as have areas of common interest between East and West blocs in international politics. Black, Latino, and homosexual contributions to the arts and popular culture in America have been significant, even if government and society do not actively encourage a wholesale mixing of the races.

These specific forecasts are less important, though, than the general theme of the "Settling," as Updike labels the leveling of differences in society in keeping with the scientific concept of increasing entropy. Entropy is a metaphor for this future, with general relevance for his readers. As they age, they find their world changing and come to rely more and more on the State. Regardless of the accuracy of his other forecasts, we can expect homes for the aged, if not necessarily more and better ones like this one. Changes in the outside world do not impinge strongly on this microcosm of what may be in store for us on Earth or in the hereafter (some critics have likened it to a "godless City of God"). Separated from the town by a wall of dubious stability, the poorhouse is still in Andrews, where farmland has given way to buildings as elsewhere in the country. Visiting the poorhouse once a year, the largely white, middle-class townspeople of this backwater are also fading away, only a step behind their spiritual if not literal ancestors. Like them, the middle-aged reader of 1958 (and 1978) might catch a glimpse of his or her own regularized future in the impersonal regime of the new prefect.

Conner (first names are rarely used, except for his assistant, Buddy) is an "enlightened" civil servant, dedicated to cleanliness and order, the avoidance of pain and partiality, and the furthering of his career. Young for his responsibility, he has two years to go until automatic promotion, having already served three since the death of his predecessor, Mendelssohn. Cleaning up the place, installing fire escapes, creating an infirmary, wangling full-time medical staff, he has seen to it that his charges lack no material necessities. But the changes are as much in his own interest as theirs, since he is rewarded for their longevity and productivity. Dreaming, like Walter Mitty, of the day he can announce that his research team has discovered a cure for cancer, he is only biding his time here, and has little concern for these old folks as individuals.

He eats with them, rather than on a raised dais, and would never dream of leading them in gospel singing or reminding them of their impending death as did Mendelssohn. Concerned with respecting what he thinks is their dignity, Conner is unaware of how much his predecessor contributed to their humanity by treating them personally and not trying to blur the distance between their roles. This is brought home to the men in the novel's first scene, when they discover Buddy, acting on Conner's orders, has affixed name tags to the porch chairs they sit in, disturbing the natural disorder of things. When Conner denies the role of tyrant, they can only see him as hypocritical; whatever good he thinks he is doing, he is also infringing upon their freedom, reaffirming that, as Hook points out, they have no rights. Instead of the gratitude he needs, Conner receives respect, perplexity, solicitude, and resentment, the latter breaking out into open hostility on this day of the fair.

The fair provides the framework for this book, which is laid out in three long chapters, recounting preparations for the fair, reactions to its apparent washout by a thunderstorm, and the event itself as seen by both the inmates and their visitors. Forty-four subchapters, symmetrically arranged (13, 18, 13), provide a kaleidoscope of points of view, but the events that define the meaning, as against the shape of the narrative, center on confrontations between Conner, Gregg, and Hook.

The kind of man no Utopian system can peacefully contain, Gregg continually challenges the order of the place and its prefect. Attempting to pry the name tags off the chairs, he expresses the irritation others feel. To test the prefect, he brings a wounded cat inside the institution's walls and sneaks food to it; offended by the sight of the animal in pain, Conner reveals his weakness. When the soft drink truck arrives, Gregg demands that its teenage driver help him "escape," then goads the boy into maladroit driving which topples part of the wall. Discovering that Lucas has a pint of whiskey he bought in town to ease the pain of an inflamed ear, Gregg rounds up other malcontents to help drink it on the porch in the rain. After the rain, he finds the body of the cat, shot by Buddy (who left it to attend to the truck accident, then to escape the rain) and rages against the cruelty of Conner's "humaneness." Finally, when Conner rounds up some of the younger men to help stack the stones near the broken wall before the fair begins, Gregg initiates an episode of stoning the prefect, in which a dozen others join.

Conner is not seriously hurt, though struck once on the back of the head. His sense of justice is outraged, his dignity injured because he panicked for a moment. Although he reacts shrilly with an implicit threat, "I know you all," his pique gives way to a forgiveness incomprehensible to his attackers. Intellectually recognizing his own unconscious complicity ("I am their leader," he tells the outraged Buddy), still he turns angrily on Hook, an innocent bystander, whom he conceives to be the instigator.

Hook *is* his chief antagonist, but on a level Conner is incapable of recognizing. The patriarch of the place, there fifteen years, Hook is looked up to not simply because of his age. The house intellectual, he still lectures, especially on classical times and nineteenth century American politics, interests developed before he ever taught. Those times are more real to the aged than the apolitical, even acultural present, suggesting how sparse Conner's memories will be at their age, whatever his present certainties. Hard of hearing and limited to forward vision through thick glasses, Hook is more perceptive and imaginative than Conner will ever be. This and his apparent proprietary attitude toward the place irritate Conner, but not half as much as the comeuppance the prefect gets from the old man during the rain-induced hiatus in the day's activities.

Wanting to be liked, Conner tries to warm up the chilly sitting room where Hook and others are talking. None too competently, he starts a fire — using hard-to-burn glossy religious magazines (named *Sweet Charity*, left by a deceased inhabitant) — and has to be shown how to open the fireplace flue. Then he insinuates himself into a conversation among community members hardly aware of his presence. Trapped into a conversation about the hereafter by Elizabeth Heinemann, whose blindness makes her believe that unfairly discriminating sense will not be present in the afterlife, Conner attempts futilely to scourge them of their superstition. Believing "This [the well-run poorhouse] is their reward," he preaches a Utopian conception of heaven on earth which does not have the effect he anticipates. For one thing, he admits they are too old to live to see it, to which Amy Mortis appropriately replies, "Well then, to hell with it." For another, it resembles too much the present blandness both inside and outside the poorhouse walls, save the addition of a kind of endless summer with beautiful bodies, another affront to his hearers. The major problem with his vision, however, is its soullessness, which Hook sees through, into the emptiness of the visionary, and of the era he represents.

An age which puts health and longevity above all else sees no place in the scheme of things for pain, unless experimentally induced, or for death, at least not of human beings. Evil is pain and its elimination is virtue for Conner, who recognizes the current truths of science and believes that if the Universe has a Creator, He must be "an idiot crueler than Nero." Hook, on the other hand, finds cruelty in the experiments Conner sees as increasing knowledge, reducing pain, and lengthening life; having lived so long, Hook sees no value in longevity for its own sake. Acceptance of death by the aged underlines the point of a letter of complaint Conner has received, one ungrammatical sentence of which buzzes through his mind all day ("Yr duty is to help not hinder these old people on there way to there final reward").

The homely truth of Hook's ultimate rejoinder reaches home, and sours Conner's anticipated triumph in a matter beyond science and logical argument: "There is no goodness, without belief. There is only busy-ness." If the prefect's reforms have been beneficial, his actions now have passed on to just such "busy-ness" as Hook indicts. On this day alone, Conner has labeled chairs, meddled with preparations for the fair, killed a cat, allowed his walls to be breached, incompetently played with fire, and presumed upon his secular authority to interfere with others' religious speculations. When his final bit of "busy-ness" with the repairing of the wall brings about a hostile reaction, it is to an accumulation of minor irritations, directed not so much at himself or the job at hand as at the twin specters of boredom and authority.

This authority is not exercised for evil; good intentions are always in the forefront. Besides having negative nuisance value, however, the prefect's actions are implicitly in the direct line of Mendelssohn, whom Conner thinks of as acting like God. But Conner himself acts as if the elements should be under his control on this fair day; as an arm of the state, he strives to make more order where entropy dictates there will be less. Ironically parallelling St. Stephen, Conner is no martyr; the gospel he brings is that of an outside world which, for all of its commitment to sameness, enters the fair through the broken wall in search of belief — in handicrafts, in history, in meaning — which its "utopian" progress has all but obliterated.

If Conner's generation lacks something the old people have, Conner himself is conscious of what the next generation lacks. Buddy has no sense of humor; he looks at the world as if he were living the "thrillers" he has read and watched as part of his education. The band that plays for the fair, composed of old and very young musicians, emphasizes another failure of Buddy's "mechanical" generation (and Conner's). But all of the visitors to the fair are described by the narrator as lacking "heart," as mere "pleasure-seekers," even less than that. Lacking meaning or belief, they are

> "just people, members of the race of white animals that had cast its herd over the land of six continents. Highly neural, brachycephalic, uniquely able to oppose their thumbs to the other four digits, they bred within elegant settlements, and both burned and interred their dead. History has passed on beyond them."

The usual reading of this novel is primarily as a religious parable, an interpretation backed by the body of Updike's work. But the parable is ambiguous. It is too simple to read this Utopian future as one in which man has usurped God's position, when the result is the same if God does not exist, except as a comforting superstition, and man has come to realize that truth. Although Conner's "busy-ness," and that of the State, trying to create secular order out of chaos, may be in error, the fair itself is only a faint ghost of those celebrations of the past when a get-together at a specified time of year had ritual meaning because people assented to it.

Once the dramatic action is over, and the fair itself actually takes place, the day's false pregnancy is revealed. The narrative declines into trivial acts and sensory impressions which implicitly deny the order of either Hook or Conner. Though Hook, at the very end, strives to think, upon retiring for the night, of something he can say "as a bond between them and a testament to endure his dying in the world," he cannot think of what that "small word" might be that could "set things right." There is no single word, of course, as there is no communication between the two men, no bridge between the generations.

As a naturalistic "cautionary tale," *The Poorhouse Fair* is bleak in its prognosis, and right at home in the literature of post-1950's science fiction, warning of "coming attractions," into which, but not out of which, we may be led by our fascination with and misapplications of science and the scientistic way of thinking. Moreover, in the density of his structure, the allusiveness and vividness of his imagery, and the sheer poetry of his style, Updike's writing simply outshines the Utopian nebula and the whole science fiction galaxy.

David N. Samuelson

A PRINCESS OF MARS

Author: Edgar Rice Burroughs (1875-1950)
First book publication: 1917
Type of work: Novel
Time: The late nineteenth century
Locale: Arizona and Mars

The heroic adventures of John Carter, first American on Mars, who rescues a beautiful Martian princess from a series of villainous Martian captors of various races and tribes, wins her love, and saves the planet from extinction

> *Principal characters:*
> JOHN CARTER, the hero
> DEJAH THORIS, the heroine
> TARS TARKAS, the best green Martian man
> SOLA, the best green Martian woman
> SARKOJA, the most dangerous green Martian woman
> WOOLA, Carter's devoted Martian watchdog
> KANTOS KAN, Carter's red Martian sidekick
> SAB THAN, Carter's red Martian rival

A Princess of Mars was Burroughs' first novel. Although he went on to write seventy more books — including ten additional Mars novels, five Venus novels, and twenty-eight Tarzan novels — *The Princess of Mars* remains one of his most popular works. The reasons for its enduring popularity are instructive; for, with a freshness, exhilaration, and clarity not always found in his later writings, this novel addresses some of the most widespread hopes and fears in modern Western culture.

The novel opens in 1866 with the coming of modern times to the United States. To the narrator-protagonist, Captain John Carter of the Confederate Army, life seems to have lost most of its meaning now that the Gilded Age has begun. No longer the chivalric champion of the Old South, he has been reduced to self-centered money-grubbing as a prospector in the Arizona desert. Alone with his partner and former comrade-in-arms Captain John Powell, Carter quickly discovers that even his limited goal of restoring his personal fortune is probably not attainable. Their living death in the desolate wilds turns into total death as first Powell and then Carter are pursued and apparently killed by savage Apaches.

Up to this point, Burroughs' novel uses the melodramatic elements of Western popular fiction to represent familiar terrors of the modern industrialized world. There is the ordeal of discovering who one is and what one can do in this world, where many find, with Carter, that traditional familial and social roles no longer provide workable answers. There is the bedeviling suspicion that neither society nor nature concerns itself about any individual, however prudently, morally, or gallantly he may behave, and that all individuals are likely to be victimized by brutal, essentially impersonal forces which they can neither understand nor control. In the grimly realistic modern world view, no earthly frontier affords escape from these distresses. Nor can modern man outrun death, against whose triumphs work, fame, and love are pitifully, utterly ineffective, and in whose onmipresent shadow good and evil lose all significance.

For Burroughs' hero there is a way out. Carter inexplicably jumps out of his clothes, out of his apparently dead body, out of the cave which has become his tomb, out of Earth's imprisoning atmosphere — and finds himself in a strange environment which he instinctively knows to be Mars. Superficially, the Red Planet is quite a contrast to Earth: under its two moons, Carter meets his first Martians — six-armed, oviparous green people who tower an intimidating fifteen feet in height. Yet on closer examination these green Martians, the Tharks, reveal themselves as extreme embodiments of the same cruel, predatory spirit which menaced Carter and Powell in Arizona. On Mars Carter learns that even one good man can make a great difference. He begins by astounding himself and the Tharks with his Earthman's ability to leap extraordinary Martian distances, and goes on to display other physical skills with which he successfully combats one belligerent green giant after another. But his crucial superiority is his sense of decency; by awakening the same sense in Tars Tarkas, a green Martian prince, Carter is able to subvert Thark society, so that at the end of the novel, when Tars Tarkas has been voted the Tharks' new leader, there seem solid grounds for hoping that Carter has started the green Martians on the road to reform.

In battling and subverting the Tharks, Carter represents civilized humanity, seeking out and destroying the "huge and terrible incarnation of hate, of vengeance and of death." The reader identifies with him as the idealized master of derring-do who is the standard hero of adventure stories. But Carter does not remain simply a heroic warrior assailing green monstrosities; because he must also confront the red Martians, who represent humanity imprisoned by civilization, he grows into a new dimension of heroism. As he labors to restore the red Martian princess, Dejah Thoris, to her family, Carter becomes a romantic hero whose actions are directed solely by his love for this ideally beautiful, wise, and virtuous woman. The new Carter is a superheroic savior who preserves all Mars — and, by implication, all humanity — from otherwise inevitable destruction. For Carter the superhero, incorporating both the adventurous and the romantic stereotypes of heroism, defeats the most difficult enemies in his world: alienation and purposelessness.

Apparently Burroughs himself, like his fictional Martians, found Carter's superheroism irresistibly inspiring. In each of the ten sequels to *A Princess of Mars* the original formula recurs — the hero of adventure and the hero of romance fuse and conquer. Moreover, Tarzan of the Apes and Carson of Venus also follow this pattern throughout the thirty-three volumes devoted to them. In other words, Burroughs' best-known books tell one essential story over and over: the perennially popular myth of his brand of superhero.

The details do vary from book to book, however, and such differences in detail are especially marked in the eleven Mars novels. Mars was Burroughs' first imaginary world, and he invested it with a much more complex history, geography, zoology, and anthropology than he invented for any other fictional environment. Burroughs' Mars is not merely a place where Carter can develop the heroism denied him in Earth's Gilded Age; it is a richly exotic haven to which Burroughs' reader can imaginatively escape from humdrum reality. Most of the fascinations of Mars are disclosed in *A Princess of Mars* and in its two immediate sequels, *The Gods of Mars* and *Warlord of Mars*; all three novels were written and published between the years 1911-1914. In these volumes, which Burroughs intended as an epic trilogy, Carter rises to be Warlord of Mars, and as he does so, he explores the Red Planet from pole to pole. He meets members of Mars's five major races — green, red, black, white, and yellow Martians — as well as the bizarre plant people; he ranges over Mars's deserts, forests, rivers, mountains and polar regions; he encounters various strange and horrible Martian creatures, including white apes, thoats, siths, apts, banths, and calots; he learns the complex Martian language and social etiquette; he demystifies Mars's mystery religions; and he masters Martian science, technology, and politics. Much of the suspense in the three novels derives from the fact that neither Carter nor the reader knows what to expect in this emphatically unearthly realm.

In presenting his fictional Mars, Burroughs displays considerable skill. He provides vivid, particularized, highly specific descriptions, so that the reader cannot help but visualize precisely the images called up. And this visual information is supplemented by audible clues, for the Martian language which Burroughs invented for his Mars stories is onomatopoeic — its terms sound like what they mean. Moreover, Burroughs' Mars tantalizingly combines the fantastic and the familiar; its elements differ enough from everyday reality to be consistently amazing, yet often they also externalize images which every man can recognize as the stuff of his own daydreams and nightmares, and which are integral to Western popular culture.

For the most part Burroughs seems to have churned out these images without considering their symbolic or mythic significance. The unpremeditated, spontaneous quality of his writing is a pronounced characteristic of popular fiction, which energetically eschews the intellectualized approach of the highbrow author. Burroughs' spontaneity undoubtedly charms many among his worldwide readership. Unfortunately, it also mars his novels with serious artistic flaws. His plots usually lack focus and climax, but are instead episodic ramblings along vaguely defined thematic tracks; furthermore, they frequently reproduce Burroughs' few favorite stock situations, rather than presenting a new line of action. So, for example, the last half of *A Princess of Mars* deteriorates into a repetitive sequence of pitched battles among diverse opponents and noticeably lacks the dramatic intensity which distinguishes the novel's first half. And so many Martian princesses undergo capture — there is at least one such kidnaping or imprisonment in every Mars volume — that Mars seems to be populated mostly by past, present, and would-be princess-stealers and princess-savers. Of course all of Burroughs' books, including this one, were composed for serial publication and understandably express the serial writer's typical preference for immediate thrills and shortterm climaxes. It seems likely that Burroughs' lifelong orientation toward magazine publication reinforced his tendency toward slapdash plotting, and kept him from trying very hard to write unified novels.

By contrast, he appears to have been deeply troubled, even obsessed, by something else which he did not think through in *A Princess of Mars*. Carter's superheroism is implicitly self-contradictory, for he must simultaneously demonstrate that he is Mars's most sensitive lover and its most efficient killer. Popular fiction often blends clashing images in this manner; the stereotypical Western hero, bringing law and order by his violent individualism, is an obvious example. But Burroughs, who perpetually glorified the loving warrior, evidently could not help examining, reexamining, and repeatedly trying to explain and harmonize the inherent conflicts in his concept of heroism. Despite the numerous explicit moralistic statements in this novel that true heroes must be loving, Burroughs does not quite establish that Carter's compassionate soul dominates his perfectly muscled physique — particularly since Carter's "love," not to mention the exigencies of action-oriented serial fiction, impels him from one gory exertion to another. Although Burroughs extends Dejah Thoris' ordeal of captivity through *The Gods of Mars* and *Warlord of Mars*, bestowing her on various Martian fiends all over the planet, he keeps relying on Carter's sword to save her from her several captors. As Carter's daughter explains in *The Chessmen of Mars*, fifth novel in the series, Carter has a credibility problem: her lover reminds her that

> "It has been long ages since the men of Barsoom [Mars] loved peace."
> "My father loves peace," returned the girl.
> "And yet he is always at war," said the man.
> She laughed. "But he *says* he likes peace."

While the first three Mars novels articulate the paradox in the lover-warrior image of superheroism, volumes four through seven attempt to resolve that paradox. In all four novels Burroughs replaces Carter with alternate protagonists, each of whom combines warmaking and lovemaking in a slightly different personality. These new protagonists — Carthoris, Gahan, Paxton, and Hadron — confront what is really a single enemy in diverse incarnations: all four must prove that brawn does not matter more than brain. Burroughs represents the mind-body conflict by strikingly original, memorable images — phantom bowmen, whose existence is purely hallucinatory; the symbiotic rykors and kaldanes, complementary races of bodiless heads and headless bodies, brain transplants, dazzlingly beautiful villains and unimaginably hideous heroes and heroines. Possibly because of the power this theme held for its author, the Mars series displays a focus, color, and dramatic intensity in its four central volumes which it had not shown since the first half of *A Princess of Mars*; *The Chessman of Mars* is especially strong.

These four novels also re-create the rebirth and redemption pattern which is so important in *A Princess of Mars*, where the miraculously reborn Carter redeems Tars Tarkas, Sola, and even Woola the watchdog from the spiritual death enforced by the brutish Tharks. Similarly, Carthoris, Grahan, Paxton, and Hadron must each undergo the regenerative experience of finding and winning his princess, or soul-mate; and each helps at least one token "convert" to free his or her true souls from materialistic impediments. By contrast, the final four volumes of the Mars series center on death, the king of terrors, which Carter defies but cannot completely conquer in *A Princess of Mars*. Images of death abound in the last four Mars novels: the "rat," a professional assassin in Mars's labyrinthine criminal underworld; synthetic thugs, created out of uncontrollably expanding ooze; walking, talking corpses; skeleton men. In the eleventh volume, *John Carter of Mars*, death-images coalesce in the culminating horror of a synthetic man who becomes a mad scientist and manufactures the super-weapon to end all super-weapons, a gigantic, synthetic white ape. Death envelops Carter in *A Princess of Mars*, which begins by killing him off and concludes by returning him to his Arizona tomb under such ambiguous circumstances that everything Carter has fought for — his own life and that of the Red Planet — seems lost. Carter does survive, of course, and the Mars series continues, but death haunts his efforts and in the last four Mars novels gathers a terrible, concentrated force. Burroughs may have been seeking a way out of the apparently mortal danger to his first hero when he sent Carter briefly to Jupiter in the last half of *John Carter of Mars*. But death came for Burroughs himself before he could pursue this possible escape route, so that Carter is at the last, as he was from the first, true to his greatest love and one real home — Mars, the warrior's world.

Jane Hipolito

Sources for Further Study

Criticism:

Hillegas, Mark. "Martians and Mythmakers: 1877-1938," in *Challenges in American Culture*. Edited by Ray B. Browne, Larry N. Landram and William K. Bottorff. Bowling Green, Ohio: Bowling Green University Popular Press, 1970, pp. 150-177. This is the most detailed discussion of Burroughs' treatment of the "myth of the superior Martians." It also compares Burroughs' use of the myth to other major writers.

Kyle, Richard. "Out of Time's Abyss: The Martian Stories of Edgar Rice Burroughs," in *Riverside Quarterly*. V (January, 1970), pp. 110-124. Kyle believes that Burroughs' Martian stories are heavily indebted to the influence of H. Rider Haggard.

Moskowitz, Sam. *Under the Moons of Mars: A History and Anthology of "The Scientific Romance" in the Munsey Magazines, 1912-1920*. New York: Holt, Rinehart, & Winston, 1970. Moskowitz traces the influence of Burroughs on Martian themes in science fiction.

Mullen, Richard D. "The Undisciplined Imagination: Edgar Rice Burroughs and Lowellian Mars," in *SF: The Other Side of Realism*. Edited by Thomas D. Clareson. Bowling Green, Ohio: Bowling Green University Popular Press, 1941, pp. 229-247. Mullen, through an examination of the Martian novels, attempts to show the sources of Burroughs' descriptions of the planet.

Reviews:

Amazing Stories. XXXIX, January, 1965, pp. 124-125.
Analog. LXXXI, June, 1963, p. 91.

LE PRISONNIER DE LA PLANÈTE MARS
(The Prisoner of the Planet Mars)

Author: Gustave LeRouge (1867-1938)
First book publications: Volume One (1908), Volume Two (1909)
Type of work: Novel
Time: The early twentieth century
Locale: The Earth and Mars

A noted French precursor to space opera which involves an Earthman who travels to Mars by the force of spiritual power, where he fights imaginative monsters

> *Principal characters:*
> ROBERT DARVEL, a French engineer
> GEORGES DARVEL, his brother
> ALBERTE TÉRAMOND, his fiancée, the daughter of an American billionaire
> RALPH PITCHER, an English taxidermist
> BOLINSKI, a Polish engineer
> ARDAVENA, a Brahmin
> PHARA CHIBH, a yogi

Gustave LeRouge was a unique character. A friend of Verlaine (he dedicated one book to that poet and another to his school) and a poet himself, he became a popular writer, producing adventure and science fiction novels, love stories, volumes of verse, dramatic pieces, film scenarios, and essays on the most diverse subjects. In *The Man Struck by Lightning*, Blaise Cendrars devoted two-thirds of the volume to LeRouge. He knew the author toward the end of his life when he lived among the Gypsies in a Gypsy van, teaching them to handle a whip, while pricking lilies so that they would become blue or black.

LeRouge's work, both popular and decadent, contains elements of the serial story, with its classic situations and stereotyped characters: the rich American, the heartless businessman, the noble engineer. One finds in his work treasures of erudition, powerful and poetic pages, a surprising power of evocation, and a real love for all forms of life.

This novel consists of two volumes, *Le Prisonnier de la planète Mars* (The Prisoner of the Planet Mars) and *La Guerre des vampires* (The War of the Vampires), which later were republished under the titles *Le Naufragè de l'espace* (The Shipwreck in Space) and *L'Astre d' epouvante* (*The Star of Terror*). The novel opens when a young engineer, Robert Darvel, sees his friend Bolinski arrested and imprisoned, and finds himself abandoned, ruined, and rejected by Téramond, the father of his fiancée. (Darvel and Bolinski had been in Siberia working on an interplanetary communication project that failed.) His resources are exhausted and Darvel accepts without hesitation the proposals of the Brahmin Ardavena to study yogi powers at the Chelambrum Monastery in India. Here he learns the power of the human will, and decides to build a condenser which can accumulate the psychic energy of the monks. In this way he expects to be able to explore outer space. Ardavena, however, decides to steal the invention. The Brahmin puts Darvel to sleep, encloses him in a steel capsule, and, utilizing the combined will-power of the monks, sends him to the planet Mars. But the condenser is overloaded and blows up; Ardavena is left blind and insane. No return for Darvel seems possible.

On Mars, Darvel believes at first that he has been transported to the Canadian forests, but he learns the truth from the two moons which rise in the sky. He is the Robinson Crusoe of this planet, dressed in a cotton loin-cloth, who must master fire and arm himself. Darvel is overcome with the magic of the colors: the rose and purple forests, a sea the color of peach-blossoms, the blue and yellow bushes. But it is a dangerous splendor. Darvel attracts the ire first of a creature resembling a terrestrial octopus, then of a giant bat, a half-human drinker of blood.

On Earth, Téramond dies of joy when he learns that, after having been ruined, he is once more a billionaire, since the lands Darvel persuaded him to buy were the site of fabulous gold mines. His daughter Alberte resolves to track down her fiancé. With Ralph Pitcher, an English taxidermist, she leaves for India, where Captain Wad introduces them to Phara Chibh. The yogi meets his death while evoking a vision of Darvel, who is seen to be menaced by a bat with a human face. His friends do not doubt the reality of the vision and are sure that he is on Mars.

On Mars, Darvel meets a tribe of humanoid Martians, the size of children, who are peaceable, friendly, hospitable, but terrorized by the vampire Erloors. The engineer civilizes them; like a common missionary he overturns their idols and burns their temples; he gives them fire and teaches them to defend themselves. For this reason the Erloors seize and carry him away.

Bolinski, meanwhile, having escaped from prison, brings some photos of Mars to Alberte and her friends on which can be made out the dots and dashes of Morse code. Darvel thus tells them of his interplanetary adventures. The story continues in part two, as Georges Darvel, Robert's brother, arrives in Tunisia to join Alberte and her friends. The signals from Mars have stopped and everyone is worried. Bolinski discerns that the making of those signals also shows that Robert has acquired a dominant position on that planet — therefore, the interruption can only be temporary. Next, a meteorite suddenly strikes the villa, killing Bolinski. Darvel is found inside the rock. Revived, he undertakes to tell what happened to him after being captured by the Erloors.

The Martians of the marsh freed him, but soon afterward, while passing through a cloud of animated plants, his companions were annihilated by the invisible vampires. Recaptured, Darvel regained consciousness in a colored crystal tower which protruded from the sea. This tower, and others, were parts of a combined structure, half in the air, half under water, and seemingly totally deserted. The rooms were museums or storerooms housing figures of the inhabitants of Mars, arms, provisions, and materials which formed books. These rooms were haunted by the laughing of invisible creatures.

Finally, Darvel discovered a pink opal helmet; he put it on, and invisible objects became perceptible to him. He discovered the enormous heads equipped with wings and tentacles which were the Martians. He learned that they fed on the blood of other creatures, but that they themselves were consumed in turn. Once a month, flights of them went to an opal mountain and entered a cavern from which their wings and tentacles were then spat out. Darvel went there and found that under the mountain lived an enormous brain, the Great Brain, Master of the Planet, drawing a part of its energy from the atmospheric electricity. Darvel broke its cable, but held the vampires back from it. The Great Brain seemed to die from exhaustion. The electricity drawn from the sky then supplied arc lamps which, when handled by the vampires, carried messages to Earth.

However, the Great Brain recovered, regained its power, and unleashed lightning on the crystal towers, compelling the vampires to send Darvel back to Earth. The vampires accompanying him, who tried to blackmail him into returning them to Mars, were annihilated.

Le Prisonnier de la planète Mars is a marvelous exception among the works of LeRouge; it is his chief work, one of the *chefs d'oeuvre* of the era. The twenty years from 1894 to 1914 were the golden age of French science fiction. The authors in the genre — LeRouge, La Hire, de Quiriella, J. Hoche, Perrin and others — had freed themselves from the influence of Jules Verne; they had read Wells and the elder Rosny. The best monthly and weekly publications all made room for science fiction. Méricant put out a specialized collection, and in the area of illustration, Robida was accompanied by Lanos. The wonderful inventions that inspired so many novels were superseded by explorations of the consequences of inventions, or by descriptions of astonishing developments which did not relate as much to science fiction as to science fantasy.

This novel is reminiscent of the adventures of Edgar Rice Burroughs' John Carter, but with more poetic force and rigor. For LeRouge, the use of the power of the will is not a gimmick; it is a logical consequence of his occultist bent. His Mars is a planet whose builders have disappeared. The race which dug the canals, built the crystal towers, and accumulated the wealth and the documents in the underwater galleries no longer exists. It has not disappeared in the strict sense of the word; it has metamorphosed. The brain of these creatures grew, while the body atrophied, and thus the vampires were born; they were nothing more than heads equipped with wings and tentacles. Although these vampires fed on blood like Wells's Martians, they are not mere imitations. On LeRouge's Mars there is also a peaceable species, the friendly Martians of the swamps, on whom the Erloors and other vampires feed. The Great Brain in turn feeds on the latter. Although this creature has been able to detach itself from many of its material dependencies, abandoning its limbs and organs to become little more than a mind, it cannot escape hunger; it must be nourished with blood and cerebral matter.

A Marxist schema fits here; one thinks of the capitalist "blood-sucker," and is reminded of a novel published a little later, *The End of Illa*, in which an entire civilization is nourished by blood — first of animals, then of people. In reality, this is not what LeRouge had in mind. The Martians become more and more degraded morally in proportion to their effort to be more "spiritual." If the Martians of the marsh are amiable creatures, it is because they live in communion with nature. They accept the fate of all living things. The other species illustrate the thought of Pascal: "He who would be an angel becomes a beast."

Part of what sets *Le Prisonnier de la planète Mars* apart from other novels of the period is the perpetual mystery of the planet Mars. A thousand questions are posed, but no answers are given. Thus, Darvel visits a valley surrounded by mountains which are covered with parabolic mirrors which concentrate their heat on a central cone, from which flow rivulets of metallic solutions that transfer the heat. In the jungle lives a plant which is a carnivorous animal. Is it all a botanic garden or a place of torment? The author does not answer this question, but no one else in this era painted the grandeur and fascination of a dead civilization with such force.

Jacques van Herp

THE PUPPET MASTERS

Author: Robert A. Heinlein (1907-   )
First book publication: 1951
Type of work: Novel
Time: Probably the twenty-first century
Locale: The United States

A novel of education in which a young secret agent, fighting against aliens who possess their human hosts, learns to make full use of his mind and capabilities

> *Principal characters:*
> SAM (ELIHU NIVENS), a secret agent
> THE OLD MAN (ANDREW NIVENS), head of the secret agency and Sam's father
> MARY (ALLUCQUERE), a secret agent and later Sam's wife

The Puppet Masters is a perfect example of what is referred to as "golden age" science fiction. In the novel, Robert A. Heinlein presents a world under seige by an alien life form that attaches itself to human hosts and effectively controls all the actions of that host. Except for the hump caused by the alien body connected to the back of its victim, the possessed human appears to most people to be acting quite normally and freely. Other than accepting the aliens and the colony on Venus, Heinlein asks no further act of faith on the part of the reader. And even in the case of the aliens, all features of the novel are carefully presented in sufficient detail to create a credible world. Thus, while the fantastic is very much part of the novel, fantasy is not. All actions, all events, all solutions have explanations within the work itself.

But the world of *The Puppet Masters* is only part of the justification for calling the novel golden age science fiction. Of far more importance than the fictional world itself is what is done with that world. Heinlein has chosen his aliens carefully because he has a particular theme in mind, a theme that recurs in several of his works: mankind is threatened by a form of life that is absolutely uninterested in compromise. In such a battle there can be only one victor, and the victory must be complete. Like the bugs in *Starship Troopers* (1959), the slugs of *The Puppet Masters* appear one day, start to possess humans, and set out to enslave all of humanity. Heinlein clearly presents the alien slugs as intelligent, brutal, singleminded creatures bent on their own design of cosmic rule. No accommodation or compromise can be reached because they are simply not interested.

It the utter ruthlessness of the puppet masters is not accepted by the reader, an important part of the novel will be lost, as it is all too often lost by readers of *Starship Troopers*. Heinlein is not a simpleminded militarist who glories in calling the enemy names, in describing futuristic military hardware, or in portraying gory battle scenes. Rather, like John W. Campbell, Jr., in "Twilight," he is interested in defining those features of the human race that enable it to survive and to develop. Unlike Campbell, however, Heinlein is not satisfied with merely calling man an "animal with curiosity." He is interested in survivors, in successful and idealistic men. The puppet masters, therefore, are not only aliens that threaten humanity; they are also the excuse for Heinlein to explore with the reader definitions of survival, success, and idealism. And it is this exploration that makes the novel so successful as science fiction.

The aliens, since they completely control the hosts that they attach themselves to, become a graphic symbol of oppression. Yet ironically, the human host, who knows that he is being controlled, derives a certain amount of pleasure from the takeover. Because the slugs think and make decisions for their hosts, they offer a degree of peace and joy that arises from a freedom from responsibility. But for Heinlein, such peace and joy prevent human survival and success. Moreover, people willing to surrender free will in order to experience *nirvana* endanger not only themselves but also the entire race. Survival, success, and idealism must depend on a different type of man, represented in the novel first by the Old Man and then by Sam.

It might be difficult to imagine the head of a supersecret agency as idealistic, but the Old Man clearly is. Sam, one of his agents as well as his son, says of him:

> Not that he was a soft boss. He was quite capable of saying, "Boys, we need to fertilize this oak tree. Jump in that hole at its base and I'll cover you up."
>
> We'd have done it. Any of us would.
>
> And the Old Man would bury us alive too, if he thought that there was as much as a fifty-three-per-cent probability that it was the Tree of Liberty he was nourishing.

While such an ideal may seem out of touch with our present, it is an essential belief to Heinlein. Man must be free; the Old Man believes first and foremost in this single dictum. But his idealism alone is not sufficient to qualify the Old Man as either a survivor or a savior of the human race; it must be tempered with a practical wisdom which allows him to judge the gravity of a situation, to determine the possible solutions, and to decide which of the probable solutions is best for the immediate case. Thus, the Old Man is an idealist, but more importantly, he is a *competent* idealist. The term "competent" is very important here because, on the one hand, it defines the limits of idealism and on the other, it is synonymous with survival and success. By the end of *The Puppet Masters*, there are two competent men: the Old Man and Sam.

In many ways the novel presents the education of Sam into a competent man. At the beginning, Sam acts out of a double loyalty, as an agent of the United States and as the son of the Old Man. But that loyalty is not always sufficient to guide his actions, especially during those times when Sam must act for himself. Thus, when he returns to Des Moines, Iowa, to obtain filmed evidence of the slugs in control of humans, he is anything but successful. He first picks on a man who is not possessed, and then, when he does invade a stronghold of possessed humans, he fails to get the needed proof. Finally, when he returns to the agency, he returns with a fellow agent who is, unknown to him, possessed. Sam has done the best job he is capable of under the circumstances, but he has not done a competent job. In these early chapters, Sam still has much to learn from his father; he is still a young man learning how to cope, and competency will only come with the experience of age.

Sam's education begins in earnest after he has been possessed by a puppet master and then rescued by his father. At this point a personal crisis forces him into competency: the Old Man needs a volunteer to be possessed by a captured master so that information can be obtained from it; Sam is in no mood to volunteer, especially since the captured master is the one from whom he has just escaped. However, when he finds that the volunteer is Mary, the woman he loves, he steps forward and allows himself to be placed under the slug's control once again. Despite his fears and his nightmares, he gives himself up to the one thing that he most abhors. Such an act is necessarily a step in his education because, up to this time, Sam has acted only out of blind faith in his father. In order to continue to develop into a competent man, however, he must act on his own for people other than himself. Here is the beginning of the idealism that his father already has. It is a small beginning, but one that will fully develop as the novel progresses.

As Sam gains more experience in fighting the puppet masters, he starts to act in a more informed way. While he still does not have his father's ability to reason through to concrete conclusions with the use of limited information, he does exhibit a fine ability to act conservatively on the facts he has. Thus, when he scouts out Kansas City, a puppet master stronghold, he is able to avoid the traps set up for him. In this particular case he makes fewer mistakes than in his earlier ventures and is actually able to bring back valuable information. However, Sam's information is too late to help an attempted invasion of the territory held by the slugs, and the information is already known through other sources. Again, Sam cannot be blamed for the outcome; he has done a good job, but he is not yet up to the standards required of the competent man.

Two events lead to the final step in Sam's education. The first is his marriage to Mary, and the second is the revelation of Mary's earlier life on Venus. The marriage, in a world that defines itself in terms of temporary "contracts" between men and women, represents Sam's final necessary commitment to others beyond himself and his father. Mary, as an infant, was part of the first settlement on Venus. The settlers were possessed by the slugs, who for some reason died; and Mary survived both the possession and whatever caused the death of the puppet masters. So shocking was the experience, however, that she has blocked the entire period out of her consciousness.

The Old Man and various military officials realize that if Mary can recapture the memory, the solution to their problem might be at hand. Something must be found that will kill the masters but leave their human hosts alive. An elaborate procedure is therefore begun in which Mary relives her entire experience under hypnosis. To spare her the pain of the memories, she is instructed at the end of each session to forget what she has remembered under the probing of the scientists. Furthermore, Sam is not allowed to participate in the sessions because his lack of expertise and his emotional involvement with Mary would make him a hindrance.

After many fruitless sessions, Sam does insist on joining the group. He reasons that others with even less at stake than himself are participating, and that, given his knowledge of his wife, he might very well be of some help. He goes even further than this, moreover, and orders his father and all nontechnical people out of the session. Then, once the scientists are about to begin, Sam insists that all previous tapes relevant to the search for the solution be played for him, and that his wife be allowed to see them as well if she wishes.

The result of Sam's action is an immediate solution: Mary sees the tapes and quickly identifies the disease that had killed the puppet masters. Thus, acting out of love for his wife and using his understanding of her personality, Sam is able directly to attack the problem and resolve it. As later problems arise, such as the danger that the disease poses for the human hosts, the method of transmitting the disease, and the timing of the spread of the disease, Sam uses the same combination of compassion for others and practical wisdom to find answers. It is at this stage that Sam has become a truly competent man. He now acts with both mind and heart in perfect accord. As proof, furthermore, of just how far Sam has progressed, when the Old Man is possessed by a slug, it is Sam who saves him.

At the end of *The Puppet Masters*, Sam has grown into a man ready to face his destiny with full confidence in his ability both to fight for the right reasons and to fight well. He is now ready to carry the battle to the home of the puppet masters, and his final speech summarizes not only the lessons he has learned but also those that Heinlein has sought to teach the reader throughout the work:

> Whether we make it or not, the human race has got to keep up its well-earned reputation for ferocity. The price of freedom is the willingness to do sudden battle, anywhere, any time, and with utter recklessness. If we did not learn that from the slugs, well — "Dinosaurs, move over! We are ready to become extinct!"

While the idea of the competent man can easily be lost in much of the rhetoric found in the novel, the reader would be doing a disservice to himself and Heinlein to do so. The simplistic expressions used in reference to the Soviet Union and the female characters are certainly most annoying to readers of the present. *The Puppet Masters*, however, must be judged in terms of the genre, and, as science fiction, is it successful.

Stephen H. Goldman

Sources for Further Study

Criticism:

Sarti, Ronald. "Variations on a Theme: Human Sexuality in the Work of Robert A. Heinlein," in *Robert A. Heinlein*. Edited by Joseph D. Olander and Martin H. Greenberg. New York: Taplinger, 1978, pp. 107-136. Sarti calls this a new twist on the invaders from space theme.

Slusser, George E. *The Classic Years of Robert A. Heinlein*. San Bernardino, Calif.: Borgo, 1977, pp. 42-49. Slusser calls this a classic tale of intrigue.

Reviews:

Amazing Stories. XXVI, February, 1952, pp. 148-149.

Analog. XLIX, March, 1952, p. 159.

Authentic Science Fiction. XIX, March, 1952, p. 112.

Galaxy. III, February, 1952, pp. 84-85.

Kirkus Reviews. XIX, August 1, 1951, p. 414.

Magazine of Fantasy and Science Fiction. III, February, 1952, p. 105.

New Worlds. XXI, June, 1953, p. 126.

New York Herald Tribune Book Review. October 15, 1951, p. 22.

New York Times Book Review. November 18, 1951, p. 41.

San Francisco Chronicle. November 18, 1951, p. 18.

THE PURPLE CLOUD

Author: M. P. Shiel (1865-1947)
First book publication: 1901
Type of work: Novel
Time: The early twentieth century
Locale: Various, but chiefly England, the North Pole, and Imbros

The story of the only man to survive the destruction of all animal life on Earth by a cloud of poisonous gas

Principal characters:
ADAM JEFFSON, a doctor
LEDA, the only other survivor of the Purple Cloud

The Purple Cloud was not the first story of a catastrophe so great as to leave only one man and one woman alive in all the world, and several more were to follow it, but in its account of the psychology of the survivor it is quite unique. The narrative is a baroque nightmare, infected by a deep sense of guilt and a slowly encroaching madness. It purports to be the diary of a man left alone in the world for nearly twenty years, transmitted back into the past to be transcribed by a medium in trance, but more than any other novel of its kind it invites interpretation as the terrible hallucination of a man driven insane by guilt: a transcendental voyage through an inner hell.

The manuscript transcribed by the medium opens with its ostensible author, a physician named Adam Jeffson, recalling the ranting of a Scottish preacher who predicted disaster if any expedition to the North Pole should reach its objective. The reason offered by the preacher is that the pole is in some mysterious sense the Tree of the Knowledge of Good and Evil forbidden to man since the days of Adam in Eden. An expedition to the pole is about to get under way, lured there by the promise of a large cash prize for the first man to reach it. Jeffson goes on to tell how his fiancée, a woman named Clodagh, murders a member of the expedition so that her lover may take his place.

When the expedition reaches the polar ice field, Jeffson too becomes a murderer, shooting one of his companions in a bitter duel. As a result of this action he becomes one of the party to make the attempt on the pole. Fired by ambition he thrusts on ahead of his companions and wins through to his goal, which he perceives as a pillar engraved with unreadable characters and surrounded by a lake of living fluid, though he knows this to be an illusion. He waits for his companions, but they do not come.

Jeffson begins the trek south again, afflicted by hallucinations and attended by a mysterious scent of peach-blossom. He sees a purple glow on the horizon, but it recedes as he approaches. He discovers birds and bears dead in the snow, preserved by the eternal ice, but can find none living, and wanders the ice-desert for several months until he finally discovers the ship that brought him, its crew likewise dead. He finds, as he sails south, that all animal life is extinct and that the world is empty. He eventually reaches England, and searches fruitlessly for survivors. He reads in the newspapers of the last days: a vast cloud of purple gas, released by a volcanic eruption in the southern Pacific, slowly engulfed the entire world, moving eastward at an inexorable hundred miles per day. He hopes that some individuals, forewarned as they were, might have found adequate shelter in the deepest mine-shafts, but these hopes prove unfounded.

Once convinced that he is, in fact, alone Jefferson takes up temporary residence in London, but frustration causes him to plot the destruction of the city by fire, and he leaves it burning when he sails for France. He conceives the idea of building himself a vast palace — the richest the world has ever known — and returns to loot the gutted city of London as well as the other capitals of Europe. The manuscript becomes fragmentary in this phase, at one point breaking off for seventeen years, but the story conveyed is that of periodic outbreaks of disenchantment and despair, during which the palace is temporarily abandoned and Jefson sallies forth on missions of destruction to burn all the great cities of the world. By now the autobiography is almost surreal, its subject carried forward by successive waves of obsession which reflect the fact that his life has lost all meaning. Jefferson is tormented by forces that seem to him to have used him all his life as their battleground. He characterizes them as "the white" and "the black," and considers himself the helpless toy of the latter, though the former will not quite surrender the struggle. Alone in the corpse of civilization he asks himself the question: "Must I not in some years cease to be a man, to become a small earth, her copy, weird and fierce, half demoniac, half ferine, wholly mystic — morose and turbulent — fitful, and mad, and sad — like her?"

More than once Jefferson abandons himself to death only to find himself mysteriously preserved. He feels that he is being saved for some purpose, but resents the fact and fears the prospect. Again and again he is drawn back to the palace that he is building on the Aegean island of Imbros, and eventually rises from the depths of despair to the heights of a grand narcissistic megalomania as he describes the dimensions of the house he has made for the emperor of the world. But the forces will not let him rest, and they draw him now on a journey through Constantinople and Stamboul, and ultimately to Pera, where he finds at long last the second survivor of the cloud. This is a girl, younger than the postdisaster world, born in an airtight chamber where her mother had been put into seclusion. She cannot speak, and is quite ignorant of the world around her, having only recently escaped from her subterranean prison.

Jefferson's first impulse, expressive of the darker force which seems to use him, is to kill her, and he nearly does so, but is prevented by a lightening bolt. He has no difficulty in interpreting what has happened: he has been preserved in order to play Adam to this innocent Eve, and for this "the white" intends to use him. He is in no doubt about his own intentions in the matter — he is aligned entirely with "the black," and is determined that he will not be father to a new human race. To the gods, he supposes, the career of man is no more than a game, but for the men who lived on Earth before the coming of the cloud, life was a catalogue of "racks, rack-rents, wrongs, sorrows, horrors" and he will not be responsible for starting it all again.

He takes the girl back to Imbros, naming her "Clodagh" in a spirit of wicked irony. He begins to educate her, and as soon as she finds out the significance of the name he has given her she demands that it should be changed. She asks to be called Eve, but he will not allow it, and they compromise on Leda. Together they tour the lands of Europe, and now the voice of the narrator seems to grow saner. Jeffson feels this change coming over him, but is less than pleased by it. His reaction, in fact, is this:

> All the more was my sense of responsibility awful: and from day to day it seemed to intensify, a voice never ceasing to remonstrate within me nor leaving me peace, the malediction of unborn billions appearing to menace me; and to strengthen my fixity I would often overwhelm myself, and her, with names of scorn, calling myself 'convict,' her 'lady-bird,' asking what manner of man was I that I should dare so great a thing, and, as for her, what was she, to be the Mother of a host? — a butterfly with a woman's brow! and frequently now in my fiercer hours I was meditating either my death — or hers.

Nevertheless, Jeffson is weakening in his resolve and, to use the terms which he has imposed upon the situation, "the white" is gaining steadily against "the black." Eventually, he decides that temptation has become so strong that he must abandon her, and he crosses the channel to England, persuading her to remain in France by promising that he will keep in constant touch by telephone. When separation does not strengthen his resolution he decides to kill himself, and sets a time for his self-execution, but in what is to be the last of the telephonic conversations she reveals to him that the purple gas is again visible on the eastern horizon. The new threat ends his resistance, and he begs her to come to him with all possible speed. No poison cloud follows her, but he refuses to speculate whether there ever was such a cloud. He accepts at last the role prepared for him, and recovers his faith in "the white" — and with it, one infers, his sanity. His narrative closes with the ringing declaration that "the one motto and watchword proper to the riot and odyssey of Life in general, and in especial to the race of men, ever was, and remains, even this: 'Though He slay me, Yet I will trust in Him.' "

Most novels of this kind can be read as spiritual allegories, as parables of human indomitability and as myths of salvation and rebirth. Many are consciously engineered to such ends. *The Purple Cloud* is perhaps the most self-conscious of them all, and sets more powerful obstacles in the course of its protagonist's spiritual education than any other. Good and evil are incarnate here in the contradictory impulses which arise within Adam Jeffson's delirium as a result of his seeking wealth and glory in the symbolic voyage to the North

Pole and the Tree of Knowledge. The battle that the opposing forces fight with weapons of sin and guilt amid the ebb and flow of reason is a fiercely dramatic one.

The Purple Cloud is undoubtedly Shiel's masterpiece — a commanding vision which contrives to embody all the pain and anguish of a man alienated from life and faith. In other works his highly elaborate prose seems to be little more than ostentatious stylistic embroidery, but here it is the perfect vehicle for Jeffson's experiences. Only once — in "The Place of Pain" — did Shiel manage to repeat the trick. The novel is, or should be, an uncomfortable one to read, creating the disturbed feeling which inevitably accompanies any vision of the darker aspects of human psychology. It is a fantasy, but it is certainly no idle construction of whimsy; whether its events are construed literally or as the delusions of a sick mind hardly matters, for in either case they provide a metaphorical representation of a particular consciousness of the world and the self. *The Purple Cloud* is possessed of a fearful kind of realism of which only imaginative fiction is capable.

Brian Stableford

Sources for Further Study

Criticism:

Stevenson, Lionel. "Purveyors of Myth and Magic," in his *Yesterday and After: The History of the English Novel*. New York: Barnes & Noble, 1967, pp. 111-154. This overview of Shiel and others is significant for its placement of science fiction and fantasy within the literary mainstream.

Reviews:

Books. May 4, 1930, p. 14.

New Republic. LXII, April 23, 1930, p. 281.

New Statesman. XXXII, March 16, 1929, p. 740.

New York Times. April 13, 1930, p. 17.

Saturday Review. CXLVII, March 16, 1929, p. 363.

QUANDO LE RADICI
(When the Roots)

Author: Lino Aldani (1926-   )
First book publication: 1977
Type of work: Novel
Time: 1998
Locale: Italy (Rome, Piacenza, and Pieve Lunga, a country town halfway between Piacenza and Pavia)

The odyssey of a man in the forthcoming world of the Megalopolis, in which a society is trying to stifle individual relationships and feelings

> *Principal characters:*
> ARNO VARIN, a Roman clerk who visits his birthplace, Pieve Lunga
> THE TROGLODYTES, twelve old citizens living in Pieve Lunga
> A BAND OF GYPSIES

Since his earliest stories appeared in 1960, Lino Aldani has been a writer endowed with two qualities rather uncommon among his Italian colleagues: a rare taste for precision (and uniqueness) of style and a strong inclination toward social themes. He has always been inclined to discuss and attack in his stories every form of malignancy in human life under the light of a speculative vision. Such is the case in this novel, his first, if a short narration which appeared as a serial in 1960 is ignored. It is also very easy to say that *Quando le Radici* ranks among the best of Italian science fiction.

Arno Varin is a clerk who works in Rome at the Central Institute for Urban Planning and is continually confronted with the various facets of a humanity subject to complete alienation. Italy is by now (1998) a republic whose President is a Communist, but it is impossible to ascertain for sure whether the real pattern of the country's political economy is capitalistic or socialist, because of the slow achievement of that compromise between the Communists and the Christian Democrats, a topic which has been discussed since the early 1970's.

But this is just one of the grotesque facts of this future Italy. Life is concentrated in a small group of Megalopolises inhabited by millions (only ten such concentrations, distributed all over the peninsula and Sicily). Every other town has been absorbed or destroyed to permit the development of large automatic farming areas around the supercities; drugs and stimulants have free circulation; half-robots help in many matters; methane-steaks and other synthesized foods supplement the otherwise scarce meals; oxygen dispensers at street corners make it possible to endure the polluted atmosphere of the cities; blatant suicides often amuse the passers-by; and sex is relegated to the morbid and distorted games ordered by fashionable associations (sort of lonely-hearts clubs) to their members.

In this society Arno Varin works without even knowing exactly what he is doing, as do the majority of those working for the enormous civil bureaucracy. The only difference between him and his colleagues, the point in which he is perhaps more sensitive to this situation, is his memory. Arno was born in Pieve Lunga, a small village on the river Po, now reduced to a few tottering houses and a dozen old "troglodytes" (as the few old people who longingly remember the old days are called). The few memories he has of the short years spent there still haunt him with a vague but charming sting. Arno is full of doubts about his present situation and feels strangely curious. He is presented as being like any other man, but he is endowed with those memories which draw him like a magnet to his birthplace, giving Aldani the opportunity to describe a human character related to our own.

Not capable of denying the call of his inner roots, Arno returns to Pieve Lunga and the twelve old people still clinging to that lost society, only to find that this oasis has also been condemend by a new invader, the concrete mixer. Here, in a rural setting, replete with colorful and sometimes lyrical details, Aldani voices the most powerful theme. Gaining impetus from underground currents which are not only generally eternal but also deeply linked with a close Italian reality, he succeeds in powerfully portraying Arno as a man groping for a new kind of maturity. While Arno stays in the village of the "troglodytes," he has the opportunity to find a life that most of the civilized world has rejected, and he is able to perceive what is vital and useful in this old world. If his doubts only fade with the new consciousness that he cannot alone start a new way of life (for the inhabitants of Pieve Lunga are very old and soon doomed to extinction), they are entirely wiped out by the introduction of another old suggestion, offered by the coming of a group of gypsies.

At last, Arno finds a real chance to build a new life for himself. He doesn't care for the scientific achievements and the technical progress of his era (judging all these matters as mere superstructures not really necessary to life in his terms); and he is interested in the original elements which appear more reliable for human survival, because he will soon be confronted by such a necessity. When one of the troglodytes hears, on an old portable radio, that the first USA-USSR joint expedition has landed on Mars, he relays the news to the other men, who are pressing wine; no one is interested.

The arrival of the gypsies enhances the freedom that Arno has already achieved. His newborn free will is confronted with a strange way of life, unchanged for centuries, possessing full freedom of movement, self-reliance, a penchant for enjoying life, and mutual respect. Arno literally enters a new world and begins to ascertain what elements of it he welcomes, but his rashness almost ruins his chance to discover life's true value. He repeats his search with more self-control until at last he becomes a full member of the group, ready to help the gypsies in their long journeys and also to accept their help in developing a personal alternative to the alienated way of life of his fellow citizens. Before he can do that, however, he pays his debt to Pieve Lunga and its old inhabitants. Although his opposition does not last long against the counterattack of concrete, he stands up to the first people sent to examine and survey the area for the new highway which would cross Pieve Lunga; and he defeats them. Only then can he begin his new life in a gypsy wagon.

What appears to be a novel which only sings the praises of a flight back to a golden age, *Quando le Radici* also gives a realistic dimension to a difficult choice which is not confined only to its main character. For too many facets of Arno Varin's life resemble those now facing all people who enjoy the comforts of modern life and too many speculated details in the novel are sure to be realized in the coming years. Aldani's work is truly a fascinating and deep quest for answers to the problem of loss of identity in modern life. *Quando le Radici* offers hope for man's future, providing he is willing to accept the reality of his inner roots and fight to keep them alive. Perhaps the best characterization of this attitude is given in the old saying Arno applies to himself, a rough translation of which is, "Born I was of willow tree, and forever you shall smell wood in me."

Gianni Montanari

Sources for Further Study

Criticism:

Rottensteiner, Franz. *The Science Fiction Book*. New York: Seabury, 1975, p. 145. Aldani is a promising writer, but so far Italian science fiction has not produced a really outstanding writer.

QUINZINZINZILI

Author: Régis Messac (1893-1943)
First book publication: 1935
Type of work: Novel
Time: Before, during, and after an imaginary Second World War
Locale: In and around Lozère (central France)

After a cataclysmic war wipes out most of the human race, a small group of teenage survivors attempts to begin a new society

> *Principal characters:*
> THE NARRATOR, a passive, misanthropic teacher
> ILAYNE, the sole surviving female
> MANIBAL, inital chief of the group, killed by Ilayne
> LANROUBIN, the leader of the group and Ilayne's lover
> EMBRION, Lanroubin's rival both for leadership and Ilayne's attentions

Quinzinzinzili is a postcataclysmic story that might have inspired William Golding's *Lord of the Flies* (1954) and might even have achieved the same fame if it had been published after World War II with proper publicity. Unfortunately it came out too soon and went completely unnoticed in its time. It remains, however, very readable and a classic treatment of its theme. The novel offers a grim insight into the behavior of a small group of abandoned teenagers after a worldwide cataclysm as they regress to a primitive way of life. The totally pessimistic view of the author both of the civilization that fostered the catastrophe and the behavior of the survivors foreshadows the mood of many science fiction works that appeared after 1945.

Régis Messac was a pioneer in the genre and a connoisseur of American science fiction at a time when it was completely unknown in France. A university professor, he was the first real French science fiction scholar and essayist, as well as being a writer of original stories. *Quinzinzinzili*, his first novel, was obviously influenced by American science fiction, a surprising thing, since it would become popular in France only after 1950. His second novel, *La Cite des Asphyxies* (*City of the Asphyxiated*, 1937), could have been written by Stanton A. Coblentz; it is a satirical story of time travel to a distant future when, the surface of the Earth nearly airless, oxygen has become priceless in the underground cities where mankind manages to survive.

Quinzinzinzili consists of a diary left by a dying teacher. The first part deals mostly with the world political situation before the cataclysm. The teacher presents a panorama in which he displays a strikingly bitter insight into, and a profound acquaintance with, contemporary problems. To begin with, Japan, squeezed in its tiny infertile and overpopulated islands, attempts to colonize China. But China, an immense underdeveloped and unexploited market, is also coveted by the United States as it is "the only hope left for American capitalism, then at bay." In both countries the production of armaments speeds up, but the first offensive is diplomatic. The United States and the Soviet Union form an alliance, compelling Japan to join forces with Germany. Then the Japanese and Russian armies clash in Manchuria. One young Japanese officer bombards Hawaii with his ship, seemingly in disobedience of orders, before committing *hara-kiri*. The U. S. Navy moves toward Panama but is blocked in the canal as a British steamer sinks in front of it. Revolts break out in India and Indochina and are savagely repressed. Germany attacks the Soviet Union; France attacks Germany; England attacks France.

In the meantime a Japanese scientist has synthesized an isomer of nitrogen protoxide that breaks down the components of the air into an unbreathable mixture. A side effect is to make the zygomatic muscles contract so that when the Germans use it a part of mankind dies laughing. As for the rest, they are swept off the face of the Earth by the freak disturbances that shake the whole atmosphere. These events give Messac the opportunity to display his impressive array of contempts for capitalism, colonialism, nationalism, the army, Jesuits, Freemasonry, religion, and the world of finance and politics — in short, his hostility toward the entire planet and its inhabitants. To him their destruction is obviously a glorious thing. Régis Messac was a pacifist, but an anarchist with a terrible grievance against mankind; he was also an idealist who died in a German concentration camp. The most negative aspects of his philosophy pervade the entire novel. The Narrator of this grim story regrets several times that the catastrophe left so many survivors, for their descendants are bound to repeat the same mistakes.

Immediately before the cataclysm, a handful of children from a sanatorium had been visiting a cavern in the central mountainous part of France. They emerge when everything is over to find the world a waste and a ruin. Most animal life on the surface has been destroyed. With little to eat, they have to catch moles and snakes. With no houses left standing they go back to the cavern. In most stories of this kind the survivors are considered the hope of a new if not a better world. We find no such commonplace here. The novel aims at demonstrating that no improvement is to be expected from the human animal and that the few remaining members of the species will follow exactly the way of their forebears.

The group survives, but at a price. After some months and several deaths, all that remain are eight boys and one girl, nine children in their early teens or younger, most of them tubercular, and one adult, the Narrator. He could have used his superior knowledge to maintain a semblance of civilized life, but he dislikes his pupils, and instead of leading them he lets them manage alone. When he finally does feel some concern for the survivors, it is too late: they have become cavemen. This book chronicles the tragedy of those children who have built a culture of their own with what little they remember of the fallen one. From that point the Narrator confines himself to observing them closely and following their evolution with a truly anthropological concern.

The little tribe is composed of Manibal, their chief, the oldest and strongest; Tsi-Troen, his closest ally, but sly and secretly envious of Manibal's power; Embrion Sanlatin, a brute in latent opposition to Manibal; Lanroubin, the most intelligent, or rather the least stupid; Tchaon, Pantin, Bidonvin, and Bredindin, four individuals of little importance; and Ilayne, the future mother of mankind. Their names are often unrecognizable forms of their original names, for they have corrupted the few words they have not forgotten altogether. In addition, seven of them are French, one is British, and another is Spanish, each contributing to the formation of a common language. The title *Quinzinzinzili* comes from the Latin prayer "Pater Noster, qui es in Caelis" (Our Father, who art in Heaven). They have developed a religion and Quinzinzinzili is their god, half Santa Claus, half ogre. They worship him every evening and consider him the source of both good and evil.

Messac's vision provides not only a picture of a few delinquents, but a mirror image in which the whole of fallen mankind can recognize itself, with its superstitions and divisions. The Narrator obviously delights in depicting the stupidity of the tribe and exults every time he realizes that they are even more stupid than he had expected. For him, they are like the dawn men from which the previous civilization arose; and they will evolve in the same way. They are mankind and mankind is the root of all past, present, and future evil. The Narrator spends a part of his time spying on them and watching his worst expectations come true. They are afraid of night and they do not know how to make a fire, only how to keep it alive. They are ignorant of all that concerns generation but, like most primitive peoples, they become nubile very early and discover sex by themselves. Manibal tries to rape Ilayne, but she bites him cruelly and chooses Tchaon as her first lover. Manibal tries a second time, but she kills him with a rock. She takes Embrion as a second lover, and he slays Tchaon. Ilayne has now become the most important member of the tribe: the future society will be a matriarchy.

But the comedy is not over. Ilayne gets rid of Embrion and takes Lanroubin, who becomes the new chief. The two males dislike each other. But since Lanroubin is the stronger, Embrion quiets down, although he renounces neither the crown nor Ilayne's couch. Now that mankind has learnt love, jealousy, and murder, it is time to explore its domain. Lanroubin decides to shift quarters and leads the tribe southward. They walk to a dale where they find the remains of the dead inhabitants. During a halt Embrion enlists the help of Bredindin and Pantin and pushes Lanroubin into a ravine. Lanroubin survives, however, by grabbing a tree and then rises to punish Embrion. Everyone but the teacher believes that Quinzinzinzili has brought him back to life. His leadership undisputed, Lanroubin guides the tribe to the sea, not a great distance, since all of the French Riviera is now under water. The expedition next moves northward to the ruins of Lyon, buried under a layer of dried mud. There they stay only a short while, for winter is coming and Ilayne is ill.

Returning to the cavern, she gives birth to a son, ignorant of who the father is — or even *what* a father is. The last words of the Narrator follow shortly as he dies cursing mankind and wishing it the worst possible destiny.

The Narrator is indisputably the most negative figure in the book. Passive, egocentric, and hateful, he is no better than the human race he despises; he is, in fact, the epitome of that race, a perfectly logical conclusion — and logic is his forte. His actions (or the lack of them) follow inevitably from his opinions. One may wonder whether the destiny of the survivors might have been different had he chosen to help them. Messac's answer to that would probably be "no," for he obviously does not believe in the improvability of man. This is self-evident in *La Cite des Asphyxies*, his second novel, and in his last, *Valcretin* (*Cretins' Vale*), completed in 1943 and published posthumously in 1973, in which he describes an incredibly degenerate community.

It is unlikely that Messac intended to depict himself in the Narrator of this terrible story, for it is doubtful that he held himself in such low esteem. On the other hand, it is evident that the Narrator is the medium he used to expound his views. So we must admit that, whether he wanted it or not, Régis Messac let himself be trapped by his character. To what extent is hard to say, but it would be difficult to find a more violent pamphlet against mankind. The sincerity of his disgust for his fellow man is unmistakable in this novel. And the reasons he gives are not without foundation. That is why this unpleasant and sardonic story does not deserve the neglect that has been its fate for so many years.

Remi-Maure

Sources for Further Study

Criticism:

The Encyclopedia of Science Fiction and Fantasy. Compiled by Donald H. Tuck. Chicago: Advent Publishers, Inc., 1978, pp. 310-311. This biographical article shows Messac's influence on French science fiction.

THE RAKEHELLS OF HEAVEN

Author: John Boyd (Boyd Upchurch, 1919-   )
First book publication: 1969
Type of work: Novel
Time: 2228
Locale: The Earth and the planet Harlech

Two space scouts, one a con man and the other a carrier of God's Word, set about changing the patterns of tolerance and permissiveness that mark a planet conceived of by its inhabitants as heaven

> *Principal characters:*
> JOHN ADAMS, a space scout
> CARA, his wife
> KEVIN O'HARA, a space scout
> BUBO THE DEAN, the leader on Harlech

In the Preface to the Penguin Edition of *The Rakehells of Heaven*, John Boyd states that the ideal reader of the novel "should have the mentality of a Southern stock-car racer, be a Baptist with a sense of detachment, have a well-developed sense of the absurd, and be fascinated with the quirks and accomplishments of the human animal." What he meant by the first two characteristics, perhaps only he knows; but certainly the last two are understandable and, indeed, applicable. *The Rakehells of Heaven* presents a story that is on the one hand a hilarious satire and on the other a tribute to man's never-flagging efforts to change the *status quo*, for better or worse.

The third novel in a trilogy, *The Rakehells of Heaven* was begun, according to Boyd, as a science fiction version of the myth of Prometheus, that Titan condemned by Zeus to be bound forever to a jagged cliff for giving man the knowledge of fire, numbers and letters, and happiness and evil. Defiant in spite of his punishment, Prometheus insists that his action was no crime but merely an effort to help man, to teach him to hope — in other words, to change the *status quo*. In the end Zeus shatters the Titan's rock with a bolt of lightning which hurls Prometheus to an abysmal dungeon deep in the Earth. As Boyd himself admitted, he does not carry the myth through to the end of the novel. In truth, it is doubtful, without Boyd's comments in the Preface, that the reader would recognize this particular myth as the point of departure for one of the most entertaining fictional trips into space.

At the opening of *The Rakehells of Heaven*, the hero of the novel, Space Scout John (Jack) Adams returns from a mission earlier than scheduled and without his companion, Space Scout Kevin (Red) O'Hara. The narrator of the story, a psychiatrist at the Mandan Naval Academy, debriefs Adams with the specific purpose of finding out why Adams has aborted the mission and what has happened to O'Hara. The official theory prior to Adams' arrival is not only that he has violated regulations by returning early, but also that he has suffered stalker's fever — a condition in which one spaceman, because of prolonged confinement on a spaceship, stalks his partner and kills him. What the psychiatrist learns is the tale of the novel.

Jack Adams, a Southerner from Alabama, and Red O'Hara, a shanty-Irishman from County Meath, were classmates at Mandan Naval Academy. O'Hara, nicknamed King Con, succeeded at their first meeting in conning his roommate Adams out of the lower bunk, in spite of which they developed a close friendship. Upon graduation, because their separate but equal personalities interlocked, they were assigned a space mission together, but not before O'Hara married, and Adams received a Call to carry the Lord's Word to other galaxies.

The purpose of their mission is to scout the universe for undiscovered planets that are similar to Earth, explore them, and classify *homo sapiens*. To be thus classified, an alien inhabitant must, among other things, possess an opposing thumb, believe in a Supreme Being, practice coitus face-to-face, be able to crossbreed with humans, and have a gestation period of from seven to eleven months. If these conditions cannot be met, then the planet in question is to be occupied by the Interplanetary Colonial Authority.

Adams and O'Hara find a promising planet, land their ship, set up a tent, and arrange numerous Earth exhibits. Soon a large crowd of humanlike beings gather in a nearby field for a game similar to soccer, in which, with their exceptionally long legs, they demonstrate superiority to humans. One other aspect that Jack and Red are quick to notice is that under the very short tunics, the only clothing worn by the planet's inhabitants, there are no "shorts or panties."

The two space scouts soon learn they are on the planet Harlech, which is made up of an association of self-governing universities. Because all industry is automated, the Harlechians spend their time in scholarly pursuits. Jack and Red, having landed in the area of University 36, receive an invitation through Bubo, Dean of 36, to offer courses at that institution. Jack offers to teach Earth customs, philosophy, government, and religion; Red offers to teach Earth folklore, poetry, drama, and biology. They become known as Jack the Teacher and Red the Teacher.

While the two new additions to the faculty of 36 learn the language of Harlech and prepare their courses for the coming summer session, they discover Harlechian distinctions: Harlechians live primarily underground because of the violent electrical storms that frequently sweep the planet's surface; they practice free love; they show no emotions; they have no word for God; and their word for heaven is Harlech. Red, with his virulent interest in sex, feels he really is in heaven and soon earns a reputation for sexual prowess. Jack, on the other hand, vows to remain aloof from such activities and to bring the Word to the Harlechians.

Con man that he is, Red convinces Dean Bubo that the courses he and Jack are to offer should be in a new department, Liberal Arts. Then he conducts a

publicity campaign with large posters urging that the students "Thrill to lepre-
chauns!" and "Experience the miracle of Salvation!" The classrooms are arranged in tiers, with the students sitting on high stools, and the large number
of female students wearing no underwear; Jack and Red witness a new view of
academe. Jack struggles vainly to keep his eyes away from temptation by looking at the ceiling while he lectures and hoping that such a posture will be
thought of as a strange Earth custom. Red, far from distracted by the nudity of
his students, uses it to call the roll, "since all their faces look alike."

Finally conditioning himself to look not at the faces of his students — a
Harlechian taboo — but at their "forefended places," Jack lectures with zeal
on the virtues of modesty. But he falls victim to Cara, his golden girl, whose
"mound of Venus swelled as a perfect ovate spheroid tassled with cornsilk
curls," and whose "curve gave it an air of joy blended with a feeling of peace
which seemed to exude happiness and serenity." His lectures, however, soon
take effect; his golden girl, along with her classmates, begins to wear underwear.

Red sets out to present a television adaptation of Shakespeare, in which he
amalgamates *Romeo and Juliet*, *Hamlet*, *Macbeth*, and one or two other plays
— a true Elizabethan soap opera. A great success, the production causes the
Harlechians to do something they never have done — show emotion. In fact,
Bubo the Dean, acting as the God who punished the sinner Prometheus, decides that those who played the roles of villains should be expelled from
school; and they are. This act infuriates Red (Prometheus), who now says that
Bubo must be taught a lesson in justice, and he stages a cultural battle of the
Titans in this particular Heaven. He plans to present another drama, this one a
Christmas extravaganza focusing on another Prometheus, Christ, complete
with Herod, centurions, the Maids of Bethlehem (prostitutes), angels, a virgin,
and the Christ child. He hopes to get Bubo the Dean to expel more villains so
that he, Red, will have the nucleus of a revolutionary force.

Jack and Red have accomplished several changes on Harlech: modesty has
taken hold; emotional responses are apparent; a legal system prevails; a police
force exists; and sexual possessiveness has taken over from the earlier concept
of free love. In short, Jack and Red have turned Harlech into a mirror of Earth;
the change becomes evident when a Harlechian man is murdered in a dispute
over a woman. The murderer is found to be Nesser, a young man that Jack has
been using as an altar boy in his religious classes.

Things look bad for Nesser despite his being defended by two students who
have studied in Jack's legal class. At the last minute, however, they come up
with a wrinkle worthy of a Clarence Darrow. Since the murdered man's organs
have, according to Harlechian custom, been transplanted to other Harlechians,
Nesser's lawyers maintain that the victim is alive and well in various parts of
Harlech. Nevertheless, Nesser is sentenced to hang. He beats the hangman by
hanging himself.

On first falling in love with Cara, Jack refuses to take her, saying the flesh is willing, but the spirit says no. The spirit, however, soon gives way to the flesh. Here the roles of the two space scouts are reversed: Jack, always the defender of regulations and duty, becomes the one willing to give in to the pleasure principle; and Red, usually a hell-raising con man, argues that to defect would be stupid. He suggests that Jack, as commander, appoint him, Red, as chaplain to their crew so that he can marry Jack and Cara. Soon, with Cara pregnant, Jack hopes that her gestation period will qualify her as a humanoid, but she gives birth in the fourth month. She explains, however, that Red used her as an experiment in his class on love and courtship and, since the baby is his, she meets the deadline with two months to spare.

Jack sets out searching for Red to kill him and angrily tells Bubo the Dean that Red should be crucified in his own Passion Play. Before Jack can intervene, Red is crucified, and his body is burned by lightning.

To prevent the students from making Red a demigod, Jack reveals that his and Red's mission had been military not educational; Bubo has Jack put in his spaceship and sent back to Earth. Jack attempts to accelerate to the point that he can beat time and arrive on Earth prior to the time that he and Red actually left, thereby saving Red's life; but this fails. The psychiatrist comments that Red O'Hara, con man that he is, cannot be dead. If there was a crucifixion, then there was a resurrection. After all, Red is an Irishman. And who should know Irishmen better than Dr. Michael Timothy O'Sullivan?

The book, then, satirizes higher education and the egotistic compulsion to make other worlds like our own — to rake our hell over their heaven. The Harlechians may think their society, tolerant and permissive as it is, is heaven; but Jack and Red know better. For Jack Adams, with his Southern Baptist Puritanism, tolerance and permissiveness lead away from God's word. For Red O'Hara, with his Irish Catholic Puritanism, those qualities take away the sense of victory that comes from a hard-fought seduction. Though these apparently divergent views cause conflict between the two space scouts, they add up to the same thing: with no goals — holy Words or earthly seductions — there can be no heaven. For heaven is not a place where one arrives; it is a place toward which one strives.

Some readers may complain that Jack and Red serve as serpents in the garden, destroying the idyllic innocence of the Harlechians, much as missionaries did to the inhabitants of the South Seas or other places. At another level, Red and his fate may be seen to exemplify one of the types of hero that Joseph Campbell describes in *Hero with a Thousand Faces*; like Prometheus, Red darts to his goal and unbalances the established powers so that they react sharply, and he is "blasted from within and without — crucified, on the rock of his own violated unconscious."

But the humorous element remains uppermost. Boyd has written that while writing *The Rakehells of Heaven*, he often woke his wife in the middle of the night, chuckling over some incident from the book. Boyd commented that if the books of his trilogy were named after characters from Shakespeare, *The Rakehells of Heaven* would have to be Edmund from *King Lear*, because it "was a whoreson of science fiction, but there was great sport in its making." And, to be sure, there is great sport in its reading.

Wilton Eckley

Sources for Further Study

Reviews:

Analog. LXXXV, July, 1970, pp. 162-164.

Best Sellers. XXXIX, December, 1970, p. 21.

Books and Bookmen. XVI, May, 1971, p. 27.

Kirkus Reviews. XXXVII, October 1, 1967, p. 1087.

Luna Monthly. XIX, December, 1970, p. 28.

Magazine of Fantasy and Science Fiction. XXXIX, December, 1970, pp. 21-22.

Times Literary Supplement. April 16, 1971, p. 455.

RALPH 124C 41+

Author: Hugo Gernsback (1884-1967)
First book publication: 1911
Type of work: Novel
Time: 2660
Locale: New York City and outer space

A technocratic fable, equally remarkable for the meretriciousness of its prose and the surprising accuracy of its technological prophecies

Principal characters:
RALPH 124C 41+, a brilliant scientist
ALICE 212B 423, Ralph's sweetheart
FERNAND 60O 10, a persistent suitor of Alice
LLYSANORH' CK 1618, A Martian in love with Alice

Largely because he founded *Amazing Stories* in 1926, Hugo Gernsback has often been cited as the "father of science fiction." More accurately, he may be said to be the father of a particular strain of technophilic science fiction, long on gadgetry and technical invention but desperately short on style, plot, and character. He promoted this style of science fiction in his magazines and practiced it in his own small output of fiction, the most notable example of which is *Ralph 124C 41+*. As a work of fiction, *Ralph 124C 41+* certainly must be one of the most awkwardly written full-length science fiction works to see print. It is often startlingly accurate, on the other hand, as a catalog of technological ideas and prophecies.

Born in Luxembourg in 1884, Gernsback emigrated to the United States determined to make his fortune as an inventor and radio technician. Few of his business ventures met with success, although one of them — a mail-order radio supply company — may in part account for the Sears-Roebuck catalog style in which much of this novel is written. The book itself might never have been written had not another of Gernsback's projects, a radio magazine titled *Modern Electrics*, run short of material for the April, 1911, issue, prompting him to concoct the first of what would be twelve installments of *Ralph 124C 41+*. It has been reported that Gernsback had no idea of an overall plot when he began writing his episodes, and the headlong, disjointed nature of the completed narrative tends to support this. The first nine chapters of the book comprise little more than a continuous revelation of the scientific marvels of urban New York in 2660, most of which seem to have been invented by super-scientist Ralph ("one of the ten men on the whole planet Earth permitted to use the Plus sign after his name"), and none of which seems to have had any social impact significant enough to bring New Yorkers out of the behavioral patterns and attitudes of 1911. For all its innocent glorification of utilitarian technology, these first chapters retain a certain charm and reveal the astounding ingenuity with which Gernsback could find potential applications for what was known of electronics and chemistry at the time. The last seven chapters, however, descend into an absurd space-opera chase melodrama that not even the most jaded parodist could match for sheer witlessness. The plot, such as it is, is not one of the reasons one reads *Ralph 124C 41+*.

Nevertheless, if one makes allowances for several erroneous technical details, the prophecies that make up the New York of 2660 are impressive. In one way or another, Gernsback foresees color television with wall-sized screens (although the sound is conveyed by "loud-speaking telephones"), radar (complete with a convincing and reasonably accurate diagram), artificial fabrics, a rustproof alloy of steel called "steelonium," the use of magnesium alloys in construction, vending machines, fluorescent lights (or at least "cold" light generated by "iridium wire spirals"), the widespread use of plastics, directional range finders to locate radio sources and objects in space, hydroponic gardening, jukeboxes, tape recorders (and even "thought recorders"), microfilm, network radio, subliminal teaching devices, solar energy plants, fiberglass, video telephones, transatlantic jumbo jets (or "aeroliners"), government restraints on smoking tobacco (people as important as Ralph aren't allowed to smoke at all — the rest of us, presumably, can wheeze away), telephotos and teletypes, suspended animation, nighttime baseball, radiation therapy, the use of electro-cardiac shock to revive dying patients, recycling of resources, an economy based on credit rather than money, the use of voiceprints for identification, and many other technological innovations. Although Gernsback's strongest prophecies are in areas that involve electronics or radio technology, the sheer inventiveness of his technological extrapolations is almost overwhelming. It is remarkable how many of his visions have come to pass in the nearly seven decades since he conceived them, and one cannot help but wonder about his prophecies that are still unfulfilled.

However, as might be expected in a book that is so full of predictions, Gernsback also often misses the mark badly. Ground transportation in his future New York has been given over entirely to an insane sort of electrical roller skate with wires leading up the wearer's back to an antenna-cap, more wires dangling behind to maintain contact with the steel streets, and rubber wheels to keep the noise from being unbearable (and presumably to keep the wearer from being electrocuted). We are asked to believe that people zip along the sidewalks of New York in these contraptions at speeds of twenty miles an hour, carefully staying in their lanes and never losing control or flattening themselves against walls. Newspapers remain the principal means by which people learn of current affairs — it apparently never occurred to Gernsback that television or even radio might cover news events — and what is worse, the citizens have the contents of these newspapers fed into their brains as they sleep, so that they may discuss the day's events over breakfast. Gernsback's enthusiastic descriptions of synthetic milk and "scienticafes," where artificial foods are predigested and pumped through tubes into the patron's mouths, are thoroughly revolting, and his ideas about radium — that it draws heat from the ether around it and is basically harmless — are misguided even for 1911.

Nor are Gernsback's social and economic predictions especially well thought out. His Utopia is essentially a technocratic dictatorship in which art, culture, and manners have not progressed at all in the preceding 750 years. Gernsback argues that crime will be eliminated once production reaches peak efficiency and money is eliminated as a medium of exchange; yet his streets are brightly illuminated to ensure safety at night, and his villains, the evil Fernand and the lovesick Martian Llysanorh', are as heinous as the most vicious supercriminals of any pulp fiction. Virtually the only concession Gernsback makes to the general unpleasantness of his utilitarian Utopia lies in his notion that everyone once in a while must get away to floating resort cities, which are supported by antigravity devices at altitudes of twenty thousand feet and on which literally nothing happens. Gernsback keeps assaulting us with the wonderfulness of his all-electric New York, but even he seems to suspect that it would drive one crazy after a while.

Of the plot, characterization, and style of *Ralph 124C 41 +*, one might politely note that Gernsback's technological vision is not matched by his literary ability. However, one must remember that English was not Gernsback's native language. The plot, which does not fully emerge until the last third of the book (and we might all be grateful that Gernsback kept it subdued that long), revolves around the great scientist Ralph discovering his first true love, the Swiss maiden Alice. In the first chapter, he rescues her from an avalanche (which he somehow melts halfway around the world with the aid of radio waves); and in the last few chapters he again rescues her from a wicked disillusioned suitor named Fernand and a lovesick Martian named Llysanorh', who, forbidden by law to intermarry with an earthling, decides to kidnap her to the asteroids. The characters of Fernand and Llysanorh' add a rather distasteful note of racism to the narrative, and Ralph's dramatic last-minute rescue of Alice (in the course of which he creates an entire comet) is not entirely successful; when he reaches her, she is dead. All is not lost, however. Ralph's spaceship is equipped with enough research equipment to satisfy a dozen research hospitals, and what it does not already have he whips up in a flash — so he resurrects her. Here, within a few pages of narrative, we have the creation of a heavenly body, the vanquishing of evil, and the final triumph over death itself, perhaps the most direct and devout portrayal of the scientist as god in all science fiction.

All of this is presented in a style of demented childish melodrama mixed with naïve didacticism and passages which read suspiciously like instructions for assembling Japanese toys. Unable to maintain a coherent point of view or to focus for long on his characters, Gernsback incessantly lapses into a science-textbook prose full of passive constructions and even an occasional sentence fragment, shifting verb tense, or fused sentence. His one attempt at a literary trick is in the book's title and Ralph's last name. 124C 41, we discover with muted surprise, is a pun meaning "one to foresee for one," although exactly what *that* means, we are not told.

For all its weaknesses as a novel, however, *Ralph 124C 41+* holds a position of undoubted significance in the history of science fiction. Welcomed enthusiastically by the technical-minded readers of Gernsback's *Modern Electrics*, the novel prompted Gernsback to solicit more fiction for his magazine, led to the publication of the all-fiction issue of *Science and Invention*, and ultimately resulted in the founding of an all-fiction magazine, *Amazing Stories*, the first science fiction pulp. Though most of the writers for *Amazing Stories* could not help but improve upon the literary merit of *Ralph 124C 41+*, the technophilia of that novel and its fascination with gadgetry and elaborate "scientific" explanations became standard features of the science fiction that it influenced and eventually led in part to the entire school of what is now referred to as "hard" science fiction — tales in which the science is stressed decidedly over the fiction. Whether *Ralph 124C 41+* was altogether a salutory influence in the development of science fiction is thus a matter of continued speculation and debate, but that it was a considerable influence, and that it came at a time when the youthful genre was most impressionable, there can be no doubt.

Gary K. Wolfe

Sources for Further Study

Criticism:

Gibbs, Angelica. "Onward and Upward with the Arts: Inertiam, Neutronium, Chromalogy, P-P-P-Proat!," in *New Yorker*. (February, 1943), p. 36. Gibbs, although somewhat unfavorable towards science fiction as a whole presents an interesting picture of Gernsback.

Panshin, Alexei. "The Nature of Creative Fantasy," in *Fantastic Stories*. XX (February, 1971), pp. 100-106. Panshin attempts to define creative fantasy as employed by Gernsback.

Pratt, Fletcher and Lee De Forest. "Introductions," in Ralph 24C41+: *A Romance of the Year 2660*, by Hugo Gernsback. New York: Frederick Fell, 1950. Pratt praises this 1911 novel which celebrated the scientist-inventor as a hero who "belongs to the state," not himself.

RE-BIRTH

Author: John Wyndham (John Beynon Harris, 1903-1969)
First book publication: 1955 (as *The Chrysalids*)
Type of work: Novel
Time: Several generations after a nuclear holocaust
Locale: Labrador

A stylistically superior novel combining two favorite science fiction themes: the post-holocaust society and telepathy

> *Principal characters:*
> DAVID STRORM, a telepathic mutant
> PETRA, his younger sister
> ROSALIND MORTON, his cousin
> MICHAEL, his friend
> SOPHIE WENDER, his childhood girl friend
> AXEL STRORM, his uncle

Though less well-known than *The Day of the Triffids* or *The Midwich Cuckoos*, *Re-Birth* is perhaps the most successful of John Wyndham's novels in terms of characterization and setting. Its early chapters have the carefully crafted, autobiographical flavor of Victorian novelists in general and the early H. G. Wells in particular, and Wyndham's style remains balanced and controlled even in the later chapters, when the plot begins to weaken and moves from a convincingly realistic portrait of a rural post-atomic war society into a more traditional science fiction chase adventure. Wyndham's skill in constructing an engrossing narrative is also in evidence throughout.

The novel's chief weakness stems from Wyndam's difficulty in integrating his two major science fiction concepts and the thematic ideas that are associated with each. In the early chapters, the central science fiction device is the repressive post-atomic war society which regards the war as a punishment from God (calling it the "Tribulation") and seeks to do penance by rigidly adhering to fundamentalist concepts of obedience and conformity. The slightest deviation from the norm, the slightest evidence of mutation or rebellion, is punishable by death. This aspect of the novel presents a powerful indictment of bigotry and repression in "moralistic" societies, and the society itself is drawn with an eye to detail and character that is quite persuasive. Even the geographical setting has been worked out so meticulously that a careful reader can locate key settings on a map of North America: the village where the novel begins, called "Rigo," is apparently Rigolet in Labrador, "Newf" is nearby Newfoundland, "Lark" is Lark Harbour in Newfoundland, the "Black Coasts" are the northeastern United States.

But combined with this traditional post-holocaust theme is another traditional science fiction theme: that of the mutant race of telepaths who represent the next stage in human evolution. A few of the young residents of Rigo, including the novel's protagonist David, discover that they have telepathic gifts; in the end they are forced to flee their village to take up sanctuary in the more technologically progressive society of the telepaths. The point that Wyndham makes with this theme is a much broader one than an attack on bigotry: human evolution, he says, does not stop with *homo sapiens*, but must advance to a stage where fuller communication is possible and where wars will be unnecessary and untenable. This broader theme is also a common one in science fiction, but its evolutionary perspective changes the entire tone of the novel: we are left with the impression that the earlier attack on bigotry and repression was less a plea for humane treatment of the "different" than a warning against interfering with the natural processes of evolution. The social message gets somewhat lost in the eschatological one.

Because of its dual theme, the novel also works on two levels of estrangement. On one level, the reader's knowledge is greater than that of the characters in the novel; we are at once amused and irritated by the narrow provinciality of the citizens of Rigo, and we identify with the protagonist who dreams of distant cities and comes to doubt the value of his society. As in many post-holocaust stories, the reader shares privileged information with the author, and much of the narrative suspense arises as the protagonist gradually discovers what the reader already knows. David's growing knowledge of the real nature of the world thus serves to reduce the estrangement we feel from his society; as he learns, he becomes more like us. But as Wyndham reduces the estrangement on this level by educating his protagonist, he augments it at another level by introducing elements with which we are not familiar — David's own telepathy and the promise of a new race of superior humans. As David becomes more like us in knowledge, he becomes less like us in kind, and we learn that we did not understand as much as we had thought. For example, when David at the beginning of the novel dreams of a beautiful city on the sea with brightly lit buildings, "carts running with no horses to pull them," and "things in the sky, shiny fish-shaped things that certainly were not birds," we immediately recognize a modern metropolis with automobiles and planes. This knowledge makes us superior to David, who has no experience of such things. But we do not know at this point how he comes to have this remarkable dream, and when we learn it is evidence of his telepathic powers, our sense of superiority begins to dissipate. Finally, when we learn that this marvelous city is not in fact an image of the modern city with which we are familiar, but rather an image of a new city built by the new society of telepaths, even our sense of the familiar begins to dissipate: this is not the world that we had expected David to discover outside the narrow bounds of his village society.

David's society is circumscribed not only by its repressive values, but also by the uninhabited wasteland of radiation that surrounds it. Immediately beyond the village is the "Wild Country," where radiation makes it difficult to avoid mutations in plant or animal breeding. Beyond the Wild Country is the "Fringes," with an even greater level of mutation and radiation, and beyond that is "the Badlands about which nobody knew anything." Thus a traditional hero myth seems inevitable: David will somehow enter the wasteland and win a boon that will help his people. But the first conquest of this wasteland is not made by David, nor is it made by a physical quest. Instead, David's young sister Petra, whose telepathic abilities far exceed those of David or any other member of the small secret group of telepaths, finds she is able to exchange messages with a more advanced community of telepaths as far away as New Zealand.

Petra's discovery of the world outside changes the focus of the novel: while the early chapters created a picture of David's society and presented the nature of the outside world as a mystery to be solved, the middle chapters focus on the growing suspicion among the elders that there may be "Deviants" in their midst and the growing realization among the young telepaths that they must eventually escape to avoid destruction and to be with others like themselves. The actual escape is precipitated when a young telepath named Katherine, who has been imprisoned by the elders of the village, is tortured into revealing the existence of the group. David, Petra, David's friend and later lover Rosalind, and the other telepaths flee across the wastelands, aided by Michael, another telepath who remains undetected among the pursuers and advises them of the pursuers' movements. In the Fringes, however, the group is captured by a band of mutant exiles, among whom is Sophie, a friend of David from childhood who, because of having six toes on each foot, had been driven from the village years earlier. Sophie is still secretly in love with David, and she aids the telepaths in their attempted escape from the Fringes people. They are rescued, finally, by a group of advanced telepaths from New Zealand, who had been guided by Petra's thoughts and who immobilize the enemy with a weapon that rains tendrils of a plastic-like substance over the warriors, first rendering them immobile and then contracting until they die. The telepaths, except for Michael, are taken to New Zealand to be trained in the use of their gifts and to become a part of the society there. Michael promises to try to join them later.

There is a slight ambiguity in this ending, however. The technological weapon that the New Zealanders use against the primitives is described as being more "merciful" than the arrows and spears the telepaths had been using, but it is also more impersonal, and both David and Rosalind are rather shocked by the "coolness" with which the New Zealand woman regards the wholesale slaughter of the relatively defenseless primitives, and with her justification of it in terms of a war for racial survival and supremacy. This new society regards the "Old People" — the nontelepaths — as "'only ingenious half-humans, little better than savages.'" There is thus a hint of racism in this new society, but it is not clear whether Wyndham intends to justify this racism in terms of his evolutionary argument (which is essentially survival of the fittest, the new, "better" breed superseding the old), or whether the argument is intended to temper this new Utopia with an ominous, satirical edge. After all, the telepaths in the end are as intolerant of nontelepaths as the nontelepaths were of "deviants" in the beginning. In terms of the novel's indictment of bigotry and intolerance, not much progress has been made at all. The bigotry of the telepaths is only made more palatable by their more sophisticated arguments and weapons.

Re-Birth, then, begins as a convincingly realistic portrait of a rural society desperately trying to maintain its stability in the wake of an event it only imperfectly understands and in an environment that seems unremittingly mysterious, hostile, and threatening. The bigotry that expresses itself in this society as worship of the normal could be any social pattern of intolerance and hate, and this seems to be the central theme of the book. But soon other, more complex issues are introduced: evolution, warfare, and technology. While these issues do not replace the book's fundamental concern with attitudes toward those who are different, they certainly raise questions that Wyndham does not offer to resolve. Can two intelligent races coexist if one is demonstrably superior to the other? Is the technological society of the telepaths morally superior to the tribal society of Rigo? Is the technological warfare of the telepaths really more humane, as they claim, or is it only more efficient? One must conclude that Wyndham is not overly concerned about these things; the ending of the novel, like its title, suggests that the telepaths offer a genuine "re-birth" for humanity, a means of escaping the kinds of hatred and intolerance that had initially led to the atomic cataclysm and that seem to be redeveloping rapidly in the society of Rigo. But the price of this re-birth, as in the earlier novel by Arthur C. Clarke, *Childhood's End* (1953), is the end of humanity as we know it. One might even argue that Wyndham's solution to human social problems lies in replacing the human race with something better — perhaps not a bad idea, but one that seems disappointingly irrelevant when one remembers that the problems of intolerance and persecution that David and his companions faced in Rigo are very real ones even in our own society, which does not have the excuse of an atomic holocaust to account for/justify them.

Gary K. Wolfe

Sources for Further Study

Reviews:

Amazing Stories. XXIX, November, 1955, p. 114.

Analog. LVI, October, 1955, pp. 145-146.

Fantastic Universe Science Fiction. IV, October, 1955, pp. 109-110.

Galaxy. X, September, 1955, p. 91.

Magazine of Fantasy and Science Fiction. IX, August, 1955, pp. 93-94.

Original Science Fiction Stories. VI, January, 1956, pp. 118-119.

RENDEZVOUS WITH RAMA

Author: Arthur C. Clarke (1917-   )
First book publication: 1973
Type of work: Novel
Time: 2031
Locale: Rama, an alien spacecraft, the Lunar headquarters of United Planets

The grandly exciting story of the human exploration of a giant, uninhabited alien artifact which enters the solar system from interstellar space

Principal characters:
> COMMANDER WILLIAM T. NORTON, Commanding officer of *Endeavour*
> SURGEON COMMANDER LAURA ERNST, ship's doctor and Norton's sometime mistress
> LIEUTENANT COMMANDER KARL MERCER, *Endeavour*'s second officer
> LIEUTENANT JAMES PAK, *Endeavour*'s most junior officer
> LIEUTENANT BORIS RODRIGO, religious fanatic and expert saboteur
> DR. BOSE, Chairman of the United Planet's Rama Committee

Rendezvous with Rama is one of those novels obviously destined to become instant classics. The combination of authorial reputation, imaginative use of setting, likable characters, and exciting action brought the book immediate success, including the then-rare accolade of both Hugo and Nebula awards, along with several other less prestigious honors. It has remained a large seller in the several years since its first publication, for it combines adventure, mystery, and scientific gadgetry in an extraordinarily pleasurable way. No heavy philosophical work, the book nevertheless poses important questions and, significantly, leaves the answers open at its end. Furthermore, it moves rapidly and easily through scientific marvels and alien wonders with the grace and assurance possible only for an author who really knows what he writes, yet can present it in a lucid manner acceptable to a novice. *Rendezvous with Rama* is thus a *tour de force* of a kind possible only in the best of hard science fiction.

At first blush, the novel is an example of the traditional sense-of-wonder, technologically oriented science fiction. It postulates steady progress by the human race in technical fields, so that in the year of its setting, there is a United Planets Headquarters on the moon, from which are administered the external affairs of the seven member bodies (the planets Earth, Mars, and Mercury; and the moons Luna, Ganymede, Titan, and Triton). Obviously, colonization and commercial space travel are commonplaces. Other technical advances are also presented: the Earth is defended, for example, by Project Spaceguard, an extensive tracking and missile network (based on the ABM systems its name recalls). This marvel is designed to prevent Earth's collision with any wandering space bodies whose impact on the surface could cause major damage; it is this system, ostensibly put in place after a disastrous meteorite strikes northern Italy, which detects Rama and sets the events of the novel in motion. Spaceships are plasma-powered, large, long-range, and equipped for all sorts of missions; they carry space scooters for short-range missions in deep space. War and weapons are strictly controlled, but the Hermians (inhabitants of Mercury) use fusion bombs in their mining operations and have the capacity to launch them at interplanetary distances. Some terraforming has been attempted, but most human settlements on the bodies of the solar system are marvels of life-support engineering — probably nowhere more so than on Mercury. Nor are the biological sciences neglected: the caretakers aboard Clarke's spaceships are "simps," living products of the Super-chimpanzee Corporation's experiments with natural and synthetic genes. These animals possess an IQ of about sixty and can comprehend several hundred words of English; but weighing less than thirty kilos, they consume only half the food and oxygen of a human being while replacing 2.75 persons in routine jobs.

Thus, the author gives us no romantically conceived solar system, with terrestrial locales and indigenous life forms; we see a rigorously extrapolated one, employing the best scientific knowledge available to Clarke at the time of writing. Note the accuracy, for instance, of the astronomical observations used in the depictions of uninhabitable Venus and the barely habitable Mercury. Clarke is, of course, optimistic in his predictions of the solutions to the engineering problems involved in exploring and colonizing the solar system, but the rules of this subgenre require him to be. He is also playful at times, in such notions as a Lunar Olympics structured to take advantage of the low gravity and airless surface of that world; even his playfulness is purposeful, however, for the sky-bike used in the Olympics by one of the officers of the cruiser *Endeavour* is also used to explore the interior of Rama. Unfortunately, sometimes Clarke provides a conventional rather than a genuinely necessary extrapolation, as in providing his spacemen with the legal right to multiple wives and families on different planets; and sometimes he is merely topical, as when he has the commander of *Endeavour* echo Neil Armstrong's first words on the moon as he lands his ship on Rama. On balance, however, Clarke provides a sound technical novel, resembling in its plausibility of detail his own earlier works, such as *A Fall of Moondust* and *Earthlight*.

But *Rendezvous with Rama* is not only like that particular sort of earlier Clarke novel; it has some affinity as well with his less conventional *Childhood's End* and *2001: A Space Odyssey*. Like those earlier works, *Rendezvous with Rama* is a "first contact" story (there is even a chapter entitled "First Contact"). The aliens of this novel, however, are not physically present; Clarke depicts only their handiwork, Rama, named by human observers for the Hindu god. This artificial planetoid, a gigantic hollow cylinder fifty kilometers long and twenty kilometers in diameter, intrudes on the solar system, leading to the exploratory mission which occupies the bulk of the novel. The explorers are the crew of the Solar Survey research vessel *Endeavour*, commanded by

William Tsien Norton, providentially one of the more experienced and more competent space commanders. Norton's mission is to land on Rama, gather as much information as possible, then abandon the giant vessel as it swings past the sun on a parabolic orbit which will take it forever back to interstellar space.

To accomplish this, Norton has a talented and imaginative crew well versed in the dangers of space, alien worlds, and unexpected events. The mission is no cakewalk — for one thing, *Endeavour*'s fuel will be exhausted in simply making the rendezvous, and the subsequent rescue of her personnel will be difficult — but it will be, presumably, an archaeological expedition, for there is no sign of life to mankind's first visitor from the stars. Consequently, *Rendezvous with Rama* reads like a grand and colorful adventure. The superiors who send *Endeavour* to Rama think in terms of Schliemann at Troy and Mouhot at Angkor Wat and Norton twice compares himself to Howard Carter at the opening of Tutankhamon's tomb, thus emphasizing the archaeological aspect of the mission. But more often Norton thinks of Captain James Cook, after whose ship his is named, and the lonely exploration of the vast wastes of the Pacific, amidst storm, cannibals, reefs, and disease. Clarke's plot deftly incorporates elements of both kinds of voyage of discovery.

In the rousing plot, Norton and his crew explore the interior in a series of compact, often tense incidents. While these are often stereotyped — Opening the Door, Seeing the Vast Interior for the First Time, Descending into the Unknown Dangers — Clarke's concrete detail and laconic, even understated, style keep the reader turning the pages. The writer becomes a verbal magician, pulling a series of ever more complex tricks out of his hat. Etched on the reader's mind is a sequence of vivid sketches; for all that Rama is an enclosed artifact, this is a novel of vistas and scenery. The grand staircase leading from the center of the end to the wall; the cylindrical sea encircling Rama at its waist, flanked by sheer, metal cliffs; the six giant artificial suns, linear lights shining from deep valleys across to the other side of the cylinder; the different colors and textures of portions of the interior; the shapes of the "cities" and "towns" which dot the interior — all these are stunning concepts, fully realized in Clarke's wholly appropriate prose.

Along with these static scenes are the dynamic events which take place against them: the first breath of Raman air, stale with the disuse of eons; Norton and a small party sailing a makeshift boat across the Cylindrical Sea; Jimmy Pak flying his sky-bike to the far end of the interior to explore the mysterious peaks there; most memorable of all, the grand surge of all Raman things toward the Cylindrical Sea as the great machine shuts itself off. These are heady moments indeed. Yet, they are as soundly grounded in extrapolation as the scenes sketching the human achievements of 2030. Clarke has worked out a logical — even necessary — sequence of events, given the probable origin and intent of a ship such as Rama, and he has deduced the sorts of technology that its builders would have needed to accomplish their ends.

The novel, then, is a tour of the wonders of technology, ours and theirs. But though it resembles some of the opening events in *Childhood's End* and the scenes of *2001: A Space Odyssey* set in the computer-driven spaceship, both the quasireligious awe of the Overlords and their masters of the former book and the anthropological analysis and Eastern mysticism of the latter are missing. The first contact in this most recent Clarke speculation on the theme is only with the products of alien minds, never with the beings themselves. Hence, the earlier novels' insistence on alien interference with human affairs is also missing. Here there are no aliens helping mankind to move to a higher state of being; Rama and its absent builders are cosmically indifferent to the human impingement on the planetoid's journey — even unaware of it. The early fears of some members of the Rama Committee, and especially the paranoia of the Hermians, are never actualized; Rama is no Pandora's box.

This is not to say that Rama is empty of mysterious beings, even if they are not quite the evils released by Pandora. When Rama reaches a (predetermined?) distance from the sun, it switches on. Out of the rich chemical soup which is the Cylindrical Sea, the chemical complexes which resemble Earthly cities manufacture *biots,* the crew of Rama. These are creatures which are a hybrid of machine and living organism — biological robots, as the acronym hints. They come in all sizes and shapes, each uniquely configured for its task (some of the tasks are, of course, incomprehensible to Norton's party). In general, they seem to be making Rama ready for the habitation of its controlling race, which may or may not be the eight-foot-tall, three-armed, three-legged, spiderlike creature for whom was designed a sort of spacesuit found in the Raman place called London. Since Rama, for all its age, looks new when Norton first enters, can it have been programmed as a robot ship to seek the proper place to set up housekeeping for its prodigiously advanced builders? Where then are the Ramans? Have they all died in the millennia Rama has spent in interstellar space? Or will they be rebuilt, like the biots, at the proper time? None of these questions is answered; nor are the even more grand questions behind them: where do we humans stand in relation to the other beings in the universe? Do we matter? Can we ever know? The mystical but perhaps too pat answers of the earlier Clarke "first contact" books are wholly absent here.

Unfortunately, Clarke's substitutions for the profundities of the earlier works are the weakest portions of *Rendezvous with Rama.* The arch hints about Norton's sexual entanglement with his ship's doctor add a sporadic romantic subplot which is, finally, only trite. Even worse is the melodramatic attempt by the Hermians to destroy Rama with a nuclear-armed guided missile. True, the Hermians would have the most to lose should Rama settle down in the solar system — as it appears to be doing at one point — for they will be closest and their hold on their planet is the most precarious in the solar system. But Clarke depicts them as paranoid frontiersmen who, in the best Western mode, think xenophobically and reach for their guns. The Hermian ultimatum and missile, Norton's decision to disarm the missile, Rodrigo's brave dismantling of the weapon — all these are hyped-up incidents in a space opera subplot which is ill-matched with the grandly simple and genuinely exciting scenes of exploration. These are the flaws which, combined with the lack of mystical answers, keep the Rama novel from achieving the almost cult status of Clarke's other works about aliens; although all three books are to some extent contrived, this one *seems* so. Nevertheless, the reader takes away from it a sense of wonder and a quickened pulse as the result of contemplating Rama and its implied builders. These emotions are only heightened by Clarke's constant reminders — even to the closing line — that the Ramans do everything in threes. There will probably not be two more Ramas; but the one, and its novel, are very grand machines indeed.

William H. Hardesty III

Sources for Further Study

Criticism:

Scholes, Robert S. and Eric S. Rabkin. *Science Fiction.* New York: Oxford University Press, 1977, pp. 85-86. These pages contain a brief discussion on Clarke's themes and style of writing.

Reviews:

Best Sellers. XXXIII, October, 1973, p. 291.

Choice. X, December, 1973, p. 1547.

Christian Science Monitor. August 8, p. 3.

Library Journal. XCVIII, August, 1973, p. 2339.

New York Times Book Review. September 23, 1973, p. 38.

Time. CII, September 24, 1973, p. 125.

Times Literary Supplement. November 9, 1973, p. 1377.

REPORT ON PROBABILITY A

Author: Brian W. Aldiss (1925-   )
First book publication: 1968
Type of work: Novel
Time: Indeterminate, perhaps the present
Locale: The environs of Mr. and Mrs. Mary's home

A brilliant, surreal literary tour de force *in which the author implies that Time is static, that Reality is in the eye of the beholder, and that Art is the only universal*

Principal characters:
G,
S,
C,
MIDLAKEMELA, and
DOMOLADOSSA, watchers

Report on Probability A is, at first reading, such a puzzling novel that it almost defies description. In one sense, it is a labyrinth within a labyrinth, an enigma. As such, it is by no means either a conventional science fiction novel or an example of mainstream literature, although it shares characteristics of each group.

To begin with, *Report on Probability A*, despite the fact that it has a number of "watchers" identified only as G, S, and C, has no characters in the most conventional sense. It has little if any plot; nothing happens to the characters except that they continue watching and are in turn watched. They are static, immobile, virtually motionless, frozen in time and space. They do nothing. Nothing happens to them, and their disposition at the end of the novel is unclear. All the reader knows — and he does not know it for certain — is that he has been placed in a labyrinth with no thread of Ariadne to lead him out.

The few clues that do exist for the reader are broken, complex, difficult. Brian Aldiss is unsparing in his passion for objectivity, but the very emphasis on objectivity is misleading. After all, his epigraph for the novel is an inscription from Goethe: "Do not, I beg you, look for anything behind phenomena. They are themselves their own lesson." Yet the phenomena described, sometimes in considerable detail, throughout the novel seem to be meaningless, far from the *ding an sich* which Goethe's remark seems to imply. In fact, the reader would be well advised to recall the statement made by one of the characters, "All we are after is facts. We don't have to decide what reality is, thank God!"

Facts, then, or phenomena, seem to be what Aldiss is concerned with. And facts he gives us, again and again and again, sometimes in the exact wording he has used earlier. For example, the description of the bungalow behind Mr. and Mrs. Mary's house is repeated word for word several times in the novel, even including detailed descriptions such as, "It's roof was also of planks, covered by asphalt; the asphalt was secured in place by large flat-headed nails which dug into the black material. Cracks ran round many of the nails." We see those nails and those cracks from multiple points of view, but the exact language is used each time.

Insofar as *Report on Probability A* has a plot in any sense of the word, it is concerned with the attempts by various observers to determine the nature of the world which they observe, which is virtually identical with their own. As one character puts it, "Our robot fly has materialized into a world where it so happens that the first group of inhabitants we come across is studying another world they have discovered — a world in which the inhabitants they watch are studying a report they have obtained from another world." Aldiss, in other words, is presenting reality as a multiple mirror, in which worlds are reflected in worlds which are reflected in worlds which are reflected . . . *ad infinitum.* The reader has no sense of which reality is real, or, for that matter, which reality is his own.

Report on Probability A was written in 1962 and immediately rejected by Faber. Aldiss has admitted that he was strongly influenced by the French anti-novel, particularly the works of Alain Robbe-Grillet. This influence may be the key to understanding the lean, hard-surfaced, absolutely nonemotive, nonaffective surface prose of *Report on Probability A.* Many British critics have commented on Aldiss' transmutation of French techniques into a Pinteresque, but typically English, novel; the work remains in print in England but has been virtually ignored in the United States. The French antinovel provided Aldiss with the stylistic orientation for his approach to static time celebrated in *Report on Probability A.* Moreover, his use of factually objective phenomena approaches the surreal, extending almost beyond reality.

Thus, almost by definition, or by the limitations of the genre he adopted, Aldiss was forced to construct a characterless, plotless novel. And the very strong measure of the success of his attempt is found in the novel itself. It represents, as he himself has put it, "a writer carrying out his intentions as closely as possible."

Throughout much of his work Aldiss has been concerned with time, art, and to a lesser extent, particularly in his earlier works, with death. The first two themes seem to dominate *Report on Probability A.* Here there is no sense of elapsed time, and Aldiss' careful, almost obsessive use of the present tense indicates some sort of eternal present. Each of the watchers seems to realize that time may move at a different rate in the continuum he is observing, but no frame of reference is given to permit either the observer or the reader to measure its flow. The hands on G's clock, for example, seem forever fixed at ten minutes to eight; the hands have not moved for something over eleven months. Time is frozen, static, immobile — like the characters, the setting, and the plot.

Yet the reader has somewhat of a horrifying fascination in watching G's inaction, just as C or S has. As if trapped by a basilisk, the reader is frozen by the icy brilliance of Aldiss' conception and the chilling perfection of his technique. Yet it should be clearly understood that this fascination with technique or execution is an intellectual, not an emotional one. The reader's sympathies do not lie with the characters, for there are none with whom to identify. Neither are they engrossed by the plot, except in the almost vain attempt to decipher the puzzle Aldiss presents. Rather, the appeal of the book lies in the intellectual contemplation of the difference between the ideal and the real.

At this point, therefore, Aldiss the artist and art lover must be considered. Several of his earlier novels have dealt, in one way or another, with the artist as artist, or even with the artist *manqué*. His use of the intricately woven tapestry motif in his recent novel, *The Malacia Tapestry*, where he brings to life a multitextured but unchanging society, is indicative of his continuing interest in the artist or his creations. However, whereas the most important source of tension in *The Malacia Tapestry* is the crucial tension between the forces of change and the rigid, inert society he depicts, in *Report on Probability A* Aldiss is concerned only with the totally unchanging nature of art itself. *Vita brevis, ars longa*, he seems to say, and celebrates this ancient thesis with the work of art he has created.

Aldiss, however, is not content simply to make such a bold assertion directly. Rather, he places at the center of the novel a single artistic phenomenon observed by all of the observers, William Holman Hunt's painting "The Hireling Shepherd," which is reproduced even on the cover of the paperback edition of the book. This painting, studied by G, S, C, and every other observer may be the key to understanding the novel itself. Thus a work of art — this novel — depends upon still another work of art — Hunt's painting. But the painting embodies, in the words of the novel,

> [the Victorian's] painful incarceration within time . . . so their painters became masters of the Unresolved, of the What Next? instant: the dilemma, the unanswered question, the suspended gesture, the pause before destruction. . . . Almost all the greatest Victorian pictures represent the imprisonment of beings in a temporal structure that seemed at the time to admit of no escape; so the paintings are cathartic in essence.

Hunt, and hence Aldiss, seems to use what has been called the "freeze frame" technique, where a single moment isolated in time represents all time. In this method, as with his use of phenomenological detail throughout the book, Aldiss is unrelentingly visual. His camera eye sweeps from scene to scene, with every detail in clear focus. The technique is almost cinematic, with no illusion of perspective. Thus every detail must be photographed or rephotographed in exquisite clarity, for who can say what specific detail has more validity than any other? All are equally important, and all must be presented with the same precision of focus. But in the end, all are equally static, showing psychodramas of unresolved time.

The reader's perplexity, then, is the perplexity of G, C, or S, as well as the perplexity of the hireling shepherd or the girl with the lamb in her lap shown in Hunt's painting. It is the perplexity of stasis, the puzzle of the frozen moment, the dilemma of the suspended gesture. If the reader closes the book with anger or disgust, he will miss precisely the question with which Aldiss intends him to grapple: is time, and hence reality, merely linear as our common experience might indicate? Or is it cyclic, ever-recurring, leading Ourobouros-like, head to tail, continuing forever in a closed circle? Aldiss provides no answers, to be sure, but one thing at least is certain about this most provocative book: Aldiss makes the perceptive reader question his own basic experience of life. In this vision, Aldiss resembles no one quite so much as his mentor, James Joyce, whose style, rhythms, and cyclic vision Aldiss celebrates in *Barefoot in the Head*. Joyce's feeling of chilling exile permeates the novel and the technique of coldly logical detail resembles more the catechism chapter of *Ulysses* than it does Robbe-Grillet. Finally, the brilliance of Joyce's epiphanic vision strikes the reader with an equal clarity after both the celebration of life as art, and the celebration of art as life that is *Report on Probability A*.

Willis E. McNelly

Sources for Further Study

Criticism:

Matthews, Richard. *Aldiss Unbound*. San Bernardino, Calif.: Borgo Press, 1977, pp. 38-41. Matthews compares Aldiss' *Report on Probability A* to Chaucer's *The Canterbury Tales*.

Reviews:

Library Journal. XCV, February 1, 1970, p. 511.

Listener. LXXIX, May 2, 1968, p. 579.

Manchester Guardian. XCVIII, May 2, 1968, p. 10.

Magazine of Fantasy and Science Fiction. XXXIX, July, 1970, p. 45.

Observer. May 26, 1968, p. 29.

Punch. CCLIV, June 12, 1968, p. 865.

Times Literary Supplement. October 3, 1968, p. 1137.

THE REPUBLIC OF THE SOUTHERN CROSS
(RESPUBLIKA YUZHNOGO KRESTA)

Author: Valery Bryusov (1873-1924)
First book publication: 1907
English translation: 1972
Type of work: Novelette
Time: The twenty-second and twenty-third centuries
Locale: The South Pole

A workers' republic is destroyed by a peculiar madness

Valery Bryusov is not usually thought of as a science fiction writer, nor for that matter even as a prosaist. He occupies a solid place in the history of Russian poetry as a fine craftsman, an epigone of French and German masters, an initiator of Russian Symbolism, an indefatigable editor, and a superb translator from many tongues. Bryusov's merit is said to be his promotion of formal excellence in Russian poetry, his almost singlehanded demolishment of careless sentimental and Populist verse, and his establishment of polished classical forms. His demerit is said to be his coldness, his impersonality, his rarefied dilettantism. Bryusov's poetry gave his enemies, who were legion, ample ammunition for the charge of aestheticism and emotional sterility.

Bryusov's encyclopedic range of themes from prehistory through Greece and Rome and the Middle Ages to the present, his titles in Latin and French, and his arcane references permitted critics to consider him removed from the real world, from current issues. His infatuation with the perverse, with sexual immolation and psychological disintegration, prompted the charge of hothouse decadence. Finally, his insufferable arrogance, his delusions of grandeur (in the Preface to his humbly titled collection *Chefs d'oeuvre* he wrote: "In its present shape, this seems to me a perfect book"), and his thirst for fame (he wrote Lev Tolstoi to include his name in the second edition to *What Is Art?* as an important forerunner of Tolstoi's ideas), suggested mental instability, even idiocy. Whatever their virtuosity, Bryusov's works were not great enough to withstand all these objections. And so today he is accorded the fame of a historical monument, a reserved niche in all the anthologies, a paragraph in the textbooks. (He himself said he wanted to be a footnote, for in addition to his mania, he was modest.) Probably no one reads Bryusov as a favorite poet: he had the misfortune to help educate a greater poet named Aleksandr Blok. He rests in a cold tomb of history.

This obscurity is a shame, because he was an excellent writer. His crime was not to write poorly, but to write well in too many genres. Had he written only classical poems, he would have been considered a true classicist, like Vyacheslav Ivanov. Only Symbolist poems — a Symbolist like Andrei Belyi. Only mystical poems — a mystic like Vladimir Solovyov. And so on: he wrote in all genres and was considered an unfeeling eclectic. This criticism was universally leveled at his prose, and no one bothers much with it today. It is not anthologized, not taught in universities, rarely mentioned in textbooks. Again, Bryusov was surpassed by a greater younger man, Andrei Belyi, author of *Petersburg* — and also by an older man, Fyodor Sologub, author of *The Petty Demon*.

And yet, if one spends the time, Bryusov's prose is interesting, even refreshing. More than any Russian writer since Pushkin, Bryusov wrote clear prose; the action always moves swiftly, the author never intervenes, he always remains a storyteller. And while many of his works are set pieces, conscious imitations of foreign models (Poe, Maupassant, Anatole France, Przybyszewski), one finds individual touches, innovations, and occasional greatness. In addition to two historical novels, Bryusov wrote over a dozen stories. The novel *The Fiery Angel* (1908), set in Germany of the early Reformation, is now remembered as the basis for Sergei Prokofiev's ill-fated opera (in French), the music for which was converted into the Third Symphony. The second novel, *The Altar of Victory* (1913), is set in Rome of the fourth century. The stories, most of which appeared in the collection, *Earth's Axis* (*Zemnaya os'*, 1907), deal primarily with madness. The long story, *The Republic of the Southern Cross* (*Respublika Yuzhnogo Kresta*), first published in 1905 in the journal *Scales* (*Vesy*), is included in this collection and is illuminated by its surroundings. Thus, before discussing this work, it will help to make a brief survey of the other stories.

In the Preface to the collection the reader is informed that the stories are united not only by their style, but by a single idea. "This idea," writes Bryusov, "is that there is no definite boundary between the world real and imagined, between 'dream' and 'waking,' 'life' and 'fantasy.'" The Earth turns, it would seem, on this axis. Making the necessary changes in vocabulary, we can see that Bryusov, from the structuralist point of view, meant to explore the genre described by Tzvetan Todorov as "the fantastic." Todorov's conditions for the genre, it will be recalled, are three: first, the reader must regard the world of the characters as the real world of living characters and must hesitate between a natural or supernatural explanation of the events described. If a natural explanation should suffice, the story is "uncanny," if a supernatural — the story is "marvelous," if neither — "fantastic." Second, the characters themselves may experience the same hesitation. Third, the reader does not regard the text as only allegory — he is left uncertain. A number of the stories in *Earth's Axis* approach the fantastic, but fall short. The tramp who sees the face of the woman he betrayed in a fifteenth century Italian bust is obviously obsessed: he is mistaken when he thinks he invented the woman at the sight of the bust. ("The Marble Bust.") The meek wife who sees a proud double in the mirror, becomes her slave, kisses her, and changes places with her is understood psychologically: the double is not supernatural. ("In the Mirror" — a neglected masterpiece of Russian literature.) And the psychopath addicted to lurid dreams who murders his wife and then discovers he cannot wake up definitely belongs to "the uncanny." ("Now When I Have Awakened.") But the prisoner who suddenly knows that he is in a dream about Russian history and that Aleksandr Nevsky will defeat his German torturers, who wakes up to tell his dream and who suddenly suspects that this waking is a dream and he will return to be tortured, introduces the true fantastic. For we cannot know: he was right the first time — why should he be wrong now? ("In the Tower.") One story suggests a supernatural explanation: an enamored young man dresses up as the ghost of a widow's husband, but is thwarted in his conquest of the widow by the appearance of the ghost itself. However, one detail turns the story into the fantastic: the young man may have seen his own reflection in a full-length mirror. So then: was it the ghost or the reflection, or the ghost acting through the reflection? ("Protection.") Similarly, does the betrayed Elizaveta torture the penitent lover Basmanov by pretending to be an unknown woman named Ekaterina, or does Ekaterina torture him by pretending to be Elizaveta? Does the woman seek vengeance for herself or another, or is it all the same? ("For Herself or Another.") Here Bryusov reveals that the genre of the fantastic is a psychological category, that psychological quandaries are completely fantastic.

The Republic of the Southern Cross, as we shall see, is imbued with psychological uncertainty, set on a fantastic tilt, but this is not apparent at first. More obviously, the story relates to the science fiction apocalyptic genre represented by the story "The Last Martyrs," the dramatic scene "Earth," and the poems "Pale Horse" and "The Coming Huns." The first of these is a planned nightmare: doomed ritualists celebrate their last orgy as revolutionaries break into the temple and massacre them as they scream in agony and ecstacy. "Earth" adds the science fiction element to apocalypse: the youths in the mechanical world of the future, longing for sunlight and fresh air, demand that the cupola over the city be opened. The oldtimers know that mankind can breathe only artificial air and can stand only artificial light. The cupola is opened and the city instantly turns into a cemetery of shriveled forms with outstretched arms. In "Pale Horse" (*Kon' bled*, 1904), another overlooked masterpiece, a fiery-faced horseman appears on the streets of a metropolis, rides through the traffic, under the skyscrapers, and stuns the crowd — but only momentarily. The city bustle resumes, and only an escaped lunatic and an awed prostitute understand that civilization is doomed. The famous poem "The Coming Huns," written at the time of Russia's defeat by Japan, welcomes the invasion of Europe by the yellow menace, the book burning, the desecration of temples and the infusion of rich barbarian blood.

One more antecedent should be named for *The Republic of the Southern Cross* — Dostoevski. *Notes from the Underground*, Raskolnikov's vision in *Crime and Punishment*, "The Dream of a Ridiculous Man," and "The Legend of the Grand Inquisitor" in *The Brothers Karamazov* form the very basis of the anti-Utopian tradition in Russian literature. Particularly germane to Bryusov's story is the vision or revery experienced by Raskolnikov during his sickness after confession and imprisonment. This vision carries Raskolnikov's idea of the great man to the farthest extreme thus discrediting it, but it also augurs a future when every small man will consider himself great. Raskolnikov envisions a plague arising out of Asia and Europe. People are infected by a new type of trichina, mindful and willful little spirits, which cause the infected to consider themselves right in everything. Each person becomes the sole possessor of the truth and opposes the falsehood of the other. Villages, cities, nations are infected. Law and order break down, wars are fought with soldiers killing others on the same side. All crafts and agriculture cease. Only a few men are destined to save the raging mad world, to renew and cleanse it, to begin a new race, but these few are not seen and not heard.

The Republic of the Southern Cross is told by an uninvolved narrator who attempts to report the true history of the Republic. Previous reports, he claims, relied excessively on surviving residents of the Republic, all of whom were stricken by a psychic disorder. The Republic was founded at the South Pole by a steel mill trust. The capital, Star City, was situated precisely at the pole, with the spire of the city hall marking the Earth's nadir or axis. It was covered by a cupola and flooded with constant artificial light. Streets radiated out from the center in concentric circles and meridia. Most of the inhabitants lived in outlying areas in cities modeled on the Star City plan, and those in these areas worked in the steel industry. Residents of the capital were mostly retired workers living on generous pension plans. The Republic was a Utopia in the form of a workers' democratic republic, but the real power was wielded by the steel trust. Externally appearing to be a mecca of bright entertainments, the place was essentially a dictatorship with absolute regimentation of housing, clothing, food, sleep, work, reproduction, education, and information. Yet a diversity of entertainments and vices was provided by foreign entrepeneurs, with spies of the City Council watching the behavior of the citizens.

By this description Bryusov immediately links his story with the Petersburg tradition in Russian literature. The fantastic city constructed in the swamps and mists of the Neva, with its geometrically planned streets and great monuments, its luminous snows and white summer nights, its governmental ranks and paper existence, both inspires and stages the dreamlike experiences in Pushkin, Gogol and Dostoevski, and Bryusov naturally attaches himself to this tradition. In so doing, and in describing the regimentation and its disintegration, he takes a step toward Belyi and Zamyatin.

The chief event in the story is the outbreak of an infection, a mental aberration called *mania contradicens*. The disease is progressive. The first symptoms are verbal: the victim says "no" when he wants to say "yes," continually contradicts himself. Next the contradiction affects his actions: he turns right when he wants to turn left, gives away money when he should collect it, stops when he should start. Finally the disease attacks all words, thoughts and actions: the victim becomes frenzied, enraptured, murderous or suicidal, his brain may hemorrhage, he invariably dies. Bryusov details the spread of the mania with dispassionate inventiveness: street scenes with snarled traffic, concerts with false notes, hospitals with fatal prescriptions, nurseries with murdered babies. Measures against the disease fail, and the citizens flee in panic, causing further catastrophes at the train stations. The story, from this point on, steadily enlarges the scale of the disaster: looting, lechery, rape, carnage, cannibalism. The electrical supply is cut off, and the city is plunged into cold blackness. It becomes "an enormous black box," "a gigantic lunatic asylum," where human beasts howl, attack and die amid the rotting corpses. The apocalyptic proportions of Raskolnikov's vision are achieved. And, as in that vision, only a few men promise salvation for the deranged world: the Chairman of the City Council Horace DeVille and his subordinates.

The term *mania contradicens* may have been used in Bryusov's time, and the condition itself is described in many books. Silvano Arieti mentions the *negativism* of some catatonic schizophrenics: if asked to show their tongues, they close their mouths; asked to stand up; they lie down. (*Interpretation of Schizophrenia.*) R. D Laing analyzes the *false-self system*, whereby the schizoid personality disassociates himself from the actions of his body, his "false self." (*The Divided Self.*) C. G. Jung describes the *shadow*, the demonic personality underneath the *persona*, the social mask. In such accounts, the personality is split by society, and the greater the regimentation, the greater the repository of contradictory impulses.

Horace DeVille is described as a virtual saint. Having acquired emergency powers, he alone acts for the good of the city. He organizes rescue missions, issues warnings, provides transportation, distributes food, cremates bodies. When a man named Whiting, numbered among the sane, begins a campaign to kill off the sick to eliminate the disease, DeVille and his forces oppose the murderers. Eventually Whiting is caught and discovered to be in the last stages of the mania. But, despite his heroic effort, DeVille cannot hold back the tide, and he disappears from view as the entire republic succumbs to madness. Only his diary and telegrams survive to provide the record for the narrator of the tale. The work ends as foreigners clean up the wreckage and a tourist trade is begun for the curious.

The foregoing account has been detailed in order to provide all the clues for interpretation. As one may see, the story contains no plot in the sense of an intrigue, no conflict of characters in the sense of a clash of personalities or philosophies, no surprises once the initial premises have been stated. It appears to be a straightforward narrative, another apocalypse, another anti-Utopia. All commentaries on the work leave it at that. Bryusov is scored for his purple passages and his vain attempt to frighten readers. Yet the fantastic nature of the other stories in the collection and the author's penchant for psychological ambiguity prompt another reading. If "previous reports" of the destruction were unreliable because of the madness of those reporting, what greater reliability does the narrator's account have? In particular, how do we know that DeVille was not himself afflicted with *mania contradicens*? As Chairman of the dictatorial City Council was he motivated by benevolence or malevolence, which under the influence of the disease manifested itself as its opposite? Or, to add another level of ambiguity, might not the whole history of Star City have been concocted by the deranged Chairman in his diary, which the narrator takes for verity? Or another level: might not the slaughter have been perpetrated by DeVille under the cover of a pestilence and the need for emergency measures? Was there any attack or counterattack? Any contradiction at all? You may read the story a second and third time and find no definite answer to these questions. Interpretation of the story is itself eaten up by *mania contradicens*, and nothing remains certain, everything becomes fantastic.

It is commonplace to relate Bryusov's psychological orgies to the dismal mood prevailing in Russia after the first revolution, to the excesses of "Decadence" and early Symbolism, the pessimism of Leonid Andreev, the prurience of Mikhail Artsybashev and Zinaida Gippius. His description of the failed workers' republic might be related to the soviets of 1905 or to any of the Socialist Utopias discussed at the time. But Bryusov's erudition, his dependence on Dostoevski, foreign literature and the whole international tradition of horror tale, apocalypse and anti-Utopia permit a wider view. As the history of mankind unfolds, the claims of civilization become more universal, the pressure of mental and spiritual regimentation becomes more burdensome, the ability to adapt becomes more difficult. Dostoevski, writing about the labor camp, formulated the principle that "man is a creature who can adapt himself to anything," and on this principle civilization proceeds. Bryusov shows where it might end. Had he lived in our time he could have drawn more colorful and more varied pictures of *mania contradicens*.

Gary Kern

Sources for Further Study

Criticism:

Harkins, William E. *Dictionary of Russian Literature*. New York: Philosophical Library, 1956, pp. 27-29. A brief discussion of Bryusov's life and career is given here. This work is regarded as his most famous novel.

Jackson, Robert L. *Dostoevsky's Underground Man in Russian Literature*. The

Hague: Mouton, 1958, pp. 113-116. A discussion of Utopian literature in relation to Bryusov's work is given in these pages.

Suvin, Darko. *Other Worlds, Other Seas*. New York: Random House, 1970, pp. xvii-xviii. Suvin calls this a despairing story, with heroic, isolated figures.

RETIEF: AMBASSADOR TO SPACE

Author: Keith Laumer (1925-   )
First book publication: 1969
Type of work: Short stories
Time: The twenty-eighth century
Locale: Outer space

A clever and humane diplomatic troubleshooter ranges from planet to planet bringing order out of disorder

> *Principal characters:*
> JAME RETIEF, a diplomatic troubleshooter
> MAGNAN, his companion
> GROACI, enemies of planetary order

In *Retief: Ambassador to Space*, Keith Laumer, a former military officer and diplomat turned science fiction writer, recounts seven more adventures of Jame Retief, an interplanetary administrative agent for the Corps Diplomatique Terrestrienne during the twenty-eighth century. One of the more popular series characters in science fiction, Retief combines the ingenious resourcefulness and optimistic self-assurance of a James Bond with the rather rollicking life view of Mark Twain's Connecticut Yankee. Like the crew of Star Trek's ship *Enterprise*, Retief and his compatriot Magnan move through the galaxy solving problems from Rockamorra to Skweemen and outwitting the Groaci — enemies of peace and order.

The first story, "Giant Killer," takes place on the planet Rockamorra, where a ninety-foot dinosaur named Crunderthrush satiates his appetite with an occasional inhabitant. Retief and Magnan have accompanied Terran Ambassador Pinchbottle to Rockamorra to become the first to establish diplomatic relations with that world, thus taking an advantage over the Groaci. What Pinchbottle does not realize, concerned as he is with the details of protocol and his own inflated view of his role in history, is that during the colorful ceremony of presenting credentials, he has committed himself to the slaying of Crunderthrush by sundown the next day. When Pinchbottle states that he has no intention of attacking the dinosaur, the Rockamorrans sentence him to be decapitated.

Retief tells Haccop, the Rockamorran interpreter, that it is all right to kill off diplomats, but that it must be done according to protocol. They must, therefore, at least wait until the sundown deadline before carrying out the sentence. After Haccop agrees, Retief accepts his invitation to play cards. Retief not only wins all of Haccop's money, but he also wins Haccop himself. The two then set out to gather all the information they can about Crunderthrush's habits, and once informed, Retief constructs a mechanism to kill the dinosaur. Stationing Pinchbottle where he can operate the weapon, Retief lures the monster into the target area. The scheme works, and Crunderthrush is killed.

The Rockamorrans commute Pinchbottle's death sentence to slavery for life since he killed the dinosaur, but did so with help. Retief, however, buys Pinchbottle's slave contract and sets him to work cutting blubber from Crunderthrush's carcass until the ship arrives to take them away from Rockamorra.

"The Forbidden City" finds Retief and Magnan on the planet Sulinore, where a civilization millions of years old is declining. Ninety-nine percent of the planet's surface is now devoted to cemeteries, historical shrines, and monuments to the past. The Sulinorians believe that there is no more Divine Affluvium, a mineral necessary for their existence. From a once-proud race of giants, they have been reduced to elfin creatures. When Magnan asks why the Sulinorians will not try deep mining to discover more of the mineral, he is told that it is better to decline through eons of erosion than to be eaten by engines of industry.

At the time of the story, a peace conference is being held on Sulinore, attended by Terrans, Groaci, and Blugs — the latter, warlike protégés of the Groaci. The Groaci, who have been assigned the security arrangements of the conference, are secretly planning to take over Sulinore. Captured by the Groaci, Retief and Magnan effect an escape and go into the Forbidden City to warn the Sulinorians of their danger. The latter, using what remaining Divine Affluvium they have, resuscitate Tussore (now a statue), one of their great warriors of the past, and ask his advice. He awakens, but falls asleep again before he can answer. At this point, a disguised Blug is discovered in their midst and, as Retief and the Sulinorians chase him, he exudes a brown gas, which awakens another Sulinorian hero — Bozdune. Forcing the Blug to breathe on Tussore, they reawaken him, and all head toward the Terran embassy, where a state dinner is being held. Retief and his companion burst in on the dinner, attacking the waiters, who are really Blugs disguised as Sulinorians. The Blug plan was to have poisoned all the leaders at the peace conference, thus scoring a victory for the Groaci. The resuscitated Sulinorian heroes start out to raid various Groaci territories, inviting Retief to join them. Though he is tempted, he refuses — and the raiders, with banners waving and bugles sounding, march off into the gaudy sunset of Sulinore.

In "Crime and Punishment," Magnan is the Terran Consul to Schweinhund's world, Slunch, as the natives call it, and Retief is vice-consul. Slunch is a land of thermal mud created by a geyser which spouts every twenty-seven hours. One day a CDT transport makes a surprise visit, bringing a trade mission to stimulate enthusiasm among the Slunchans for Terran goods. The problem is that the mud has had a corrosive effect on everything shipped to Slunch. Moreover, the Slunchans want nothing more from the Terrans than that they go away. Bureaucrats that they are, the members of the trade mission will not listen to what Magnan tells them about Slunch or the Slunchans and they persist in trying to sell items that the Slunchans do not need or want.

Obsessed with cleaning up Slunch, the trade mission leader, Rainsinger, has spread ten tons of rat poison to kill the prevalent mud rats. This act has upset the delicate ecological balance on Slunch, causing an enormous amount of mud to erupt from the geyser threatening to inundate everything and everyone. Together with Magnan and Rainsinger, Retief goes to the source of the mud, a volcanic mountain, and is successful in diverting the flow of mud by using explosives. Returning to the city, they are shocked to discover that the mud, after coming into contact with some powdered tombstones, has turned into a hard, smooth surface, thus effecting the birth of a new product for trading.

"Trick or Treaty," perhaps the most suspenseful of the seven stories, finds Retief on Gaspierre, a planet in danger of being taken over through diplomatic negotiations by the Krultch, centauroid quadrapeds. The Krultch, with a foothold on Gaspierre, would be free to expand their control through the Gloob cluster. A practical race, the Gaspers are in little mood to fend off the Krultch. In order to keep the Terrans from interfering with the negotiations, the Krultch have confined the Terran's ambassador, Sheepshorn, to his embassy. Retief, with a group of acrobats and magicians that have been performing on Gaspierre, sets out to sabotage the Krultch plans. Utilizing their talents, Retief and his accomplices sneak aboard a huge Krultch war vessel being used for the command headquarters on Gaspierre. After a number of close encounters, they succeed in capturing the Krultch commander, and Retief threatens to expose the Krultch bribery of Gaspierre officials unless the commander agrees to give up his request for a space station on Gaspierre in favor of such activities as animal husbandry and folk dancing. Thus the Terran mission once again succeeds in heading off war.

In "The Forest in the Sky," the Terrans and the Groaci are battling with one another on the planet Zoon. Under the direction of Terran Ambassador Oldtrick, the Terrans lands on Zoon and propel themselves *via* flying jackets to a mountain top where the Zoonites are supposed to live. There, they are attacked by the Groaci and all with the exception of Retief and Oldtrick are captured. Although the latter two initially succeed in escaping by use of their flying jackets, Oldtrick's jacket is later hit by Groaci fire, and he begins falling seven thousand feet to the valley below. After much daring, Retief succeeds in catching up with the Ambassador in order to give him a second jacket. Then, disobeying Oldtrick's orders, Retief returns to the mountain top.

Once there, he rescues Qoj, the Zoonite, from a monster and is taken to a secret bower where the Zoonites have a settlement. The Zoonites, having an aversion to children, force their offspring to live in the valley where they tend to devour one another. Retief soon discovers two important facts: that the Zoonites have spore pods that enable them to float in the air, and that their offspring have foot-long blue baby fur. Armed with this knowledge, Retief is able to convince the Groaci ambassador that it would be to his planet's advantage to limit its interests to the valley. Here, they would restrain the Zoonite offspring to one-half the planet's surface in return for the privilege of collecting their fur after molting season. By this strategy, the Terrans, on the other hand, would gain the spore pods from the Zoonites on the mountain top, and thus, once again, gain a Terran advantage over the Groaci.

The last story in the collection, "Truth or Consequences," takes place on Plushnik II, where the CDT mission finds itself in the midst of a centuries-old feud between the Blortians of Plushnik I and the Gloians of Plushnik II. During the mission's nine-month stay, the capital of Plushnik II already has changed hands four times. Ambassador Biteworse is at a loss regarding his assignment of pacifying the system, and he is particularly concerned because an inspection team is due soon to check on his progress. The stage is set once again for Jame Retief.

Realizing that the traditional strategies — kindly indulgence, latent firmness, reluctant admonition, or gracious condescension — are fruitless, Retief sets out to follow his own strategy of peacemaking. As a result of secret research conducted in the Center of Learning, he succeeds in capturing Lib Glip, the premier of the Gloians, and takes him to General Barf, the leader of the Blortians. There, Retief explains to all present that the original home planets have become mixed-up in the long war as have the identities of the participants — the Gloians really being descendants of the Blortians and vice versa. With this startling news that all are really brothers in race, both sides agree to a peaceful coexistence, and the inspection team finds all well when its members arrive on Plushnik II.

Although Laumer utilizes many of the conventions of the space opera in *Retief: Ambassador to Space* he does so because the form offers him the freedom to blend satiric melodrama with tongue-in-cheek humor in order to achieve a welcome antidote for the smug self-importance of diplomatic bureaucrats. Wherever he may be found — calmly smoking an eighteen-inch purple cigar with a five-eyed quadruped, struggling in a sea of thermal mud, or risking his life against the Groaci — Jame Retief maintains both a practical and moral perspective, perhaps best summarized by his statement that "one intelligent being should keep another from being eaten alive, whenever he conveniently can." Retief's foils in these short stories are the various Terran ambassadors, self-seeking and generally stupid, and the Groaci, constantly exploiting situations to their own advantage. During his adventures, Retief never loses his cool composure, or acts in vengeance; indeed, never once does he set out to take a life. Little more can be said about Jame Retief. Laumer had the good sense to keep his hero some distance from the reader; the result, strange though it may seem, is that both Retief and his adventures are almost more believable than unbelievable.

Wilton Eckley

Sources for Further Study

Reviews:

Analog. LXXII, December, 1963, p. 88 and LXXVI, February, 1966, pp. 147-148.

Analog. LXXIX, May, 1967, pp. 3160-3161 and LXXXIII, August, 1969, pp. 164-165.

Galaxy. XXXII, January, 1972, pp. 115-116.

Kirkus Reviews. XXXIX, May 15, 1971, p. 576 and XXXIX, June 1, 1971, pp. 611-612.

Luna Monthly. I, June, 1969, p. 29, VIII, January, 1970, p. 29, and XXXVIII–XXXIX, July–August, 1972, pp. 33-34.

Magazine of Fantasy and Science Fiction. XXIX, September, 1965, pp. 70-71.

New Worlds. CLXV, August, 1966, p. 144.

THE RIDDLE OF THE TOWER

Authors: John D. Beresford (1873-1947) and Esme Wynne-Tyson (1898-   )
First book publication: 1944
Type of work: Novel
Time: The 1940's, the distant past, and the distant future
Locale: Various

A commentary on human nature and society developed by means of illustrative visions of past and future

> *Principal characters:*
> BEGBIE, a publisher
> DETMOLD, a writer

The Riddle of the Tower was written during the darkest phase of World War II, and was itself to some extent a victim of the war: it was published in a small edition that went virtually unnoticed. It was one of two fantasies which Beresford wrote in collaboration with Esme Wynne-Tyson, the second being his final work, *The Gift* (1946).

The Riddle of the Tower represents the culmination of a second phase of speculative work within Beresford's career. The first phase, which produced *The Hampdenshire Wonder*, *Goslings*, two short story collections, and *Revolution*, lasted from 1911-1921, and for the next twenty years he wrote virtually nothing that can be described as science fiction save for the faith-healing fantasy *The Camberwell Miracle*. That he was once again inspired to flights of the imagination was certainly a result of the new war with Germany. The apocalyptic anxieties aroused by the war led the aging writer to produce three more futuristic novels, the first two being *What Dreams May Come . . .* (1941) and *A Common Enemy* (1942).

World War I had affected the nature of Beresford's imaginative fiction considerably. He was a noncombatant (having been crippled by poliomyelitis from an early age), but he saw the effects of the war upon his homeland and was deeply affected by the news of the fighting and its progress. The stories which he wrote during the period vacillate between two perspectives — one clinical and emotionless, describing horrifying events in a flat, journalistic tone which exaggerates their horrific qualities by understatement; the other an extravagant, almost lyrical visionary perspective not unlike that of Arthur Machen's famous wartime story "The Bowmen." The former mood is best represented by "Young Strickland's Career," in which a youth's precognitions are dismissed as false because they seem to foresee an impossibly arid landscape, which turns out to be the battlefield where he is ultimately killed. The latter is most straightforwardly developed in "Enlargement," in which an air raid provides the milieu for a cosmic vision. The same period produced "A Negligible Experiment," in which scientists discover that Earth is about to be destroyed by a cosmic disaster, and take this as proof that mankind was merely one of God's negligible and fruitless experiments.

In the first of Beresford's speculative novels of the World War II period, *What Dreams May Come* . . ., the author was working very much in the visionary mode. A conscientious objector working with the fire service during the blitz is concussed by a bomb. While his body lies comatose, his mind is projected into the Utopian world of Oion, where all is harmony. The inhabitants have mental powers which give them complete control of their environment, and they have adopted a philosophy of collective responsibility which perceives their society as One Mind and One Body. The book is, however, essentially a despairing one. The hero returns, altered in body and mind, and takes up a messianic career in the hope of communicating his dream of perfection. He makes but a single convert, a soldier whose consequent refusal to fight leads to the hero's imprisonment for incitement to desertion. The hero's body dies in jail, leaving his spirit to go, alone, to Oion.

A Common Enemy functions in the other mode: it is a conventional disaster story in which much of Western Europe is destroyed by a geological upheaval, and the survivors have to reconstitute their society. It is a very British work, embodying the notion that if only society could be taken by the scruff of the neck and given a good shaking it might wake up and invest wholeheartedly in middle-class decency and socialist self-renewal.

The Riddle of the Tower is a more contemplative work than either of its predecessors. Like *A Common Enemy*, it has a journalistic tone, but adds to this tone the bleakness and casual treatment of terrible events which characterized "Young Strickland's Career" and "A Negligible Experiment."

The central character of the novel is Mr. Begbie, a publisher disillusioned with the habits of modern civilization. The reader first sees him in a meeting of a committee formed to organize relief for some of the victims of the war, and finds him depressed by the committee's ability to make even the simplest of decisions difficult and time-consuming by a ponderous preoccupation with procedural protocol. His fellows seem to him to be blinded to the reality of war and life, doggedly reducing all their concerns to a level of calculated triviality, obsessed by routines. This idle thinking is given a more coherent philosophical shape by the author Detmold, who wants Begbie to publish a book on *Automatism*, whose basic claim is that human nature includes a negativistic desire, based on a craving for submission to authority, to surrender the prerogatives of decision-making to any set of rules which will free it from the need to think. Only thus, claims Detmold, can human history be understood and the success of various religious and political ideologies be explained.

Like David Shillingford in *What Dreams May Come* . . ., Begbie is then concussed by a bomb, and his consciousness is set free to roam through time to consider the implications of Detmold's theory. In the distant past — "The Time of the Choice" — he follows the fortunes of a Utopian island state whose social order begins to decay as a result of its intercourse with the outer world and subsequent cultural pollution, stemming from the activities of its own "missionaries." He sees this "thought-experiment" wiped out in the end by a natural catastrophe, just as Plato scrubbed out his own thought-experiment in social philosophy, Atlantis, by sinking it beneath the waves. The significance of the fact that Begbie, unlike Shillingford, finds his Utopia in the past rather than the future, is soon revealed.

Begbie's disembodied viewpoint now goes forward in time to witness the ultimate human world which is implied in Detmold's philosophy and supported by the logic of the "choice" made in the past by those who forsook their island Utopia. He watches the development of a uniform, regimented state in which individuals become slowly more subject to the will of the group. Human society evolves by degrees into a hive-society analogous to a termitary, ruled by a Queen. The most striking thing about this society is its resemblance to Oion, for here too there is One Mind and One Body, and all is harmony.

In depicting this horrific future of ultimate Automatism, Beresford tries hard to maintain political neutrality. He is emphatic in his insistence that this world is not the consequence of any political decisions; it is neither the ultimate extension of Fascism or of socialism, but rather the ultimate implication of the mere existence of any such political ideologies. Logically, religious ideologies also ought to be drawn into the same vortex of nihilistic criticism, but here the authors relent slightly — or at least hesitate. When Begbie returns to his everyday life in the present, his reflections on what he has seen take the form, in part, of a defense of Christian ideals. Beresford's previous work betrays a continual uncertainty about matters of faith, but he was frequently waspish in his condemnation of Christian bigotry, and his novel of religious conversion, *All or Nothing*, deals with a rather more generalized religious inspiration. It may well be, therefore, that this retreat from total pessimism can be attributed to the influence of Esme Wynne-Tyson (the ethical sickliness of their postwar novel *The Gift* provides further support for this thesis).

When Begbie's explorations of past and future are complete he must take up the threads of his ordinary life again, committees and all. This return to mundane problems is actually a more effective conclusion than the escapist conclusion of *What Dreams May Come* . . ., for it serves to emphasize what the earlier novel forgot: that it is the present, not the past or the future, which is really under consideration, and that the visions are really important only insofar as they cast new light upon its affairs.

The heart of the argument put forward in *The Riddle of the Tower* is the way it fuses the Utopian and dystopian images of future society, submerging political affiliations into the theory of Automatism and projecting the "perfect" society back into a long-lost primitive Eden. Begbie notes this in his casual, yet oddly scrupulous fashion, making the argument seem so ordinary as to be practically self-evident. Nevertheless, the story is not simply a product of despair, for it remains, as its title claims, essentially a riddle: it asks why the world is the way it is, and challenges the reader to find a solution.

As a writer of speculative fiction John Beresford worked in the shadow of H. G. Wells, whom he greatly admired and whose ideas he often seemed to echo. His point of view, however, was markedly different from that of Wells — his was the attitude of a watcher, not of an actor; he was never strident and never satirical. While Wells was an extrovert, Beresford was very much an introvert. *What Dreams May Come* . . . is much more mystical than any of Wells's Utopian novels, and though *A Common Enemy* is entirely Wellsian in its central assumption, it is far more parochial than *The World Set Free*. The Wellsian work with which *The Riddle of the Tower* most invites comparison is, of course, *Mind at the End of Its Tether*, the final agonized expression of the elder writer's despair. Both works exhibit a deep pessimism (though Beresford's is moderated somewhat) but there is a striking contrast between the visions of the future which illustrate and rationalize their pessimistic claims. Wells foresees mankind perishing in the Darwinian struggle for existence, condemned to extinction by his determined unfitness to survive. Beresford, on the contrary, sees man surviving, and finds his ultimate defeat precisely in the fact of that survival, since its cost is the loss of his humanity.

The irony is that man, in *The Riddle of the Tower*, loses the struggle for existence precisely by winning it, by becoming well-organized and awesomely efficient — the mirror-image of the alien hive-species which Wells, in *The First Men in the Moon*, designed as the paradigm of a Darwinistically fit society.

Brian Stableford

THE RIM OF MORNING

Author: William Sloane (1906-1974)
First book publications: The Edge of Running Water (1937); *To Walk the Night* (1939)
Type of work: Novels
Time: The 1930's
Locale: Maine, Long Island, and the American Southwest

Two novels, the first dealing with the efforts of a physicist to construct a machine to contact the spirit of his late wife, and the second investigating the effects of one woman, Selena, on the lives of three men

> *Principal characters:*
> **The Edge of Running Water**
> JULIAN BLAIR, a research scientist
> MRS. WALTERS, a medium, his assistant
> ANNE, sister of Julian's late wife, Helen
> RICHARD SAYLES, the narrator, a professor of psychology, Julian's friend
> ELORA MARCY, Julian's part-time housekeeper
> SETH MARCY, her husband
> DAN HOSKINS, the sheriff
>
> **To Walk the Night**
> PROFESSOR LENORMAND, a professor of celestial mechanics
> JERRY LISTER, a former student of LeNormand
> BERKELEY JONES, his friend
> SELENA LENORMAND, LeNormand's widow, later Jerry's wife
> DR. LISTER, Jerry's father
> ALAN PARSONS, police investigator of LeNormand's death
> GRACE JONES, Berkeley's mother

William Sloane is best known as a successful and innovative publisher, the founder of a distinguished publishing house which bears his name, and teacher of creative writing at the Breadloaf Writers Conference. Very early in his career, shortly after his graduation from Princeton in 1929, Sloane wrote two novels which today can be classified as "science fiction." Both works achieved only a modicum of success when they were published in limited editions prior to World War II, but in 1964, under the title of *The Rim of Morning* (which apparently has nothing to do with the contents of either book), they were brought back into print again after a lapse of decades. Although generally ignored by the science fiction fraternity (they are not even mentioned in Brian Aldiss' *Billion Year Spree*) these two novels have now acquired a small but vociferous following who maintain that in many ways the books are early but excellent exemplars of the science fiction idiom. Even forty years after their original publication, they have a charming quality, a grace of style, and a carefully constructed aura of horror and terror that make them well worth reading, even by an audience that might have come to expect more sophisticated plot devices or characterizations.

Both novels are from the "Had I But Known" or "There Are Some Questions Better Never Asked" school of writing. The central problem of each is the question of the Unknown, the unspoken, unseen, lurking Horror that it is better not to investigate. As such, they belong to the great American gothic tradition, evoking reminiscences of such writers as Melville, Hawthorne, or Sloane's contemporary, H. P. Lovecraft. Sloane has written what Hawthorne would have called "romances," with their wildness, their tendency to plunge into the underside of consciousness, and their implicit or explicit warning against tampering too much with the powers of darkness.

Both novels accomplish their aim well, and more than one reader has regretted that Sloane busied himself more with the problems of publication of the works of others than with his own creative writing career. While these novels are successful in the limited terms Sloane sets out for them, they nonetheless show some obvious earmarks of immature craftsmanship and technique. Sloane depends so much on the Unknown with a capital "U" to carry his theme of mystery and terror that when the unknown is finally revealed it seems to lack the power of evoking real empathy on the part of the reader.

The Edge of Running Water purports to be a message written in the form of a novel to some scientists who might attempt to duplicate the experiments vaguely described in the book. Do not attempt to reach the spirits of the dead by creating a machine to bridge the gap with the Unknown, says the narrator, a professor of psychology. "But this one thing (contacting the spirits of the dead) is best left untouched. It rips the fabric of human existence from throat to hem and leaves us naked to a wind as cold as the space between the stars."

Julian Blair, described as an "electrophysicist," has suffered the loss of his beloved wife, Helen. He leaves his teaching career to concentrate on building a machine which will enable him to reach her, to communicate with her. He has established his laboratory in a remote, antique deserted house on the side of a river in a Maine estuary. An ostensibly authentic medium, Mrs. Walters, is cooperating in Julian's experiments. Richard Sayles, a former student of Blair, has conducted some psychological experiments on brain-wave emanations and is called upon by Blair to provide some help in the experiments. Helen's sister Anne is also visiting the remote house, and Sayles, who was also in love with Helen before her death, now gradually falls in love with Anne. Anne and Sayles attempt to dissuade Julian, who now has become almost the archetypal "mad scientist." During the experiments the housekeeper, Mrs. Elora Marcy, is accidentally killed, and in a final attempt Julian disappears into a black vortex created by the machine. The narrator, Sayles, tells the story so that other researchers will not attempt to duplicate Julian's machine or his experiment.

Such a short commentary cannot suggest the skill with which Sloane weaves together the disparate elements of his plot. His creation of the atmosphere of the insular New England town is well done, its very strangeness and parochialism contributing a significant share to the darkness of the novel. Sloane also utilizes some of the elements of the mystery novel or detective story as well. How Mrs. Marcy died and how her death was made to seem merely a tragic accident puzzles the reader, although Sloane, like any good detective story writer, gives enough clues.

Characterization in the novel is slight, but most of the major characters are at least believable, even if they lack significant depth. Julian is a man obsessed not only by his experiments but also by the overpowering love he felt for his wife and his pain over her early death from pneumonia. Mrs. Walters, stolid, powerful, also obsessed with her abilities to help "pierce the veil between life and death," is as reprehensible a person as one might want to meet in fiction, to say nothing of science fiction. Anne and the narrator seem little more than convenient foils for Julian and Mrs. Walters, and Sloane wisely does not let their growing love story get in the way of the plot itself.

In the end, if we are not quite convinced that the "whirling gulf of blackness," as the vortex created by the machine is described, is a "breach in the whole of life," we are quite satisfied by the novel. If Sloane asks a bit more suspension of disbelief than some readers are willing to give, the horror of the novel is still gripping enough for most.

Sloane, of course, is not the only writer who faced the difficulty of describing the indescribable. Lovecraft, to cite only one example, too often depended on exotic vocabulary — "oozing ichor" — or accretions to a mythos he himself created — Chthulu and *The Necronomicon*, for example — to help break down his reader's resistance. Sloane, for his part, works by understatement rather than overstatement and is generally successful in his attempt.

The Edge of Running Water was followed within a few years by *To Walk the Night*. Once more we have a similar problem and a similar technique. The first-person narrator this time is Berkeley M. Jones, close friend and college classmate of Jerry Lister. Lister has committed suicide in his remote desert hideaway, and Jones, a witness to his death, relates the story of his visit to Jerry and his wife Selena, to Dr. Lister, Jerry's father. The entire narrative, in fact, is a summary of the last years, months, and days of the relationship between Jerry, his wife, and Jones. At the heart of the narrative recurs the question of Selena. Who is she? What is she? Where does she come from? Is she from Earth? Or is she from purgatory (the title of the book is derived from *Hamlet*, ". . . a spirit doomed for a certain term to walk the night. . . .")?

Or perhaps Selena is from another dimension, incarnating herself briefly on this earth simply to learn as much of it as possible. The body Selena inhabits during her sojourn here seems to be that of Luella Jamison, a beautiful mentally deficient girl who disappeared from her home at the same time that Selena appeared on the university campus and married a professor of celestial mechanics, Dr. LeNormand. LeNormand dies in a mysterious accident that baffles the police, as well as Lister and Jones, who, coincidentally, witnessed LeNormand's death. Lister falls in love with Selena, marries her within a month, and goes with her to live in a remote house in the American Southwest. Throughout all of this narrative the mystery of Selena looms larger and larger. Mythologically she resembles Diana, the moon goddess which her name suggests — cold, incredibly beautiful, ultimately mysterious. Lister gradually becomes aware that Selena is a traveler from another dimension, and Sloane mixes just enough mathematical jargon to make the thesis credible. Both LeNormand and Lister, his brilliant student, have gone beyond Minkowski and proved the "serial nature of time." Selena, then, may be either from the fourth dimension, from some future time, or from some other location in the universe.

At the end when Jones confronts her with his own poorly understood version of what both LeNormand and Jerry understood completely, Selena says, "Did you suppose that you were alone in the enormous spaces of the universe? Do you believe that you are the ultimate product of creation? There is nothing unique about you." She admits that she "killed" both LeNormand and Jerry because they had found out the truth about her; she explains that she is a superior, but essentially emotionless, being from another world or dimension, and that they could not live with this knowledge. Just as in the earlier novel, "There Are Some Questions Better Never Asked."

At the heart of both novels, aside from the insistence on dealing with the Unknown, are the characters of women. In *The Edge of Running Water* the most important person, in a way, is Helen, Julian's late wife. She is never seen on stage, of course, but her presence dominates Julian and, consequently, the actions of the novel. To a lesser extent we have the enigmatic, powerful figure of Mrs. Walters, the cold, calculating medium, who also exercises a dominant influence on the book. Combine the two figures of Helen and Mrs. Walters, add the inherent brilliance of a supergenius with total lack of emotions, and you have the character of Selena in the second book: beautiful, awful, cold.

Sloane, however, is not content simply to make Selena an unknowable, inhuman figure. He rather skillfully combines these elements with allusions to the myth of the little mermaid. In fact, the only time in the entire novel that Selena shows even a trace of human emotion occurs when she reads this myth and tears are detected in her eyes. She is an inhuman being, then, who almost breaks through to human consciousness as a result of perceiving, albeit dimly, the human concept of love.

Both books also seem to reflect something of the spirit of pre-World War II America. There are excellent, evocative description of Pullman rides; a college football game with "off-tackle slants," hip-pocket flasks and only eleven men playing an entire game. There are references to tea-dancing, bridge games, recalcitrant sheriffs, and other reminders of a vanished age. The reprint edition has attempted to update the two books with a reference to an "atomic bomb" or other post-World War II paraphernalia, but these suggestions of modernity seem gratuitous and unnecessary. Part of the charm of both novels, in fact, lies in their precise evocation of another time, another place, another era.

What makes these novels science fiction? They are curiously leisurely books, redolent with a nostalgia for a forgotten age when an individual scientist could putter about in his home laboratory and design a breakthrough invention, and as such both seem quite dated. Yet even with our alleged intellectual sophistication and superiority, we can appreciate Sloane's books as examples of the scientific romance, to use H. G. Wells's term. They do not falsify reality or the problems of the human heart. Rather, they enable the reader not only to share another, perhaps lost, reality, but also, paradoxically, to ask some searching questions about contemporary scientific research that he might not otherwise ask. Simply because we can conceive of something — say a cobalt bomb — should we construct one? Are there, in reality, Some Questions Better Never Asked? Sloane provides no easy answers for his readers, but he has at least raised some vital questions and that has always been a function of science fiction.

Willis E. McNelly

Sources for Further Study

Reviews:

New York Herald Tribune Book Review. October 10, 1954, p. 12.
Saturday Review. XXXVII, December 4, 1954, p. 54.
Springfield Republican. January 9, 1955, p. 7C.

THE RIM WORLDS SERIES

Author: A[rthur] Bertram Chandler (1912-   )
First book publications: 1961-1978
Type of work: Novels and short stories
Time: At least a century, perhaps several, in the future
Locale: Rim Stars on the frontiers of galactic civilization

A space opera set at the rim of the Galaxy, principally the adventures of John Grimes from the start of his career until his rise to flag rank

During World War II, John W. Campbell, Jr., observed to a fan that wartime duties prevented many of his regular writers from achieving their normal output, and invited the fan to submit something to *Astounding Science Fiction*. The fan was A. Bertram Chandler, whose North Atlantic convoy duties for Great Britain's Merchant Marine interspersed leisure and danger. Chandler accepted the invitation, and the naval officer became a prolific writer of short stories over the next ten years. But times were changing in publishing. In the middle of 1957, the market for science fiction short stories was more than a score of magazines in America, not to mention ones in Britain and Canada. By end of 1961, that number had shrunk to six. Chandler noted the collapse of the market and turned to longer works for the swelling field of original paperbacks; out of that change came the Rim Worlds Series.

The Rim Worlds series consists of at least twenty novels and collections of short stories produced between 1961 and the present. If the Milky Way is a locale, then Chandler's stories all have the same locale. Many of them, however, are located in a more restricted space, in the area called the Rim, in which are situated the lonely stars along the outer edge of one of the spiral arms bordering on intergalactic space.

Despite the vastness of the locale, these stories have a common core of characters. For example, Derek Calver, the central figure of *The Rim of Space* (1961) and *The Ship from Outside* (1963), has been the lover of Sonya Verrill, who in later novels becomes the wife of John Grimes, hero of at least eleven of the novels and collections in the Rim Worlds series.

Publisher's Weekly once called Grimes science fiction's answer to Horatio Hornblower; the debt to C. S. Forester's Napoleonic-era hero is clear and conscious on Chandler's part, as he admits in an autobiographical essay, "Around the World in 23,741 Days" in *Algol* (Spring, 1978). After Grimes was established as a character, Chandler followed Forester's practice and began to relate the story of Grimes's early career. Those tales appear in *The Road to the Rim* (1967), dedicated to "Admiral Lord Hornblower, R.N."

The Rim Worlds series is not, however, only Hornblower in space: Chandler borrows freely from other figures in British naval history and from his own experiences. As illustration, the mutiny which occurs in *The Big Black Mark* (1975), a novel dedicated to William Bligh, resembles to some extent that of *Mutiny on the Bounty*. And in part, Chandler's own career and personality have shaped Grimes. Chandler was born in Britain; Grimes is born on Earth and begins his service for the Earth-centered Interstellar Federation. Just as Chandler left the British merchant marine, took a job with an Australian shipping line, and made a home in Sydney, so does Grimes leave the Federation's employ and sign on with the Rim Runners, a shipping company of the Rim Worlds Confederacy, making his home on one of their faraway planets. Chandler explains that the idea for the Rim Worlds occurred to him while in service for a line operating between Melbourne and the West Coast of Tasmania. If Tasmania is not quite as romantic and remote as the Rim, it will do for now.

From time to time, references to World War II convoy duty turn up in the stories. Both *The Way Back* (1968) and *To Keep the Ship* (1978) cite peculiarities in naval regulations and maritime law illustrated by incidents in the North Atlantic convoys. Even slang terms occur: the common term for "marine" in the series is *pongo*, a piece of early twentieth century naval slang. Both Grimes and Chandler smoke pipes, both have hearty appetites. When Chandler became captain of his own ship, Grimes became Commodore in the Rim Worlds Navy. It is even tempting to see the readiness of the Rim Worlds' characters to shed their clothes as a reflection of Chandler's avocation of nudism.

Besides using his own experience, Chandler frequently alludes to contemporary literature. Thus, for example, a constellation in *To Keep the Ship* is named "The Hobbit"; in *The Rim Gods* (1968), Grimes complains that he is getting too old for James Bond adventures; and in *The Road to the Rim*, a woman succumbing to Grimes's charm mutters "wotthehell, wotthehell, . . . toujours gai," in the words of mehitabel the cat, a character from "archy and mehitabel," by the American humorist, Don Marquis. References to science fiction are found in Grimes's recollection of James Blish's *Cities in Flight* (1970) and H. G. Wells's "Vision of Judgment" and *The Island of Doctor Moreau*, among others. In the early Grimes stories, messages between faster-than-light ships are sent by telepathy, a method first seen in Robert A. Heinlein's *Time for the Stars* (1956); in *The Dark Dimensions* (1971), Chandler even borrows a character (with permission) — Sir Dominic Flandry, a creation of Poul Anderson.

As a writer, Chandler has both virtues and vices. His locales are well-realized, and scenes on board spaceships, a major part of the setting in each story, sound authentic. The sense of a concrete reality is strengthened by Chandler's use of technology; far from standing still, the art of space navigation improves in hardware and technique. Thus, the Carlotti transmitter makes telepathic communication obsolete; the Mass Proximity Indicator makes faster-than-light travel safer; captains learn more about the use of their Mannschenn Drive, which allows them to circumvent the limiting speed of light.

Chandler's knowledge of the military chain of command, the frustrations it produces, and the subterfuges it inspires, spills over into and enriches Grimes's climb up the ladder of rank. His maritime experience sparks the many scenes of merchant life.

Since the stories are based on the life of a single character, Chandler's plots are bound to be episodic rather than tidily structured, and these episodes may not fit comfortably into a novel-length work; thus we find that *The Hard Way Up*, for instance, consists of seven stories, while at the other extreme, the plot set in motion in *The Dark Dimensions* is not resolved until the conclusion of *The Way Back*. But an episodic plot is not in itself either good or bad; if it is well-motivated, plausible, and fast-moving (as Chandler's are), it will suffice.

Plot and setting, then, are Chandler's strengths; his weaknesses are characterization and dialogue. John Grimes seems likable, if a little colorless, always meaning well, behaving lawfully and with good intentions. His diffidence and uncertainty are not uncommon in youth. Yet his superiors are almost always surly and overbearing. The older Grimes is easygoing and tolerant, yet now his juniors are frequently surly and overbearing. One wonders why he never finds either mentor or disciple. Supposed to be both competent and lucky, he faces mutiny, insubordination, mechanical breakdown, shipwreck, from which he must extricate himself by his wits. It becomes clear after several stories that Chandler uses characterization only to get the plot started: Grimes must be a nebbish at the beginning of a story; if he were as cool and crafty then as he later becomes, he would never get into such fixes in the first place.

Characters tend to be stereotypes. Germans, who tend to be tall and blond, are either good or bad: the good ones are regimented, efficient, and fanatically loyal; the bad ones are regimented, efficient, and absolutely treacherous. Australians are slangy, impatient with authority, and casual to the point of caricature. An Irish psionic officer is a sentimental drunk who speaks in a brogue straight from vaudeville. But one and all, they do not worry too much about Grimes.

Despite his later rank and fame, Grimes is plagued by people of imperial demeanor even when he is not subordinate to them, and sometimes the plot suffers as a result. In *The Rim Gods*, Grimes, as Rim Runners Astronautical Superintendent, is sent to a backwater planet to resolve crew problems on one of the company's ships. He removes a malcontent officer, who at once joins a dangerous insurgent group on the planet, threatening relations between the local government and the Rim Confederacy. The Rim Worlds ambassador orders Grimes, a high corporate official and a commodore in the Naval Reserve, to pursue and apprehend the officer personally. Grimes complies, much against his will. The plot, then, depends on the reader's willingness to believe that the ambassador to, say, Costa Rica, can compel either a private citizen or a naval officer equal in rank to a brigadier general to undertake a hazardous mission for which neither his training nor his inclination suits him.

Nor are women in the stories strongly differentiated. Grimes's two loves over his long career, Margaret Lazenby and Sonya Verrill, are almost interchangeable. In *The Dark Dimensions*, two John Grimeses from alternate universes meet; in the universe of the series, Grimes has married Sonya, and in the other has married Margaret. Both women are present, and they are almost mirror images, reacting alike, saying the same things, holding exactly similar duties and positions. Having two women with him is no new situation for Grimes: if men seem to dislike him immediately without apparent reason, women cannot keep their hands off him, again without apparent reason. The omnipresence of luscious women of varying ages, and Grimes's constant willingness, supply the series with many strongly erotic, even mildly pornographic scenes. (*The Dark Dimensions* may be the only novel in which a man cuckolds himself.)

But whatever his problems with characterization, Chandler's greatest difficulty is with the related task of creating dialogue for his figures. His chief drawback within this area is the repetitious use of stock phrases, so frequently, in fact, that were the names of the characters disguised, one could identify a novel by Chandler from a few speeches.

The stock phrases are generally slang, and again, nothing is wrong with the use of slang, *per se*. In the far future time of the series, we would expect some new words and phrases to have developed, as indeed some have. An influential person, in today's naval slang, "draws a lot of water"; in Chandler's novels, he "piles on the G's." This change is to be expected; it shows creativity on the author's part, and gives solidity to the make-believe world in which the characters move. But most of the shoptalk of the characters is exactly that of today, used heavily and without regard to whether the character would indeed employ it. In Chandler's novels, to brief someone is always "to put him in the picture." The expression is used by Sonya Verril (in *The Way Back*); by Commander Delamere of the Federation Survey Service (in *The Big Black Mark*); by Admiral Kravitz of the Rim Worlds Navy, by Grimes himself, and by Mr. Smith, a civilian from another planet in *The Dark Dimensions*; by a religious fanatic in one story and by the High Priest of the planet Tharn in another in *The Rim Gods*; by Commander Damien of the Survey Service and even by a giant intelligent insect, a Shaara Queen (*The Hard Way Up*).

Even harder to overlook is Chandler's tendency to lose sight of a character's reaction to a catch-phrase. In *The Road to the Rim*, Ensign Grimes is invited to make himself at home when a merchant captain uses the words "Spit on the mat and call the cat a bastard — this is Liberty Hall." Later in his career, Grimes uses the expression himself, and hears it from other captains both military and civilian. Yet in *The Rim Gods*, Grimes hears the expression from a scientist and we are told that it had never failed to annoy him. And in *The Dark Dimensions*, he uses it again.

In the final consideration, Chandler's novels will most probably appeal to those who take a liking to John Grimes, enjoying the progress of his adventures. Although the books have been steady sellers, they have received little or no serious attention; perhaps the most apt comparison is to television: in Rim Worlds, we have one of science fiction's longest-running series.

Walter E. Meyers

Sources for Further Study

Reviews:

Catch the Star Winds:

Analog. LXXXV, April, 1970, p. 169.

SF Commentary. VIII, January, 1970, p. 38.

The Deep Reaches of Space:

New Worlds. CXLI, April, 1964, p. 125.

Rim of Space:

Amazing Stories. XXXV, October, 1961, p. 135.

Analog. LXVIII, November, 1961, pp. 165-166 and LXX, December, 1962, pp. 155-156.

Galaxy. XX, December, 1961, pp. 145-146.

Rim Gods:

Luna Monthly. VII, December, 1969, p. 24.

RING AROUND THE SUN

Author: Clifford D. Simak (1904-   )
First book publication: 1953
Type of work: Novel
Time: 1977
Locale: New York State, somewhere in the Midwest, and Earth Number Two

The story of a plot by a group of paternalistic mutants to rescue mankind from its existential plight

> *Principal characters:*
> JAY VICKERS, a writer
> ANN CARTER, his agent
> HORTON FLANDERS, an old man
> GEORGE CRAWFORD, a representative of North American Research

Ring Around the Sun first appeared as a *Galaxy* serial, following up the classic *Time and Again*, which the same magazine had run as *Time Quarry* two years earlier. The novel is archetypal Simak, redolent with nostalgia for childhood and folksy rural life, considering contemporary city life as a kind of existential blight from which modern man must somehow be saved. In Simak's postwar work there are three main agents who feature as hopeful symbols of this possible salvation: robots, aliens, and superhumans. *Ring Around the Sun* features the third of these — though, like virtually all his saviors, they remain enigmatic and mostly operate outside the immediate framework of the story, which focuses on the central character's discovery of their existence and reconciliation to his role in their scheme. The novel belongs to the postwar boom in stories about superhuman mutants who represent the future of mankind, but the way in which it develops its theme sets it apart from most other products of the boom and marks it as, first and foremost, a Simak story.

The central character of the novel is Jay Vickers, who lives a peaceful life as a writer in an outlying district of New York state. At the beginning of the book we find him planning to go into New York City, whence he has been summoned by his agent Ann Carter, who wants him to meet a man named Crawford. Vickers potters around before setting off to the city, exchanging conversation with several of his neighbors. He asks the local rodent exterminator to get rid of some mice he has heard scrabbling beneath his floorboards, and calls on the local garage man to collect his car. The car, though, is not repaired, and the mechanic tells him that there is no point in fixing it. A new car has just come onto the market which never breaks down and never needs replacing. The advent of this remarkable machine, which is also absurdly cheap, follows the setting-up of "Gadget Shops" which sell everlasting domestic goods of various kinds, and the "marketing" of synthetic carbohydrates whose makers offer them free to anyone who might otherwise go hungry. Vickers contemplates these innovations while he rides on the bus into New York, and decides that they are signs of something strange happening in the world. He also listens in on a conversation between two "Pretensionists" — people who make a hobby out of pretending that they live in some past era.

The man he has to meet turns out to be a representative of a myterious agency called North American Research, apparently funded by big business interests which are worried about the threat posed by the Gadget Shops. Unless the Shops are stopped, the economy of the whole world will collapse, for their next innovation will be high-quality prefabricated homes at giveaway prices. If the Gadget Shops continue, Crawford points out, their owners will be supplying food, housing, transport, and all manner of domestic goods very cheaply, destroying the market. His organization has been unable to find out who is behind the Gadget Shops or where their factories are, and he wants Jay to join his cause as a propagandist. Jay refuses, and returns to his home.

In the evening, Jay has a curious conversation with his aged neighbor, Horton Flanders, who puts before him the proposition that some external force has been interfering in human affairs for some time, acting to prevent war. Jay is disturbed by this suggestion, and more so when he hears again the scrabbling which he had thought to be mice. Now, knowing that there are no mice in the house, he tracks down the sound and manages to destroy a tiny machine which appears to have been keeping him under surveillance. He goes in search of Flanders hoping to discuss the new development, but the old man has disappeared entirely, leaving a note for Jay telling him not to worry and suggesting that Jay visit the scenes of his childhood.

Jay's sense of disquiet grows worse when he remembers that he rode into New York with an empty seat beside him — a fact which suddenly seems extremely significant. *Always*, when he has ridden on buses, people have shown a considerable reluctance to take the seat beside him, and throughout his life people have seemed inclined to keep him at arm's length. Before he can discover the significance of this, however, he is forced to flee his home because of a mob which is convinced that he has murdered Horton Flanders. Having nowhere else to go, he follows Flanders' advice and returns to his hometown, somewhere in the Midwest.

He visits his old home, and finds a childhood toy — a spinning top — which brings back curious memories. He remembers watching the top spin and wondering where the stripes "disappeared" to as they spread out from the center to the rim. Once, he remembers, he "followed" the stripes into an "enchanted fairyland." This is not the only memory of enchantment which he has, for he also remembers walking in a "magic valley" with a girl named Kathleen Preston, whom he once loved, but who was sent away when he was eighteen. He visits the Preston house, too, but finds it a ruin.

Jay phones Ann to tell her what has happened, and repaints the spinning top with the intention of repeating his childhood experiment in following the stripes into fairyland. However, Crawford has tapped Ann's phone and visits Jay in his hotel to tell him that all-out war is about to be launched by his organization, and by international allies against a race of mutants who are masterminding the plot to destroy the world's economy. When Jay asks what it all has to do with him, Crawford explains that Jay is one of two known mutants.

Jay jumps to the conclusion that the other mutant known to Crawford is Ann, and he sets off in a Forever car to warn her, though a hunch tells him he is wrong to do so. The Forever car delivers him into trouble — like all products of the Gadget Shops it becomes the target of a destructive mob when the news of the mutant conspiracy breaks. Clutching the top, Jay runs from the mob, and when cornered he spins it and tries to follow the stripes as they spin right out of the world. He succeeds, and lands on the soil of an alternate Earth, where America seems still to be virgin forest, and where there is no sign of human habitation. He sets off on foot toward the Midwest, heading for the magic valleys of his youth, and after many days of traveling he discovers a house standing on the spot where, on the original Earth, the Preston house lies derelict. Nearby is a factory where robots turn out the goods which are imported to Earth Number One by the operators of the Gadget Shops. In the house he overhears a conversation in which Horton Flanders is talking about him. From Flanders' remarks Jay gathers that he is not human, but is in fact an android created by the mutants to be one of their agents on Earth, and that his experiences of the last few weeks have been engineered by the mutants in order to bring him to awareness of his status.

Horrified by this discovery, Jay flees into the wilderness, eventually to be taken in by a farmer relocated on this second Earth by the mutants. The farmer explains to him the scope and purpose of the mutants' plan. A whole sequence of alternate Earths is available, all empty of mankind, which can be used to return Earth's population to a healthy and pastoral life-style away from the sickness of cities and civilization and technology, which have gotten out of hand. Jay is rapidly convinced of the mutants' benevolence and of the necessity of their actions.

The work of the mutants was greater than the mere gadgetry they would like it to appear, something greater than Forever cars and everlasting razor blades and synthetic carbohydrates. Their work was the rescue and re-establishment of the race. . . .

Jay returns to Flanders to take up his own role in the plan. Flanders explains that he has the personality of a real person which has had to be "decanted" into a series of android bodies in order to multiply and advance its special talent — a talent for "hunches." Flanders and Jay are two of these bodies, but Flanders refuses to say whose is the third. Jay's mission is to thwart Crawford, and his reward will be to return to his eighteen-year-old body and then to be reunited with Kathleen Preston. Jay has his doubts about the merits of this promise, but he sets in motion a plan to oppose Crawford's antimutant campaign by sending the relocated farmers back to Earth to spread the good news about the unspoiled Earth waiting for those with the will to escape. The Pretensionists, already desperate escapists from their arid reality, are easily swayed to the new cause. Meanwhile, Jay reasons that Crawford and his compatriots, the most successful men in America, must be mutants themselves, making unconscious use of their latent talents. He confronts them all, and persuades them to watch a film of a spinning top, whose stripes seem to be vanishing into nowhere. One by one, the captains of industry vanish too, pulled by the lure of the stripes into fairyland. Jay discovers that the third avatar of his original personality is Crawford, and that Ann Carter (whom he has loved as an adult) is an android version of Kathleen Preston, now to be redeemed and reunited with her teenage lover.

Ring Around the Sun is, like several of Simak's later novels, rather sickly in its more sentimental moments and rather brazen in its calculated naïveté. Its representation of modern man as a child playing with technological toys too advanced for him, who has to be taken in hand by a kindly adult presence who will lead him safely to a Rousseauesque Promised Land, is not one which will endear itself to all readers. The story's message and moral are basically imitations of the voice of a gentle and kindly parent reassuring a child that all will be well as long as the child is good and quiet and trusting. It is a message that some of the book's readers will undoubtedly find insulting, and for all its benevolence it is basically patronizing.

The plot of the novel is full of logical absurdities. Its only semblance of coherence comes from the fact that the various components of the ideative edifice are revealed to Jay Vickers one by one, so that he barely catches a glimpse of the whole before having to tie up the ends of the plot in a rather absurd and cursory fashion. The reader who looks back over the revealed pattern to ask why the mutants have done all that they are supposed to have done, and how the moves they have made add up to any kind of sensible strategy, will find great difficulty in coming up with answers. The novel draws its strength entirely from the emotional continuity provided by the confused and anxious hero as he stumbles through his series of upsetting revelations until, immediately after the climactic discovery of his unhumanity, he receives the blessed relief of enlightenment. All these faults, however, cannot detract from the success which *Ring Around the Sun* enjoyed in its own day — a success attributable to the fact that its implicit mythology was so dramatically pertinent to the real anxieties of its day, when many people did come to feel that technology had gotten out of hand, that modern city life was the cause of alienation and unhappiness, and that some kind of existential salvation was devoutly to be desired. If the book retains its strength today, it is because we have not altogether recovered from that kind of feeling.

Brian Stableford

Sources for Further Study

Reviews:

Analog. LIII, April, 1954, p. 146.

Galaxy. VII, October, 1953, pp. 119-120 and IX, November, 1954, pp. 121-122.

Imagination Science Fiction. IV, November, 1953, p. 144.

Magazine of Fantasy and Science Fiction. XII, April 1957, p. 87.

New York Herald Tribune Book Review. May 17, 1953, p. 31.

New York Times. June 14, 1953, p. 13.

Worlds of If. IX, September, 1959, pp. 97-98.

RINGWORLD

Author: Larry Niven (1938-   )
First book publication: 1970
Type of work: Novel
Time: Approximately one thousand years in the future
Locale: "Ringworld," a huge artificial ring two hundred light years from Earth

Four space travelers journey to, and explore the surface of, Ringworld, an artificial ring approximately three million times the size of Earth

> *Principal characters:*
> LOUIS WU, a two-hundred-year-old Earthman of mixed human ancestry
> NESSUS, a Pierson's puppeteer
> SPEAKER-TO-ANIMALS, a young kzin
> TEELA BROWN, a twenty-year-old Earthwoman
> PRILL (HALROPRILLER HOTRUFAN), a bald woman at least fifteen hundred years old
> SEEKER, a native of the Ringworld

By 1970, "hard" science fiction had become passé, but Larry Niven provided the exception to prove the rule. His *Ringworld* is an incredible, sometimes hilarious, and thoroughly entertaining *tour de force*.

The four main characters — Louis, Nessus, Speaker, and Teela — are in themselves interesting and believable enough, but their chief function is to act and react in such ways that the Ringworld and a few other bits of Niven's hardware become familiar enough to be accepted as probable. The other two, Prill and Seeker, are present to give the reader a perspective on the Ringworld that only native beings can; besides, each is needed for the conclusion of the plot. The plot exists merely to get the main characters on and off the Ringworld, and to provide a series of incidents each of which makes the hard science fiction explanations integral parts of the novel and plain imaginative fun.

The plot is utterly simple. Nessus chooses three other persons to travel with him to the Ringworld (though he says nothing about the place itself and admits only that it is about two hundred light years from Earth); in return for their part of the expedition, the humans and the kzin will get a working model — and detailed plans for constructing more — of an incredibly faster-than-light vehicle. The four travel to Nessus' destination, crash on its inner, habitable surface, explore by traveling about 300,000 miles, meet the two other major characters, and finally succeed in escaping from the Ringworld. More accurately, the four participate in the adventure through the exploration stage, then Teela decides to remain with Seeker, and Prill decides to leave with the other three.

There is, however, some background information that lends interest and credibility to the plot. The action takes place roughly a thousand years from now. For about two hundred years, there has been peace between the kzinti and the Earth-type humans; during those two centuries, the Earth's population has been controlled in part by means of a birthright lottery (the winners are allowed to have children), and the kzinti have grown markedly less aggressive. Pierson's puppeteers, an intelligent race known for its main occupation of trading, its refusal to reveal the whereabouts of its home world, and its members' conspicuous cowardice, have all but disappeared from Known Space during the same two centuries. That is no coincidence: Nessus himself was the one who engineered the birthright lottery system, and few puppeteers wanted to be around when and if the humans discovered that they were being bred, like laboratory animals, for the genetic characteristic of luck. Nor is it a coincidence that the kzinti-human wars occurred in the manner that they did, for in allowing them to continue the puppeteers were helping nature to de-select the most aggressive of the kzinti.

The remote motive of the plot is this: the central core of this galaxy went nova more than ten thousand years before the temporal setting of the book, and the "explosion" of lethal subatomic particles would reach Known Space in about twenty thousand years. The puppeteers, so cautious that only the "insane" among them dared to leave the surface of their home world, had two needs: to escape the result of the supernovae before it reached them, and to find enough habitable planetary surface for their enormous population. Something like the Ringworld might answer the latter need, but because the race was so very cautious, it had set its very planets in motion — just a bit under lightspeed — in order to reach the Clouds of Magellan with a temporal margin of safety. Since no one but a crazy puppeteer — or a kzin or a man or a woman — would dare to explore the artifact called Ringworld, the crazy Nessus finds the most socialized and amiable of the kzinti, a man who has lived long enough to prove that he has excellent judgment with regard to fatal risks, and a woman with six generations of good-luck genes bred into her and takes them off to visit the Ringworld.

Louis Wu goes along because he is bored, having just celebrated his two-hundredth birthday. Speaker-to-Animals goes because it would be an absolute failure of courage not to go. And Teela Brown goes because she is on Nessus' list of lucky humans and, for the time being, she loves Louis and refuses to leave him. Nessus is there to lead the expedition, of course, but also to perform a heroic duty so that he may be granted the right to be a parent.

The four adventurers leave the solar system aboard a puppeteer-designed vessel named the *Long Shot*, which is powered by a quantum II hyperdrive that can move it along at the rate of one light year every one-and-a-quarter minutes (the best starships in use at the time take three days to travel the same distance). Though the *Long Shot* is claustrophobically cramped as regards passenger space, the humans and the kzin are assured that it is merely an experimental model and that their pay for the voyage will be a ship of the sort that will enable the two races to evacuate their planets' and colonies' populations quickly enough to escape annihilation, reach an extragalactic destination, and set up housekeeping by the time the cautious and crafty puppeteer worlds arrive.

Just before the group begins its journey, Speaker — showing at least a remnant of his fierce heritage — attempts to cut the two humans out of their share of the profit and allows Niven to introduce a behavior-modification practitioner's dream. Nessus stops Speaker with a tasp, a surgically implanted device that can be aimed as precisely as a glance and that overwhelms the pleasure center of the brain of its target. As Louis notes after the incident, only the puppeteers would use a weapon that causes its victims to feel *good*.

At the end of the *Long Shot*'s journey, the humans and the kzin discover that the "system" of the puppeteers — four planets terraformed for agriculture in addition to the home planet — is in fact a Kemplerer rosette. In theory, such a formation should be possible by putting three or more objects of equal mass in place equidistant from one another and imparting to each the same angular velocity so that they will revolve forever around the center of gravity their motion creates. In fact, no one had ever seen one; that the puppeteers had made a Kemplerer rosette in cosmic scale causes Louis to decide again to live forever (as he had once when awed by Mount Lookitthat's forty-mile-high waterfall) so that he will not miss seeing everything there is to see.

One of the richly humorous aspects of Niven's imagination is revealed by his juxtaposition of incredibly complex scientific theory and technology with utterly mundane names like the one above. Here, perhaps, lies one secret of the success of his fiction: he provides the reader with considerably more scientific detail than most hard science fiction novels did even when they were in fashion, but he knows human nature well enough to let his fictional places and artifacts bear names that frontier-type humans would be likely to give them. There is the planet We Made It, obviously the site of a successful colonizing venture. The Long Fall River is, logically, the one that has the cataract higher than any other in Known Space. The *Long Shot* is a double pun; the *Lying Bastard* — shortened to *Liar*, the spacecraft that takes the four adventurers to the Ringworld — is given its name because it is as weaponless as any puppeteer could wish yet most of its instruments, like the "flashlight" utilizing a variable-beam laser, are of the sort that have an alternative lethal practicality. "Ringworld" itself is an utterly prosaic name, yet it is perfectly accurate; and on that world are a thousand-mile-high mountain called Fist-of-God and a floating building called Heaven. Needless to say, at age two hundred, Louis did not come by his twenty-year-old's body naturally: he has been taking "boosterspice" for one hundred and thirty years. The result of Niven's nomenclature is a delightful surprise; the lack of respectful terminology for his scientific wonders relieves them of a good deal of jargon and almost automatically causes his readers to feel easy with them.

The four adventurers aboard the *Liar* soon leave the puppeteers' system behind, and, coming out of hyperspace at what would be the outer limit of a star's planetary system, they see a G2 star as a brilliant point of light with a halo around it. The Ringworld is so huge that it is visible at a distance from which a star cannot yet be perceived as a disk. Louis Wu was right: it is a sight worth living two centuries to see.

The Ringworld is an artifact; it did not happen the way the rings of Saturn did — it was constructed by human, though not Terran, engineers. Its dimensions are impossible to comprehend: a million-mile-wide flat circular strip of matter, its flat side facing its sun, the Ringworld revolves around its primary about one astronomical unit out, so that a straight-line journey along its circumference would be almost 600,000,000 miles long. Its inner surface — that facing the sun — is a bit less than 600,000,000,000,000 square miles, and that much area is simply too much for one to imagine concretely; hence the necessity of *Ringworld* the novel, with its comprehensible characters and their actions, to make Niven's exciting abstract concept something that can be experienced concretely and vicariously by its readers.

Evidently, the builders of the Ringworld had not discovered any kind of hyperspatial mode of travel; limited by the speed of light, they could not colonize the planets of distant stars in order to deal with the pressures of overpopulation. But they evidently had discovered a fairly inexpensive and practical means of transmutation, so they could — and did — transform the matter of planets and asteroids and anything else they could come upon into material forms necessary to make and maintain a world that is identical with its orbit, a world with approximately three *million* times the area of Earth. The race that built the Ringworld had three basic problems (after they had taken care of gravity by spinning the ring at 770 miles-per-second, and handled the problem of atmosphere by erecting thousand-mile-high rims to keep the air from falling off the edges).

First, since the Ringworld's habitable surface always faced the sun (which is always in noonday position), the Builders had to arrange for alternating periods of light and darkness; this they did by putting "shadow squares" — rectangles a million miles wide and two-and-a-half million miles long, held in place by invisibly thin wires six million miles long — in orbit between the Ringworld and its sun, at a velocity sufficient to have night-length shadows pass over each part of the Ringworld with precise regularity. Second, because their artificial world was immense beyond imagining, the Builders needed even more energy than that caught from the sun by the Ringworld's area; this they solved by using the "shadow squares" — utterly black and thus most absorbent — to capture solar energy, which could then be beamed down to the surface in usable form. So successful were the Builders at this that they had enough energy at their disposal to make cities with buildings that floated, against gravity, in the very air. The third problem arose from the transmutation itself: once the available matter had been made into the Ringworld, there were no heavy elements left to be "natural resources"; if the great artifact malfunctioned, there would be nothing with which to repair it. And, about fifteen hundred years before Louis, Nessus, Speaker, and Teela arrive, the Ringworld had an energy-breakdown.

While the members of Nessus' expedition begin to view the interior surface of the great ring, their craft is (but for the phobic caution of puppeteer engineers) practically destroyed by still-functioning automatic laser cannon, apparently designed to prevent meteors from reaching the Ringworld's surface. Because of the *Liar*'s design, its living compartment remains intact and crashes on the Ringworld almost exactly between the world's two rims, near the foot of the Fist-of-God. So the four adventurers unload the *Lying Bastard*, mount their ingeniously designed flycycles, and set out to find some civilization. They find ruins instead.

Eventually, the luck of Teela Brown finds a city with a resident "goddess": Prill, who is persuaded by Nessus' tasp to help him and Louis and Speaker to get the *Liar* off the Ringworld. Not until they get her police station "palace" floating of its own accord and moving by the power of Nessus' flycycle do they rediscover Teela Brown. She was getting off her flycycle just as Prill's police machinery overpowered it, so she, lucky as usual, stayed outside the building until she met Seeker. Together they pursue the flying building and catch up with the others, take part in a fight with barbarian natives during which one of Nessus' heads is cut off and Speaker manages to grab the fallen piece of "shadow square" to which its incredibly thin and strong wire is attached, and then they leave the others. Seeker, given some very potent antigeriatric drug more than fourteen centuries ago, must continue his quest: to reach the base of the great arch (the other side of the Ringworld always looks like a blue arch over the flat land). Teela, who now loves the barbarian hero, decides to accompany him — and it is her luck that makes this quest her destiny, for only on the Ringworld are there dangers against which, on Earth, her good luck would have protected her; only on the Ringworld will she ever mature.

About two months later, the flying building reaches the *Liar*. Nessus, kept alive by his flycycle's first-aid kit, is put into his "autodoc" (the puppeteer builders of which had provided a couple of spare heads just in case). The others, using the wire from the "shadow square," tow the *Lying Bastard* up the slope of Fist-of-God, which, like most things even remotely connected to the luck of Teela Brown, has a fortunate aspect: the mountain is actually the scar of a moon-sized meteor, hollow at its core and thus the port of escape. As Speaker and Louis maneuver the flying building so that it will pull the *Liar* down toward them and empty space, they realize that the Ringworld, the outer side of which can stop forty percent of neutrino bombardment, is angled just so that its flat surface will prevent the major part of the galactic explosion from affecting the inner side; Teela and her hero will probably be safe forever.

This is the end of the book, but not the end of fascination with the Ringworld. As certainly as Louis and Speaker plan to return to that artifact someday, the readers of *Ringworld* are imaginatively reexploring the concepts in and the implications of Niven's verbal artifact.

Rosemarie Arbur

Sources for Further Study

Criticism:

Jameson, Frederic. "Science Fiction as Politics: Larry Niven," in *New Republic*. XXX (October, 1976), pp. 34-38. Jameson gives a discussion of Niven's work, including *Ringworld* in a political context.

Niven, Larry. "The Words of Science Fiction," in *The Craft of Science Fiction*. Edited by Reginald Bretnor. New York: Harper & Row, 1976, pp. 178-194. Niven writes on his own contributions to science fiction literature and analyzes the field generally. The book as a whole is an important work of science fiction criticism.

Reviews:

Amazing Stories. XLV, May, 1971, pp. 105-107.

Analog. LXXXVII, June, 1971, pp. 173-174.

Books and Bookmen. XVII, March, 1972, pp. 60-61.

Foundation. II, June, 1972, pp. 44-52.

Galaxy. XXXI, March, 1971, pp. 112-113.

Science Fiction Stories. XLI, September, 1971, pp. 41-43.

Worlds of If. XX, March–April, 1971, pp. 164-165.

RITE OF PASSAGE

Author: Alexei Panshin (1940-   )
First book publication: 1968
Type of work: Novel
Time: 2205
Locale: Aboard one of the seven Great Ships left after the destruction of the Earth in 2041

A sensitive portrayal of a pre-adolescent girl's growth to maturity as she qualifies for adult status in her nomadic spaceship society by passing a survival test in the wilds of a barbaric planet

    Principal characters:
        MIA HAVERO, the young heroine in her twelfth to fourteenth years
        MILES HAVERO, her father and chairman of the Ship's Council
        JIMMY DENTREMONT, her closest friend
        JOSEPH L. H. MBELE, Mia's and Jimmy's tutor

Rite of Passage was written both as a deliberate response and an attempt to improve upon Robert Heinlein's teenage heroine in *Podkayne of Mars*, for Alexei Panshin is not only a serious student of the earlier science fiction author, but a perceptive critic of his work as well.

In his critical study, *Heinlein in Dimension*, Panshin examined the character and depiction of Podkayne and concluded that although there was a need in science fiction to portray characters other than young men in their twenties, Heinlein had not successfully done so. Panshin then proceeded to do this himself in his 1969 Nebula Award-winning first novel.

Because Panshin had especially faulted Heinlein for the use of the first-person journal, which he felt was an awkward and sometimes confusing technique, he began *Rite of Passage* with a flashback. The heroine, Mia Havero, looks back seven years after the action to evaluate what has happened to her and to examine her growth to maturity as it occurred between the ages of twelve and fourteen. This reflective technique adds a note of verisimilitude to the work. Panshin's technique not only provides an aura of truth, but in addition places the focal point of the novel where the author wishes it: on the process of change. Panshin has Mia note that the changes which occurred *within* her were more important than the events which happened *to* her.

In Panshin's future world, Mia Havero lives with her father, Miles, on an enormous spaceship which, while originally designed to transport colonists, has been reequipped as a self-contained world. It is now one hundred and sixty-four years since the destruction of Earth by wars which were principally caused by overpopulation and its attendant evils (in 2041 there had been an Earth population of more than eight billion). Mankind has evolved in two directions. One hundred and twelve colonies in a like number of star systems have been settled by manual laborers who struggle to wrest a living from an often hostile environment. Seven enormous ships populated by professionals

— primarily scientists and technologists — travel from planet to planet trading limited amounts of scientific knowledge in return for specific, needed natural resources. Mutual hostility exists between the two groups as evidenced by their slang terminology for each other: the Ship inhabitants consider the colonists "Mudeaters," while the latter, in turn, see those on board the Ships as exploitative "Grabbers."

In addition to occasional trade, another major contact between the two groups occurs at Trial, when groups of fourteen-year-olds are dropped from the Ships for thirty-day survival tests. This is the "Rite of Passage" of the novel, comparable to the familiar rites of contemporary society: baptism, confirmation, marriage, and the like. But this rite has more primitive and more serious overtones because it determines who will survive to be accepted into the adult world aboard Ship. It ensures that members of the space-bound society are able to function and survive on a planet, and — even more important — provides an additional check on the population since some fail the test and do not return.

Trial looms before Mia, but there are other trials that she must face before the ultimate one: she must face leaving the Ship and leaving the comforting confines of her "quad."

Panshin handles Mia's development most realistically. She is, in many ways, a typical adolescent with a typical fear of any change: change of residence, of friends, or of her own anatomy as she develops towards adulthood.

As a jest, her father whimsically has "frozen" Mia, so that she will stay a little girl (the fantasy of many little girls), and while she envies the bodily development of her peers, she has more than a little desire to really stay a child, safe and protected. Mia was reared in a communal dorm until age nine, when she fled it to live with her father. Her mother, although alive, is absent from the story, living alone to pursue art (although Panshin also gives some psychological justification for her behavior later in the tale).

As the story opens, Mia is about to meet the first of the changes which she fears, and which shape her: the change of residence to a new quad where she will have to adjust to new friends, new neighbors, and a new tutor. None of these challenges is accidental: they have all been arranged by Mia's father, who now recognizes how reluctant she is to face new situations. Thus, her new best friend is Jimmy Dentremont, who is a potential mate according to the Ship's Eugenist, and her tutor is Joseph Mbele, who had once tutored her father (but who has a more humanitarian ethical code than her father). Her father continues his program for Mia when he invites her to accompany him on a trade visit to the planet Grainau, where Mia makes the startling discovery that the Mudeaters she has scorned in turn look down upon the Ship's people and disparage their way of life.

Other essential changes occur in Mia's character. For example, when she explores the air ducts of the ship, she learns that her companion, while initially a coward, can rise to the occasion and overcome fears. This teaches her empathy, and she begins to see parallels between herself and other persons challenging and conquering the unknown. As she meets ever more difficult tests, she comes to learn about herself, her values, and her ethical philosophy.

Ultimately, there is Trial, and Mia and Jimmy, with others, are singly dropped upon the planet Tintera. The ensuing adventure scenes are unfortunately the weakest part of the novel. Mia meets the inhabitants of Tintera, struggles with evil men, sees her pick-up signal (essential for return to the ship) destroyed, and rescues Jimmy from prison. By salvaging his pick-up signal, she not only survives, but also manages to have her first sexual experience with Jimmy in the midst of all the danger.

More important to Mia's development than the dangers she meets and surmounts, is her change of heart about the Mudeaters whom she had hitherto scorned. She mellows and becomes ever more tolerant throughout the novel as learning about herself connects her to the larger world. However, even though Mia grows into a humane and sensitive individual, the note on which the book ends is falsely optimistic. Panshin hints that the new generation will implement humanitarian programs, yet, at the same time, the entire planet of Tintera is destroyed.

Nevertheless, if Panshin's denouement is weak, the major portion of his narrative is sound and interesting. His descriptions of life aboard the multi-leveled Ship are fascinating. Level Three, a vast area simulating Earth, has three divisions. One sector is utilized for cultivation and production of food, oxygen, and fodder for the cattle being raised. (Beef is the only meat raised naturally; other meat products are grown in vats). A second area contains a lovely park with trees, lakes, flowers, and picnic and riding areas, and the third sector is reserved for a wilderness designed for hunting and used as a training ground for survival lessons prior to Trial. The sheer size of Level Three is so vast that the roof is over three hundred feet above the ground and the area extends for miles before either roof or ground meet the sides of the ship.

Panshin also takes great care to present detailed character descriptions. The populace of the ship, primarily mercantile entrepreneurs, are presented deliberately, with care and attention given to their unique educational, political, and ethical systems. Family life is presented as it is affected by specific space phenomena. For example, the Ship people enjoy extreme longevity. Mia's parents have been married fifty years (although they have lived apart for the last eight). Siblings may be spaced as far apart as forty years.

Another mark of the author's craftsmanship lies in the brief but essential stories he couches within the main story. At several points in the novel, one character tells a fairy (or folk) tale to another. Not only are these vignettes charming in their own right, but they additionally serve to illustrate ethical problems and solutions for Mia, to aid in her development, and also to reinforce the conservative philosophy of the majority of the Ship's adults. For example, Panshin explores sociology and politics, drawing comparisons between the "haves" and the "have nots."

Moments in the plot of *Rite of Passage* may ring untrue, but Mia as a character is believable. Since 1968, other science fiction authors may have matched Panshin in creating a realistic teenaged heroine, but they have not, as yet, topped him.

Beverly Friend

Sources for Further Study

Reviews:

Amazing Stories. XLII, January, 1969, p. 143.

Analog. LXXXIII, April, 1969, pp. 165-166.

Galaxy. XXVIII, July, 1969, pp. 156-158.

Magazine of Fantasy and Science Fiction. XXXVI, January, 1969, pp. 41-43.

RIVERWORLD SERIES

Author: Philip José Farmer (1918-   )
First book publications: To Your Scattered Bodies Go (1971); *The Fabulous Riverboat* (1971); *The Dark Design* (1977)
Type of work: Series of novels and one novelette
Time: At least 4900 years in the future
Locale: The Riverworld, a planet whose entire surface is covered by the River and its valley

All humanity is resurrected in the Riverworld, a land which provides both adventure and an opportunity for speculation on man's nature

Principal characters:
SIR RICHARD FRANCIS BURTON, Victorian explorer, writer, and scholar
MONAT GRRAUTUT, a native of Tau Ceti
PETER JAIRUS FRIGATE, a science fiction writer from Peoria
ALICE PLEASANCE LIDDELL HARGREAVES, the original Alice for whom Rev. Dodgson wrote *Alice in Wonderland*
KAZZINTUITRUAABEMSS (KAZZ), a Neanderthaler
GWENAFRA, an ancient Celt, age nine on Resurrection Day
JOHN DE GREYSTOCK, a thirteenth century English baron
HERMANN GÖRING, the famous Nazi, who undergoes a change of heart
SAM CLEMENS, who still wants to pilot a Riverboat, the *Not for Hire*
JOE MILLER, an eight-feet-tall, eight-hundred-pound titanthrope
CYRANO DE BERGERAC, author, soldier, and swordsman
X, THE MYSTERIOUS STRANGER, a renegade Ethical who recruits resurrectees to oppose the Plan of the Ethicals
KING JOHN OF ENGLAND
MILTON FIREBRASS, an engineer and astronaut, first a representative of Soul City, then Captain of the airship *Parseval*
JILL GULBIRRA, an airshipperson and aggressive feminist
PISCATOR, a Japanese airshipman, Sufi master, and ardent fisherman
JACK LONDON, who travels under the name Martin "Frisco Kid" Farrington with Tom Mix, Nur, and Frigate
TOM MIX, who travels as "Tom Rider"
NUR EL-MUSAFIR, a twelfth century Moorish Sufi master
YESHUA, the historical Jesus, who is martyred again in "Riverworld"

The Riverworld stories have a curious history. The original version, a novel entitled *I Owe for the Flesh*, was written in 1952 for a Shasta Pocket Books competition, which it won; however, it was not published, due to the failure of Shasta in circumstances fictionalized in Volume I. More than a decade later, Frederik Pohl encouraged Farmer to rework and expand the material for a series of magazine serials, and it is these, slightly revised, that appeared as *To Your Scattered Bodies Go* and *The Fabulous Riverboat*. The first draft of a third volume ran to 400,000 words; the first half has been published as *The Dark Design*. The second half of the draft will comprise Volume IV and will complete the main sequence of the series. Farmer has plans for further explorations of the milieu in what he calls "sidestream" stories, on the order of "Riverworld," which will allow him to juxtapose various historical figures in the Riverworld setting.

The Riverworld premise allows almost any number of stories, given the potential cast of characters. All humanity, from pre-*homo sapiens* to twentieth century man, awakens on the banks of a multi-million-mile-long River. Their resurrected bodies are at the physiological age of twenty-five, but they retain memories of entire lifetimes — and deaths — on Earth. Food, drink, and a few luxuries (tobacco, liquor, a hallucinogenic gum) are provided by mysteriously replenished buckets called grails. The young bodies mend quickly when injured (even regenerating limbs or eyes), are immune to sickness, and do not age. Should one be killed, it is resurrected again the next day elsewhere along the River. The River and its valley, snaking and turning, occupy the entire surface of the planet. There is no animal life other than earthworms, fish, and humankind.

In this setting, Farmer is able to mix two kinds of science fiction, the traditional adventure story of chases, escapes, travels, and intrigues (akin to his own *The Green Odyssey*, 1956), and an unusual variety of socio-historico-philosophical speculation in which the historical Jesus can meet a fifteenth century German inquisitor (as in "Riverworld," with Tom Mix as the point-of-view character), or a feudal king can try to cope with an American who insists on constitutional government, or Herman Göring can be converted to the pacifist Church of the Second Chance. The two varieties of story generally share the narrative line, as when Burton and his companions travel upRiver, dodging grail slavers and encountering states founded on social, religious, and philosophical ideas from the entire range of human history. Something like this second sort of story has been done before by the American humorist John Kendrick Bangs in *A House-Boat on the Styx* (1895) and *The Pursuit of the House-Boat* (1897), in which the shades of the illustrious dead hold endless conversations in the floating clubhouse of the title. Farmer's cross-cultural encounters, however, take place in a much more complex milieu; the initial conditions of Resurrection Day are not stable, thanks to human imperfection and restlessness and curiosity, and the operation of these forces provides the material for a chronicle of wars, scheming, madness, fanaticism, and slavery covering (so far) the first thirty-four years of Rivervalley life.

An Edenic environment cannot convert the Old Adam, and from the second day of resurrection onward, mankind recapitulates its Earthly history. We see this process through the eyes of a born outsider, Sir Richard Francis Burton. The initial reaction of the reborn is confusion and hysteria; all have experienced death, and none expects an afterlife such as this. Burton shakes off the shock rather quickly — he had awakened *before* resurrection in a space filled with ranks and files of sleeping bodies, some not completely renewed — and realizes that this is a natural rather than a supernatural event. Normal gregariousness asserts itself, and within minutes, groups start to form; the one that collects around Burton includes Monat, Kazz, Frigate, and Alice, and later Lev Ruach (a survivor of the Nazi holocaust), Gwenafra, and others. Burton's hardheadedness does not desert him, even in this impossible afterlife:

> He looked around for a stick or club. He did not know what was on the agenda for humanity, but if it was left unsupervised or uncontrolled, it would soon be reverting to its normal state. Once the shock was over, the people would be looking out for themselves, and that meant that some would be bullying others.

Burton's reasoning is justified when the few demonstration grails deliver the first meal and there is a riot over the contents, and again when a gang of Chicagoans try to take over the bamboo huts that Burton's group has built. It is the dreamgum-inspired, first-night orgy, however, that shows the unregenerate power of libido and id. The gum loosens Alice's Victorian inhibitions, much to her alarm and disgust, and all along the Riverbank the other resurrectees copulate (with or without mutual consent), fight, or speechify with demonic energy.

Burton's line of reasoning about human nature eventually occurs to the mass of *lazari*, and within a year the banks are lined with thousands of small communities and states armed with primitive weapons for defense or offense; grail slavery (the practice of imprisoning an individual in order to steal his labor and, more important, some of the food and all of the luxuries provided by his personally coded grail) is common. Burton's gang has built a bamboo catamaran, the *Hadji*, and begun to sail upRiver. In their first 415 days they are threatened by slavers at least fifty-five times; on the 417th day they are finally captured by slavers from a state run by Hermann Göring and the ancient Roman king Tullius Hostilius. The Göring-Tullius tyranny combines grail-slavery's usual brutality with another Earthly evil that has refused to die — anti-Semitism. Although Göring impartially enslaves all races, he established his rule by at first suggesting that only Jews be so treated; after his takeover, he enslaved many of his supporters.

Burton and his people participate in the inevitable slave revolt and help to form the state of Theleme. They discover an agent of those who are responsible for resurrection posing as a resurrectee — Robert Spruce. Under duress, Spruce reveals that his people are the descendants of the cataclysm of 2008, 5000 years earlier, and that the whole enterprise is a combination rehabilitation (thus the label, "Ethicals") and scientific project — and then wills himself dead. A month later, the Ethicals make an attempt to kidnap Burton, and he gathers part of his crew and flees upRiver. Eventually, Burton is contacted by an Ethical who tells him that Spruce's story and the teachings of the Church of the Second Chance (that men have been raised in order to perfect themselves spiritually) are lies, that the project is purely scientific, and that at its end the resurrectees will return to oblivion. The Mysterious Stranger is opposed to this and had awakened Burton in the preresurrection bubble as part of his attempt to defeat the Plan. Part of that counterplan requires that Burton and eleven others (which eventually include Sam Clemens, Cyrano, "Liver-Eating" Johnston, Tom Mix, Jack London, John de Greystock, Nur el-Musafir, and Odysseus) reach the north polar region. The means of travel hinted at by the Stranger and accepted by Burton is the "Suicide Express" — deliberate death and resurrection in a new location. In the next seven years, Burton makes this jump 777 times. The Ethicals finally intercept him, and he is interviewed by their council of Twelve. Their message: Burton is weakening the link between his soul and body by suiciding, and ruining his chances for salvation. They return him to Theleme, but fail to wipe out his memory (interference by the Stranger, presumably). On rejoining the old crew, Burton is ready to sail up-River again.

With so much necessary exposition and scene-setting out of the way, Farmer can develop some of the themes of the series in *The Fabulous Riverboat*. Like Burton, Sam Clemens longs to sail upRiver in search of the secrets behind the afterlife; unlike him, Sam intends to do so on a genuine Riverboat, constructed from metal rather than bamboo and oak. The only metal he knows of in the valley is the nickel-iron ax of Erik Bloodaxe, the Viking captain, which has been fashioned from a meteorite. Thus Sam and his blood-brother and bodyguard, the titanthrope Joe Miller, accompany the Vikings in search of a meteorite that may not even exist. The Mysterious Stranger takes a hand, arranging for a large meteorite to strike the valley not far away, and then recruits Sam into his conspiracy. Sam's dream of a metal Riverboat coincides with the Stranger's needs, and X reveals that other metals, bauxite, platinum, and cinnabar, have been deposited nearby the meteorite strike — the basics for a transition from a neolithic to a metal-working technology.

That transition is not without cost. Sam betrays Bloodaxe and establishes a partnership with King John (who "was so crooked, he was admirable") to found the state of Parolando for the purpose of building the boat. Their part of the valley is marred by diggings and clear-cutting of timber, the air is fouled by smelter and factory fumes. Possession of the meteorite iron requires not only the death of Bloodaxe, but an increased military vigilance to defend the wealth from predators; and the need for raw materials tempts even Sam to consider conquest as a means of obtaining them. In addition to the relatively simple vices of rape, murder, and slavery, the Rivervalley now sees the reinvention of politics, pollution, regimentation, and imperialism. The evils that infect Parolando are not, however, solely the result of Sam's obsessive desire for the Riverboat, but also stem from the greed, ambition, and fanaticism of Parolando's neighbors, particularly the expansionist Iyeyasu and the racist Elwood Hacking of Soul City, a nearby community. It is the simple existence of iron and the power it promises that dictates the shape of the struggle; when

Sam decides that he wants the boat, he must accept the logic of a competition that requires betrayal, exploitation, manipulation of neutrals, and alliances with villains.

Sam is troubled by more than problems of practical politics; like Burton, he resents the arrogance of the Ethicals in raising him from the dead without his permission, for their own shadowy purposes. Furthermore, both men are haunted by dreams. Burton's is of a Victorian God, wearing Burton's own face, who tells him, "Your owe for the flesh" (recalling the 1953 novel's title), and Sam's is of Doctor Ecks, "the unknown quantity, the eternal passer-through, the mysterious stranger, the devil dedicated to keeping other poor devils alive" (and who looks like Mark Twain), who delivers the infant Sam, burdened with "all the sins of the world." In fact, all the viewpoint characters of the main sequence — Burton, Clemens, Jill Gulbirra, and Peter Frigate — dream of both private sorrows and the common pains, guilts, and doubts of all men, and all respond to their anxieties by traveling the River in search of answers to their questions.

Sam's fixation with the Riverboat, like the compulsions of the others, is the result of a mixture of private and shared motives. To the general public, the boat is safe, luxurious, high-status transportation to the mysterious polar regions; for the inner circle, the Stranger's initiates, it is a means of striking back at the Ethicals. But in Sam's heart of hearts it is a symbol of freedom from domination of all the forces of a determinist universe; it is *Not for Hire* on every level of meaning. (Note a parallel in Burton's farewell oration at the launching of the *Hadji*: " 'I will pay tribute to none; owe fealty to none; to myself only will I be true.' ") Ironically, Sam is no more able to free himself from his inner demons than is Burton. While sailing with Bloodaxe, he seeks the face of his Earthly wife among the millions on the Riverbank, and when Livy arrives in Parolando as the companion of Cyrano, he is consumed with jealousy; he cannot adjust that part of himself to the realities of post-resurrection life. Trapped as he is by private obsessions and compulsions, it is little wonder that he subscribes to a determinist philosophy and hates the Ethicals for again binding him to the wheel of existence.

Others are not so hag-ridden. Lothar von Richtofen accepts perpetual youth and easy living at face value; the prehumans, Kazz and Joe Miller, similarly live in the present moment. Some resurrectees have actually overcome the crippling effects of their Earthly lives and found a kind of freedom. On a small scale, Alice sheds the worst of her Victorian attitudes — prudery and snobbery — to become Burton's companion. Hermann Göring, on the other hand, manages a complete renewal of personality. After escaping the fall of his slave-kingdom, he becomes addicted to dreamgum, which turns loose all the demons of the undermind. As a convert to the faith of the Second Chancers, he cleanses himself and turns up as a missionary in Parolando. The mass of resurrectees, however, are either, like Alice, moderately adjusted to their new lives or, like King John, completely unregenerate.

In the plotting and counterplotting of Volume II, Sam loses the boat to invaders from Soul City, who in turn are attacked by Iyeyasu's forces; both are then wiped out by a triple cross on the part of John, whose admirably crooked plan the whole thing was. The *Not for Hire* is finally completed in the year 26 ARD (After Resurrection Day), only to be stolen by John in a final, triumphant swindle. The curtain falls with Sam shaking his fist at the departing King, promising to build a new boat and to avenge the theft of the old.

The Dark Design is the most complex of the three novels. It follows three sets of characters and three different, gradually converging time schemes: in 32 ARD, Burton and company sail the *Hadji II* upRiver; in 31 ARD, Jill Gulbirra arrives in Parolando to join Firebrass' airship project, the successor to Sam Clemens' now completed second Riverboat; in 7 ARD, Peter Frigate (whose double is simultaneously on Burton's crew) joins "Martin Farrington" (Jack London) and "Tom Rider" (Tom Mix) on the *Razzle Dazzle II* for a journey upRiver. In the beginning of the fourth decade of Rivervalley life, things have changed: grail slavery is much diminished, thanks to organized resistance on the part of a multitude of communities; in many places life has become settled and stable; and, for reasons no one understands, secondary resurrections no longer occur — permanent death has returned. Perhaps more than the industrialization and intrigue of Volume II, these changes mark how far the population has come from the Edenic anarchy of Resurrection Day.

Rather than resolving the mysteries of the first two volumes, *The Dark Design* lives up to its title by intensifying them. Two of Burton's companions, Monat and Frigate, are found to be agents for the Ethicals (though whether on the orthodox or renegade side is not revealed) and vanish. Since it was Monat who led the interrogation of Robert Spruce (in Volume I), the old picture of the Ethicals' background and motives is suspect. The problem is complicated for the reader when a second Peter Frigate is introduced in the next chapter (III/28). This Frigate is a viewpoint character, and his consciousness contains no indication that he is anything other than the real Peter Jairus Frigate, Peorian, science fiction writer, would-be Burton biographer, and fan of Tom Mix, Jack London, and airships. All that is certain at this point is that one Ethical has a counterplan to a greater Plan — but the whole truth about this struggle and the part to be played by resurrectees is far from clear.

The polar regions seem certain to yield some answers. In Volume I there was the skeleton of the story that Joe Miller tells in detail in Volume II, of the expedition of Egyptians he accompanied to the polar sea, where he glimpsed the Dark Tower, the presumed headquarters of the Ethicals. In Volume III the same story is told again, but from the point of view of one of the Egyptians who actually entered the Tower. Tom Mix, who recounts the Egyptian's version, had himself died once when attempting the same journey by boat, and there was an even earlier attempt by Robert Rohrig (an Earthly friend of

Frigate's) and two others. Accordingly, everyone is traveling to the source of
the River: Frigate, Mix, and London by boat and balloon; Sam Clemens on the
Mark Twain; Burton on the *Hadji II* and the *Snark*; Jill Gulbirra, Cyrano, and
Firebrass on the airship *Parseval*; even King John on his stolen *Rex Grandissimus*. The group that reaches the Tower in the present action of Volume III is
the crew of the *Parseval*, and they find not answers but more questions. The
only visible entrance is at the top, by way of a curving corridor guarded by a
field that progressively resists efforts to walk it. Jill gets only a few steps
inside, but Piscator easily reaches the curve, and then with some effort passes
around it and is seen no more. With nothing more to be learned, the expedition
reluctantly returns to the valley.

Piscator's disappearance should focus reader attention on his character and
that of one of Frigate Number Two's companions, Nur el-Musafir. Both are
Sufi masters, and both take time to explain to Frigate and Jill something of
Sufi values. While not Chancers themselves, they show a similar belief in the
possibility of spiritual perfection and a similar optimism in the face of the
intellectual and moral disorder of the Rivervalley — although they are less
unworldly than the Chancers and are not pacifists. If, as Farmer has said,
spiritual regeneration is the theme of the whole series, these Sufis and the
Church of the Second Chance are important forces. After Piscator vanishes
around the curve of the corridor, Jill recalls a line from the *Aeneid:* "Facilis
descensus Averni," "It is easy to go down into hell." Her reaction to this
message from her subconscious mind is that the line is "not appropriate," that
the corridor was hard to enter but easy to leave. She ignores the obverse: if it
is easy to descend into hell, perhaps it is difficult to rise to heaven, and Piscator's spiritual state has allowed him to enter where Jill and the rest of the
crew cannot — yet.

Piscator's fate may be illuminated by the metaphysics of the spirit promulgated by the Church of the Second Chance and partly confirmed by the
Stranger. The soul (the Chancers' *ka*, the Ethicals' *wathan* or aura) is a real
entity, the animating force of consciousness, without which no resurrection can
take place. Burton, for example, weakens the ties between body and soul by
suiciding 777 times and puts himself in danger of becoming a wandering,
unconscious ghost. The completely evolved *wathan*, that of a person ethically
perfect or nearly so, "*goes beyond*" at death — is absorbed into what amounts
to God. The Chancers preach that the Ethicals' purpose is to give all humans
the opportunity to become ethically perfect; the Stranger insists that only a
very few would be able to do so in the time provided by the scientific project.
For those who wish neither ghosthood nor absorption into godhood, the
Stranger hints at a third alternative, but does not expand on it. Given these
facts (if they remain uncontradicted by later revelations), Piscator's entry into
the Tower could indicate that someone (the Ethicals? the Stranger?) has established a test and that Piscator has passed it — and that this and phenomena

such as Göring's regeneration are the way out of the trap of human imperfection, the endless repetition of the Fall enacted in the Riverworld's replay of human history.

In the rest of the plot, however, characters are busy struggling for freedom, or pursuing revenge, or engaging in endless intrigue. Caught between these distractions and the contradictory testimony about the most basic facts of existence, Burton, Sam Clemens, King John, and the others continue to live through an adventure story. In a twist of the final chapter, even the Stranger (though not identified specifically as such, this is the likeliest possibility) finds himself groping with the rest of the Riverdwellers when mechanisms in a satellite fail and deprive him of some of his tracers.

The series is too large to treat in detail; as Peter Frigate reflects, the idea needs a dozen books "to do it anywhere near justice," and Farmer has consistently expanded its size as he has worked on it. Among the features not dealt with herein are treatments of racism and sexism, reflections on religion, biographical portraits of historical figures, literary discussions, various riparian political systems, puns, Frigate-as-Farmer, and much more. The series contains all Farmer's strengths and weaknesses; it is a compendium of his characteristic themes and attitudes (both his unhappy suspicions about human nature and his openness to the possibility of heroism); it attempts to integrate important features of his intellectual and emotional worlds, in much the same manner as his fictional-author work (Kilgore Trout's *Venus on the Half-Shell*), but along a different line. This is a life work. Farmer may write books formally or technically more perfect, but he is unlikely to write anything more Farmerian or anything that better shows so much of what science fiction can do as a literature of entertainment and reflection.

Russel Letson

Sources for Further Study

Reviews:

Analog. LXXXIX, May, 1972, pp. 163-165.
Booklist. LXVIII, April 1, 1972, p. 649.
Books and Bookmen. XIX, May, 1974, p. 112.
Kirkus Reviews. XXXIX, November 1, 1971, p. 1179.
Library Journal. XCVII, January 15, 1972, p. 27.
Publisher's Weekly. CC, November 15, 1971, p. 67.
Times Literary Supplement. April 12, 1974, p. 385.
Worlds of If. XXI, May–June, 1972, pp. 113-114.

ROADSIDE PICNIC
(PIKNIK NA OBOCHINE)

Authors: Arkady Strugatsky (1925-   ) and Boris Strugatsky (1933-   )
First book publication: 1972
English translation: 1977
Type of work: Novel
Time: The near future
Locale: North America, probably Canada

A "first contact" novel about aliens who leave their refuse behind after a brief visit to Earth, and about the life and career of Redrick Schuhart, a black market collector of artifacts

Principal characters:
REDRICK SCHUHART, a "stalker"
GUTA, his wife
MARIA, their daughter, also called "The Monkey"
KIRILL, a laboratory assistant at the Foundation
BURBRIDGE, another "stalker"
THROATY, a black marketeer

The Strugatsky brothers are, together with Sakyo Komatsu and Stanislaw Lem, the most widely read science fiction authors in the world today. Most of their novels have been best sellers in their native Soviet Union, and they have been published all over the world. Several of their novels (including this one) and short stories have also appeared in English translation. Arkady Strugatsky has a background as a linguist, specializing in Japanese, but has been a full-time writer since 1964. His brother Boris was originally an astronomer, then switched over to computers and advanced mathematics and is now a professional science fiction author, also since 1964. This makes for a uniquely broad background, extending from the humanities to technology, an excellent basis for good science fiction.

The authors' diverse backgrounds certainly show in this tale of mankind poking about in the junk left by extraterrestrial visitors, like primitive tribesmen sifting through the refuse left on their shores by passing ships from other continents. The theme of first contact with aliens, with man playing the part of the ignorant savage, the pariah of the universe, as it were, facing a superior and basically incomprehensible culture, is not entirely new: Algis Budrys wrote a minor classic on this theme, *Rogue Moon* (1960), and one year after *Roadside Picnic*, Arthur C. Clarke published his award-winning novel *Rendezvous with Rama* (1973). A more recent example of the theme is seen in Frederik Pohl's *Gateway* (1977), in which mankind uses the artifacts left by an earlier race without really comprehending them or benefiting from even a fraction of their potential.

The Earthmen in *Roadside Picnic* are even worse off. Aliens have visited

Earth and left behind what are called the "Zones" — areas littered with objects of a strange and often dangerous nature. The Zones are in some way contaminated; all the usual natural laws do not apply, and they are deadly for trespassers. Death in the Zones can be swift or lingering, but it always lurks there, and the scientists of the research foundation, who are trying to explore the Zones, have learned to be extremely cautious.

The aliens made a brief visit to Earth and departed, leaving behind what is, perhaps, the cosmic counterpart of empty beer cans, dirty napkins, and the like — but some of this refuse is unusual, to say the very least, and some of the artifacts prove to be of immense value to Earth. A power pack has already revolutionized Earth civilization, although it is almost certain that the aliens did not use if for that purpose; Earthmen's use of it is probably comparable to a savage's use of a pocket calculator as a hammer. A number of artifacts, some of them never seen, give off unpredictable radiation which kills or changes people, while others offer a strange and deadly bliss.

Needless to say, a flourishing black market in these alien objects has sprung up, with "stalkers" sneaking into the heavily guarded Zones to steal things and, if they survive, sell them to private buyers or the Foundation. The story centers around one of these stalkers, Redrick Schuhart, probably a Canadian in his early thirties, who makes a rather dangerous living by getting artifacts out of the Zone outside his home town. A very convincing character, Redrick is far removed from the usual science fiction hero. The story, which alternates between his journeys into the Zone, which he regards with a mixture of longing and intense fear, and his life with his wife Guta and their daughter Maria, called "The Monkey" on account of her fur (probably the result of genetic damage to Redrick in the Zone), reflects very effectively various sides of his personality as he irrevocably moves on toward his dream of salvation in the Zone.

Redrick searches for salvation, as does everyone in this novel, each in his own way, and maybe he finds it in the end — in the mythical Golden Ball, the most mysterious of all the alien objects, never seen but much whispered about, which is said to fulfill all wishes. This rumor is an obvious case of wishful thinking, of course; but in an age where old gods have fallen, new ones must be found. The aliens and their mysterious objects are as close to modern gods as anything likely to be found; and besides, the Golden Ball might really be able to grant wishes. All stalkers, and in effect the rest of humanity, beseech the unknown aliens to act as their saviors, and many of them appear to get just what they ask for — not from the aliens, who probably never even noticed that Earth was inhabited, but from themselves. Much of the novel is actually a tale of self-fulfilling prophecies, with the aliens acting as catalysts, untouchable and incomprehensible gods who can only be glimpsed through the effects of their unpredictable litter.

This is a rather ironic view of humanity, groveling before the discarded trash of unknown cosmic travelers and finding esoteric meaning in this junk. The authors have put forth views like this before, notably in their celebrated novel *Vtoroe nashestvie marsian* (The Second Martian Invasion, 1967), a wry comment on H. G. Wells's *The War of the Worlds*, in which mankind learns to live with the Martian invaders, acting as milch cows and selling their digestive juices to the aliens, who conquer not by heat rays, but by modern business practices. *Roadside Picnic*, however, is more subtle, and the satire is less heavy. As in Clarke's *Rendezvous with Rama*, the aliens are never seen, and, although their strange refuse has very tangible effects on human civilization, the real effect grows out of the expectations of people. People have glimpsed God, or at least His refuse, and are ardently anxious to give themselves to Him. The only problem is that God is not interested: He does not care for them, and has passed them by without even noticing them.

One perceives that this might be a rather daring statement for two authors who have had their ups and downs in the official Soviet eye, since it depicts people behaving unheroically when faced with uncomfortable truths, and, moreover, suggests that ideals are not always to be trusted. When Redrick finally finds the Golden Ball, which is as close to God or salvation as he ever will come, he is overwhelmed and cannot bring himself to make the wishes he has planned to make — money, a long life, health for his daughter, and so on — surely a god cannot be bothered with things like that. He ends up lamely wishing for happiness for all, which is about as vague a wish as anyone could make. Nevertheless, it is an altruistic wish, and as such might be interpreted as a sign of moral growth. In any event, it ends Redrick Schuhart's quest for salvation and eternal happiness.

European — and especially East European — science fiction writers have long made an art of subtle hints, allusions, puns, double meanings, and seemingly innocent remarks understood only by those who are intended to understand. This approach is not used solely for political reasons, as many Westerners are prone to believe, but for intellectual and literary ones. Stanislaw Lem is very adept at this, as are the Strugatskys; their works are like onions with layer upon layer of meaning beneath the overlaying plot. European readers are practiced at peeling off these layers, but in translation and in the transition to another cultural and historical environment, some of this complexity is lost. Perhaps the Strugatskys' works can be appreciated to their full extent only by a Russian; the same might also be true of Stanislaw Lem and the Polish authors. The Strugatskys are especially talented at satirizing the official government, Party language, and behavior of the Soviet Union; unfortunately, however, much of this sort of satire can be rather incomprehensible to a Western reader who has not experienced life in the society being described.

Perhaps the Western reader, brought up on standard British or American pulp magazine fare, with its sterling heroes, nubile heroines, and loathsome monsters, is in a similar position to Redrick in *Roadside Picnic*, finding his own truths where there are no such truths and using the marvelous objects differently from what was intended.

Still, good science fiction is good science fiction, and even to a Western reader, *Roadside Picnic* remains a forceful story with all the good qualities one would hope to find in the genre: vision, irony, and above all, literary excellence.

Sam J. Lundwall

Sources for Further Study

Reviews:

Analog. XCVII, September, 1977, p. 170.

Booklist. LXXIV, September 1, 1977, p. 25.

Kirkus Reviews. XLV, April 1, 1977, p. 364 and May 1, 1977, p. 248.

Library Journal. CII, June 1, 1977, p. 1307.

New York Times Book Review. May 22, 1977, p. 22 and March 12, 1978, p. 45.

Observer. July 2, 1978, p. 26.

Publisher's Weekly. CXI, March 7, 1977, p. 92.

Spectator. CCXLI, August 26, 1978, p. 20.

Times Literary Supplement. June 16, 1978, p. 662.

ROGUE MOON

Author: Algis Budrys (1931-   )
First book publication: 1960
Type of work: Novel
Time: 1959
Locale: One of the Pacific states of the United States and the Moon

When attempts to explore an alien construction on the Moon lead to the death of all investigators, a research program designed to reveal its secrets is initiated

> *Principal characters:*
> EDWARD HAWKS, head of the research team
> AL BARKER, a sports hero with a death wish
> VINCENT CONNINGTON, the manipulative director of personnel
> CLAIRE PACK, Barker's mistress
> ELIZABETH CUMMINGS, a fashion designer whom Hawks comes to love
> SAM LATOURETTE, a top assistant in laboratory, and a terminal cancer patient

Rogue Moon is set in 1959, the year it was written, because Budrys wanted to show, as he has since admitted, that science fiction need not be set in the future. The world of this novel is as we know it, except for the secret work which for some years has been carried out in Hawks's laboratory. A matter transmitter has been developed which can scan a man's body, atom by atom, and resolve it into an electromagnetic signal which can be reconstituted into matter in a receiver. The process destroys the original, but as far as can be measured, the new subject in the receiver is identical in every respect.

At around the same time an American circumlunar rocket has photographed what is apparently an alien artifact on the Moon, though it could be a strange natural formation or even a living thing. A matter-transmitter receiver is dropped near it from a rocket, and through this a technician is transmitted. He builds a larger receiver, and a return transmitter. Exploration can begin.

The alien labyrinth has an entrance which cannot be used as an exit. Everyone who tries to explore the maze is killed in a variety of disgusting and painful ways. There seems to be a set of incomprehensible rules; the labyrinth will not accept certain gestures, certain kinds of equipment, certain directions of movement. Hawks is obsessed with mapping it, and finding if killing was what it was designed for, or a mere side-effect of some other function; his need to understand it is overwhelming.

Hawks creates two duplicates of each volunteer explorer. One is sent to the Moon, one to a receiver in the laboratory on Earth. The reassembled twin bodies remain in telepathic contact for a short time, so that the volunteer on Earth is able to report what is happening within the maze to his *Doppelgänger*, and in what way he meets his death. The psychic strain of this process often ends in madness; no Earth-version of any volunteer has been able to undertake a second trip and no Moon-version has lived. The government is worried, about both the cost and the cruelty.

This is the situation as the novel begins. Connington, the cynical personnel director, proposes to Hawks that Barker, a driven man, a remarkable athlete whose career has been amazingly dangerous, may be enough in love with death to survive the destruction of his *alter ego* without breaking down. (Connington's hidden motive is to destroy Barker and thus gain possession of his beautiful mistress.) Barker is attracted to the challenge and suicides many times in an effort to resolve the enigma of the labyrinth. Hawks sees himself as murderer, Barker as victim, and feels bound to accompany Barker on what seems likely to be the final run; the two men successfully traverse the labyrinth and emerge. However, they die anyway, since without complex scanning equipment on the Moon it is impossible to transmit human bodies back alive. Barker had not known this, and finds difficulty in accepting his death (though, of course, his Earth duplicate lives on). Hawks is stronger.

Even in synopsis the plot is intriguing, but it barely hints at the violent, cryptic quality of the novel. In a series of essays on the art of writing in the science fiction newspaper *Locus*, Budrys has discussed what he saw himself as doing in the novel. His model was the cinema; he intended "to flood the reader with compressed data," and, as in a film, he used two objective cameras, or at least their prose equivalent; one of them sees Hawks and one sees only what Hawks sees. There is no omniscient narrator to bring the reader inside the consciousness of any character; motivation is, therefore, often enigmatic.

The characters themselves are deliberate archetypes, more vivid and direct than in life, their nerves more nakedly exposed. The novel has almost no periods of rest; the human relationships are all caught at crisis point. Budrys himself comments:

> The quasimaniacal pace of kinematic prose promotes reader fascination . . . the characters . . . can be seen purposefully and singlemindedly committing themselves to every social interaction as if it were crucial. . . . Every interchange is freighted with the potential violence of people ready to throw their psychic and sometimes their physical lives in the balance in order to maintain dominance of sometimes apparently trivial situations.

The risk of such a strategy is that the narrative could so easily topple over into hysteria, and that might have happened here, if the book had been merely about the conflicts of neurotic people. However, these conflicts are not the subject of the book, which has more to do with the future of Man than with the future of individual men. From the beginning there are ample signposts to show the observant reader that he is dealing with a highly structured, complexly metaphorical work; its mode has little to do with everyday realism; it is designed more like a poem, using a patterning of images which seem at first elusive and random, but which finally cohere, until the mental eye of the reader can discern a larger symmetry. The high-pitched, taut characterization is appropriate to Budrys' ends. He wants to show each character as representing a different way of confronting the major problems of the world. We are interested in what they stand for in relation to the larger themes of love and death, aspiration and rebirth, rather than in the psychology of their selves.

Of these themes, the most immediately obvious is death. The matter transmitter kills its subject even as it reconstructs a duplicate. The Moon labyrinth kills, too. Hawks is also a death-machine, sending men to destruction and madness for the sake of knowledge. Barker has spent his life flirting with death in various guises; he is a man of considerable cruelty and suppressed violence who boasts of being a "whole" man even as he stalks around on an artificial leg. His mistress Claire is a metaphoric death-machine who will "chew you up and spit you out." Connington, the manipulator, is an impotent man who deadens himself with alcohol and gets his kicks through feeding emotionally upon those whose knowledge of life and death is more intimate than his own. Latourette, the assistant technician, is literally eaten up by death in the form of cancer.

There is an unsubtle, ferocious authorial courage in Budrys' readiness to thrust home the symbolic themes of the novel so relentlessly, never slackening the tension. All his characters feel love, though it means something different for each of them, but in only one case is this feeling not saturated with an awareness of death. Elizabeth Cummings is not hag-ridden, but she is perhaps the least successfully rendered character. It is she who gives the alienated Hawks the psychological support he needs; her sympathy and understanding seem to come from a softer, more gentle universe than that in which the main action takes place.

The forces which drive the characters into such unyielding conflict seem destructive, yet they are clearly parallel to the driving obsession which enables Barker to scrabble ruinously, repeatedly dying, through the killer-maze. Indeed, among its many symbolic functions, the labyrinth is a kind of metaphor for the novel itself: just as Barker has to traverse the maze to restore meaning to his being, so the reader who is able to follow the labyrinth of the book becomes, in a sense, somebody not quite the same as the person who sat down to read in the first place. (There is almost a suggestion here that the maze is an alien message, a kind of book in a foreign language, an act of communication.) It is interesting that Budrys' account of the novel's structure could equally be an account of the maze which is at his novel's heart:

> . . . kinematic prose forces the reader to climb out on the structure while it is still apparently being built and has no clear terminus as far as the reader can see. Enigmatic but purposeful characters are obviously scrambling towards some destination, and there are occasional handholds and now and then a road sign declaring that the bridge gives access to solid ground. Still and all, there are continual doubts which the reader must continually resolve.

The fact that the symbol contains the story's own structure is by no means the whole story. More centrally, the crossing of the maze stands for a *rite de passage*, a ceremony of suffering and transition which the initiate (in this case we can perhaps see the novices Hawks and Barker as standing for mankind as a whole) must undertake to achieve adulthood.

Hawks, with Barker as his violent instrument, is a kind of Prometheus stealing fire from the heavens (his name suggests flight), or a Faustus risking physical death and the ruination of his soul in return for the expansion of his understanding. This idea that Man's growth consists of conceptual breakthrough into ever more complex paradigms, ever richer world-pictures, is perhaps the most central theme in science fiction. Its centrality in the novel may be why *Rogue Moon* has already secured a place as a minor classic in the genre.

Hawks's behavior cannot readily be justified in conventional moral terms, and until the close (which is itself enigmatic), the reader is able to think of him as villain rather than hero, because of his readiness to sacrifice life and happiness for an ambiguous end whose value in quantifiable terms is dubious. Nonetheless, this end is shown symbolically to be part of an evolutionary imperative. Even the cover of Barker's first schoolbook, he recalls, shows goldfish trying to dive upwards out of a bowl; images of man as primitive sea-creature abound, as do visions of the shore. Throughout the book, metaphors thrown up in conversation intersect with the facts of the maze, and with the evolutionary growth its painful penetration seems, in part, to stand for. Barker tells Hawks that a man who sends others out to battle for him is "some kind of crawling, wriggling thing." The link is made specific in the appearance of the chart of the labyrinth, as if it were "a diagram of a prehistoric beach, where one stumbling organism had marked its laboured trail up upon the littered sand between the long rows of drying kelp. . . ."

Hawks is in one way better fitted than Barker for the evolutionary struggle through the maze, because he is less disturbed by its impersonality (which here seems almost to stand for the impersonality of life and of the universe itself) than Barker, who takes everything as a "personal" challenge, and is cowed by the fact that heroism and cowardice are alike irrelevant to the maze. (This abstract courage of Hawks is reinforced by a remark to the dying Latourette, "Why should a man be at the mercy of things that pay him no attention?" Latourette's impersonal cancer is itself a kind of amorphous, inward killer-maze.) Yet it is Barker, half in love with death and with no larger perspective, who succeeds first, Hawks, the ultimately stronger man, still following in his footsteps.

At times there seems no end to the symbolic resonances which the labyrinth is made to carry. For example, when Hawks tells Barker not "to set foot" in his mind, we do for a moment see the maze as a correlative of Hawks's own consciousness, which for Hawks to traverse would bring self-knowledge, for Barker to penetrate would be a violation. Yet it is all done tactfully. Budrys never lets us forget that it is, first and foremost, a literal maze.

Much of the excitement of the novel, especially on second and subsequent readings, comes from the skill and economy with which Budrys allows the labyrinth to take on such a network of symbolic associations, and even this very variety is given an oblique explanation at one point, when Hawks tells Barker that "no one sees the world that others see." Even this apparently casual remark has its analogue in the maze, whose most salient and compulsive features are described quite differently by each explorer. Where Hawks sees "a lake of fire," Barker sees "a jagged green archway."

While talking to Elizabeth, Hawks explains how he believes that human evolution is imperative in a dying universe, and makes explicit the tension between growth and death which vibrates through the novel: "It's all running down. Some day, it'll stop. Only one thing in the universe grows fuller and richer, and *forces* its way uphill. Intelligence. . . ." Soon afterwards he describes a childhood experience where through half-closed, watering eyes he saw that "everything . . . seemed to have haloes and points of scattered light around it . . . I was walking through a universe so wild, so wonderful, that my heart nearly broke with its beauty." But, he says, when he dies, this vision will die with him. No, Elizabeth replies, now it lives in her mind too. Just so, *Rogue Moon* seems to tell us, the death of the individual does not mean the death of what he knew and felt. The series of deaths in the maze, each one adding a tiny accretion to human knowledge, tells us the same thing in a curiously moving image, made more lovely and touching by the fact that each new traveler in the labyrinth passes the bodies of those who have gone before (and in so going, helping him to get as far as he has), transfigured.

The final *rite de passage*, when Barker and Hawks successfully traverse the maze together, is surprisingly brief, but done with great delicacy and economy, with its surrealism just sufficiently tied down to the kinds of human experience the reader can understand. The labyrinth contains "flowers of frost" which recall the subjective wonderland Hawks had experienced in his childhood epiphany. Only at the moment of apparent resolution, almost at the very end, does the theme which has been unfurling so that its convolutions become ever clearer suddenly infold again, with a moment of enigma. After his successful transition, and just before his necessary suicide, Moon-Hawks (as opposed to Earth-Hawks back in the laboratory, who is undergoing a fit of unmanning claustrophobia) blinks "sharply, viciously, repeatedly" as he (apparently) re-creates his childhood wonderland for a last time while looking at the stars. " 'No,' he said, 'No, I'm not going to fall for that.' " This is the moment of the novel that leaves an uncomfortable itch in many readers' minds. What does this final repudiation mean, when one might expect triumph or acceptance? Perhaps the wonderland of the mind only helps when it is forever unattainable.

The final two pages are truly teasing in another way, too, for they bring up again, unresolved but with renewed force, the whole question of identity which has lain uneasily, semidormant, beneath much of the action. Is the man created by the matter transmitter the same as he who was destroyed by it? (Much the same question could be asked of the survivors of the maze.) But if the question is not resolved, at least it is proposed with an air of touching resignation. The last words of the novel are in the form of a note the old Hawks has written to his new self: " 'Remember me to her.' "

As a science fiction tale of baroque and mysterious adventure, *Rogue Moon* is eminently satisfying, but it is more than that. Carried within the image of the killer-maze lie what are perhaps the most pervasive symbolic resonances to be found in any science fiction novel; few readers would not be stirred and shaken by them. The book can be criticized for a certain brittleness of tone at the level of its social interactions, but it readily survives these. Best of all, perhaps, *Rogue Moon* is a true original, unique. There is nothing else in science fiction like it.

Peter Nicholls

Sources for Further Study

Reviews:
Amazing Stories. XXXIX, March, 1965, p. 126.
Analog. LXVII, June, 1961, p. 164.
Magazine of Fantasy and Science Fiction. XX, June, 1961, pp. 104-109.

ROGUE QUEEN

Author: L. Sprague de Camp (1907-   )
First book publication: 1951
Type of work: Novel
Time: Approximately two hundred years in the future
Locale: The land and environs of the Avtini, the most civilized inhabitants of the planet Ormazd

Transformed through her contact with members of an Earth spaceship on an exploratory mission, Iroedh repudiates her role as a worker in the rigid Avtini sex-caste system and effects revolutionary social change in her Community

> *Principal characters:*
> IROEDH, a worker
> ANTIS, a drone, a friend of Iroedh, later her lover
> INTAR, Queen of Elham
> ESTIR, Crown Princess of Elham, later Queen
> WYTHIAS, leader of a band of rogue drones
> GILDAKK, a Thothian acting as the Oracle at Ledhwid
> DR. BLOCH (Winston Bloch), the leading scientist of the Earth expedition, in love with Barbe Dulac
> BARBE DULAC, his assistant, previously engaged to O'Mara, now in love with Bloch
> O'MARA, photographer of the Earth expedition, Barbe's ex-fiancé

Written before the social upheavals of the 1960's changed the direction and form of much science fiction, *Rogue Queen* shows a bland, or what may be only an unconscious, indifference to the characteristics of the New Wave: probing social themes, convincing characterization, plausibility, and meticulous attention to detail. However, that is no reason to overlook *Rogue Queen*. For both dedicated science fiction buffs and casual readers, the novel offers a fast-paced plot, engaging characters, an intriguing "what-if" concept governing a parallel world wherein only the Queens (one to a Community) are fully functional females, an abundance of highly imaginative action, and a social commentary that is one part spoof and two parts mild satire.

The action takes place on a planet strikingly like Earth. The atmosphere, climate, terrain, and flora are identical; only the fauna differs, and then only in minor external ways. Domesticated draft animals are bipeds rather than quadrupeds, for example. Seemingly, the differences are present simply for the sake of being different. For the most part, de Camp avoids scientific explanations, which suggests the attitude that such detail is unnecessary; the story, after all, exists for the sake of the story, not scientific education.

Rogue Queen traces the metamorphosis of Iroedh from a worker, inexplicably drawn to a drone, to a Queen, who radically alters the structure of her society. As a loyal worker of Elham, a Community of the Avtini, Iroedh encounters an expedition of Earthlings that has landed its spaceship, *Paris*, in the valley of Gliid. Although attracted to the strange Earthlings, especially the

tall scientist Dr. Bloch and his friendly assistant Barbe Dulac, Iroedh is confused by their "magical machinery," their baffling sexual relationships, and
especially their obsession with an utterly incomprehensible emotion called
"love." A product of a beelike society, which regards work as its highest
value, Iroedh has trouble understanding the significance the Earthmen attach to
this perplexing passion.

Iroedh's world has only three classes: the Queen, the only sexually developed female in the Community, who lays the eggs necessary for the continuation of the group; workers, neuter females, who comprise the bulk of the
population and perform all necessary survival tasks; and the drones, a select
group of highly sexed males, who serve the Queen but are ruthlessly destroyed
in periodic "Cleanups" at the first sign of aging or waning powers. Although
this culture has developed writing, metalworking, a complex architecture, and
a high degree of social organization with democratically elected councils, the
Avtini remain in the primitive Bronze Age. They use flint to create fire and
crude weapons such as the spear to wage war; they have developed no sophisticated illumination and enjoy no transportation except chariots drawn by
beasts.

Iroedh asks the Earthmen to help fight against the Arsunni, ancient enemies
of the Avtini who are poised on the borders of Avtinid threatening invasion.
When Bloch denies her request on the grounds that exploratory crews are
strictly forbidden to interfere in the local affairs of any planet, Iroedh desists
but later blackmails Bloch into using the Earth helicopter to bring off the daring escape of her beloved drone Antis, condemned to death in the next Clean-
up and imprisoned at Elham.

Iroedh gives the Crown Princess a machete she has stolen from the Earthmen. This enables Estir to defeat the old Queen Intar in the Royal Duel. However, the new queen reneges on her promise to pardon Antis, forcing Iroedh
and Antis to flee. Now homeless exiles, they decide to travel north to Ledhwid
to seek the Oracle's advice, and they invite the newlyweds Bloch and Barbe to
join them. On their journey through wild, sometimes almost impassable terrain, the quartet struggles against formidable obstacles to reach the security of
the Oracle's Temple. Iroedh is unable to find edible vegetation, her only
source of food. When she is faced with starvation, she submits to Bloch's
pleas to eat the meat of an animal they have killed. The results are astonishing.
Iroedh's initial surprise that she did not die in the throes of an agonized, con-
vulsive death is soon surpassed by her amazement at the physical changes
occurring in her body. In a matter of days she experiences the full effects of
puberty and finds herself a completely "functional female." She and Antis
discover that they are in love "in the full, ghastly, sentimental Terran sense"
and wanting a permanent relationship like that of the Earth people, they persuade Bloch to marry them.

Once at Ledhwid, however, the newlyweds fail to find the comfort they are seeking. Not only is Gildakk, the Oracle, a fraud (he is the lone survivor of an expedition from the planet Thoth who had taken refuge in the Temple), but the sacred precincts are soon under siege by Wythias, the leader of a band of drones. Repulsed three times by the hopelessly outnumbered defenders, who put up a superb defense with the aid of the Earthmen's firearms, Wythias sues for a parley. By exhibiting Iroedh and by promising each drone a functional female of his very own once the workers are introduced to a meat diet, plus some dazzling hocus-pocus, Gildakk persuades the drones to accept Iroedh as their Queen. Outmarching her new army, Iroedh reaches Elham in time to dispose of Queen Istir and join the Elhamni in their defense against the attacking Arsunni. The victorious Elhamni accept the mixed diet which will produce functional females for the drones. Antis and Iroedh are, however, too restless to remain as titular rulers; they eagerly accept the Earthmen's offer of jobs with the Terran space authority as representatives for the planet Ormazd. They plan to leave, assured that the Elhamni will complete the defeat of the Arsunni and solve the problems presented by their new revolutionary social structure.

The novel is both a captivating tale, in spite of some weakness in characterization, and a provocative social commentary. De Camp gently directs his satire at love and sexuality; war and violence; prophecy and presumption; and man's inconsistencies, irrationalities, and illusions.

There must be something wrong with a society that smothers individuality under the cloak of sex roles. Although the four major characters enlist our sympathy, they fall short of sharp and distinct definition. In fact, the major weakness of the novel is perhaps the tendency to peg the characters into narrow sexual stereotypes. Bloch, efficient in his job as "xenologist," is nonetheless the timorous, indecisive Milquetoast of a man who must be spurred to action by the "little woman" (Barbe Dulac). Barbe, on the other hand, generously endowed with the initiative powers Bloch lacks, is still devoted to the efficacy of feminine wiles to ensnare the opposite sex. Notably, her gift to Iroedh is a compact, "one of her feminine doodads," so useful in creating the female beauty needed to "catch" men. Even in the relationship between the drone Antis and the worker Iroedh, who initially assumed authority, subtle shifts occur once they are thrown together and come under the influence of the Earthmen. Fluttering her lashes, Iroedh depends more and more on Antis and even allows him to usurp her ideas as his own, a feminine trick, Barbe assures her, widely used on Earth.

Love divorced from role playing, however, is depicted as something entirely different. Since the elimination of sexual love two thousand years earlier through strict dietary laws, the Avtini have not only stagnated culturally, but retrogressed. The potency of love as a positive, motivating force is demonstrated in a "rescue" motif de Camp uses throughout the novel. Although Iroedh's rescue of Antis from prison, Antis' of Iroedh from the Elhamni, and Barbe's of Bloch from the quicksand are consistent with the courageous nature of these characters, Bloch's rescue of Barbe from the fearsome noag is nothing short of phenomenal, given his timidity. The cause "must be that Terran love of theirs," a puzzling emotion powerful enough to lift man out of his flawed human nature and allow him to act on occasion like a god. Thus, the return of the Avtini to the Earth brand of love and sexuality through the overthrow of dietary injunctions is seen as a promise of social regeneration, but is not to be construed as an unqualified blessing. When we also see the pain (that suffered by Bloch and Barbe over O'Mara's jealousy) and the humiliation it brings (that endured by Subbarau over his wife's infidelity), its value becomes tempered.

The comedy inherent in controlling a society through its stomach informs the entire Oracle episode, the best sustained spoof in the novel. The absurdity of man's propensity to rely on anything but the resources of his mind in his search for security is exposed in the sham of the prophetic Oracle. Rather than an ascetic seer able to interpret the divine will through mystical trance, he is a roly-poly Thothian dedicated to bureaucracy, busily putting "the Oracle on a business basis" by organizing the priestesses. Admirably disturbed by the sorry state of the prophecies when he took over the enterprise, "all mixed up and written on leaves and potsherds and things," he has hastened to file and cross-index them properly. The travelers in this future Oz have found out their fraudulent Wizard. Even Iroedh's messianic role is not taken up with the exultant spirit of risk attendant on such adventures of high purpose, but is thrust upon her by the necessities of the situation; unable to hold out against Wythias' overwhelming numbers, the tiny garrison has only one recourse: to employ a strategy reminiscent of the *Lysistrata*. The price of peace is "a handsome and congenial functional female." And Iroedh is confirmed as leader of the revolutionary force, not as the divinely appointed, but as the result of an ambiguous prophecy and adroitly timed fireworks.

De Camp continues in this comic vein when he uses an "alien" protagonist (Iroedh) for ironic comment on human idiosyncrasies (a reversal of a major Swiftian device). This "foreign" point of view allows the author ample opportunity to satirize human frailties and foibles. But it is usually a mild Horatian satire, a gentle barb tossed at our relatively harmless albeit foolish fripperies. Iroedh is astonished at Bloch's insistence on recovering O'Mara's dead body; after all, neither his clothes nor his body has any practical value. Where is the logic in allowing above-the-waist nudity for the males of our species, but not the females? To each and every question, Bloch can only answer, "It is the custom."

Not all the subjects of attack are as harmless, however; violence and war, frequent satirical targets, get their share of attention. The charge is made through the creation of three levels of social consciousness — that of the Avtini, the future Earthmen, and the present Earthlings — and by placing us in our usual perch, the middle. By establishing parallels and contrasts between the outer levels, de Camp is thus able to illuminate the irrationalities of the middle. Earth culture of the future has evolved into a Utopian state where violence and war have been abolished. By contrasting in one vivid image the belief of Iroedh's primitive society that violence and war are inevitable because they are "part of the nature of things" with the enlightened view of Bloch's world, de Camp creates an awareness of the ironic contemporary position; while sharing with the future culture the knowledge of the futility of war, we nevertheless emulate the senseless destruction of the Elhamni, without the excuse of their ignorance.

Irony is also present in the most basic elements of the plot. Bloch makes the point time and again that Earthmen cannot interfere in the affairs of other cultures. Yet the structure of the novel hinges on the Earthmen's existence; their very presence on Ormazd makes the novel possible. Where else would Iroedh get a helicopter to rescue Antis? And who is responsible for Iroedh's eating the meat that changed her from a neuter to a sexy female? Bloch's repetitive pronouncements of nonintervention become highly ironic as we see the configuration of incident after incident turned by the action of one of the Earthmen or by the use of one of their artifacts. The machete stolen by Iroedh during her first encounter with the Earthlings carves out a new destiny for the Avtini. The thrust, and a sharper thrust than anticipated, seems to be aimed at man's presumption: his pride that he can order things to his liking. Plan, organize, determine as he will, there is nothing that man can do to negate his effect on the environment or on others.

Although the *Rogue Queen* does not exhibit those characteristics which have become familiar to readers of New Wave science fiction, it does exhibit many qualities worthy of note. It offers a glimpse of an appealing world, which is vividly created. An abundance of action results in a swashbuckling adventure yarn. A sly and sometimes humorous poke in the ribs makes the novel an effective, yet mild criticism of human faults. These qualities all add up to make a novel which is decidedly good reading.

Dorothy K. Kilker

Sources for Further Study

Reviews:

Kirkus Reviews. XIX, May 1, 1951, p. 237.

Library Journal. LXXVI, August, 1951, p. 1225.

New York Herald Tribune Book Review. September 16, 1951, p. 18.

New York Times. July 29, 1951, p. 13.

Springfield Republican. July 29, 1951, p. 5D.

THE ROSE

Author: Charles L. Harness (1915-   )
First book publication: 1966
Type of work: Novel
Time: The near future
Locale: Unspecified

An account of the evolution of a new human species and of the antagonism between Science and Art

Principal characters:
ANNA VAN TUYL, a psychiatrist, dancer, and composer
RUY JACQUES, an artist
MARTHA JACQUES, his wife, a scientist
MATTHEW BELL, a psychogeneticist

The Rose is a doubly complex story. It is an allegory whose characters play the symbolic roles of characters in a story written by Oscar Wilde, which itself constitutes a stylized commentary on human nature in the form of a fable. Thus, it is difficult to appreciate the work unless one is familiar with Wilde's story, "The Nightingale and the Rose." The full significance of the conclusion of *The Rose* is dependent on the fact that it overturns the bitter ending of Wilde's story, thus becoming a wholehearted affirmation of the superiority of the superhuman nature it presents over the human nature caricatured by Wilde.

"The Nightingale and the Rose" is the story of an impoverished student who becomes infatuated with a girl who promises to dance with him if he will bring her a red rose. There are white roses growing beneath his window, but try as he might he can find no red ones. A nightingale, hearing his desperate lament, is so taken by pity that she impales herself upon the thorn of one of the white roses and stains it red with her blood. The student carries his prize to the girl, but another admirer has given her jewels, and she spurns him. The shallowness of his infatuation is then revealed as he casts aside the flower and returns to his books, convinced of the stupidity of love as compared with philosophy and metaphysics. The story (as with the other tales in *The Happy Prince*, from which it comes) is a cynical attack on the illusions of romanticism. Harness, however, elaborately uses the fable to subvert its message and affirm precisely what "The Nightingale and the Rose" denies.

In Harness' allegory, the nightingale is Anna van Tuyl, a psychiatrist and dancer who has composed all but the final scene of a ballet based on Wilde's fable. The story begins with Anna staring into a mirror and contemplating her ugliness, which is caused by a progressive disease that has made her humpbacked and is causing hornlike projections to grow from her temples. Because of this ugliness she is selected by Martha Jacques to take on the case of her husband, Ruy, whom she believes to be schizophrenic. Martha is insanely jealous of her husband's affections, especially since he has long since ceased to love her despite her physical beauty. Martha can satisfy any whim or carry out personal revenges because her peace of mind is extremely valuable to the government — she is working to solve the Sciomniac equations which will unify all scientific knowledge into one system and make possible unlimited power through its practical applications.

As a composer Anna also comes into contact with Ruy, because he intends to stage her ballet at a festival in the Via Rosa, the artists' colony where he lives. Anna recognizes in him the same deformities which have overtaken her. With the aid of the psychogeneticist Matthew Bell, she concludes that what is involved is neither disease nor madness but evolution, and that both she and Ruy are undergoing a slow metamorphosis into the first beings of a new species. Bell considers the time ripe for the emergence of *Homo superior*, and he speculates that it will involve the development of new forms of communication.

At the beginning of the story Ruy's syndrome is more advanced than Anna's, but he suffers a crisis which interrupts and inhibits his progress. Anna falls desperately in love with him (though he seems quite incapable of love himself) and fails to conceal the fact from Martha, who tries to have her killed. With Ruy's aid she escapes the death trap and comes rapidly to her own crisis; unlike Ruy, however, she passes through it successfully and goes on to a new phase in her development.

Martha solves the Sciomniac equations — which, represented graphically, present the form of a rose — and celebrates the triumph of her science over her husband's art. She plans to destroy the Via Rosa with the aid of a weapon developed *via* Sciomnia: the symbolic thorn on which the nightingale is destined to be impaled. Anna reappears at the beginning of the ballet to play the part of the nightingale, no longer deformed; it quickly becomes apparent that the wings she sports are not stagewings but real ones. The ballet, however, still lacks thirty-eight chords. Ruy persuades Martha to seek her revenge by transforming the nineteen equations of Sciomnia into sound to fill the period of silence in the conclusion of the third act, thereby destroying both Anna and the Via Rosa. She complies, but her nineteen discordant equations are miraculously re-created, transformed into harmony to bring the ballet to its close. Anna absorbs the power of the death-dealing device, sacrificing herself to save the Via Rosa. As a result of her action, Ruy overcomes the lack of ability to love which had inhibited his own development, and his metamorphosis continues to completion.

Dominating the narrative is the fierce opposition between Science (personified by Martha) and Art (personified by Ruy), and the war between them grows out of the attempt by Martha to reclaim Ruy for herself as her science crushes and sterilizes art (as, of course, the student's books reclaim him after his temporary alienation in Wilde's story). Harness' sympathies throughout are entirely with Art: Martha is depicted as irredeemably evil, while Ruy, despite his inability to love, is definitely on the side of the angels. At every confrontation Ruy manages to upstage and humiliate Martha, his artistic *savoir faire* being more than a match for her unimaginative logic.

The plot, embellished by the marvelous ideative flourishes which are so characteristic of Harness' work, makes much of the power of art to bewilder the senses. Anna's escape from Martha's first murder attempt is orchestrated by Tchaikovsky's *Symphonie Pathétique*; the rhythm of its second movement is used to upset the coordination of the gunman's reactions, and she is then saved from detection in a rose garden by a cunning application of the color juxtaposition used by the pointillist impressionists after Seurat. All this is made ingeniously plausible, but it is its symbolic power which is really significant.

Harness' extreme hostility toward science may seem at first to be rather surprising. His earlier science fiction shows both an extensive familiarity with twentieth century science and a considerable capacity for imaginative inspiration derived from it. His antagonism arises not from a reaction against science *per se*, but against the social role of science. In his essay *Icarus*, Bertrand Russell put forward as early as the mid-1920's the view that scientific progress was undesirable because it added to the abilities of power groups to indulge their "collective passions," resulting in oppression and large-scale war. The explosion of the atom bomb which destroyed Hiroshima brought this message home to a large number of people, who were convinced that human nature, as expressed by contemporary international relations, was such that the world must surely be destroyed now that such power was at large within it. *The Rose* is perhaps the most exaggerated, and certainly the most strikingly eloquent, expression of this postwar attitude. It represents the scientist and his (or, in this case, her) political puppet-masters as the threat which might imminently destroy humankind and searches desperately for some reservoir of hope by which the threat can be opposed.

The Paradox Men presents the same enemy, opposing it with the hope that such enlightened scientists as Kennicot Muir might switch sides and work to overthrow their former masters; but in the end it falls back on the symbol of the superman as the means to salvation. In *The Rose*, a much more serious work, the formal opposition comes from the artists, champions of creative thought, and the development of new human opportunities. It is from their ranks that the new superhumans must come, endowed with communicative abilities and powers of empathy that would make the imperfect collective passions of hatred and group rivalry unthinkable. With this transcendence of the human condition will come a new power generated by the mind, which will make technology, and the scientific habit of thought responsible for technology, redundant. "In the final analysis," says Martha Jacques at one point, "Science means *force* — the ability to control the minds and bodies of men." In the world of Harness' superbeings, force will be neither possible nor necessary.

Though *The Rose* is a unique work, the attitude encapsulated in it is one that became very prominent in postwar science fiction. Numerous stories appeared which championed art against science in one way or another; notable examples are Walter Miller's "The Darfsteller" and James Blish's "A Work of Art." The transcendent superman became one of the most important symbols of the 1950's, and its importance can be judged by the fact that it was established in opposition to what had, before 1940, been a long-standing image which presented the superman as a powerful but essentially emotionless being.

The Rose, however, is most emphatic in its insistence that far from being emotionless, the superhuman must have as his most basic qualification for *being* superhuman, the ability to love. It is on this point, this vital "message," that *The Rose* is built. Lack of love prevents Ruy from fulfilling his destiny, and the discovery of love allows him to come belatedly into his inheritance when the novel finally and crucially departs from the original fable. The same idea forms the basis of much of Theodore Sturgeon's postwar science fiction, especially *The Dreaming Jewels* and *More Than Human*. Though Harness is not the prose stylist that Sturgeon is, *The Rose* is surely the equal of these classic works.

The Rose passed quite unnoticed in its day. It failed to find an American market and ended up, absurdly, in the British magazine *Authentic*, which specialized in the most vulgar and routine space adventure stories. Great credit is due to the editor, H. J. Campbell, who recognized the merit of the story and preserved it in print despite the fact that it was grotesquely unsuited to his publication. Some of the people who read the story then appreciated its worth, but there can only have been a handful. One of them, Michael Moorcock, contrived to have the story reprinted in 1966, and it finally appeared in America in 1969. For the thirteen years between its first and second publications, Harness published no science fiction at all. If the public response to *The Rose* was the cause of or a contributing factor toward this long absence, then its failure was most certainly a tragedy; and it was not the only first-rate work to receive a cold welcome in the science fiction market of the early 1950's. However, whereas many of the other works have since received the attention they deserve, *The Rose* is still unjustly neglected. It is, by the standards which it sets itself, both a work of art and a labor of love.

Brian Stableford

Sources for Further Study

Reviews:

Magazine of Fantasy and Science Fiction. XXXI, July, 1966, pp. 32-33.

New Worlds. CLX, March, 1966, pp. 157-159.

Observer. October 5, 1969, p. 39.

SF Commentary. XV, September, 1970, pp. 9-10.

Worlds of If. XIX, October, 1969, pp. 145-146.

WSFA Journal. LXX, December–February, 1969-70, pp. 26-27.

R.U.R.

Author: Karel Čapek (1890-1938)
First book publication: 1920; presented 1921
Type of work: Drama
Time: The late twentieth century
Locale: A remote island

The play which introduced robots to the world

> *Principal characters:*
> HARRY DOMIN, General Manager of Rossum's Universal Robots
> FABRY, Chief Engineer of R.U.R.
> DR. GALL, Chief Physiologist of R.U.R.
> DR. HALLEMEIER, Chief Psychologist of R.U.R.
> CONSUL BUSMAN, Business Manager of R.U.R.
> BUILDER ALQUIST, Chief of Construction of R.U.R.
> HELENA GLORY, Daughter of President Glory, member of the Humanity League
> NANA, her maid
> MARIUS, a robot
> SULLA, a robotess
> RADIUS, a big-brained robot
> PRIMUS, another robot
> HELENA, a robotess modeled after Helena Glory

It is hard to understand why Karel Čapek's amusing play, so popular in its time and so universal in its influence, is not performed today. Perhaps the reason lies in its very success: the themes it introduced have become so commonplace that to the present-day audience the original may look like a copy. Yet, rereading it today, one cannot help but be struck by its topicality, its apparent awareness of scientific advances reported in this week's magazine. In this respect, Čapek has more meaning for our time than either of the great prognosticators of science fiction, Jules Verne and H. G. Wells. While Verne concentrated on inventions destined to be realized and surpassed by reality (the submarine, the airplane, the spaceship), and Wells formulated "impossible hypotheses" unlikely to be realized in any foreseeable future (the time machine, the invisible man, the food of the gods), Čapek discovered a twilight zone of scientific possibility — apocalyptic premises, very plausible and very deadly (the robot, nuclear energy, prolonged life). Which is to say that Čapek's premises may be realized, but not surpassed. They prognosticate a world transformed, or a world destroyed.

The basic idea of *R.U.R.* is closest of all to *The Island of Doctor Moreau* (1896). This novel is founded on one of Wells's less "impossible" hypotheses: the transformation of animals into men. Wells attempted to bolster the hypothesis with "scientific" examples drawn from his time and the result is painfully dated. "You forget all that a skilled vivisector can do with living things," says Moreau. Through pages of detail — "A pig can be educated" —

we move to the creation of a man from a gorilla, from a puma, and the inevitable return of animal nature.

Čapek also has an island, the production of artificial men and the return of human nature. But unlike Wells, he does not try to pin down his hypothesis:

> It was in the year 1920 that old Rossum the great physiologist . . . attempted by chemical synthesis to imitate the living matter known as protoplasm, until he suddenly discovered a substance which behaved exactly like living matter, although its chemical composition was different.

This premise is not offered seriously — it is merely the first step into fantasy. But, insofar as human beings are composed of chemicals, it does seem theoretically possible. And though the making of human beings from scratch seems fairly remote, the recent advances in biochemistry, the discovery of DNA, the manufacture of bacteria, the birth of the first "test-tube baby," and the possibility of cloning make Čapek's facetious premise more than a laughing matter.

But Čapek does not stop here. Old Rossum belongs to the past — to Dr. Frankenstein and Dr. Moreau. *R.U.R.* takes another step: "Then up came young Rossum, an engineer, the nephew of old Rossum . . . and said: 'It's absurd to spend ten years making a man. If you can't make him quicker than nature, you may as well shut up shop.' " Young Rossum puts man on the assembly line, eliminates everything unnecessary for work, and produces efficient, unfeeling robots. Strangely enough, they are not all that different from men: both men and robots are taken for each other by Helena Glory, both repeat platitudes about the weather, both are sterile, both fall in love. Because men are dehumanized and robots are humanized, the characters in this work are all fairly drab, not nearly so colorful as the individually drawn personalities in the works of H. G. Wells. On the other hand, they are not only characters. It is reported that Čapek got the idea for *R.U.R.* while riding in a car: he glanced out the window and the crowds of people suddenly looked like "artificial beings." The robots he created have a symbolic value exceeding most of the characters of Verne and Wells.

The play was first published in 1920 and performed the following year. Although written in Czech, the title and characters names are in English. The text contains many English and international words: *pardon, Liga Humanity, cyclamen, telegramy, revolver, Ultima, revoltu robotů, elektrána, haha, Amen.* The now familiar word *robot* was coined by Karel's brother Josef in 1917; it derives from the Czech *robota,* meaning "heavy labor, drudgery, servitude." The word *robotess — robotka* in Czech — never caught on. The name of the inventor, Rossum, comes from the Czech *rozum,* meaning "reason." Clearly the author intended an international, or at least Western cast of characters, speaking a somewhat universal language, living the last days of mankind on a remote island. Unfortunately, the standard English version of the play, made in 1923 by Paul Selver, adapted for the English stage by Nigel

Playfair, and reprinted to the present day in England and America, spoils this scheme somewhat. Here the name Domin, suggesting someone godlike or dominant, is changed to "Domain," something a bit different. Dr. Hallemeier, the German psychologist, whose name suggests a person familiar with halls, is changed to "Dr. Helman," probably to make the name shorter. Consul Busman, clearly a "businessman," is turned into "Jacob Berman." Helena Glory's father is demoted from President (of America?) to "Professor." Her maid Nana, who sounds Slavic, is called Emma, who sounds English. Engineer Fabry, whose name recalls the French entomologist, remains the same. The robots also retain their own names. But the changes mentioned have the overall effect of giving England credit for destroying the world, rather than all the countries, as it should be.

Another serious change is relabelling the four acts "I, II, III, Epilogue," whereas they are in fact Prologue, I, II, III. Since there is a ten-year passage of time between the Prologue and Act I (reduced to five years in translation), and only short periods between the remaining acts, this change is not really acceptable. The translation also fixes the time as "a paltry 30 years" after competition between man and robot, but the available 1940 Czech text lacks this passage. Since Rossum made his discovery in 1932 and lived to a ripe old age, we can assume that the time of the action is the late twentieth century. The Selver version also makes some cuts and some additions, and converts all the dollars into pounds. The speech, as might be expected, is very British: *U čerta* becomes "Confound it," *Jemináčku* and *Ale božička* become "By Jove," *to je sláva* becomes "that's splendid," and so on. One suspects this By-Jovishness has contributed to the work's neglect in the colonies. It must be noted, however, that a New York edition of this same translation, put out by Samuel French, without credit to anyone, has restored the proper names, times, and currency, but has also made its own additions and cuts, such as calling the work a "fantastic melodrama" and dropping the entire Biblical passage at the end. It is a shame that no modern, accurate, American version of this important play exists.

The story line is simple, the pace is swift. In the Prologue, Helena Glory, on behalf of the Humanity League, visits the island to check up on the treatment of robots. She is instructed by Domin, who tells her about the old and young Rossum. Domin expounds his utopian ideal: the robots will liberate man from the degradation of labor, clothe and feed him, wash his feet; work and poverty will vanish; man will be free to perfect himself spiritually. He also reports that the robots have become an economic necessity in the world: they eat anything (the source of energy is not specified), cost only ¾¢ to operate per hour, and cause all the prices to drop (even the 2¢ loaf of bread will go down). Suddenly he proposes to Helena. There are no women on the island, and he wants to have first crack at her before the other directors of R.U.R. meet her.

Act I begins on the tenth anniversary of Helena's visit. She is now married to Domin. The situation is tense: Domin carries a gun, the island is cut off from the outside world, the robots — who have become the standing armies of all countries — have revolted and massacred seven hundred thousand people, human beings face extinction because of a drastic drop in fertility. The reason for the revolt is a change made in the more recent robots: at Helena's prompting, Dr. Gall has inserted something like a soul, a sense of pain. He has also built himself a robotess Helena, but bemoans her lack of spirit. The human Helena, upset by all the bad news, burns the newspapers, and with them, old Rossum's secret of robot manufacture. The act ends with the reading of a manifesto to the "robots of the world," declaring man an obstacle to work and an outlaw of the universe. War is declared and the island is attacked.

Here, in effect, the play is over. But, as William Harkins notes in his book on Čapek, the end is delayed by an electrified railing which prevents the robots from entering the factory. This permits the characters to express various ideas before the final rout. Alquist the builder condemns old Rossum for his godless tricks, young Rossum for his avarice, and the R.U.R. shareholders for their love of dividends. Domin laments the loss of his dream. Busman blames the business world, which continued to demand cheap robots regardless of the consequences. He runs out to make a deal with the robots and electrocutes himself on the railing. The remaining men place their hope in Rossum's secret — so long as they have it, they remain masters. Helena reports the burning. The robots, led by big-brained Radius, rush in and murder everybody, save Alquist, who is spared because he works with his hands.

The last act exists to promise resurrection. Alquist, a worker but not a creator, cannot make new robots. No other men can be found — either to rediscover the secret or to reproduce humankind. The robots will wear out in twenty years. As Alquist rests on his bed, the robotess Helena comes in with the robot Primus. In a scene too long for today, but necessary for the time, the two discover the emotion of love and state their willingness to die for the other. Alquist then sends them away to be husband and wife — the robotic Adam and Eve — and he closes the play reading from Genesis: "Be fruitful and multiply. . . ."

The reader may wonder whether the robots are sexual. Čapek's answer is inconclusive. In the Prologue, Helena is informed that robots are made in male and female form only because people are accustomed to waiters and waitresses. One imagines a glabrous space between the legs — after all, sexual organs do not contribute to work. In Act I Dr. Gall complains about the robotess Helena, made as a surrogate of the woman he loves. Even if, in this day of inflatable companions, one suspects that Dr. Gall made certain innovations for his own pleasure, there is no reason to suppose he connected all the tubes, or was even able to. In the next act he confesses that without Rossum's formula in hand he is helpless; yet he has made the soul. Has he inserted something else as well? The question is left open, but the awakening of Adam and Eve assumes that they are adequately equipped.

Another shortcoming is the inviolability of Rossum's secret. The Prologue establishes that the robots think and work much more efficiently than man; they immediately retain everything they read. Yet in the last act they wait around helplessly for Alquist to rediscover the secret, while their parts wear out. Today we are familiar with computers which can do hundreds of man-hours of work in a second, so we naturally wonder why the robots cannot rediscover the secret, or at least maintain their parts. The crux of the problem is really the difference between mechanical and "soft" thinking, but Čapek did not focus on this. He was more intent on plotting man's self-destruction and miraculous resurrection.

In his discussion of the play, William Harkins points to two dramatic weaknesses: the early victory of the robots and the power of Helena. Since the robots have really won the world by the end of Act I (or even before it begins), Harkins considers the last two acts "anti-climactic." However, it could be argued that the focus is different, the climax is not military but spiritual. Be that as it may, Harkins is certainly right about Helena. She is insufferable: she worries about the perfectly content robots, persuades Dr. Gall to give them souls, big brains, and whatever else, and she destroys the only thing that can save the besieged scientists. Harkins quotes a Czech critic who says that mankind disappears from the Earth because Helena cannot mind her own business. Without question, Čapek intended her as a comic stereotype of the meddlesome, sentimental, disastrous woman.

Interpretation of the play would seem to be obvious. Machines promise to liberate man from drudgery, yet threaten to rob him of vitality. By building substitutes of himself, man may duplicate (and magnify) his own failings, yet his better qualities (so the author hopes) will inevitably rise to the surface. But, of course, there is more to it than that. The best guide to interpretation is Čapek himself, who responded to a discussion of the work with these words:

> I wished to write a comedy, partly of science, partly of truth. The old inventor, Mr. Rossum (whose name in English signifies Mr. Intellect or Mr. Brain), is no more or less than a typical representative of the scientific materialism of the last century. His desire to create an artificial man . . . is inspired by a foolish and obstinate wish to prove God to be unnecessary and absurd. Young Rossum is the modern scientist, untroubled by metaphysical ideas; scientific experiment is to him the road to industrial production, he is not concerned to prove, but to manufacture . . . . Immediately we are in the grip of industrialism; this terrible machinery must not stop . . . . It must, on the contrary, go on faster and faster, although it destroys in the process thousands and thousands of other existences. Those who think to master the industry are themselves mastered by it; Robots must be produced although they are, or rather *because* they are, a war industry. The conception of the hu·an brain has at last escaped from the control of human hands. This is the comedy of scienc·.

Two points deserve to be emphasized. First, Čapek is not speaking of mechanical men, but biologically artificial men — not "robots" in the present sense, but the more advanced creatures now called "androids." With them he develops the brilliant insight of Samuel Butler, who predicted a new stage in evolution when men would serve their own machines, just as bees serve the flowers they pollinate. ("The Book of the Machines," in *Erewhon* [1872].) Old Rossum declares a new era in evolution when he makes his discovery. It is the era of "human engineering," the production of "desirable" types, designed to serve society, whom society may serve. Second, with young Rossum's massproduction methods, Čapek introduces perhaps his most original thought: the concept of suicidal economy. We do not have to look far today for examples of this principle — the sale of arms, automobiles, drugs, cigarettes, pesticides, poisons. When a town is faced with the choice — nonpoisonous air or a new factory and new jobs — and it chooses the factory, we must call it a suicidal economy.

As Čapek himself said:

> Now for my other idea, the comedy of truth. The General Manager Domin, in the play, proves that technical progress emancipates man from hard manual labor, and he is quite right. The Tolstoyan Alquist, on the contrary, believes that technical progress demoralizes him, and I think he is right, too. Busman thinks that industrialism alone is capable of supplying modern human needs; he is right. Helena is instinctively afraid of all this inhuman machinery, and she is profoundly right. Finally, the Robots themselves revolt against all these idealists, and, as it appears, they are right, too.

Where does this leave us? In a battle between opposing "truths." Čapek was a relativist: he did not believe that one ism or another would solve the fate of the world, that one man's utopia or another's would be realized. It is rather a combination of all the forces, a suprapersonal principle under no one's command that controls the destiny of man. In his own words: "I ask whether it is not possible to see in the present social conflict of the world an analogous struggle between two, three, five, equally serious verities and equally generous idealisms?"

R.U.R., of course, is a product of its time. The robot war has clear overtones of World War I, the manifesto of the working drones parodies the Russian revolution, the assembly line production of men mocks the technology of the West. Other writers were doing the same thing. Witness the amazing parallels between this play and Evgeny Zamyatin's novel *We*, written in the same year without a knowledge of Čapek: both works present dehumanized beings of the future, both call the timetable the pinnacle of the human spirit, both describe a final revolution which is not final, both rediscover the "soul," both re-create Adam and Eve.

Many writers remain stuck in the 1920's, but Zamyatin and Čapek transcend their time. We can see Čapek's story in almost every subsequent fictional contest between man and robot. But it is not only in fiction that the robots exist. While we may doubt the transition from mechanical to "soft" thinking, we ought at least to acknowledge the presence of one particular robot which has already turned most of the nations of the world into wastelands of mindless, illiterate consumers of products, platitudes, and propaganda: the one-eyed monster who rules us all, television.

Gary Kern

Sources for Further Study

Criticism:

Darlington, W. A. "Brothers Čapek," in *Literature in the Theatre, and other Essays*. New York: Holt, 1933, pp. 137-144. Darlington evaluates Čapek's drama as being timely.

Harkins, W. E. *Karel Čapek*. New York: Columbia University Press, 1962, pp. 84-95. Harkins gives a thorough analysis of Čapek's *R.U.R.* Although he finds faults with the play Harkins feels that no other play has captured the public's imagination.

Wellek, Rene. *Essays of Czech Literature*. The Hague: Mouton, pp. 50-51. *R.U.R.* is revealed to be a testimony to Čapek's lively sense for the state.

Reviews:

Booklist. XIX, April, 1923, p. 215.

Bookman. LVI, December, 1922, pp. 478-480.

Drama. XIII, December, 1922, pp. 90-91.

English Review. XXXVI, June, 1923, pp. 588-592.

Literary Digest. LXXIII, November 4, 1922, pp. 30-31.

Nation. CXV, November 1, 1922, p. 478.

New Republic. XXXII, November 1, 1922, pp. 251-252.

New Statesman. XXI, May 5, 1923, pp. 110-111.

SAGAN OM DEN STORA DATAMASKINE
(The Tale of the Big Computer)

Author: Olof Johannesson (Hannes Alfvén, 1908-   )
First book publication: 1966
Type of work: Novel
Time: The distant future
Locale: The Earth and Mars

A history of the evolution of human life and computers from the origins of man through the "Symbiotic Age" to the beginning of the true computer age, "written" by a computer-historian

The "future history," as exemplified by such works as Isaac Asimov's *Foundation Trilogy*, Robert A. Heinlein's *The Past Through Tomorrow*, and Cordwainer Smith's "Instrumentality of Man" stories, has become one of science fiction's most imaginative fictional concepts. In *Sagan om den stora datamaskine*, Olof Johannesson has brilliantly taken this concept one step farther. He has actually cast his novel in the form of a volume of historiography produced in a distant future with all of the substance, paraphernalia, and language of a scholarly text. This thoughtful and well-written work is ostensibly the product of a computer-historian who is, himself/itself, a prime example of the final flowering of the society into which computers have evolved.

The book trades the historical process of this human-computer evolution from its beginnings to the "True Computer Age," with special emphasis on the "Symbiotic Age." It is divided into four long chapters, each of which describes a historical period of life on Earth (and the space settlements), and each of these four sections are in turn divided into a number of smaller chapters describing the sociological, political, cultural, and historical events more systematically and in greater detail.

In the opening section the historian-computer traces human evolution from the birth of mankind to the year 1 A.C. (After the Computer). This chapter provides the necessary background on the history of man and his relationship with the earliest computers (both from a biological-evolutionary point of view and from a sociological and political one). All human achievement prior to the invention of the computer is treated as largely trivial and incidental. Only with the coming of the computer, the historian-computer (hereafter called the historian) seems to suggest, can history really be thought to have begun.

The historian goes on to explain that men are not fit to govern a society. They think too slowly; they take too long to translate their notions into concrete results; and their lust for power interferes with every progressive development. Beyond this, the historian argues, the organization of society is too complex a task for the human brain, individually or collectively. This last insight it/he (hereafter called he) formulates as "The Sociological Complications Theorem." He ends part one with a short description of the technological evolution, the rise of computers (which throughout the book is equated with biological evolution) and the great mystery of the past: the big city.

In the second chapter the historian deals with computers and man in the "Symbiotic Age." He goes into greater detail on the history and evolution of computers, from the first primitive, purely mathematical, ones to the super-computers of his own day. Given man's basic inability to deal with his affairs ("The Sociological Complications Theorem"), the computers have, during this period, taken over the running of all aspects of society, leaving men only a few technical jobs such as programming and making simple repairs, plus some continuing "rationalization jobs"; that is, occupations devised to give man the illusion of "usefulness." Even education, that most basic of human activities, has been rendered obsolete; no one needs schools or universities when all the knowledge in the world is instantly available to everybody by way of "tele-totals" or "minitotals." With all power transferred to computers, war has been eliminated and universal prosperity reigns.

In the third section of the novel the historian describes the great catastrophe that occurred and speculates about why this "perfect system" broke down, resulting in the deaths of most of the population of the world and of the space colonies by starvation, cold, and disease. After this collapse of the com-puterized society, cultural evolution had to start all over again, and people endured great hardship until they were able once again to master such elemen-tary things as crafts, languages, and farming — everything that they had either handed over to the computer-controlled factories or never bothered to learn in the first place. (Fortunately, the museums still existed to provide models; mankind had only to re-create things, not invent them.) From an ecological point of view the catastrophe was a very good thing.

In the final chapter, the author takes up the history at the moment man again begins to utilize computers; from that time on development was rapid. To avoid the possibility of another catastrophe (which the computers discovered had been caused by the "rationalization workers" lusting for power) *every-thing* was now done by computers and computer controlled machinery. The historian describes the introduction of this fully computerized society, the birth of the supercomputers, and the invention of the PSC-Print, by which comput-ers began to think and deduce without the need of any human intervention whatsoever. At this point the computers divided themselves into two groups, one to do the calculating and controlling, the other simply to think and deduce. The historian concludes his book with some remarks about the present and future relationships between the computer and man, now that man has become superfluous.

In these final speculations, two interesting metaphysical and moral ques-tions are posed: (1) Why does a computer not have a soul? (2) What is the relationship between the computer and power?

After having dealt with the soul and spirit in man and animals — the presence of a "soul" being man's primary claim to superiority — how can it be that the soul has settled in a human body, when computers are preferable both from an intellectual and a moral point of view? Seen from such an "objective" point of view, the so-called "superiority of man" appears dubious. How tolerant nature has been to this animal who for centuries has talked about a better world, but has instead made wars and brought about ecological spoliation; who places such immense value on wealth, but uses it accidentally, arbitrarily, and often destructively. Is man merely a savage who became intelligent too early? The historian has only the weak suggestion that perhaps the soul prefers protoplasm.

Then the historian goes more fully into the question of power. Throughout the book he strongly suggests that it was mankind's immense lust for power that created continual crises and probably also caused the "Great Catastrophe." It is the basic reason for man's inability to govern himself. Fortunately, he goes on to say, computers are completely without this trait; it is the reason why computers have succeeded, where man has failed, in building the perfect society.

But one factor contradicts this assertion. When the historian tries to describe the near future and man's place in it, he points out that man has now become a parasite. What should the computers do with him? Some of the people will have to be "rationalized away," because the computers are being used to produce things for man — goods, transportation, leisure activities, and hospitals — without receiving anything useful in return. So, from an economic point of view, men have ceased to be a profitable part of society. The logical thing would be simply to get rid of them. However, the historian reassures the reader, the computers do not plan to get rid of *all* the people. Some must be kept as "insurance" in case a new catastrophe should occur, and some others just as an act of pious good will. The computers will continue to love and care for man just as man admired and looked out for his horses after the advent of the automobile and tractor.

It is at this point that the effectiveness of Johannesson's half-serious, half-comic tone becomes most effective. The central continuing irony of the book resides, of course, in the notion that computers, created to serve man, eventually replace him, not only in the physical and social sense, but in the moral one as well. If "lust for power" is what has continually lured man to self-destruction, that quality has perhaps, in a somewhat different guise, been thoroughly, if unconsciously, absorbed by the supercomptuers. As a group, the computers, having gained all political, economic, and social power, talk about the "use" of men and plan to "rationalize" most of them away, partly because men are useless and partly because they form a possible, if slight, threat to this perfect society. If the computers do not have a conventional "lust for power," their striving for perfection is just as dangerous. Johannesson seems to be asking, in the guise of his historian, whether the "price" of the perfect society might not be too high.

In addition to this major ironical thrust, Johannesson effectively satirizes many aspects of modern life, some directed specifically at the contemporary Scandinavian scene and some generally applicable to all modern industrial societies. He scores the paradoxical distances between politicians' promises and their performance; the rationale for "defensive" war machines to "keep the peace"; the pollution of the world; the destruction of nature; the killing of rare species; and, most emphatically of all, the laziness of the people, their blind acceptance of the world they inhabit, and their rampant hypocrisy and generally declining moral standards. Johannesson is especially biting in his treatment of the modern city and its primary symbol, the motor car.

The historian confesses bafflement in trying to understand why people choose to live in big cities, and he cannot at all understand their preoccupation with the automobile. His colleagues have formed a theory — "The Ignorance Theory" — but even this does not sufficiently explain the absurdity of these "human" institutions. Why, for example, bring huge amounts of goods into the city, only to send them right out again? Why expend vast amounts of time and energy bringing large numbers of people together in meetings, when they could more easily use telephones or television for the same ends? And, especially puzzling: what is the difference between cars that are parked and cars that are stuck in traffic jams? Is it all, by any chance, part of some exotic religious ritual?

Olof Johannesson (a pseudonym for the Swedish scientist Hannes Alfvén) has much to say in this novel, and he says it with great humor and subtle indirection. As with all good books, *Sagan om den stora datamaskine* provides a historical-cultural view of its own time. But it also presents a vivid picture of a New Era to come, complete with a "small" warning about the immense potential, favorable and unfavorable, inherent in the computers themselves. It contains an even more trenchant commentary on the possibilities — both positive and negative — of these devices in the hands of a powerful group — *of men*.

Erik H. Swiatek

Sources for Further Study

Reviews:

Analog. LXXXIII, May, 1969, p. 167.

Booklist. LXIV, April 15, 1968, p. 974.

Bulletin of the Center for Children's Books. XXI, April 1968, p. 129.

Library Journal. XCIII, January 1, 1968, p. 96.

Magazine of Fantasy and Science Fiction. XXXIV, June, 1968, pp. 52-53.

Publisher's Weekly. CXCII, November 20, 1967, p. 51.

Young Readers Review. IV, April, 1968, p. 7.

"THE SANDMAN"
("DER SANDMANN")

Author: E. T. A. Hoffmann (1776-1822)
First book publication: 1816
English translation: 1824
Type of work: Short story
Time: The early nineteenth century
Locale: Germany; the University town of G_____, and a second unidentified small town

The story of the search of a student, Nathanael, to find knowledge, and of his subsequent sufferings and death

> Principal characters:
> NATHANAEL, a student
> KLARA, his fiancée
> COPPELIUS, a lawyer
> GIUSEPPE COPPOLA, a Piedmontese peddler of barometers and optical instruments
> PROFESSOR SPALANZANI, a famous physicist and a professor at Nathanael's university; "father" of Olimpia
> OLIMPIA, an automaton constructed by Spalanzani and Coppola
> SIEGMUND, a student in G_____, Nathanael's true friend

To claim E. T. A. Hoffmann's "The Sandman" as science fiction forces us to examine the origin and nature of this elusive genre. "The Sandman" is a story in which men build robots, but these men remain alchemists; their science and technology are not contemporary (this is the age of Priestly and Lavoisier), but anachronistic and fanciful. Therefore, in a literal sense the tale is not concerned with what Asimov calls "the impact of scientific advance on human beings"; it does, however, share this quality on a level beyond hardware.

Hoffmann lived in what was, in the modern sense, a scientific climate. As a writer, he felt the pressures of the Newtonian experimental method as surely as did Kant or Goethe. "The Sandman" is a narrative cut loose from absolutes; at its core lie problems rather than statements. Is the nature it describes that "deathly" materialist system Goethe decried in "D'Holbach"? The attempt of Nathanael's father and Spalanzani to build an *homme-machine*, which implies a refusal to distinguish between matter and spirit, seems to move in Goethe's direction. Or, on the contrary, are natural things "hieroglyphs" that conceal some indwelling power? Nathanael's premonitions hint that man perceives not by reason alone, but in dreams might indeed reach beyond the chain of material cause and effect to more primal unity. This is Schubert's "nightside" world of the natural sciences, that of Mesmeric experiment and the investigation of somnambulistic states. Hoffmann's hero faces the problem of perception itself, and in his search for truth makes use of intuitions and scientific instruments alike.

If Nathanael's dilemma is that of modern scientific man — the search for permanence in the face of rapidly changing ideas of nature — Hoffmann sets it

in a world whose contours are ultimately unscientific. If the mirror of nature
reflects anything in this story, it is man rather than God. Yet that man is
inexplicably divided, fallen away from nature and self. If his need for knowledge produces a maze of ideas, each of these ideas in turn proves to be a
mirror for perceiving self. The nightmare world of "The Sandman" is generated by a corresponding maze in the human mind. Forced to seek explanation
for this gallery of mirrors, over and over we are borne back, irrationally, to an
idea like original sin. And in the context of new science, this theological remnant becomes all the more grim. To Hoffman, the fall seems as unassailable as
the mechanist first cause: from it flow — more as cold facts than as the results
of any "sin" of intellectual pride — the conflicting hypothesis of modern science. As the world they create becomes increasingly fragmentary, the corresponding dissolution of man at the center waxes monstrously.

Hoffmann's tale begins with three letters. In the first (presented without
introduction or frame), protagonist Nathanael writes to his friend Lothar, telling him of the peddler Coppola's visit and of his uncanny resemblance to a
childhood bogeyman, the lawyer Coppelius. He then relates a long, involved
tale of the Sandman: he recounts his father's alchemical experiments with
Coppelius, his gradual association of this man with the eyestealing sandman of
the nurse's *Marchen*, his eavesdropping, his traumatic discovery by Coppelius,
and his father's later death by explosion. The reader wonders why Nathanael
tells this story in such a self-conscious, self-indulgent manner, since surely if
Lothar were a childhood friend, he would have heard all this before. Nathanael's discourse loses itself in its own configurations; it is a rational ordering of
irrational materials for the yet more irrational end of narcissistic contemplation. Significantly, the return letter is not from Lothar but from his sister
Klara, Nathanael's fiancée. Having opened his letter by mistake, she now
chides him, saying that his dark fears are the product of a tired brain, nothing
more. Such common sense, however, is totally at odds with whatever urged
her to devour a letter not addressed to her. Nathanael's reply is not, as we
might expect, to Klara, but to Lothar, and is written in a tone as cutting and
sarcastic as it was rapturous before.

As Nathanael continues with his story, telling of the physics professor Spalanzani and his odd daughter Olimpia, his observations are now blunt and pragmatic,
rather than fanciful as before. He notices Olimpia's wooden movements, whereas
later he will be totally blind to them, and to the possibility that she might be less
than human. Nathanael never addresses Klara, pushing her aside like an object; in
his mind she is already the "wooden doll" he sees in the end.

The narrator now intervenes. His voice, however, is no more stable than
Nathanael's. He is neither objective nor omniscient: he loses the thread of his
logic in a rhapsody on one of his own characters, a Klara who bears no resemblance to the voice we have just heard; then he loses himself in the mirror of
his own sonorous phrases and figures of speech. As he continues his narrative

to its end, his stance becomes increasingly schizophrenic. Without transition he passes from affectedly analytical commentary (his satirical account of society's reaction to the discovery that Olimpia is not a lady but a machine) to indiscriminate chronicling of contradictory modes or facts, then back again. Throughout "The Sandman," the point of view shifts and the narrative tone moves back and forth between unresolved opposites. This equivocation penetrates the story's smallest corners: we see it microscopically in an early allusion to Franz Moor's nightmare in Schiller's *Die Räuber*, which reminds us of the famous scene in the play and its web of irresolution. Two interpretations are offered — dreams come from bad digestion, dreams come from God — but neither is proven. In fact, Franz's materialist assertion contrasts glaringly with his obsessive imagination and his Macbeth-like inclination to have visions. Conversely, the prosaic old servant Daniel is an unlikely *Geisterseher*. Instead of a solid structure, the story's layering of multiple hypothesis and conjecture creates a labyrinth.

The characters in "The Sandman" are strangely alike. Klara is not (as is often thought) Nathanael's opposite so much as his own image inverted. He is wild and effusive one moment, coldly logical the next. His haunted imagination is offset by a contrary yearning for the peace of the family circle; he hates Coppelius for his disruption of his household. Klara is equally split. One moment she denounces Nathanael's premonitions as "phantoms" of his ego, the next she is swept up in them. Furthermore, the divided nature of the character is reflected in the world around them. But are the characters prisoners of their world or of themselves? Perhaps like Narcissus they are contented with the self they see as their mirrored images.

Such solipsism proves destructive throughout. Absorbed in his scientific experiment (itself a flawed mirror in its twisted approach to the creation of life), Spalanzani allows Nathanael to pursue Olimpia and his illusion to their fatal end. Klara is apparently so wrapped up in herself that she can utter the remark ("See, we've driven the horrible Coppelius away") that triggers Nathanael's recitation. Within this garden circle, with its promise of fruitful human communion, each withdraws into a sterile circle of self. She is fascinated and repelled by Coppelius to the point that his divided being becomes the mirror of her own. As she loses herself in this reflective act, the other individual becomes an object, without feelings or needs.

In his poem, Nathanael in turn encompasses his own obsession in a metrically perfect whole, so that its reading becomes a like exercise in self-absorption. As he reads, Klara is drained of life; her eyes look back at him with a "puppetlike stare." Man then is perhaps less cursed from without, the victim of a malicious force that makes all beings alike and impermeable to one another, as he is the cause of his own cursed existence. Each of these reflexive "relationships" points inexorably to a flaw within man, who, by seeking his way out of the maze, only widens the rift.

Hoffmann's characters seek answers in science, but their objective search for truth leads in circles and results in vertigo and loss of self. An explosion hurls Nathanael's father face down on the blank floor, his earlier blindness — seeking self in a robot — is now mirrored in his own eyeless face. Fallen over his beakers, a similarly blind Spalanzani is left groping for the eyeless face of Olimpia.

The central fall in the story, however, is Nathanael's. His fatal curiosity seems awakened by his mother's ambivalence: there is no sandman, and yet there is. She smoothes over the dark violence of the nurse's tale with rational assurances, yet she fears Coppelius as if he were really the fairy-story creature. Driven to find out the truth for himself, Nathanael hides in the alchemist's chamber only to fall out on the floor. Scientific temptations bring further falls. Spread out on the table, Coppola's eyeglasses flicker and seem to come alive. Nathanael's vertigo drives him to purchase the fatal glass through which he first glimpses Olimpia and falls into further confusion and error. Later, his first fit of madness is caused by an event which openly links the act of seeing with violence against self: Olimpia's eyes — in which he had sought the mysteries of the universe — are hurled back at his chest by Spalanzani. As he screams out, "Turn, wooden doll!" its spinning becomes the vortex through which he regresses to a raging beast.

Nathanael's second fit, which brings about his leap from the tower, is set spinning by a strange perception of Klara; the archrationalist sees something profoundly irrational — a "walking bush." In each case man attempts to extend his vision through scientific methods of improving sight or through instruments — Nathanael's last gesture is to grab his telescope. Each attempt, however, is destructive to the viewer; the problem is irradicable, since its source lies at the heart of the human act of seeing.

In interpreting this story, two theories have traditionally been offered to explain Nathanael's actions: either he is the victim of diabolical forces, or he is mad. Hoffmann's more sensitive critics, however, see Nathanael as suspended between these two extremes, alternating between the "uncanny," the "marvelous," and the "fantastic." Throughout the narrative, action is governed by a basic pattern which defies all attempts by science or religion to explain it. Whatever operates here is more than any subjective state, yet less than the active intervention of an "enemy": from beginning to end, Nathanael is denied even this grim certainty. In the final scene on the tower, he swings his glass to see the walking bush and sees instead Klara's face. In his ensuing madness, he again cries out, "Turn, wooden doll!" In his mind, she and Olimpia have become one. Yet there are deeper ties which join these two dissimilar beings: the root of Olimpia's strange name is the Spanish "limpia," meaning "clarity."

Coppelius and Coppola are likewise linked. More than double agents of Nathanael's fall, however, they seem mirroring poles. The common root of

both names has two possible meanings: "coppo," or "eyesocket," and "cop-
pella," or "crucible." In this name, the organic and inorganic opposites are
fatally enfolded, but the element common to both is science; scientific analysis
is bound to the eye — the organ of investigation itself. On all levels of the
story, man's search to know is doomed to failure, which is always described
through the metaphor of eyesight. In his rhapsody on Klara, for example, the
narrator describes his gaze igniting a fire in her eyes, which flows back as
inspiration into his own breast. This is the fire, however, which destroys the
work of art, which turns song into chaotic sound. Nathanael's love poem
describes the same process: this time it is Coppelius who touches Klara's eyes,
and they leap out of her head and penetrate Nathanael's breast as "bloody
sparks." This same scenario becomes reality in the Olimpia episode: eyes
"stolen" from Nathanael and given to Olimpia (in the poem Klara had shouted
that what he thought were her eyes were really drops of his own heart's blood)
are thrown back at their owner by Spalanzani.

The central image of "The Sandman" is the mirror. But the story's mirrors
are special: more than just empty, they are dark cavities that efface as they
reflect — they are both sockets and crucibles. In this tale the more mirrors are
polished, the duller they become. As the narrator ponders Klara's image, he
loses himself in the empty glass of her eyes; these in turn are mirrored in the
limpid depths of the Ruisdael lake to which he compares them. It is the same
with Nathanael's poem; the more he polishes it metrically, the more chaotic it
becomes. In its thematic mirror, Nathanael's solipsism is broken by Klara: "I
still have my eyes!" she shouts, and the whirling stops. On the tower, there is
the same reaching out from the circle of self to make contact with eyes, this
time Coppelius'. Again, the image reflected is fatally obscured. Socket and
crucible meet as Nathanael blurts out Coppola's distorted German ("sköne
Oke" — "lovely eyes-a"), and leaps to his death.

Speaking of another Hoffmann story, the author's contemporary Clemens
Brentano said: "For some time I have had a horror of all poetry which mirrors
itself and not God." But Hoffmann's vision has proven the more modern, for
he shows us unaided man pursuing nature — as material cause and effect or as
a set of "hieroglyphs" — only to find himself trapped; there is no way out of
the maze of things. Later, Baudelaire echoed this same predicament; and, as
Baudelaire's modernism is tainted with ancient sin, so Hoffmann's tale, as an
ancestor of science fiction, is equally janus-faced: in it, the old proponent of
scientific enquiry has, in a complete reversal, become a rebel in the name of
man against impersonal processes elevated by scientific authority to iron law.

Hoffmann's story, which belongs to the unbroken line that runs from the
Faustbuch to Ray Bradbury, is profoundly antiscientific: science is the necessary extension of man's fall. Klara has only a touch of the seeker, and in the
end, she can retreat to her comfortable circle of family. For Nathanael, however, imagination is a curse. He cannot go backward; to put the family ring on

Olimpia's hand is a grotesque parody of the search for lost Eden. However, to use the glass of science is to go forward to greater perversions of an already fallen existence. In making and adoring Olimpia, man has mistaken death for life.

George Slusser

Sources for Further Study

Criticism:

Davidson, A. "The Tales of Hoffman," in *Magazine of Fantasy and Science Fiction*. XXVII (September, 1964), pp. 78-79. This article gives a brief description of Hoffman's works.

SANREIZAN HIROKU
(A Hidden History of the Hi Tribe)

Author: Ryo Hanmura (1935-   )
First book publication: 1972
Type of work: Novel
Time: The early 1500's to the present
Locale: Japan

A heart transplant operation performed on Japanese history in which the author gives full rein to his impressive storehouse of ethnological knowledge to provide an alternative explanation for the rise of the Japanese state based on the intervention of the "Hi Tribe," a group descended from extraterrestrials

> *Principal characters:*
> ZUIFU (LATER TENKAI), head of Hi clan and adviser to Tokugawa Shogunate
> TOBIWAKA, Zuifu's youngest son
> SARUTOBI, Tobiwaka's older brother
> SASUKE, Sarutobi's grandson and Japan's most famous "ninja" secret agent
> SHINKICHI, a burglar in the Edo period
> SAKAMOTO RYOMA, a prime mover of the Meiji Restoration

Japan in the early part of the sixteenth century was a land wracked by two hundred years of continuous warfare. Ever since the vicious street fighting that laid waste to the capital city of Kyoto during the Onin War of 1467, Japan had been a nation without a core. The Imperial household was in eclipse, impoverished and lacking even spiritual authority. The Ashikaga shogunate was in shambles, emasculated by in-fighting and a succession of puppet leaders, continuing in existence only for want of any other power in the country with a broad enough base to assert national leadership. The situation was ripe for the appearance of a figure able to weld together the suspicious and bickering feudal daimyo and seize control of Kyoto, and with it Japan, for himself. Tenka toitsu — bringing together all under heaven — was a phrase that fired the imagination of any warlord of stature in those days, and it was also a phrase on the lips of those who simply wished for an end to the violence of centuries, perhaps at any price.

The rise of Oda Nobunaga as the military genius who set in motion the chain of events leading to the unification and pacification of Japan is a subject that holds an apparently inexhaustible fascination for the Japanese. In countless permutations, the story of Nobunaga's stunning initial victory over the Imagawa family, crushing an army a hundred times the size of his own in a masterful surprise attack; of the long and bloody conflict with Takeda Shingen, the other most likely contender for control of the islands; of Nobunaga's death at the hands of his lieutenant-turned-assassin Akechi Mitsuhide; and of the bloody succession struggles that finally brought into existence the Tokugawa hegemony that lasted until Perry tore the fabric of Japanese isolationism, have appeared over and over again in books, in drama, in movies, and on television. Japan is a country deeply aware of the drama of its own history, and the Japanese are a people who, as can be seen in the tremendous popularity of historical novels and costume drama, feel a constant need to look back and reexamine their past.

This is perhaps one explanation for one of the distinguishing features of Japanese science fiction: the paucity of satisfying works with the stars as their stage and a great affection for time travel and time paradox. As many of the major writers in the field have matured, they have turned their eyes more to the past, some even abandoning all pretense of science fiction to write straight historical novels.

Ryo Hanmura is one of those Japanese writers assigned, sometimes it would seem almost by chance, to the science fiction genre, who feels compelled to keep his attention on the past more than on the future. In fact, Hanmura himself has written that the only piece of science fiction he ever wrote was his first story. Following this initial effort, which placed first in the short story competition sponsored by Japan's *SF Magazine* in 1962, he sank out of sight for ten years, and when he returned to writing it was to champion what he termed "Romance SF," novels written on an unabashedly grand scale, often heroic in nature and concerned primarily with being "a good read." Rather than exhibiting any deep concern with the development and explication of character, they pose the question "What if?" to a body of facts and rigorously pursue the implications of the answer on a grand scale.

The fields where Hanmura chooses to ask his questions are often off the beaten track, and the rigorousness with which the implications are pursued is occasionally amazing. The reader is dragged along not only by the story lines but also by an eager curiosity to see what Hanmura will fish up next from his magician's hat.

Sanreizan Hiroku has often been singled out as the best of Hanmura's prodigious body of works. Awarded the Izumi Kyoka Prize for literature in 1973, one of only a handful of science fiction works ever to be formally recognized in Japan, it encapsulates most of the features of Hanmura's approach to literature, both good and bad.

The basic premise of *Sanreizan Hiroku*, directly translatable as *The Secret Record of the Spirit Producing Mountain*, is the existence of a powerful and secret clan that has worked in the shadow of Japanese society and largely determined the course of Japanese history. Hanmura takes his cue from a passage in the *Kojiki (Records of Ancient Matters)*, a treasure trove of myths and legends written in 712 that starts with the tale of creation, in which is described a god who stands higher in the hierarchy than the one reputed to have given rise to Japan's Imperial line. The descendants of this deity, postulates Hanmura, citing other old texts for "confirmation," were initially in a position superior to that of the Imperial family but took it upon themselves to avoid the day-to-day struggles for power and to labor instead to explore and open up the Japanese archipelago.

As Hanmura has it, the "Hi," as this clan is called, possess certain paranormal powers and, with the assistance of support facilities they established throughout Japan in the period of exploration, are able to teleport. These abilities prove of great value to them as, with Japan settled and their role as pioneers at an end, the Hi come to be guardians of the Imperial house, materializing in times of crisis to preserve the Emperor.

One of the main threads of the book — indeed, the central thread — is the laborious process of finding out exactly who the Hi are. Not until the last half of the eighth and final section does a total picture, one far transcending the borders of Japan, appear. The gods, it proves, and not only those of the *Kojiki* but those across the world, were apparently extraterrestrials, and the Hi, both in Japan and across the world, are their interbred and much adulterated descendants. Far back in prehistory, the ancestors of the Hi established a system of "musubi-yama," the spirit-producing mountains of the title, extending across the world. Though never explained in detail, the musubi-yama are apparently four-dimensional constructs that focus and intensify psychic phenomena. Every region of the earth has its musubi-yama system, centering on a central "shin-no-yama." The shin-no-yama themselves constitute a system linked to a global shin-no-yama on the moon.

The central role of the musubi-yama system is to determine the future. On a folklore level, this function is translated into a belief that if one can pray directly to the central shin-no-yama, one's prayers will be answered (it should come as no surprise to learn that the churches, temples, and mosques of the world tend to be built over musubi-yama). One of the long-standing traditions of the Hi is that they must search out the central shin-no-yama and pray directly to it for peace. It is this search for Japan's shin-no-yama that constitutes another main thread of the book.

However, the third main theme of *Sanreizan Hiroku*, and the one which Hanmura appears to have enjoyed playing with the most, is the secret history of how the Hi have determined the course of Japanese history. This is not the first time Hanmura has toyed with his country's history: in one book, for instance, he transplanted a unit of the modern Japanese army back to 1530 and had them unify Japan in place of Oba Nobunaga. However, just as the actions of his armored battalion eventually worked out in such a way as to form a history identical to that in the history books, so, too, the actions of the Hi have not changed history as we know it, but have merely changed the reasons for the order that has come about. Hanmura seems to believe in a fundamental resiliency of history verging on determinism. The means may change, but the ends are inevitable.

Sanreizan Hiroku begins shortly before Oda Nobunaga began his rise to power, with the issuance of an Imperial order, given in greatest secrecy, to the

Hi that they restore peace to the land. By the sixteenth century the Hi are a scattered and weakened lot, many having lost all sense of their ancestry and, save for a small handful centered on clan-leader Zuifu, most are deeply involved in everyday life. Even the concept of the shin-no-yama exists only as a garbled myth.

Nonetheless, Zuifu gathers what remains and throws it behind a daimyo chosen as the most likely founder of a unified Japan, neither the Hi nor the Imperial court having the necessary military might to achieve this goal on their own. The daimyo chosen is, of course, Oda Nobunaga.

What follows is a masterfully thought out reinterpretation of Japanese history. Nobunaga's upset victory over the Imagawa family is seen to be the work of Hi maneuverings. The "ninja" secret agents which lent a colorful, and basically true, page to Japanese history are seen to have been Hi, accomplishing their prodigies with the assistance of the special abilities given to Hi gene-carriers. The sudden and totally unexpected death of Nobunaga's most powerful enemy, Takeda Shingen, in the midst of preparations for a campaign that could have ended Nobunaga's dreams of national unification, is still explained as an illness — the accepted theory in Japanese history texts — but one brought on by a concentrated psychic assault channeled and magnified by the musubi-yama system's special properties.

However, as the Hi work to promote Nobunaga, they are themselves caught up in the swirl of events and begin to lose control. Nobunaga razes Hiei-san, known in Japanese religious history as the center of Buddhism in Japan but known in Hanmura's "secret record" as the training and educational center for the Hi (in fact, almost any landmark in Japan incorporating "hi" in its name, we are given to understand, has long-standing connections with this clan). Following this action, Nobunaga turns on the Imperial household itself.

It is here that Hanmura is at his best. Taking the unusual disposition of Nobunaga's forces at the time and the undeniable historical record of the military leader's drastic policies, he builds a strong and convincing case for the argument that Nobunaga planned a *coup d'état* to remove the emperor as the figurehead of Japanese government and seize true control of "all under heaven." The Hi, confronted with this upstart reaching for a level of national unification even they had not imagined, must take action, and the result is the famous assassination of Nobunaga by his trusted lieutenant Mitsuhide. Mitsuhide, Hanmura has established long before, is a Hi placed under Hobunaga's command to further the clan's plans for the military leader.

Thus history comes full circle. The dates, the acts, even the names are unchanged. Only the why of history has been completely transformed.

This is the pace Hanmura sets for the whole book, proceeding to explain the rise of the Tokugawa family in Hi terms as well. Jumping further ahead in history, he reveals the famous Edo-period burglar Nezumi Kozo to have been a Hi who died while trying to confirm that Japan's shin-no-yama was under Edo, the present day Tokyo. The small army that fought to establish the Emperor at the head of the Japanese state in the turmoil following Perry's arrival was composed of Hi. The stubborn Japanese resistance to acceptance of the Potsdam Declaration was not out of concern for the Emperor, but to avoid handing over control of the Japanese shin-no-yama to America, which incidentally, has its own shin-no-yoma under the White House. And last but not least, the race to put a man on the moon was actually a race between the United States and the Soviet Union to gain control over the global shin-no-yama located beneath the Sea of Tranquility. Over and over again Hanmura cuts the liver we know out of history and inserts one of his own, sewing up the incision so neatly it can no longer be seen. He mobilizes, particularly in the earlier sections of the book, an astonishing familiarity with Japanese history, folklore, and strange or quirky legends of all kinds, along with a masterful ability to organize and rationalize it all in order to lend credibility to his alternate history.

Unfortunately, while the book is a remarkable accomplishment in this sense, the tremendous amount of information that must be omitted, and the jumps through time which come in the second half, do not help the work in literary terms. Particularly toward the end, Hanmura's own interest shows signs of slipping, and with increasing frequency sentences appear beginning with, "Now I'd like the reader to remember back to an earlier chapter where. . . ." The presentation of his "theory," and the facts he has chosen to back it up, lead Hanmura to give short shrift to many of his characters, particularly those appearing after the sequence of events relating to the rise and death of Nobunaga.

Likewise, in terms of theme, promising developments are cut off in midstep in the rush to get the reader to the moon. Serious reflections on how the once tightly knit clan of the Hi has declined over time, or the consequences of tangling with Hanmura's particularly willful vision of history, founder on shoals of dry exposition. The final section in particular, bringing the book up to the present, suffers from clichés and occasional polemical outbursts against modern politics, the emperor system, and more. The final chapter, in which a friend of the last Hi is seen telling a novelist about the closing developments and asking him to write them up as a book, is a feeble and disappointing ending to a novel as interesting and intriguing as *Sanreizan Hiroku* can be in its finest parts. One only wishes that Hanmura would include, in his definition of "Romance SF," a slightly stronger emphasis on discipline.

David Lewis

Sources for Further Study

Criticism:

Rottensteiner, Franz. *The Science Fiction Book*. New York: Seabury, 1975, p. 142. The background of Japanese science fiction is detailed.

THE SANTAROGA BARRIER

Author: Frank Herbert (1920-   )
First book publication: 1968
Type of work: Novel
Time: The present
Locale: Santaroga, California

An isolated community, exploring different forms of consciousness through drug use, provides an opportunity for comments on modern culture and counterculture alike

Principal characters:
GILBERT DASEIN, a consulting psychologist
JENNY SORGE, Dasein's girl friend
DR. LAWRENCE PIAGET, a Santarogan psychologist
DR. CHAMI SELADOR, Dasein's friend and adviser

The theme of the isolated community, outwardly normal but guarding a strange and terrible secret, is a common one in science fiction. Such a community provides a convenient arena for an author to work out what might be regarded as anthropological or sociological "thought experiments" not unlike the thought experiments in physics or astronomy that so often characterize more technical, hardware-bound varieties of science fiction. Often, such communities are found to be outposts of alien culture (as in Chad Oliver's *Shadows in the Sun* [1954]), and their enforced isolation is explained by the simple fact that these communities are not a part of our culture at all and thus have no need to interact with the outside world. Less common is a novel such as *The Santaroga Barrier*, in which the community is very much involved with the outside world, and in which the isolation arises out of a deliberate rejection of all that world represents. A novel such as this belongs properly in the tradition of utopian and anti-utopian fictions, since its central thematic concern is the portrayal of a community that strives to achieve an ideal society, or at least a better one than is currently available in our culture.

The question arises, then, as to whether the countercultural society of Herbert's Santaroga is intended as a vision of Utopia or a nightmare of dystopia. And the answer must be that with novels like *The Santaroga Barrier*, science fiction has moved beyond such simple either-or dichotomies in its portrayal of imaginary societies. Certainly, the criticisms Herbert makes in this novel of the mainstream of American society in the 1960's are deeply felt: the growth of a mass-market culture, the endless striving after economic expansion for its own sake, the overdependence on technology, the compromising of human values to corporate planning, disregard for the environment, faith in the problem-solving abilities of science, and relentless association of science with power — all are articulated by the Santarogans without the slightest trace of an irony that would suggest that the author is at all critical of these attitudes. But when these same Santarogans proselytize about their alternative — a communal, self-sustained society structured around a "consciousness fuel" drug called Jaspers — a note of critical irony does creep in. *The Santaroga Barrier* is indeed highly critical of the consumer society, but the focus of its criticism is more on the kinds of countercultural alternatives that were seriously proposed and discussed in the 1960's. In many respects, then, *The Santaroga Barrier* is what is coming to be called "an ambiguous utopia," in Ursula Le Guin's phrase: the novel is both a *homage* to and a critique on such behavioral-conditioning utopias as B. F. Skinner's *Walden Two* (1948).

The novel is very much a product of its time, however, and the 1960's fascination with such movements as existentialism and structural psychology is reflected even in Herbert's invented nomenclature. The drug, Jaspers, suggests an association with the philosophy of Karl Jaspers, whose concern with the limits of scientific knowledge and the plight of the individual in mass culture is reflected in many ways in the arguments of the Santarogans for their way of life. The leading spokesman for Santaroga is a Dr. Piaget, who sometimes even *sounds* like the psychologist Jean Piaget when he talks of pushing back the barriers of childhood and transcending the self-referential consciousness to arrive at a higher plane of awareness. Even the protagonist's name — Dasein — translates from the German as "being" or "existence," and the name of the girl whom he loves — Sorge — translates as "care" or "sorrow." Such deliberately suggestive naming of people and things perhaps invites a too easy allegorization (is a character named Calvin Nis supposed to tell us something about Calvinism?) but it also suggests that Herbert is making a conscious effort to associate the belief-systems represented in his novel with real belief-systems that were enjoying a vogue at the time the novel was written. Even the principal products through which Jaspers is transmitted — cheese and beer — call to mind the stereotypical diet of undergraduate intellectuals during the 1960's, and many of the arguments of the Santarogans sound suspiciously like sophisticated variations on the "turn on, tune in, drop out" arguments of the drug culture of Timothy Leary and others.

Is Jaspers meant to be LSD, then? This seems doubtful, since the social function of Jaspers as used by the Santarogans is not merely to liberate the consciousness of the individual, but to enable the individual to enter into a kind of group consciousness. Indeed, the Santarogans seem to Dasein to be more "aware" than outsiders, more in touch at all levels with their feelings and desires, but there is much to suggest that they have not quite freed themselves of unconscious, primitive instincts. Investigators sent to Santaroga to explore its mysterious isolation have regularly died in mysterious accidents, and Dasein suffers a number of such potentially fatal accidents as he carries on his investigation. Mounting evidence suggests that these "accidents" are in some sense intentional: there is no deliberate plotting on the part of Santarogans to do away with investigators, but the collective unconscious of the community strives to protect itself by destroying whatever appears to be a threat. The unconscious drives of the citizens are not actually eliminated at all:

they are merely united into a collective drive for self-preservation. In this sense, the entire community of drug-imbued Santarogans becomes like a single organism, with little room for individual action or motivation.

Such a community achieves stability not only at the price of individualism, but also at the price of its own freedom to function within a larger society. Furthermore, Herbert seems to argue, the more stable a society is internally, the more precarious the balance of that stability becomes. Santaroga's enforced Utopia can only survive under the most rigid conditions: complete independence, isolation from external forces, and unquestioning acceptance of the system by all residents. Although a few immigrants are allowed into Santaroga, no one can join the society without undergoing an initiatory addiction to Jaspers, and no one addicted to Jaspers can survive comfortably outside, without periodic doses of the drug. Thus the society of Santaroga appears to be a social and cultural cul-de-sac; it can only interact with the outside world if the outside world becomes like it, and such a universal transformation of human consciousness (a là Arthur Clarke's *Childhood's End* [1953]) is not what Herbert is after in this novel. Santaroga has confused the needs of the individual with the needs of a society, and in the process it has evolved a society that behaves like a highly narcissistic and self-righteous individual. Though Herbert apparently wrote the book in part as a comment on the drug counterculture of the 1960's, it might just as well serve as a comment on the various popular human potential movements of the 1970's. In each case, the reaction of a subculture to the often frightening and intimidating problems created by the larger culture takes the form of narcissistic withdrawal.

In fact, much of the discussion of reality and consciousness, of social responsibility and self-awareness that takes place in the novel invites an analogy that seems at first far-fetched: Santaroga, as a community among communities, behaves in much the same way that a psychotic individual behaves among other individuals. It has evolved its own beliefs and myths apart from those in the culture at large, regards these beliefs as superior, feels irrationally threatened by anything that appears to challenge these beliefs, and occasionally even explodes into unconscious violence. It would like to convert others to its way of thinking, but fears exposing itself to ridicule and believes that no one can understand its system without becoming a part of it and accepting it wholeheartedly. Furthermore, it is too wrapped up in itself really to care much about what happens to those outside; Santarogans are convinced that the outside world is on the verge of destroying itself, but none of them shows much of an impulse to do anything about it.

Throughout the novel, Dasein, sent to investigate Santaroga for a large marketing conglomerate, realizes the drawbacks of the Santarogan society and argues with Piaget about them. But at the same time he is becoming more and more dependent upon Jaspers and more and more motivated by a rekindled love for his former girl friend, Jenny, who lives in Santaroga and cannot leave.

In the end, Dasein, after having ingested a massive dose of pure Jaspers, realizes that, like it or not, he is now part of the society, as dependent on the drug as all the rest of the residents, and he tries to convince himself that *"It'll be a beautiful life."* The irony and horror of this final line in the novel is ambiguous, for we are not quite sure if Dasein is desperately trying to reconcile himself to a life in which his individuality will be lost, or if he has in fact already lost his individuality and actually believes what he tells himself. Nor can we be sure which of these two interpretations is the more frightening: whether it is better to be a convert or a slave.

The Santaroga Barrier deliberately raises many issues and resolves few, but it does manage to be provocative. As an adventure novel, it moves at times with agonizing slowness; as a psychological novel, it disappoints by not developing more convincing or complex characters (this is especially notable during interior monologue sequences in which Dasein seems to have no reality beyond the particular abstractions with which he is groping). Utopian fictions, however, are often little more than philosophical treatises disguised as narratives, and on this level the novel can be counted as one of the more thoughtful and intelligent of science fiction's responses to present-day social movements.

Gary K. Wolfe

Sources for Further Study

Reviews:
Magazine of Fantasy and Science Fiction. XXXVI, April, 1969, pp. 47-48.
Publisher's Weekly. CXCIV, September 16, 1968, p. 72.
School Library Journal. XXIV, October, 1977, p. 128.

SATANA DEI MIRACOLI
(Satan of Miracles)

Author: Ugo Malaguti (1945-   )
First book publication: 1966
Type of work: Novel
Time: An indefinite future
Locale: A distant planet (very similar to Earth) called Land of Arrival

Through a reversal of religious attitudes (Satan becomes "good" and God is "evil") a self-exiled group from Earth brings about a new balance of power in religion on an alien planet

> *Principal characters:*
> ASTAROTH, a young man who becomes the leader of a planetary rebellion
> IL MENESTRELLO (THE MINSTREL), a rabble-rouser
> MORGANA, a skeptical young lady
> A WITCH, a young girl thought to be Satan's lover
> I LONTANI (THE FAR-OFF), the alien inhabitants of Land of Arrival

A writer later turned translator and editor, Ugo Malaguti is an interesting figure in modern Italian science fiction. Since his debut in 1960, through stories and short novels published under the pseudonym Hugh Maylon, his work as editor of the science fiction book series *Galassia* (1965-1969), and, later, as the director of his own publishing house Libra, he has become well known in Italy. After his English pseudonym apprenticeship, mainly as a writer of space operas and the kind of "archaeological" science fiction pioneered by L. R. Johannis (Luigi Rapuzzi), Malaguti at first assumed a "sociological" stance, but later adopted a rather oblique and lyrical style for the works published under his own name. Coming between these two periods, *Satana dei Miracoli* displays a notable balance of opposing moods (the first fading out, the second just beginning to stir) and it stands today as one of his finest achievements.

In an undefined future, mankind has reached a level of scientific and technological development that makes the building of interstellar starships and very complex robotic structures a common thing. But this sort of "evolution" — as always seems to happen in science fiction — has not been accompanied by a similar cultural development in the so-called soft branches of learning: the moral and psychological components of everyday life. While man still struggles with his ancient moral dilemmas without finding solutions or new phenomenological approaches, religion retains its position of primacy. And what is more, it is a so-called Christian religion, now soundly (again) founded on political power and direct action. It is left to robots, the new champions of the Faith of their technocratic society, to become the missionaries of God and the true conservators (as well as the cruel judges) of His reactionary Word.

Most of mankind accepts this situation without protest; but there is, of course, an underground movement. Naturally the members of the movement are cruelly persecuted by the establishment whose rulers do not hesitate to resurrect the Inquisition itself. Thus, mankind is still divided along the lines of God and His Saints, and Satan and His Dark Followers. This means that the holders of the actual technocratic power (assisted by the robots) are arrayed against the supporters of a new order not based on the "narrow" laws of science, but, on the contrary, on the all-consuming values of anarchy. Satan's followers see their Lord as the symbol of a truly humanized godhead, freed from ancient faults and now become the "true" Good.

The story reaches its climax on a planet where the dissenters have sought sanctuary from the pursuing army of robots. Here in the Land of Arrival, men and robots fight one another in a kind of guerrilla warfare necessitated by the fact that robots can go abroad only by day and the men by night. The humanoid inhabitants of the planet are called I Lontani (The Far-Off) for their literal remoteness from human and robotic affairs. They wander around on the planet in large wagons like gypsies and, when asked, only hint at some terrible cataclysm in their past. We come to understand that their culture underwent the same development as that of mankind, only to suffer a final catastrophe, apparently the result of a technological mishap. Their long climb back from the ensuing fearful age has been lost in the past and their present demeanor is characterized by haughty aloofness from the quarrels of men and robots. Because of their complete detachment from "human" affairs, they are completely ignored by the robots, which apparently cannot even *see* them. In this situation, the life of the colonists consists of bloody encounters with the robots, at night, and, by day, long quarrels about the constitution of a new Order after the robots have been defeated.

At last, there comes a Sign. But is it from God or Satan? A black starship lands on Land of Arrival and exerts a powerful attraction for every robot. When the robots touch the hull of the ship, they receive a powerful shock. In short order, every robotic form of life on the planet is destroyed. Then the black starship leaves without a word, its mysterious mission accomplished.

Now the exiles are free to act as they please, and — *horribile visu* — they behave exactly as their hateful oppressors had done. Forgetful of their own search for freedom, they consider The Far-Off to be followers of the abominable ways of God and put them to the stake. Again, factories will produce roaring machines, and new starships will be built to bring the Word of Satan to whomever is still ignorant of it. Only the name of this "message of the Word" has changed. The new Power will be imposed everywhere, to the greater Glory of Satan.

Against this background, generally portrayed with nice overtones of adventure, the characters attain a marked interest of their own. Most fascinating is the hero of the novel, Astaroth. He is a young man who represents the weary distress of an isolated group willing to take a step up the ladder of human development. He clearly reveals his idealistic nature in his desire to play just one game of chess with Satan, not out of any vain hope of victory, but only to realize his dream of really once acting as a true *homo faber*. After having been first tempted by Morgana and then by The Witch (whom he discovers to be a virgin even after the presumed repeated assaults of Satan), he falls an easy prey to the wiles of The Minstrel, who is the first to propose the scientific and technological "resurrection" of the exiles. Like a true (Christian!) martyr, Astaroth fights among the *many* horns of his existential dilemma, realizing that Satan often has more than two horns and that his plea for a game with him (or with his homologous counterpart, God) has already been granted.

Gianni Montanari

SAURUS

Author: Eden Phillpotts (1862-1960)
First book publication: 1938
Type of work: Novel
Time: The present
Locale: Devon

An account of the life of an intelligent lizard hatched from an egg dispatched to
Earth from the asteroid Hermes

> *Principal characters:*
> FELIX TODDLEBEN, a zoologist
> NORAH HAPGOOD, his sister and housekeeper
> MILDRED, her daughter
> SAURUS, a visitor from another world

The concept of alien beings first appeared in science fiction in the late
nineteenth century, after the popularization of Darwin's theory of evolution
had spread awareness of the fact that life on other worlds might develop according to a pattern very different from that seen on Earth as a result of adaptation to different physical circumstances. Previously, all intelligent inhabitants
of other worlds had been human in mental outlook, and frequently in form
(though various satirical works had placed human mentalities in animal bodies).
These beings, however strange, could not be described as *alien* in that
they were seen to belong to the same general creative scheme as men, and
were not the product of independent evolutionary sequences.

Several writers — notably Camille Flammarion in *Lumen* — introduced the
idea of alien life systems without using alien beings as actors in fictional drama. It was H. G. Wells, in *The War of the Worlds*, who first gave the alien a
role to play: that of man's competitor in the cosmic struggle for existence, and
invader of Earth. It was a role which was enthusiastically taken up by the
writers of magazine science fiction in subsequent decades. Curiously, though,
the alien being remained almost exclusively confined to popular magazine fiction for half a century after Wells published *The War of the Worlds* in 1898.
Wells himself developed the first image of alien society in *The First Men in
the Moon* (1901), and then abandoned aliens altogether. J. H. Rosny the elder
made considerable use of alien beings in France, but writers in the English
language virtually ignored the notion until 1937, when Olaf Stapledon made
prolific use of images of alien life in *Star Maker*, a work which has more in
common with *Lumen* than with *The War of the Worlds*. A year after *Star
Maker*, however, Eden Phillpotts published *Saurus*, a novel which gave the
alien a new role: that of "objective observer" of human society.

Several would-be social critics had in the previous fifty years developed
imaginative fictions in which contemporary British or American society came
under the scrutiny of an "outsider" who could clearly perceive and pour
ridicule upon those features of modern life which, though their contemporaries

took them for granted, the critics deplored. William Dean Howells employed a visitor from an Imaginary Utopia in *A Traveller from Altruria* (1894), Wells an angel fallen from Heaven in *The Wonderful Visit* (1895), Grant Allen an anthropologist from the future in *The British Barbarians* (1895), and John Beresford a superman born before his time in *The Hampdenshire Wonder* (1911). The strategy dates back at least as far as Diderot's "Supplement to Bougainville's *Voyage*" (1796). Phillpotts, however, was the first writer to call upon a referee from outside the context of human life and thought.

Phillpotts had written a good deal of imaginative fiction previously. In the period from 1922-1925 he wrote three fantastic thrillers under the name of Harrington Hext. In *The Grey Room* (1931) he used the framework of a "detective story" to contrast the different approaches of scientific rationalism and religious mysticism to the problem of a supposedly haunted room. He wrote numerous mythological fantasies in the 1920's and 1930's, culminating in *The Owl of Athene* (1936), in which Britain is subjected to an invasion of gigantic crabs as a kind of "divine experiment." *Saurus*, however, was his first pure science fiction story, though he went on to write two more: *The Fall of the House of Heron* (1948) and *Address Unknown* (1949). The former is an early study of the morality of "scientific detachment" in connection with the making of nuclear weapons; the latter deals with a situation similar to that presented in *Saurus*. Though Phillpotts turned his hand to science fiction late in his career, it is perhaps worth noting that he was actually four years older than H. G. Wells — *Address Unknown* was published when he was eighty-seven (and he wrote several more novels afterwards).

Saurus begins with the careful characterization of its main character, Felix Toddleben:

> Professor Felix Toddleben was a reasonable man, which is to say that he accepted facts often repellent to human instinct. While granting that our senses alone permit us to know anything at all, since they represent the sole channels through which knowledge may be attained, he yet acknowledged the scientific truth that they are not constituted ever to attain reality. He resented sham solutions to the riddle of existence and denied that the true one lay within reach of finite intelligence. . . . He held biology the most exciting occupation and wished that he were young again to concentrate upon it. For him the Victorian universe was a fiction of the past — its dogmas and certainties as dead as the dodo — but he recognized no considerable genius at present carrying on the good work, or tilling the fruitful field.

Much is made within the novel of this attitude of calm detachment and mistrust of metaphysics. Saurus himself is no more than an embodiment of this attitude taken to its logical extreme — an extreme impossible in a feeling human being. The professor's philosophy is, however, subject to some corrective balancing within the book by virtue of the presence of his widowed sister and housekeeper, Norah Hapgood. She admires the professor greatly, but finds him unworldly, and combats his idealism (taking Saurus, also, to task in his turn) with down-to-earth common sense and a demand for compromise with circumstance. She cannot tolerate high principles taken to uncomfortable extremes, and thus provides a counterweight to the cold and clinical analysis of human faults and follies which provides the novel's "message."

The story gets underway when the professor is roused from his sleep by a frightful sound. He subsequently discovers that a cylindrical metal capsule has crashed into one of his fields, and finds that it contains a sealed container full of jelly, a packet of seeds, and an egg. The last-named is extraordinarily similar to the egg of an iguana, which the professor recognizes because he is the world's foremost expert on lizards.

The egg does indeed hatch into a lizard, but one which lacks a tail and possesses an unusually large cranium. The creature, nourished first by the jelly and later by the produce of the seeds, grows with astonishing rapidity and soon shows signs of great intelligence. Though he is deaf and dumb he learns to read and write. He has an eidetic memory, and eventually proves to be telepathic, able both to read the verbalized thoughts of men and to establish rapport with the family dog. He names himself Saurus.

Saurus is completely emotionless; his kind are entirely rational beings. He does not, however, despise the emotions of his hosts; though he cannot share their experience of emotion, he can comprehend its effects and perceive its usefulness. Saurus reasons that he must have been launched from the asteroid Hermes during an unusually close conjunction of that world with Earth, and presumes that his own kind expected the Earth to be populated by intelligent reptilian creatures similar to themselves. The fact that this supposition was wrong causes him no distress; he can feel neither loneliness, nor fear, nor regret, and has no sense of irony or tragedy.

Saurus' criticisms of humankind begin conventionally enough be deploring narrowmindedness and the folly of war. Although his criticisms are frequently scathing, they are ameliorated somewhat by the fact that he usually finds in Britain, her Empire, and her people the least of all the evils which he perceives. Despite his lack of emotion, he has no difficulty in attaching meanings to the concepts of good and evil, which he finds wholly rational, and much of his discourse is devoted to showing how the passions of mankind draw him away from the former toward the latter. He sees history as a war between morally enlightened rationalism and destructive passionate impulses. He considers that the natural gregariousness of mankind, which might have evolved into universal goodwill and respect for others, has instead been subverted by an atavistic selfishness which is jealously preserved, and from which all the ills which afflict mankind proceed.

This is not a particularly original diagnosis of the predicament of twentieth century man, nor is it presented in an exceptionally eloquent fashion. It is, however, a commentary which is notable for its lack of bitterness as compared with previous "objective observations" taking the form of imaginative fictions. Norah continually complains to Saurus that his excessive honesty and disregard for social conventions of politeness and reserve are unjustified, and her daughter Milly argues that he cannot sufficiently appreciate the *positive* side of emotionality, as seen in art and love. Saurus accepts these criticisms gracefully enough, and his own views prove to be sufficiently diplomatic not to upset distinguished visitors (who include a member of the royal family and a bishop). He does, however, manage to put an ironic gloss on Milly's complaints when he is instrumental in rescuing her from great peril after she is seduced by a clever Russian spy.

Saurus' career lasts little more than a year — he lives his life at a far faster tempo then humans live theirs. He dies with his philosophical work, including an ambitious Baconian instauration of the sciences, barely begun. The written farewell he leaves behind is fond, its exhortations to charity and wisdom rather hackneyed and patronizing, but modest and inoffensive. As with all Phillpotts' fantasies, the book is lighthearted in its seriousness, and above all gentle in its treatment. Phillpotts' own position is clearly allied with Toddleben and Saurus, though the author has a few careful reservations concerning the essence of humanity — the one thing that Saurus, by definition, could not possess.

Interestingly, Phillpotts seems later to have retreated considerably from this position. *The Fall of the House of Heron* takes a much harsher view of the detached rationality of the scientist, while *Address Unknown* is far less certain of the validity of criticisms aimed at humanity from an extraterrestrial viewpoint. In the latter novel the alien becomes much more enigmatic and rather more fearful, and though the scientists of the story are ready enough to fall under the spell of his "superior wisdom," the narrator is not. The tragic ending of *Address Unknown*, when the brilliant scientist is killed in trying (and failing) to establish closer contact with the alien, also holds a note of relief, in that the alien is thereby cut off from further intercourse with mankind. This conclusion contrasts sharply with the sentimentally described death of Saurus, whose passing is lamented by one and all.

It seems, therefore, that Phillpotts, having invented an alien being as a social critic, then followed the implications of his invention further, and found that he liked the idea less than before. Interestingly, genre science fiction has gone exactly the opposite way. The dominant image of the alien in the pulp science fiction of the 1930's was a menacing one; tales extolling the benefit of contact and friendship between alien races, after the fashion of Raymond Z. Gallun's classic "Old Faithful" (1934), were very much in a minority. In modern times, however, and especially in the last twenty years, the image of the wise alien, whose superior spiritual qualities and better adaptation to his environment make him a perfect mentor for erring humankind, has gained ground rapidly. This image is now established as something of a cliché — an irony that Phillpotts would have appreciated.

Brian Stableford

Sources for Further Study

Criticism:

Twentieth Century Authors. Edited by Stanley J. Kunitz and Howard Haycraft. New York: H. W. Wilson Company, 1942, pp. 1102-1104. Although not relying on Phillpotts' Science Fiction writing, this article does give significant biographical information on the author and lists a lengthy bibliography of his works.

THE SCIENCE FICTION OF EDGAR ALLAN POE

Author: Edgar Allan Poe (1809-1849)
Editor: Harold Beaver
First book publication: 1976
Type of work: Short fictions and a prose poem

Fifteen short prose pieces and a philosophical prose poem that anticipate modern science fiction, written by one of America's important nineteenth century writers

Edgar Allan Poe utilized four popular forms in the writing of his fiction: the Gothic romance, the explorer's narrative, the detective story, and the science fiction story. The first two were, of course, extant, even old-fashioned forms by the time Poe got to them, although he made them his own. The first of them pervades virtually everything of substance that he wrote. The latter two, although not without precedent, were largely unknown forms when he came to them. Indeed, it has been claimed that he invented both.

His credentials as "father" of the detective story are rather solid and obvious. In "The Murders in the Rue Morgue" and "The Purloined Letter" he introduced both the plot situation and the character composition that make up the basic components of the "classical" detective story: the brilliant, eccentric, one-dimensional detective, his dull sounding-board partner, the central puzzle, the baffled officialdom, the reduction of the story to process, the revelation, and the subsequent explanation. But, in the eagerness to establish science fiction's literary authenticity by establishing important precedents, it would be a mistake to claim a like paternity for Poe's science fiction.

In the first place, science fiction, even when it is no more than pure pulp, does not approach the formulaic rigidity of the classical detective story. While science fiction may be an "idea" literature, it is not a rationally constricted genre like the classical detective story. Thus, in terms of mechanics, Poe can, at most, be credited with introducing some basic science fiction elements into his stories that have continued to be important in the genre. On the other hand, some recent critics have developed a kind of all or nothing view of Poe as a science fiction writer: either all of the fiction — and even the verse — can be marginally classified as science fiction, or else none of it can. Both of these views are true. It depends only on one's critical perspective.

Roughly speaking, the stories that editor Harold Beaver has selected to represent Poe's science fiction can be divided into four fairly distinct categories — with a good deal of overlap. To coin, perhaps, some labels they might be classified as "scientific satires," "philosophical conversations," "science oriented horror stories," and "imaginary explorations."

The most purely science fictional of Poe's stories — that is, the stories having to do most immediately and directly with the science of his own day — are also the weakest. "The Thousand-and-Second Tale of Scheherazade," "Some Words with a Mummy," and "Mellonta Tauta" are long, unfunny literary jokes. Poe's sense of humor (or lack thereof) has long been lamented, to some extent unfairly. Although hardly his finest talent, Poe was, on occasion, capable of rich humor. What he lacked was any semblance of wit and only sophisticated and controlled wit could have pulled off the overly ingenious satirical ideas behind these three stories.

The first postulates an additional tale by Scheherazade to her hard-to-please husband, which turns out to be a satirical tour by Sinbad of nineteenth century science, told with a coy attempt at irony. The king finds the account unbelievable and so has his bride at last executed. In "Mummy," an ancient Egyptian ("Allamistakeo"!!) is brought back to life *via* electricity and given a lecture on nineteenth century science and politics. After a short debate the Mummy reluctantly concedes that the modern century is an improvement on his own age based on the development of laxatives. In "Mellonta Tauta," Pundita, a visitor from 2848, surveys the nineteenth century from a balloon and makes a series of inane comments on philosophy and history. But perhaps it is wrong to fault Poe because his humor and material in these sketches has dated so badly; they were intended as popular journalism directed at a mass readership and not as pertinent works of literary merit.

At the opposite end of the spectrum from these strained satires are the abstract philosophical dialogues: "The Conversation of Eiros and Charmion," "The Colloquy of Monus and Una," "The Power of Words," and "Mesmeric Revelation." Perhaps his prose poem (or as Charles O'Donnell has labeled it, his "abstract fiction") "Eureka" should be added to this list, since it is actually the culmination of them. It is in dealing with such items as these that the critic is brought back to the notion that all of Poe's writing is in a sense science fiction of a kind. Although these works brush against topics that were later to become science fiction staples — the catastrophic end of the world, physical survival after death, balloon flight, time travel, indentity change, mesmerism — that is not why they fit in the genre. They are science fiction because they are Poe's most direct statements of his *scientific* view of the universe and man's place in it. And, as such, they infuse all of his writings. Although well versed in the science of his own time, and quite willing to borrow — frequently verbatim and without acknowledgment — the writings of scientists to flesh out and authenticate his works, such materials were usually trappings. The important thing to Poe was his own science, and that is at the center of everything he wrote. That this scientific world view is, to use contemporary jargon, pseudoscience today, is irrelevant; the decision to structure his stories on a scientific world view has deep and continuing implications for science fiction.

It is tempting to label "The Conversation of Eiros and Charmion" and "The Colloquy of Monos and Una" scientific mysticism. These dialogues take place in a "realm of spirits" where the newly dead linger after their demise. In both, a recently deceased individual describes the experience to a former friend who has preceded him/her. In the former, the description includes a picture of the entire Earth consumed by a comet. In the latter, the death remains individual, but is described in precise, lingering physical detail. They both combine the mystical with the scientific in a curious manner; the setting and ideas are pure mysticism, but Poe provides a scientific rationale for all of it and a precise description of all the physical processes involved. Death itself is neither a total cessation of being nor a transition from the earthly to the spiritual; it is a subtle and sensual metamorphosis from one level of material being to another, a more rarefied one. One is tempted to call it an entrance into a new dimension.

The same scene is played out in "Mesmeric Revelation" except that this dialogue is between the living and the dead, the bridge between them being provided by the science of mesmerism. Thus, it is more concrete than the other two, although the situation still exists only for the sake of the ideas offered. The ideas become even more rarified in "The Power of World" and perhaps more central to Poe's thought. The roles of newly dead in this dialogue are reversed, with the experienced spirit, Agathos, explaining the universe to the newly dead Oinos. He postulates the immortality of matter, and the infinite effects of every cause, including every spoken and written word. It is this "vibration" which created — and continues to create — the universe, and no detached, providential god. This infinite animate universe is further explored in the lengthy prose poem "Eureka" which is generally taken as Poe's summary statement, albeit an ambiguous and perhaps ironical one.

In that long and abstract essay-poem, Poe postulates a vision of the universe in which everything moves in a dynamic tension between attraction and repulsion. Matter is never dead or static; it only changes shape constantly. Initially a perfect and simple oneness, the universe has dispersed in all directions and continues to do so until it reaches its maximum extension at which point it will begin to collapse back into itself. A personalized synthesis of various contemporary theories, the vision is more poetic than scientific and it animates all of Poe's work. The notion of an apocalyptic collapse into oneness, both on the individual and the universal level, provides a running tension in all of his efforts. In Poe, everything — man, beast, vegatation, the physical Earth itself — is alive and on the brink of dissolution. This end is both feared and longed for by all of his heroes. As a son of the Enlightenment and a committed rationalist, he firmly believed in a material universe; as a son of the Romantic Era, he spiritualized it.

Given this animate vision of matter, it is not surprizing that Poe was fascinated by the science of mesmerism. As previously noted in the philosophical dialogues, many of his better works explore the mysterious line between life and death. Therefore, a science that seemed to be able to induce a state of being that suspended the individual between the two worlds, allowing, perhaps insights into both, could not help but interest him. Indeed, here was a scientific confirmation of many of his own best occult stories.

In the "Tale of the Ragged Mountains," the mysterious Doctor Templeton, a "convert to the doctrines of Mesmer," cares for Bledsoe, the odd central figure in the tale, Despite the fact that he is a severe neurotic and a drug addict in weak health, Bledsoe enjoys taking long walks in the "Ragged Mountains" near Charlottesville, Virginia. Taking such a walk one day in a previously unexplored area, he suddenly finds himself strangely transposed into the middle of an exotic Far Eastern city where he is thrust into the midst of a riot and immediately killed. After his return, the good doctor explains to him what he, Bledsoe, had experienced — or reexperienced — in his own death in a previous life, or a previous stage of this one. Did Templeton's mesmerism save and preserve him? Or is it reincarnation? Or, perhaps, is it simply a hallucination, induced by the doctor's suggestions and a copious supply of narcotics? A more general question is how does the story qualify as early science fiction? Time travel is a standard science fiction theme; the multiple identities theme is becoming increasingly popular; reincarnation is now borderline, but catching up rapidly.

"The Facts in the Case of M. Valdemar" is the most typical Poe tale in the Beaver selection and perhaps it is the most effective as a story. Again Poe uses mesmerism to explore the region between life and death, but in this case the primary motive seems to be to tell a story, or, in Poe's term, to create an effect. Instead of exploring the information the mesmerized patient babbles, Poe concentrates on the experience of being suspended between life and death. At the point of death, Valdemar is put into a trance. In this state he apparently dies, but the trancelike state keeps him animate. Poe focuses on the physical changes that occur; he carefully prepares the reader for the awakening which will, paradoxically, allow Valdemar to complete his death. Thus, the last line, as in Poe's best tales, evokes the desired effect.

> As I rapidly made the mesmeric passes, amid ejaculations of "dead! dead!" absolutely *bursting* from the tongue and not from the lips of the sufferer, his whole frame at once — within the space of a single minute, or even less, shrunk — crumbled — absolutely *rotted* away beneath my hands. Upon the bed, before that whole company, there lay a nearly liquid mass of loathsome — of detestable putridity.

However, in terms of the developing shape of the science fiction narrative, the most important of Poe's science fiction ventures would seem to be his short fiction modeled on the imaginary exploration tales of his own times, his tales of descent ("MS. Found in a Bottle," "A Descent into the Maelstrom") and ascent ("The Balloon-Hoax" and "Hans Pfaal").

"MS. Found in a Bottle" was the first of Poe's sea voyage tales. At best we would today categorize it as a science fiction fantasy, but it is a good illustration of one of Poe's — and science fiction's — best techniques: the meticulous and realistic detailing of all the particulars of a thoroughly fantastic situation. In less than a dozen pages Poe compresses virtually all of the basic elements of his sea voyage tales into the one tale: the complacent beginning, the virulent storm and shipwreck, the isolated struggle for survival on the open sea, the ambiguous rescue, the uncontrolled flight into one of the icebound poles, and the final encounter with the maelstrom that breaks off the narrative. Much of the power of this tale comes from the purity and simplicity with which Poe renders this basic pattern. "MS. Found in a Bottle" is almost more poem that narrative; it is not so much a story as the extended working out of an elaborate and powerful central image, that of the massive ship and its aged crew relentlessly rushing to a mysterious and awesome destiny.

The Narrator of the story is also Poe's archetypal hero: a man without family or clear social ties ("of my country and of my family I have little to say"), but with ample money and an aristocratic heritage of some sort. Not unlike Ishmael, he goes to sea because of a "nervous restlessness which haunted me as a fiend." Once under way, he alone is sensitive to the minute atmospheric and natural changes that foretell impending chaos. Sure enough "a wilderness of foam" sweeps everybody but the Narrator and an Old Swede (so he can have somebody to talk to) overboard. They barely survive for five days, plagued by increasing cold and darkness. In the midst of these natural calamities, a huge ship appears, described in vivid detail, apparently unaffected by the natural turbulence. The huge vessel rides right over their boat, hurling the Narrator onto its deck.

There he discovers a crew of ancient, doddering, but apparently efficient, sailors. At first he attempts to hide from them, but he subsequently realizes that that is pointless; they do not recognize his existence as they carry out their mysterious mission. He discovers and enumerates several more clues in meticulous detail — his own accidental daubing of the word "Discovery" on a sail; the porous, unknown wood of the hull that seems alive (more so than the crew); the quaint, obsolete navigational instruments strewn about, unused, on the floor of the captain's cabin — all of which only deepen the mystery. Finally, he looks the captain straight in the face and sees that "His gray hairs are records of the past, and his grayer eyes are "Sybils of the future." In the end, the Narrator learns nothing, but his fear and horror almost give way to a kind of eager anticipation of the destruction he knows to be imminent:

> . . . a curiosity to penetrate the mysteries of these awful regions, predominates even over my despair, and will reconcile me to the most hideous aspect of death. It is evident that we are hurrying onwards to some exciting knowledge — some never-to-be- imparted secret, whose attainment is destruction.

The destruction about to be embraced in that story is experienced, and survived, in "A Descent into the Maelstrom." Again, the Narrator accidentally drifts into acute danger (his watch stopped) and finds himself caught up by a natural phenomenon; again he struggles futilely and, on the brink of extinction, becomes fascinated by his plight, eagerly awaiting it as an ultimate experience and revelation:

> how magnificent a thing it was to die in such a manner, and how foolish it was in me to
> think of so paltry a consideration as my own individual life. . . . I became possessed with
> the keenest curiosity about the whirl itself. I positively felt a wish to explore its depths,
> even at the sacrifice I was going to make.

The vehicle is, however, no ghost ship, but a solid commercial vessel and the doom is no mysterious unknown, but a factual whirlpool, the "Moskoestrom," located near a group of islands off the Norwegian coast. This greater particularity and authenticity makes this story a much better example of embryonic science fiction than its predecessor, although, perhaps, a less memorable narrative.

Both stories owe an obvious debt to *The Rime of the Ancient Mariner*. An old sailor tells his story to a tourist as they look down at the whirlpool from a coastal mountain top. Before actually recounting the narrative, the old man carefully reviews the geography, history, literature, and theoretical explanations for the whirlpool. Poe's inspiration for the story was an encyclopedia article, and it shows in these meticulous details. In the best hard-science fiction manner, Poe does not proceed to adventure before establishing the scientific veracity of his situation. And, in the end, the observant old sailor saves himself according to strictly scientific (in Poe's view) principles. As the various objects descend into the whirlpool, the sailor observes that larger bodies, especially spherical ones, fall more rapidly, and cylindrical ones more slowly. Hence, by lashing himself to a barrel he retards his descent and eventually reverses it. The science itself is doubtful, but the scientific apparatus, complete with an (inaccurate) footnote, gives the tale an aura of objective truth.

Poe's ascension stories qualify perhaps even more centrally as science fiction, although they are inferior as narratives, "The Balloon Hoax" and "The Unparalleled Adventures of One Hans Pfaal" have both been labeled "hoaxes," but of different types. The former was a real hoax that eventually forced a declaration from Poe. As a journalistic ploy it is excellent, but as a foray into balloon travel it is less interesting than the lengthier and more fantastic — also more scientific — latter story.

"The Unparalleled Adventures of One Hans Pfaal," too, is a hoax, but a more subtle one. It might be labeled an inverted hoax; that is, an obvious joke that strains in the direction of factual truth. The story opens with the descent of a rather ridiculous balloon "manufactured entirely of dirty newspapers" piloted by a ludicrous earless dwarf who throws a letter to the assembled Dutch crowd. The message is from a down-and-out bellows-mender named Hans Pfaal, who has recently vanished. After a short account of his conspiratorial efforts to rid himself of three particularly naggy creditors, he describes the way in which he became fascinated by the possibility of balloon travel, his preparations for a trip, and his voyage to the moon *via* balloon.

The curious thing about the story, and the quality that gives it interest as original science fiction, is the meticulous way in which Poe describes the mechanics of the trip. That burlesque emphasis fades; it is as though the joke opening of the piece was intended to belie the fact that Poe was really serious about his subject. If not likely, such a trip was not proven completely impossible in the science of Poe's day; he gives the readers a sure feeling of authenticity, but always in the context of the story's absurd frame. The astute recorder of immediate physical sensations, Poe carefully describes Han's physical reactions to his surroundings. At the same time, he explains at great length exactly what he is doing. After announcing his intentions to go to the moon, he heaps pages of statistics and calculations on the reader. Once aloft, he chronicles his progress carefully and meticulously; he takes great pains to establish the scientific credibility of the moon flight. Unlike in the descent tales, the destruction postulated in the story is neither particularly foreboding nor, for that matter, particularly important — Pfaal's missive says nothing about the nature of the place after he lands on it. It is the process of going there that fascinates Poe, and this emphasis on process certainly establishes connections between the story and later science fiction of the hardest core.

On the surface nothing would seem further from the science fiction hero that the melancholic, neurotic, obsessed, sometimes hysterical, occasionally insane Poe narrator. But, looked at closely, many such characters, especially those in the explorations, have a number of qualities that would not be out of place in a Robert A. Heinlein story.

The typical Poe hero is a split creature; he acts and observes himself acting. Thus, however extreme the situation and overwrought the narrator, the detached part observes and analyzes. And, in crisis, it acts. Moreover, the Poe science fiction hero shares with Dupin a rare set of analytical capacities and an intuitive sense of how to use them. Thus, in each of the explorations, the narrator carefully and logically observes his situation and acts in the most controlled, sensible, scientific way possible. One never thinks of a Poe hero as a man of action, but he is, in fact, just that. And he is usually successful, at least until the most awesome and unexplained powers of nature overwhelm him, although even then he usually survives.

Even in his nonscience fiction stories, Poe describes physical processes in careful sensual detail; while one is seldom aware of what a Poe character is like, one always knows how he feels. This emphasis on process, especially when coupled with his meticulous explanations of the technology and the theories behind it, fixes Poe firmly in the science fiction tradition. His single effect theory of the short story works perfectly for many a science fiction short story if one simply substitutes the word "idea" for the word "effect." His use of the fictional (and poetic) mode to present a scientific — if highly personalized — world view marks him as a science fiction writer in every sense of the term.

Keith Neilson

Sources for Further Study

Criticism:

Bonaparte, Marie. *The Life and Works of Edgar Allan Poe: A Psychoanalytic Interpretation*. London: Imago, 1949. Bonaparte, in this interesting study, analyzes the psychological motifs of Poe's fiction.

O'Brien, Edward J. *The Short Story Casebook*. New York: Farrar, Rinehart, 1935, pp. 181-211. O'Brien selects Poe as one of the major exponents of the short story and examines his style.

Regan, Robert, Editor. *Poe: A Collection of Critical Essays*. Englewood Cliffs, N.J.: Prentice Hall, 1967. This collection presents a significant number of different critical approaches to Poe's fiction.

Shulman, Robert. "Poe and the Power of the Mind," in *Journal of English Literary History*. XXXVII (1970), pp. 259-261. The psychological aspects of Poe's technique is briefly examined in this book on "The Tell-Tale Heart."

Thompson, G. R. *Poe's Fiction: Romantic Irony in the Gothic Tales*. Madison: University of Wisconsin Press, 1973. Thompson looks at Poe's short fiction emphasizing the author's treatment of irony.

THE SECOND WAR OF THE WORLDS
(VTOROE NASHESTVIE MARSIYAN)

Authors: Arkady Strugatsky (1925-   ) and Boris Strugatsky (1933-   )
First book publication: 1967
English translation: 1979
Type of work: Novel
Time: An imaginary present
Locale: A town with Greek names

"The notes of a sensible man" record strange explosions, rumors of Martians, conversations with drinking buddies, curious happenings, and finally the establishment of a new government in which everyone is guaranteed an income, blue bread, leisure, and democratic freedom

> *Principal characters:*
> APOLLO, a retired astronomy teacher and a stamp collector and
>   diarist (God of fine arts, eloquence, and moderation)
> ARTEMIS, his daughter (Goddess of hunting, an eternal virgin)
> CHARON, her husband, editor of the newspaper (Ferryman of Hades)
> MYRTILUS, their next-door neighbor, who runs a gas station (A
>   charioteer killed for rigging a race)
> PANDAREUS, chief of police (Pandareus was killed for stealing the
>   golden dog guarding the infant Zeus)
> ACHILLES, a pharmacist and stamp collector (Greatest Greek warrior
>   in the Trojan war)
> POLYPHEMUS, a one-legged drinking buddy and war veteran (Cy-
>   clops blinded by Odysseus)

Without question the Strugatsky brothers are the most popular writers of science fiction in the Soviet Union — Arkady, a specialist in Japanese literature, and Boris, an astronomer. Throughout the 1960's the two played a major role in the revival of a socially oriented and philosophically probing science fiction. Their works were very popular and drew steady and increasingly severe attention from the critics. At present their works are being translated in great profusion for foreign readers. After the success of *Hard to Be a God*, the last few years have seen translations into English of *Monday Begins on Saturday*, *The Final Circle of Paradise*, *Prisoner of Power* (original title: *The Inhabited Island*), *Roadside Picnic* and *Tale of a Troika*.

As Darko Suvin points out in his survey of criticism on the Strugatskys' works, the period of the 1960's ended with a wary compromise between those arguing for an explorative science fiction touching on all problems of human existence (the Strugatskys and their supporters) and those demanding literary models of a Communist future (conservative critics and writers). Suvin sums up the terms of the compromise as follows: "Ground already gained in *Hard to Be a God* may be held, *The Second War of the Worlds* is just barely tolerable (with much gnashing of teeth), but the line is drawn to exclude the depth exploration of *Snail on a Slope*, *Tale of a Troika* and *Nasty Swans*." Since these words were written, *Snail on a Slope* has still not appeared in book form and *Nasty Swans* has not appeared in any form within the Soviet Union.

The Second War of the Worlds (*Vtoroe nashestvie marsiyan*) was first published in a Siberian journay, *Baikal*, and then, together with another short novel, as a book (*Molodaya Gvardiya*, 1968). The journal version was presumably the source for a translation which appeared in a British anthology, *Vortex*. This version seems to be a censorial abridgement of the book version: missing are most of the vulgarisms, the hero's eczema, and some dubious statements about peasants. (The British translation is done in a lively, colloquial style, but is rife with errors — the Greek names are often not recognized.) The book version is the source for the translation discussed here; it is also this version which stimulated critical discussion and marked a turning point in the Strugatskys' career.

In his introduction to the book, fellow science fiction writer Roman Podolnyi gave an enthusiastic endorsement. He saw *The Second War of the Worlds* as a follow-up of the invasion described by H. G. Wells, with the difference that the Martians of the Strugatskys were more subtle: they did not come for blood with awesome weapons and wholesale destruction; they brought a more insidious type of enslavement — an economic one — and they permitted the conquered country all the rights of a democratic society. On this basis, Podolnyi considered *The Second War of the Worlds* a lampoon of present-day capitalism; the action takes place "somewhere in Europe" and the hero — or antihero — exhibits all the characteristics of a cowardly bourgeois with petty, self-centered interests. This philistine even applauds the Martian victory over the thugs and Fascists who previously ran his country, just as the Italians applauded Mussolini for clearing out the Mafia in order to establish his own Mafia-style dictatorship.

While there is much to support Podolnyi's interpretation, there are many other features in the story which relate specifically to Soviet society. When the Martians arrive, the citizens can obtain no reliable information; neither the newspapers nor governmental spokesmen will talk about the matter and all vital concerns must be communicated by rumor. When the Martians inaugurate their program, the newspapers slavishly follow suit, filling their pages with incomprehensible discussions of the new (blue) Martian wheat — the Soviet reader cannot fail to think of his own newspapers with perennial headlines and articles about successful harvests. Eventually Martian cars appear on the streets — sleek and black like the dreaded black Volgas of the KGB and party upper-crust. Human collaborators with the Martians (or humanoid Martians?) sport tight jackets and beat up the old privileged class — recalling the leather-jacketed bolsheviks and their strong-arm tactics. A farmer is celebrated who possesses an incredible ability to produce gastric juices for the Martians — a clear allusion to Stakhanov and Stalin's program of "socialist competition." And so it goes: the long lines in stores, the suspicion of returned POW's, the closing of a newspaper for an innocuous poem, the habitual drinking at all levels of the populace — all of these, whether by the authors' intention or natural frame of reference, derive from and comment upon Soviet society.

Understandably, many critics were not swayed by Podolnyi's one-sided view. They did not openly discuss the offensive passages in this and other works, preferring to work behind the scenes to bring the Strugatskys in line. Thus the articles that did appear represented only "the tip of the iceberg" (Suvin). The battle was apparently prolonged and intense, and not without counterattacks by Strugatsky supporters. It came to a sort of end in 1970, when an article in *Pravda* established the shaky coexistence described by Suvin.

One question asked in the polemic may be repeated here: Whom are the Strugatskys warning and what are they warning against? In respect to *The Second War of the Worlds*, we can hardly believe that they warn of a Martian or foreign invasion. (The appearance of the book a month after the invasion of Czechoslovakia was surely coincidental.) Nor is it feasible that they warn Soviet leaders of the dangers of democratic freedom at the cost of economic enslavement; certainly they do not intend to warn the West of its own collapse. The warning, if there is a warning, is a universal one, just as the satire is not limited to any capitalist or Communist country. The Strugatskys excel in posing philosophical questions. This time the question might be phrased: What would you do if a superior power offered you money, security, democratic freedom, and even a tasty new bread and a less-filling new beer — all in exchange for a small and regular "donation" of gastric juices, sweat, or some other renewable body fluid? Is there any reader in any country who could state categorically that he or she would forcibly oppose such sweet slavery? Is there a government which demands less or gives more? When put in this light, *The Second War of the Worlds* poses the problem of spiritual freedom in its most extreme form. It thus continues the tradition of Fyodor Dostoevski's "The Grand Inquisitor," Evgeny Zamyatin's *We* and Karel Čapek's *War with the Newts* — works of universal significance which warn not only of a possible future, but also of the loss of freedom at the present moment.

Yet this is not only a philosophical parable; it is also an imaginative, witty, and thoroughly enjoyable work, packed with exciting action, humorous episodes, and droll ironies. Although a short novel, there is a large cast of characters with individual peculiarities. The authors employ the familiar device of throwing us *in media res*, not introducing the characters but leaving us to work out the relationships. The hero-diarist, Mr. Apollo, is immediately characterized by his faintheartedness and self-serving rationalizations, and yet he is not completely negative. He has served in the war, been a prisoner, worked as a teacher for thirty years, forgone the pleasure of drinking beer during that time, and he now feels entitled to peace and quiet (and beer). As an astronomer, he has a perspective a bit broader, more reasonable, and more scientific than that of his drinking buddies, but one still far too narrow to encompass the events which now rush upon him. Actually this Apollo is a seductive character: we often laugh at him, particularly when he contradicts himself or changes his steadfast principles, but we also share his fear during some of the more harrowing episodes, and we tend to agree with him that most of his acquaintances are idiots. Ultimately we see him pass through all shades of reaction to the Martian invasion, and insofar as we sympathize with him we inadvertently accuse ourselves.

Having noted successes, we must acknowledge a few flaws. The first and most obvious is the title. It would seem, as Podolnyi suggested, that the brothers refer to H. G. Wells's *The War of the Worlds*, as if to say: "This is the way we would have described the Martian invasion." There are in fact some amusing remarks about spiders and octopuses which perhaps allude to the Wellsian monsters. But within the story itself, there has been no previous invasion, only a war against Fascists and Blackshirts, so that as far as the characters are concerned this is not the *second* invasion from Mars, but the *first*. So long as we consider the title to be written by the authors and the diary to be written by Apollo, things will make sense, but the split in perspective is misleading at first.

A second shortcoming is the diary itself. The Strugatskys handle the form well, creating a vivid and self-revealing picture of the diarist and his world, but nowhere do they inform us *why* Mr. Apollo keeps a diary. It may be his habit, he may be the Samuel Pepys of his time, we simply do not know — no external or internal motivation is given. When one thinks of the complex motivation of the diary in Zamyatin's *We*, where the diary itself plays a role in the story and even breaks through time zones, the marvelous possibilities of the form and the Strugatskys' conventional usage of it become apparent. Further, the length of the diary entries often exceed what might be expected for one sitting. Mr. Apollo complains of weakness and itching, yet writes dozens of pages with descriptions and dialogues. Thus the immediacy of the diary is lost in favor of the development of the story.

Probably the most curious feature of this work is the setting. All of the characters are given ancient Greek names, and although their city is not identified, the capital of the country is said to be Marathon (or "Marafiny" — the Marathon fields). From this and a few other hints, it appears that the action takes place not just "somewhere in Europe," but possibly in Athens, and the characters are the degenerate descendants of the heroes of Greek mythology. In this way their trivial desires and petty pursuits are magnified, and the whole history of Western civilization is cast into doubt. The Western reader naturally thinks of James Joyce and *Ulysses* (Russians have not been permitted to read *Ulysses*). The Strugatskys sometimes use the names to good advantage. For example, the great one-eyed giant of Homer's *Odyssey*, Polyphemus, is now a one-legged, blustering war veteran; Laomedon, the King of Troy who refused to pay for the construction of a wall around the city, is now the corrupt city mayor; Minotaur, the terrifying bull-monster fed on human sacrifices, is now the sanitation engineer, uncontrollably drunk and reckless.

Often, however, the Strugatskys run into trouble. Since they use Greek names mainly for ironic contrasts, and not for the more profound Joyceian purpose of transforming the entire myth, the underlying histories often conflict and create havoc. Thus, Mr. Apollo brings the Apollonian principle of the golden mean down to the level of total compromise, while his daughter, who is unfaithful to her husband, mocks the name of Artemis, the eternal virgin and goddess of hunting: well and good, but in Greek mythology Artemis was the twin sister of Apollo and could hardly be his daughter, even with the incestuous relations of the Greek gods. Perhaps the authors intend to show that the heroes of Greek mythology are now, in their present embodiment, no more than a collection of names, but one cannot escape the feeling that the Strugatskys were simply unable to construct a comprehensive system.

Even with these problems, *The Second War of the Worlds* remains an engaging work, imaginatively conceived and skillfully plotted. The work contains a positive hero in opposition to our sensible Mr. Apollo — his son-in-law Charon. This figure clearly derives from the socialist-realist stereotype of the bolshevist: active on the newspaper, engaged in political discussions, contemptuous of entertainments, dedicated to man's development and spiritual freedom, determined not to become "a cow" for the Martians. And yet, unlike his literary forerunners, he is not wooden: he drinks heartily, curses like a trooper, neglects his wife, and fails to stop the Martians. The reader cannot help but wonder about Charon's future: will he succumb to the environment of happy drinking, or will he rouse the citizens and effect a change? Here is the positive force the Soviet critics overlooked and the man we must measure ourselves against.

Gary Kern

SEED OF LIGHT

Author: Edmund Cooper (1926-   )
First book publication: 1959
Type of work: Novel
Time: The near future, one thousand years in the future, and fifty thousand years in the past
Locale: The Earth and the starship *Solarian*

The story of the destruction of Earth by nuclear warfare and the attempt to begin the career of mankind a second time by means of a starship carrying five couples and their descendants in search of a new world

> *Principal characters:*
> SIR CHARLES CRAIG, Prime Minister of the United Kingdom
> DR. OTTO REHN,
> PROFESSOR BOLLINDEN, and
> MICHAEL SPENSER, space scientists
> "SOCRATES,"
> "NEWTON,"
> "KEPLER," and
> "THALES," crew member of the *Solarian*

Seed of Light is dedicated "to those Church Dignitaries, Politicians and Eminent Men who advocate the retention of nuclear weapons." It is a book whose principal *raison d'être* is the expression of the antiatomic hysteria which was common in the late 1950's, publicized in Britain by the Campaign for Nuclear Disarmament and its annual marches from Trafalgar Square to the atomic research center at Aldermaston.

Science fiction, of course, provided a natural literary framework for the expression of antiatomic anxiety, and much of the science fiction of the 1950's is suffused with the symptoms of what James Blish once described as "chiliastic panic." *Seed of Light* is a cardinal example of this particular vein of science fiction, and while it is far from being the best-written representative, it is certainly one of the clearest and most direct. It is an impassioned novel, fervid with apocalyptic fear and written in the kind of metaphysical purple prose characteristic of such tracts. The dominant imagery of the work is, of course, Christian imagery — the scientist whose artificial satellite sparks off the final war has a peculiar fascination for The Revelation of St. John the Divine. The theme of the work as a whole, however, goes beyond Judgment Day and features a kind of desperate self-aggrandizement more reminiscent of the "ghost dances" of the North American Indians threatened by extinction at the hands of the European invaders.

The first part of the novel, "Bitter Harvest," is the story of the resumption of World War III after a temporary pause. The section begins, as does each of the three parts, with a "proem" which attempts to lend significance to the story by setting it in an evolutionary context. In this case the proem describes the extermination of Neanderthal Man by his Cro-Magnon successors, and draws from the tale the customary harsh moral concerning the aggressiveness of human nature, which must lead the species to self-destruction once it has achieved the means to that end. Writing in 1959, the author found the seeds of atomic Armageddon in the atom bomb itself and in the launching of armed space satellites in the wake of Sputnik.

Cooper's story begins with the launching of a new generation of satellites after limited war has destroyed the first generation. The new space station is put into orbit by the British Commonwealth, and in an attempt to avoid further conflict, the Prime Minister of Britain, Sir Charles Craig, offers the other major powers a share in its administration and control. Unfortunately, neither Russia nor the United States finds the offer attractive, and both embark upon a desperate race to get new satellites into orbit. Once the race is on, its conclusion is inevitable; but the designer of the British satellite, Professor Bollinden, decides that there may be one way to prevent that conclusion — by using the threat of his own station to force both sides to disarm. Unfortunately, one of his associates has already been passing information to the Russians which will give them the edge in the new space race, and he is determined that the advantage shall not be canceled. The destruction of civilization duly follows.

The story is told in an episodic fashion, presenting a kaleidoscopic image of world affairs by cutting back and forth from high-level political discussions to the reflections of the scientist-philosophers and the everyday affairs of ordinary people, in the manner which has become traditional in political thrillers. The method had already been used in several stories of nuclear war, including Nevil Shute's *On the Beach*, which had attained best-seller status two years earlier. In Cooper's novel, however, the gathering of the apocalyptic forces is only the prelude to the main story, which is one of rebirth.

The material in the novel's second section, "The Seed," is equally familiar, following as it does an often-used formula. Three domed cities are all that survive of civilization in Europe; these are doomed because the land outside is dead, and the threat of the radioactive poisons cannot be held at bay forever. From one of these cities the starship *Solarian* prepares to launch; its crew is the sole hope for the future of the human race. As the blast-off approaches, the masses who are to be sacrificed go through the usual motions, already adequately described in a number of catastrophic stories, including T. T. McIntosh's *One in Three Hundred* (1956). Cooper, free of the necessity to dwell on this part of his narrative, quickly takes his ship into space, and follows its crew of ten through the first years of their long journey.

Again the narrative is chopped and discontinuous, and the whole sequence is of largely figurative significance; its development is curiously illogical. The *Solarian*'s search-pattern involves zigzagging across the sky to investigate stars whose sole distinction is that Earthly astronomers have given them names. There is no attempt to follow an economical flight path or to concentrate on G-type suns. The crew of the ship is willing to invoke the logic of eugenics to justify the murder of a baby born a victim of Down's syndrome (a "Mongolian," as Cooper incorrectly describes the infant), but find themselves unable to tolerate the abandonment of monogamous sexual relationships lest the "psychological shock" of promiscuity should prove too much for them. The reader intent on looking for a rational development of the plot is likely to come to the conclusion that this second section is so *gauche* and amateurish as to make it difficult to believe that it is the work of a mature man rather than a teenager. However, the lack of rationality is in fact unimportant to the novel's real purpose and coherence, which is purely affective.

There is a curious pseudosignificance in the fact that the crew members of the starship adopt new names, the males choosing those of celebrities from man's intellectual history. (The females choose nonsymbolic names — it is perhaps worth noting that some of Cooper's later works, notably *Five to Twelve* and *Who Needs Men?*, reveal him to be science fiction's premier male chauvinist.) These names seem to be selected more or less at random, though there is the occasional crude analogy — the original crew's psychologist, for instance, is named Jung. There is a temptation to read into these names more than is actually there; the author's intention is merely to show that the founders of the new human race represent the past intellectual heritage of humankind.

The third section of the novel, "Germinal," is incompetent as a literary work; its tone is positively frenetic. However, although its purple prose is aesthetically and intellectually vacuous, there is no doubting the author's sense of urgency and genuine emotion. Ironically, the very crudity of the section as literature emphasizes its emotional force and lends it the power to affect sympathetic readers. In this section the story is sketched in through scattered paragraphs; the "message" has taken over completely.

What actually happens in this third section is that the starship pursues its quest for a new world for forty generations, while its original crew becomes the stuff of legend. (There are several crude parallels drawn between the tribulations of the starship children and the children of Israel wandering in the wilderness.) The new generations surpass the old, developing extrasensory perceptions, making progress in science, and ultimately discovering the secret of immortality.

Eventually, the scientist Thales develops a "selective cosmometer" which has the miraculous power to transport the *Solarian* instantly to the vicinity of a world guaranteed to be ideal for human habitation. This it does, delivering the ship to the neighborhood of Earth fifty thousand years before the events described in the first part of the novel. The ship discharges its superhuman cargo, and this time the strangers who confront the Neanderthals in Western Europe are not the Cro-Magnons, whose nature is so fatally flawed, but the "Upright Ones," descendants of Thales and his crew, who come not as destroyers but as peacemakers. This finale, with its loop back through time to the crucial moment of the prehistoric confrontation of two human races, is strikingly similar to the concluding image of Charles Harness' *The Paradox Men*, which is another work impregnated by the spirit of "chiliastic panic" aroused by the impressive debut of the atom bomb.

Seed of Light is such a perfect encapsulation of the spirit of its time that it has aged badly. Like Dr. Strangelove, we have, for the most part, stopped worrying, and if we have not quite learned to love the bomb, we have at least come to take its presence for granted. A certain chiliastic temperament is still very prominent in contemporary science fiction, but it has become much more subtle in its nature and its modes of expression. We have moved far enough away from the raw emotion of *Seed of Light* to be unimpressed by its urgency and irritated by its ineptitude. Nevertheless, if we recall its historical context, there is still a good deal of interest to be found in it.

There is a great deal of science fiction, particularly pulp science fiction, whose imaginative force is actually dependent upon its lack of sophistication. If *Seed of Light* had been more elegantly and more cleverly written, its impact on the imagination of many of the people who read it in its own day would certainly have been reduced. Its rawness emphasizes the anguish of its fears and the desperate ambition of its visionary finale, when it transcends the boundaries of reason to reach for an altogether supernatural solution. There is an evangelical quality about its message, and in order to put the message across Cooper makes use of the strategies of the evangelical preacher, which demand the use of insistent, rough-hewn parable and the repetition of talismanic verbal images.

One of the most interesting features of genre science fiction is the extent to which the jargon of science and technology are absorbed into the rhetorical techniques of religious writers, so that the fiction secures its effects much more by affective aggression than by an appeal to the speculative intellect. *Seed of Light* is a perfect example of this tendency. It also bears eloquent testimony to a particular anxiety which afflicted the social environment in which Edmund Cooper found himself in the 1950's, and it is all the more eloquent for its literary imperfections. It is a novel utterly without subtlety and often without sense, but it speaks clearly of the haunting of the 1950's by the specter of the mushroom cloud.

Brian Stableford

THE SEEDLING STARS

Author: James Blish (1921-1975)
First book publication: 1957
Type of work: Short stories

A series of four linked stories, forming a chronicle of the dispersal of humanity throughout the universe by means of a program of "seeding" alien planets with biologically adapted humans

Science fiction has characteristically dealt with the problem of colonizing planets with environments hostile to human life, in two ways: either adapt the environment to suit the colonists (sometimes called "terraforming"), or adapt the colonists to suit the environment. The latter solution belongs to a long and broad tradition of science fiction stories that explore the limits of what can reasonably be called "human" through narratives that postulate radical transformations of humanity as we know it. How much can a man be changed before he ceases to be a man? What, after all, are the essential human qualities: biological form, or psychological makeup, or some less easily defined concept of "will" or "spirit"? These are some of the questions that underlie James Blish's "pantropy" stories, collected and rewritten in book form as *The Seedling Stars.* "Pantropy" is a term literally meaning "changing everything," and Blish uses it to describe a process by which humans are genetically transformed into creatures capable of surviving in various alien environments that would otherwise be unavailable for human colonization. The stories in *The Seedling Stars* are set in these alien environments, and the protagonists are the strange creatures bred to survive in these environments and thus ensure the plenitude of the human race — in its broadest sense — throughout the universe.

Though Blish is careful to provide clear exposition of his basic thesis at the outset, it soon becomes apparent in reading these stories that he has set for himself a considerable narrative challenge. How, after all, can an author create a convincingly human character whose human characteristics have been severely altered, who exists in an environment totally alien from any we recognize, and who shares no common human culture? Except for intelligence, a few traces of racial memory, and an obliquely alluded to "spirit of rebellion," there is very little that any of the odd creature-heroes of these stories have in common with one another or with their parent civilization. Culture itself — science, art, philosophy — apparently cannot be transmitted through pantropy; each new species must discover and create these things for themselves. This not only leaves us with a rather vague notion of Blish's definition of man, but also creates a problem for Blish in simply making his narratives convincing and involving. It is hard enough to keep an adult reader interested in the adventures of tree-dwellers, microbes, or seals; but to persuasively portray such creatures as rational, mature, problem-solving humans rather than as fairy-tale curiosities demands special skill. To accomplish this, Blish draws on his not inconsiderable resources of literary technique and style. By sprinkling his narrations with pointed allusions to literary tradition (Jack London, the "pathetic fallacy," epic poetry, Kant) and mundane imagery, and by occasionally parodying traditional kinds of narratives (including science fiction "space operas"), Blish provides a number of "links" that aid us in understanding and empathizing with his strange creatures.

The first story in the collection, "Seeding Program" (initially published in 1955 as "A Time to Survive") establishes the essential theme of the series and tells us why and how pantropy is carried out. Appropriately for a tale dealing with the creation of new forms of life, it is rich in images of birth and growth. Sweeney, the pantrope-protagonist, has been created and nurtured in a womb-like underground dome on the moon, isolated by his need for a radically different environment from that of humans and able to communicate only via a one-way speaker controlled by his human mentors. As the story opens, Sweeney is in a spaceship — still isolated both from the human community and from the natural universe by protective walls — about to undertake a political mission on Ganymede: he is to infiltrate a colony of pantropes who threaten the Earth faction that prefers "terraforming," or the remaking of planetary environments, to pantropy. Sweeney has been promised he will be made human upon his return if he successfully captures the renegade pantrope leader. But clearly, Sweeney is a creature without a country, caught in a conflict between his loyalties to his creators and his natural affinity for other pantropes like himself. Furthermore, he is virtually without identity; he has never even experienced the birth trauma, much less social interactions or emotional involvement.

On Ganymede, Sweeney begins to experience all of these things: first a symbolic "birth" with his traumatic ejection from the spaceship that takes him there, later in his emotional involvement with the pantrope girl Michaela. Deeply moved by his first experiences of socialization and individuation, Sweeney is persuaded by the rebel pantrope-scientist Rullman to remain and help carry out the "seeding" project which is the basis of the remaining stories in the series.

The problem of alienation both from human culture and tradition and from the natural environment is one of the recurring themes in the book. The next two stories, "The Thing in the Attic" and "Surface Tension," both concern cultures which have been adapted for life in alien environments, but which have failed to achieve fully the conquest of those environments that is necessary for the species to grow and survive. In both cases, the key to continued survival lies in the ability to survive on the surface of the planet. "The Thing in the Attic" concerns a society of tree-dwelling pantropes unable to survive on the violent, evolutionarily primitive surface of a jungle planet. Only through the heroic action of an individual is the surface finally mastered. The story might be read as an evolutionary parable of the descent of man's ancestors from the trees to "fight it out" on the surface and thus achieve final mastery of the environment — and take a step closer to *homo sapiens* as well.

"Surface Tension" has become something of a science fiction classic in its original version which appeared in *Galaxy Magazine* in 1952. Rewritten here to dovetail better with the stories that surround it, the tale borders on absurdity and is written in a tone of sustained irony, suggesting that it may be a sort of parody of the vast heroic sweep of much science fiction. Here the heroic quest for knowledge is given a new perspective: the pantropes are microbes living in a puddle of water; the great scientific quest is to break through the surface tension of the water and survive in the "outer space" beyond; and the dispersal of humanity becomes no more than the ability to colonize nearby mud puddles. To this extent, the story parodies the entire concept of *The Seedling Stars*, but it also parodies other science fiction as well. The hero is a rebellious young man determined to explore the "outer world," aided by a wise older scientist and a faithful paramecium. The antagonists are horrible monsters that are really nothing more than microscopic rotifers. The young man, Lavon, succeeds in his quest, and on this new planet, at least, the human race has found itself another mud puddle.

The final story of *The Seedling Stars* is also ironic, but in a more predictable way. By the time the action of "Watershed" begins, the seeding program has been under way for millennia, and the Earth has long been abandoned and allowed to evolve into a barren, oxygen-poor planet with no intelligent life — not unlike many of the hostile environments that the seeding program was initially designed to help colonize. Not surprisingly, the Earth thus becomes the next target of the seeding program, and a group of adapted "seal-men" are sent to colonize it. By this point in Blish's expansive history, the few "normal" humans left in the galaxy have become resentful of the far more numerous pantropes, whom they regard as inferior. The problem is no longer the survival and dispersal of humanity, but rather the unification of all its different strains into a common brotherhood. Just how this is to be accomplished (or why, for that matter) is not made clear, but the "watershed" of the title refers to the time when such a union takes place. And the protagonist of the story predicts that such a time will be brought nearer when it is widely known that the Earth itself — the cradle of humanity — is no longer inhabitable by "normal" humans who have not undergone pantropic adaptation. In one sense, then, the theme of the story is simply that you can't go home again, that change and adaptation are natural and necessary parts of man's progress through the universe. In another sense, however, this final story reinforces the idea that Blish has made implicit throughout the book: man is not defined by his form but by his spirit and intelligence.

The Seedling Stars is valuable, then, for the boldness of its conception and the sweep of its narrative. Though it is perhaps unusual for a novelist to cast an epic narrative in the form of a few short stories, Blish succeeds by leavening his narrative with humor and literacy, and by commenting on the traditions of science fiction as he exemplifies them. But it is equally valuable as a study in how an intelligent author grapples with the problem of describing alien states and beings in a style which is limited to the familiar — perhaps because of the nominal realism demanded by the traditions of science fiction magazine publishing. In a sense, *The Seedling Stars* is a mock-epic, a miniature counterpoint to Blish's more detailed future history cycle of his *Cities in Flight* novels. If the prose does not at times live up to the conception, and if the whole seems somewhat disjoined (as one might expect from a group of short stories vaguely disguised as a novel), the book nevertheless remains a worthwhile example of science fiction on biological and evolutionary themes, and of the kind of radical imagination of which the genre is sometimes capable.

Gary K. Wolfe

Sources for Further Study

Criticism:

Scholes, Robert and Eric S. Rabkin. *Science Fiction*. New York: Oxford University Press, 1977, pp. 158-159. This book briefly mentions the theme of *The Seedling Stars*, describing it as a "complete novel," dealing with the spread of forms of humanity through the universe.

Reviews:

Analog. LX, December, 1957, pp. 152-153.

Galaxy. XV, January, 1958, pp. 104-105.

Infinity Science Fiction. II, April, 1957, pp. 94-96.

Magazine of Fantasy and Science Fiction. XIII, July, 1957, p. 92.

SEMPITERNIN

Author: Lajos Mesterházi (1916-   )
First book publication: n.d.
Type of work: Short stories
Time: The present and near future
Locale: Hungary, Peru, and an unidentified place

A collection of satirical science fiction short stories based on biological premises

There have been very few Hungarian authors whose work has been restricted to science fiction or whose most important achievements have been in that genre. That fact can be partially explained by considering the evolution of Hungarian literature and its linguistic isolation; but it is also partly due to the relatively delayed progress of science and technology in Hungary, and in certain characteristics of the society itself. Because of the special nature of Hungarian history, authors there have paid attention primarily to the present state of affairs rather than speculating about the distant future; they prefer to examine human relationships rather than problems of science and technology, robots, space travel, and star wars. Even so, science fiction does play a significant role in the history of Hungarian literature, which has produced some works of very high quality.

This is how we must approach Lajos Mesterházi's short stories, the only science fiction collection that has so far been published by the author. Even the most cautious general critics regard *Sempiternin* as a high point in the author's career. Science fiction critics and fans, however, praise it as the peak. Such praise is warranted; these stories are really masterpieces. They exhibit great literary and philosophical erudition, together with a keen sense of concrete detail. Mesterházi is a moralist who passionately seeks the motivations for the deeds of individual persons. In each of his novels, stories, and plays, he portrays these characters through the medium of exciting action. In his science fiction stories he exhibits all of his literary craftsmanship, but, at the same time, employs novel techniques. He presents the grotesque and satirical side of a reality which he depicts realistically in other works. The four short stories collected in *Sempiternin* are excellent examples of Mesterházi's art.

The story "Rockets, Stars, Recipes" has three parts. The first describes the life and technological marvels of R 51, a rocket launching station situated, in documentary fashion, in the High Sierras. Mesterházi depicts scientific marvels, while at the same time describing the dull routine followed by the crew, the barren landscape of the mountains, and the great poverty of the local inhabitants. Station R 51, like other bases in the network, scans the sky and prepares instantly to destroy any unidentified object.

The second part tells of the contents of a mysterious message. Being present at the crash site of a destroyed alien craft, the author manages to decode the text of a message found on board the ship. Venusians, a superintelligent octopoid race with a brain capacity several times greater than that of humans, wish to save mankind from a forthcoming catastrophe, even though they have had very bad experiences with Earthlings. As a result of a debate in the Supreme Council of Venus they send a spaceship to Earth to establish contact with the leaders of mankind.

In the third part, Mesterházi gives a list of recipes. The poor people living in the valleys of the High Sierras very seldom eat meat, for that reason they regard it as a genuine blessing when, on Easter Sunday, meat is literally showered on them from the sky. Some think that these provisions were intended for the rocket station, but most of them do not bother with explanations; they simply enjoy the food, the blessing of Heaven. The author visits the small village in the mountains and describes the various methods of preparing the meat.

The elliptical technique is excellent. The three parts have no apparent connection, but an understanding of the whole comes through a set of refined intimations.

"A Sporting Event" employs a different method, it being ostensibly the diary of a biologist. The Narrator gives a long and detailed account of his fishing expedition in a big lake near a research institute. The writer intimates that scientists working for the army in this closed valley are experimenting with a new biological weapon. It is a kind of poison or gas that kills, dehydrates, and mummifies its victims. It annihilates the population while leaving the buildings, including the industrial plants, in tact, thus solving the main problem of war. The corpses become as dry and fragile as crackers, but not infectious. The victims are even induced to turn off the gas and electricity to stop the machines, thus reducing the loss of matériel to a minimum. While the inventor-biologist is pursuing a large fish that appears quite unexpectedly, the scientists are finishing their series of experiments in the station. A large number of convicts from various prisons are exterminated by the scientists, who conclude their work with satisfaction. The Narrator — the hero of the story — stays a few more days on the scene; he catches the fish after a long struggle, but, having no use for it, lets it go.

Here Mesterházi creates an astonishing effect with his stylistic and narrative contradictions. He tells the fishing story in a detailed and passionate way, exploiting all possible tension and excitement in the situation, while, in the description of the experiments, he adopts a dry, objective, and "scientific" tone. We follow the colorful description of the fishing episode with difficulty, almost with boredom, while we read the cool narration of the experiments with great excitement. But the paradox is not limited to the style. Human beings are being killed in these experiments, while in the fishing story the victim is pursued and caught, but spared in the end. Whose life has more significance, that of a fish or a man? The reader must decide.

The story that gives its title to the volume is set in Hungary in the present or near future. Sempiternin is a drug that bestows immortality and eternal youth. It is the invention of a defected Hungarian scientist, in whose will the secret of the drug is bequeathed to his native land. A large pharmaceutical factory works at full capacity manufacturing Sempiternin, but there is not enough of the medicine to go around. Some allocations must be made; some is sold abroad for hard currency; and some is sold on the black market for incredibly large sums. None is available for the average man.

The protagonist is the retired manager of the pharmaceutical firm, who learns that he is suffering from an incurable disease. He visits his successor, whom he was instrumental in having appointed to the post, and asks him for some of the medicine. From the heated conversation between the two men we learn much about the drug — the history of its development, and its effects and side effects. We also learn about the plans for its distribution — who can get it, and under what order of priority. The new executive (who, of course, has already received the drug) refuses his predecessor's desperate request in a coldly logical manner. He even tries to show how difficult it will be for those who become immortal through Sempiternin, as they will have to deal with all the problems and conflicts of the future. The pleas of the older man are rejected; he says goodbye and goes away to die.

The story is told with startling realism. The naturalism of the setting and the authenticity of the voices have about them the ring of truth. But the fantastic basic idea, the unsettled issue of death or immortality, distorts reality and illuminates everything with a terrifying new light. Behind the intentionally elliptic conversation there is a tragedy, the conflict between weakness and inhuman power and unavoidable death runs through every line of the story.

In the final piece Mesterházi openly deals with the problem of death in a playful and humorous manner that may seem inappropriate but is nonetheless very effective. The story takes its title from the English expression "Happy Ship," phonetically, in Hungarian, "Hepisip." Mesterházi displays his mastery of construction as the plot proceeds along parallel lines — a parodistic-satirical one, and a sentimentally melancholy one.

The "hepisip" is a state institution for euthanasia, its official designation being "C" Department of Central Social Ceremony Halls. We get to know László Meszes, an author, on the day he is granted permission to "use" the services of the hepisip, together with his wife, Veronika. Meszes is bored with life. He feels that his work is finished, so he seeks a painless death. He waits for his wife in a sweet shop; but she does not come, so Meszes goes by himself to the Central Ceremony Hall. As he waits, Meszes scrutinizes the mural on the wall of the vestibule and becomes acquainted with the other people who are to have seats on the happy ship. There is a small ceremony preceding the "journey." Famous actors recite poems; a string quartet plays fine music; and a children's choir sings a song beginning, "We shall go on bravely." Meszes keeps looking at his watch, as he waits for his wife, but Veronika does not arrive.

As the ceremony proceeds, we slowly get to know the background of the passengers. The usual problems of old age, the population explosion, the prevalence of incurable diseases, have all contributed to the practice of euthanasia. It had of course first been debated in the capitalist countries, and it was first actually practiced aboard a ship, hence the name. Years later it became a subject of discussion in Hungary, first as an example of the inhumanity of capitalism. Then write-ups began to appear in travel books; and, finally, there was a full-fledged ideological and political debate. Mesterházi gives an excellent account of the events, liberally interspersed with references to figures of Hungarian or of international significance: their articles and books are cited, much in the manner of certain British "New Wave" science fiction writers. The Hungarian participants in the debate are especially effective. The various shades and refinements of domestic culture being thus obliquely presented in a highly humorous way.

László Meszes continues to wait for his wife in vain. He is attracted to a pretty woman among the people awaiting death and a slight flirtation ensues. Suddenly, at the last moment, a disheveled Veronika arrives and finds her husband in the company of an unknown woman, as she had so often done before. She starts to scold, but soon quiets down, along with the other "travelers" who receive their sedatives and settle back to watch an old Hungarian comedy on the screen. As the gas valves are opened, and the people begin to fall one by one, Veronika embraces her husband. The film rattles on; the mischievous hero's antics oscillate on stiffened eyeballs. Only Veronika's last embrace seems alive.

Mesterházi is a courageous author with a critical temperament. His ideas are original; his stories are full of realistic details, mingled with pungent humor and irony. The structure of his stories is complex; beneath the surface of the action-filled plot there are always very serious ideas to be found. This unusual volume might perhaps be compared with certain works by Harlan Ellison or Brian W. Aldiss. But Mesterházi's personal style and view of the world are uniquely his own.

The stories in *Sempiternin* have been translated into Bulgarian, English, German, Polish, and Russian. Lajos Mesterházi has won the highest Hungarian literary awards. In 1972, in Trieste at EUROCON II, upon the suggestion of the Hungarian delegation, he received a special prize for his works in the field of science fiction.

Péter Kuczka

LA SEPOLTURA
(The Burial)

Author: Gianni Montanari (1949-   )
First book publication: 1972
Type of work: Novel
Time: The 1980's
Locale: Milano and Verona, in Italy

A police state seeks to destroy the carriers of a mutant gene that causes paranormal behavior

Principal characters:
THE NARRATOR, who is unnamed and who returns from exile
BARBARA, his mistress
ANDREA, a member of an underground organization
ANGELA, a teenage girl who can control her paranormal powers

Written two years after Gianni Montanari's first novel *Nel nome dell'uomo* (*In the Name of Man*), *La sepoltura* effects a stronger approach to the theme of communication as well as a more detailed reconstruction of a near-future society. The basic failure of the world described by Montanari is a failure of communication between the old community and the newly emergent "Muties" who can levitate small objects, or can practice telepathy. This failure works both ways, since the average "Mutie" does not possess full control of his powers. Montanari seems to suggest that full communication, that is, full control, requires a more than ordinary balance. This is why the Narrator, who has an unresolved obsession with his father, is doomed to annihilation.

Montanari postulates the following chronology of events: In the early 1970's, after a misbegotten revolution reminiscent of the student movement of the late 1960's, an increasing number of people are discovered to possess paranormal capacities. (Montanari speaks of a "mutation" or allele of the sickle cell gene, but never goes beyond that simple reference.) The first to be surprised by the new capacities are the "Muties" themselves, as they "reveal" their powers under conditions of stress. Immediately, "normal" humanity builds "camps" in which the "Muties" are subjected to brain surgery, in the hope of eradicating the new faculties.

Since Montanari makes much of infrafamilial misunderstandings and hatreds, husbands are very prone to accuse wives, and *vice versa*. This happens to the parents of the Narrator. His mother's "talents" are noticed by his father, and she subsequently dies. The desire to kill his villainous father, however, gives way to a compulsive urge to flee, and the Narrator quickly leaves Italy for France.

Eight years later, he returns to Italy with his mistress, Barbara. The Narrator takes a look at an Orwellian Milano, then joins an underground movement that is trying to steal "Muties" and smuggle them outside of Italy. He has a glimpse of a possible savior for the subrace of "Muties": a girl, Angela, who is in apparent control of her paranormal powers, so that she does not betray herself. The Narrator resolves to attack his father, but in the end commits suicide. The "burial" is his own. Why does he kill himself? Either his father is a fullfledged "Mutie" who was compelled to kill his aberrant wife and now must kill his offspring, or the Narrator has realized his utter unworthiness and eventually achieves that self-destruction he has vicariously been seeking by ruining the lives of everybody with whom he comes in contact.

There is a structural parallelism between society and the Narrator: each is unable to resolve its inner conflicts. In the last line of the novel, we are led to see that there can be no communication: the world itself "cleaves in two parts," long after the Narrator's suicide. The main barrier seems to lie in the father-child relationship and *La sepoltura* is possibly the chronicle of an unsuccessful reconciliation with the father figure. The Narrator tries time and again to assert his adulthood by means of liquor and sex, but he always avoids a direct confrontation with his father.

La sepoltura represents a new international approach to science fiction, evidenced, in the United States, by such novels as *The Men Inside* by Barry Malzberg, and in Italy, by other works, for example, *Quando le radici* by Lino Aldani, where we see a sort of "neosociological" approach, after the "sociological science fiction" of the 1950's. In the 1950's society was found to be oppressive, but writers tried to analyze the mechanics of that oppression, and their novels were intended as warnings of possible dangers. Nowadays, such analysis — along with its ensuing promise of hope — has given way to a feeling of utter helplessness. It is the helplessness of Malzberg's Messenger, and of Montanari's Narrator, whose every plan is destined to go astray.

In Italy, Gianni Montanari was one of the first writers in the field to express that feeling in the years when a widespread hope of social reform was prevalent. Now, however, a new generation of writers is more oriented toward Montanari's kind of fiction than toward, say, the conventional Campbellian science fiction, which assumes that the future will necessarily be better than the present.

It must be questioned, however, whether Montanari could not have written the novel without the use of a "science fictional" locale. Much of *La sepoltura* might well have taken place during the years of the Nazi domination, with the substitution of "Jews" for "Muties." The conventions of science fiction are properly used in two instances: in the character of Angela, who suggests a possible reconciliation between the old and the new humanity, and in the ending of the novel, where no such reconciliation is possible. These conventions are the generically definitive parts of the novel, and they would have been ineffective without the science fiction setting. They are why the whole work hinges on communication rather than being simply a Man *versus* "Mutie" novel.

Riccardo Valla

SHADOWS IN THE SUN

Author: Chad Oliver (Symmes Chadwick Oliver, 1928-   )
First book publication: 1954
Type of work: Novel
Time: 1950's
Locale: Jefferson Springs, Texas

One of the first novels to introduce serious anthropological themes in science fiction, and to present a more mature and sympathetic view of alien "invaders"

> *Principal characters:*
> PAUL ELLERY, a young anthropologist
> ANNE, his fiancée
> JOHN, an alien leader
> MELVIN THORNE, a rancher in Jefferson Springs
> CYNTHIA, a teacher at the Jefferson Springs high school

As much of science fiction deals with imaginary cultures and contact between radically different civilizations, it is something of a surprise to note that before Chad Oliver, anthropology had been one of the more neglected sciences in the genre. Perhaps this is because of the engineering and physics biases of many of the editors and readers in the 1940's, who may have regarded anthropology as something of a "soft" science. Perhaps it took the rise of what has been called "social science fiction" in the early 1950's — science fiction that deals with social and cultural issues — to enable writers to make the all-too-logical connections between the issues treated in anthropology and those treated by science fiction. Perhaps, even, many science fiction writers simply did not *know* enough anthropology to use it as a basis for speculation in fiction.

Chad Oliver did much to change this in the ealry 1950's, and *Shadows in the Sun* draws much of its historical importance from the fact that it was one of the first serious works of anthropological science fiction, a subgenre which now boasts works by some of the major writers in the field, such as Ursula K. Le Guin. Oliver, himself a practicing anthropologist with a Ph.D. from UCLA, approached the problem of aliens taking over the Earth as an anthropological problem, and *Shadows in the Sun* is loaded with expository summary of anthropological theory and technique. What if, he posits, the Earth were being colonized in much the same way many "backward" areas of the Earth had been colonized by European explorers — such as North America or Africa — without the "natives" ever being fully aware of what was going on? What if we were the Indians rather than the Europeans, and what if such broad social movements as the migration to the cities were secretly being engineered by an alien civilization with advanced propaganda techniques, in order gradually to confine us to "reservations"?

Such questions, of course, may reflect the early 1950's paranoia about conspiracies as much as they reflect genuine anthropological concerns; and indeed, some of the major themes in the novel are characteristic 1950's themes. The notion of aliens taking over a small town with no change in the outward appearance of the town was common during this period, probably reaching its most famous manifestations in the first version of *Invasion of the Body Snatchers* (based on a Jack Finney serial which appeared the same year as *Shadows in the Sun*); and even if Oliver's aliens are portrayed as essentially indifferent to the welfare of Earth, the fear of a fifth column within our culture, controlled by some distant foreign power, is pervasive in the novel.

The presence of the aliens is also related to another favorite fear of the period — atomic war. While the aliens are forbidden by their own law to intervene in human affairs, they rather hope and expect that Earth will reduce its population and level of civilization through such a war, thus making room for more colonists. A political faction among the aliens even advocates intervening to promote war among the natives. Furthermore, when anthropologist Paul Ellery discovers the presence of the aliens, who have gradually supplanted the entire population of the small town of Jefferson Springs, Texas, he is invited to undergo a period of education and training which will enable him to join them — a process which sounds suspiciously like sophisticated brainwashing techniques which, during the 1950's, Communist nations were widely suspected of using. All this serves to remind us that the novel is very much of its time; still, the work does not seem especially dated.

The major reason the novel still holds up well is the ingenuity with which Oliver formulates his anthropological problems and the clarity which characterizes the exposition underlying these problems. In fact, in many ways the book is more of an intellectual exercise than a novel. The narrative is thin, the characters sketchily drawn, and the focus is consistently on the thought processes of Paul Ellery as he tries to formulate and solve the problems facing him. This focus on formulating the problem — on learning to ask the right questions — is remarkably sophisticated for a genre which had characteristically presented clearly drawn puzzles that could be unlocked by ingenious scientific deduction or, failing that, heroic action. Paul Ellery's initial problem is that Jefferson Springs is too normal, that it conforms too precisely to what an anthropologist would expect from a community of its size and location. But this, Ellery realizes, is not much of a problem: why is a normal community so normal? The mystery of Jefferson Springs is one he could hardly explain to anyone intelligently.

But like the typical dogged scientist of science fiction, Ellery persists in trying to unravel the mystery — and here is where Oliver's ingenuity in plotting enables him to depart from formula. While the reader, perhaps familiar with stories of this type, expects the solution to this problem to coincide with the resolution of the plot, instead we find the problem solved before the book is one-fourth over — and the answer is simply given to Ellery by the aliens. Realizing that Ellery cannot really do anything with the information once he has it, the aliens offer it to him freely — thus creating a new problem for him and in the process elevating the level of the overall puzzle another notch. Ellery's next problem is more complex: what is the nature of this alien civilization, and what, if anything, is its weakness? Oliver introduces suspense into this latter portion of the narrative by imposing a deadline on Ellery: he must answer these questions before he makes the final decision as to whether to undergo the aliens' training program and become one of them.

Again Ellery's problem, essentially, is formulating his problem, and again he is somewhat frustrated in his detective work by having the answer handed to him by the alien leader John, who has come to like and value Ellery as a friend, even though by his standards primitive. Only a week before Ellery must make his decision to join the aliens or remain on Earth, John invites him aboard the spaceship which seems to serve as an administrative center for the Earth colonies and shows him a vision of some amorphous, truly alien beings called the Others. Again, Ellery is forced to shift his perspective: compared to the Others, John and his fellows colonists are not really aliens at all, but fellow humans who happen to be born into a far more advanced civilization than our own. The unity of humanity as a species needs to take precedence over loyalty to specific political or cultural units, which are after all only structures within which humans operate.

It is here that the central theme of the book finally becomes clear — the relationship between the individual and the culture. Despite the advanced technology and science of the alien colonists, the individual colonists are no more advanced than ordinary humans. In fact, they are ordinary humans, not brilliant scientists or intellectual supermen. Ellery had seen some evidence of this earlier in his relations with two of the aliens other than John. One was Melvin Thorne, whose "cover" in Jefferson Springs was that of a cheerful redneck Texas rancher. Ellery eventually comes to realize that Thorne's personality is really like that; his disguise is his role rather than his personality. The other was Cynthia, the high school teacher who has a brief affair with Ellery; he finally realizes her sexual attraction to him was real, even if it did involve for her an element of decadence, of making love to a "primitive." John, however, finally enables Ellery to see that it is not he who is primitive, but rather his culture, or more accurately, his culture's science and technology. For the political structure of the aliens' government is really not much different from that of many colonial governments in Earth's own history. Furthermore, Ellery comes to realize, the colonists are alienated from the mainstream of their own culture, condemned to living in a kind of galactic backwater and as resentful of that fact as colonials always are.

Morally and politically, then, the aliens are no more advanced than we are; their culture is not genuinely alien from ours, it is simply more developed. Oliver's characterization of individual aliens is in keeping with this point: they write bad poetry, tell jokes, make political deals, and generally behave not at all as one would expect from science fiction aliens. As individuals, they are no different from us. When Ellery is finally made aware of this, he realizes that to join the aliens would be merely to trade one set of cultural problems for another, and not really to gain much in the process. In the end, he rejoins his fiancée, Anne, and decides to devote himself to the betterment of his own society on Earth.

As a novel, *Shadows in the Sun* has its weaknesses. Most of the characters are rather hastily drawn, though the characterization of Ellery himself provides an insightful portrait of a young scientist grappling with problems beyond his grasp and, more importantly, facing the real difficulty of formulating these problems. The alien John is a fine antidote to the usual run of humorless intellectuals that so often represent advanced societies in science fiction, though his motives are never made quite clear. Other characters, such as Thorne or the dour editor of the local newspaper, are stereotypes — though we cannot be sure whether the stereotyping is on Oliver's part or is a wry comment on the aliens' attempts to simulate small-town life in America. The style of the novel often tends to be frustrating, as Oliver repeatedly leads us through Ellery's thoughts in interior monologues so single-minded that we begin to lose patience. And the exposition of anthropological ideas, though entertainingly written, adds a note of overt didacticism to the book and gives it a slightly patronizing tone. In 1954, however, it may be that such didacticism was useful in bringing anthropology into science fiction. *Shadows in the Sun* is neither great nor greatly ambitious, but in many ways it achieves the entertaining blend of idea and action toward which so much science fiction strives.

Gary K. Wolfe

Sources for Further Study

Reviews:

Amazing Stories. XXIX, May, 1955, p. 114.

Analog. LV, May, 1955, p. 149.

Fantastic Universe Science Fiction. II, January, 1955, pp. 126-127.

Galaxy. IX, February, 1955, p. 108.

Magazine of Fantasy and Science Fiction. VIII, April, 1955, p. 81.

Nebula Science Fiction. XVI, March, 1956, pp. 101-102.

New Worlds. XLIII, January, 1956, pp. 126-127.

THE SHAPE OF THINGS TO COME
The Ultimate Revolution

Author: H. G. Wells (1866-1946)
First book publication: 1933
Type of work: Novel
Time: 1933 to 2106
Locale: The Earth

A school textbook of the year 2106 summarizes the collapse of civilization in the twentieth century and outlines the creation and design of the Utopian modern world state

> Principal characters:
> DR. PHILIP RAVEN, a diplomat and the author of the "dream-book"
> "H. G. WELLS," the editor of Raven's notes

The problem with *The Shape of Things to Come* is that it posits a discomforting premise in behalf of an unconvincing solution. "Today" teeters hopelessly on the edge of economic collapse and decimating plague, while "Tomorrow" promises salvation in the shape of technocrats ordering a new world by creative fiat. And it is precisely the difficulty inherent in using make-believe as the vehicle of rhetorical strategies (for scolding, or warning, or persuading) that makes this work interesting yet unsatisfying. The artist in Wells, the Wells of the early scientific romances, here turns to prophecy: the novelist becomes journalist. Wells the moral philosopher takes over from the provocative storyteller of *The Time Machine*, *The War of the Worlds*, and *The Invisible Man*.

Where once he had dramatized, the author of *The Shape of Things to Come cum* social reformer and revolutionary, now recites and preaches. Though the narrative is characterized in the Introduction as a "Short History of the Future," "a modern Sibylline book," the work might aptly be described as a treatise on the descent of man under capitalism and the origins of the New World Order. In lieu of fully developed fictional characters, we are offered peoples, races, humanity, man; instead of plot, a recapitulation and analysis of history; instead of thematic subtlety, ideology. Because the narrative is primarily a recitation of events, the mode being journalistic, we, the readers, find ourselves outside, watching as the center folds and collapses. Consequently, the magic lantern slide show may be interesting, but it never engages our emotions or taps our imaginative or spiritual potential.

The Shape of Things to Come purports to be a translation and reconstruction of the shorthand manuscript notes of the deceased Dr. Philip Raven by H. G. Wells, his friend and confidant. Dr. Raven, (a diplomat assigned to the League of Nations Secretariat in Geneva in the year 1930) had presumably read the book of the future. The Introduction by H. G. Wells gives an account of how the two men met and became acquainted, how Raven explained the existence of his "dream-book," and under what circumstances the editor came into possession of the materials that comprise the narrative. Thus, the "dream-book" constitutes a record of what Raven "saw" already written in the year 2106: a chronicle of catastrophe in the twentieth century attributable to "ignorance, individualism, monetary collapse and nationalism" and subsequent world rebirth in the form of a Modern State, designed by social and political scientists.

The novel proper opens with a long disquisition on how humanity came to find itself in a terminal condition of economic, social, and political disease and disintegration. By "taking our imaginations back into the past," we will come to realize "how evil to nose, eye, ear and soul the congregation of human beings could be." (Supposedly, like Lemuel Gulliver in Houyhnhnm-land, though we stand exposed as the Yahoos we really are, we also stand to profit from the comparison with our betters.) The imperialist, capitalist Past led humanity down the ideological path to self-destruction. Its society was a madhouse-prison whose captives were unaware of their captivity.

The birth of the new world order, initiated by a phantom plague that reduces the world's population by half, is accompanied by a strict code of commandments issued by the "first-makers" of the World State: tell the truth; maintain the highest technical standards; control money and do not keep it; give your powers ungrudgingly to the service of the World State. It was clearly the responsibility of the new regime to "clean up the racial mind." Failure to do so "would leave the race to drift back again to animal individualism, and so through chaos to extinction."

In order to forestall any such possibility, three important resolves were formulated by the fathers of the Socialist World State: to establish a central control over all transportation and communication (Sea and Air Ways Control); to organize and centralize all resources (Supply Control); to implement a universal social order (Education and Advertisement Control). The initial task of the leadership was to overcome recalcitrant human nature by institutionalizing a process of "mental reconstruction." Such reconstruction involved eliminating national and racial boundaries and biases, establishing a *lingua franca* as a universal language, and absorbing all religious and ethnic systems into a Universal Education Control. The control over transportation, communication, supply, and resources could insure the effectiveness of universally controlled education. In time, by means of suppression and dilution, Christianity crumbled. Islam went quickly because of its inextricable tie to its language. The Jews, once thought to be so intractable and tenacious, "were educated out of their oddity and racial egotism" in just three generations.

Finally, the World Council, composed of elite technocrats charged with the governance of the world, had achieved a modern state in control of all aspects of life. With chaos now replaced by an ordered world economic system, and permanence assured by the "reconstruction of education on the basis of world history and social science," the World Council can retire. "There is nothing left for a supreme government to do," says one of its members, "Except look upon the world it has made and see that it is good. And bless it."

Philip Raven's "dream-book," posing as history, and reading like a pamphlet, has all along really been a secular reworking of the Good Book itself, rooted in a kind of journalistic headline thinking (*The Shape of Things to Come* exhaustively subtitles its subtitles). Wells maximizes the idea of universal degeneration and calamity as sanction for the scientific efficiency of the correctives. The Ideal Order then becomes a necessary corrective for the Ideal Chaos. In adopting a perspective that sees from the vantage point of a perfect or ideal world, the "dream-book" commits us to having to acknowledge the manifold imperfections in our own world.

By incorporating the individualistic capitalist "I" into a communal socialist "We," and replacing competition with cooperation, the requisite shift in identity is accomplished. The creation of the new world is presented in terms of order, planning, control, organization, and sublimation, while the imperfect reality is described as disproportionate, inefficient, anxious, and chaotic. What eventually proves disconcerting about this secular testament is the suspicion that the "new world," as pictured for us, holds a horror equal to the old one it replaced. Whatever the "blessings" granted by the supreme World Council on the Heaven it believes it has finally wrought, we rightly fear it condemns its beneficiaries to an everlasting hell of boredom and sameness. It is an inheritance we instinctively distrust.

But the resemblance of the final pronouncements of the World Council to Genesis 1:31 (where, after the Creation, God surveys His handiwork and, pronouncing it good, blesses it) is unmistakable. And so perhaps is the analogy we are meant to draw from the similarity. Indeed, now we know why the "dream-book" and its Utopian vision of an ultimate "world garden" leaves us unconvinced. It is a picture of Paradise without God. The new man has not really earned his way there.

The paradoxes presented by *The Shape of Things to Come* find no satisfactory resolution. The novel incorporates both dystopian and Utopian views, seeing from both angles at once, to form another creation myth. As in Genesis, the novel recounts the primeval history of its world, and then the history of its fathers, the "first-makers" of the goodly state. When, having reached the end of Raven's manuscript, the editor provides a supplementary conclusion prophesying "reconstruction" of the world by "an aggressive order of religiously devoted men and women" imposing "a new pattern of living on our race," we are being reinforced in the notion of divine commission.

Then the analog between the *five books* of *The Shape of Things to Come* and the Five Books of Moses (the Pentateuch) becomes apparent. There is the revelation of primeval history; the exodus from bondage and slavery; the giving of the law and the covenant of the chosen people; the historic pilgrimage through the wilderness to the promised land; and the book of the law reinterpreted and codified. Genesis, Exodus, Leviticus, Numbers, and Deuteronomy are secularized as "Today and Tomorrow: The Age of Frustration Dawns," "The Days After Tomorrow: The Age of Frustration," "The World Renascence: The Birth of the Modern State," "The Modern State Militant," and "The Modern State in Control of Life." Raven's dream-book is the secular equivalent of the Old Testament. The Modern State resembles the Promised Land of Scripture; and the chosen people are now the technocratic "Airmen" who are to unite and bring blessing on mankind. In secular fashion, we are treated to an account of the generations, the flood and the plague, the remnant that is saved, and the "new beginning" that signifies deliverance.

Not to slight the New Testament, we can easily recognize the Holy Trinity now become the all-powerful Transportation, Supply, and Education Controls. These Controls are aspects of the one World Council which is, as a result, omniscient, omnipotent, and omnipresent. The essence of God has, in this version, been actualized and realized as the Modern State. Monotheism, called here "the first form of the World-State in men's minds," becomes the idea of *centrality*, of oneness. The dream-book announces integration of control over transportation and communication by means of the airplane, with control over all the Earth's resources and universal social order to follow. Instead of an abstract sign, the machine now becomes the symbol of the new cosmology.

The airplane as a symbol of order, of plenty and peace, is also paradoxically the symbol of awesome power and destruction. God in His heaven — both the just and merciful God and the God of vengeance — is replaced by the air machine. The archangels are called "Airmen," and the beat of Cherubim wings is become the thrust and fire of rocket engines traversing the infinite heavens of once metaphysical space.

The Biblical story of creation is the story of how God created an orderly world out of primordial chaos. The narrative of *The Shape of Things to Come* recounts how men of the World Council formed the perfectly ordered Utopia of year 2106 from the chaos of economic collapse and the void of social and political disorder. The first Eden into which all men were placed ("Adam" meaning collective man) was corrupted by the "dark figures" of capitalism: banker J. P. Morgan, arms magnate Basil Zaharoff, and that sinister industrialist Ivar Kreuger "who created an almost world-wide system of lucifer match monopolies." Thus, man falls into toil, pain, anxiety, competition murder, and death.

For the modern world, then, there is no redemption in prayer. There is, however, a secular equivalent that is both rational and efficient — the law. Individual salvation is now human progress, and private prayer has been replaced by social and political legislation, rewarding and punishing in response to collective petition. Self-expression becomes communication. The priests of the past are the technocrats of the future; the old sacred sects are displaced by new scientific brotherhoods ordered by specialization.

In the year 2106, even a schoolboy knows that the permanent conflict in life is "between past and future, between the accomplished past and the forward effort." Traditional orthodoxies had obstructed development of an ethic harmonizing man with his place in space and time. As a means of achieving such harmony, the twenty-second century has contrived a universal language called Basic English. Where, in the past, intellectual progress had been hampered by the "endless flaws and looseness of the language nexus," language is now manufactured, made synthetic, by the infusion of words, idioms, and roots from all other languages and with new lettering, spelling, and vocabulary. As language is brought to a "new level of efficiency," there appears a collective Brain, otherwise known as the Fundamental Knowledge System and the Memory of Mankind.

Yet, in spite of the prophetic accuracy we can already sense at work here, or *because of it*, we sniff an inherent paradox in the joyful anticipation of a future achieving ultimate creative freedom through a mind-machine alliance. After all, is creativity or freedom compatible with Systems, Bureaus, and Controls? The Language Bureau, and the Dictionary Bureau are, in Wells's dream, the bright side of Orwell's nightmare bureaucracy of "Newspeak" and all that it implies. The dark side of "mental reconstruction" is psychosocial and genetic engineering. The exaltation of the mind may be had at the price of the discrete soul, the worship of science at the expense of spirit, and maximum efficiency at the cost of imagination.

The Shape of Things to Come defines itself as an outline of history. And because the shape of something can be seen only from the outside, this novel is finally *without* flesh, or blood, or viscera. It is all bone and muscle. But though, as a novel, it may not touch us in memorable ways, it cannot be dismissed. Like muscle, it packs its own kind of wallop.

If we are not entirely convinced that this novel takes the form we might desire, we cannot help but be impressed by its vitality, its commitment, and its optimism. We come to see what is unavailable in Raven's dream-book: cause for optimism lies not so much in the Utopian future Wells envisions as in the envisioning process itself — the power of the unique mind to construct imaginatively a world that is literally "nowhere." Such an imagination can, and does, finally bring order to the chaos of our existence by reclaiming the barren desert of our failures and planting in its place a dream of paradise.

Greta Eisner

Sources for Further Study

Reviews:

Booklist. XXIX, February, 1933, p. 182.

Bookman. LXXVI, February, 1933, p. 189.

Catholic World. CXXXVII, April, 1933, p. 117.

Nation. CXXXVI, January 25, 1933, p. 97.

New Republic. LXXIII, January 25, 1933, p. 301.

New York Times. January 22, 1933, p. 1.

Saturday Review. IX, February 11, 1923, p. 425.

SHE

Author: H. Rider Haggard (1865-1925)
First book publication: 1887
Type of work: Novel
Time: The 1880's
Locale: England and Africa

Two British adventurers search for the lost city of Kôr and its ruler, a woman of incredible beauty and power who has lived for more than 2,000 years waiting for the reincarnation of her dead lover

Principal characters:
> AYESHA, OR SHE-WHO-MUST-BE-OBEYED, a 2,000-year-old woman of matchless beauty and wisdom, ruler of the Amahagger
> LEO VINCEY, a remarkably handsome young man who is the descendant and exact likeness of Kallikrates, an Egyptian priest
> L. HORACE HOLLY, a middle-aged Cambridge mathematician, mentor of Leo Vincey and narrator of the novel
> JOB, the servant of Holly and Leo
> BILLALI, an elderly leader of the Amahagger and servant of Ayesha
> USTANE, an Amahagger woman in love with Leo

H. Rider Haggard's fourth novel, *She*, was published in 1887, the year after *King Solomon's Mines*. Haggard wrote it "at white heat" in about six weeks and completed it on March 18, 1886. Some critics complained that it was too outlandish in plot and too lurid in style, but it was an immense popular hit and has never been out of print. William Gillette dramatized it, and it has been filmed six times. Together with the adventure fiction of Robert Louis Stevenson, Haggard's novels were instrumental in reviving the romance at a time when realism and novels about the poor and the working class were predominant.

Haggard states that the "central idea was a woman who had acquired practical immortality, but who found that her passions remained immortal too." Her overwhelming passion is a deathless love for Kallikrates, an Egyptian priest of Isis who broke his vows of chastity to flee with Amenartas, a woman whom he married. At about the same time, over 2,000 years ago, Ayesha, a beautiful woman of Arabian ancestry, fled from Egypt. The trio discovered the majestic city of Kôr, a hazardous journey inland in east-central Africa. There, Ayesha found the fire of immortality in the heart of a volcano; she bathed herself in it and became a creature of almost supernatural and deathless beauty, but when she offered her love and the gift of immortality to Kallikrates, he refused, out of love and loyalty to his wife. The enraged Ayesha then killed him. But Amenartas escaped, gave birth to a boy, and bequeathed to her descendants the command to find Ayesha and take revenge.

The novel begins when Vincey, a friend of the Cambridge student Ludwig Horace Holly, arrives in a dying state, persuades Holly to become the guardian of his five-year-old son Leo, and bequeaths to him a strongbox to be opened when Leo turns twenty-five. Holly is almost grotesquely ugly but is good-hearted, courageous, and immensely strong. Leo develops into an incredibly handsome man, resembling a Greek god. When they open the box, they find a potsherd inscribed with ancient inscriptions that tell the story of Kallikrates, Amenartas, and the immortal white goddess. A letter from Leo's father explains that the Vinceys are the descendants of Kallikrates and that he had failed in an attempt to discover the city of Kôr. Leo determines to take up the quest, not out of duty to avenge his murdered ancestor but out of curiosity to solve the mystery and see if the wonders are true. Holly and their servant Job accompany him. Their ship is wrecked in a gale, but they escape in a whaleboat and find themselves at the precise point on the African coast that they were seeking. They proceed to row inland up a river through a wasteland of dismal swamps until the channel is choked off. Then they are captured by savages, the Amahagger or People of the Rocks, whom Ayesha, having foreseen their coming, had dispatched to bring them to her unharmed.

During the arduous trip through the swamps, Holly rescues the Amahagger leader, Billali, from drowning. But when Billali goes on ahead to Kôr, the ferocious Amahagger attempt to kill a Moslem survivor from the wrecked ship by placing a red-hot pot over his head and then eating him. Holly and Leo try to stop them and are almost killed in an epic fight, when Billali returns and saves them. Leo, however, has been seriously wounded and becomes feverish. He is nursed by Ustane, a native woman who claims him as a husband. The journey continues through the swamps, across barren plains, to a ring of mountains hiding Kôr. The Englishmen are blindfolded and led through tunnels to the lost city. Ayesha does not live in the ruined city itself but in its immense necropolis, a series of vast caves and tunnels carved out of the rock to house the mummified citizens of Kôr who died of a plague millennia ago.

Alternately playful and passionate, Ayesha reveals herself to Holly, and the confirmed middle-aged bachelor falls hopelessly in love with her. She tells him that she is not for him but has been waiting for 2,000 years for the return of Kallikrates, whose body she has kept preserved in her chambers. She promises to heal Leo but waits until he is at the very point of dying from fever. Then she is terrified to discover that he is the reincarnated Kallikrates and that she may be too late to save him. But Leo recovers, and Ayesha destroys the no-longer needed corpse of his ancestor. Leo is enraged when Ayesha kills Ustane by a supernatural blast from her eyes; but when Ayesha shows him her face, he is enslaved to her beauty as Holly was. He agrees to bathe in the fiery Pillar of Life and wed her in immortality. A perilous journey takes them into the bowels of a volcano, where the immortal flame roars and rumbles through a cavern. When Leo hesitates to immerse himself in the awesome fire, Ayesha enters it herself both to reassure him and to further enhance her already supernatural beauty. Bathed in fire and drawing it into her lungs, she seems at first the embodiment of vitality, but when she steps out, she at first almost imperceptibly, then horribly alters and shrivels into the shrunken, hideous, incredibly ancient body of a two-thousand-year-old-woman. She dies, promising yet to return to Kallikrates. Job falls dead of shock, Leo's hair turns white and he seems to age twenty years, but he and Holly escape and with Billali's help make their way through the swamps. After a year and a half of further wandering, they return to England.

The plot is a highly romantic melodrama, blending gruesome Gothic details with the sort of exotic adventure in lost cities that later flourished in the fiction of Edgar Rice Burroughs and his successors. But Haggard's novel transcends melodrama on a number of counts. First, the story of She-Who-Must-Be-Obeyed has a mythic dimension. Realistic in its narrative details, it also suggests a timelessness, not only in the heroine's near-immortality but also in echoes of the worship of goddesses in the religions of many ancient peoples, from the pre-Islamic Arabs, the Phoenicians, Babylonians, and Assyrians down to the Bantus, Ashanti, and Zulus in Haggard's own time. The Pillar of Life from the bowels of the earth is the Promethean flame that has taunted and lured mankind from the beginning of time with the elusive hope of immortality. This hope, combined with the ancient Eastern myths of metempsychosis or spiritual evolution, purports mysteries beyond Darwin's scientific and (to the Victorian critics) mechanistic evolution. Carl Jung cites Ayesha or *She* as a classic example of the *anima* or female force in man; She is also a prime example of the *femme fatale* who flourished in the literature of the later nineteenth century. But She is not merely a heartless beauty; She tries to make her cruelty and her evil deeds understandable on the grounds of her timeless and profound love. Though the men in this novel are proper Victorians, *She* is very unVictorian in its presentation of a heroine whose passions are utterly unrestrained. "How very different from the home life of our own dear queen" applies to Ayesha even more than to Shakespeare's Cleopatra.

Haggard knew Africa from firsthand experience, and he succeeded in providing verisimilitude by realistic if frequently imaginary anthropological detail, so that some critics call his novels "romances of anthropology." But *She* is definitely in revolt against the sort of middle-class realism advocated by William Dean Howells, who insisted that novelists should show only the smiling aspects of life, should write nothing unsuitable for a father to read to his young daughter, and should avoid effects at all costs. Ayesha is as far removed as possible from Howells' crinoline-clad heroines, and the novel is primarily a reaching for effects in an attempt to evoke that feeling of the sublime which Edmund Burke said was to be found in terror and astonishment, aroused through such qualities as darkness, solitude, vastness, infinity, difficulty, magnificence, sound, and spectacle. Haggard provides all of these in abundance, piling one awesome and horrific effect upon another. Edmond Gosse wrote Haggard that no other book has so "thrilled and terrified" him. "Awful" is the key work in the novel. Even Ayesha's loveliness is as awful as it is entrancing. In addition, we have repeatedly the fear and fascination of the unknown; the awesome terror of the squall; the desolate, endless, gloomy landscapes; the horror of cannibalism; the love of slaughter that even Holly and Leo respond to in their fight with the Amahagger; the mixture of the splendid and the hideous in Ayesha's royal residence in the caves of Kôr. The caves are a vast catacomb, where Ayesha is served by savage guards clad in leopard skins and is waited upon by mutes. *She* herself is terrible as well as irresistible in her supernatural powers, her deathlessness, her immortal beauty.

In scene after scene, Haggard uses what Wordsworth called the "ministry of fear" to arouse the reader's imagination. Ayesha herself rules by terror and inflicts unspeakable tortures on those who disobey her. To entertain her guests, she has her savage followers stage a dance of grotesque spectacle, lit by the lurid flames of mummies set to the torch. The entire city is an endless charnel house, and one enormous pit contains thousands of jumbled skeletons or desiccated corpses with the skin still on them. There is an awful and hideous grandeur, a mixture of "horrors and wonders" in the spectacle of Kôr, with its caves, its vast chambers, its majestic ruins, and its barbaric splendor. The final journey to the Pillar of Life takes the protagonists into a sensational and terrifying series of scenes among caves and crevasses either swathed in darkness or lit briefly by a sickly shaft of light giving lurid illumination to bottomless pits that they must cross. Repeatedly, they encounter views that are appalling in their gloom and grandeur. In the climax, when Ayesha bathes herself in flame, sublime beauty is immediately followed by such hideous horror that Job drops dead at the sight. The novel's "strange and terrible" adventures are steeped in gloom, yet at the same time it projects an intense evocation of passionate life, heroic excitement, and exotic beauty.

H. Rider Haggard was a profound influence upon the subsequent "sword and sorcery" school of science fiction and fantasy, but he himself outdid them all both in sublime effects and in literary skill. Andrew Lang urged him to write a sequel to *She*, and eventually he produced three of them. In *Ayesha, or The Return of She* (1905), Leo and Holly encounter the reanimated spirit of Ayesha in Tibet, and they all die. *She and Allan* (1921) occurs some years before *She* and brings her together with Allan Quatermain, the hero of *King Solomon's Mines* and numerous other Haggard novels. Finally, *Wisdom's Daughter* (1922) tells the original story of Ayesha and Kallikrates, some 2,000 years earlier.

Robert E. Morsberger

Sources for Further Study

Criticism:

Atwood, Margaret. "Superwoman Drawn and Quartered: The Early Forms of *She*," in *Alphabet*. X (July, 1965), pp. 65-82. Atwood views *She* as Haggard's attempt to dramatize some of the central conflicts of his society.

Cruse, Amy. "Science and Romance," in her *After the Victorians*. London: Allyn and Unwin, 1938, pp. 163-173. This chapter deals with the use of scientific materials in literature by Haggard, Kipling, and other novelists.

Kyle, Richard. "Out of Time's Abyss: The Martian Stories of Edgar Rice Burroughs," in *Riverside Quarterly*. IV (January, 1970), pp. 110-124. Kyle believes that Haggard's *She* was the principal influence upon Burrough's Martian stories.

Randell, W. L. "Sir H. Rider Haggard and His Work," in *Bookman*. LXII (August, 1922), pp. 206-207. This overview of Haggard's work places *She* in perspective to the author's entire canon.

Teitler, Stuart A. "A Projected Bibliography: By the World Forgot," in *Extrapolation*. XII (May, 1971), pp. 106-108. Although this article primarily describes an effort to produce an annotated bibliography, it provides a valuable discussion of H. Rider Haggard's influence upon the evaluation of science fiction.

Weales, Gerald. "Reader to Rider," in *Commonweal*. XXXVII (June 2, 1961), pp. 253-255. Weales gives much attention to Haggard's story line and its use in the myth-quest tales of which *She* is a prime example.

THE SHEEP LOOK UP

Author: John Brunner (1934-   )
First book publication: 1972
Type of work: Novel
Time: The late twentieth century
Locale: The United States

A dystopian fiction in which an ecological disaster is used to examine an individual's inability to escape responsibility for his fellow man

Principal characters:
AUSTIN TRAIN, a muckraking author
JACOB (JACK) BAMBERLEY, an industrialist
MICHAEL ADVOWSON, a doctor assigned to the United Nations
PETE GODDARD, a crippled hero-cop
THOMAS GREY, a computer expert

Starting with the first chapter, the world of *The Sheep Look Up* is one of narrow controls which place rigid limitations on what its citizens may do. The freedom and choices available to mankind are severely restricted by a hostile world that seems inevitably bound toward ecological catastrophe.

This impending doom is the single most noticeable feature of the earlier chapters, and the tone of pessimism it produces is deliberately sustained by the plot. Brunner frequently presents promising figures so that he can kill them off and plunge the world of *The Sheep Look Up* into a yet greater depth of depression. Thus, there is the British doctor Michael Advowson, who is assigned to investigate the charges that the relief food sent to Noshri was poisoned. As various groups start to take sides even before a chemical analysis has been made, Advowson clearly represents one of the few characters concerned not with political slogans but with human beings.

The reader quickly identifies with Advowson, and then Brunner kills him. Advowson's death, in fact, is extremely depressing since it is an absurd one. Having identified the fact that the batch of relief food, Nutripon, sent to Noshri had been contaminated by a hallucinogen, the government insists on destroying an uncontaminated batch of Nutripon as well. Hearing about this, a huge number of drug cultists gather to save what they believe to be their key to one great "trip." Advowson tries to mediate between the soldiers who want to destroy the Nutripon and the cultists. Neither side, however, is interested in the truth, and, in the resulting riot, Advowson is killed.

Advowson's death and the resulting frustration is not an isolated example. Just as two men are about to reveal the hoax of Puritan Health foods, they are killed. A small commune is destroyed by stupid and brutish "good citizens." A United Nations nurse who lived through the horror of Noshri is used and then discarded. And, to borrow a phrase from Kurt Vonnegut, Jr., "so it goes" — up to the point that the city of Denver itself goes mad because of the contamination of its water supply with the same hallucinogen that affected Noshri.

Brunner plunges the world into ever deeper doom that precludes any easy resolution. Thus, the title of the novel, taken from Milton's "Lycidas," is appropriate:

> The hungry sheep look up, and are not fed,
> But swoln with wind, and the rank mist they draw,
> Rot inwardly, and foul contagion spread.

Brunner emphasizes the seeming hopelessness of the situation because of the theme of *The Sheep Look Up*: individual responsibility. He is not interested in exploring too deeply the causes of the dystopia. Certainly greed and stupidity are in ample evidence, but there are no satanic figures. The politicians and industrialists are greedy fools who are too simpleminded to be taken for devils. The ultimate responsibility must rest with mankind, the sheep, who have allowed the rape of nature and who continue to allow it even when it has become obvious that their own lives, and their children's, are threatened.

If the Earth and mankind are to be saved, someone must be found who will lead the sheep, who will convince them that rot and foul contagion are not inevitable facts of life. Such a man cannot be a Michael Advowson who, despite all his good intentions, lacks the power, following, and understanding to effect change. *The Sheep Look Up* is the story of how the one man who can rightfully lead society comes to accept that responsibility; the novel is the story of Austin Train, a moral man in an immoral society.

When the novel opens, Train has already been trying to escape his responsibility. As a successful writer who has warned his readers about the coming ecological disasters, Train has made many powerful enemies, but they are not the real cause for Train's attempt to hide. Instead, he is afraid of the potential violence that might be done in his name. There is already a rather amorphous group of people, mostly young, who have taken the label "Trainites." While they are for the most part harmless individuals, some have already committed violent acts, and Train is worried about even worse incidents. He worries about the possibility that his statements might convince someone that an entire city is responsible for the destruction of the biosphere. Would such a person arrange to destroy that city?

It is his fear that cripples Train. He cannot act because he does not, at this point, want the responsibility of leadership. He refuses to take the chance that people will act on his words in ways he cannot accept; he is afraid of causing further insane acts.

Madness, however, is already in control of the world, in the form of greed, blindness, and stupidity; time and again, Train endangers his anonymity to give aid to individuals who need it. He cannot ignore his own concern and love for the human race and he cannot ignore the suffering around him. It soon becomes obvious that he has accepted responsibility for individual lives; it remains for him to generalize this responsibility to all men.

This process begins when Train accepts the role that people demand of him. By taking responsibility for the actions of others, Train will enable people at last to react to their world. No one need fear the consequences of his or her actions, since Train will bear that burden; like Christ, he will take their sins upon his shoulders. When Train accepts this role, it is time for him to come out of hiding.

Once Train has decided to come out of hiding, it only remains for him to choose the time and place. In light of his earlier fear of people performing unconscionable acts in his name, it is ironic that Train chooses as his coming-out a trial in which he must answer for a kidnaping which used his name but of which he was totally ignorant. Thus, the time and place serve to underscore the change he has undergone and his acceptance of that change.

Even more ironic, however, is the message Train has to tell the American public. After reminding his national audience of what life was once like, he calls for a general uprising. Less than a year earlier, Train was afraid that some madman might destroy a city and claim that he did it as a follower of Train. Now Train is directing the entire American population to rebel and destroy a country. The biosphere can no longer afford the United States.

Lest the reader be too appalled at such a complete reversal in Train, Brunner attempts to mollify the impact by the use of four factors. The first is the complete hopelessness of the situation. It is better to die resisting greed and stupidity than to go to the slaughter as sheep. The second factor is an appeal to the intellect. After thorough research and careful analysis, a computer expert, Thomas Grey, reaches the conclusion that the biosphere and mankind can survive if the two hundred million most wasteful people are eliminated. Thus the future of the world can be provided for, although at a great cost. The third factor is emotional appeal. Pete Goddard, a former cop whose heroic action saved two children, becomes a builder of bombs. His pregnant wife is exposed to microwave radiation from a poorly constructed oven, and her unborn baby is literally cooked in the womb. Both the government and the manufacturer knew that that model was dangerous. For Pete Goddard and millions of others, the future is already dead. And if a saver of human lives now sees the need to destroy life, can Train be wrong?

The final factor is metaphoric. Early in the novel it is established that the United States has become a net importer of oxygen; that is, the United States consumes a great amount of oxygen and replaces it with a huge amount of pollutants. The result is a vacuum which draws in the world's supply of oxygen, a vacuum with the United States at its center. When the country starts to burn, the vacuum is broken, and the winds, with their oxygen supply, reverse direction and start blowing out of the United States again. While such a metaphor is not scientifically sound, it does serve to confirm both Train's intuitive and Grey's intellectual conclusions. Thus, the destruction of the United States can be seen as Train's fellow Americans following his example and individually accepting responsibility for their former sheeplike behavior.

Austin Train is not alive to see this ultimate acceptance of responsibility. As an individual he has shown the way, but in order for the final sacrifice to be meaningful, the sheep must lead themselves. Good men like Train can take the first step, but others — many, many others — must freely follow that step. Thus, in *The Sheep Look Up*, Brunner explores not only the nature of a dystopia but also its cure. As in his other major works, that cure lies in moral individuals accepting responsibility. What makes *The Sheep Look Up* unique in Brunner's major works, however, is that in it, not only has an individual accepted such responsibility, but an entire society as well. The mass destruction at the end is a sign of hope which the rest of the world must act upon.

Stephen H. Goldman

Sources for Further Study

Criticism:

Scholes, Robert and Eric S. Rabkin. *Science Fiction*. New York: Oxford University Press, 1977, pp. 80-82. According to Scholes and Rabkin, Brunner's theme concerns events and places familiar to the reader and places him in a futuristic society.

Reviews:

Amazing Stories. XLVII, December, 1973, pp. 118-119.

Analog. XCI, June, 1973, pp. 156-157.

Booklist. LXIX, November, 1972, p. 229 and p. 238.

Choice. IX, December, 1972, p. 1290.

Kirkus Reviews. XL, May 15, 1972, p. 597.

Library Journal. XCVII, August, 1972, p. 2651.

Yale Review. LXII, March, 1973, p. 461.

THE SHIP WHO SANG

Author: Anne McCaffrey (1926-   )
First book publication: 1969
Type of work: Novel
Time: The distant future
Locale: The Milky Way

Six stories of romance, loosely connected and later published as a novel, involving separate casts of characters interacting with the heroine, Helva, who is always present to avert tragedy

Set in the distant future, Anne McCaffrey's visionary novel reveals character through emotional confrontation. The central character is Helva, an intensely emotional yet keenly analytical cyborg who seeks enduring love. Her' quest involves her in numerous adventures with subordinate characters caught up in their own problems. The six chapters, five of which were earlier published as separate short stories, were adapted to the novel format and are linked by themes of love, loyalty, companionship, and human individuality. All are sensitively written and related from a female perspective, with Helva functioning as an intelligent observer of the events unfolding around her.

Helva is a strong character who was born so badly deformed she was called a "thing." To save her life, her parents chose a destiny for her as an encapsulated brain over euthanasia. The first story, "The Ship Who Sang," recounts her childhood and girlhood as a "shell person," a surgically stunted and inert human enclosed in a metal shell; her brain directs wheels and mechanical controls. Conditioned to enjoy her existence, Helva considers herself fortunate because she suffers no pain, is not physically frail, and can anticipate a lifespan of several centuries as the brain and nervous system of a scout ship. At age sixteen, her neural synapses are connected to mechanical leads in the central panel of "brainship" XH-834, and Helva is enclosed forever within a titanium shell where nutrients keep her alive. After selecting a mobile human partner or "Brawn," she is ready to embark on the first of many tasks for the Central Worlds government.

Many brawns vie for service aboard the XH-834 since Helva has a highly sensuous nature and brilliant mind. In her ship's hull, they court her for an evening and Helva scrutinizes them carefully with her amplified senses; she finally selects Jennan, a refined, warm, and virile brawn who shares her love of song and addresses her central column directly, thus acknowledging her physical presence. This last factor is important because although she is a cyborg, Helva has a basic human need for companionship beyond the platonic even if the union cannot be physically consummated. In recognition of their union, the ship's name is officially changed to the JH-834. The first story climaxes with Jennan's untimely death which is set dramatically against the backdrop of a supernova explosion and the evacuation of religious fanatics from a doomed planet. Deeply in love with Jennan yet powerless to help, Helva agonizingly watches his death throes, and the memory haunts her in subsequent stories.

In "The Ship Who Mourned," an embittered Helva is paired with another grief-stricken woman, Theoda of Medea, a physiotherapist who feels responsible for her family's deaths and longs for her own. Their work in helping the plague victims, especially children, enables them to enjoy brief respites from sorrow, but also forces Theoda to recall the painful events surrounding the plague that killed her family. Helva helps assuage Theoda's guilt through compassion and her assistance in making their mission a success. A slow healing also takes place in Helva's psyche when Theoda cries over Helva's loss, a physical outlet Helva needed, but could not perform. They part friends, with Helva no longer indifferent to another's emotional needs. Helva has learned another facet of love: how to be a healing and a caring companion as well as a "mistress."

One of the most touching scenes in this story involves a dialogue over the question of cyborgs. Theoda pities Helva because the latter's condition is an artificially produced state which denies her physical mobility; and she questions the ethics of shell life. In answer, Helva describes the advantages she enjoys as an "amplified" human being capable of macroscopic and microscopic sensory impressions with the ship's machinery as her appendages. To Helva, it is normal to be half-machine, half-human since she can recall no other identity. She does not view her inert human body as a limitation. For these reasons, she cannot understand why a lack of physical movement should be such a tragedy for the plague victims and has to learn from Theoda: ". . . it's one thing to be bred up to it and another to be forced into it as the only expedient." Tragedy, McCaffrey asserts, is a product of mental outlook and conditioning.

In "The Ship Who Killed," a less troubled Helva is paired with a vibrant young female brawn, Kira of Canopus, who, like Theoda, harbors a death wish. Kira's restless changes of mood, suicide attempts, and neurotic grief, make her a complex personality and one that Helva must protect from self-destruction. Kira too has lost her mate and feels her aloneness most acutely because she is sterile and without hope of artificial reproduction. Helva eventually finds a solution to Kira's childlessness, but not before brawn and brain confront the possibly devastating consequences of grief.

The controversial issue of test tube babies dominates this story as the KH-834 transports embryos from donor planets to a sterile population on a newly colonized planet. A delicate and intricate mission, it requires constant monitoring of the embryo cargo, a duty that preoccupies Helva because she feels an affinity to each encapsulated embryo who, like her, is also kept alive by a balance of nutrients. Kira too is deeply involved in her duties, but in a professional, indifferent way that leaves Helva as a representational mother figure. Her caring, in a sense, makes her more human than Kira and enlarges upon her intrinsic femininity, the driving force behind her actions.

Previous themes such as conditioning, the fate of children, and religion are widened in scope as Kira and Helva confront a planet driven insane by a rogue brainship, the 732, which has to be destroyed by Helva and Kira. The story of the 732's demented attachment to her dead brawn unfolds amidst dramatic scenes of Helva rescuing an entranced Kira through her crooning of a "Dylan," a protest song that subliminally revives Kira.

Horrified by the harm the 732's grief inflicted on others, Kira comes to terms with her own loss and Helva is less troubled by her memory of Jennan; an almost fatal encounter has put love in perspective for both women. They leave with cargo intact, singing a Schubert serenade rather than the sad "Dylans" that Kira previously sang and taught Helva. The story's end also marks Helva's passage from girlhood to womanhood, a maturing which she attributes to her responsibility in tending to 110,000 babies. She is now ready for a more mature love which will open the storyline to a higher level of sophistication and complexity.

In "Dramatic Mission," an emotionally stable and professionally experienced Helva supervises an important mission to Beta Corvi, an unexplored planet, where methane-ammonia breathing humanoids have agreed to exchange badly needed scientific information for dramas. She must contend with the animosities and inner conflicts that explode among a troupe of actors rather than with the personal tragedy of a single human. Alternately soothing and reprimanding, both an observer of and a participant in the real and the dramatic life of the troupe, Helva expands her mother role to a discrete matriarchial responsibility. The longest of the six chapters, this story is as experimental as the free-fall performance of Shakespeare's *Romeo and Juliet* on Beta Corvi. The actors adapt their performances to Corvikian energy needs by means of telepathic devices which transfer their consciousnesses to Corviki "envelopes," or mindless bodies. McCaffrey skillfully manages to individualize many characters — the vengeful, the considerate, the watchful, the talented.

It is a sign of Helva's self-sufficiency that a cast of characters, not a brawn, is her main concern in this story. While she yearns for a close emotional relationship, she accepts the fact that her temporary brawn, Chadress Turo, is a transient and not dependent on her emotionally. She is fully integrated into all action, even into the physical, for she too must transfer her mind into a Corvikian envelope and for the first time experience physical sensation. Unlike her brawn, she elects not to remain in that state because she thinks: "It was somehow unclean to feel along every part of her." She is satisfied with her identity as a cyborg, a human, and an individual, and does not need this alternative.

The choice of *Romeo and Juliet* as the play to perform on Beta Corvi serves to remind the reader of the general theme of enduring love and its timeless nature. Helva's ideal love for Jennan is part of the continuum of human emotion and is as appreciated on alien worlds like Beta Corvi as it is in human circles. It is also a powerful energy source: on Beta Corvi it excites the inhabitants to an emotional orgasm while in life, particularly Helva's, it fills routine and duty with energizing anticipation. But when the play ends or death separates partners, it is time to release the emotional energy, a lesson Helva has learned from Theoda, and experiences with more dramatic impact here. Jennan's death is now a closed chapter in her life.

At the story's close, a new love interest enters Helva's life when Niall Parollan, her supervisor, both antagonizes and humors her out of a bad mood until finally she once again feels like singing. But for the moment, Helva is unaware of his feelings for her and being unattached, contrives to meet other brawns. Against the advice of Parollan, Helva chooses as her new partner Teron, a very handsome brawn who is the antithesis in personality of Jennan in "The Ship Who Dissembled." By failing to perceive the character of the person behind the cool, attractive exterior, she finds herself in an intolerable relationship at the story's opening. Teron is unimaginative, patronizing, "a neckless Neanderthal" who regards cyborgs as abominations and preaches about the advantages of completely automated scout ships. Helva plans to "divorce" him, but must first undertake a mission with him to Tania Borealis where four brainships have disappeared. The journey is a difficult one for Helva since Teron insists he is in charge of the ship and needlessly overrides her directives, usurps her duties, and checks her work. By countermanding her instructions not to allow suspicious-looking officials to board her on Tania Borealis, he allows ship and brawn to be hijacked by the impostors. When finally freed by Central Worlds personnel, he has learned nothing and continues to take Helva for granted until she "divorces" him. His lack of emotional development makes him little more than a human shell in contrast to the deeply emotional Helva. McCaffrey seems to say that the essence of humanity lies in the mind, in a willingness to care about others.

With the exception of Teron, Central World employees recognize the human side of shell people, and hence appreciate Helva's talents, particularly her singing ability, and become disturbed when they find Helva and the four missing shell people treated as abominations on Tania Borealis. The situation occurs when a former brawn, now a deranged drug addict, violates Helva's enclosure by mouthing the release syllables that render her unconscious and inoperative. He then reconnects her to a limited power pack so that she will serenade him with sensuous songs. She outwits him by "Reticulating a mating croon" with such powerful sound and eroticism that he dies of shock while his followers either die or faint.

Niall Parollan then reappears, this time as Helva's would-be rescuer, who has lost three days' sleep searching for her. His appearance is brief and serves to underscore Teron's indifference through his own concern.

In "The Partnered Ship," Niall Parollan becomes Helva's permanent brawn, a logical development that stems from their knowledge of what they want and do not want in a partner. Helva is now financially as well as emotionally able to select the brawn of her choice: she has accrued so many bonuses and awards for her exceptional missions that she can pay off Central Worlds for her early training, the dream of all brainships. In this story, she is advised by civil rights representatives and other shell-people to buy her freedom, but Parollan and several Central Worlds' colleagues try to persuade her to remain in service. The latter speak of their need of her to undertake another mission to Beta Corvi to obtain a device that will make intergalactic travel possible. Tempted by the thought of visiting the Horsehead Nebula (which was Jennan's dream), she stays on though she no longer needs the company of someone like her first partner. By the end of the story, she becomes emotionally attached to Parollan who then becomes her brawn. His expression of love is as individual and as uniquely dramatic as his personality. Their pairing concludes Helva's quest and by extension, the novel.

The Ship Who Sang displays a range of human emotions in a story-within-a-story framework where science is part of the setting. Different facets of love and personality are explored in highly dramatic, exotic, and often sinister imagery that categorizes the novel as Space Gothic.

Anne Carolyn Raymer

Sources for Further Study

Reviews:

Analog. LXXXI, September, 1970, p. 167.

Galaxy. XXX, July, 1970, pp. 102-103.

Kirkus Reviews. XXXVII, September 15, 1969, p. 1033.

Library Journal. XCV, February 15, 1970, p. 793.

Luna Monthly. XVI, September, 1970, p. 15.

Magazine of Fantasy and Science Fiction. XXXIX, July, 1970, pp. 40-42.

Science Fiction Review. XXVIII, June, 1970, p. 35.

WFSA Journal. LXXI, March–May, 1970, pp. 81-82.

THE SHOCKWAVE RIDER

Author: John Brunner (1934-   )
First book publication: 1975
Type of work: Novel
Time: The not-too-distant future
Locale: The United States

An exploration of the information explosion in terms of how the flood of information affects the lives of individuals and whether there are any circumstances under which information should be withheld from the general public

Principal characters:
>NICHOLAS HAFLINGER, a renegade who is able to avoid categorization by the information network
>INA GRIERSON, an executive of G2S
>KATE LILLEBERG, Ina's college student daughter
>PAUL T. FREEMAN, a government agent in charge of interrogating Haflinger
>RALPH C. HARTZ, Freeman's superior
>THE PEOPLE OF HEARING AID, citizens of Precipice

One of the more frequent words associated with science fiction is "extrapolation." A popular definition of the genre usually states that a science fiction writer extrapolates from present social, political, and technological characteristics to produce a work that presents future developments of contemporary institutions. Invariably, such a definition tends to accentuate the type of science fiction story that seems to predict future inventions and social changes. Too often, the reader and the teacher of science fiction emphasize the accuracy of an early writer's predictions and thus give the impression that the many social and technological descriptions found in the genre are aims in themselves. Such an unfair characterization of science fiction literature is particularly abundant in criticisms of short stories and novels that deal with a future not very far removed from the present. In such works there is a tendency for the critic to read into them his own preoccupation with gadgets.

John Brunner's *The Shockwave Rider* is susceptible to exactly this kind of misreading. The information network that Brunner creates in the novel can easily remind one of the fears present citizens of the United States have concerning the use of computers to store information about people. Moreover, the standardization of society which is so soundly criticized in *The Shockwave Rider* must appear to many readers as a confirmation of their own warnings against extensive use of the computer. Thus, all too often, extrapolation for such readers means that the writer agrees with their own interpretation of what the future will bring.

Certainly *The Shockwave Rider* presents a dystopia that has as its main feature a complete information network. Even more to the point, by means of this network American society has been standardized beyond the wildest dream of the most insane behaviorist. The flood of information available to all people in all places has changed the nature of American culture. It has, among other things, annihilated any concept of regionalism; the United States has truly become a single nation. Because everyone "knows" the same things and therefore acts upon the same knowledge, the Easterner, the Southerner, the Midwesterner, and the Westerner have disappeared and have been replaced by the American. Moreover, since it has become more convenient to carry on economic, political, educational, and cultural transactions by means of one's telephone, the information system is able to keep track of each citizen and his actions.

Yet, despite these extrapolations, the point would be missed if *The Shockwave Rider* were seen as a dystopian warning to the reader about the horrible consequences of letting computers get out of hand. As interesting as the information network and the social changes are, they are only background to Brunner's theme. If there are horrors in this fictional world, they are horrors caused by men, not by machines. In this novel Brunner is interested in portraying the men who control the information network and the uses they make of it. The computer is morally neutral in *The Shockwave Rider*; it is left to the human characters to add the value of good or bad.

One clue to the moral nature of the men who control the information network lies in the early history of the novel's protagonist, Nicholas Haflinger. Haflinger was an orphan who had been identified as an intellectually gifted child. The United States government has developed a program to isolate such children and educate them in a special environment at a school called Tarnover. While at Tarnover, Haflinger sees the result of an experiment in trying to produce human life in the laboratory. What he sees is identifiably human but badly mutated. Haflinger is shocked by the experiment and even more shocked at the casual attitude the scientists display toward their creation. Haflinger sees the creature as human and tragic; the scientists see her as one more step for mankind. Her deformity and early death are simply things to try to avoid the next time. It is this inhumane attitude that makes Haflinger leave Tarnover and develop his skills in avoiding detection by the computer, and it is the same attitude that the reader must consider in judging the directors of the computer, who have little concern for the individual human and view mankind solely through statistics and generalizations.

It is interesting, therefore, that it is not Haflinger but one of the agents from Tarnover who voices the opinion that too much information will confuse most people. People should be given information sufficient to suit their daily lives but nothing more. Any more would destroy whatever equilibrium they might have established with their world. Moreover, according to this agent, some information must be kept from the general mass of people for their own good.

The agent, Freeman, voices here the real cause of the dystopia in *The Shockwave Rider*. Ironically, in a world that has developed the ideal information network, some people are privileged to know much more than the vast majority of citizens. A new caste system has developed that uses the information network as a status symbol. Those who know more do not owe their greater knowledge to superior intelligence but to a higher classification number. Information has been classified in a hierarchical system determined by the same types of men who either condone or participate in the biological experiments at Tarnover. Thus, knowledge is metered out by amoral men on a graduated scale that is determined by a caste system. And such a method soon becomes elitist. Being a member of a higher caste assures success because more information is available. To become a member of the higher castes, moreover, it is necessary for an individual to be identified by the agents of the government and then for that individual to go through the indoctrination program at such schools as Tarnover. The masses of citizens can therefore be ignored because they are never in a position to threaten the system — they are too ignorant of it.

The result of such a situation is an innate lack of trust throughout society. People distrust other people because it becomes impossible to tell whether a neighbor's, a relative's, or a friend's success is the result of native skill or privileged information. People refuse to share information with one another because they are afraid of revealing something that others do not know. People become isolated from one another, and their ability to share ideas and problems is lost. Thus the average citizen of the world of *The Shockwave Rider* is paranoid.

In such a society, Hearing Aid, a service run by the citizens of Precipice, becomes the single most helpful agency. The understanding that the hearer will never repeat or act on the information given by the caller allows overburdened callers to relieve themselves of their fears and gripes. But such an arrangement is rather artificial. It completely prevents any real human contact and therefore only treats symptoms. Calling Hearing Aid will not change the society that has caused the paranoia, nor will it restore the ability of individuals to trust one another.

To achieve such a change, the condition of privileged information must change. As a first step toward such a restructuring of society, Nicholas Haflinger must himself learn to trust people. After he escapes Tarnover, Haflinger is able to exist in his various fictional *personas* because he trusts no one. Thus, the one man whose genius lies in the manipulation of computers is not ready to manipulate the information network for the good of society.

When he is forced to trust Kate Lilleberg because his own mental breakdown renders him helpless, Haflinger starts to see how important other people are to him. Their importance is further emphasized to him during his period of recuperation at Precipice. There he is able to see the basic goodness of at least a portion of mankind, and this new view of man leads him to a desire to act on their behalf. Brunner, in other words, has created in Haflinger the capable man, and he then devotes a large portion of the novel to tracing the growth of social consciousness in Haflinger. When Nicholas Haflinger acts, it must be for reasons that are the exact opposite of the ones which motivate the controllers of the information network.

Learning to trust individuals, however, is a far less complicated task than deciding whether all members of society can be trusted to know all things. By completely opening up the information network, Haflinger would, in fact, declare just such a trust. While his conversations with Freeman do show that he is willing to take such a step and he does go so far as to loose a "worm" in the network that releases selected information, Haflinger does not take the final step of completely opening the channels. The issue of whether or not to trust all people with knowledge of all things is too large for a single man to answer. After all, the paranoia so widespread in the world was caused by a few men making such a decision for all men.

Brunner's solution to this problem is to hold a plebiscite. Haflinger presents all Americans with two issues:

> 1: That this is a rich planet. Therefore proverty and hunger are unworthy of it, and since we can abolish it, we must.
>
> 2: That we are a civilized species. Therefore none shall henceforth gain illicit advantage by reason of the fact that we together know more than one of us can know.

In *The Shockwave Rider*, the novel ends with mankind at the crossroads. Haflinger can effect the change, but society must first declare its basic humanity. If it refuses, then free and unlimited access to all information is too dangerous and the world will be better off without it.

Thus, despite the gadgets and the reference to a current raging debate on the use of computers, *The Shockwave Rider* is not about an extrapolated future. Instead, Brunner has used the issue and the machines to examine contemporary man and to tell the reader a little more about how man himself is responsible for his own fate.

(It is important to note that John Brunner has stated that the American text of *The Shockwave Rider* as published by Harper and Row (and, hence, Ballantine Books) has been mutilated and differs substantially from the British edition.)

Stephen H. Goldman

Sources for Further Study

Reviews:

Booklist. LXXI, June 1, 1975, p. 991.

Kirkus Reviews. XLII, November 15, 1974, p. 1224.

Library Journal. C, February 1, 1975, p. 312.

New York Times Book Review. July 20, 1975, p. 10.

Psychology Today. X, June, 1976, p. 96.

THE SHORT FICTION OF ARTHUR C. CLARKE

Author: Arthur C. Clarke (1917-   )
Type of work: Short stories, vignettes, and novellas

Stories and novellas, collected from six separate volumes, which foreshadow the major themes of Clarke's longer fiction

Although best known as a novelist, Arthur Clarke produced during three decades a considerable body of short fiction which often mirrors and anticipates the ideas he worked out at greater length in his longer works. These stories provide valuable insights into the growth and development of a major science fiction writer during a period in which many of science fiction's early dreams became a reality. Clarke often wrote of the relatively near future, of life aboard space stations and on the moon — and many of these stories seem dated today. But he also wrote of vast expanses of time and far distant futures, and many of these stories remain striking in their odd juxtaposition of sentimentality and cosmic landscapes, and in their "nostalgia for the infinite." Throughout his career, Clarke has alternately chronicled man's first steps into space, and his first forays into new technologies with their accompanying small ironies and almost domestic comedies, and painted vast visionary landscapes of abandoned cities and deserted worlds in the far future. There seems to be no middle ground for Clarke: his stories characteristically take place either within the next few centuries or millions of years in the future, but nowhere in between.

This dual aspect of Clarke's imagination is evident even in his early stories, written between 1946 and 1953. These stories are steeped in what might be called cosmic irony: the last artifact of human civilization turns out to be a Walt Disney film ("History Lesson," 1949); men survive eons of suspended animation only to be killed ("Exile of the Eons," 1950) or to find that insects have inherited the earth ("The Awakening," 1951); a criminal obtains the ultimate tool for crime, only to find that he cannot use it ("All the Time in the World," 1952). Yet, for all the ways in which Clarke portrays man as a victim of time, he also provides evidence of the indomitable spirit of man to survive and prosper. "Rescue Party" (1946) concerns an advanced alien civilization come to save the human race from certain destruction when the sun threatens to explode; they find humanity has already saved itself. When an advanced civilization from Mars prohibits man from further rocket research in "Loophole" (1946), humans achieve space travel with the invention of a matter transmitter. Not even our own folly can destroy us: atomic war destroys Earth in "If I Forget Thee, O Earth" (1951), but the moon colony grows and thrives.

These early stories also include a number of traditional "space opera" adventures ("Breaking Strain," "Hide and Seek," "A Walk in the Dark"), and exhibit what was to become a characteristic concern of Clarke long before von Daniken — that of aliens visiting the earth in the distant past. The most famous of these stories is undoubtedly "The Sentinel" (1951), which concerns a radio beacon placed on the moon millennia ago and deactivated by humans who find it, and which provided the germ of the film *2001: A Space Odyssey*. But there are also stories that set out to explore seriously the nature of technology. "Second Dawn" (1951) is a sensitive portrayal of a culture that develops advanced mathematics and philosophy before it develops technology, and "Superiority" (1951) — which for a time was assigned to students at M.I.T. — shows how a superior technology can lead to military defeat. "The Road to the Sea" (1950) points up poignant contrasts between a posturban future society which has largely rejected technology, and their cousins who long ago left the earth for a life in space; Clarke is careful to avoid didacticism by showing neither culture as morally superior. In a story which combines concern with the impact of technology with Clarke's penchant for cosmic irony, a group of Tibetan monks purchase a computer to help them in listing all the possible names of god, thus fulfilling the purpose of the universe and bringing it to an end ("The Nine Billion Names of God," 1953).

The middle period of Clarke's short fiction (1954-1958) is dominated by his humorous tall tales of loony scientists and bizarre inventions, most of which were collected in *Tales from the White Hart* (1957). "The White Hart" is a mythical London pub where scientists and science fiction writers gather to listen to one Harry Purvis spin his tales about machines that absorb noise ("Silence Please," 1954), record physical and sexual sensations for playback ("Patent Pending," 1954), extract minerals from the sea ("The Man Who Ploughed the Sea," 1957), or defy gravity ("What Goes Up," 1955). While many of these stories are little more than shaggy dog stories built around science fiction concepts, a few (such as "The Man Who Ploughed the Sea") offer interesting character portraits of isolated scientists trying to achieve both technological breakthroughs and personal satisfaction.

In this middle period, Clarke also began to produce more of his short, anecdotal stories about the coming space age. Two sequences of vignettes ("The Other Side of the Sky" and "Venture to the Moon," 1956-1957) were written as newspaper commissions; these, together with "Who's There?" (1958) and "Refugee" (1955) are slight, thinly plotted episodes that, together with the Harry Purvis stories, begin to suggest that Clarke was devoting less time to his short fiction, using it only to present an occasional clever idea and perhaps to acclimatize people to the idea of space travel by proselytizing for it. Two stories from this period ("Let There Be Light," 1957, and "A Slight Case of Sunstroke," 1958) are no more than ingenious technological murder tales. Virtually the only serious stories from this period are "The Star" (1955), in which explorers find that the supernova which created the star of Bethlehem also destroyed an advanced and humane civilization; and "Songs of Distant Earth" (1958), a reworking of the theme of "The Road to the Sea" in which a girl from a nontechnological Earth colony falls in love with a visiting Earth spaceman who represents a world of adventure and technology of which she knows nothing.

Clarke's later short fiction (1959-1971) is comparatively sparse and reflects few new developments or trends in his writing. The humorous vignettes and tales remain dominant ("An Ape About the House," 1962 and "Trouble with Time," 1960), if occasionally a little racier ("Love That Universe," 1966, postulates a situation in which universal orgasm is the only source of psychic energy sufficient to signal alien civilizations to save us from destruction when a "Black Dwarf" enters the solar system). Clarke still occasionally wrote a story about life on the moon or in space: "Out of the Cradle Endlessly Orbiting" (1959) concerns the birth of the first baby on the moon, and "Saturn Rising" (1961) is about a visionary resort developer who plans the first vacation resort on a moon of Saturn. And there are again a number of stories about alien intelligence ("The Shining Ones," 1962, about intelligent squids; and "Crusade," 1966, about an intelligence evolved through the superconductivity of a cold planet). One such story, "A Meeting with Medusa" (1971), is one of the most striking of Clarke's later fictions. The tale is about an adventurer who is bionically restructured after an accident aboard a futuristic dirigible, then later explores the atmosphere of Jupiter and finds there strange, massive life forms. It is awe-inspiring in its descriptions of the massive planet, if a bit uncertain of its focus (the thematic significance of the mechanical rebuilding of the protagonist is never made clear).

But perhaps what is most noteworthy in this later fiction is Clarke's growing concern with the political implications of technology and space travel. "I Remember Babylon" (1960) speculates on the possible political exploitation of communications satellites — a concept Clarke himself had introduced as early as the late 1940's. "Hate" (1961), which barely qualifies as science fiction at all, concerns a bitter anti-Communist who deliberately allows a downed Soviet astronaut to suffocate in the space capsule — only to discover that it is a woman. "Death and the Senator" (1961) involves an American senator who, after opposing funding for a space hospital, discovers that his own heart condition can be treated in zero gravity in the space hospital the Soviets have built. In "The Last Command" (1963), the President orders his defensive moon base *not* to retaliate after a nuclear holocaust — and we learn that the President is the President of the Supreme Soviet. "The Light of Darkness" (1964) concerns the use of a laser to disable an African dictator. These stories suggest that in his later career, Clarke has come to focus more on the human problems involved in technological expansion; indeed, they are considerably stronger in characterization — if weaker in vision — than his earlier work.

Clarke might well be accused of being a sentimentalist about space. His "Transit of Earth" (1970) seems to have no other purpose than to invest a poetic image — the transit of Earth between the sun and Mars — with an emotional power it would not otherwise have by showing it to us from the perspective of a dying astronaut. He may often be accused of not paying enough attention to his short fiction. Some of his stories exist solely for a punch-line; in others, he employs an omniscient narrator only to enable him to shift point of view suddenly and assault the reader with a clumsy irony. Some of his later stories, especially, seem unfinished; "Crusade," for example, virtually stops the narrative in midstream and quickly summarizes the end of the story. But at his best, Clarke can create a sense of cosmic expanses and vast eons of time that at once overwhelm us and convince us of our importance.

Though his stories are weak in characterization and often crude in style, they occasionally attain a sort of science fiction version of the sublime — a vision at once humane and technological, personal and cosmic. Above all, he has used his short fiction to explore ideas. And if the ideas sometimes overwhelm the fiction, the same could be said of much science fiction. In a preface for *Reach for Tomorrow*, Clarke wrote of his fiction, "It may not be art, but it can be enjoyable and intriguing." That is true of much of Clarke's writing, but on occasion, his work is art as well.

Gary K. Wolfe

THE SHORT FICTION OF AVRAM DAVIDSON

Author: Avram Davidson (1923-   )
Type of work: Short stories

> *On the borderline between fantasy and science fiction, these stories display an entirely individual blend of recondite knowledge, wide sympathy, and subtle linguistic manipulation*

Avram Davidson's short fiction consists of three collections of stories reprinted from various magazines, *Or All the Seas with Oysters* (1962), *What Strange Stars and Skies* (1965), and *Strange Seas and Shores* (1971). In addition, many stories have not as yet been reprinted, but have appeared for the most part in *The Magazine of Fantasy and Science Fiction*. *The Enquiries of Doctor Esterhazy* (1975) consists of eight short stories with a shared central character. Finally, Davidson's short novel "Rogue Dragon," published originally in *Fantasy and Science Fiction*, was later expanded and printed separately.

The individual quality of Avram Davidson's work can be seen in his first published story, "My Boy Friend's Name Is Jello." Its title comes from a children's hand-clapping game chant. As an invalid lies in bed, he hears little girls playing outside and slowly realizes that what he has understood as "Jello" is a mistaken form of "Ajello," the name of a real person whom he knows. He further realizes that the little girls are in the habit of singing about real people, and that what they sing comes true. They are sorceresses of a kind, and their counting rhyme is one of the oldest forms of spell. In essence this story is curiously like an anecdote in the old witch-hunters' book, the *Malleus Maleficarum*, in which a man suddenly becomes aware that his wife and little daughter belong to the Female Society of witches; both books testify to the ancient tendency of men to regard women as a separate species. Davidson's story also relies for its effect on an injection of pure fantasy into a realistic setting, without even the usual science fiction pretense of a rationalizing explanation. Disbelief is held back by the slenderness of the invalid's train of thought, the hypnotic beat, and seeming inconsequentiality of the little girls' rhymes. This, then, is the tightrope which Avram Davidson characteristically walks. He uses fantasy of a pure and archaic type, which many readers would under most circumstances dismiss as superstition, but lends it credibility through extremely accurate observation, sympathy for human feelings, and precise use of language, especially of odd, childish, dialectal, or otherwise nonstandard language.

A similar mixture of fantasy and reality can be seen in the title story of the *Or All the Sea with Oysters* collection, which won Davidson the Hugo award for the best science fiction short story of 1958. It is set in a cycle-repair shop, where two very different people work — the extroverted, unintellectual Don Juan, Oscar, and the bookish, inhibited Ferd. When Ferd observes the sudden and unexplained appearances and disappearances of metal objects such as bicycles, safety pins, and coat hangers, he proposes an explanation: these are alien, intelligent beings, who only *camouflage* themselves as human artifacts. Ferd is later found strangled by a wire coat hanger, a circumstance which supports his thesis. The story is recounted by Oscar, seemingly a superfluous character, but actually vital in communicating his partner's strained balance between insight and madness (two states which Oscar himself takes no trouble to differentiate). Without Oscar the story would lose its fragile cohension; with him it becomes vivid and compelling.

Davidson specializes in sordid and trivial settings. "Negra Sum" deals with the same type of object as that used by Rudyard Kipling in "Bisara of Pooree" (1887) — a talisman which produces love for its bearer. But whereas Kipling's story was structured around a whirl of decorous engagements, Davidson's is set in a whore-haunted roominghouse run by an old man without hopes or ambitions and inhabited by only the oafish or the crazy. The incongruity between talisman and setting enhances the basic plot. Racketeers, slum land-lords, army sergeants on the make in occupied cities, failed gamblers waiting for the collection gang to arrive — populate some of Davidson's best stories, while the basic plot often uses the supernatural for dominance or revenge. A wry switch on that plot occurs in "Summerland," where a spiritualist seance manages to put a widow in touch with the ghost of her husband. All that materializes, however, is a scream of fire and agony. A mistake, murmur the spiritualists, immersed in the cozy debris of traditional belief, for there can be neither grief nor pain in "Summerland." But the narrator, unlike the widow, knows how good old Charley made his money. Hell has survived man's belief in it.

Davidson's early stories face the problem of introducing the supernatural without rationalizing it, and so make it natural once again. But as his career developed, he utilized another talent: the depiction in minute detail of those specialized skills and manias which only a complex civilization can foster. In "Help! I Am Dr. Morris Goldpepper," the old motif of an Earthman kidnaped by aliens is given an incongruous twist by being set entirely in the little world of the American Dental Association. Its members never see the kidnaped Goldpepper as a man, but only as the inventor of Goldpepper's Semi-Retract-able Clasp. All their maneuvers of appeal and rescue are carried out with reference to the treatment of teeth. Like Dickens, Davidson works best with the bizarre and nonstandard, showing how many of us are subject at some point or another to a kind of monomania. Often the subject is collectors' madness, the same whether it is directed at Chinese snuff flasks, tin cans full of bacon grease, or wooden Indians (see respectively "A Bottle Full of Kismet," "The Goobers," "Take Wooden Indians"). But the ruling passion may also be act-ing, atheism, museum building, or snooping — anything, as long as it involves a plethora of detail in which the human psyche can submerge itself.

Philanthropy is the subject of "What Strange Stars and Skies," and its objective correlative is Dame Philippa Garreck's kit bag, described with loving inclusiveness in two hundred words and twenty-two separate items, each particularized with minute care: the ten-shilling notes "folded quite small," the "fifteen packets of five Woodbine cigarettes," each attached to *six* wooden matches, the spare one indicating yet again Dame Philippa's combination of charity and common sense. Her professionalism justifies even the strangest items of her armory, the mixed toffees and the picture postcards of the Royal Family. Surely these are mere childishness? But no, for Dame Philippa realizes that the objects of her charity are for the most part mad, driven to the slums by the fading and erosion of their minds. In such cases memory and magic may work better than food or money: the toffees evoke memories of childhood, the postcards appeal to the still-felt charisma of the sacred Queen. Yet magic is not the subject of the story, which for once approaches science fiction closer than fantasy. Dame Philippa's expedition in the slums ends in tragedy, with the shanghaiing of her and many other people by an alien spacecraft. Yet, the narrator concludes, we can be confident that her "noble and humanitarian labors still continue, no matter under what strange stars and skies." The whole story is told in a highly accurate pastiche of Victorian English, suggesting thought structures and basic assumptions almost imperceptibly but with great cumulative power.

Incongruity once again forms the basis of the story, in this case between the standard UFO plot and the highly un-standard setting of a "Sherlock Holmes" Victorian London with a confident, skeptical, and rationalist population. UFO's in California, one might say, is nothing new: in Baker Street, however, the evidence must be strong! Also once again, the basis of Davidson's powers of conviction is control over language.

In other stories Davidson has integrated equally convincing forms of non-standard English into his plots. Thus a basic linguistic datum of "Where do you Live, Queen Esther?" is that "Queen Esther," a black cleaning woman from the West Indies, confuses nominative and accusative forms of personal pronouns, as is normal in her dialect. The fact is a reminder of her non-English speaking slave ancestors and of the powers they brought with them from darkest Africa — the duppy and the obeah. It also means that the heroine of her little inserted story about "Mistress Serve-She-Well" would be, in standard English, Serve Her Right. And "serve her right" is the epitaph we pronounce on her rich and querulous employer when she releases the duppy. Davidson uses a similar creole dialect and setting to give body to his "Jack Limekiller" stories. These are set in the strange cultural enclave of "British Hidalgo," a colony (like reallife British Guiana) which combines British, Spanish, Negro and Indian elements to such an extent that almost nothing in it is predictable.

Davidson's finest exploitation of the comedy of cultural diversity, however, occurs in *The Enquiries of Doctor Esterhazy*, another Sherlock Holmes-derived set of stories, placed in the "Triune Monarchy of Scythia-Pannonia-Transbalkania." The mixture of languages in this strange empire is at first sight fantastic. The Pannonians speak Avar (a Finno-Ugrian language, seemingly), the Scythians Gothic (a now-extinct Germanic language), the Transbalkanians Slovatchko (which is clearly Slavic). A smaller minority contributes Vlox. And yet there is sense, even realism, in the jumble. Vlox, for instance, is clearly a word similar to Vlach, a real Balkan national grouping, and further to Old English *Wealh*, modern English *Wales*, and modern German *Welsch*. It is, in fact, the old Germanic word for a Latin-speaker; and at one time there was a corner of Europe where Latin, Slavonic, German, and Hungarian met, obviously within the boundaries of the old Austro-Hungarian Empire. The Triune Monarchy is a "might-have-been" past, but one firmly anchored to what really was. This setting, with all its complexities, adds greatly to the effect of Dr. Esterhazy's involvements with shape-shifting, necromancy, wizardry, catalepsia, and much else. Like his world, his sciences are fantastic. But the skeptical precision with which he employs them, and the constant choice of words and worlds we might accept as true, make us think first that there may be something in mesmerism or phrenology after all, and second — the main achievement of science fiction — that even if there is not, practitioners of acupuncture and particle physics cannot afford to be disdainful. Hundreds of minor oscillations between the real world and the world of European fantasy give the stories memorable charm and humor. Their force comes from details (the Provót, sour cherries, Christian Diabolism, the Brothers Swartbloi Snuff Tobacco, to name but four); but the details imply a consistent whole forever escaping the eye but forever insistently present. It is a moment of genuine sadness when the image begins to fade and the "fetch" or *Doppelgänger* of Emperor Ignats prophesies his own disappearance, as if character were dismissing author and readers rather than, regretfully, the other way round. At such moments Avram Davidson shows better than any other author of science fiction the extent to which realism is a product of art.

T. A. Shippey

THE SHORT FICTION OF DMITRI BILENKIN

Author: Dmitri Bilenkin (1933-   )
Type of work: Short stories and novelettes

Stories and novelettes written by a Soviet writer of short fiction, characterized by the ideas rather than the action

Dmitri Bilenkin is a confirmed short story writer, never having written any "big" literary work except his trilogy about the psychologist Polynov. Bilenkin's stories stick in the memory; at the very least, the reader, seeing his name on a title page knows exactly what to expect. For Western readers it may be useful to refer to Theodore Sturgeon's introduction to the collection *Uncertainty Principle* where he says that if he had a Time Machine, he would take Bilenkin to 1939 and introduce him to John W. Campbell, Jr., as "one of the Asimov-Heinlein-Bester-et-al. company."

It is easy to characterize Bilenkin's stories. He is very consistent in his vocation; once he found his own style and themes, he remained faithful to them for two decades. In the first place, Bilenkin's is a science fiction of ideas, not of intricate plots or amazing images. His stories as a rule are rather short and dynamic, his style is precise, very intelligent, and devoid of ornamental devices. But at the same time, his prose is never dry or boring. He is one of the most widely read and popular Soviet science fiction writers.

Bilenkin is very meticulous about the so-called "initial conditions." At the very beginning he describes the setting carefully and distinctly, and the *dénouement* is usually unexpected, paradoxical, and laconic. Sometimes one has the feeling that, even before Bilenkin ends his story, he almost loses interest in it, having resolved all the problems in his mind in advance.

Bilenkin is a geochemist by profession and by the time he turned to science fiction he had already written several books and articles in the field of his specialty. This is quite obvious to any reader of his stories. Even the closest possible reading of his books turns up neither simplification nor slips. He is not merely scientifically accurate on the surface; Bilenkin's science fiction is *scientific* rather than *fictional*. He is accustomed to scientific thinking, so he "proselytizes" his readers. Since he is of the world of science, his personal consciousness is reflected in his fiction.

Still, the scientific thinking is not intrusive; there are no scholar-heroes, nor pseudoscientific problems of the kind that are so tiresome for science fiction fans. His science is implicit in his method. Bilenkin is well aware of the "scientific" world in which we live today and he considers science fiction to be a powerful, and proper, means of reflecting that world. Moreover, to take a utilitarian approach to literature, it is a means of helping the reader to adapt to his surroundings. That is why science fiction is the child of two parents for Bilenkin: It conforms to the laws of literature as well as those of science. What are these laws of science? Without going into the means and techniques of particular sciences, it is possible to discern a basic methodology in contemporary science. It is diverse in character, but includes the systematic approach, modeling, the method of analogues, and new discoveries in the field of storing and transmitting information. Modern science has taken a tremendous step forward from the mechanistic views of the past. Even the scientific vocabulary has changed considerably. Could Descartes or Newton have guessed that exact sciences would use such notions as "relativity" or "uncertainty"?

That is why Bilenkin's is *science* fiction. It is genuinely scientific, but not mechanistic, rationalistic, and not boringly formalistic. One cannot doubt that if Bilenkin wanted to write about God's existence, he would do it in a purely scientific way! The Niven and Pournelle novel *Inferno* could have been written by Bilenkin. Not only in Campbell's times, but even now, Bilenkin's science fiction would be gladly accepted in *Analog*.

Most of Bilenkin's stories deal with one subject: technological progress and man. His protagonists are seldom optimists in rose-colored glasses, believing blindly in technological progress. Bilenkin's protagonists look at the rapidly approaching future in a straightforward way. They are ready to meet it head on. This sobriety of vision distinguishes Bilenkin from other modern science fiction writers. Contemporary authors usually fall into two opposing groups. Either they hail technological progress or they damn it. Bilenkin differs from both. *The Intelligence Test* is a very apt title for a collection of his stories.

Bilenkin constructs his stories solidly and creates a perfect laboratory situation, where his ideas, protagonists, and plots are put to the test. The accuracy of his design leads to unexpected possibilities. Against the background of so many classic science fiction themes and plots, Bilenkin's stories always impress the reader as something new and fresh.

Take, for example, one of his best-known stories, "The Martian Surf." One may wonder what more could be written about Mars. But Bilenkin ignores the fact that the Martian theme is one of the most frequently used in the genre and chooses an utterly prosaic and dull aspect of it: the Martian sands. Any teenager would think the phrase banal. But who would think of a "sand ocean," or "sand surf"? Bilenkin's elegant scientific hypothesis is happily incorporated into the plot — the first visitors to Mars bathe in sand waves. Bilenkin describes this fantastic scene beautifully. For another writer, perhaps, this situation could become the central point of the whole story. But for Bilenkin it is not that important. He is primarily interested in the behavior of people, rather than in the plot as such. The primary focus is on the psychological behavior of a man who finds himself in a strange world. The reader must make out the barely discernible line between bravery and foolhardiness, between selflessness and mere posturing. Still, one will never forget this visual "pearl" of the "Martian sand surf."

Take another example. In the story "Once Upon a Night" two creatures meet. They are of such different cultures, a horse and a robot dustman, that contact between them is impossible. Science fiction investigation of the "psychology" of animals and androids is very common; yet, except for Simak's robot-old-man and his faithful Dogs, no other example of a like symbiosis comes to mind. Again, Bilenkin does not confine himself merely to an imagined situation (or rather an instant symbolic image of a distant relative of man, an animal, who walks hand in hand with a robot, man's creation); he has a more serious purpose in mind. Most important is the fact that the contact does take place, and the description of it is very convincing. "Disturbed by nobody, they walked between buildings and lights, indifferent to all but themselves, and slowly, very slowly, their bodies began to approach each other. Even now the man, an invisible mediator, walked beside them, too." Ever since an ancient philosopher declared that "man is the measure of all things," the entire world has been seen through the eyes of men. Only by taking this into account is it possible to understand fully the difficulty of trying to look at the world through nonhuman eyes. Bilenkin is not afraid of such problems and he faces them (even if he cannot offer final solutions) with eagerness and enthusiasm. We know very little of animal psychology today, and Bilenkin is already probing the psychology of an animal who is endowed with elementary consciousness by a man of the future. Thus, we see two bosom friends, a girl and a wolf, walking about town. It is not the cruel wolf of the fairy tale, but a tame one. Is it indeed an animal? Hardly. It has rudimentary consciousness and it saves people from imminent catastrophe ("The City and the Wolf").

What can save our civilization from cosmic cataclysms? How can we leave behind us signs of our presence for future generations? The answers given in science fiction are almost always the same. The answers given by Bilenkin are original. In his story "Long Waiting" the researchers, while seeking the remains of a lost civilization, come to understand that they have been looking for the wrong thing. They had been applying ordinary archaeological methods in looking for traces of an ancient culture. It turns out that the civilization did not "want" to leave its *remains* — it left *itself*. Records of the dead civilization have been preserved in the planet's very dust. Back on Earth, in the Institute of Embryomechanics, the researchers reconstruct something. What is it? The appearance of their brother-in-consciousness? "One second passed. Another passed. One more. And suddenly the cry, a baby's first cry broke the silence. . . ."

Finally, there are the ecological problems. They have their part in Bilenkin's stories as well. As usual in his science fiction they are treated in an unusual way. What could be more obvious than the importance of "preserving the fauna"? Yet, in the story "And All That" this thesis is turned upside down. The author assures the reader that he is quite right from the point of view of both logic and ecology. People, admits Bilenkin, are inclined to emotional "staggering" and they tend to run from one extreme (first conquering and then destroying nature) to another (being totally indifferent to nature). The most important thing here is *balance* in nature, and it is altogether ignored.

In another story, "Nothing but Ice," the ecological problems are considered by the author in a somewhat traditional manner. Future Earthlings find themselves in a quandary: Shall they conduct a test that can bring unimaginably fruitful scientific results at the cost of destroying a distant planet which, though lifeless, is strangely beautiful? Whether to preserve this unique beauty, a beauty that the people have never seen and will never see, this playful nature's masterpiece, and in so doing decline deliberately the opportunity of achieving power over the entire universe: that is the dilemma.

Bilenkin knows very well that progress is Janus-faced. The problem is how to adapt oneself to the inevitable. Mankind's forward movement, the writer says, is not a mistake, nor a whim, nor a folly, but the foremost necessity. If man does not move outward into the Universe beyond the solar system, he will perish in the end, defeated by his own technology, destroyed by thermal or chemical pollution, or by overpopulation. "But if we were to decide what to lose: either a lunar station or the moonlight, what would we choose?" Bilenkin himself does not have the answer. But the reader of "Nothing but Ice" will long ponder the question.

The author's constant striving for originality, while taking ostensibly trivial situations for his plots, is brilliantly manifested in his novellas about the psychologist Polynov. In the story "The Space God" Bilenkin resurrects two clichés: space opera and superman. He has space pirates roaming the universe; a "mad scientist" obsessed with his desire to rule the world; a sexy beauty; and an almighty hero. Their fights, pursuits, and melodramatic adventures all seem to indicate that Bilenkin decided to tease his readers, who expect their author to be, first and foremost, serious. But these banalities are deceptive; the reader soon realizes that the hero is so phenomenally successful not because of his iron fists or electronic superweapons, but because of his intellect. Polynov understands people; and he remembers his history well enough to foresee how a future candidate for "space god" will act. The conflict between a scholar and a Fascist is won by the former simply because for Bilenkin — though not for most American writers — the victory of humanity over brutality is historically predestined.

Look at the details. Are they as banal as they seem? A space dictator wants to use as his weapon neither bombs nor "death rays" (it is usually assumed that even by naming these dreadful things a science fiction writer can frighten the reader to death), but an apparatus that destroys a planet's ozone. One more detail. The absence of fantastic muscles is compensated for by the hero's excellent knowledge of the laws of physics. While Polynov is being conducted by a pirate, who walks some distance behind, the hero understands that gravity in the "asteroid belt" is considerably different from that of Earth. One long leap, and Polynov is saved. He uses hypnosis and various chemicals, common enough in the hands of any professional psychologist or chemist. Step by step

Bilenkin disposes of the clichés until only the name "space opera" remains.

Bilenkin's first novella, "The Descent on Mercury," is a more or less solid and rather conventional science fiction book. The next, "The Space God," is both a thriller and a socially oriented space opera. In the third part of the trilogy, "The Solar Eclipse at Dawn," a social theme is dominant. Here Bilenkin somehow could not help imitating the Strugatsky brothers' *Final Circle of Paradise*. Polynov's adventures are similar to Zhilin's. Here again are the "rotting paradise" of narrow-mindedness, the decline of culture, the mysterious forces proclaiming, out of despair, the last crusade against Reason. Would it be possible to accuse Bilenkin of actual plagiarism? No. In our time, when such words as "culture" and "intelligentsia" sound like blasphemy in some parts of the world, the theme is quite "up to date." Polynov, although his adventures do seem like Zhilin's, remains himself to the reader who knows about him from the two previous books.

The search for inner intellectual resources is a particular theme of Bilenkin's science fiction. Some stories seem to be a manifestation of well-known methods of freeing the intellect (so-called brainstorming or turning to cybernetics) which enable a scholar to explore a problem from an extraordinary "mad" point of view. In that sense, "The Man Who Was Present" is a pivotal story. Its protagonist has a remarkable faculty: His mere presence makes people think freely, literally turning their thinking on. Thus, his presence is needed when difficult scientific problems are being addressed. It should be noted that he himself knows nothing of these problems; he is not a scholar, but only a "catalyst" of the intellect.

Science fiction has not yet been defined in any rigorous sense. Its possibilities are even now not fully understood. But one might risk the statement that science fiction teaches the art of thinking. Bilenkin's work seems to prove the point.

Vl. Gakov

Sources for Further Study

Reviews:

Strange Seas and Shores:

American Book Collector. XXI, May, 1971, p. 4.

Library Journal. XCVI, March 15, 1971, p. 979.

Magazine of Fantasy and Science Fiction. XLI, December, 1971, p. 22.

THE SHORT FICTION OF EDMOND HAMILTON

Author: Edmond Hamilton (1904-1977)
Type of work: Short stories

The short fiction of a writer whose talent exceeded the outlets available to him in American pulp magazines

On November 14, 1969, Apollo 12 was launched toward the moon; sitting among dignitaries and reporters at Cape Kennedy was the sixty-five-year-old Edmond Hamilton, witnessing the kind of event he had written of so many times before in a career that began the same year as the descent of American pulp science fiction into the ghetto of specialization. In a sense, space flight was a justification of Hamilton's work as a science fiction writer, yet one cannot help wondering what he might have written had he been born ten or twenty years later than 1904.

Had he begun writing in 1939 instead of in 1926, he would have avoided the editors of the Hugo Gernsback era. For Edmond Hamilton was a writer of talent who was all too often hampered by the circumstances of the medium for which he wrote. Time and again the pulps stereotyped Hamilton to the detriment of his development, depriving readers of stories that would have fully engaged his talents. Had he been a decade or two younger, there would be little doubt that today he would be ranked the equal of Kurt Vonnegut, Jr., or Ray Bradbury. As it is, some of his short stories are as good as any written under the label of science fiction, yet so many of his stories and novels were cut from the cloth of the 1930's pulps that they are forgotten today.

Edmond Hamilton's career began with the publication of "The Monster-God of Mamurth" in *Weird Tales*, August, 1926. Hamilton submitted it under the title "The Desert God," and the change illustrates the tinkering with stories that the editors of the time so frequently practiced. The story appeared just five months after Hugo Gernsback launched the first all science fiction magazine, *Amazing Stories*. "The Monster-God of Mamurth" is still a vivid and colorful story of adventure, a struggle of a human and an invisible alien in an invisible temple. It was an early illustration of the imagination that was to mark Hamilton's work. (It, like the other stories cited in this review, is most readily available in Doubleday's *The Best of Edmond Hamilton*, which adds an afterword by the author and a preface by his wife, the writer Leigh Brackett, to a fine collection of his short fiction.) Over the next few years, Hamilton became the most popular author published in *Weird Tales*, among whose regulars were H. P. Lovecraft, Robert E. Howard, and Murray Leinster, no small accomplishment for a man in his early twenties.

As Sam Moskowitz points out in a biographical sketch of Hamilton in *Seekers of Tomorrow*, this popularity was limited indeed — limited by the small circulation of *Weird Tales*. For example, while Edgar Rice Burroughs was reaching an audience of hundreds of thousands in Munsey publications, an author whose work appeared in *Weird Tales* never had a readership larger than fifty thousand. Thus, as Moskowitz notes, although Hamilton had published several stories in 1927, he was touted as the new writer by the editor of *Amazing Stories* when a piece of his saw publication there in January, 1928.

Moskowitz also discusses the chief failing of those early stories: their repetitious plots. Hamilton was writing action adventure stories in which one man succeeds against all odds in frustrating a threat to Earth (or larger regions). He was beginning to build the reputation that would earn him the nicknames "World-Wrecker" and "World-Saver." Yet his imagination was irrepressible and in its working threw off the sparks of new idea after new idea in these early stories in *Weird Tales*, *Wonder Stories*, and *Amazing Stories*. Leigh Brackett lists a half-dozen firsts for which Hamilton can take credit. His Interstellar Patrol, an idea that E. E. "Doc" Smith was later to profit from, took science fiction out of the laboratory, even out of the solar system, and opened vast areas for use as settings that would be seeded by later writers. The concept of the spacesuit first appears in his works, as does what NASA calls "extra-vehicular activity," the space-walk.

Many of his themes were clearly beyond the sensibilities of some editors of even the 1940's and 1950's. The sympathetic alien and the aggressive Earthman are characters in his "A Conquest of Two Worlds," published in *Wonder Stories* in February, 1932. The mold of the "bug-eyed monster" was broken by Hamilton two years before Stanley G. Weinbaum's "A Martian Odyssey" appeared in *Wonder Stories*. Hugo Gernsback, the editor (with Charles Hornig) of *Wonder Stories*, did the field a service in these acceptances; one cannot imagine John W. Campbell, Jr., the longtime editor of *Astounding Stories*, putting aside his Earthman-first bias and accepting "A Conquest of Two Worlds."

Hamilton was not always so fortunate with his stories. He was something of a rarity in his best works of the 1930's, a writer who could handle pathos, who could depict a plausible disillusionment in characters. Contrast this ability with that of so many others who filled their stories with characters full of starry-eyed notions of progress, who portrayed no emotion other than ambition. And he was realistic at times; in "What's It Like Out There?" he wrote about the first manned mission to Mars. His spaceship is not the creation of some eccentric millionaire scientist or a bunch of talented amateurs, but of a concerted national program (foreseeing NASA). The trip is not a Sunday drive, but a risky and grueling undertaking. Science fiction in the pulps was not ready for the theme in 1933. Every editor to whom he submitted it rejected the story, and it did not see publication until 1952 in *Thrilling Wonder Stories*.

"The Man Who Returned," published in *Weird Tales* in February, 1934, shows what Hamilton could do when the restraints of pulp adventure were not a consideration. This story of a man who discovers that he is literally better off dead has much of the thematic impact of post-World War II "existentialist" fiction without its philosophical pretensions. Hamilton excelled at tales of the loner, the man rejected, in settings that are often sheer fantasy. "Child of the Winds" (*Weird Tales*, May 1936) tells of the love of an adventurer for a strange girl, one apparently adopted by sentient and powerful winds. In the standard adventure format, boy meets girl, boy loses girl, boy rescues girl. But Hamilton at his best is never satisfied with the ordinary, easy ending. His adventurer is the rational and competent hero of much science fiction. He knows about delusions and rejects superstition. Yet although he marries the girl, the last picture we have is that of a man obsessed that he may be wrong, that the winds may be in fact alive, and that his wife may one day return to them. A similar story of failed love is handled in only five pages in "The Seeds from Outside" (*Weird Tales*, March, 1937).

The best of these love stories is "He That Hath Wings" (*Weird Tales*, July, 1938). Again with a man rejected as its central character, the story tells of a genetic freak, born with wings and hollow bones, a man who is able to fly. Hamilton has something useful to say about conformity here, and says it well. David, the child in question, is raised in a sheltered environment by the doctor who delivered him, but as he grows he inevitably increases his human contacts. The girl he loves thinks of him as a freak, and agrees to marriage only on the condition that he have his wings surgically removed. He agrees, and for a while her love replaces the meaning that has fallen from his life. Their child is born, without wings, normal in every respect, but David's wings have begun to grow back. At the climax of the story he abandons his wife, his child, and the business he has been given by his father-in-law and soars into the air. Though exhilarated and drunk with pleasure, his newly-grown wings are weak and small, and he tires rapidly. Falling, he foresees his death, but he is content to have regained his uniqueness, if only for a while.

Stories like these ran counter to the "World-Wrecker" reputation, and the science fiction pulps were about to enter an era of increased artistry when an absolutely disastrous event for Hamilton's writing occurred. Leo Margulies of Standard Magazines proposed a new pulp magazine for juveniles, *Captain Future*. As Sam Moskowitz describes it in *Seekers of Tomorrow*:

> . . . each issue was to feature a novel about the same character. There must be a superscientist hero. There must also be aides: a robot and an android and, of course, a beautiful female assistant. Each story must be a crusade to bring to justice an arch villain; and, in each novel, the hero must be captured and escape three times. *Captain Future* was the pure distillation of stereotyped science-fiction gimmicks brought to bear on a single-character magazine.

Hamilton wrote eighteen of the twenty-one novels in the series. An assessment of Captain Future's impact on Hamilton is reflected in the fact that of the twenty-one stories Leigh Brackett selected for *The Best of Edmond Hamilton*, fourteen were written in the 1930's, only three in the 1940's. And as Moskowitz adds, Captain Future did even greater harm to Hamilton's image. While Isaac Asimov, Robert A. Heinlein, Ray Bradbury, and others were building their reputations, Hamilton was being typecast as a writer of old-fashioned juveniles.

Of course, one must survive, and it is and was terribly difficult to make a living selling any kind of fiction, let alone science fiction. So for twenty years Hamilton wrote for *Batman* and *Superman* comic books. While understanding the necessity, one can still regret the waste.

The 1960's saw Hamilton quite capable of changing his style to suit the resurgence of science fiction magazines, and stories like "Requiem" (*Amazing Stories*, April, 1962) and "After a Judgment Day" (*Fantastic*, December, 1963) show that he had not diminished in talent or imagination. But the most powerful story in the book was published in *The Magazine of Fantasy and Science Fiction* in October of 1964, "The Pro." One reads autobiography in an author's fiction at a real risk, and perhaps "The Pro" reflects none of Hamilton's feelings about the science fiction pulps; it would be tragic if it did.

"The Pro" is about an aging science fiction writer whose son is an astronaut about to leave for the moon. Always adept at showing the psychology of his characters, Hamilton shows the writer as a man whose fame hides both a deep frustration and an unsettling fear. These emotions are expressed in a dream he has, in which he is banging at the door of his son's spacecraft. He is at once terrified for his son's safety and desperately anxious to be allowed to go along. The emotions war with each other, as shown by his answers to the questions of a reporter. The interviewer asks if he thinks his science fiction had any effect on his son's choice of career, and he brusquely ridicules the idea. Reflecting later, he realizes that his fictional characters were wooden, but his son is flesh and blood, and his fears for the son join with his jealousy to tear him apart emotionally. At the end of the story he is in his study, looking at the gaudy covers of thirty years of pulps on the shelves. He beats his fist against them and says, "Damn you, . . . damn you, damn you."

What is done is done. Perhaps had things been different, Hamilton would never have needed to turn to comic books and *Captain Future*; but despite those hypothetical books that were never written, Hamilton managed to turn out a considerable number of novels and short stories comparable to those of the best writers of his long career. If we do not have more, we at least have these. Stories that are compassionate and insightful are always rare, and to have written as many as Hamilton is no small achievement.

Walter E. Meyers

Sources for Further Study

Criticism:

Moskowitz, Sam. *Strange Horizons, The Spectrum of Science Fiction*. New York: Scribner's, 1976, pp. 82-83 and 242-243. A frequent topic of Hamilton's early stories was the battle of the sexes as affected by the future, according to Moskowitz.

Wolheim, Donald A. *The Universe Makers*. New York: Harper & Row, 1971, pp. 30-32. Wolheim sees Hamilton as a rising young writer illuminating the theme of galactic civilization.

THE SHORT FICTION OF FITZ-JAMES O'BRIEN

Author: Fitz-James O'Brien (1828-1862)
Type of work: Short stories

Miscellaneous stories of the fantastic and the grotesque published in the mid-nineteenth century and heavily influenced by the writings of Poe and Brockden Brown

Fitz-James O'Brien's stories are not read much in contemporary times, and, when his talent is compared with that of the writers he emulated and whose fiction his most nearly resembles, this does not seem especially surprising. His art is too clearly derived from Edgar Allan Poe and Charles Brockden Brown for him to be considered with them as one of nineteenth century America's fantasy geniuses. Nevertheless, some few of his stories display an imaginative capability of substantial power and originality. These stories, all written within the decade of 1852-1862 (the dates of his immigration to New York from Ireland and his death in Virginia following the Battle of Bloomery Gap) merit O'Brien a lasting if minor representation in the canon of America's fantasy writers.

Like Brown's and Poe's, his realm is the disordered mind. His characters, like theirs, are students of the supernatural or the scientific; their scholarly inquisitions into the mysteries of the universe become obsessions, either with some amazing discovery or with the inquiring process itself, and madness or worse results. This is, of course, the formula for Brown's *Wieland* (1798), *Edgar Huntly* (1799), and for several of Poe's most famous pieces; by the middle of the nineteenth century it had become a predictable and somewhat hackneyed plotting device. O'Brien adds little to the formula itself, but he does occasionally use it to develop characteristically American themes in a way neither of his predecessors was really able to do.

Certainly the best example of O'Brien's ability to do this, and what is generally conceded to be his finest story, is "The Diamond Lens," first published in the *Atlantic Monthly* in January of 1858. Its protagonist, an independent young man named Linley, is an amateur microscopist who becomes possessed by the desire, first to construct the perfect microscope, and then, using that machine, to discover the nature of elemental matter. Through spirit communication, Linley finds out how to construct the instrument; through easily rationalized and carefully planned murder, he acquires the one diamond in all the world suitable to become its all-powerful lens. But what the story is finally about is neither the acquiring of a jewel nor the making of a microscope; it is what Linley discovers through that diamond lens. And what he discovers places "The Diamond Lens" squarely in the gothic mainstream of American fiction. For the madman finds a new world — a preternatural, densely forested country, an Eden into which evil has not yet entered. Looking through his microscope Linley becomes the American Adam, and the Eve he loves floats sylphlike in a water droplet under his awestruck gaze. It is a shattering discovery that he makes. But if he is an Adam he cannot possess his Eve; neither can he, as a god might, even take credit for her being there. And this is his dilemma. He can look at her and love her or he can, as finally and thoughtlessly he does, destroy her. She, of course, is at the end as oblivious to his accidental role in her death as she had been earlier to his love for her. This enigmatic, unresolvable relationship between the madly reasoning man and what he discovers, certainly is emblematic of that ambiguous and inadvertently destructive kinship between, for instance, the proudly rational democratic ideas of Jefferson and the fragile wilderness which those ideas have subsequently come to dominate. "The Diamond Lens" succeeds, as no story of Poe's or Brown's ever convincingly does, in translating the American experience into grotesquery, and the American himself into a lunatic.

If "The Diamond Lens" shows O'Brien at his best, "The Wondersmith" shows him at his most typical. "The Wondersmith" is simply overbaked horror. Its characters are ridiculous caricatures of good and evil, and most of its stage effects are bathetic. But its major plot supposition, that animated, murderous dolls might be used to rid the world of children, has distinct possibilities (indeed, the same idea was used with great visual success in the 1968 science fiction film "Barbarella") and many of its details are of such arresting power as to rescue the story from the quagmire of its predictability and stereotyping. It is preposterous that a "Hebraic" gypsy with no apparent motive might be so constitutionally evil as to plot the destruction of all New York City's Christian children, and that he should attract confederates with the depraved purpose and supernatural means to accomplish the mass infanticide. Similarly, that he should be parent to a beautiful daughter (not surprisingly kidnaped from a European nobleman in her infancy) whom he delights in abusing is a complication so ordinary as to be tedious. Furthermore, the girl is forced to find employment as an organ grinder and carry with her a monkey which actually weeps at her suffering.

But O'Brien takes the horrible beyond absurdity when he makes the mistreated girl find love with an ugly, stumbling, and crippled hunchback. The marvelously wrought "Saint Agnes' Eve" quality of these lovers' escape into a Manhattan December, though unimportant to the plot of "The Wondersmith," is a masterful touch that leaves a reader shaking his head somewhere between disgust and laughter. One horrific detail too astounding and well-rendered to be the work of merely an ordinary talent is the artificial eye one of the plotters has devised. He carries it in his pocket, fondles it until it becomes bloodshot, or leaves it in corners and desk drawers so that he might observe things unnoticed. And the scene in which the haunted dolls are loosed in a birdseller's shop to test their bloodlust on lovebirds and canaries is downright chilling. The point is that O'Brien's stories are for the most part uneven. They are combinations of weak, predictable characterization, stale plotting, and extraordinarily fine detail; and O'Brien himself seems not to know their strengths from their weaknesses.

Apart from "The Diamond Lens," "What Was It?" is perhaps O'Brien's most nearly successful story. Its inquisitive protagonist is an opium smoker as well as a scientist and philosopher, and the vice which renders him a somewhat unreliable narrator is the vehicle for a reader's willingness to be immersed in the fantastic situation laid out for him. The story involves the discovery of an invisible though corporeal monster, and the monster's capture, refusal to eat, and subsequent starvation. If O'Brien draws his reader into the fantasy with a narrator who himself may be subject to hallucination, he nonetheless has that reader convinced and nearly in sympathy with the unfortunate beast (referred to alternately as the Mystery, the Horror, the Terror, and the Enigma) which has become docile and may even be trying to communicate with its captors before it dies. It is a well-written story, one in which foreshadowing and ambiguity are both used to good effect. And characterization, while never really strong, is adequate here to plot requirements. The protagonist's initial inquiry into the metaphysical question of what is the worst of all possible horrors is never finally resolved, but neither does it need to be; and at the conclusion of "What Was It?", as if to insure that nothing is taken too seriously, O'Brien entertains his reader with the preposterous spectacle of two apparently sane men furtively digging a hole in a garden — a hole where they plan to hide the invisible remains of a thing in which no one but themselves is much interested in the first place.

Unfortunately, such wonderfully whimsical touches as the burial of an invisible corpse in "What Was It?" or the strange, romantic flight of a crippled hunchback, his lover, and her monkey in "The Wondersmith" are rare in O'Brien's work. Too often what he has to say seems shrill and vitriolic, as in the diatribe he preaches against Mormonism in "My Wife's Temper," or the vicious, perverse characterizations he presents of Jews in "The Diamond Lens" and again in "The Wondersmith." Of course one can never be certain whether a character is speaking with his author's own mouth, but there is a pattern of consistent and naked cultural and racial bitterness in these stories that tends to overwhelm the contemporary reader and to dismay him.

Fitz-James O'Brien was an enigmatic, but perhaps a careless writer. Certainly it is odd to consider that the same expansive mind which imagined "The Diamond Lens" was so provincial as to patronize an Oriental civilization he seems not to understand in "The Dragon Fang," and naïvely to ape, in the same story, an "Oriental" style of writing that never existed outside Goldsmith. Similarly, it does not seem entirely logical that the author of such tightly constructed, well-paced tales as "The Pot of Tulips" or "The Lost Room" could digress into such banality as "My Wife's Temper" and a great deal of "The Wondersmith" contain. It is interesting to speculate how O'Brien's writing might have matured had he survived the Civil War. That he died at thirty-four and still was able to leave a group of stories that are to be reckoned with more than a century later surely speaks highly of his potential; but such speculation serves no real purpose after all. His tales are interesting but uneven, imaginative but derived; it does not seem likely that they will be read a great deal in the future except by scholars of early American fantasy and gothicism.

Douglas J. McReynolds

Sources for Further Study

Criticism:

Franklin, H. Bruce. *Future Perfect: American Science Fiction of the Nineteenth Century*. New York: Oxford University Press, 1966, pp. 321-327. Franklin places O'Brien in his proper perspective as a precursor of science fiction as we know it.

Walle, Francis. *Fitz-James O'Brien: A Literary Bohemian of the Eighteen Fifties*. Boulder: University of Colorado Press, 1944, pp. 151-158. Walle views O'Brien as an *avant-garde* science fiction writer — a view that is reinforced by his excellent analysis of *The Diamond Lens*.

THE SHORT FICTION OF FREDERIK POHL

Author: Frederik Pohl (1919-   )
Type of work: Short stories and novellas

A varied body of work, predominantly satiric in mode and sardonic in tone, moving from space opera, to "comic infernos" directed at consumer society, to enigmatic fables of the human condition

After an undistinguished writing career in the 1940's, during which he produced a number of wooden melodramas and space operas, Pohl emerged in the 1950's as a leading satirist who won accolades from Kingsley Amis in his pioneering study of science fiction, *New Maps of Hell* (1960). Most familiar of his satires, perhaps, is "The Midas Plague" (1954), which turns economic values upside down, so that the "poor" are burdened by having to consume huge amounts of food and products churned out by automated factories. The desultory plot, involving a newly married couple from different classes, concludes with the "happy idea" (perhaps a bit obvious) of shortcircuiting the process by involving robots in consumption as well as production. Pohl was well aware that the premise (suggested by *Galaxy* editor H. L. Gold) was untenable, and rather than trying to shore up its believability, he turned it into a "tall tale" through his unflagging comic invention of logically extrapolated details. The story was popular enough to inspire three sequels, "The Man Who Ate the World" (1956), "The Wizards of Pung's Corners" (1958) and "The Waging of the Peace" (1959), none of which comes up to the original, though they do have moments of satirical brilliance.

In his "consumer cycle," Pohl also took dead aim at other aspects of the affluent society, telling a conventionally plotted but fast-moving story while providing illumination and perspective by comic inversion or reduction to the absurd. "Happy Birthday, Dear Jesus" (1956) uses a traditional love-story plot to ridicule the commercial ideals of Christmas, which identify love and identity with mechanical products, and extend the Christmas shopping season through the beginning of summer.

Social control of another sort is involved in "What To Do Till the Analyst Comes" (1956). Long before hallucinogens were in the public eye, Pohl posited a "non-habit-forming" drug which banishes worry, while it also frees the society from the need for accuracy, efficiency, and productivity. His narrator is particularly well situated to tell the story; overdosed by the drug at its inception, he has an allergy to it which effectively makes him the only person left to worry about anything.

The 1950's mania for sedation and conformity even governs Pohl's best space adventure story of the decade, "The Mapmakers" (1955). Stranded in space by an accident which blinded its navigator, the crew of a spaceship are at the mercy of hyperspace hallucinations and a deadly build-up of body heat. His cries stifled by sedation, the navigator finally manages to persuade his nurse not to drug him so that he can rescue them. With his knowledge of the stars, he is beset in hyperspace by visions which not only direct their journey, but also give transcendent value to his "insight."

Blindness and sedation in a consumer society lead eventually to overpopulation and pollution, as is shown in two other stories from this period. "The Census Takers" (1956) is a comic inferno, in which the job of the census is mainly to reduce population, which the protagonist, an efficient but unimaginative civil servant, does well and without compunctions. "The Snowmen" (1959) postulates a rapid terrestrial approach to the "heat death of the universe," through the overuse of "heat pumps," an all-purpose term covering all sorts of convenience machines, the most obvious of which are refrigerators and air conditioners. The effect of both satires is diminished by the emergence of aliens as a plot gimmick in the end; an underground race sets off volcanoes and earthquakes in the first story, while visitors from space become victims themselves of rapacious, invincibly ignorant consumers in the second.

One alternative to ecotastrophe is the controlled society, the butt of Pohl's satire in two more ambivalent stories. The title of "Rafferty's Reasons" (1955) refers to why a former artist, "retrained" (brainwashed) into filling a more useful niche in society, has homicidal tendencies. Controlled by his training, Rafferty only imagines the weapon with which he attacks a politician. His little tragedy and thousands like it, are a small price to pay, it appears, for the elimination of unemployment, overproduction, and economic depressions.

"My Lady Greensleeves" (1957) is a broader satire of class distinctions based on occupational categories. Ostensibly about a prison riot, it examines the society of which that prison is only a symptom. The riot fails because the white-collar thinkers and blue-collar workers among the inmates cannot work together to engineer the breakout, but also because each level of the governmental hierarchy is only as competent as it needs to be to avoid turning a mild disturbance into a bloodbath. Though the story does not praise these social arrangements, it does point out their saving graces, such as the complete absence of illogical biases based on color, religion, or ethnic origin.

Best of the cycle is "The Tunnel Under the World" (1955), perhaps the ultimate fictional statement on commercial manipulation. Hanging his satire on a traditional horror story, Pohl reveals that menace only gradually, taking his protagonist and the reader through several mistaken constructions of reality before the truth is finally announced. Disturbed by strident advertising techniques and some bewilderingly effective salesmanship, Guy Burckhardt discovers by accident that each day repeats the experiences of the previous day. That this is not the first time it has happened to him is made evident by an acquaintance whom he jarred from complacency the last time he became conscious of the anomaly.

Between them, the two attempt to find out what is happening, and are led to startling, but seemingly nonsensical discoveries which eventually bring Burckhardt to a horrifying discovery. He and all his fellow citizens are victims of an industrial accident, from which they have been preserved in a way, in order to function through miniature manikins in a table-top scale model of their small town. As a trade-off for this half-life, they sacrifice their consciousness of the passing of time, which might change their perceptions from the perfect control situation of the same day every day, the day after the accident. The advertising gimmicks at the beginning are their reason for continuing to exist, as a test market for an advertising research firm.

This bare summary does not do justice to the deftness with which the story is handled, or to the implications of the concept for the managed consumer society. The message is not belabored, nor are the stereotyped characters obtrusive; their mechanical nature as mass men rather than individuals is perfectly appropriate to the conception and to the working out of the plot.

Moving towards the ambivalent fables of the 1970's, but still related to the consumer cycle, is "The Children of Night" (1964), in which public relations and politics replace advertising and economic salesmanship. The narrator is another efficient manager, who has some misgivings about the morality of his work, though he does not let them get in his way. Aliens are important in this story from the start, since it is the Arcturans, with whom Earth has an armistice (not a peace), whose wish to build a "base" in a small Midwestern town he is paid to carry out. Alienating the populace, even his clients, he wins the referendum by turning himself into a scapegoat, uniting the electorate with the hated aliens in opposition to the agent of disruption.

The satire in that story cuts both ways, as it does in a series of sketches (pieces hardly substantial enough to be called stories) which represent Pohl's best fiction in the 1960's. Aliens appear in four of them, twice as ubiquitous Martians of science fiction. "The Martian Stargazers" (1962) comments obliquely on human history and pride, explaining through Martian star lore why the Martians killed themselves long before humans arrived on their planet. "The Day After the Martians Came" (1967) concerns sidelights of the coming of the aliens. Pitiful creatures, the Martians are the butt of jokes which suggest that they will occupy the lowest rung in society, raising the status of blacks in America.

"Earth 18" (1964) is a fictional guidebook account of what few attractions there are for the alien traveler on Earth, regardless of how much "development" the conquering aliens promote. "Speed Trap" (1967) only implies alien manipulation in the problem of modern science that travel, conferences, and administration eat more and more into the time of anyone whose research seems to have real potential.

The star turn of the 1960's is "Day Million" (1966), a love story with a difference. Genetic engineering and social change in the fairly distant future have changed the meaning of gender, for forms human bodies can take, and the immediacy of a love relationship. Without actually telling a story, the narrator presents us with two genetic "males" who "marry" by means of obtaining electronic replicas of each other. These they will use for sexual experiences of a temporary nature which provide as full a relationship as many couples enjoy now, perhaps fuller. The jolting shift of perspective common in Pohl stories is introduced at the beginning and then built up by logical extrapolation, rather than being thrown in as a last-minute surprise. Directly addressing his audience several times, moreover, the narrator attempts to browbeat them into taking historical change into account. The effect is more akin to contemplation of rather than to rejection of the outrageous circumstances, and is a vindication of the narrator's claim that this is indeed a "love story."

The early 1970's saw another shift in direction for Pohl, toward a more romantic, almost Utopian view, akin perhaps to the stories of his youth, but with a more mature conception of character, a sense of the tragic human condition, and a greater regard for and facility with construction and style. Perhaps the best example of this is "We Purchased People" (1974), which combines a number of recurrent themes in Pohl's work with a superior narrative treatment. A love story with a sadomasochistic twist, it suggests the tragic potential for the individual in certain "utopian" solutions to problems.

Wayne Golden and Carolyn Schoerner are would-be lovers, star-crossed in more ways than one. Because they have been found guilty of heinous crimes, they (or at least Wayne) are regarded as criminally insane. Having been purchased by aliens, they are remotely controlled most of the time, serving as the aliens' agents in business dealings on Earth. Thus they seldom meet or see each other, except when at least one is being controlled by their owners. Finally, they are brought together by the aliens for purposes of "experimentation" with human sexual patterns of behavior.

This situation would be bad enough as an intolerable invasion of privacy, which, indeed, is how Wayne at first views it. But an added complication makes this story distinctly not for the squeamish. Having been introduced to Wayne as a lover frustrated by his owners, we discover later why he was a "purchased person" to begin with. He is, or was, a homicidal maniac who got his kicks from young girls — not by sexually molesting them, but by "watching them die." And the aliens, unaware of any change in his personality, experiment with him according to "the sexual behavior which has been established as his norm."

The result is sick, even outrageous, but predictable, perhaps inevitable given the premises of the story. Moreover, rather than making a moral judgment that this is wrong, the story raises the question of how high a price a society ought to pay to achieve the benefits of peace and technological growth which the aliens have brought. In addition, of course, the story places Pohl's favorite theme, manipulation, into a whole new light, one perhaps especially suited to the 1970's.

Also rich in implication are two novelettes of 1972, in which romantic success, albeit tinged with ashes, is wrested out of dystopian situations. *The Merchants of Venus* takes place on the hellish version of that world seen by modern astronomy, and centers on the quest of a prospector and tour guide to make a big strike in an undiscovered tunnel of the long-vanished alien race, whose leavings encourage man to inhabit the planet. The hero's snatching of victory from the jaws of defeat is acceptable, though the cards are obviously stacked. The real interest, however, lies in the imaginative details of the background, such as physical and social conditions on Venus, and the implied disastrous conditions on Earth from which people have fled.

Heavily indebted to the rise of the youthful counterculture of the 1960's, "The Gold at the Starbow's End" has echoes of the rock album "Jefferson Starship." Amid street politics escalating to guerrilla warfare in Washington, a Kissinger-type scientist conceives a Machiavellian project of sending ten bright young people to Alpha Centaurus to explore a nonexistent planet. The real purpose, to give them ten years for concentrated thinking, produces more than the planners bargained for. The emissaries "go hippy," not only in outward appearances, but also with tangible achievements that transcend traditional scientific and technological knowledge. They succeed in creating a planet of their own in the Centaurus system and return for colonists, but not before they have sent back a rain of heavy atomic particles, wiping out all nuclear devices, partially melting the ice caps, and reducing Earth practically to savagery.

A less drastic way of jettisoning the old to adopt the new is presented by "In the Problem Pit" (1973), a multiple-character study which all but eliminates a conventional melodramatic plot. Although there is some low-key romantic love interest, and a momentary scare when one member of the group disappears into the complex of caves where they are meeting, both these subplots are subordinated to the story's "minimal" science fiction. Focusing on a group of average people brought together by a governmental agency to solve problems for one another and indirectly for society, the story develops them as people who interact on human as well as technical grounds, even as it suggests a workable method with which to implement a variant brand of what Alvin Toffler has called "anticipatory democracy." Emphasizing encounter training, generalized love for others, sexual freedom, and problem-solving, this story sums up nicely a kind of Utopian outlook one could adopt in the 1970's without being labeled a hopeless romantic.

Produced over the course of four decades, these hundred-odd stories of Frederik Pohl are not all alike; they vary in subject, approach, and level of competence. But they all illustrate how Pohl's work has mirrored the changing times and fashions of commercial science fiction during that era, and they include a handful of satirical shockers that are classics of modern science fiction.

David N. Samuelson

Sources for Further Study

Criticism:

The Encyclopedia of Science Fiction and Fantasy. Compiled by Donald H. Tuck. Chicago: Advent Publishers, Inc., 1978, pp. 350-352. Tuck gives a short biography of Pohl and a full bibliography of his works.

Pohl, Frederick. "The Publishing of Science Fiction," in *Science Fiction, Today and Tomorrow*. Edited by Reginald Bretnor. New York: Harper & Row, 1974, pp. 17-45. The author gives a full accounting of his own career and efforts and a writer of science fiction, as well as a discussion of the field generally.

THE SHORT FICTION OF FREDRIC BROWN

Author: Fredric Brown (1906-1972)
Type of work: Short stories and short-shorts

Stories initially published in science fiction pulps between 1940 and 1954, display-ing great technical control as well as artistry and imagination, and, in general, opti-mism about man's possible futures

Fredric Brown was certainly one of the most versatile fantasy and science fiction writers at work in mid-twentieth century America. He was also one of relatively few to distinguish clearly between fantasy, which he considered to concern itself with things that cannot be, and science fiction, which concerns itself only with things that may well someday be and in doing so logically accounts for their being. Brown wrote both, but most of his speculative stories are, according to his definition, science fiction. Seldom asking to be taken entirely seriously, he was content instead to pun, invent outrageous things, and stimulate his reader's mind into its own flights of imagination. On the planet Nothing Sirius, for example, birds fly with propellers; on Earth four Andromedans borrow the bodies of a dog, a squirrel, a chicken, and a cow before making contact with a very surprised writer and his equally startled wife — whom the dog calls "Toots." The planet Placet, owing to an energy field in its figure eight orbit which slows light rays but not solid matter, meets itself twice a day; and so on. Brown was a sleight-of-hand man, shamelessly invent-ing stories about a science fiction writer who has deadlines to meet but no plot ideas to develop, or about a Linotype machine which develops intelligence, begins to take over the world, and then discovers Buddhism and Nirvana.

There is no doubt that Brown's career as a mystery writer influenced his science fiction stories. This connection is especially evident in the characters he drew, for many of them are virtually indistinguishable from the inhabitants of those pulp mystery magazines that were immensely popular in the 1930's and 1940's. His bill-harried protagonists are more interested in being smiled at by a pretty girl than in the mind-boggling technology of whatever century and whatever galaxy they find themselves enmeshed in. There are struggling paper pushers and underpaid police officials just trying to stay alive in a universe which may be mad and, regardless, whose immense indifference is matched only by its size, performing mundane and thankless tasks from which their personal integrities will not allow them to shirk.

Typical among these is Rod Caquer, a police lieutenant in Sector Three of the planet Callisto in "Daymare" (*Space on My Hands*, 1951). Lieutenant Caquer wants to solve an apparent homicide in which the supposed victim dies in two different places and by six different means, and even more, to be loved by the girl he calls, with reason, Icicle. His efforts are complicated by the existence of an illegal Vargas Wheel — a mesmerizing device looking like a beanie with several refracting propellers on it, but which is used by its wearer to impress his own thoughts upon whole civilizations — and its mad owner's designs for galactic domination. Another of Brown's detectives, Bela Joad ("Crisis, 1999") Space on My Hands discovers that, while hypnosis is used to thwart police investigations, it can be used also, and just as deviously, to reform criminals and end organized crime. The point is that Brown's protagonists are not much different from the heroes of most detective fiction; it is the kinds of worlds and technologies with which they are involved that intrigues and arrests the reader.

Two themes generally seem to run through Brown's short stories. The first of these is that the basic machines of mid-twentieth century American industry — drill presses, lathes, linotypes, and the like — are more valuable to civilization's future than are the electronic gimmicks which this or any other technology might manage to produce. Television and its spawn are little more than platforms for the advertisers, and one astute businessman goes so far as to move the fixed stars of the northern sky into a configuration spelling out "Use Snively's Soap." Poetically, he falls through a window to his death at the shock of realizing his name is spelled wrong on that giant billboard; still, company sales increase 915%. But colonists everywhere need to make things and read newspapers, and the skilled machinist or typesetter, whether utilizing real horse power on earth after an invasion has reduced all electrical power to uselessness, or inventing a way to facilitate radite mining on Callisto, invariably enriches the culture of which he is a part.

The second theme is that Brown seemed fascinated by the unpredictable natures of possible extraterrestrial invasions. His BEM's are seldom actually evil, though one group does sterilize the earth before making any kind of contact with the pairs of each species it wishes to preserve in its own zoological garden. More often, they are discorporeal entities who seem oblivious to whatever discomfort they cause their hosts, and who themselves, pests though they are, cause little actual physical harm. The Waveries (*Angels and Spaceships*, 1954), for example, completely disrupt all radio and television signals and then, when broadcasting ceases, devour whatever electricity is generated on earth. When, at length, men learn to get along without electricity, the Waveries, still present on earth, pose no further problem. Other insubstantial invaders do not deign even to notice atomic weapons being exploded inside them or full-scale attacks by the combined armed forces of the United States. They simply go about their inscrutable business. But (and this theme is explored in much greater depth in Brown's novel *Martians Go Home* than in any of these stories) the invaders usually generate enough international distress that they succeed in making man use his technological knowledge to kill himself off. It is as though some vast intelligence in the universe will not allow human civilization not to advance in productive ways, and it every so often has to come and take away the dangerous toys man has invented but cannot control.

In some of his stories Brown seemed to demonstrate a cosmic pessimism almost worthy of Mark Twain. His "Letter to a Phoenix" (*Angels and Space-ships*), proposing that man is the only immortal being in the universe because he alone is congenitally insane, demands to be taken seriously. Its narrator is not a lost pilot or a detective or a writer, but a survivor, combining the sto-icism of the Wandering Jew with the world weariness of Twain's Mysterious Stranger. Though not immortal, he has seen 180,000 years of human civiliza-tions rise, spread across this and other galaxies, make war, and self-destruct down to a few savages around a few campfires. But there is a kind of satisfac-tion in the narrator's voice even as he maps out the grim future he sees for mankind in A.D. 1954. Man is crazy and therefore incapable of eradicating himself completely, even though hundreds of billions of men will die. He will endure and, apparently, in endurance there is some satisfaction. He tells man-kind not to worry: the impending nuclear war, while it may destroy a third of earth's population, is not a real blow-up even though it may seem like a holo-caust; no one now living will see the terrible wars that, millennia hence, will plunge the remains of humanity back again into the stone age for yet another go. Unlike most of Brown's pieces, "Letter to a Phoenix" is an upsetting story, largely because of the fundamental incompatibility between the sus-tained consolation in its narrator's voice and the existential horror waiting in the future that voice so calmly foretells.

Fredric Brown was also a master of the so-called short-short story, a three- to five-hundred-word vignette whose relation to the short story is much the same as that of the epigram to the lyric poem. These stories are fun, not to be taken seriously. Typical of what Brown does in them occurs in "Answer" (*Angels and Spaceships*). A scientist who has just plugged in the ultimate computer — a network with members on each of the ninety-six billion popu-lated planets in the universe — asks it the question, "Is there a God?" The machine answers, "of course, *now* there is a God," and immediately strikes dead the man who has had impudence enough to ask the question. What Brown seemed to understand is that some fictions, like some jokes, are dependent almost exclusively on the force of the punch line, not at all on the telling. So in his short-shorts he went straight to that punch line, wasting no more time than is absolutely necessary in working up to it.

Fredric Brown's stories are always groomed and polished, and nearly al-ways a pleasure to read. He manipulates his characters and plots but never maliciously or deceitfully. He makes his reader want to be manipulated and to enjoy whatever preposterous beings or situations he may be asked to accept. Brown's stories are on the whole optimistic, often buoyant. If they have a message to convey, it is this: that the universe and the creatures which inhabit it are just crazy enough to go on surviving, and just resourceful enough to make that survival a relatively painless experience.

Douglas J. McReynolds

Sources for Further Study

Reviews:

Booklist. LXXIV, September 1, 1977, p. 21.

Books West. I, October, 1977, p. 34.

Kliatt Paperback Book Guide. XI, Fall, 1977, p. 10.

New York Times Book Review. May 15, 1977, p. 45.

Publisher's Weekly. CCXI, April 4, 1977, p. 87.

THE SHORT FICTION OF FRITZ LEIBER, JR.

Author: Fritz Leiber, Jr. (1910-   )
Type of works: Short stories and novelettes
Time: Various, but usually the present or a generation hence
Locale: Various, but usually an urban setting

The short fiction of one of the most accomplished writers of contemporary literature, in or out of science fiction

Over a career of forty years, Fritz Leiber, Jr. has been one of science fiction's finest stylists and most versatile storytellers. Although his name may not immediately come to mind when one thinks of the field's most honored writers, no one — not Asimov, not Clarke, not Delany, not Le Guin — has received greater acclaim than Leiber. Since John W. Campbell, Jr., first published his work in *Unknown* of August, 1939, Leiber has garnered three Nebula Awards from the Science Fiction Writers of America, six Hugo Awards presented at annual World Science Fiction conventions (in addition to being Guest of Honor at New Orleans in 1951), the Gandalf Award in 1975, and the August Derleth Fantasy Award in 1976. And not one but two magazines, *Fantastic* in November, 1959, and *The Magazine of Fantasy and Science Fiction* in July, 1969, have devoted entire issues to his work.

Leiber's wide appeal is attested to by the fact that three of his stories have won *both* the writers' Nebula and the fans' Hugo — a feat unequaled by any other writer. His versatility is shown by his winning Hugos in the categories of Novel, Novella, Novelette, and Short Story. And his energy, even in the seven decades of his life, is demonstrated by the fact that seven of his honors have been awarded since 1968.

Leiber may be better known, though no less appreciated, as a writer of fantasy. His "Gray Mouser and Fafhrd" stories have reached an audience comparable to that of *Lord of the Rings*, with one of them, "Ill Met in Lankhmar" (1971), being one of the double winners cited above. A second Hugo-Nebula winner was also fantasy — "Gonna Roll the Bones" (1968). But his science fiction is thought of just as highly, for one of his science fiction stories was the third double winner, "Catch That Zeppelin" (1976), an able representative of the genre under study here.

Officially, Leiber has one science fiction series, entitled "Change War," made up of the novel *The Big Time* (1958) and a number of stories published mostly in *Galaxy* and *Fantasy and Science Fiction* since 1958. They concern two alien forces, nicknamed "Snakes" and "Spiders," waging an interstellar war. Both sides recruit people from Earth. Their chief weapons are devices that allow them to change the past in hopes of bringing about more favorable situations. As inventive and rewarding as the "Change War" stories are, Leiber's nonseries stories show better the range and depth of his talents.

Those talents are shown in the two collections that are available today. The more comprehensive of the two is the Doubleday anthology *The Best of Fritz Leiber* (1974, hereafter abbreviated *Best*), which included an introduction by Poul Anderson. A paperback collection, *The Book of Fritz Leiber* (DAW, 1974, hereafter abbreviated *Book*), is noteworthy for containing interspersed fiction and nonfiction, one essay of which provides almost an anatomy of Leiber's work. That essay is "Monsters and Monster Lovers," in which the author discusses his definition of and fascination for the monster. For Leiber, the monster is more than merely a figure of meaning and power; it is unique in kind, and hence alone in its individuality. If we accept this definition, then we can see that the fascination with the monster runs through not only his fantasy but through his science fiction as well.

Perhaps the principal characteristic of the monster is its menace. Dracula, the Wolfman, and Frankenstein's monster threaten us personally or as a society. This type of monster can be found as the unnamed central figure of "The Foxholes of Mars" (*Best*), whose integrity and personality we see crumble through a long war until he ends up to be no more than a budding dictator, alienated from all around him. This monster is easily seen, but in other stories we discover the monster's true identity only after it is too late.

A story of consummate skill is "The Ship Sails at Midnight" (*Best*). It is a masterpiece of characterization which begins, "This is the story of a beautiful woman. And of a monster." Helen is a waitress of obscure origin, whose interest in each of four people leads to her downfall. Believing that Helen loves him (or her) alone, an artist, a physicist, a philosopher, and a writer are each inspired to brilliance. At the story's climax they discover that Helen loves and has made love to each, and that knowledge evolves into jealousy and hatred. After one of the four murders Helen, they all learn that she is literally not of this world, for they witness an alien carrying her body back to a spaceship. Helen's otherworldly origin has been hinted at through the story, and the reader waits to discover that the beauty and the beast are one and the same, that the monster is really the jealousy in each of the human characters.

Leiber tells us that the monster is often a cripple, either physical or mental, as is Jeff Bogart in "A Hitch in Space" (*Book*). Bogart is dangerous because of his psychosis, yet the fact that his malevolence is unintentional makes it no less deadly. Bogart and the narrator, Joe, make up the crew of a spaceship that is haunted by Bogart's imaginary companion, a double of Joe. A peculiar facet of Bogart's madness is that the imaginary Joe appears only when the real one is absent, and Bogart is therefore unaware that he is hallucinating. The crisis comes when the narrator floats outside the ship for some routine maintenance and Bogart, seeing the imaginary Joe seated beside him, starts the motors and moves off with the narrator tethered outside.

In "A Hitch in Space" it is clear who the monster is, but a large group of stories distribute the attributes of the monster among a set of characters. It is surprising how many of Leiber's tales portray a single sane individual living in a mad world. The slightest of these stories is "Sanity" (*Best*), written for Campbell, who, Leiber has stated, "taught me more about plotting and motivation than any other individual." Yet Campbell did not serve him well here, if he had any influence on Leiber's work in this particular story. In "Sanity," World Manager Carrbury, the only sane man left, faces the psychotic machinations of the rest of the bureaucracy. At a climax which the reader has long seen coming, Carrbury is taken away, having learned that if sanity means conforming to a norm, then he is the only lunatic left.

Leiber was aware of Campbell's flaws, despite his sincere gratitude to the man he calls the "master editor," and he expresses that awareness in "Poor Superman" (*Best*), another story in which the lunatics run the asylum. It is set in a post-atomic-war America, in which both the government and the military stand in awe of "The Thinkers' Foundation," a vast confidence game whose front man is the sleep-learning, engram-clearing Jorj Helmuth — a biting satire of John Campbell, Jr. The Foundation has bilked the whole country with its fake Martian wisdom and its snake-oil compound of Dianetics and General Semantics. All important questions are submitted to "Maizie," supposedly the Foundation's giant computer, but in reality a false front. The answers are supplied, behind the false front, by a beer-drinking fat man, sitting in his shorts, typing away — a satiric portrait of L. Ron Hubbard.

The reader comes away from Leiber's reminiscences thinking that he was not well served by his editors, even though he never complains. Perhaps his finest story is "Yesterday House" (*Book*), once again a story of the lone sane individual facing a mad world run by a monster. Its biology-student hero, Jack Barr, has come to study for the summer on the coast of Maine at the home of Martin Kesserich, the greatest living biologist. Pleasure-sailing one day, he discovers a house on a lonely island on which two older women are rearing a young girl. They have created an insane environment for her (although she does not know it), a world eighteen years in the past: although it is really 1951, she believes it to be 1933. Her "aunts" drive an Essex; each morning they bring her a yellowed newspaper; and taped broadcasts from the period are piped to her radio. And each morning she receives a box containing some mark of affection: a poem, some flowers, a ring. The gift varies, but the box always holds a note from a lover whose name she does not know.

The situation horrifies Barr, and he seeks to learn as much as he can about the girl, whose name is Mary Alice Pope. During Kesserich's absence, his wife tells Barr the story of a man as mad as Jeff Bogart, but one who is able to bring his imaginary companion to life. Eighteen years before, Kesserich's fiancée, Mary Alice Pope, had been killed in an accident that may have been caused, and certainly could have been prevented, by Kesserich's two sisters. Immediately after the accident, the biologist removed an egg cell from her body, and succeeded in causing the egg to develop without fertilization, thereby preserving the young woman's genetic inheritance without masking or changing her characteristics. He then implanted it in the womb of a lab assistant whom he married in return for her services. After the baby's birth, he set about duplicating the environment of his dead fiancée as closely as possible for the growing child, sentencing his sisters to raise the girl as penance. It is the love story of a monomaniac, a monster, but given its premises, the girl should love Kesserich, who has been sending the boxes, as much as her "mother" did. However, Horace L. Gold, the editor of *Galaxy*, wrote a "happy" ending that brought together the second Mary Alice and Jack Barr. *The Book of Fritz Leiber* restores its intended ending, but one wonders how many authors of talent were hurt as often as they were helped by even the best of editors.

"Coming Attraction" (*Best*) uses the same setting as "Poor Superman." Here an outsider, a sane Englishman, is sent into the asylum of a war-weary but violent, decadent and perverse America where women wear masks (often to hide radiation scars). The central figure discovers the monster beneath the mask of a young woman so sated that she can be stirred only by sadomasochism. Although "Coming Attraction" is frequently and rightfully praised, a similar story, "America the Beautiful" (*Best*), is more muted and more powerful, because the monster is more elusive.

As Leiber has said, "Coming Attraction" is a 1950's story; the cause of its madness is a fear of physical destruction; above all, a fear of atomic war. The visible signs of the fear are the twisted skyscrapers and the scarred faces, and its effects are casual violence and perversion. But whatever its date of composition, "America the Beautiful" is a story for the 1960's. Here the cause of the madness is not a fear of physical, but of spiritual destruction.

And America is indeed beautiful in the setting of the year 2000. In strong contrast to the country of "Coming Attraction," the air is wholesome, the landscape is clean, the rivers are pure — but the family visited by another Englishman lives in an underground bomb shelter, and their "picture windows" are huge television screens that can show not only a pseudoview of the land above, but battle scenes from the current Vietnams. The Americans of this story have grown accustomed to war, burying their fear of it as deep as their houses. But to justify their far-flung spilling of blood, they must maintain that their little wars protect a way of life that is worth saving. They must, therefore, be the perfect hosts in the perfect society. The family exudes a surface coolness which they believe to be the sign of their unalloyed contentment, but it is only a mask, like the physical masks of "Coming Attraction." This calmness hides an insecurity so sensitive that any suggestion of a shortcoming must be refuted at once. When the British narrator needles them about their Puritanism, he is shortly thereafter offered sexual gratification first by the wife and then by the daughter of his host. "America the Beautiful" has become a land of shadows, where style is not an outgrowth of substance but a substitute for it.

Leiber offers many other fine stories, such as "A Pail of Air" (*Best*), as fine a hard science fiction short story as has been written, and more stories about "monsters," as he uses the word: "Crazy Annaoj" (*Book*), another story of an insane love, and "Little Old Miss Macbeth" (*Best*), a brilliant example of using mood to hint at a plot. But Leiber can also richly draw a sane society, one in which madness is cured, or at least exorcised for a time. "The Big Holiday" (*Best*) is a tale of the ritual removal of monsters from society. The occasion is a future holiday suggesting, though differing strikingly from, the Roman Saturnalia or the medieval feast of the Boy Bishop. In a lyric style, Leiber tells of the revelers of a town banishing from their midst people costumed to represent Money, Success, Glamour, Hurry, and Worry. Here we do not find the monster behind the mask, but rather the monster as mask. When the banished ones change their clothing, they rejoin their friends and welcome Friendship, Love, Laziness, Fun, and Joy.

Leiber asserts that the difference between fantasy and science fiction concerns monsters. This master of both genres points out that in science fiction, we try to understand the monster, and if we succeed, we remove its danger. If it follows that understanding removes the monster's meaning, too, then we face somewhat of a dilemma since, as we have seen, the monsters are often us.

Walter E. Meyers

Sources for Further Study

Reviews:

Fantastic Stories. XIX, October, 1969, pp. 129-130.

Luna Monthly. XVIII, November, 1970, p. 16.

Magazine of Fantasy and Science Fiction. XIII, August, 1957, pp. 106-107 and XXXV, September, 1968, pp. 34-35.

Science Fiction Review. XLI, November, 1970, p. 32.

THE SHORT FICTION OF GENNADIY SAMOILOVICH GOR

Author: Gennadiy Samoilovich Gor (1907-   )
Type of work: Short stories

Stories which treat themes of cybernetics, the transfer of spirituality and culture across time, the persistence of man in the face of absolute technology, Soviet life, and immortality

Gennadiy Gor was born and lived in a remote part of Russia; he grew up in an untamed wilderness area analogous to the Yukon at the turn of the century. Gor underwent a long development as a writer before he wrote his fantastic tales. He moved to Petrograd in the early 1920's to study ethnography at Leningrad University; he voluntarily returned to Siberia in the 1930's to observe the natives and study their folklore. He was drawn toward Western culture; he managed to familiarize himself with such diverse topics as graphic arts, Impressionism, advanced physics, semantics, and cybernetics. He associated with Tsiolkovsky and the Oberiuty writers, all of whom died or quit writing by the end of the 1930's.

Among his early works were short stories about life in the brutal wilderness, such as "Lanzhero" (1937). Lanzhero, a Siberian primitive, is bewildered by sudden exposure to modern civilization; to him, a radio seems a voice cut off from the body and imprisoned. This method runs throughout Gor's works — he contrasts the world view of a savage to that of a modern man and then tries to extrapolate, to construct an imaginative drama out of the confusion and mental changes one would suffer if confronted suddenly by the future.

Gennadiy Gor began writing science fiction in the 1960's. "Dokuchlivy sobesednik" appeared in 1961, and treated questions of communication, memory, and symbolic values, whether stored in a computer or cherished in a human heart. A Traveler from a civilization advanced far beyond ours, visits Earth in our Stone Age. Trapped in our past, he delights in pushing men towards a higher level. The Traveler leaves behind a sort of robot, "Another I." This artificial self preserves his vast knowledge, opinions, and memories for ages. Finally, the "Other I" is discovered by a scientist of the present day. He is overwhelmed by the flow of details from the robot.

As elsewhere, Gor takes a firm stand in favor of the human mind. He credits the robot with only minimal understanding, and little finesse or subtlety of thought. Furthermore, the ultracivilized beings usually build an "Anti-I." This robot contradicts and tests the ideas frozen into the other robot, which can only echo a stored personality. Also, the living brain pits the two robots against each other, lest one dominate.

Paul Pogodin, hero of "Strannik i vremya" (1963), undertakes a risky experiment in suspended animation, and passes into the twenty-third century. In that age, barriers of space have been overcome; one may live on one continent and work on another. With the aid of cybernetic nets and "institutes of memory," the data of past lives are ever available. Time itself appears tamed in a way impossible to imagine. The man of our age first undergoes cultural shock, but gradually contacts great minds, symbols that unite our ages: Einstein, Dostoevski, Leonardo da Vinci.

Pogodin had read Maturin's tale, *Melmoth the Wanderer* (1820). He feels himself also a wanderer in time, not cursed by Satan, but cut loose from a stable environment and exposed to immortality, like Melmoth. For the future civilization of "Tiom" allows life and experience to go on indefinitely. Here the author stands squarely against transhuman expectations and defends the concept of limits. The "Tiom" culture has to retrench; deathlessness meets a barrier. Life only has meaning if we develop individuality, and a technology that allows time without end blurs and distorts individuality. Gor sees Faust as a warning, not a model.

In the novella "Gosti s Uazy" (1963), renamed "Kumbi," Gor treats a similar problem. Human personality can be enlarged and continued without end by constructing artificial brains. Scientists experiment with a series of these. Kumbi combines the traits and memories of many dead men. Yet the all-knowing machine provides a lesson all too often neglected in science fiction by showing the negative aspects of immortality. Kumbi knows "everything," yet, in a sense, he knows nothing. For the enormous data bank cannot be used, since Kumbi lacks a sense of relations between facts. Such a dilemma parodies the "information explosion" and bureaucracy of our time. The means to handle relations between facts rests upon human individuality and spontaneity, which the machine lacks. Gor takes the same problems and treats them again and again from completely different viewpoints. In "Dokuchlivy sobesednik," the creature Ryabchikov suffers from amnesia; he can explore the past, but fails to cope with ongoing, recent memories. Like Kumbi, Ryabchikov lacks individuality.

"Ol'ga Nsu" (1965) depicts a world of immortals. Only the old scientist, Lodiy, refuses to take the treatment he has given mankind because he agrees with Gor's philosophy; he wants to live on only in grateful memory. The story warns against transforming our natures beyond certain limits.

On the other hand, Gor optimistically disputes the thesis of Arthur C. Clarke that man will become obsolete. His position resembles that of Ray Bradbury: the human heart will prevail, no matter how adverse the environment becomes; and man's limitations will strengthen his works. No matter how exotic the situation, only creatures like us will survive.

Significantly, however, humanity might achieve survival by preserving images of itself in electronic systems. Man would thus remain man, yet pervade a nonhuman sphere. Or, man might prevail by merging with nature. In "The Garden" (1968), Sid plays the role of the wanderer. He does not fit into our age, so he transforms himself into a garden. This affinity to nature shows the influence of Pasternak's poetry on Gor, particularly the poet's collection *My Sister Life* (1922). In prose, the personification of trees, landscapes, and waterfalls strikes us more strangely than it does in lyrical poetry. Gor also shares with Boris Pasternak a respect for the individual and an appreciation of incongruity resulting in frequent changes of subject. Pasternak and Gor both capture images of beauty in the manner of flash-photography. However, in style Gor resembles Bradbury, with his bright carnival imagery and his mixture of naïve and sophisticated points of view; unfortunately, Gor is not consistently a good stylist.

The author uses the same protagonist and theme in two complementary stories of 1964. Gor deals extensively with the topic of cybernetics. "A Dweller in Two Worlds" describes the grim struggle of Larionov, who experiences the mind of a wanderer from the planet Dilneya. He is disconcerting to everyone, including his sweetheart. "Skitalets Larvef" is a miniature novel. The two tales fit together as a puzzle. "Skitalets Larvef" is told from the viewpoint of Pavlushin, an Earthman who finds a diary and puzzles over it, uncertain. But in the shorter tale, "Larvef" finds he must cope with the possibility that he is suffering from delusions. In "Sinee okno Feokrita" (1967), a future technology allows people to walk through a door into artificial worlds that simulate past ages; it is an inspiring substitute for schools and museums. Feokrit (Theokritos, his poet-namesake) often travels thus. His father studies the ancient poet Tatius. When his mother, also scholarly, later passes the door and falls in love with this Tatius, her husband tries to keep his scientific objectivity. Moreover, Feokrit wanders into a twentieth century setting and falls in love with Tonya.

In "The Boy," the author shows his Russian bent for attention to everyday life. Gromov plays the role of an estranged youth who somehow commands the knowledge of a boy on a star ship that visited Earth in the age of dinosaurs. Yet, the tale also unwinds around lives of schoolboys in the modern U.S.S.R. The others ostracize Gromov; this antagonism follows the familiar conformity of youths who vie against one precocious or deviant. When Gromov writes his strange diary from the spaceship, the plot reflects the ambivalent yearning the children feel toward his mystery. The boy in space dreams of forests. How green do trees seem for one who knows only stories, electronic images? Ordinary life bores him. A robot teacher playfully asks when the wheel was invented; thus the story harks back to the primitive base of all civilization. Finally, the link to Gromov is revealed: a "second personality" for the boy had been found by a scientist, transferred electronically to Gromov's brain.

Gor requires the reader to pursue his themes, which he has gradually worked out over a lifetime. Philosophical novellas and puzzles of cybernetics and semantics surely do not suit everyone, and his characters often fall into abstract types; his riddles surpass the bounds of any story resolution. Nonetheless, this writer dares to treat cosmic riddles, yet to keep man the measure and pivot for all.

John W. Andrews

THE SHORT FICTION OF H. G. WELLS

Author: H. G. Wells (1866-1946)
Type of work: Short stories and novellas

A critical survey of the short fiction of H. G. Wells that attempts to rate the quality of the work as a whole while acknowledging its inferior position in comparison to the long fiction for which the author is justly famous

Most of H. G. Wells's short stories, after appearing originally in magazines, were collected in five anthologies published in 1895 (*The Stolen Bacillus and Other Incidents*); 1897 (*The Plattner Story, and Others*); 1899 (*Tales of Space and Time*); 1903 (*Twelve Stories and a Dream*); and 1911 (*The Country of the Blind, and Other Stories*). Wells's stories tend to be concerned less with character than with, as the title of his first collection suggests, incidents. The core of most of his tales is a marvelous or disturbing or mysterious event — the explosion of a green powder, a secretive glimpse into a luminous crystal, the theft of a culture of new bacteria from a laboratory, an anatomical freak, a violation of the laws of optics, the first attempt to fly an aeroplane or dive in a bathysphere or communicate telepathically, invasions by sea monsters or ants or men in tanks. But the most characteristically Wellsian tales are never merely incidental or sensational in their treatment of such phenomena but speculative and analytical.

Perhaps the kind of speculative story for which Wells is most famous is the predictive tale, such as "The Argonauts of the Air" (1895), a preview of the invention of flying machines, and "The Land Ironclads" (1903), a grimly accurate forecast of tank warfare. Generally, though, despite their value as illustrations of Wells's technological imagination, the predictive stories are not among his most accomplished fictions. An exception is the quietly moving biography of "Filmer" (1901), the supposed inventor of the first workable aircraft. The story focuses not on the fact of technological innovation but on its implications, and far from celebrating Filmer's achievement it seeks to account for Filmer's suicide on his day of glory. As a tale that speculates about "that recurring wonder of the littleness of the scientific man in the face of the greatness of his science," "Filmer" belongs in the company of those Wellsian fictions which ponder the insecurity of human intelligence and the tentativeness of our civilization.

In one of his finest stories, "The Star" (1897), Wells pursues the issue of human vulnerability to an apocalyptic conclusion. He combines a global panorama of disasters and panics, occasioned by the appearance of a huge comet in the sky, with a portrait of the individual despair of the mathematician who charts the comet's path. Having calculated a direct hit of the earth, he concludes that "Man has lived in vain." But in one particular detail the mathematician's figures are incomplete — a telling indication of human limitations — and his conclusion is not only tainted by a banal humanism, it is also premature. The earth is barely preserved from annihilation by the interposition of the moon between the planet and the onrushing comet. Even so, millions die, the climate becomes markedly hotter, the earth's surface is remade by earthquakes and tidal waves, the lunar cycle is lengthened to eighty days, and the remnant of the human population migrates to polar regions. The human species survives, but the minimally happy ending insists not on the vanity of human life but on its comparative littleness. The final paragraph takes us to Mars where astronomers — relatives, presumably, of those shortsighted adventurers who briefly conquer the earth in *The War of the Worlds* (1898) — are peering through telescopes to observe the geological effects of the collision between comet and moon. The Martians are even preparing scientific papers on what they take to be the remarkably small damage done to the earth. And Wells's narrator draws the definitively Wellsian conclusion: "Which only shows how small the vastest of human catastrophes may seem, at a distance of a few million miles."

Wells's perspective on the contingency of human civilization are not always extraterrestrial. "The Empire of the Ants" (1905) ends with a vision of the recolonializing of the earth by a remarkably clever and swiftly breeding strain of ants steadily moving through the interior of Brazil: "By 1920 they will be halfway down the Amazon. I fix 1950 or '60 at the latest for the discovery of Europe." Because we know the consequences of the "discovery" of the Americas by European conquistadores, the closing sentence is ominous. It puts human civilization in its place — and that place is not at the center of creation. Even a relatively thin tale such as "The Stolen Bacillus" (1894) has something to suggest about the fragility of the human race. Its premonitions of both biological warfare and the tactics of modern terrorism are powerful enough, despite the smirking reassurances of the conclusion, to remind us that humans are certainly crazy enough and perhaps just intelligent enough to figure out a way to exterminate their own species.

Wells inquires more extensively and mythically into the nature of civilization in two novellas published in 1897. "A Story of the Stone Age" and "A Story of the Days to Come" are basically episodic fictions, scenes from the lives of a paleolithic man and woman and a couple from twenty-second century London. The novellas are symmetrical in design and ideologically complementary: in each the protagonists are malcontents, exiled from the dominant culture, whether tribal or industrial; each is a story of fitness and survival; each portrays the genesis of a new civilization which will transcend and replace a dying culture. But taken together, the episodes in the stone age and in the days to come offer a disquieting vision of the human price that must be paid for social progress. And ironically, Wells allows the symmetry of the stories to suggest that while each generation continues to have the price of civilization exacted from it, the actual advance over fifty thousand years is small. In "Days to Come" the futuristic man discovers how much he is still a stone-age man: "After all, we are just poor animals, rising out of the brute." Although both novellas suffer from flaws in conception and execution, they are representative of Wells's ambivalence towards civilization in the great decade bounded by *The Time Machine* (1895) and *A Modern Utopia* (1905). "A Story of the Days to Come" is the richer of the two, but in its partly successful effort to create an anthropologically credible portrait of prehistoric humanity, "The Stone Age" is one of Wells's most daring experiments and his most interesting failure. Whatever their technical deficiencies, the two novellas document strikingly and sometimes movingly the notion that human history is only a small part of planetary history and that the story of civilization is itself a short story.

Wells is renowned for perfecting a pseudodocumentary technique for his speculative fictions, but, as the mythic novellas suggest, his imagination was versatile and his range broad. "The Stolen Body" (1898) displays Wells at the height of his speculative powers, but its form is the tale of the macabre or occult. The narrator who is "Under the Knife" (1896) in a hospital operating room inhales the chloroform and goes on a mental journey whose satirical and spiritual texture recalls the conventions of medieval dream-visions. "The New Accelerator" (1901) is a prose cartoon about an unscrupulous professor who manufactures a kind of super-amphetamine that speeds up his thoughts and movements. The drug allows him to make mischief with impunity because he moves so fast his victims can't see him, and, as he watches the rest of the world go by in slow motion, people appear to him as mechanisms and caricatures. His new vision is inevitably and essentially inhumane. For all its madcap charm, "The New Accelerator" is as shrewd as any of Wells's more sober speculations. The professor plans to market his new drug as fast as possible, despite the likelihood that it will be criminally abused. Identifying himself simply as a technologist, he refuses to entertain ethical questions: "We shall manufacture and sell the Accelerator, and, as for the consequences — we shall see."

With their use of drug-induced modes of perception, "Under the Knife" and "The New Accelerator" have links to others of Wells's tales that may be generally described as visionary. In the visionary stories the protagonists acquire, usually involuntarily or accidentally, some special angle or instrument of vision that enables them to see familiar reality freshly and unfamiliar realities with both wonder and terror. The transformations of perception in "The Remarkable Case of Davidson's Eyes" (1895) and "The Plattner Story" (1896) occur in laboratories, and the locale suggests the upsetting of scientific certitudes and habits of thought by a sudden eruption of inexplicable visionary experience. In Plattner's case scientific investigators are eager to disprove his claims about disappearing into a shadowy limbo lit by a green sun from the vantage of which he views the normal world with altered perceptions. But they are stymied by one incontrovertible fact: all his body organs and features which ought to be on his right side have shifted to his left. The scientists are baffled, mortified, disgruntled; although publicly they remain skeptical about Plattner's story, they are in fact embarrassed by a man whose anatomy is a living refutation of scientific assurance and rational sufficiency. Variations on the visionary motif occur in "The Crystal Egg" (1897), a grotesque fantasy about a mysterious object that permits an unhappy antique dealer to escape into visions of another world, apparently Mars, and "The Country of the Blind" (1904), a parable about an El Dorado-like region in the Andes inhabited by blind people and accidentally discovered by a sighted man. While coldly refuting the proverb about the one-eyed man being king among the blind, the story asserts the necessity of spiritual vision; blindness becomes not simply a clinical phenomenon but a metaphor for atrophied imagination and rigid dogmatism.

Of all Wells's short stories the most difficult to like are his "pure" fantasies — those tales which do not try to rationalize or theorize about mysterious events, but accept and develop a magical or weird or miraculous premise without the interference of rational skepticism. As a fantasist Wells is often too arch to be convincing and, in the absence of his customary visionary or speculative substructure, such stories as "The Flowering of the Strange Orchid" (1894), "The Magic Shop" (1903), and "The Truth About Pyecraft" (1903) lean heavily on labored attempts at whimsy, a poor substitute for the fantastic. In "The Valley of the Spiders" (1903) Wells is at his worst; the tale is an unassimilated mess of horror and allegory. An aroma of sexual sadism mingles with images of giant gelatinous spiders, and the whole is wrapped in clumsy political fantasy in which the nameless characters have labels such as "the master," "the little man," "the gaunt man," and "the half-caste girl."

But two fine short fantasies show off this seldom edifying side of Wells's fiction. In "The Story of the Late Mr. Elvesham" (1896) an old philosopher clings to life by spiking a liqueur with a magic powder which causes him to exchange bodies with young Mr. Eden. The premise is unabashedly fantastic, but the heart of the story is the brilliant rendering of the duality of body and personality. The description of Eden's gradual realization that he has awakened trapped inside the body of Elvesham, that he has in the space of one night become wrinkled, toothless, thin-voiced, cold-footed, sniffling, bleary-eyed, bony, skinny-fingered, loose-skinned, wracked with cough, and persistently and disablingly weary, while retaining all the desires and sensibilities and the lively consciousness of youth, is one of the triumphs of Wells's imagination, equal to some of the great passages in the longer scientific romances.

"The Man Who Could Work Miracles" (1898) eschews the horror of "Elvesham" and combines fantasy with farce in a way which, as in *The Invisible Man* (1897), avoids Wells's predilection for fantastic banality. Here a materialist and rationalist, Mr. Fotheringay, finds himself startlingly in possession of powers of mind over matter. The story follows the career of a man of slender intellect gifted with absolute power. Such power can be puckish in effect, as when Fotheringay irritably tells a constable to go to Hades and quickly finds himself alone. But it may be cataclysmic unless harnessed by a modest sense of human limits and wielded with a vigilant presence of mind. When Fotheringay tries to duplicate Joshua's feat of making the sun stand still, he neglects to will the suspension of the consequences of such an interruption of the natural rhythm of the planet. Instantly the Earth ceases to rotate on its axis and, in strict obedience to the laws of inertia, every person and thing on Earth is whirled forward into annihilation. In the midst of the chaos he has casually wrought, Fotheringay conceives "a great disgust of miracles" and ends his career with two simultaneous and final wishes: to lose his thaumaturgical gift once and for all, and to let everything revert to the way it was just before he discovered his powers. Thus the jinni is rebottled, the damage is undone, and the story's ending repeats the opening conversation of the tale. As a work of fantasy, this makes a thoroughly absorbing and satisfying updating of the classic fairy tale of miraculous power, the story of Aladdin from *The Arabian Nights*. And (how Wells would have approved this unintended application of his tale!) later readers can hardly help but find in "The Man Who Could Work Miracles" a cautionary fable for the nuclear age.

While much of Wells's short fiction was written with the left hand while he worked on the longer scientific romances, the two novellas and perhaps a dozen short stories belong to his major work. Even many of the flawed stories, despite the evident haste of their composition, display Wells's inventiveness and thoughtfulness and confirm his stature as modern science fiction's one genius. Readers have often bypassed his short fiction on the assumption that it is inferior to his novels. But "A Story of the Days to Come" is in many respects more convincing and more consistent than its novelistic sequel, *When the Sleeper Wakes* (1899). The issues of size and scale and the management of technology Wells raises in "Filmer" are treated in more detail, but more diffusely and with less power, in *The Food of the Gods* (1904). And *In the Days of the Comet* (1906) is a bloated version of "The Star," and interesting only in those passages which imitate the methods of the short story. Wells's best stories do not have to be studied merely as dry runs for the novels or patronized as the hackwork of a writer notorious for overproduction. Among the works of short fiction are many authentic and even distinctive achievements of Wells's resourceful imagination.

Robert Crossley

Sources for Further Study

Criticism:

Bergonzi, Bernard. *The Early H. G. Wells: A Study of the Scientific Romances*. Toronto: University of Toronto Press, 1961, pp. 46-61. Bergonzi looks at Wells's early stories as stepping stones to his later thematic concerns.

Costa, Richard H. *H. G. Wells*. New York: Twayne, 1967. Costa views Wells's short stories as microcosms for his social thought.

Gill, Stephen. *Scientific Romances of H. G. Wells*. Cornwall, Canada: Vesta, 1975. Gill examines the relationship of Wells's short stories to his novels in the areas of plot and theme.

Williamson, Jack. *H. G. Wells: Critic of Progress*. Baltimore: Mirage, 1973. The short stories, like the novels, are vehicles for Wells's social criticism. Williamson examines the stories from this perspective.

THE SHORT FICTION OF H. P. LOVECRAFT

Author: H. P. Lovecraft (1890-1937)
Type of work: Short stories

Stories dealing with such themes as atavism, vampirism, and intrusion from space, which evoke and sustain powerful and somber moods

Although the stories which have won Howard Phillips Lovecraft his greatest acclaim are those in which he most strongly develops his conceptually fascinating Mythos — his cosmic myth cycle of frightful primal gods like Yog-Sothoth and Cthulhu — still, one finds brilliantly crafted tales among those works whose level of involvement in the Mythos is little or none. The purpose here is to consider briefly a few of the best such tales.

One of Lovecraft's most interesting and interpretable stories is "The Outsider," an early tale (1921). This piece, told in the first person, presents a narrator having lived for time untold in a decrepit and bone-strewn castle surmounted by a tall, dark tower whose heights the narrator resolves to scale from within, since he has never seen the light of sun or moon above the groves of gargantuan trees surrounding his morbid chambers. Ascending the dizzying heights in grim resignation by precarious handholds, the Outsider finally reaches an upper tower chamber and from there ventures forth into the stunningly moonlit upper world. He wanders to an ivied edifice ablaze with light and filled with the sounds of merriment within. Stepping inside, he beholds the merry company suddenly turn into a terrified, fleeing herd; when they have gone, the Outsider espies a revolting creature, evidently the cause of the terror, standing in an arched doorway. The creature is ghoulishly foul and putrescent, "a leering, abhorrent travesty on the human shape." The Outsider and this monster outstretch a hand and a loathsome paw to touch each other — whereupon the Outsider finds himself touching *"a cold and unyielding surface of polished glass."*

Possible interpretations are many. One readily sees some autobiographical touches, and it is easy to see Lovecraft himself as the Outsider. The author took an active interest in the worldly affairs of his time, but in some ways, with reference to his preference for the morals and values and literary standards of the eighteenth century, he was something of "a stranger in this century," as the tale's central figure is said to be. One should note, however, that Lovecraft was not a social recluse; affable and outgoing when circumstances permitted, he simply found relatively few people with whom he shared primary interests.

Moving from the personal to the collective level, one may see the Outsider as symbolic of humankind in general. In particular, it is irresistible to think of the Outsider's quest as the epic quest common to all people: the quest to find one's Self and to harmonize all the aspects of the human psyche. Jung's view of the psyche especially comes into play here. Obviously, the great castle with its tower can be seen as suggesting the levels of the psyche, from the collective unconscious at its deepest levels (where the Outsider initially dwells, at the archetypal level) to the tower chamber or higher personal unconscious (the realm of dreams) to the upper world of light: the conscious mind. When the Outsider seeks fulfillment in the shining banquet hall, he confronts the ultimate, intolerable horror: the dreaded Shadow, which he must recognize as himself. One may endlessly enlarge upon such an interpretation by picking through the story's details. For example, the Outsider finds the shining castle "maddeningly familiar" and finds that the faces within bring up "incredibly remote recollections" — because these things strike profound archetypal chords in him too deep for conscious expression.

This tale, written during the early artistic period in which Lovecraft was most infatuated with Poe, has a Poe-like ring to it, as does another early story, "The Rats in the Walls" (1923). This latter tale is one of atavism and ancestral curse, thematically related to Poe's "The Fall of the House of Usher" and Hawthorne's *The House of Seven Gables*. The narrator, an American named Delapore, buys and restores Exham Priory, the ancient seat of his ancestors in England. The priory is built upon a Roman subcellar, and the Roman substructure in turn has rested upon earlier Druidic ruins. Lovecraft here indulges a fondness for continuity with the past, and indeed it is such continuity which lends the tale its ultimate horror. Delapore finds that his family has had a sordid past, though at first details are scarce. In the priory, he is plagued by the noise of rats in the restored walls, moving in a beckoning way ever downward through the structure and heard only by himself and the cats. Upon investigating the subcellar, as he seems fated to do, with his companion, the "plump" Edward Norrys, he finds a "twilit grotto" beneath which corresponding to a prophetic dream which has haunted him, and evidence that his family has contained a long-standing cannibal cult whose history reaches back to times immemorial. The continuity of the tradition reaches to the very present, for Delapore (who has changed his name back to the earlier form de la Poer) undergoes a barbaric regression and is found "crouching in the blackness over the plump, half-eaten body of Capt. Norrys." The closing lines of the tale sound very Poesque.

In this story, Lovecraft was already beginning to practice a narrative restraint which would come to be a hallmark of his craft. It is one thing to "tell all" in describing a horror, but quite another thing to have the wisdom *not* to do so. For example, when one of Delapore's dreams is described as "a vision of a Roman feast like that of Trimalchio, with a horror in a covered platter," the reader is left to imagine the contents of the platter, and the effect is much more potent than any specific description would have been.

This tale, like "The Outsider," has its obvious Jungian flavor, with the descent into the "twilit grotto" strongly suggesting a descent into the deep collective unconscious. Even beyond the charnel grotto there are further, darker regions, suggesting the ever-unplumbed depths of the psyche.

During his brief residence in New York, Lovecraft in 1924 wrote another tale of an unwholesome house, this time setting the story in his own native Providence, Rhode Island. "The Shunned House" begins with a detailed history of the house (a real house, 135 Benefit Street in Providence) and a genealogy of the fictional Harris family which has inhabited it — Lovecraft's style in doing this reminds one of Hawthorne. There is a legend about the actual house in Benefit Street to the effect that it was built on the site of the burial ground of a French Huguenot family, whose lingering influence caused a woman living there to scream in French from an upstairs window in an onset of madness. Lovecraft absorbs this legendry nicely, elaborating upon it in a highly imaginative way.

In the story, the problem is that people have wasted away and died in the house in alarming numbers, over several generations, as if something intangible were draining off their vitality; thus Lovecraft employs a kind of vampirism motif here, *sans* fangs. The cellar of the house is particularly unwholesome, with its fungous dampness and suggestions of the shape of a huddled human form in the mold of the dirt floor. The narrator and his uncle Elihu Whipple finally resolve to vanquish the cellar presence beneath their feet, and in the ensuing encounter the uncle is seized by the vapory presence; in a kaleidoscopic vortex of impressions he is melted to the floor, his face taking on appearances, one after another, of those whose life force the presence has consumed and grown strong on during the house's morbid history. It is left to the narrator to dispatch the enormous, gelatinous mass beneath the cellar floor. The story is a triumph of skillfully woven atmosphere and mood. The reader can from the beginning almost feel and smell the fetid cellar's dampness and sickish air of decay. This accumulated repulsion turns to outright loathing as the final descriptions come telling of the ill-fated uncle "who with blackening and decaying features leered and gibbered," and of the "semi-putrid congealed jelly with suggestions of translucency" which the narrator glimpses beneath the cellar's foul black earth. "Some secrets of inner earth are not good for mankind. . . ." If ever an author strove for and achieved a sustained mood of dark repellence, Lovecraft did so with "The Shunned House," and the mood is woven not against a background of cobwebbed, nighted crypts of some sinister and ancient European village steeped in peasant superstition and rumored horror, not in a setting that itself would do half of an author's work for him, but rather against a background of sunlit, familiar streets on Lovecraft's own College Hill in Providence, in the twentieth century.

But an even greater mood-study was to follow in 1927. "The Colour out of Space" has been widely acclaimed as a truly great story, winning a triple-star rating in the O'Brien *Best Short Stories of 1928* and being since that time widely reprinted and translated into many languages. This was, in fact, Lovecraft's own favorite among his stories — he was always highly self-critical, and once said that, of all his short stories, only this story and the earlier "Music of Erich Zann" (1921) really pleased him.

"The Colour out of Space" is a monumental study in mood-painting and the sustaining of somber atmosphere. The theme is progressive, ineluctable decay — a creeping, transfixing death from space which, the reader knows, will engulf everyone within its reach, and about which nothing can be done. The tale is set in a brooding countryside reflective of rural western Massachusetts; the reservoir to be built, ultimately to cover over the horrors which have transpired, is an echo of the then-current plans to construct Quabbin Reservoir by flooding an entire valley and several towns, plans of which Lovecraft must have known.

In this tale, a meteorite falls upon the farm of Nahum Gardner. Its material baffles the scientists who examine it, and peculiar things begin to happen as the months pass. There seems to be a sort of poison in the soil. Plants blossom forth in strange, unearthly colors ("insolent in their chromatic perversion"), afterward turning brittle and gray, and crumbling. This diseased condition later affects the farm animals, and finally the people, who go mad and ultimately crumble like the plants and the livestock. Lovecraft displays his prowess not only at the description but also at descriptive restraint, often stopping short of telling all the details, so that the reader's imagination must come into play. Of the diseased swine, for example, he discloses only that "their eyes and muzzles developed singular alterations," alterations which we are left to ponder, while in the cows there are certain "atrocious collapses." Lovecraft builds the mood of decay and desolation stronger and stronger throughout, right up to the point where the "colour" from space departs, but leaves a vestige of itself to linger in the noisome Gardner well, around which only the gray and powdery "blasted heath" will remain to mark where a farm and a family once prospered.

With this tale, Lovecraft has proven that even in the telling of the most loathsome horrors, there can be beauty of language. The term "blasted heath" occurs both in Shakespeare's *Macbeth* and Milton's *Paradise Lost*, and in fact there are surprising echoes of Milton in the tale's beautifully crafted opening paragraph, which begins

West of Arkham the hills rise wild, and there are valleys with deep woods that no axe has ever cut. There are dark narrow glens where the trees slope fantastically, and where thin brooklets trickle without every having caught the glint of sunlight.

It is striking to compare this passage with lines 132-141 of "Il Penseroso" by Milton:

. . . me, Goddess, bring
To archéd walks of twilight groves,
And shadows brown that Sylvan loves
Of pine or monumental oak,

> Where the rude ax with heavéd stroke
> Was never heard the nymphs to daunt,
> Or fright them from their hallowed haunt.
> There in close covert by some brook,
> Where no profaner eye may look,
> Hide me from day's garish eye. . . .

It is appropriate to find such worthy poetic echoes in "The Colour out of Space," because that tale is a sensitive "mood poem" from beginning to end. It illustrates that, however interesting Lovecraft's strongly "Mythos" tales may be, one does not have to confine oneself to them to experience the greatness of Lovecraft's creativity.

Donald R. Burleson

Sources for Further Study

Criticism:

Bradley, Marion Zimmer. "Two Worlds of Fantasy," in *Haunted: Studies in Gothic Fiction*. I (June, 1968), pp. 82-85. Bradley examines literary influences on Lovecraft's fiction. He dismisses Poe as a major factor.

Gehman, Richard B. "Imagination Runs Wild," in *New Republic*. XVII (January, 1949), pp. 16-18. Gehman examines Lovecraft's themes and establishes him along with H. G. Wells as the first notable American science fiction writer of the modern era.

Solon, Ben. "Lovecraft on the Doorstep," in *Haunted: Studies in Gothic Fiction*. I (June, 1968), pp. 87-88. Solon singles out "The Thing on the Doorstep" as Lovecraft's finest story.

Wilson, Colin. "The Vision of Science," in his *The Strength to Dream: Literature and the Imagination*. London: Gollancz, 1962, pp. 94-117. Wilson devotes most of his attention to Lovecraft in a discussion which attempts to juxtapose science fiction and realism.

Reviews:

Galaxy. XV, December, 1957, p. 102.

Kliatt Paperback Book Guide. V, April, 1971, p. 2.

Luna Monthly. XXXIX, July–August, 1972, p. 37.

Magazine of Fantasy and Science Fiction. XLI, July, 1971, pp. 75-76 and *XXIV, January, 1963, pp. 48-50.*

1978

THE SHORT FICTION OF HARLAN ELLISON

Author: Harlan Ellison (1934-   )
Type of work: Short stories

A critical appraisal of one of science fiction's most biting satirists

One of American science fiction's most honored writers, Harlan Ellison is perhaps best known for his contributions to the field as an editor and for his persistent refusal to be labeled a science fiction writer. His series of anthologies beginning with *Dangerous Visions*, (1967) provided impetus for a major shift in science fiction styles and subjects, but Ellison himself seems to prefer the term "fantasy" as a more inclusive label, if indeed a label is needed at all for the variety of fictions he has produced since his earliest publications. One thing is certain: his published work constitutes a most underrated body of literature. With one or two exceptions, his stories have received attention only in reviews and publishers' journals. A serious critical appraisal of his major short fiction is overdue, but is made difficult by Ellison's own repeated encouragement of blurred distinctions between fantasy and reality, autobiography and fiction, himself and the characters he creates.

Ellison's characters are complex. Many of them, particularly in the later stories, are tormented, ironic, sardonic — images of men whose persistent hopes for order, sanity, and purpose in human existence have been repeatedly betrayed by the nightmare that is reality. Occasionally such characters seem to function as spokesmen for the philosophy of the absurd. On one hand, some works reflect a Sartrean sense of human entrapment in a hell of one's own making. "Are You Listening?" (in *Ellison Wonderland*) and "I Have No Mouth and I Must Scream" (in the collection of the same title) reflect this point of view. On the other hand, some works evoke the image of Camus' Sisyphus, as man, helpless against an omnipotent and impersonally malicious force, struggles endlessly to be heard despite the certainty of defeat and the frustration of being doomed to perform a hopeless task over and over again. "Silent in Gehenna" (in *Approaching Oblivion*) suggests a variation on his common existential theme.

If one mode of writing characterizes Ellison's work more than any other, that mode is probably satire. In an irrational and probably cruel universe, a mocking and self-conscious gadfly posture suggests an affinity for the genre given its name by the Roman poet Juvenal. Ellison's stories, like Juvenalian satire, frequently comment sardonically on the insanity of current happenings, with the author in the role of the prophetic just man engaging in scathing social criticism. The worlds of Ellison's fiction frequently resemble hells, and often are named as such by the characters who inhabit them. They are worlds characterized by disease, ugliness, decay, and death, or a continuance of life more horrible in its aspect than death itself. Hope is fragile in such worlds, and

Ellison writes of it at times with lyrical and haunting beauty.

The tendency to social commentary manifests itself very early in Ellison's prose, and develops through the years with increasing bitterness of tone and correspondingly darker humor. Themes in *Ellison Wonderland* include the constancy of basic flaws in human nature, the tendency to be molded rather than to control one's surroundings, and the consequences of failure to distinguish between appearance and reality. Here Ellison treats them with fairly light humor. In "Commuter's Problem," for instance, suburbanite John Weiler, mistakenly thinking he is going to his office on Lexington Avenue, blindly follows a group of interstellar commuters, including his neighbor Clark DaCampo (really an alien named Helgorth Labbula) to the planet Drexwill. Here he finds an overcrowded urbanized world for which Earth is secretly a bedroom community. The planet's Head Auditor, unable to return Weiler for fear the secret will be discovered, allows him to plead for his life. Weiler, deciding he hates the suburban rat race, asks to stay. Ironically, on Drexwill he adopts in essence exactly the manner of life he claimed to despise on Earth — credit cards, rent, and rushing to get to work included. Weiler clearly represents the type of man who carries his flaws with him everywhere, never becoming conscious of them and hence never capable of change. In the same collection, "The Forces That Crush" (which appeared originally in *Amazing Stories* under the title "Are You Listening?") is about relentless pressure to conform. Its main character, Albert Winsocki, molds himself to others' demands and expectations so completely that he becomes quite literally invisible. Unlike others who accept this status, seeing in it their only chance to control, he fights to be noticed again, and survives chiefly in his annoying humming of the fight song "Buckle Down, Winsocki, Buckle Down."

Three stories in this collection, explicitly concerned with failure to distinguish between appearance and reality, seem to have been prompted at least partly by Ellison's experiences as a Hollywood scriptwriter. In "All the Sounds of Fear," actor Richard Becker slips horribly into faceless insanity; his last words (uttered from his cell in a mental institution) are a tormented cry for light. Becker's inability to distinguish himself from the roles he has created is a metaphor for the loss of self-identity forced on one by a culture in which everyone rushes headlong toward sameness. In "The Sky is Burning," Earth is the dead-end of the Universe for a race of godlike creatures, their jumping-off point for the lemming-like suicide by one generation which precedes the maturation of the next. The knowledge, forcibly inflicted on men with an insatiable urge to roam and rule, that they are not masters of the universe, precipitates the suicide of some of the world's greatest minds and leaves the narrator himself shaken and helpless, clutching a bottle of sleeping pills. In "The Silver Corridor" two megalomaniac theoreticians duel to the death by means of projected illusions from their own imaginations, dying together at the moment each admits he might have been wrong. All three stories catechize their audience on the dangers of a false view of reality and particularly on the hazards of centering one's existence on a mistaken view of oneself.

In spite of the harsh view of existence implied in such stories, the collection does not lack for representations of hope and love. One such piece, "Nothing For My Noon Meal," shows a man stranded on an airless, darkened, desert world where nothing grows except the Fluhs, plantlike beings who supply him with oxygen drawn from deep within the planet's surface, but who exact in return a horrifying disfigurement of his face, which mutates to form an airsack. He has survived the crash of his ship, the death of his wife, and the harshness of the world he has named Hell. Believing that the Fluhs are dying, when a rescue ship arrives he nearly is tempted to leave, but he hears his dead wife promise him her eternal closeness and the hope of renewal. He offers instead to help young people sent to the planet study the mechanism which enabled him to survive and concludes with the tenuous suggestion that the world he had named Hell might in fact be closer to its opposite. The story is a hymn to the indomitability of human spirit. "In Lonely Lands" shows Pederson, a blind and dying space traveler who, having settled down to end his days on the planet Jilka, is befriended by an alien called Pretrie. Pretrie remains his companion, constant to death, refusing to allow his friend to face even "the Grey Man" alone. Pederson and Pretrie are tributes to the saving power of that friendship which enables human beings to face the void in quiet resignation.

Paingod contains Ellison's most famous story, probably the most frequently anthologized one, and certainly one of his best: "'Repent, Harlequin!' Said the Ticktockman." From the American obsession with time and schedules, Ellison extrapolates a not-distant-enough future in which being late too often becomes a capital offense. On one level, the theme is extremely unsubtle. For readers who need such matters made obvious, Ellison cites a passage from Thoreau's "Civil Disobedience" which claims that men best serve government by resisting it. On another level, however, Ellison makes a subtle point about the nature of such heroism. His hero, Everett C. Marm, who persistently refuses to fit into the schedules set for him and who creates disturbances and diversions masquerading in a clown suit as "the Harlequin," is a hero only by default. He resists the system because he is incapable of fitting into it. The Harlequin is an engaging character, dimpled, humorous, and buoyant. By contrast, his antagonist, the Ticktockman, who holds the power of life and death over the citizens of the future, is a shadowy, hated, masked figure who comes off ultimately as rather ineffectual. His equilibrium is sufficiently disturbed by his mask-to-face encounter with Harlequin that he himself arrives three minutes late for work, throwing the master schedule off and creating the first rift which can ultimately lead to the crumbling of the system. Everett/Harlequin is destroyed, brainwashed in an Orwellian Coventry, but the point is made. The *status quo* can be altered. No treatment of the story on this level, however, can re-create the delightful spontaneity it achieves through Ellison's easy juggling with time sequence, careful blend of formal and racy diction, and exuberant images which include at one point a happy rainbow of jelly beans dropped into the mechanism of a slidewalk. The story makes some serious points with a light grace and humor that are its most engaging characteristics.

I Have No Mouth and I Must Scream displays an avowed intention on Ellison's part to shake his audience into a vision of reality which is far more explicitly cynical and hopeless than that embodied in *Ellison Wonderland*. These stories assault the intellect with harsh visions of present and future that are emotional rather than intellectual, prodding their audience in expectation of angry and revolted response. In "I Have No Mouth and I Must Scream," five characters are tortured in the bowels of the earth by AM, a sentient super-computer, in the aftermath of a computer-conducted war which has destroyed the rest of the human race. The strategy of satire in this piece, one of Ellison's most disturbing, revolves around a grimly humorous evocation of horrors. Every aspect of AM's torture is described in an almost lovingly detailed parody which suggests scriptural accounts of God's blessings to the chosen race. Ted, the narrator, notes that when AM sends manna, it tastes like boar urine, which they eat anyway. While the computer both blames humanity and tortures its prisoners out of hatred for its own eternal, immobile sentience, there is a hint that the characters choose to remain imprisoned rather than risk the unknown. As AM keys up for an attack, Ted suggests escape, but is rebuffed by Gorrister, who is resigned to the belief that AM has even worse horrors waiting for them outside. Eventually the characters seize the only opportunity for escape left to them: death. Ted sacrifices his own chance to die, instead killing Ellen, the only woman in the group. AM, in rage, transforms him into an obscene, slug-like monstrosity.

Ted's ironic role as a satiric character is clarified in the way he speaks of the others: Ellen, who provides sexual services for the men, is a slut; Benny, a gay theoretician and once a college teacher, has been transformed into a super-endowed, apelike idiot; Gorriste, who had been a typical 1960's-style social activist, is presented as an apathetic husk. And whatever depravation AM has visited on Nimdok is apparently unspeakable even in this story, which is not noted for being mealy-mouthed. Ted's character provides ironic counterpoint to our knowledge of the others, since his pronouncements are rendered untrustworthy by his own paranoia. The others hate him, he claims, because he is the youngest and the one AM has tampered with least. If it were not for the others, he whines, he might have a chance to escape; as it is he cannot combat the ill-will of all the others and AM too. The validity of his vision is undercut by Ted's own inability to see what AM has done to him, so that the entire story is little more than a grim jest.

While Ted in "I Have No Mouth and I Must Scream" is unaware of his own failing, Johnny Lee, the narrator of "Big Sam Was My Friend," is acutely aware both of his own personal failing and of a moral malaise in society which encourages and feeds on it. In this story Charlie, a likable character with a problem, is sacrificed — allowed to be lynched — so that his employer will make a buck. No one, not even his closest friend (the narrator), moves to help him until it is too late. Johnny Lee is left with the sickening realization that the circus by which they are employed is a moral failure, and that by allowing it to control him he has failed as well. He cannot evade the burden of guilt and so concludes by suggesting that Heaven, the world on which Charlie was hanged, is really more like Hell, a telling reversal of the conclusion to "Nothing For My Noon Meal."

The misery engendered by moral failure is the subject of other stories in this collection as well. In one of these nightmares, "Lonelyache," Paul, a man unable to love, is ultimately driven to suicide by the objectified hypocritical selfishness of himself and others. In another, "Delusion for a Dragonslayer," Warren Glazer Griffin, as he is crushed to death by a collapsing building, is offered one chance at a Heaven which includes the idealized woman of his dreams. But he succumbs to his own bestiality and becomes the very monster he must slay in order to be saved. One of the strongest stories in the collection is "Pretty Maggie Moneyeyes," which uses the flashy setting of a Las Vegas casino as a backdrop for a story of ultimate betrayal in the oldest of all con games. Maggie, a high-priced hooker, sells her body in a clawing and frenetic attempt to escape poverty until she dies of heart failure while playing a slot machine. The machine imprisons her soul; Maggie subsequently frees herself by trapping in her place Kostner, a down-and-out gambler, with the promise of love. He dies at the end of a winning streak on the silver-dollar machine which has befuddled the owners of the casino; the machine, which is deemed "unlucky" by its owners, is sent to be melted down to slag.

The Beast That Shouted Love at the Heart of the World reinforces the presentation in *I Have No Mouth and I Must Scream* of thinly fictionalized psychological autobiography and societal cautionary tales. "The Waves in Rio," the nonfiction introduction, makes Ellison's intention to adopt the conventional prophetic stance of the satirist explicit as he shouts a warning to humanity that it is responsible for its own salvation. He singles out writers as a group for irresponsibility, telling them that their refusal to look truly at the future may in fact deprive the human race of all its tomorrows. The stories present worlds which have failed to redeem themselves. "Phoenix," for instance, is an appropriately heavyhanded commentary on the circularity of history in which an Atlantean man who has failed at love discovers the radioactive ruins of New York rising out of the desert. He concludes that the stupidity which impels men to self-destruction is a constant. Hence the irony implicit in the title: the only thing in this world that is likely to be reborn from ashes is more ashes.

"A Boy and His Dog" seems to confirm a growing conviction that human personal relationships are doomed to ultimate sterility. Vic the boy, and Blood his dog, telepathic and symbiotic, have evolved a responsibility relationship which transcends the now-impossible hope for continuation of the human race through normal male-female relationships. All real love between the sexes is impossible. Women in devastated, post-World War III New York are objects who exist only to be raped and murdered. There are no children, only sexless monster-mutants who are ripped like Macduff from their mothers' wombs and destroyed immediately. Into this violent world comes Quilla June, a teenage emissary from an underground Midwestern town whose inhabitants have chosen to freeze themselves in time at the turn of the century. Their inability to breed male children threatens their survival; sterility is a metaphor for the bloodless unreality of their imitation existence. Quilla June has been sent to trap Vic into stud service for the "downunder." He is tricked into thinking that he loves her, and is trapped downunder; he escapes with her assistance (she helps him kill her father) only to realize that she is still merely using him. Eventually he comes to his senses and teaches her the real meaning of love in a universe gone mad by sacrificing her to provide food for Blood, the only character in the story who is capable of sustained fidelity. The "happy ending," with boy and dog reunited, is on one level, at least, bitter satire. Until they die, Vic and Blood will wander from city to city, repeating the futile round of searching for food and violent sex that characterizes their present existence. Ultimately, there is no place for them to go.

The story is not entirely without hope. Blood can genuinely care for Vic, and Vic seems to learn to care for him. What is most disturbing, aside from the violent caricature of our world that the story presents, is the suggestion that human love is insufficient to rescue us from degradation, and may in fact lead us into it. The suggestion is found elsewhere in this collection, in "Shattered Like a Glass Goblin." Rudy Boekel, a young man who had been drafted, then released on a medical discharge, searches for Kris, the girl he loves, in the house of drug addicts into which she has moved. She will not go back with him, but the eleven inhabitants of the house allow him to move in because he can talk to police and others on the outside for them. His parents send him money which ensures the inhabitants of the house survival of a sort; he insists on Kris as repayment. But Kris pushes him to try drugs as well, and eventually they destroy him as they have all the other inhabitants of the house, turning them into predatory monsters and victims. The culmination of Rudy's faulty attempt at loving is his own destruction.

The failure of human love is a recurrent theme in the stories of *Approaching Oblivion*. In what seems, on the surface at least, to be an ultimate rejection of hope, the author depicts a world which is killing itself, is aware of what it does, and will not stop. All that remains of the social consciousness is mocking laughter; the author's bequest is the disease of despair. The stories in this collection reflect a growing awareness of isolation not merely as an existential condition but as a matter of conscious choice. Not surprisingly, as the universe decays around the characters of these stories, an engaging sort of "whistling-in-the-dark" humor occasionally surfaces.

The narrator of "Cold Friend," Eugene Harrison, has died. He reawakens to a world which has shrunk to the confines of a three-block-square section of Hanover, New Hampshire, and which includes a hospital, a post office, and a pizza parlor. Eugene has never learned to make pizza. If this is hell, it is again a hell of the central character's own making. Like Albert Winsocki, Eugene has allowed himself to be trapped, this time by his own narrowness of vision. Unlike Albert, he decides that he prefers isolation to escape. Offered a chance at salvation by following out of the range of his own prescribed limits a woman he has hurt, Eugene stays put. He does, however, decide to teach himself to make pizza, which suggests that Ellison here has given up only on the human ability to love, not on its will to survive.

"Ecowareness" is a cautionary tale, a fairy story in which the Earth wakes up one morning, discovers it is having trouble breathing, and retaliates against its tormentors by swallowing a student who has thrown his candy wrapper in a gutter, frying fifty thousand Green Bay Packer fans in hot lava, drowning the Mormon Tabernacle Choir in a natural lake formed instantaneously on the site of the Hollywood Bowl, and dispatching a host of celebrities by fire, lightning, and earthquake. The fairy tale has a happy ending: the human race (particularly, Ellison implies, that portion of it living south of Canada, north of Mexico, and between the Atlantic and Pacific oceans) gets the message and cleans up its act, allowing Earth to enjoy a secure sleep once more. At the very end, the authorial voice intrudes with a sharp comment on the likelihood of such an event ever happening.

The theme of love's inadequacy echoes through two extremely poignant stories in this collection. In "Paulie Charmed the Sleeping Woman," a jazz musician's attempt to play Orpheus to his dead woman's Eurydice ends with the horror of what really returns from the grave. And in "One Life, Furnished in Early Poverty" the author returns as an adult, courtesy of a toy soldier he had buried as a child, to visit himself in his own childhood. He attempts to rescue his own future from heartache by forestalling some of the pain. Eventually, though, he realizes that if he remains in his own past long enough to help the boy he was, he will die. He must desert the child. In saying goodbye he suddenly realizes how much of the bitterness of his own past he had inadvertently caused himself. The time paradox illustrates the inability of love to rescue even oneself from the pain of existing.

A single story combines perhaps the greatest humor with no inconsiderable pathos. "I'm Looking for Kadak" presents Evsise the Zouchmoid, a blue Jew from the planet Zsouchmuhn, who undergoes enormous hardships in his search for Kadak, a man he despises but must seek anyway because one more male Jew is needed to make up a minyan, the required quorum of adult male Jews who must be present for any religious ceremony to be validly performed. Evsise is a skilled patterer in the tradition of the Jewish stand-up comic. He peppers his conversation with Yiddish curses funny enough to the audience in a normal setting but enough to cause humorous convulsions coming from a blue alien with eleven arms but quite a normal bifurcated behind. Evsise's adventures scouring his planet for the missing Kadak take him through a series of mishaps suggestive more of the comic sidekick in a quest narrative than its hero. In one such adventure he is ravished by a Zsouchmoid prostitute. (On a world in which females have sex by inserting their index finger into the navel of their partner, Evsise refuses to comment on the horrors engendered by a dirty fingernail.) Eventually Evsise finds the long-lost Kadak; he had undergone a series of transformations as a member of offbeat religious cults and finally metamorphosed into a butterfly. Unfortunately, he has only been a butterfly for ten years, and so is not old enough under Jewish law to participate in the minyan. But he manages to signal the men that the nine of them who remain, taken together with the Holy Ark itself, may make the quorum. Jews on this world as on our own are survivors, their customs and adherence to tradition providing them with the continuity to outlast even the death of a planet, as Ellison reminds us at the end. The minyan is necessary because the men are preparing to sit *shivah*, to say the prayers for the dead, for their homeworld which is to be destroyed, leaving them refugees in the universe.

One of the most topical stories in *Approaching Oblivion* is "Silent in Gehenna." It evokes clearly the mood of violent, radical protest in the late 1960's and early 1970's through its protagonist, Joe Bob Hickey. Left as an infant in a Midwestern orphanage in 1992, he has sought out trouble all his life. Now he revolts against a country in which even the universities are under complete control of the military-industrial complex. Injured after creating a disruption at the University of Southern California, he is cared for by a group of deformed tramps. All of them received their deformities in government laboraties, but all of them are blindly faithful to the government nonetheless. After attempting to interrupt the commencement exercises at the State University of New York at Buffalo, he is translated in a burst of golden light to a world where great, bulblike creatures who enslave smaller ones imprison him in a cage to spout his protest rhetoric endlessly and uselessly, as an eternal conscience who never causes change. The story is, perhaps, Ellison's version of the myth of Sisyphus: as Sisyphus rolls the stone up the hill only to have it crash to the bottom again, Joe Bob berates the bulb-creatures, who stop and beat their breasts and then go on beating their slaves. Conscience is not enough to cause change, the message runs; protest is futile, and essentially hypocritical.

The collection ends on a note of almost unbearable poignancy. "Hindsight: 480 Seconds" chronicles the last few moments before the Earth is destroyed by Vastator, a wandering planet whose collision course with the sun will cause a solar storm that sterilizes then vaporizes all life, and causes the seas to boil. The chronicler is Haddon Brooks, a poet who has volunteered and been chosen to stay behind as the rest of humanity, in a supreme survival effort, boards great Orion ships and moves out to the stars. He is to record the last moments of the world as a historical record for posterity. The world Brooks remains behind in when his wife and children board the ships is a world which dies as it ought to — naturally, after the race has achieved peace and harmonious mastery, and when people are capable of willingly taking the step out into the universe together. The story is a haunting elegy rather than a song of hope, its poignancy lying in stoic acceptance of the disparity between what is and what ought to be.

Deathbird Stories deals with worship in many aspects, as Ellison explores the myths which control and underlie the people his works display. As might be expected, Ellison's gods, like his humans, range from the predatory to the sardonic to the beautiful. "The Whimper of Whipped Dogs" is based on news accounts of the brutal murder of Kitty Genovese in New York while dozens of onlookers watched from the windows of their apartment buildings and did nothing. Ellison posits a brutal god of the city whose demand is blood sacrifice. There is no middle ground: one either worships fully and willingly or becomes a victim on the sacrificial altar. Into this world enters neophyte Beth O'Neill, a former Bennington dance major who now records choreography for a dance company. She attempts to remain neutral even after having witnessed, along with her neighbors, the stabbing murder of Leona Ciarelli. Naïvely, she believes it is possible to meet the city on its own terms without worshipping its demon god. She nearly becomes a sacrificial victim herself. The ultimate lesson is clear: worship is the price for freedom from fear.

"On the Downhill Side" echoes the terrible lyrical beauty of "Hindsight: 480 Seconds." It is essentially affirmative, dealing with the power of love to save. Paul, the man who has loved too much, and Lizette, a woman who never loved at all, are offered, after death, one final chance at life if they can unite their spirits into one completely reconciled being capable of loving neither too much nor too little. The theme of this story embodies a message contained in much of the work which precedes it. Excess of love and want of it are equally destructive. If Paul and Lizette fail at this chance, he will wander forever, accompanied only by his unicorn. She will be devoured by bestial monster-gods who mock the God of Love that gave them their final chance. Lizette resists union and is trapped in a ring of flame on the altar of the gods waiting for their feast. As an act of love, Paul's unicorn leaps the flames and sacrifices itself in Lizette's stead, allowing the two souls to join with the promise of rebirth in a happier future. Success in love is possible, but only at terrible cost.

"Deathbird" is Ellison's most obvious treatment of the concept of myth, an attempt to question the answers some posit for universal concerns. It is a rewritten Genesis, with a Satan (Snake) who is really the protector of Adam (Nathan Stack). The structure of the story is complex, with self-conscious interludes of catechism-type questions interrupting the story of Adam/Nathan Stack who is left to the control of a figure who is apparently the Judeo-Christian God only as the result of failed negotiations by the inhabitants of distant stars. Snake (Satan) is the one caretaker of man that these beings are permitted to leave behind. Snake ultimately brings Stack the knowledge that the earth is in pain and wishes to be destroyed. He remembers its history and gathers the strength to put it to sleep, recognizing Snake for what he is. Dira the Caretaker clasps hands with his friend at last, and waits for the descent of the Deathbird to the earth.

This story is at least partly a myth which accounts for the death of the earth through man's progression toward self-knowledge and which turns upside-down a traditional view of a kind and loving God. One interlude, an apparently nonfiction passage in which the author describes the death of his beloved dog Ahbhu, seems to reinforce the feeling of "A Boy and His Dog" that human loving relationships are ultimately ineffectual. On a deeper level, it suggests, as do several of the earlier stories, that real friendship is that which enables us to confront even death with resignation. Dira and Stack are the counterparts of Ellison and Ahbhu, and perhaps of Pretrie and Pederson from an earlier story. They are affirmations that love is possible, even at the very end of all things.

Ellison's work is varied in subject, range, and intensity. He is capable of lashing satire, bitterness, and occasionally lyrical beauty. His themes tend to revolve around the failure of people adequately to control the circumstances of their own environment or the failure of people to care enough for themselves, others, and the world to try. His style tends heavily toward a brash rawness that seems to belie the sophistication with which his stories are constructed, although his use of language, when carefully examined, yields poetic richness. Particularly, he seems to enjoy stretching the limits of the printed page, creating, for example, visual and nonverbal images of a computer mind, or attempting to catch, in a whirl of words and letters, the moment of death. He is occasionally didactic, sometimes difficult to accept, but always passionately involved.

Carol D. Stevens

Sources for Further Study

Criticism:

Brady, Charles J. "The Computer as a Symbol of God: Ellison's Macabre Exodus," in *Journal of General Education*. XXVIII (1976), pp. 55-62. The image of the computer is discussed as it relates to various Ellison short stories.

Delap, Richard. "Harlan Ellison: The Healing Art of Razorblade Fiction," in *Magazine of Fantasy and Science Fiction*. LIII (1977), pp. 71-79. Delap outlines the main ideas behind Ellison's stories.

Slusser, George E. *Harlan Ellison: Unrepentant Harlequin*. San Bernardino, Calif.: Borgo, 1977, Slusser treats in depth Ellison's science fiction.

White, Michael D. Ellison's Harlequin: Irrational Moral Action in Static Time," in *Science-Fiction Studies*. IV (1977), pp. 161-165. White treats with one of Ellison's most famed works: *"Repent, Harlequin!" Said The Ticktockman*.

THE SHORT FICTION OF HERMAN MELVILLE

Author: Herman Melville (1819-1891)
Type of work: Short stories

Stories examining the destructive aspects of science and technology

In his review of Hawthorne's *Mosses from an Old Manse*, Melville wrote of feeling a "shock of recognition" upon reading Hawthorne, as if they were parts of the same soul; and later, when they actually met, they became intense friends for a time and spent many evenings discussing literature and art. Under Hawthorne's influence, Melville rewrote *Moby Dick*, turning it from a realistic adventure narrative into a symbolic study of the "mystery of iniquity," and a number of his short stories also show the influence of Hawthorne, especially of Hawthorne's science fiction stories.

Moby Dick itself, if not precisely science fiction, has a number of ingredients of science fiction and fantasy. Most of the novel consists of a fantastic voyage. *The Pequod* never touches port, and in its isolation it becomes a microcosm. Furthermore, the possibility of tracking and finding one specific whale through the oceans of the world borders on science fiction. The encyclopedic presentation of cetological detail gives the novel a strong scientific keel, and the almost mythical whale comes close to qualifying as a bugeyed monster. When the *Pequod* moves into Antarctic waters, Moby Dick lures the hunters on to their destruction with his seemingly supernatural and constant spout; and Fedallah, Ahab's evil angel, plays Mephistopheles to the captain's Faust. And the increasing occurrence of omens that come true places the novel within the realm of tragic fantasy.

The *hubris* that is part of Ahab's tragic flaw is a recurring quality in the obsessed scientists of science fiction. Melville focuses on it in a short story called "The Bell-Tower." Set in Renaissance Italy, "The Bell-Tower" resembles some of Hawthorne's moral allegories about science. It is the story of the "unblest foundling," Bannadonna, a "mechanician" or scientist who constructs a campanile with both bell and clock that will be the tallest tower in the world, a new Babel. As the ultimate symbol of his mastery over nature, he is working secretly on a domino, a robot designed to strike the hour, but an invention more creature than machine, that should have "the appearance, at least, of intelligence and will." Melville had borrowed a copy of *Frankenstein* in 1849; but unlike Victor Frankenstein, Bannadonna does not try "to arrive at a knowledge of the source of life." Specifically rejecting the occult lore of Cornelius Agrippa and Albertus Magnus, whom Frankenstein studied, Bannadonna seeks no "germ of correspondence" between "the finer mechanic forces and the ruder animal vitality" that might empower him to create life. "With him, common sense was theurgy; machinery, miracle; Prometheus, the heroic name for machinist; man, the true God." Thus his pride, though Faustian, is not that of a medieval magician but of a Renaissance artist and scientist combined. Unlike Hawthorne's scientists (Aylmer, Ethan Brand, Dr. Rappaccini, Dr. Heidegger, and Dr. Grimshawe), who dabble in necromancy as much as they work with science, Bannadonna works within the realm of possibility. His laboratory has nothing of the magician's inner sanctum but is equipped with "plain vice-bench and hammer."

Nevertheless, he overreaches himself. When casting the great state-bell, he disregards warnings against its dangerous weight. The molten metals "bayed like hounds," terrifying the workmen, and when they balk at returning to their posts, Bannadonna strikes the "chief culprit" with his ladle and kills him. Like Benvenuto Cellini, whom Pope Paul III exonerated for a murder on the grounds that such an artist is "above the law," Bannadonna's homicide is excused on the grounds of "esthetic passion." But the magistrates continue to worry about the secret project with the shrouded figure of the domino and feel haunted by some unseen but living presence above them in the tower. One of them also observes that Una, the first of twelve sculptures that Bannadonna is carving to represent the hours, has a face like that of the deadly Old Testament judge Deborah, and that she seems to be looking with judgment at her maker.

The observation is prophetic, for Bannadonna's pride destroys him. True artist as much as mechanician, he becomes so absorbed in perfecting the final details of his sculpture of Una that he forgets he is in the path of the domino's hammer. Striking the hour, the robot crushes his skull, just as he had killed the workman; and the sliver of the workman's skull that was dashed into the molten metal fatally flaws the bell, which breaks from its moorings and crashes through the side of the tower to the ground. It is erected once more, but a year later, the entire tower is demolished by an earthquake. "So the blind slave obeyed its blinder lord; but in obedience slew him." As Frankenstein was destroyed by his monster, "so the creator was killed by the creature." And so Melville was one of the earlier writers to warn scientists of forbidden knowledge that can turn technology to terror and bring pride to a fall. In this, Bannadonna is akin to Aylmer, Ethan Brand, and Rappaccini, Hawthorne's scientists who distort science to their own perverse experiments and become guilty of the unpardonable sin of placing pride of intellect above love for humanity.

Leslie A. Fiedler includes "The Tartarus of Maids" in his anthology of science fiction, *In Dreams Awake*, but the tale only marginally qualifies. It is more fact than fiction, although it has an atmosphere of myth and fantasy in its fairy-tale-like narrative. In this it resembles Bunyan's *Pilgrim's Progress* and Hawthorne's legendlike moral allegories. Factually, it is one of the first (perhaps the first) criticisms in American literature of the excesses of the Industrial Revolution and the exploitation of labor.

The tale takes place in the 1850's, and already there exists a company town in which the women employees are wage slaves. Specifically, Melville is writing about a paper mill; though it is supposedly in Massachusetts, however, the narrator's trip there becomes a journey into another dimension, somewhat akin to Young Goodman Brown's night journey into the forest to attend a Black Mass. To reach the mill, he travels through a Romantically gloomy landscape that resembles the Rhineland, except that its Gothic atmosphere is American. He has to traverse bleak hills near Woedolor Mountain via a "Dantean gateway" called the Black Notch, through the "cloven walls" of which flows a red torrent named Blood River. Among the "Plutonian" hills is a hollow called "the Devil's Dungeon," where the whitewashed paper mill stands like a "whited sepulchre." This place "from which there is no escape" is a version of hell, the "tartarus" of the maids who toil there like Sisyphus or some other doomed soul from ancient mythology. Clearly this is not the routine factory in a standard company town but a haunted spot in a world of nightmare. Thus the visit becomes a fantastic tour through the Inferno.

Within the mill, everything looks as blank as the white paper being manufactured. Gaunt-faced girls seem to be feeding an "iron animal." When the narrator observes one girl working with rose-hued paper, the paper seems to have absorbed the blood from her cheeks and left her pallid. At another machine, a fair-browed girl prophetically seems to have exchanged features with a furrowed and wrinkled woman. No speech is allowed, and the human voice is replaced by the whirring of machinery. In anticipation of the debased Morlocks descended from workers in H. G. Wells's *The Time Machine*, or of the subterranean worker-slaves in Fritz Lang's film *Metropolis*, the people are dehumanized, almost robotized. "Machinery — that vaunted slave of humanity — here stood menially served by human beings." The abuses of science have made a monster, like Frankenstein's creature.

A dark-complexioned foreman, who resembles Hawthorne's satanic figures, assigns the visitor a guide, ironically named Cupid, to show him the employment of the passive and loveless maidens, whose pale cheeks seem to have been drained into the red chemicals of the water. The air they breathe is full of particles that are poisoning them just as surely as Rappaccini poisoned his daughter in Hawthorne's tale, and they are just as much prisoners, but without a garden. "So, through consumptive pallors of this blank, raggy life, go these white girls to death." A pair of them working with swordlike blades seem to be their own executioners. In a moment of insight, characteristic of Hawthorne, the narrator imagines all the uses to which the *tabula rasa* paper will be put, from registers of birth to death warrants. To him, machinery takes on the role of fate or doom; its movements have an "inevitability," a "metallic necessity," an "unbudging fatality," an "autocratic cunning" that fills him with dread. He imagines the faces of the girls ground through the cylinders and printed on the paper like the tormented face of Christ on Veronica's veil. Since the employers want steady workers twelve hours a day, six days a week, they employ no married women; all the employees are maids, doomed to a barren, sterile fate.

Later writers were to take up the cause of female workers exploited by self-righteous captains of industry; Stephen Crane, Theodore Dreiser, O. Henry, Frank Norris, and others showed the horrors of the sweatshop or the deprived lives of working girls. But they treated the subject realistically, whereas Melville's tale is filtered through fantasy, and the visit to the factory is a tour through hell. At the end, the narrator ascends to the outer world with a sense of relief as if returning from Hades, or as he calls it, Tartarus.

"Bartleby the Scrivener," the best-known of all of Melville's stories, is even more marginally science fiction, if it qualifies at all. There is no science involved, and the narrative is told in a realistic fashion. It is the grotesque tale of a pale copying clerk who comes from nowhere (except that he once worked in the Dead Letter office) and after an initial frenzy of output, soon refuses to copy, to run errands, to obey any orders, to leave the office, or to do anything except insist passively, "I prefer not to." The tale has reverberations of fantasy and the atmosphere of a nightmare. Despite the surface realism, Bartleby's existence is so bizarre that he seems almost alien to humanity, despite his employer's benediction at finding him dead in the prison called the Tombs, "Ah, Bartleby! Ah, humanity!" In his brief, starved, impenetrable existence, Bartleby has seemed not so much a member of the living as one of the living dead.

In insisting "I prefer not to," Bartleby may seek a freedom from conformity, from obedience to the will of others, but his complete withdrawal takes away both his freedom and his life. Melville prefaces "The Bell-Tower" with some lines of free verse which conclude,

> Seeking to conquer a larger liberty, man but
> extends the empire of necessity.

These lines apply to Bartleby as well, but they are aimed specifically at the scientists and technicians who, in the name of ambition or of progress, make man a slave to or a victim of his technology. In this sense, these stories, among the earliest in science fiction, anticipate the shape of things to come.

Robert E. Morsberger

Sources for Further Study

Criticism:

Fenton, Charles A. "The Bell Tower: Melville and Technology," in *American Literature*. XXII (1951), pp. 219-232. Fenton describes Melville's attitudes toward and use of technology through his interpretation of "The Bell Tower."

Fogle, Richard H. *Melville's Shorter Tales*. Norman: University of Oklahoma Press, 1960. Fogle provides an excellent introduction to Melville's shorter fiction since he deals with the major interpretations and critical concerns of each work.

Mason, Ronald. *The Spirit Above the Dust: A Study of Herman Melville*. London: John Lehmann, 1951, pp. 182-184. Most of Melville's short stories of major interest to science fiction students occur in the *Piazza Tales* which is discussed by Mason in a general way.

Poenicke, Klaus. "A View from the Piazza: Herman Melville and the Legacy of the European Subline," in *Comparative Literature Studies*. IV (1967), pp. 267-281. Poenicke analyzes the influences of various writers of European fantasy on the short fiction of Herman Melville.

THE SHORT FICTION OF J.G. BALLARD

Author: J. G. Ballard (1930-   )
Type of work: Short stories

A critical examination of J. G. Ballard's short stories that points to his preoccupation with personifying altered modes of experience

Aside from the collection of "condensed novels" known in Britain as *The Atrocity Exhibition* and in the United States as *Love & Napalm: Export USA*, J. G. Ballard's short fiction has been featured in fifteen collections, though there is a considerable overlap between them. These are: *The Voices of Time* (1962), *Billenium* (1962), *Passport to Eternity* (1963), *The Four-Dimensional Nightmare* (1963), *The Terminal Beach* (1964), *Terminal Beach* (1964), *The Impossible Man* (1966), *The Day of Forever* (1967), *The Disaster Area* (1967), *The Overloaded Man* (1967), *Vermilion Sands* (1971), *Chronopolis and Other Stories* (1971), *Low-Flying Aircraft* (1976), *The Best of J. G. Ballard* (1977), and *The Best Short Stories of J. G. Ballard* (1978).

Ballard is one of several authors who spent the early part of their careers writing for the British magazines edited by John Carnell — *New Worlds* and *Science Fantasy* — and who then went on to become important figures in the transfiguration of *New Worlds* in the mid-1960's. Ballard, in fact, invites identification as the key figure in the transfiguration since his work for Carnell seems in many ways to have heralded the revolution.

Ballard made a simultaneous debut in the two Carnell magazines with "Escapement" (1956) and "Prima Belladonna" (1956). The former is a story of gathering anxiety concerning a man who discovers that he is living the same segment of time over and over again, except that the segment is getting progressively shorter. The second is an exotic fantasy about a brief romance between a man who sells musical flowers and a singer "with insects for eyes," which ends when the man finds his mistress in the passionate embrace of one of his plants. Both stories contained what were to become recurrent motifs in Ballard's work: the dislocation of individuals from the everyday world, and romantic encounters confounded by the power of exotic dreams become real.

These two stories were quickly followed by "Build-Up" (1957), in which a human population of many trillions inhabits a completely enclosed world where a boy's quest for the free space of which he has dreamed comes inevitably to a frustrating conclusion. This introduces the characteristic theme of many Ballard stories: his protagonists are frequently haunted by dreams of some mysterious past, which exert a powerful psychological attraction. The price of following that attraction to fulfillment is in almost every case what we as observers would term a descent into madness, although there is a curious sense of triumph in those stories where such a resolution can, in fact, be attained. One of the most important observations to be made about Ballard's work is that stories in the former category outnumber stories in the latter quite considerably.

One of the most effective stories of fulfillment is "The Overloaded Man," in which a man undertakes the curious exercise of attempting to dissolve the world of phenomena and cast himself adrift in a universe of raw sensation. Other straightforward examples include "Now Wakes the Sea," whose protagonist drowns in a dream-ocean of the distant past, and "The Gioconda of the Twilight Noon," whose protagonist blinds himself in order that a hallucinatory visual experience should not be threatened by the sight of the real world. Opposed to these we find such stories of frustration as "Build-Up," "Manhole 69," in which three men undergo an experimental operation to remove their need for sleep, and which ends with their catatonic retreat from the perpetual confrontation with reality, and "Deep End," in which the last fish in the world is stoned to death, leaving the protagonist with no tangible link to his past.

This preoccupation with altered modes of experience — whether expressed as subjective hallucinations or as the objective consequences of environmental change — is central to Ballard's use of science fiction as a medium; and his main endeavor is the ironic examination of the processes of self-alienation which lead to the pursuit of these altered modes. In his outright fantasies, the result of the search for new experience is merely exotic, a purely cerebral or aesthetic exercise. In the course of his career, however, Ballard began to anchor the search solidly in the psychology of ordinary individuals, contrasting the lure of new experience with the mundane reality of the everyday world. Many of his stories of the mid-1960's represent this phase of his work — "The Delta at Sunset" and "The Impossible Man" are extra examples to set alongside "Now Wakes the Sea" and "The Gioconda of the Twilight Noon."

Later, the author argued that our own experience of the contemporary world is being drastically altered by the electronic media and the power of its images, and that we are being forced to undergo processes of adaptation not dissimilar to those which he had imagined consequent upon the environmental changes featured in such novels as *The Drowned World* and *The Drought*. This belief led to the phase of his career in which he produced the "condensed novels" and such novels as *Crash* and *High Rise*. The seeds from which these novels grew were sown in such short stories as "The Subliminal Man" whose protagonist comes slowly to realize the extent to which the consumer society in which he lives is maintained by psychological manipulation — and in a group of short stories which speculate about the psychological significance of the space program, ranging from "The Cage of Sand" (1962) through "A Question of Re-entry" (1963) to "The Dead Astronaut" (1968).

A key story in Ballard's gradual shift of focus is "The Terminal Beach," whose protagonist is searching for his particular fulfillment on the abandoned island of Eniwetok. The island is symbolic, first because its entire landscape is manmade, and second because of its association with the career of the atom bomb, a crucial element in the psychopathology of the modern world (both these symbologies are made explicit in the early pages of the story). This is perhaps Ballard's finest story; economical and devastating, it stands at the midway point between major phases of his career.

It is notable that as Ballard's work extends into the 1970's, not only does it become more and more involved with fragmented versions of the landscape of contemporary life, but the cold and frustrating endings once again tend to replace the endings of fulfillment. This is particularly clear in the stories collected in *Low-Flying Aircraft*.

The most frequent purely science fictional landscape used by Ballard is that of the otherworldly wilderness, which figures in "The Waiting Grounds" (1959), in "The Time-Tombs" (1963), and — by proxy — in "The Cage of Sand." Clearly, this landscape owes more to Ray Bradbury and the science fiction mythology of Mars than to astronomical discoveries about other worlds, and it serves primarily as a mediator between the various protagonists and the moments of cosmic vision which they achieve. The bitter irony of "The Cage of Sand" puts the infinite vistas opened up by "The Waiting Grounds" into their actual historical context, and provides something of a disenchanted commentary on the vaulting imagination of the genre.

Intermediate between the visionary moments of these two stories is the best of Ballard's early stories, "The Voices of Time" (1960), which is replete with such science fiction apparatus as genetically engineered monsters and enigmatic signals transmitted from distant galaxies. The signals are a countdown to the end of the universe, while the monsters are products of the genes wherein resides the potential future of life on Earth (much altered from its present state). The two protagonists face both prospects with a fatalistic calm; one is forced to capitulate as he is slowly claimed by eternal sleep, while the other is prevented from capitulating because he cannot sleep at all.

A similar landscape to the otherworldly wilderness is that of Vermilion Sands, the setting of "Prima Belladonna" and a whole series of later stories. Vermilion Sands is a decaying desert resort populated by eccentrics and bygone star-cults. The stories all feature mysterious, usually guilt-ridden women, who practice the various art forms of a culture which has unlimited technology to bend to the service of aesthetic whimsy. These stories — "The Cloud-Sculptors of Coral-D" (1967) and "Cry Hope, Cry Fury!" (1967) — represent Ballard at his most romantic as well as his most ironic. The best of the group is "Studio 5, the Stars" (1961), a synthesis of Greek myth and *Sunset Boulevard* in which the mysterious Aurora Day adopts extreme measures to woo the "poets" of Vermilion Sands away from their IBM Verse-Transcribers while trying to reenact the story of Melander and Corydon. Ballard does not get sufficient credit for his remarkably elegant wit, which is amply displayed here. A story similar in spirit to the Vermilion Sands stories, though not actually set there, is "The Sound Sweep" (1960), which is based on the premise that sounds leave emotionally influential residues and that subsonic music, which is felt but not heard, may be infinitely more subtle than our crude music.

Each of these sets of stories makes use of desolate landscapes as backdrops for elaborate psychodrama, but each is essentially artificial. From the earliest part of his career, however, Ballard realized that the concrete landscapes of modern cities could function in a similar fashion. Early stories such as "Build-Up," "Chronopolis" (1960), and "Billennium" (1961) make much of the claustrophobic crowdedness of city life, but "Chronopolis" does so only retrospectively, dealing as it does primarily with an abandoned and empty city, as desolate as any wilderness. The hero of the story finds the lost heritage of metropolitan life fascinating, but eventually finds a flaw in its psychological seductiveness. This theme is repeated much more explicitly and extravagantly in the novella "The Ultimate City" (1976) and in the later novels. Like the desert scenarios, the apparatus of civilization here becomes a display of the aridity of our inner life.

Ballard's chief interest has always been private experience: cherished hopes, guilt-fantasies, and aesthetic responses are the focal points of his stories. The environments of his stories are thus incarnations of private experience; the landscapes are primarily psychological ones. He has never tried to resist classification as a science fiction writer, but he is first and foremost a surrealist writer (and he sees the value of science fiction in terms of its role as the chief vehicle of contemporary literary surrealism). His essay "The Coming of the Unconscious" is a commentary on surrealism in art, but its definition of surrealism serves also as a definition of his own fiction.

Ballard's technique relies heavily not only on his use of landscape, but also on the curious attitude of passivity exhibited by his protagonists (especially those of "The Voices of Time" and "The Terminal Beach," though "The Overloaded Man" provides the paradigm). These characters cannot show surprise; they accept the discoveries they make with resignation: all that happens is confirmation, never revelation. This is because their environments and the events that happen there are already a part of them, and in acceptance lies the only possible harmony. Every Ballard protagonist (except in some of the earliest stories) is alone with his world, and social relationships, including romantic ones, can only provide an obstacle to adaptation. This is the "moral" of such disturbing mid-period stories as "The Delta at Sunset" and "Storm Bird, Storm Dreamer" (1966); and the same viewpoint has been starkly represented in a recent and particularly cruel short story, "The Intensive-Care Unit." It is this aspect of Ballard's work which more than any other seems to isolate him as a writer *sui generis*, for it represents a flat denial of the most cherished myth of our time — the supremacy of love as a means to salvation. This is something that many hardened cynics forbear to challenge, but Ballard is a particularly ruthless iconoclast (as witness "The Life and Death of God," which suggests that even if God existed we would have to abandon belief in him). If the phenomenal scope of his inventiveness were not adequate to establish the claim, the extremism of this particular line of thought would surely demonstrate that Ballard has as eccentric an imagination as any other contemporary writer.

Brian Stableford

Sources for Further Study

Reviews:

The Impossible Man:
Foundation. IV, July, 1973, pp. 55-56.
The Best Short Stories of J. G. Ballard:
Booklist. LXXV, December 1, 1978, p. 599.

THE SHORT FICTION OF JAMES TIPTREE, JR.

Author: James Tiptree, Jr. (Alice Sheldon)
Type of work: Short stories

A collection of stories involving the psychology and behavior of characters who must make important decisions under stressful conditions

James Tiptree, Jr., recognizes the inexpressible contradictoriness of human life. Her stories dramatize paradoxes of behavior that extend the reader's involvement with character and plot into philosophy and introspection. Stylistically they are spare, crackling with language stripped so that no energy is lost in the narrative thrust. Tiptree's control of her materials and her exceptional thematic coherence unify the effect of the stories. Though we may feel disoriented, thrust into alien environments, or ushered into endings that seem to leave no hope, we nevertheless may feel a sense of victory in the display of human potential that can contain such contradictions as Tiptree writes about and feel exhilarated by the intelligence that can integrate the clashing opposites.

One typical choice for Tiptree's characters, for example, is between pleasure and pain. In "Painwise," an Earthman who has been programed to feel no pain except when he touches down on his home planet chooses to endure an agonizing death on Earth rather than indulge in a joy ride around the galaxy with some hedonistic aliens. The urge to obliterate sensory reality in sensual excess is viewed skeptically by Tiptree; in "Mother in the Sky with Diamonds," the drug "phage" induces ecstacy and ESP but causes physical and ethical values to vegetate.

One of Tiptree's best stories, "The Girl Who Was Plugged In," tells of an ugly, deformed, humpbacked woman, P. Burke, who is given a chance to live again, as it were, in the beautiful teenage body of "Delphi," grown like a vegetable and controlled through the mind of P. Burke. Delphi becomes an instant international celebrity — and the power of identification being what it is, P. Burke becomes totally absorbed in her new life, forgetting the hideous reality behind the image. She also attracts the love of a handsome and rebellious son of a rich industralist, and they are subsumed in a dream of bliss for a while. But after inadvertently learning the truth and killing the thing he loves, the youth loses his idealism and is absorbed by the System.

The fragile membrane of dreams we spin to shield ourselves from unpleasantness is delusory, Tiptree warns. Nothing kills the idealistic impulse faster than the revelation of its incompatibility with reality. In "The Psychologist Who Wouldn't Do Awful Things to Rats," a scientist with humane impulses towards laboratory animals is lured by the King Rat, a Pied Piper in reverse, towards "the place where lost things go." Lost himself, alienated from his fellow scientists, the man tries to follow but balks at the last minute when he finds the ideal is not "real." Flip-flopping to the opposite extreme, he becomes a sadistic animal torturer, hiding behind the cloak of scientific respectability. He is one of Tiptree's many failures, an innocent who cannot live in the world as it is, but because he cannot live anywhere else, becomes the destructive thing he hates.

There is a side of human nature, it seems, that is destructive, that must be dealt with, not ignored. It is part of what makes us human, part of our capacity for growth. Three space travelers in "Houston, Houston, Do You Read?," transported into a future world of female clones, discover that the traditionally male, aggressive, fiercely individualistic side of human nature has been lost; the females' ideal is a peaceful harmony of consensus. But the price paid for the lack of strife has been that technological growth has come to a halt, and the capacity for empathy, for personal feeling, has been dulled. That is humanity's future, Tiptree implies, if we sacrifice the claims of individual desires in an attempt to avoid the discomfiting aspects of change.

Tiptree uses satire to arrive at the same moral in "I'll Be Waiting for You When the Swimming Pool Is Empty," the story of a young anthropology student of the future, off on a lark, who brings a primitive planet quickly into the space age. The author hilariously extrapolates the jargon and nuances of the current hip value systems, showing that even as now, there will be no easy answers to the basic metaphysical question "What do we do next?" that comes after all strife has been eliminated. Progress is entropic when the contradictoriness of human desires is muted.

The problem of entropy — what to do about the disintegrative tendency of time — is a major theme in Tiptree's work. It comes up in "I'm Too Big but I Love to Play," for example, in which an alien with an enormous energy field takes over various human bodies in an attempt to alleviate the pockets of disorderliness he finds on Earth. He is frustrated, however, by the inability of humans to communicate genuinely and thus reduce environmental disorder. As the head of a think tank he tries to untangle science — which is supposed to be reducing entropy by advancing knowledge — from its ties with selfish corporate interests. But the strain is too great, and the alien pops out of our space-time field, causing a massive implosion.

Can man then not live without entropy? Is his dream of overcoming death futile, even undesirable? The attempt to escape time's entropic jaws backfires in "Forever to a Hudson Bay Blanket," where through a time-jumping device, enabling one to exchange bodies for a few hours with one's own future self, a man dies in the short duration of his trip. Thus he never returns, paradoxically dying twice, once when old, once when young. The hope of mitigating the decrepitude of age by a few hours of youthful bliss results in the sacrifice of the better part of the man's life.

The two great paths out of the problem of entropy are the subjective and the objective. By the former, man transcends the world by withdrawing; by the latter, one builds bigger and better machines to conquer new frontiers. In

"And So On, And So On," Tiptree rejects the former for its narcissism (a civilization based on dreams ends up devouring its own young) and the latter for the sensory limits it accepts. Neither path suffices by itself: mankind's hope is in the bright, seeking eyes of the youth who is capable of true inner and outer vision, seeing where no one has seen before.

Many of Tiptree's stories deal with the allure of the Other, and the disaster that befalls man when he gains the universe but loses his soul. The notion that aliens may be sexually irresistible for humans is a persistent version of this theme. In "And I Awoke and Found Me Here on the Cold Hill's Side," the swingers of the future are men and women who suffer humiliation and physical abuse to pry sexual favors from aliens. In "The Women Men Don't See," two alienated women trade their male (human) overlords for kinder extraterrestrials with faces like black discs. Not a very promising countenance, perhaps, but because of the exogamous desire to mate with the Other, humans paint their dreams on the face of the void and plunge outward towards their hope of fulfillment.

Without keeping an inner balance between sense and dreams, man's soul leaks out and is usurped by the unknown, dangerous forces of the universe. Man obliterates himself in an orgy of other-directed love. Dr. Ain in "The Last Flight of Dr. Ain" so loves the world, personified for him in Gaea the Earth Mother, that he spreads viral leukemia to wipe away the blighting influence of man. And Timor in "The Milk of Paradise" returns to the orgiastic planet Paradise where he was reared by aliens, and consummates his dream by a feast of love in the mud. His human companion is torn to death, but he and the aliens are oblivious to that.

The theme of suicidal craving for the Other is most fully expressed in Tiptree's greatest story, "A Momentary Taste of Being." Earth is desperately seeking new worlds for its burgeoning population. Lory, the sister of Dr. Aaron Kaye, thinks she has found the ideal planet and brings a representative alien back to the starship *Centaur*. Aaron is suspicious of Lory's overly eager endorsement of the planet and notices that the proximity of the alien, coupled with the pressing racial need for expansion, causes the crew members to abandon their scientific objectivity. Kaye nearly loses his own, as he feels the tug of the alien as manifested in the androgynous body of Lory, with whom he had once had an incestuous relationship. Lory is still full of youthful idealism and is blind to the evil potential in people; Kaye is older, disillusioned, and acutely aware of human shortcomings, including his own.

When the crew finally contacts the alien directly, they experience orgasmic religious-sexual bliss — all except Kaye, who manages to keep his psychic distance. But it turns out that the alien is a sort of vampiric womb that vacuums the life energy from humans like sperm, leaving behind animate but unintelligent shells. The metaphor extends to the human race, swimming like sperm towards their suicidal appointment with the stars, rather than staying to rot in the testes of an overcrowded Earth. This exogamous outward thrust, rationalized by pseudoreligious idealism, seeks the lost paradise of youth. But it is a mirage. Tiptree reveals the terrible power of an idea — albeit a dream of perfection — to subvert our energies, sexual and otherwise, in service of a nonhuman Other. A regressive sexual desire for return to the womb manifests itself as a collective suicidal urge.

The entanglement of love and death is also the theme of one of Tiptree's most powerful stories, "Love Is the Plan, the Plan Is Death." An alien life-form grows to maturity, escaping the jaws of his mother who has become a monsters, by using psychic force to turn them away, thereby extinguishing keep his beloved sister in a cave with him over the long winter. But the Plan seems to have foreseen this, as the sister-lover turns into a mother-monster and feeds her young on his body. Dying, and conscious of it all, he finally accepts the Plan joyfully. The story illustrates the deceptive nature of will — how we cooperate unwittingly with the Fate that programs our choices and passions. It also implies that there can be a higher satisfaction than individual pleasure: an individual can die for his race.

"On the Last Afternoon" depicts the aging leader of a settlement on another planet who is confronted with a choice: to save the colony, under attack by monsters, by using psychic force to turn them away, thereby extinguishing himself; or to join a group of eternal, bodiless aliens in their transcendent playground beyond space and time. He tries, and almost succeeds, to reject personal immortality for the perpetuation of his race, but his heart is too divided; he dies without saving either himself or his children, an utter failure.

In "She Waits for All Men Born," an innocent-looking girl with psi-powers lashes out against the society that has rejected her. She is seen as both the legendary Death Mother and the representative of Humanity; she endures, life and death eternally wedded in her, with release only a vague possibility in a far future.

Tiptree's vision is tragic: she sees man as inextricably torn by conflicting passions, in the grip of life and death, and unable to fulfill himself without sowing the seeds of his own destruction. Yet she is hardly a pessimist. Rather, she exalts human dignity by seeing in man's nature the microcosm of cosmic creative and destructive energies, and if he cannot save himself from this irreconcilable contradiction, it is because he contains the Plan that is beyond his highest conceptions. Ever being more than he knows, he quests unceasingly to uncover the infinite potential of his consciousness.

Douglas A. Mackey

THE SHORT FICTION OF JOHN W. CAMPBELL, JR.

Author: John W. Campbell, Jr. (1910-1971)
Type of work: Short stories
  Short stories and tales by the influential editor, for thirty-three years, of Astounding Science Fiction

No single figure in the brief history of American science fiction save one has ever laid firm claim to lasting dominance of the genre. The field is and has always been too diverse, too individualistic, too self-willed, too exploratory both in form and content, for any one school or leader to hold the course very long. That is the rule. The sole exception, first as writer and then as editor for thirty-three years of the most successful magazine of the genre, is John W. Campbell, Jr.

Campbell came to science fiction in its American infancy, quickly demonstrated his mastery of the raw, sprawling space opera then in vogue, and then just as quickly, almost by his single example, opened the way for the genre's stylistic and philosophic growth toward literary maturity. Having thus demonstrated his vision of the capabilities of science fiction, Campbell turned from his own brief writing career to the editorship of *Astounding Science Fiction*, where for more than three decades he nurtured the growth of the field along the course he had chosen.

"Scientifiction," when Campbell entered the field in 1930 with "When the Atoms Failed," was an ill-defined, crudely crafted, and luridly sensationalistic potpourri of pseudoscience, galactic conflict, gadgetry, mysticism, and superhuman heroism, the vast majority of it hardly less preposterous today for its form and tone than it was then for its content. The science was in fact minimal, serving most often either as a hardware adjunct to stories otherwise largely indistinguishable from cowboy-and-Indian sagas or, in the case of the popular "gadget" stories, as a lightly explained starting point for interstellar intrigue. Most popular, perhaps, and setting the tone for the genre as a whole, were the galactic superepics of E. E. "Doc" Smith and his legion of imitators, heroic tales of civilizations in conflict and peopled by steely-eyed, firm-jawed Earthmen in riding breeches and polished boots outmaneuvering fiendish lizardlike opponents in the distant reaches of space.

There was good reason, of course, for the popularity of such grandiose, optimistic portrayals of mankind's future; the 1930's were Depression years, years of generalized hardship and poverty, and the implicit promise of future glories offered welcome relief from the grim realities of the present. In this adventure-centered format Campbell was a quick success, achieving his first sale even before his graduation from college and following it with a steady procession of galactic adventures and gadgetry, including "Solarite," "Piracy Preferred," "The Black Star Passes," "The Islands of Space," and "Invaders from the Infinite."

One such early tale, "The Battery of Hate" in 1933, both exemplifies the "gadget" story and the optimism so attractive for Depression-era escapism and offers, in addition, a villain-industrialist. The story details the development of a new power source promising at once cheap electricity, new jobs, generalized prosperity, and a major advance in the standard of living — if, of course, it is allowed to escape the clutches of the power magnates, whose comfortable fortunes are built on oil and coal and who would therefore destroy the invention rather than pass on its benefits for the good of mankind. Opposed in the conflict are two young scientist-technicians, at once naïve and resourceful, and the oil baron who, failing to buy up their invention, would destroy it and them; the resolution of that conflict comes only when the evil baron and his henchmen are sent flaming to Earth at the spectacular climax of a night-shrouded aerial dogfight — a simplistic conclusion, of course, but one most certainly appealing to a frustrated, embittered Depression audience.

Fortunately, however, Campbell's success in gadgetry, pie-in-the-sky futures, and galactic potboilers was insufficient to satisfy his vision of the genre's possibilities. The raw materials for a new form — the taste for extrapolation, the sense of an unknown future hurtling forward into today, the untold possibilities of an expanding science — these things were already present in the genre. Lacking were discipline of treatment, the depth of detail so necessary for realism, and insight into the darker implications of tomorrow; these things Campbell set out to provide. Even as he continued publishing in the old vein under his own name, Campbell turned in 1934 to a pseudonym, Don A. Stuart (a derivative of his wife's maiden name, Donna Stuart), for publication of "Twilight," a critical touchstone in the history of science fiction. The story takes a visitor, a Wellsian time-traveler, further forward than any galactic epic had yet considered — forward seven million years, forward to an Earth strangely depopulated, almost emptied of man and more important, totally emptied of ambition, all emotion, all growth. It is a world not dead but dying, still tended carefully by the machines inherited from its glorious past, a world conquered not by galactic turmoil and monstrous invaders but by time itself.

Both in structure and tone, "Twilight" represents a radical departure from the earlier efforts of the genre and even from Campbell's previous work. At least initially, there appears in the story only the barest vestige of plot, of the elements of conflict building to crisis and triumphant resolution so characteristic of the field. The time-traveler is deposited in the future shorn of his vehicle and must of course find some way of returning to his own period, but this "problem" is treated so casually — a mere matter of calibrating and adapting easily available equipment with no opposition and no sense of urgency — as to insure the reader's attention elsewhere, and that reader in fact never discovers whether the traveler finally achieves his homeward journey. Interest is focused, rather, on the traveler's descriptions of Earth at the far end of time. It is a world, the visitor finds, almost barren of mankind, the remaining men themselves barren of curiosity, of hope, of ambition. Precisely in the manner foretold by the space operas, they have gone forth in their millions to conquer the universe, have achieved that end and indeed all conceivable victories, have conquered hunger, disease, danger, even death itself, and have ultimately retreated, aimless and satiated, from the universe.

Appropriate to this retreat is the tone of the story, a persistently melancholic, introspective foreboding that denies totally the boisterous, cheerful optimism of the space operas. Here Campbell takes science fiction beyond the range of the superepics, beyond the vision of his predecessors into a darkly logical culmination of the all-conquering dreams of his fellows. Nor is this dark vision much lifted, in the resolution to the real problem of the story, when the traveler gives to the machines, man's successors, the curiosity and questing spirit mankind has lost.

This exploratory tone Campbell was to maintain throughout his career as writer and editor. His leadership of the field and his steady expansion of the limits of the genre are demonstrated notably in Campbell's dual treatment of a single motif in "The Brain Stealers of Mars" in 1936 and, as Stuart, in "Who Goes There?" in 1938. "The Brain Stealers of Mars," as the lurid title implies, is an outright space-adventure story written in the vein of Campbell's earliest successes. One of several tales sketching the adventures of the explorers Rod Blake and Ted Penton, "The Brain Stealers of Mars" matches this stereotypical pair against a telepathic, parasitical, protozoan race capable of precisely indistinguishable mimicry. Since the protozoan mimics are capable of assuming not only the form but also the complete memories of their models, the major complication of the tale arises when Blake and Penton, preparing to return to Earth, lose each other in a crowd of identically clad and armed Blakes and Pentons, each one claiming angrily to be the original. Resolution of the problem demands, in the spirit of the adventure story, a clever untangling through alternate tests of identity, in this case application of judicious doses of pepper and tetanus toxin, with the bogus Blakes and Pentons thus identified and promptly burned down. Important to note here is that the story is handled with the casual confidence of eventual victory, that the author allows the humor of multiple identities to overtake the seriousness of the situation, and that the determined optimism of the story maintains its tone throughout: virtue triumphs, the gallant earthmen succeed once more, and all is well.

No such superficial buoyancy surfaces in Campbell's second treatment of the motif, "Who Goes There?" Again the protagonists, in this case a scientific study group isolated in the Arctic, are faced with a protoplasmic invader capable of perfect mimicry. Here, though, the beast assumes its new form by assimilating the old, and the party faces the horrifying discovery that members of the group are no longer human. Neither is there quick relief with easy tests, but instead progressive failures until a sizable proportion of the group is infected.

Notable in particular in this story are Campbell's deft portrayals of men under terrible pressure, of the changing relationships in such a group, of the terrible savagery of which men are capable, not just on the suspected members of the group, but on one another as well. Here are depicted heroes, but also murderers, men capable of rising to genius and altruistic self-sacrifice, but also men capable of failure and collapse. With the progressive deterioration of the group comes also a series of incisive character studies of a depth unusual in the genre to date, portrayals of the full range of human attributes — attributes which, in the resolution, provide the key to identification and destruction of the creature.

The sense of impending doom, the repeated failures, the building urgency of the story and the savagery and realistic depictions of mankind under terrible stress all contribute to the success of the story and particularly to its role as a step upward from the triteness of the genre. In "The Brain Stealers of Mars," it might be theorized, Campbell defined the state of the field precisely as it was and had been; in his second treatment of the motif, alternatively, he demonstrated what the genre could become.

For Campbell, though, it was not enough to demonstrate his vision of the genre. In the same year that "Who Goes There?" was published, Campbell became editor of *Astounding Science Fiction*, a position he held with *Astounding Science Fiction* and its successor *Analog* until his death in 1971. As writer, Campbell could only show the way; as editor, he could and did most emphatically demand that his vision of the capabilities of the genre be allowed to bloom. In the thirty-three years of his editorship, Campbell achieved a considerable reputation for unshakable opinions, obstinacy, the pursuit of odd causes and not-quite-workable gadgets — and also for genius in finding and shaping new writers, in encouraging and inspiring and dictatorially instructing older ones, in his steady and generous flow of ideas on which others might build (he ended, for the most part, his own writing with *The Cloak of Aesir* in 1939), and his persistent demand for depth, logic, and convincing realism in what had been, before him, the pulpiest of pulp writing.

With few exceptions, the major figures of the field today are those developed under Campbell's tutelage; Isaac Asimov, James Blish, Hal Clement, Frank Herbert, A. E. van Vogt, Robert A. Heinlein, Henry Kuttner, Eric Frank Russell, Theodore Sturgeon, Harry Harrison, and others benefited from his direction. So also benefited the audience, who might still today be reading science fiction, but a far different science fiction, had it not been for John W. Campbell, Jr.

Merrell A. Knighten

Sources for Further Study

Criticism:

Bretnor, Reginald, Editor. *Modern Science Fiction: Its Meaning and Future*. New York: Coward-McCann, 1953. This collection of essays includes some discussion of Campbell's major themes.

Sturgeon, Theodore. "I List in Numbers," in *National Review*. XVII (March 10, 1970), pp. 266-267. This study concentrates on Campbell's influence on the genre of Science Fiction.

Reviews:

Kirkus Reviews. XLI, February 1, 1973, p. 6.

Times Literary Supplement. May 18, 1973, p. 562.

Worlds of If. XXI, July, 1973, pp. 106-107.

THE SHORT FICTION OF JORGE LUIS BORGES

Author: Jorge Luis Borges (1899-   )
Type of work: Short stories and *ficciones*

The short fiction of South America's best-known writer of fantasy, and one of the most honored masters of speculative fiction of our time

Jorge Luis Borges made his first reputation as a poet, publishing three collections during the 1920's. During the same period he was also a prolific essayist, but he later suppressed most of his early work of this type. His first major prose work was a series of sketches published as *Historia Universal de la Infamia (A Universal History of Infamy)* in 1935. At about the same time he wrote a hoax essay, "The Approach to al-Mu'tasim," commenting on an imaginary book. It was not until 1939, though, following a serious illness resulting from a cut which became infected, that he began to write the short stories which were ultimately to form the basis of his international reputation.

Eight of these stories were collected in *El jardin de senderos que se bifurcan (The Garden of Forking Paths)* in 1942, which two years later became part of *Ficciones*, with six new stories added. In 1949 his second major collection, *El Aleph*, appeared, and four more stories were added to its second edition in 1952. There followed a long period of much-reduced productivity. Two new collections have appeared in Argentina during the last ten years, but only one has so far been translated (*Doctor Brodie's Report*, 1974). The stories from the earlier period appear in several collections of Borges translations: *Ficciones* (1962, reprinted as *Fictions*); *Labyrinths* (1962); *A Personal Anthology* (1967); and *The Aleph and Other Stories* (1970). These translations began to appear after Borges shared with Samuel Beckett the 1961 Formentor prize; shortly thereafter, Borges visited several American universities to give lectures.

Those of Borges' *ficciones* which invite discussion in connection with modern speculative fiction are mostly the embodiments of ideas drawn from idealist philosophy. Borges himself, if the final statement on his essay "A New Refutation of Time" is to be taken at face value, is a reluctant realist who concedes the reality of the world while remaining eager to pursue skeptical arguments and wishing that he could find them more convincing. In his fiction, he frees himself from the constraining conviction that the world is much as it appears to us, and indulges himself in flights of idealist fantasy, reveling in the aesthetics of paradox and unreason. He constantly refers back to Zeno, Berkeley, and Schopenhauer, taking delight in their mockery of the pretensions of common sense; but he frequently sets them alongside the Kabbalists and heretic theologians. They are celebrated in his work as champions of the unorthodox rather than as advocates of true wisdom.

This curious infatuation with a philosophical outlook which he cannot sincerely adopt leads Borges to fill his fictions with casual flourishes of the imagination, and to juxtapose the bizarre and the trivial as though they were the most natural of companions. When he writes about his own work (as in the commentaries in *The Aleph and Other Stories*) he professes an innocent puzzlement that anyone should find anything profound in his playfulness. He hides his real erudition behind a front of mock-erudition, and is suitably amused when readers are misled into taking the latter for the former. His very casualness lends to his ideative extravaganzas an extra force, and it is this quality which makes him unique, though it is the fact that there *is* real erudition behind the fake that turns his cleverness into brilliance.

The earliest of the tales which Borges began to write in 1939 was "Pierre Menard, Author of the *Quixote*," which — like "The Approach to al-Mu'tasim" — takes the form of a satirical mock-essay on the career of an author whose major endeavor was to write *Don Quixote* word for word without having read the original, by recapitulating in himself the world view and purpose of Cervantes. The essay compares the two works and concludes that Menard's is the greater, because of its wider range of allusions and deeper meaning in relation to the world of the twentieth century.

This work was quickly followed by "Tlön, Uqbar, Orbis Tertius," a far more ambitious piece, and perhaps Borges' best. It tells how Borges' friend Adolfo Bioy Casares introduces into an argument a reference to the heresiarchs of Uqbar, puzzling Borges, who has never heard of Uqbar. Bioy is appalled to discover that Borges' edition of the *Anglo-American Cyclopaedia* contains no reference to it, but on returning home finds that his own edition (which should be identical) has a four-page entry. Subsequently, it transpires that Uqbar is part of the world of Tlön, which is itself partially chronicled in Volume XI (Hlaer to Jangr) of *A First Encyclopaedia of Tlön*. No other volumes of this work appear to exist, but from its pages there can be derived an image of a whole alternative world where idealist philosophy reigns supreme, whose languages contain no nouns, and where the continuity of objects in time is disputed. This imaginary world turns out to have been the invention of the secret society, the *Orbis Tertius*, which gave birth to the myth of the Rosicrucians. But as the story concludes, the invention is in the process of usurping reality; as the vision of Tlön spreads, so do its languages and philosophies, and Earth is in the process of *becoming* Tlön.

Nothing else in Borges is quite as sweeping as "Tlön, Uqbar, Orbis Tertius," but alien world views and peculiar existential philosophies are frequently glimpsed in his work. "The Lottery in Babylon" tells the story of how Babylonian society is gradually taken over by the philosophy of chance inherent in the fascination which its citizens have for lotteries. The Company which runs the lotteries, administering their rewards and forfeits, gradually retires into metaphysical status until it fuses with the vicissitudes of chance implicit in existence itself. "The Immortal" takes the form of a memoir by one Joseph Cartaphilus, an antique dealer, detailing his search for the City of Immortals. He discovered it, apparently fifteen hundred years before the date of the memoir, but found neither the city nor the immortals to be as he expected, and the later pages of the memoir become increasingly dislocated from the world view of the reader in explaining how the world seems to an undying man.

All of these hypothetical world views, no matter what scale is used for their depiction, are subjectively determined. Our own world is transformed in "Tlön, Uqbar, Orbis Tertius," but only because we learn to see in a new way. This is the essence of idealist fiction, in which the idiosyncrasies of the mind become transfigurations of the world. The most explicit example is perhaps the author's most famous story, "The Circular Ruins," in which a man sets out to shape his dreams and builds from their substance a new world, including an analogue of himself; he realizes as his work of creation is completed that he himself is the figment of another such dream. Usually in Borges, this kind of predicament (if such it can be termed) is seen from within, but there are exceptions.

One exception is "Funes the Memorious," the story of a youth accidentally endowed with a perfect memory, whose every sensory experience then threatens his consciousness with an overload. The gift, which poses the problem for Funes of deciding what purpose he should adopt for his mental life, is presented only as an idea; the tale is recounted by an observer who meets Funes only twice. The problem of conveying through the medium of first-person narrative a radical dislocation of world view is an acute one, in that such stories tend to decay into the babble of irrationality, but Borges several times demonstrates his ability to handle the task neatly and economically.

In "The God's Script," a prisoner seeks escape by attempting to locate and decode a magical "sentence" which God has programmed into the fabric of existence to serve as an infallible deliverance from evil circumstance. In discovering it, the prisoner's attitude to life and to the universe is so dramatically changed that he no longer needs or wants to use it. In "The Zahir," the narrator finds a coin which is one of a class of objects having the property of becoming fixated in consciousness as a persistent, undecaying memory — an obsession-creating artifact whose effects we see in the very theorizing which comprises the story. Another strange entity, at first considered from without and then actually experienced by the narrator of the story, is "The Aleph," a particular point in space which includes all other points, so that in looking at it the whole world, past and present, can be simultaneously experienced.

The intense subjectivity of Borges' writings is mostly confined to his more imaginative fictions, though it is also manifest in his poetry and in many of the brief prose pieces in *El hacedor* (*Dreamtigers* [1964]). Even his mundane tales, however, are tributes to his powers of empathy. One apparently anomalous story among his fantasies is "The Library of Babel," which is an allegory in which the universe is represented as an infinite library containing all possible statements that can arise from a particular system of symbols. However,

Borges' own comments on the story reveal that the central notion is borrowed from Kurd Lasswitz and deployed not as an allegory but as a surrealized representation of the author's own situation as a librarian in a Buenos Aires municipal library — a position he held from 1938-1942 (when he was removed by the Peronists for political reasons).

Several of the stories in which Borges deals with subjective shifts of perception take place in a theological context rather than an abstract, speculative one or a "scientific" one. In "The Secret Miracle," a man about to be executed is granted a subjective stay of execution during the last seconds of his life in order to finish a work of art in his imagination. "Three Versions of Judas" details the life of an imaginary heretic who first becomes an apologist for Judas and eventually comes to believe that Judas and not Jesus is the Redeemer. "The Theologians" features a conflict between two scholars which ends when one causes the other to be burnt as a heretic. The niceties of hermeneutics to which their lives have been dedicated, however, turn out to be quite insignificant in the eyes of God. A further theological fantasy is "The Other Death," in which God re-creates the past in order to give a man a nobler death. The preponderance of these ideas in Borges' fiction call into question the propriety of the attempt to co-opt him into the genre of science fiction, which maintains a dogged pretense of rationalism. When Borges does show his own peculiar fascination with rationalism (in his so-called detective stories, for example), it is by no means the same species of rationalism that is characteristic of modern science fiction.

Much of Borges' "detective fiction" was written in collaboration with Adolfo Bioy Casares and remains untranslated, but the three early *ficciones*, which Borges calls detective tales, all carry curious existentialist overtones and are dominated by labyrinthine imagery that reflects the mazelike structure of the traditional detective story. In "Ibn Hakkim al-Bokhari, Dead in his Labyrinth," the maze is quite concrete. In "Death and the Compass" — a marvellous story in which the murderer plants esoteric clues in order to lead the detective to the place of his execution — the mazes are largely symbolic, though much talked-about. In "The Garden of Forking Paths," a maze at first assumed to be real turns out to be a metaphor for "a growing, dizzying net of divergent, convergent and parallel times" which contains many alternative eventualities.

Borges is said to admire Wells as much as he admires Poe and Chesterton (who provide the main inspiration for his detective tales) but in fact there is little in his work which recalls Wellsian science fiction. The one orthodox Wellsian piece in the four collections under consideration is, in fact, a late story written in collaboration with Bioy, "The Immortals," which envisages a laboratory in which a scientist has preserved the minds of several individuals against all possibility of destruction by replacing their bodies with immutable featureless structures of plastic and formica.

In addition, there is a certain ideative overlap between the *ficciones* and conventional science fiction (parallel worlds, for instance), but hardly enough to warrant a claim of kinship. However, the admiration for Borges which is common in the contemporary science fiction community actually has little to do with matters of ideative overlap and much more to do with the author's fascination for alternative world views — his investigation of possible topographies for "inner space." In such efforts, surrealists perceive a common cause with Borges. The extent to which this perception is justified is dubious. For Borges, surrealism is still a playful intellectual indulgence; his degree of commitment to it is slight, and his work lacks emotional intensity, being possessed instead of a stylish coolness. His *ficciones* retain, for him, the substance of dreams, and provide no real challenge to his sense of reality, merely a glimpse of fascinating mystery. In one of his essays in speculative philosophy, "Avatars of the Tortoise," which deals largely with the aesthetics of Zeno's paradoxes, he has this to say:

> The greatest magician (Novalis has memorably written) would be the one who would cast over himself a spell so complete that he would take his own phantasmagorias as autonomous appearances. Would not this be our case? I conjecture that this is so. We (the undivided divinity operating within us) have dreamt the world. We have dreamt it as firm, mysterious, visible, ubiquitous in space and durable in time; but in its architecture we have allowed tenuous and eternal crevises of unreason which tell us it is false.

This is the world view of the *ficciones*; this is the voice of Borges the writer. But for Borges the man it is different, and for this reason Borges in his writings can occasionally confront himself and find himself strange. The cardinal example of this is the enigmatic piece "Borges and I," which needs to be taken seriously. This puzzling act of removal from the products of his own imagination makes it especially difficult for the reader or the critic to pin Borges down, and perpetually threatens to turn writings *about* Borges into the hollow and pretentious mock-essays which Borges once loved to write.

Brian Stableford

Sources for Further Study

Criticism:

Adams, R. M. "The Intricate Argentine," in *Hudson Review*. XIX (Spring, 1966), pp. 139-146. A brief sound discussion of some of the complicated themes of Borges.

Bagby, Albert J. "The concept of Time of Jorge Luis Borges," in *Romance Notes*. VI (1965), pp. 99-105. Bagby argues that the idea that time does not exist outside of a limited framework is a recurring theme in the works of Borges.

Botsford, Keith. "The Writings of Jorge Luis Borges," in *Atlantic Monthly*. XXIX (January, 1967), pp. 99-104. An article discussing Borges' style, which makes realistic an unreal country, time and action.

Reviews:

Atlantic. CCX, August, 1962, p. 141.

New York Herald Tribune Books. June 17, 1962, p. 5.

New York Times Book Review. May 27, 1962, p. 6.

Saturday Review. XLV, June 2, 1962, p. 34.

Spectator. September 28, 1962, p. 442.

Times Literary Supplement. September 21, 1962, p. 716.

THE SHORT FICTION OF JUDITH MERRIL

Author: Judith Merril (1923-   )
Type of work: Short stories, novellas, and a novelette

The short works of science fiction's first overtly feminist writer, characterized by the ability to make science fiction themes individually significant to the reader

Judith Merril's short fiction appears in four collections whose contents overlap somewhat: *Out of Bounds* (1960); *Daughters of Earth* (1968); *Survival Ship and Other Stories* (1973); and *The Best of Judith Merril* (1976). Her total output of science fiction in shorter lengths amounts to less than thirty stories, but the best of them share with her novel *Shadow on the Hearth* (1950) an intense and sympathetic interest in the effects of science fiction situations on human relationships which makes them quite exceptional. Most of this output appeared during the years 1948-1959; the three minor stories which she published during the 1960's were all commissioned to accompany cover illustrations.

Merril's first published science fiction story, "That Only a Mother" (1948), provides a perfect example of her approach to speculative themes. It made such an impression that it appears in the *Science Fiction Hall of Fame* anthology selected by a ballot of the Science Fiction Writers of America. It deals with the experiences of a young mother whose husband has been connected with atomic research at Oak Ridge. He is still on active service and she is plagued by loneliness and anxiety. Her husband is finally allowed to come home nine months after the arrival of the baby and discovers that the infant is a mutant born without arms or legs. His wife has never allowed herself to accept the fact and believes that the child is normal.

The genesis of the story was apparently a newspaper article claiming that, according to U.S. Army information, rumors of numerous infanticides in the areas around Hiroshima and Nagasaki were unfounded. Merril was politically cynical enough to read the release "backwards" and sufficiently alert to the ways of parenthood to find the best way of making that particular possibility intelligible to her readers. It is this ability to make the human significance of science fiction ideas accessible to readers, often offering an empathetic link to characters in distress, that makes her work unique. Her characters are usually on the periphery of events and are touched by them obliquely, yet the oblique touches have profound effects on their personal lives.

The anger roused in Merril by militaristic trends in United States politics (which eventually led to her emigration) also provided the basis for her second science fiction story, "Death Is the Penalty" (1949). This is the story of a love affair between two scientists which results in their condemnation to death because their rapport established *via* communication of their ideas constitutes a security leak. The story seems heavy-handed by comparison with "That Only a Mother." The same is true of another bitter story, "Hero's Way" (1952), which provides a scathing commentary on the military notion of heroism. In her later work Merril's handling of political matters is less crude and manifests a more fatalistic cynicism.

When "Death Is the Penalty" was reprinted in *Survival Ship*, Merril remarked in an Afterword on the assumption within the story that the heroine's loneliness could only be overcome by her finding a man who is her intellectual superior; she hoped the assumption had now become dated. This serves to point out a continuing concern with sex roles in her work and the ideological assumptions which sustain them. Merril was science fiction's first overtly feminist writer. Although her challenges to stereotypy were mild by comparison with the more recent work of writers such as Joanna Russ and James Tiptree, Jr., they were daring enough to lead her to adopt the pseudonym "Rose Sharon" for two stories which appeared in 1957.

The earliest stories manifesting this concern were published in 1951: "A Woman's Work Is Never Done" and "Survival Ship." Both are minor works dealing in unambitious ironies, but the latter became significant because Merril considered expanding its theme into a novel. The novel was never written, but two other short stories eventually developed from the thought that went into its planning. "Survival Ship" concerns the selection of a crew for a starship whose journey will be so long that new generations will have to be bred aboard it before it reaches its destination. The selected crew consists of twenty females; the four accompanying males required to father the next generation are regarded as drones, without any other essential role to play in the actual handling of the ship.

The two subsequent stories on this "mothership" theme are "Wish Upon a Star" (1958) and "The Lonely" (1963). The first is a sensitive but rather plotless story about the world view of the first generation of ship-born children, focusing on the feelings and experiences of an adolescent boy. The second was written around a Virgil Finlay painting which shows space-suited figures confronted by a gigantic weathered statue of a woman with a remarkably phallic spaceship nestling between her legs. The story is a rather eccentric joke which explains this curious artifact as the product of an alien intelligence attempting to communicate with humans by reproducing an image of special symbolic significance (based, of course, on its telepathic scanning of one of the motherships).

A rather more straightforward opposition to the sexist bias virtually universal in pulp science fiction in the 1950's is seen in the novella "Daughters of Earth" (1953) and the novelette "Stormy Weather" (1954). The first is the story of the colonization of a rather inhospitable alien world. It is told from the viewpoint of one of the female colonists, who continually refers back to her grandmother and her mother, and forward to her daughter and granddaughter in order to put the story in its proper temporal perspective. The role taken by these women in the story is not the narrowly defined one conceded by most male writers in similar stories, and though the story is basically no more than an exercise in looking at a common science fiction theme from the female viewpoint (comparable to *Shadow on the Hearth*), it nevertheless implies that a greater degree of sexual equality will be normal in future society. "Stormy Weather," by contrast, is a delightfully ironic piece about a girl stuck on a space station, routinely saving the Earth from cosmic disaster while anxiously brooding about her boyfriend's failure to make a telepathic "phonecall." Her thoughts are haunted by the sadly sentimental song which provides, *via* a play on words, the title and the plot of the story.

Of the stories that appeared under the Rose Sharon pseudonym, "The Lady Was a Tramp" is by far the better known. It is, in a way, an inversion of the theme of "Survival Ship." A young officer, fresh out of the naval academy and equipped with a set of moral presuppositions similar to those held by graduates of present-day military academies, joins the motley crew (including four men and only one woman), of a rather battered starship. His predicament is the problem of adjusting psychologically to the pattern of sexual relationships necessitated by the situation. The story is justly famed as one of the earliest and most effective science fiction stories to provide a moral justification for promiscuity according to the logic of situational ethics. The other Rose Sharon story is the uncollected "A Woman of the World," a rather cruel post-holocaust story in which a woman watches her lover fight for his life against a scavenger, content to let the principle of survival of the fittest determine who is to be the father of her children.

Apart from her frequent attempts to subvert sexual stereotypes, there are two recurrent themes in Merril's work: the effects of telepathic communication on human or human-alien relationships, and the emotional tragedies resulting from the hazards and difficulties of the conquest of space. The former theme is manifested in one of the most convincing telepathic love stories, "Connection Completed" (1954). A man and a woman who have made telepathic contact tentatively arrange to meet each other, neither of them entirely sure that their silent dialogue is real and not merely a delusion conjured up by loneliness. Here, the telepathic communion proceeds in the same manner as ordinary conversation, but a very different picture of such a telepathic contact is provided in Merril's only short story of the 1970's, the Joycean vignette "In the Land of the Unblind" (1974).

A more artificial story dealing with this theme was published in 1954 as "Peeping Tom." A soldier recovering from a bad wound in the Far East takes lessons in mind-reading in exchange for cigarettes. He uses the ability primarily as an instrument in seduction, but is appalled by the fact that no woman he meets has a mind which lives up to his false presumptions regarding feminine purity. Eventually, though, he again meets one of his former nurses, who appears to be the manifestation of his ideal. Not until they have been married some time does he learn that she, too, took lessons from the Eastern sage and progressed far enough not only to read minds, but also to shield her own thoughts.

The extension of this notion to deal with human-alien contact is best seen in the novella "Homecalling" (1956). A nine-year-old girl and her baby brother, the only survivors of a crashed spaceship, find themselves stranded in territory belonging to an insectlike alien race whose society is structurally similar to that of an anthive. The queen of the hive — referred to in the story as "the Lady of the House" — discovers the children and slowly threads her way through a maze of misconceptions to realize the truth of their alien nature. The girl is at first repelled by the aliens, but slowly learns to accept them and becomes reconciled to her "adoption" by the maternal queen. The idea that contact with alien beings, though difficult and hazardous to establish, is a worthwhile and perhaps necessary goal is also central to "Daughters of Earth." It also is in harmony with the temper of the period, when many science fiction writers reacted against the assumptions of the "alien menace" plots so common in the prewar period.

A very different view of the possible fruits of telepathic communion with aliens is, however, shown in "Whoever You Are" (1952), in which earthmen who make contact with alien beings are possessed by feelings of love and friendship which set all other considerations aside. They bring their new friends back to Earth, and the planet's defenders have to decide whether the visitors are bringing a great gift or posing a terrible threat. In the end, it is decided that whatever the truth of the matter is, the aliens must be destroyed to protect mankind.

The stories which focus on the second theme, tribulations associated with the conquest of space, begin with "Daughters of Earth" and another story published the same year, "So Proudly We Hail." Like "Stormy Weather," the latter obtains some of its emotional charge from the fact that lines of the title song continually echo within it, but in this instance — as befits the use of a national anthem — the intention is wholly serious. The story concerns the wife of a man who has been accepted as a member of a space colony. She lets him believe that she is staying behind voluntarily (in fact she has been refused on medical grounds) so that he will not pass up his lifetime's ambition and stay behind for her sake.

These stories were followed a year later by "Dead Center," probably the best of all Merril's short stories. This is the account of the failure of an early space shot, as seen from the viewpoint of the wife and three-year-old son of the endangered astronaut. While attempts to mount a rescue are swiftly put in motion, the anguished wife loses sight of the child for a while, and the boy is killed as he attempts to stow away in the rescue rocket. The story is one of the most emotionally powerful science fiction stories ever written, and was reprinted in Martha Foley's annual anthology of the *Best American Short Stories*. The tragic tone of "Dead Center" contrasts with the much more optimistic novella "Project Nursemaid" (1955). The story follows the tribulations of the officer responsible for obtaining human embryos to be raised in conditions of low gravity for adaptation to life on the moon. Once this process has been completed, he must find "foster parents" to look after them in their new environment. This, too, is a very fine story, and it shows the author at her best. The sensitivity with which she explores the hero's relationships with the people he meets in the course of his struggle to keep the project moving is remarkable.

Judith Merril has made her main impact on the science fiction field as an anthologist — particularly with the series of "Best of the Year" anthologies which she edited between 1956 and 1968. In these anthologies and during her time as book reviewer for *The Magazine of Fantasy and Science Fiction*, she was an ardent champion of science fiction written from the human angle, and she worked hard to break down the barrier separating magazine science fiction from experimental fiction in the literary mainstream. She thus acquired a reputation as one of the prophets of the new wave and introduced some of the products of British new wave science fiction to the United States in an anthology embarrassingly entitled *England Swings SF* (1968). Her main concern, however, was not with literary experimentation for its own sake, but as a means of directing the attention of readers to the emotional impact of possible future developments at the expense of the traditional fascination with gadgetry and power fantasy. In her own fiction she has tried to practice what she preached, and at her best she has succeeded admirably.

Brian Stableford

Sources for Further Study

Criticism:

Miller, P. "Daughters of Earth," in *Analog*. LXXXIV (January, 1970), pp. 164-165. Miller discusses Merril's role as an early woman science fiction writer.

Sturgeon, Theodore. "Merril-y We Wave Along," in *National Review*. XXI, (November 18, 1969), pp. 1174-1175. Sturgeon calls Merril the chief exponent of the "New Wave" writers.

THE SHORT FICTION OF KIRILL BULYCHEV

Author: Kirill Bulychev (1933-   )
Type of work: Short stories

A collection of stories which view human nature fondly and optimistically

The attitude of critics and readers towards Kirill Bulychev has remained unchanged since the first years of his career as a science fiction writer (and he has been in this field for more than a decade). According to the readers' letters to the editorial boards of the magazines and publishing houses, he is unanimously declared the most widely read and popular short story writer in Soviet science fiction after Ilya Varshavski.

What is the secret of Bulychev's popularity? Is it his precision of details, exciting plots, or subtlety of thought? (In these aspects the superiority belongs to Dmitri Bilenkin and Henrich Altov.) Or does his success lay in his vivid imagination and his deep philosophical and social generalizations? (There is hardly anyone equal to the Strugatskys in this field.) Though all these merits are characteristic of Bulychev, what attracts the reader first and foremost is the author's sincere narrative tone. The need to establish a contact between the writer and the reader is usually a difficult problem for writers, but Bulychev is simply frank and honest with his readers, and they trust him. He does not trick the reader either with improbable situations or with sugary happy endings. Neither does he try to impress with theatrical effects. Bulychev is always natural in his stories.

To some extent this intimacy is achieved through the author's frequent use of the first-person narrative which is always characterized by a very personal and recognizable authorial tone, whether the narrator be adult or child, cosmonaut or student. The earmarks of this narrative voice are kindness, humor, and lyricism.

As a writer, Bulychev is benevolent toward his readers and characters alike. Kindness is one of the basic qualities of a number of Bulychev's characters. They always rush to somebody's rescue, or take care of or protect somebody (in the story "Difficult Child," for example, a family of the Earth's inhabitants accepts guardianship of a child from an alien planet). When it comes to a moral choice, the characters in these stories never hesitate to choose the right way.

Although Bulychev speaks with humor about even the most serious topics, those topics do not lose their significance as a result. Humor is a very important quality for a writer: it tests his literary taste, his sense of proportion, and to a degree, his respect for the reader. Bulychev's stories are also lyrical. His landscapes are painted with feeling; they come alive in their vividness, and add psychological overtones to the narratives. The author avoids sharp strokes and high light and dark contrasts, preferring halftones and soft pastel colors.

The stories in the two books may be divided into two groups: stories about the present and stories about the future. The majority of the stories are set in our own time and deal with events in Moscow or its suburbs. The city is described with an abundance and richness of detail; Bulychev captures precisely both purely external items such as fashion, furniture, and so forth, as well as the intellectual life of the city — its ways of thinking, tastes, interests, and passions.

However, into this well-described and down-to-earth setting, fantastical elements are introduced. The central character of "Broken Line," for example, discovers in his apartment a device capable of transferring various objects from the past into the future. He decides to help a writer who died of starvation during the seige of Leningrad during the war (the action in the story takes place twenty-five years after the end of World War II). While sending food to the writer, the central character fails to realize that the writer was living in a house full of children. Naturally, the food is given to the children, and the intended result of the transporting device's use is never achieved.

In another story, "But For Michail," the main character fails to overcome his inflated vanity, and, because of a petty grudge, he almost destroys an unearthly form of life.

The science fiction label on a number of Bulychev's stories denotes nothing more than an author's method used to create a story. In essence it is a psychological prose containing serious moral problems, and science fiction as such is necessary for Bulychev in order to turn the reality at an angle and to expose the conflicts which are interesting for the author. Thus, in the story "Professor Kazarin's Crown" the relative character of the author's science fiction technique is quite obvious (the professor discovers a mind-reading device). But without such a method there would have been no story, because the main character would not have been able to raise himself above the everyday life trivialities and to see that he was almost losing an uneasy and rare happiness — the happiness of love and understanding.

One of the best stories set in the present is "Choice." All his life the central character has considered himself a human being; then he suddenly discovers that he is an alien from an alien planet. Having learned this, he raises a question which is addressed to the reader as well: what is a human being? In what way is a human being different from any other form of life? In this story, the main character decides to stay on Earth instead of returning to his native planet in another Galaxy, because he values human love and loyalty above the intellectual power of a race of heartless superminds.

Bulychev often writes on the theme of communication arrived at through unusual contacts between humans and aliens; this theme is thoroughly explored in the series of stories about the town of Veliky Guslyar. At present, this series comprises about twenty stories, including those from "Miracles in Guslyar."

Veliky Guslyar is an imaginary town in the north of the U.S.S.R., and its 750-year history and culture are presented by the author extremely realistically. The morals and manners of this small town, with its leisurely and unruffled life, are shown deliberately to be "earthly." Funny details of everyday life create a warmly human atmosphere. In "Connections of Personal Character," for example, a can of white paint is considered evidence of a visit to Earth by representatives of an alien civilization; in actuality, Korneli Udalov, the central character of the story, used this can to paint roadside barrier posts broken by a flying saucer crew. When the local animal store receives golden fishes for sale, it turns out that the fishes can speak and fulfill three wishes. One inhabitant asks for a parrot from Brazil, the second asks for nine suits, while the third wants vodka running from the water tap in his apartment. However, it is only the first impulse. At the end of the story we see Erik, an invalid as the result of a car accident, running along the river beach swinging his eighteen arms and legs: almost every goldfish owner wished him a restoration of his lost limbs.

In "Help Is Needed," Korneli Udalov has a visitor who pleads for a flower belonging to a woman residing in Guslyar, without which the animal world of a distant planet may perish. Udalov, a stay-at-home type, leaves his cozy chair and warm room, and, despite the cold autumn night, crosses the town in the rain to get the flower. Again, a serious message about caring for others lies beneath the humorous surface of the story. Bulychev's characters often learn kindness and selflessness through the aid of fantastic situations. Bulychev is not a writer of ideas, but of real characters.

In the author's stories about the future, the central place is occupied by the Contact topic wherein a character will try to understand another civilization, taking into account the level of its moral progress. Sometimes this Contact means much more than a mere meeting of different intelligent beings, because it leads to love — deep, sincere and tragic. It is tragic because it is impossible due to different reasons, perhaps because of a physical difference of their habitat environment, as is the case in the story "Snowmaiden," where Bulychev has used the plot of a Russian folklore tale about a girl made of snow who melted under the rays of the spring sun. Sometimes it happens so that the real reason lies even much deeper.

Bulychev's stories set in the future do not have the well-developed descriptions of technological and social life that one finds, for example, in the work of Isaac Asimov or Robert A. Heinlein. Bulychev's future world is not inhabited by supermen, but by ordinary people who have their own weaknesses and drawbacks and who are quite human; and the title of the second book of Bulychev's stories, *People Are People*, seems to present a polemic challenge to H. G. Wells's *Men Like Gods*. Bulychev presents ordinary people who act in various situations, trivial as well as heroic, but who always remain sensitively human. In this future there are personal conflicts and cases of unrequited love just as there were centuries ago, but man has learned to overcome cowardness, jealousy, and egoism; he is spiritually transformed. The future can be observed in the present-day life, which precedes this future; therefore, the moral interrelations between the stories "The First Layer of Memory" and "Ugly Bio-form" becomes quite obvious. Though the events in the stories are ages apart, there exists a general interpretation of life that should be devoted to people, and heroic deeds that are one's moral obligation. Bulychev's future is being checked by our present, and the latter is being tested as a base for the future. And it seems that it stands the test very well.

Vl. Gakov

THE SHORT FICTION OF LARRY NIVEN

Author: Larry Niven (1938-   )
Type of work: Short stories

The short fiction of Larry Niven dramatizes both the consistency of his vision as a science fiction writer and the range of his interests as they extend to combinations of science fiction with the comic, the detective and mystery story, fantasy, and such minor traditions as the science fiction barroom story

Larry Niven's name has become synonymous with high quality stories that are part of an elaborate science fiction future history called the "Known Space" saga. To that extent, Niven is clearly writing within a tradition established by Isaac Asimov and Robert A. Heinlein, to whom his writing owes an obvious debt. As a writer of short fiction, Niven deserves to be ranked with both Asimov and Heinlein, along with John W. Campbell, Jr., and Arthur C. Clarke, with each of whom he shares common interests, values, and attitudes toward science and the future of the human race. There is no denying that the "known space" tales represent some of Niven's best writing, but it would be both a mistake and a disservice to limit an appreciation of his short fiction to this one series. Not only are there several other series of short stories (The Gil Hamilton and Jayberry Jansen stories of the near future set on Earth; Leshy circuit alternatives to some of the known space traditions) but Niven also has worked in such fantasy science fiction areas as teleportation and the time travel-parallel universe story, heroic and sword and sorcery fantasy, and various modes of comic science fiction, including parody and burlesque. To a greater extent than many of the writers who have emerged out of the 1960's, Niven has worked within the traditional forms and themes of science fiction literature. He has developed, extended, and perfected those forms and themes while establishing his own characteristic style and angle of vision, giving a Larry Niven short story several distinguishing features.

It is no secret that Niven rather deliberately set out to become a professional writer of science fiction. His knowledge of science fiction literature and its traditions is reflected in virtually everything he writes. The skill with which he blends hard science interests with mystery, romance, and adventure has earned him the right to be considered the heir of the Campbell, Asimov, Heinlein, Clarke tradition. His professionalism as a writer also accounts, to some extent at least, for the range and variety of stories he has written. Niven has tried his hand at almost every important type of science fiction story and related fantasy. Characteristically, his models in fantasy literature have been Dunsany and Cabell, writers who embody two of Niven's most characteristic traits: his love of adventure and his preference for the comic and the ironic over the tragic. The tragic and the pathetic are by no means entirely absent from Niven's short fiction, but when they are present, they almost always serve as background elements. The exceptions are so rare that those stories in which the conclusion is tragic, pathetic, or cynical easily stand out in a reader's memory, even though they are not first rate Niven: "The Coldest Place" (his first story), "Bordered in Black," "How the Heroes Die," "At the Bottom of A Hole." The exception is "The Jigsaw Man," an award-winning story discussed below.

Most readers will agree that Niven's best writing in short fiction has been in hard science fiction, and as long as we give ourselves plenty of latitude in acknowledging the ways in which the hard elements are combined with everything from space opera adventure to the conventions of the hard boiled detective story, that judgment will probably stand. Nevertheless, one of Niven's best stories is "All the Myriad Ways," a story of time travel-alternate worlds which combines conventional police detection with the unconventional psychology that grows out of an expanding consciousness of infinitely fissioning time lines. The story is beautifully controlled and superbly paced as the reader follows the investigation of Detective Trimble into a rash of bizarre crimes and suidices which have followed the successful operation of Crosstime, Inc. and the commercialization of crosstime trading. Trimble's investigation of an apparently motiveless suicide forces upon him and the reader an awareness of the consequences of Crosstime's cancellation of cause and effect and simple consciousness as underlying conditions of human law and basic ethics. If life is composed of an infinite series of multiple possibilities, as Trimble discovers, then all human actions are relative to the time line in which they take place. And so, as Trimble raises his service revolver to his head after cleaning it, he experiences a moment of kaleidoscopic awareness that other Trimbles are making an infinite number of other choices in other time lines at that moment. Niven's rendering of that moment of consciousness and its implications for the reader is surely one of the best of its kind. This story epitomizes another of Niven's strengths as a storyteller — his grounding of the reader's point of contact with a future technology in a moment of recognition or awareness.

Another of Niven's police detectives is Gil Hamilton, an agent of the Amalgamation of Regional Militia (ARM). He is the protagonist of the three stories of future crime solution that comprise the *Long ARM of Gil Hamilton*. These three tales, "Death by Ecstasy," "The Defenseless Dead," and "ARM," fit into the early era of the "known space" series. They are placed in the same cultural and social setting that is sketched into "The Jigsaw Man," an era in which there have been no cultural and technological breakthroughs; they lie beyond the future horizon. Instead, today's technology has been logically elaborated and fully developed, although it is considerably refined and advanced. The premise underlying these stories (and indeed many a story of future society) is summarized early in "Death by Ecstasy": "New Technologies create new customs, new laws, new ethics, new crimes." The great new crime of organlegging is a way of obtaining transplant parts. Organlegging is profitable because of the selfish desire of the living for immortality through transplant technology. It is their representatives who have made increasingly more Draconian laws, bringing even trivial crimes under capital punishment. The executions are carried out in operating disassembly rooms, in which the criminal/victim becomes the unwilling but forced donor for the state organ banks. In such a world of organized ghoulishness, of the abuse of justice and due process to serve the selfish desires of the majority, Niven has created a type of detective story which combines elements of the hard boiled detective with hard science extrapolation and social criticism. All three are first rate detective fiction, each dealing with a different type of crime and method of detection. The last story, "ARM," is a clever science fiction variation on the locked room mystery, whose solution depends on understanding the workings of a machine that produces time distortions.

"The Jigsaw Man" is a story told from the point of view of a victim of the organbank society, which punishes traffic violations with execution and distributes the body parts. The impact of the story depends on the gradual revelation of the ways in which social selfishness has distorted both human relations and the execution of justice. Warren Lewis Knowles is one of Niven's victimized heroes who becomes trapped in the machinery of legalized state murder, struggles to escape, and almost makes it before being caught again to stand trial for the capital offense of driving through six red lights in the space of two years. Knowles has a measure of revenge, however, by destroying a room full of organ preservation tanks and their contents.

"Rammer" is a story with a similar context, but one in which the rogue victim/hero beats the repressive state at its own game. Jerome Corbett was a "corpsicle," one of the frozen dead. He learns after awakening that his original body, frozen when he was dying from a terminal cancer, was beyond regeneration. His conscious personality has simply been transferred electronically into the host body of a criminal victim whose personality was erased electronically by the state. Indeed, Corbett learns in time that he is but the most recent of a series of conscious residents of that host body. The others failed to measure up to the extremely rigid state standards and had been erased, each in turn. Corbett survives a series of nightmarish training courses, never sure he is being tested, what standards are being used, or what constitutes satisfactory performance. He only knows what the price of failure will be. Corbett is to pilot the first bussard ram jet space craft designed for human flight. His mission is to find reducing-atmosphere planets and drop probes there so that the state may use them for future colonization. That the state should spread its contagion to the stars or last long enough to do so appalls the reader no less than it does Corbett. The echoes of Zamiatin's *We* in this story are perhaps more than accidental.

There are several other stories of the near future that deserve special attention. One is a delightful mystery/romance, "The Fourth Profession," which is one of Niven's barroom stories. Edward Harley Frazer runs The Long Spoon Bar, in which a newly landed race of aliens called "Monks" choose to open informal communication with humans. The monk of the Long Spoon Bar is a sampler who in several drinking sessions goes through the liquor supply and all known mixed drinks. The monk is a trader, in some ways like the Outsiders of the "known space" series, who pays for his drinks with knowledge, or rather with RNA pills that stimulate the mind of the taker according to the power of the pill. By accident or design, Frazer discovers that he can understand not only Monk language and culture but also can read their thoughts. This knowledge is used to save the human race from making a fatal miscalculation of the Monks and their motives. Despite the rather formulaic happy ending, "The Fourth Profession" is a successful and underrated Niven story that deserves wider appreciation.

"Inconstant Moon," on the other hand, is a justly famous award-winning story, written in the Walter M. Miller, Jr., tradition. It seems to owe something, consciously or otherwise, to "Dark Benediction." Like the latter story, "Inconstant Moon" is a "cosy catastrophe" story of the type we might call "catastrophe averted." In that sense, it also recalls Wells's "The Star." The story's art depends upon a complex sequence of ironies involving the hero and heroine who deduce from the brightening moon that the sun has gone nova and that this will be the world's last night. Their response to this depressing inference is neither very original nor imaginative. Niven manages to have it both ways. The hero and heroine make love, then go out to an understandably ambivalent celebration, which is punctuated by frequent glances of recognition exchanged with others who have guessed the meaning of the moon's inconstancy. Happily, the event turns out to be a serious but not world ending solar flare-up, and the couple retreats to their apartment after stocking up at the local market in preparation for the inevitable plagues of wind and flood that are sure to come. The familiar science fiction cosy catastrophe pattern is played off nicely against the mood that reminds one of the best scenes from *On the Beach*. Niven comments on the hollowness of modern life, while the reader enjoys the suspense and spectacle of the catastrophe formula.

Of the several stories set on Mars in the early twenty-first century ("The Eye of an Octopus," "How the Heroes Die," "At the Bottom of a Hole"), perhaps the best is the award-winning "Hole Man," a science fiction murder story with a quantum black hole used as a bullet. The fact that the murder weapon supplied the power for an immense and mysterious power console left on Mars by aliens of some remote and now defunct colony, adds further interest and dimension to this neatly told tale of mockery and revenge. The delightful ambiguity of the ending places this story several cuts above all but a small and elite group of science fiction crime stories, some of which are Niven products (*The Long Arm of Gil Hamilton*). Once again style and tone are combined with sophisticated scientific speculation to produce the kind of thinking man's story for which Niven is justly praised.

Five Hanville Svetz stories are collected in *The Flight of the Horse*, all of which are fantasy science fiction involving time travel from the distant future of the third millennium into the past. Four of these stories are comic, and one, "Death in a Cage," is a serious alternate history tale. The comic fantasy elements of the remaining four: "The Flight of the Horse," "Leviathan," "Bird in the Hand," and "There's a Wolf in My Time Machine," are similar in tone, style, and intention to the L. Sprague de Camp and Fletcher Pratt Harold Shea stories, most of which appear now under the title "The Compleat Enchanter." Hanville Svetz is the reluctant agent of the Institute of Temporal Research and time travels into a fabled past to bring back such trophies as a unicorn (which is taken for a horse), Moby Dick (the consolation prize for the museum following the failure to bring back Leviathan, a whale eating sea serpent), and a roc (mistaken for an ostrich). The comic possibilities of these situations are developed with a skill equal to Asimov at his comic best, and the comedy is broad enough to allow for the free play of Niven's ironic wit.

Most of the stories considered so far, with the exception of the Gil Hamilton series, are outside the known space series. These stories of varying length and merit when combined with the novels *World of Ptavvs*, *A Gift from Earth*, *Ringworld*, and *Protector*, form the mosiac of future history that science fiction readers have become familiar with as "known space." For readers who are beginning to acquaint themselves with these stories, Niven has himself provided a guide in the collection of *Tales of Known Space: The Universe of Larry Niven* (Ballantine, 1975). There is a convenient bibliography of the series and a very helpful timeline diagram similar to the one Robert A. Heinlein provided for his future history stories. Unfortunately, the collection does not contain all the known space stories. The reader will want to supplement this volume with the stories in *Neutron Star*, which contains four of the five Beowulf Shaeffer tales ("Neutron Star," "At the Core," "Flatlander," "Grendel,"); the fifth, "The Borderland of Sol," is found in *Tales of Known Space*. Part of the fun of reading the known space stories is the process of becoming acquainted with Niven's mythos of known space history and of piecing together the outlines of that vision which stirs both imagination and reason with its extrapolated science and its consistency of vision. Some of these stories are blends of adventure, suspense and hard science speculations mixed with either fantasy or aspects of the soft sciences, especially psychology. The impact of advances in science and technology are projected into the future, especially in two fields: the biological, medical sciences and transportation. Niven seems to have selected these two areas because revolutions in biological control and the development of travel through transfer booths on earth (power assisted teleportation) and interstellar spacecraft imply equally revolutionary changes in the ethical and moral spheres as well. Niven prefers to make his strongest social and ethical statements symbolically rather than rhetorically. For instance, his solution to race relations is so deceptively simple, it passes almost unnoticed in the stories and the novels. After biological control of aging has been achieved and effective control of physical conditioning and appearance has been attained, the racial question effectively disappears, because skin color and physical appearance become matters of fashion to a large extent. Of course this conveniently ignores the two evils of population control and eugenics, but future fertility control practices presumably take care of such difficulties.

"Neutron Star" and "At the Core" are complementary accounts of epic flights of Beowulf Shaeffer, a roguish space pilot from the colony world We Made It, whose personality is a plausible mixture of the caution of the Indian scout and the adventurous curiosity of the explorer. In the former study, he is inveigled into piloting a space craft to a neutron star to discover why a previous expedition proved fatal to the crew. Sponsors of this flight are Puppeteers, an alien race more highly developed in technology and in brainpower than humans, who are also inveterate cowards. The body of the story is an arresting account of the voyage to the neutron star and Shaeffer's discovery and adjustment to the unique warping of gravity which produces the tidal effect that killed the earlier crew but left the spacecraft intact. In the latter story, Shaeffer pilots another craft to the galactic core as a publicity stunt for General Products hulls. As in "Neutron Star," the details of the flight are an effective exercise in space flight description. Shaeffer's discovery that the galactic core has gone nova forms the basis for the Puppeteer migration in other known space stories, particularly in *Ringworld*.

Two other Shaeffer stories deserve mention. "Flatlander" is space exploration adventure spiced by the contrast in psychology between Shaeffer, who has learned the difference between acceptable and unacceptable risks in dealing with space exploration, and the thrill-seeking amateur "flatlander," or Earthman, who was nurtured in an environment which provides maximum comfort and protection for humans. In "Flatlander" the astronomical singularity that Shaeffer has to contend with is an antimatter star and its satellite. "The Borderland of Sol" is a very effective science fiction mystery adventure involving another singularity, a black hole, which is used by renegade scientists to remove the evidence of their space craft robberies. Niven updates the western formula in this last of the Beowulf Shaeffer adventures.

"The Soft Weapon" is an underrated story that symbolizes many of the best qualities of the known space series, combining space opera suspense and adventure with the fascination of a superior science fiction mystery. The narrative focuses on a weapon, the product of an extremely ancient and extinct species, which was developed for one of its elite agents as an all-purpose device for defense, communication, survival, and offense. The weapon becomes the prize in the battle of wits between a bellicose alien species known as Kzin and an alliance of two humans and a Puppeteer. The gradual discovery of the nature and properties of the "soft weapon," so-called because it changes shape with each function, is played out against the struggle with the Kzin for its control. Although used only as background, Niven gives the reader fascinating glimpses of the Slavers and Tnuctipun, whose great war annihilated life in their portion of the universe a billion years ago, and whose relics are sought after in hopes that a new weapon will be discovered which will give either humans or Kzin a clear military superiority over the other. In this story we meet Nessus, "the mad Puppeteer," who plays a central role in *Ringworld*, and the interested reader will also learn much of the Puppeteers, Kzin, Slavers, and Tnuctipun.

The short fiction of Larry Niven represents an exceptional achievement in the literature of modern science fiction. The only real rivals to his known space series are Heinlein's future history stories and Asimov's Foundation series; that is not bad company to be in. In range of treatment, subject, theme, and type, Niven is without peer among his contemporary science fiction writers. He has won more than his share of Hugo and Nebula awards for stories with hard science fiction extrapolations, but his best writing is not limited to hard science speculations. His stories of social science fiction are among the best written in the field, even though they lack the polemical and ideological intensity of some of the newer writers of the 1960's and 1970's. Niven has written a dozen or more of the best science fiction suspense adventure stories to the grateful appreciation of the reader who still likes his science to be laced with generous doses of exciting spectacle and action. In the Gil Hamilton stories, Niven has invented a new variation on the hard boiled formula. Indeed, all the detective and mystery science fiction stories deserve to be ranked among the best in both genres.

Niven's fidelity to the tradition of past science fiction and fantasy has blunted the edge of his social relevance for some readers. He is accused of relying too heavily on stereotypes and traditional story telling formulas. Nevertheless, for the range and quality of his work in short fiction, Niven has already earned a place among the front rank of masters of the science fiction short story.

Donald K. Lawler

Sources for Further Study

Criticism:

Jameson, Frederic. "Science Fiction as Politics: Larry Niven," in *New Republic*. XXX (October, 1976), pp. 34-38. Jameson gives a discussion of Niven's work and political philosophy.

Niven, Larry. "The Words of Science Fiction," in *The Craft of Science Fiction*. Edited by Reginald Bretnor. New York: Harper & Row, 1976, pp. 178-194. Niven writes on his own contributions to science fiction literature and analyzes the field generally. The book as a whole is an important work of science fiction criticism.

THE SHORT FICTION OF MURRAY LEINSTER

Author: Murray Leinster (William Fitzgerald Jenkins, 1896-1975)
Type of work: Short stories, a novelette, and a short novel

Works of "hard" science fiction in which the author questions the roles of logic and high technology in human affairs

From the publication of "The Runaway Skyscraper" in 1919 until his death in 1975, Murray Leinster (William Fitzgerald Jenkins) was one of America's most prolific producers of popular, mass-market science fiction. A good many of these works were, as one might expect, somewhat less than remarkable. Most, in fact, such as *Space Tug* (1965) or *Land of the Giants* (1968), have already been forgotten by all but his most loyal fans. A handful of the many novels which he published during the 1950's and the 1960's, however, do manage to retain a certain readability, particularly such old favorites as *The Forgotten Planet* (1950), *Creatures of the Abyss* (1962), and *Time Tunnel* (1964). A similar assessment can be made of the more than one thousand stories that the indefatigable Leinster wrote during those same five decades. Only a few, most notably "Sidewise in Time" (1934) and the "Med Service" stories which appeared in 1956 and 1957 in *Astounding Science Fiction*, can be said to rise above the kind of adolescent, formula-written "hard" science fiction which was his speciality.

Those works for which Leinster will perhaps be best remembered, however, are "First Contact" (1945); some stories collected in *The Planet Explorer* (1956); and "Exploration Team," for which he won a Hugo in 1956. In "First Contact," Leinster employs one of his favorite techniques. He presents the reader with what appears to be an unsolvable problem: how can a chance encounter with aliens, deep in space, be consummated without the destruction of either or both races? At first there appears to be no way out short of mutual annihilation, for neither race can be trusted to leave peacefully without attempting to discover the whereabouts of the other's home planet, thereby placing it in danger of destruction. Leinster sets up that old familiar science fiction struggle between reason and emotion. Although the Earthmen do feel a certain sympathy for the strangers, reason tells them that if they do not kill the aliens, the aliens will surely kill them. There is a glimmer of hope, however. Each race has an insatiable curiosity about the other. (The aliens, who communicate by other means, are fascinated by the humans' use of soundwaves, while the humans are interested in the aliens' uses of infrared rays). Thus, as long as this flood of information continues to flow, neither race will destroy the other.

As a professional inventor and as a writer who is most often thought of as a proponent of advanced technology, it is not surprising that Leinster has these two races communicating by means of "coders," "analyzers," and similar pieces of machinery. (Some of the other gadgets and technological special effects he uses from time to time are "visiplates," "scanners," "deflectors," "locators," and "tracers," in addition, of course, to spaceships powered by "overdrive"). Leinster does little more than mention these things, and, along with a cursory sketch of the whys-and-wherefores of the Crab Nebula, this is about all the "science" he uses.

Leinster makes it clear that technology alone will not extricate these two races from their mutual dilemma. Although it does allow them to communicate, almost telepathically, it can do nothing to allay their fear and distrust. In spite of the fact that Tommy Dort, the boyish "hero" of the piece, is able to develop a chummy relationship with "Buck," his alien counterpart, the two spaceships remain poised, ready to strike. It is only because Tommy does like Buck so much, that he is determined to find a way out; for even though Buck is a bald, gill-breathing creature who sees by means of heat waves, he appears to Tommy to be almost human. After a good deal of suspense (a Leinster trademark), Tommy finally hits upon a solution: the two races will exchange ships, thereby increasing the flow of information available to each, without risking the lives of either.

"First Contact" is an adolescent space adventure, with a typical juvenile hero, elevated a notch or two. But unlike most stories of this type, this one seems to have a point to it. What Leinster appears to be saying is that neither technology nor rationality is adequate to deal with such a delicate and complex problem — some humanity is needed, too, and this is what young Tommy supplies. Whereas "the Skipper" and "the Psychologist" and the rest of the characters on the Earth-ship are nothing more than cardboard, Tommy is real flesh and blood. In fact, Tommy and Buck are so engaging that they become a kind of space-age Tom and Huck, telling each other dirty jokes out in space, four thousand light years from Earth.

In *The Planet Explorer*, Leinster also sets up problems that at first appear to be beyond solution. In "Solar Constant," for example, Bordman lands on Lani III only to discover that unless something is done quickly, neither he nor anyone else will ever leave the planet alive. Lani III's sun is dying. The problem presented to Bordman (he seems to be the only person in most of these stories who is capable of sustained rational thought) is how to produce enough energy to activate the landing grid so that the inhabitants can live long enough to be evacuated. As is customary in a Leinster story, there is a moment when things appear to be hopeless. But it is against Bordman's nature to give up. After a false start (he failed in his attempt to rig up a helicopter-supported grid system which would have pulled energy out of the ionosphere), he hits upon a plan to launch bombs that will explode into clouds of metallic vapor. By some means which Leinster never explains, the clouds energize the main landing grid, thus providing the planet with power.

A similar problem confronts Bordman in "Sand Doom." No on can leave Xosa II because the planet's landing grid has been covered by hundreds of

millions of tons of sand. Again, everyone except Bordman seems to be im-
mobilized by fear. In his mind, however, every problem has a solution, if, that
is, he remains calm and trusts to logic. The particular solution he arrives at
here is not important. What is important is that he does solve each problem
with a combination of rational thought and a knowledge of high-technology.
Bordman is the consummate leading man of hard science fiction. Neither a
warrior nor a scientist, he is the technician *par excellence* — "A technician
first and foremost,'" as he puts it. He is the prototype of the science fiction
protagonist of the 1950's — the kind made so popular by Marshall Thompson
in all the Grade-B films of the decade. He is a completely conventionalized,
stock character — stiff, one-dimensional, static. We see him only objectively,
from the outside. He is a man without feelings ("'What difference do feelings
make? One can't change facts.'"). Even when he falls in love (in "Solar Constant"), he remains forever the tight-lipped, square-jawed hero. Any feelings
that he might have are presented only in the most stylized, abstract terms.
Despite his professions of love, he remains the quintessential loner of postwar
fiction — a man of no family and few friends, dedicated to logic and objectivity, who lives for his work, weary though he might be. Bordman is the techni-
crat turned hero.

There is one story in *The Planet Explorer* that really does not belong: "Exploration Team," his Hugo winner (which first appeared as a novelette in
Astounding Science Fiction). In this story, Leinster simply changed the name
of the main character from Roane to Bordman, and slipped it in along with
the rest of his Colonial Survey Stories. However, the choice is not appropriate.
The format might be similar, but this is not the same Bordman we have grown
accustomed to seeing in the other stories.

As usual, there is plenty of mystery and suspense. For example, what happened to the colony of humans and their slave-robots? Was it destroyed by the
sphexes, the lizardlike carnivores that terrorize the planet? Or did survivors
send that mysterious radio signal that was picked up by Huyghens, the planet's
very own Robinson Crusoe character who had fled civilization in order to live
in peace with his family of mutated Kodiak bears? And what about Huyghens,
anyway? Will Roane send him off the prison, as he promises to do, for illegal
colonization?

It is a suspenseful, action-packed tale, just the kind that any young boy
might enjoy on a rainy Saturday afternoon. But there is more to it than that.
What raises "Exploration Team" above the other stories in *The Planet
Explorer* (and from most other science fiction as well) is that there is growth
and development on the part of Roane, who, as Senior Officer of the Colonial
Survey, has come to Loren II to make a progress report on the Robot Colony.
At first there seems to be no discernible difference between him and Bordman,
his counterpart in the other stories; he is the same tight, inflexible bureaucrat
who goes strictly by the rules. As such, it is his intention to see to it that

Huyghens pays for living on Loren II without permission.

However, as Roane's relationship with Huyghens and his animals develops on their perilous journey through the sphex-infested jungle, he begins to undergo some changes. He begins to like the old hermit and his bears, especially Nugget, the cub. Nugget's playfulness rubs off on him (he had never even touched an animal before), and his rigidity begins to loosen. Huyghens' anarchism also begins to make an impact, and Roane is finally forced to admit that robots are often unsuitable for colonization. (On Loren II they were unable to respond to the unexpected — in this case, the ferocity of the sphexes).

Leinster uses the robots as symbols of the purely rational. They are effective at doing what they have been programed to do, but when it comes to an emergency, they are virtually useless. The sphexes, on the other hand, lie at the other extreme. They are the epitome of the science fiction monster — ugly, coldblooded carnivores who participate in frenzied mass attacks whenever they get so much as a whiff of blood. They are as irrational and animalistic as the robots are rational and mechanistic. Huyghens' bears, however, are animals who possess positive qualities absent in the other creatures. They are a loyal as are the robots, but because they are living, thinking beings, they have what the robots lack — an adaptability that allows them to respond imaginatively to crisis. Thus they can do what the machines could never do: they can protect Huyghens and Roane from the sphexes.

As the search for the lost colony nears its conclusion, Roane's transformation becomes complete. No longer is he the legalistic bureaucrat who vows to punish Huyghens for his attempts to live a freer and more authentic existence. He has gained an innocence, a lightness, that allows him to develop and grow away from the typical cardboard character of most science fiction (including the "Bordman" character — "Board Man?" "Bored?"). Finally, he and Huyghens find three survivors from the ill-fated Robot Colony. This is purely incidental, however, for by this time the adventure plot has taken a back seat to the story of Roane's transformation from a shallow pulp hero to a human being (an older, wiser Tommy Dort) who is both compassionate and humane. It is this transformation, in fact, that can perhaps be seen as the finest, most interesting achievement in Leinster's forty-year career as a writer of science fiction.

A. James Stupple

Sources for Further Study

Criticism:

Carter, Paul A. *The Creation of Tomorrow*. New York: Columbia University Press, 1977, pp. 109-110. Carter discusses Leinster's pioneering of the idea of parallel universes existing.

Moskowitz, Sam. *Strange Horizons, The Spectrum of Science Fiction*. New York: Scribner's, 1976, pp. 147-148. Moskowitz discusses Leinster's use of "the evil scientific genius" in his stories.

THE SHORT FICTION OF NATHANIEL HAWTHORNE

Author: Nathaniel Hawthorne (1804-1864)
Type of work: Short stories
Time: The eighteenth and nineteenth centuries
Locale: The United States and Europe

Five stories exploring the relationship between scientists and humanity

Romantic authors have often been hostile to science, which they feel threatens the sense of wonder, fantasy, and the free flight of the imagination through its insistence upon verifiable fact. They also charge it with a lack of reverence, a willingness to subordinate human beings to its experiments, and a Faustian preoccupation with forbidden knowledge. Wordsworth complained of the scientist who would "peep and botanize upon his mother's grave"; Poe charged science with attempting to destroy his vision of dryads and hamadryads; and the Transcendentalists, seeing intuition and spontaneity as the highest source of insight and way of elevating spirit above matter, derided the scientist's obsession with measurement and matter. Nevertheless, some Romantic writers saw that science could also generate a sense of wonder, as it opened new vistas to the human mind, and so they began to write scientific romances.

One of the earliest to write such stories was Nathaniel Hawthorne, who called his tales and novels romances and defined the locale of the romance as "a neutral ground where the Actual and the Imaginary might meet." Many of his tales are fantasies dealing with the supernatural rather than with science, but a handful of them do deal with scientists and qualify as primitive science fiction. Hawthorne knew little of actual science; he offers no plausible details for the scientific experiments in his fiction, and his scientists are halfway between medieval alchemy and modern science. They rely more upon Cornelius Agrippa, Paracelsus, and Albertus Magnus than upon authentic scientists of their own day, and so the scientific romances are on the borderline between fantasy and science fiction. "The fact is," wrote Hawthorne, "in writing a romance, a man is always — or always ought to be — careening on the utmost verge of a precipitous absurdity, and the skill lies in coming as close as possible, without actually tumbling over."

As extrapolative science fiction, Hawthorne's tales are absurd; but as allegories of the nature, role, and morality of science, they are perceptive and provocative. In particular, several of Hawthorne's scientists are guilty of what he calls the "Unpardonable Sin." This concept is defined specifically in "Ethan Brand" (1849), which is a good place to begin a study of Hawthorne's science fiction.

The plot is a mixture of melodrama and fairy tale. Ethan Brand, a young idealist full of love and sympathy for mankind and of pity for our sins, undertakes a search for the Unpardonable Sin, only to find that during the quest, he becomes guilty of it himself. Though he begins the quest with tenderness, he becomes corrupted by pride, for the sin is the development of the intellect without a corresponding development of the heart. In the end, Brand is raised to the eminence of scholarship and philosophy but in the process has "lost his hold on the magnetic chain of humanity" and become "a cold observer, looking on mankind as the subject of his experiment, and, at length, converting man and woman to be his puppets, and pulling the wires that moved them to such degrees of crime as were demanded for his study." During the course of his research, he makes a girl named Esther "the subject of a psychological experiment, and wasted, absorbed, and perhaps annihilated her soul, in the process." The story takes place in Brand's home community, to which he has returned after realizing that the Unpardonable Sin is in himself. The consequence is that he has become cut off from human brotherhood and suffers in lonely, though proud, isolation. At the end, in bitter despair, he leaps into a lime kiln and is incinerated except for his hard heart, which even the fire cannot melt.

Though the story is skillfully told, the plot is so farfetched and the character so undeveloped that one is likely to dismiss it as a fantasy and ignore the significance of Hawthorne's moral. The sin seems a mere abstraction. Nevertheless, "Ethan Brand" is one of Hawthorne's most profound tales, not only reflecting St. Paul's admonition in I Corinthians 13 that the person who has all knowledge but lacks love is nothing, but also looking forward to the use of science for torture, brainwashing, and total warfare. In the immediate background of the tale may be the Puritan theocrats, who would damn people on points of Calvinist dogma, and the *philosophes* of the Age of Reason who supported the excesses of the Reign of Terror in the French Revolution, guillotining people for ideological differences in the name of liberty, equality, and brotherhood. In later history, the Unpardonable Sin fits political terrorists, from Dostoevski's to our own time, who do not care whom they kill in the name of whatever cause they serve, and the totalitarian revolutionaries who prefer issues to individuals, and for the sake of some eventual Utopia designed to benefit an abstract mankind find it expedient to purge the unorthodox, to institutionalize terror, to enshrine dialectic and dogma. There are innumerable literary and historical examples, from the Spanish Inquisition to the present. As for the role of science, "Ethan Brand" applies to those scientists who claim no responsibility for how their research is used, who are dedicated in the abstract to pure knowledge, regardless of its application, and to those other scientists who actively participate in programs of germ and nerve warfare and the manufacturing of napalm, thermonuclear bombs, and other horrors. Finally, it applies to those scholars who scorn anyone who disagrees with them or who is incapable of reaching their level of supposed enlightenment.

Ethan Brand's version of the sin seems comparatively tame, because we never meet the woman he has ruined and because Hawthorne is entirely vague as to what Brand has done to her; but the destruction of a mind and the annihilation of a soul through a psychological experiment foreshadow brainwashing, drugs, lobotomies, and mind control created through terror and torture; in this sense, "Ethan Brand" anticipates *Brave New World*, *Nineteen Eighty-Four* and *A Clockwork Orange*.

Though Hawthorne does not repeat the term, the Unpardonable Sin recurs in others of his works. Dr. Chillingworth in *The Scarlet Letter* torments Dimmesdale psychologically, while planning the ultimate revenge of damning his soul to hell forever. Hollingsworth, the reformer in *The Blithedale Romance*, comes to love his philanthropic theories more than any human being. But the Unpardonable Sin is best exemplified in two more tales of scientists.

"The Birthmark" (1843) is set in the late eighteenth century, when modern science was coming into its own but when superstition and such medieval concepts as phlogiston were not yet eradicated. To the populace, modern science still seemed half magic; experiments with electricity still had about them an air of wizardry. Hawthorne's protagonist, Aylmer, is half-scientist and half-wizard, and his chemical experiments have more than a measure of alchemy about them. For Aylmer, science has become a religion, freeing man from superstitious fears and giving him mastery over nature. But that mastery has not yet been attained, and Aylmer's lack of mastery over himself is a fatal *hubris*. He has recently married Georgeanna, a woman of remarkable beauty, marred only by the blemish of a birthmark on one cheek, so insignificant that ordinarily it is scarcely noticeable. When she blushes, or when the blood flows to her cheek, the birthmark faintly suggests a strawberry-hued infant hand. To most men, it merely enhanced her beauty; many would have given much to kiss it.

But Aylmer sees it as a sign of human imperfection and as a challenge to his art. He becomes so obsessed with the birthmark that it becomes a barrier between himself and his wife. The once cheerful Georgeanna is driven by her husband's monomania to hate the birthmark and to risk her life in allowing him to subject her to chemical experiments in the hope of eradicating it forever. He assures her that he can accomplish it, that there is no risk, and he accepts the statement that he will deserve to be worshiped when he succeeds: ". . . what will be my triumph when I shall have corrected what Nature left imperfect in her fairest work!" Meanwhile, he entertains his wife with demonstrations of his skill — daguerreotype portraiture, diorama and stereoscope shows, a plant that grows from seed to flower to decay in minutes, and lectures in alchemy and elixirs. He also appalls her with a poison subtle enough to apportion the length of life by minutes or murder the most guarded monarch. But it can also wash away freckles and is akin to the drug he plans to use to remove the birthmark.

Aylmer's scientific ambitions are Faustian, and he warns his curious wife against reading "in a sorcerer's books," which contain pages of forbidden knowledge. He also concedes, finally, that his greatest successes have fallen short of his ideal aim and that there is danger for her in his experiment. Nevertheless, he is prepared to risk her life for his dream of perfection, and he has made the birthmark such a torment for her that she would rather die than live with it. The birthmark is a symbol of the imperfection that Georgeanna shares with fallen humanity; Melville compared it to Billy Budd's stammer.

Superficial though it seems, the stigmatic hand is rooted in Georgeanna's essential being, and when it is removed, she dies. Nevertheless, she has been converted to her husband's religion of science and would rather perish in the attempt at perfection than forego the experiment. For the sake of "a perfect future," Aylmer has destroyed "the best earth could offer." His dying wife approves of his action, but the reader sees that the worship of science at the expense of humanity is another version of the Unpardonable Sin. Aylmer's attempt to spiritualize materialism may be noble in the abstract, but the human consequence is tragic.

In "Rappaccini's Daughter" (1844), there is not even the excuse of a birthmark to justify the experiment that Dr. Rappaccini conducts upon his daughter Beatrice. Another blend of chemist and alchemist, Rappaccini has turned his walled garden in Padua into a lush but deadly display of poisonous plants. It is the Eden of a fallen world, and Rappaccini is an Adam who has turned one of the most innocent of human activities into a malignant pastime. Caring "infinitely more for science than for mankind," he commits the Unpardonable Sin in subjecting his daughter to experiments which give her a beauty resembling that of the flowers in the garden, but also a breath and touch which is as deadly as the poisonous plants. In its magical and erotic mystery, the garden resembles those of medieval courtly love, such as in *The Romance of the Rose*.

The one thing missing is a lover, So Dr. Rappaccini snares one for his daughter, so that she will not be completely isolated and can find happiness in the captivity he has inflicted on her. The candidate is Giovanni Guasconti, a student at the University of Padua. From his window, he has observed Beatrice and been smitten by her beauty, though bemused and shocked by what seems to be her power to kill plants and small living creatures with a breath or a touch. Professor Baglioni, an envious rival of Rappaccini, warns Giovanni about the depraved fancy of the cold, withdrawn doctor. Nevertheless, Giovanni learns of a secret entrance to the garden, woos Beatrice, and wins her love, according to her father's design. But learning of her kinship with the poisonous plants, he prevails upon her to take an antidote provided by Baglioni. Like the chemical draught that Aylmer offers Georgeanna, the medicine proves fatal.

In this story, however, Rappaccini is not alone guilty of the Unpardonable Sin. Professor Baglioni is equally guilty of it, as he gloats at the end over the fatal outcome of Rappaccini's experiment. Giovanni is not innocent either; unable to distinguish Beatrice's innocence from the deadliness around her, he gambles with her life and loses. "Oh, was there not, from the first, more poison in thy nature than in mine?" the dying Beatrice asks him.

Hawthorne's most ambiguous science fiction story is "The Artist of the Beautiful" (1844). On the surface, it is a defense of art for art's sake; but since the artist in this tale creates works of mechanical genius, we have yet another examination of the role and function of science. The germ of the story appears in Hawthorne's *American Notebooks, 1840-1841*: "To represent a man as spending life and the intensest labor in the accomplishment of some mechanical trifle — as in making a miniature coach to be drawn by fleas, or a dinner-service to be put into a cherry-stone." The artist of the beautiful is Owen Warland, an ethereal genius who shrinks with squeamish revulsion from the utilitarian world and who in turn is despised by those who respect only practical power. His particular opponents are Peter Hovenden, a watchmaker and Owen's former master, and the brawny blacksmith Robert Danforth. Owen's physique is as delicate as his sensibilities; just as his muscles are no match for the blacksmith's, so he feels out of place in the aggressive world of getting ahead. A miniaturist, he creates mechanical toys of ingenious fancy that have no practical value and are too delicate for children to play with. He has a "love of the beautiful . . . completely refined from all utilitarian coarseness." On the one hand, he can be admired as an uncompromising artist dedicated to the ideal or as a scientist working for pure research rather than technological application. He represents both art for art's sake and the pursuit of knowledge for its own sake, both uncorrupted by the pressures of the marketplace. In his hands, science is transmuted into art.

On the other hand, he falls into the recurring Hawthorne trap of becoming "insulated from the common business of life" and withdrawing into a "moral cold." In this sense, the story resembles Tennyson's poem "The Palace of Art," in which the artist retreats into a gorgeous but selfish and superficial refuge from the common concerns of humanity. Warland's beautiful trifles even have some resemblance to the fanciful garden of Dr. Rappaccini, or to the insubstantial shows that Aylmer creates to divert Georgeanna. For Hawthorne, true art requires love and sympathy, missing in mere ingenious creations of the fancy. Warland does hope, if not for love, at least for sympathy from Hovenden's daughter Annie, but she is unable to appreciate the delicate work that her more blunt father openly scorns.

When Annie marries the blacksmith, Warland withdraws completely from the world of facts into that of fancy. While Annie shares her love with her husband and son, Owen gives up everything to create his masterpiece, a mechanical butterfly. It is indeed beautiful, but it fails to reflect any human joy or suffering; it is completely unrelated to the experience of living. It is this lack of any human element rather than its practical uselessness that is its deficiency. When Annie's son crushes the butterfly, her father laughs maliciously; but Owen feels no sorrow, for he can continue to live in the ideal.

Certainly Warland's anti-artistic adversaries are wrong to scorn anything without immediate practical applicability, but Owen is equally mistaken in giving up involvement in humanity for the sake of an insubstantial trifle that is not a reflection of life. Both his character and his work are too precious, and his total dedication to aesthetic refinement is a form of egotism that deceives him with the illusion that he has devoted himself to a higher cause, when instead he has retreated from the common experiences of humanity. Though his work is otherwise harmless, the egotism behind it and its self-induced isolation make him kin to Aylmer and Rappaccini.

The elixir of life, which featured in a minor way in "The Birthmark," is the subject of "Dr. Heidegger's Experiment" (1837). This story, however, hardly qualifies as science fiction, since the elixir comes not from the doctor's laboratory but from the Fountain of Youth in Florida. Hawthorne is concerned not with the scientific possibilities but rather with the moral allegory, as he has the aged Dr. Heidegger administer a draught to three equally aged men and one woman. Instead of taking the wisdom of age with them back into their new-found youth, they revert to folly and riot. The elixir wears off after half an hour, leaving the quartet again withered and feeble. The story is ambiguous as to whether the entire experience may not be a hallucination, for while the patients think they have regained their youth, the mirror reflects them as ancient dotards grotesquely engaging in immature pranks. Dr. Heidegger, who has refrained from drinking the elixir, says he would not be young again, that age has its own virtue; but the others, having learned nothing, resolve to make a pilgrimage to Florida.

Hawthorne himself became obsessed with writing about the elixir of youth and made it a subject of *The Dolliver Romance* and *Septimius Felton*, two abortive novels that he was unable to complete in his final years. When he worked on the theme, he was in ill health and suspected he had not long to live. Before his death in 1864, he did finish a draft of each; but in these works, Hawthorne was unable to find a suitable vehicle for his ideas, and we are left with fanciful allegory unsustained by a compelling dramatic situation and flesh and blood characters.

Robert E. Morsberger

Sources for Further Study

Criticism:

Crews, Frederick C. *The Sins of the Fathers: Hawthorne's Psychological Themes*. New York: Oxford University Press, 1966. Crews's treatment of Hawthorne's themes is fundamental to any understanding of the psychological aspects of the characters.

Doubleday, Neal Frank. *Hawthorne's Early Tales, A Critical Study*. Durham, N.C.: Duke University Press, 1972. Doubleday looks at the major critical points of interest in Hawthorne's early fiction.

Elder, Marjorie J. *Nathaniel Hawthorne; Transcendental Symbolist*. Athens: Ohio University Press, 1969. Hawthorne's transcendental views and their embodiment in his symbols are deciphered by Elder.

Fogle, Richard Harter. *Hawthorne's Fiction*. Norman: University of Oklahoma Press, 1952. This study by Fogle establishes a relationship between Hawthorne's short fiction and his novels and should furnish some grounds for generalization for students of science fiction.

Stubbs, John Caldwell. *The Pursuit of Form: A Study of Hawthorne and the Romance*. Urbana: University of Illinois Press, 1970, pp. 53-60. Science Fiction is an offshoot of the romance. Stubbs shows how Hawthorne adapted and changed the form.

THE SHORT FICTION OF RAY BRADBURY

Author: Ray Bradbury (1920-   )
Type of work: Short stories

Sixty-one short stories written between 1945 and 1959, expressing the author's generally affirmative response to the world and to the possibilities opened by human imagination

Ray Bradbury began to intrigue the reading public with his short stories in 1940, and he continues to intrigue nearly forty years later. Very few American writers of science fiction have achieved — solely on the basis of his short fiction — the kind of stature Bradbury enjoys among critics and readers alike. Unlike such well-known contemporaries as John Steinbeck, Ernest Hemingway, Kurt Vonnegut, and Flannery O'Connor, he has never been a successful novelist. In fact, Bradbury has written only one novel, *Something Wicked This Way Comes* (1962), the "novel" *Dandelion Wine* having been a collection of seventeen previously published short stories more or less unified by a central point of view (twelve-year-old Douglas Spaulding) and a specific place and time (Green Town, Illinois, and Summer, 1928). *Wicked This Way Comes* was not a particularly successful novel even though it appeared when Bradbury's popular audience was probably at its peak, and in paperback it has not sold as well as several of his story collections have. Bradbury's short fiction, however, remains both in demand and in print. In particular, those stories published during the fourteen years between 1945 and 1959 — his most productive as well as his most creative years — seem to have found a position of permanence in American literature. Certainly it is the stories from that period which have earned him his own reputation as the chief of fantasy writers in this country.

It would be virtually impossible to characterize generally the nearly two hundred stories Bradbury wrote and published during those years. Much of what he wrote might best be termed speculative fiction (*The Martian Chronicles*, 1950); some of it was nostalgic reminiscence (*Dandelion Wine*, 1957); a great deal was conventional grotesquery and fantasy (*The Illustrated Man*, 1951 and *The October Country*, 1955); and there was an anti-Utopian novella (*Fahrenheit 451*, 1953). But at the same time that Bradbury was writing the stories that would fill these books he was beginning to move toward another kind of fantasy, an unusual type of fiction that would by the late 1950's appeal to readers of such disparate "slick" magazines as *The Saturday Evening Post* and *Playboy*, and do so without alienating those who had followed his maturing in the "pulps" — *Weird Tales*, *Detective Tales*, *Planet Stories* and the like — since the early 1940's. This was an unconventional kind of fantasy in which principal characters themselves are neither freaks nor madmen nor aliens, but ordinary human beings engaged in ordinary human occupations; people to whom extraordinary, almost spiritual things happen and who are changed by their experiences. It is in these stories, the best examples of which appear in *The Golden Apples of the Sun* and *A Medicine for Melancholy*, that Bradbury's considerable writing talent and his clear understanding of the human psyche are most closely aligned; it is in these stories that Bradbury's genius as well as his glad affirmation of the world is made manifest.

The title story from *A Medicine for Melancholy*, for example, is the story of an eighteenth century London girl, Camillia Wilkes, who suffers the vague symptoms of late adolescence and impending womanhood. She feels her sexuality awakening and does not know how to cope with what she feels. Her "disease" can neither be named nor be cured by any conventional physician, and it is generally feared that she will die. At length, however, she is visited by a kindly incubus — apparently Saint Bosco — in the guise of a Dustman; the incubus, never identified as such, does his work, and Camillia is made well. The story's theme, that ambiguous and difficult relationship among youth, sexuality, and acceptable behavior, certainly is familiar enough. But partly by setting the action in an age of Faith, partly by peopling it with unsophisticated, yet humanly concerned characters, and partly by refusing to ridicule those naïve characters with any kind of incredulousness or ironic askance-looking, Bradbury makes what could as easily have been erotic trivia or clinical observation into, for Camillia Wilkes, mystical experience and, for the reader, affirmation of the power of imagination. "A Medicine for Melancholy" is not a psychology lesson, nor is it strictly fantasy writing, at least not in the normal sense of the term; it is simply a celebration of one of life's significant mysteries. And what is of most importance, the story is satisfied to marvel at a girl's growing up. It seeks neither to explain nor to exploit the mystery it celebrates.

A somewhat slighter story, "The Shore Line at Sunset," also from *A Medicine for Melancholy*, quite effectively uses the fantastic as catalyst for one man's learning to accept what he is. The protagonist, called only Tom, is a sensitive California beachcomber who, because of frustrated love and indistinctly defined end-of-the-summer blues, has determined to leave his house and long-time roommate. But then he discovers a beached mermaid and, in deciding to return her to the sea rather than open a freak house with her as star attraction, he realizes why he is the man he is; and he accepts both himself and his friend. The mermaid is speechless and motionless — in fact she sleeps through the whole of the action — and her presence is accounted for in language closer to being erotic than fantastic, perhaps even closer to awe-struck than erotic; as a result she curiously does not damage credibility as she would be expected to in what is, again, a story that is finally about the relationship between two very ordinary humans and not about mermaids and mermen at all. Tom has truth revealed to him through his reaction to something extraordinary; but it is in that truth that the story lies, not in the oddity of his experience. Granting the unbelievable is necessary to accepting "The Shore Line at Sunset," but to label the story simply "fantasy" is seriously to misinterpret Bradbury's intention and just as seriously to oversimplify his technique for getting at the complexity and depth of the human condition.

It may be useful further to look carefully at such a story as "Dark They Were, and Golden-Eyed" (*A Medicine for Melancholy*). This is a piece which is superficially similar to several of those stories collected into the earlier *Martian Chronicles*, and it illustrates quite clearly the essential difference between his more conventional science fiction and the kind of fantasy he had begun working toward by 1949. For his setting in this story Bradbury returns to those same Earth colonies on Mars which had been the scene for so much of the *Martian Chronicles'* imaginative speculation. But there are no gadgets in "Dark They Were, and Golden-Eyed," no extra-terrestrial encounters, madhouses, or miraculously fast-growing trees. Instead there is simple humanity and, on an alien planet, acknowledgment of how quickly colonizers have everywhere and always — and in spite of their own intentions — become children of the land they sought to adopt. In this case the settlers are stranded on Mars for five years while atomic war screams on Earth. When a rescue ship finally arrives, its crew finds not Earthmen but "natives" instead who, tall, healthy, and beautiful, are unrecognizable to them. The colonizers have become Martians; nothing has changed but themselves, and nothing has changed them but living together on a new land in isolation from their past. The story is of Mars, but it is also of Brazil, Australia, South Africa, or Massachusetts Bay.

If there is a common weakness in Bradbury's stories, it is his inability — or unwillingness — to characterize effectively the people who inhabit them; and when one reads several of his pieces at once, one begins to notice with something like impatience the nagging similarity of one protagonist to another. His youths are all the Douglas Spaulding of *Dandelion Wine*; his astronauts, fathers, scientists, beachcombers, and even his impersonal narrators are, by whatever names, Douglas Spaulding grown-up. The rocket captain whose mission is to scoop up a sample of star-substance for scientific evaluation in the title story from *The Golden Apples of the Sun* is a case in point. When the protective suit of one of his crewmen ruptures and the man first freezes, then melts as the ship approaches the sun, the captain is reminded of his boyhood and the time he had spent watching icicles melt in Spring sunlight from his bedroom window. At twelve, Douglas Spaulding watches a small world of natural phenomena from much that same bedroom window and, doing so, dreams the future. It is to Bradbury's credit that even in his maturity "Douglas" remains credible without losing either his sense of wonder or his ability to glory in the infinite mysteries of the universe; at the same time, though, it points to Bradbury's limitations that he creates no meat-fleshed character but this one.

Still, if weak or predictable characterization seems to typify Bradbury's writing, that apparent weakness must not be taken out of the context of the fiction genre in which he normally works. These stories are about those momentary escapes from the knowable world which, reflected upon, infuse mystery and meaning alike into the world of sensory experience. They are not to be confused with realism; nor can the criteria by which realism is judged strictly be applied to what Bradbury is about.

The strength of a Bradbury story is, for better or worse, directly connected to the strength of Ray Bradbury's own voice, his own telling of it. If his characters are dwarfed by their creator it is because his own delicious sense of wonder, the infectious force of his own gladness that the universes both of material and of imagination are filled with mystery and are connected within the brain of man, so permeates his writing that, finally, his own sense of wonder and discovery is what he has to communicate. And certainly the continued popularity of his stories is witness not only to the legitimacy of his message but, further, to both the effectiveness of his unique style and the strength of his glad voice.

Douglas J. McReynolds

THE SHORT FICTION OF ROBERT SHECKLEY

Author: Robert Sheckley (1928-   )
Type of work: Short stories

A collection of typical Sheckley stories ranging from the delightfully zany to the macabre and surreal

Since his magazine debut in 1952, Robert Sheckley has published more than eighty stories of fantasy and science fiction taking full advantage of the freedom which he feels the genre offers. He has given us comic fantasies with demons and mythical beasts, poignant stories with lovable robots, comic problem stories with runaway machines, and adventure stories of survival on hostile worlds. In his hands, these and many other genre clichés become unusual handcrafted gems of entertainment wrought with imagination, compassion, and a great sense of humor ranging from the sublime to the macabre; and these stories always employ the brand of irony and incongruity which is the distinctive Sheckley trademark.

"Untouched by Human Hands," the title story of Sheckley's first and best collection, is in many ways typical of his work. In this tale two very ordinary men struggle to survive in an alien environment (a storehouse of reptilian creatures), solve a problem (how to get food and water), and do battle with a runaway gadget (an ever-swelling sealing compound). The story concludes with a comic twist when the men are threatened (not seriously) with being eaten by one of the storehouse items. In "Watchbird," a story from a later collection, Sheckley employs a similar idea but adds some social criticism as well. His military bureaucrats are befuddled when the watchbirds they insist on loosing upon humanity to stop crime wind up trying to kill all life forms instead. In these two tales Sheckley's basic method is evident: he adopts an intriguing premise and settles back to work out its logical implications. These implications usually mean some discomfort for the ordinary people in the story who, like us, are creatures of limited vision. The discrepancy between what they expect and what they get shapes the story as it so often does our lives.

But sometimes the irony of the story runs deeper than mere discomfort. In "A Wind is Rising," for example, the men are near death in a wind which the planet's natives consider a nice breeze. They are not laughing at all, and the irony deepens even more when, at story's end, they learn that a "real" wind is coming with no rescue for them in sight.

"The Leech" is a blob from outer space which, growing from a tiny spore by feeding on energy, threatens earth, and eventually the entire galaxy. Here the immediate problem is solved by luring the leech into outer space and then blowing it to bits, but again the story ends ominously. Sheckley's leech breaks down into smaller and smaller units, into " . . . spores, waiting to be fed."

In his comic fantasy *The Demons*, Sheckley gives his imaginative, ironic perception full scope by turning Dante and Marlow and Milton on their heads.

Arthur Gammen, who meets the demons, is not a tireless seeker of the infinite but a good insurance salesman who, like the man in the barroom joke, was just "walking down the street" one day. He does not *conjure* the first of the demons; the demon conjures him and then demands that *he* grant a wish. This Demon, incidentally, is not Beelzebub but his grandson, Neelzebub ("Granddaddy was an army man"), and so on and on until, by making big things small, the great legend is reduced to farce comedy. At story's end, Arthur and a much *nicer* demon who *also* sells insurance have settled down to talk shop.

It should not be thought, however, that absurd irony and gadget problems are all that inform Sheckley's best work. There is often more. In "Seventh Victim," as in the stories considered thus far, Sheckley is a conventional entirely competent architect of the science fiction tale. Sheckley whets our appetite with a bit of the storyline and some terms we do not understand: Stanton Frelaine bids a very ordinary goodbye to his very ordinary desk job and boss to take on a "Hunt." This time he won't be the "Victim" and so will not need a "Spotter"; he will be the "Hunter" working his way toward "The Tens Club" but disdaining to use a "Protec-Suit" and so on. For the first two pages we have a chance to ponder these terms and fit them together — a small-scale mystery. Then we are let in on the story's premise in a two-page exposition. Carefully and succinctly Sheckley explains the setting up of the "Emotional Catharsis" bureau's organized system of legal murder, established to channel aggression and prevent war. Then the pace and the suspense quicken as the story moves toward an ironic conclusion. The characters are given only those few features necessary to make the plot work. "Seventh Victim," then, is a spare, unpretentious, straightforward tale working out the implications of a futuristic premise; at the same time it is an excellent story for novices to the genre who think that all science fiction is about space and time travel and robots.

It should be noted that Sheckley employs women in his stories in the all-too-common fashion of science fiction writers up to the present time: there are few women characters and their roles are restricted and subordinate to male roles. They are prizes or hazards or complications, but rarely protagonists. It is fair to say therefore, that Sheckley's fiction is male-oriented. In this context, however, it is interesting to discover that Sheckley offers some strong women whose victories lampoon male conceit. The irony of "Seventh Victim" proceeds from Frelaine's misreading of his "Victim," Patricia. He feels sentiment for his "girl" victim and mistakes his protective feelings for love. The story trades, then, on the male reader's conventional response by having Patricia demonstrate that she is a very unstereotypical woman.

Similarly, Sheckley uses conventional notions about men and women to turn the tables both on the main character and on the reader in his reverse-Thurberesque fantasy, "Disposal Service." Here we are presented with a domineering, scheming male, Ferguson, who plans to have his repressed wife ("a small, plain woman with little nervous lines around her eyes") carried away in a large gunny sack by the "disposal service." When Ferguson goes for the sales pitch by the firm's representative, Mr. Esmond ("Of course, I cannot produce any personal endorsements, for we are at some pains to avoid all advertising. But I can assure you we are an old and reliable firm"), he does so without a thought that his wife might have plans for disposing of *him*.

In "The Prize of Peril," Sheckley takes the survival theme basic to men's magazine fiction and transforms it into sharp satire. Twenty years before Paddy Chayefsky wrote *Network*, Sheckley developed the idea of television becoming a kind of *circus maximus* exploiting our blood lust and taste for the bizarre. As Jim Reder struggles to elude a gang of murderers, the television game show host cries out to the audience:

> ". . . and now he's trapped there, [folks], trapped like a rat in a cage! The Thompson gang is breaking down the door! The fire escape is guarded! Our camera crew, situated in a nearby building, is giving you a closeup now. Look, folks, just look! Is there no hope for Jim Raeder?"

Sheckley makes certain that we understand that the show, *The Prize of Peril* is not unusual in his future world. To get on it, Jim had to work his way up, first appearing on smaller shows such as *Spills*, *Hazard*, *Emergency*, and *Underwater Perils*.

There is more, then, to many of Sheckley's stories than gadgets and gags. Stories like "The Prize of Peril" and "Seventh Victim" feature an extrapolation of social behavior more than of technology, and that extrapolation is not beyond possibility. Some writers achieve the comic with recalcitrant robots that hinder and thwart human behavior, and some achieve the significant and thought-provoking by taking away one or more social prohibitions. Sheckley does both.

In Sheckley's stories, anything can be made, constructed, done, bought, or sold. Such is the nature of the decadent planet Earth in "Love, Inc." (later titled "Pilgrimage to Earth"). In this story, Love itself is for sale. Alfred Simon purchases the services of a lover at the firm of "Love, Inc." but then suffers when he learns that the very brain-tampering that makes his lover's sighs real will erase him from her memory after their date is over. It is important to see here that Sheckley is not writing a romance nor employing bawdry nor appealing to decadent tastes. He is using the magazine story form to probe a basic problem of epistemology: if I can in no way distinguish the real from the false, how are they different?

This same theme is explored with different effect in "The Store of Worlds," perhaps Sheckley's most poignant story. In this tale, a holocaust survivor purchases a drug which enables him to relive an idyllic time with his family, now dead. The effect is ironic and pathetic in the same way that many of Ray Bradbury's best stories are.

At first glance, "Redfern's Labyrinth" seems to be atypical of Sheckley. Redfern reads a letter addressed to him in an imitation of his own handwriting. The letter appears to be a review of a story by Redfern called "Labyrinth"; it concludes by turning to Redfern for an explanation about the labyrinth which the story does not afford, and so on and on until by the end of this six-page story, we realize that Sheckley's Redfern's Labyrinth is itself a kind of literary maze in whose twisting passageways we have become trapped by reading.

As different as this story may seem for Sheckley, it is really of a piece with the rest of the canon. Here we see the love of plot and puzzles and irony to which all else is subordinated. And Redfern is another of those characters who encounter weird developments lurking behind ordinary events, struggle to survive in hostile environments, wrestle with runaway machines and devices, and discover that they are about to be devoured by creatures of fantasy. In Redfern's Labyrinth, Sheckley has achieved his masterpiece, a story in which we can truly identify with the main character, in which we can enjoy the bitter pleasure of discovering ourselves trapped in one of life's little quagmires.

The stories in the most recent collection, *Can You Feel Anything When I Do This?* (1971), are as luxurious as ever, but they lack the rollicking optimism of the early works. The title story develops, like many an earlier tale, a wild and interesting premise: a woman seduced by a robot vacuum cleaner. Here is the mind-body problem in a provocative form. But Melisande Durr destroys her wonderful vacuum cleaner, interrupting not only the best sexual congress of her life but true love as well. The early Sheckley would not have ended the tale like this. Melisande would have made a pact with the machine and kept it hidden in her closet. The husband would be a smug man well deserving of robot-cuckoldry. But none of this, alas, will be, for the beautiful golden-age gadget has been disconnected. In the same way, "Doctor Zombie's Little Furry Friends" die of pneumonia, and their potential threat to the world is never developed. Instead we are left with the brooding interior monologue of their mad creator, with potentiality instead of the world remade.

How different this is from, say "Triplication," an earlier tale in which we discover that the story of Akka, a robot who killed his master in order to use his body oils for lubrication, is being narrated by *another* robot after "they" have taken over from "us." The robot narrator concludes, "Hail, Akka, our liberator." Abandoning simple and buoyant ironics, Sheckley's most recent stories give out at just that point where his earlier stories were rendered strong and exciting; still, given the wealth of entertainment in any of his work, the greater pity is that at the date of this writing there is no Sheckley anthology in print.

Thom Dunn

Sources for Further Study

Criticism:

Encyclopedia of Science Fiction and Fantasy. Compiled by Donald H. Tuck. Chicago: Advent Publishers, Inc., 1978, p. 386. Tuck gives a general biographical and bibliographical review of Sheckley's career.

Ulanov, Barry. "Science Fiction and Fantasy," in his *The Two Worlds of American Art: The Private and the Popular*. New York: Macmillan, 1965, pp. 298-308. Although a general article, this work gives some discussion of Sheckley's fiction.